JEFF ALWORTH

THE
BEER
BIBLE

WORKMAN PUBLISHING · NEW YORK

....

For Sally,
to whom I owe the world—
or, at the very least, Italy

....

Library of Congress Cataloging-in-Publication Data is available.

ISBNs 978-0-7611-6811-9 (pb); 978-0-7611-8498-0 (hc)

Cover design by John Passineau
Interior design by Lisa Hollander
Photo research by Bobby Walsh

Workman books are available at special discounts when purchased in bulk for premiums and sales promotions as well as for fund-raising or educational use. Special editions or book excerpts also can be created to specification. For details, contact the Special Sales Director at the address below, or send an email to specialmarkets@workman.com.

Workman Publishing Co., Inc.
225 Varick Street
New York, NY 10014-4381
workman.com

WORKMAN is a registered trademark of Workman Publishing Co., Inc.

Printed in the United States of America
First printing July 2015

10 9 8 7 6 5 4 3 2

ACKNOWLEDGMENTS

WHEN YOU LOOK at the cover of a book, there's usually just one name there. Often an author will mention some folks who supported him or helped along the way. In the case of *The Beer Bible*, it would have been literally impossible for me to complete the book without the help of dozens of people. Folks like the English writer Zak Avery, who helped me contact British breweries to set up visits. Or importers Wendy Littlefield, Matthias Neidhart, and Michael Opalenski, who did the same for me in France and Belgium, Germany, and Italy. Wendy and Michael were wonderful in sharing their impressions of the Belgian and Italian brewing worlds, helping educate me as well as connecting me with brewers in Europe. I want to give a special *děkuji* to Max Bahnson, who spent two days giving me a tour of Prague, and another to Patrick Emerson, who not only joined me on the trip around Great Britain, but had the courage to take the wheel of the Vauxhall.

I had personal advisors who used their years of experience to illuminate and guide me on this long road: the writer Stan Hieronymus, who has done more to advance our understanding of beer than anyone in the past decade; brewer Alan Taylor, the hardest-working man in beer at Pints Brewing, Ponderosa Brewing, and (soon to be) Zoiglhaus Brewing, who helped me overcome my fear of lagers; and Portland, Oregon–based chef Paul Kasten, who revealed some of his alchemical secrets. You spent far more time than you needed to answering what must have seemed like obvious questions.

Another revolution in our understanding of beer has come thanks to a cohort of exceptional historians. These folks have looked at primary sources in the brewing record going back centuries, and have help loosen our attachment to persistent old myths. I'm thinking especially of Martyn Cornell and Ron Pattinson, both of whom graciously agreed to look over my history sections to prevent any howlers from getting out in the world. Richard Unger and Ian Hornsey have also done indispensable work. Closer to home, Maureen Ogle's history of American brewing has been essential reading.

If you look at the end of the book, you'll see the names of more than fifty brewers who took the time to speak with me about the beer, of which three dozen took me on tours of their breweries. Some of those names are the most esteemed in the business, and one of the enormous pleasures of writing this book was spending time looking inside mash tuns and up at towering conditioning tanks. In České Budějovice (Budweis), Adam Brož guided me by flashlight through a brewery darkened by electrical work. Standing with John Bexon under Crown Street in Bury St Edmunds, England, in a tangle of pipes running to the bottling line, conspiratorially, he said, "Not many people have been down here." Showing up on the wrong day at Belgian brewery Rodenbach and having Rudi Ghequire give me a tour, anyway. Standing in the mists made by hot wort pouring into the cool ship at Cantillon, drinking aged Vintage Ale in the cellars at Fuller's, dining with the folks at Lambrate, sampling *sticke alt* from the tanks at Uerige, smelling the fresh yeast of open fermenters at Schneider, meeting Teo Musso's mom, discussing German guilds at Schlenkerla. These memories (and many more) are treasures I'll carry a lifetime.

The list goes on. James Emmerson not only manages a large American brewery (Full Sail), but he checked my technical sections for accuracy. Evan Rail made sure I didn't get Czech beer wrong. Jo and Jerry Lane, Gene Alworth, and Sally Alworth all remember the fitful progress that led to this book—coming in on two decades now—and were there to hold my chin up along the way.

Finally, I want to thank the folks at Workman Publishing for entrusting me with *The Beer Bible*. I worked closely with Kylie Foxx McDonald for a year before signing the contract to write the book and for the nearly four years it took to bring it to publication. I thank her especially, but also all those who were guiding things along behind the scenes.

Whatever richness you find in this book, think of them when you appreciate it. I do.

Portland, Oregon
May 2013

CONTENTS

HOW TO USE THIS BOOK

N 2001, the wine educator Karen MacNeil published a book called *The Wine Bible.* A conceptual triumph, it manages to take more than nine hundred pages of information and put it into a form that is instantly understandable by even the layest of laypeople. MacNeil's steady voice, lyrical and accessible yet authoritative, guides you through the rolling hills of Italy's Piedmont and the Maipo Valley of Chile. Wine is a drink of place, the grapes that make it defined by the heat of the sun and elements in the earth. MacNeil acts as an expert guide on a world tour.

Beer is a little different. It is also a drink of place, but not in the same way. Culture and history exert at least as great an influence as where the barley and hops are grown. Beer types or styles are manifestations of these influences, and act as the organizing principle of *The*

Beer Bible. Mostly. It turns out movement is also the nature of beer styles. Porters jump seas and become stouts; pilsners cross borders and become hellesbiers. Places like the United States, Italy, and France pick up brewing almost from nothing and rebuild it like immigrants do, borrowing this, dumping that, scrambling x and y. Styles mutate and change. Remember that as you read about these styles, and recall that even though we wouldn't dare to question the legitimacy of Munich's famous helles beer now, once a pale lager was so radical that the city's brewers nearly had a civil war over it. Today's abomination is tomorrow's treasured tradition.

WHERE TO BEGIN

Some people who come to this book will be new to beer, perhaps enticed by the burgeoning world of craft beers; others will be old hands who want a little more information about their favorite styles. Whoever you are and whatever your reasons, you'll thumb around and drop into sections that interest you. The book is designed to be read in pieces; Karen MacNeil had the insight to structure *The Wine Bible* that way, and I happily followed her lead (though this book is segmented by style, not region). The first part of the book will give you some of the important background to understanding beer, but you might prefer to dip into it elliptically, to backfill as necessary. You may not be compelled to read through descriptions of the strange flavors of beer, for example, until you encounter something unexpected. Or perhaps the history of beer won't be interesting to you until one afternoon, as you're sitting behind a pint of abbey ale, you wonder what in the world monks have to do with brewing. If you prioritize any sections of Part One, I recommend "Tasting Beer Like a Brewer," starting on page 58—that's where you'll find the concepts and terms important to the sensory experience of beer that are repeated in nearly every chapter.

WORLD BREWING TRADITIONS

I'm an American, but this is not a book solely or even centrally about American brewing. Even though breweries in the United States now make every style of world beer, I've written about the traditions from their origin points. There are lots of American pilsners and abbey tripels, but when you flip to chapters about those styles, you'll find a discussion of Czechs and Belgians. Craft brewing has sparked a renaissance in countries throughout the world, but this book does not spend a lot of time talking about all the various international interpretations of each style.

THE BEERS TO KNOW

Following each beer style chapter is a list of "Beers to Know." These highlight examples that give a good sense of the classic contours of the style in question. I selected them based on a few criteria: They should be regular or seasonal beers, likely to still be in production a year or two after the book's publication. Since there was usually a surfeit of good beers

in each style, I tried to select brands so that wherever you live, at least one should be available for you to taste. When choosing foreign beers, I limited the selection only to those that are imported to the United States—though not all imported beer is available in every market. If you're like me, you'll scan the names to see if I got it right—and no doubt wail when you see I omitted a beer like, say, the cult favorite Three Floyds Dark Lord. The Dark Lords of the world may score very highly among critics, but it has such a constrained release that very few people will ever have the chance to sample it.

A NOTE ON NAMES

Place names can be a political topic. To call India's large western city Bombay instead of Mumbai is a political act. Throughout the book, I've used the American standard for place names even when it carries the aroma of politics. Köln is rendered as Cologne (uncontroversial), but České Budějovice is Budweis even though the city itself, like Mumbai, has made a conscious decision to leave that name behind. I did this solely to reconcile names with American usage.

Beer names are less controversial but just as confusing. By tradition, convention, and uneasy agreement, we have come to an agglomeration of titles that don't always serve the purpose of clarity. To try to restore some, I have condensed a few categories. There were once two distinct styles of red and brown beers in Flanders, but even around the West Flanders town Roeselare, home to Rodenbach, they call them one style: "red/brown" Flanders beers; I've settled on "tart ales of Flanders." The world's most popular beers, such as Budweiser, Foster's, Sapporo, and Heineken, are called everything from light lagers to American adjunct lagers, usually with several subcategories. In this book they're all "mass-market lagers." Craft breweries in Europe and the United States are experimenting with a range of ales made with wild yeast and bacteria; these I call "wild ales," and they're not brewed to a particular style.

BREWERY BIOGRAPHIES

Scattered throughout the book are more than a dozen short biographies of breweries. They follow and are meant to further illuminate elements of the preceding style chapter. For example, after the weizen chapter is a description of the most important Bavarian wheat beer breweries, G. Schneider and Sohn. Orval follows abbey ales, Samuel Smith after bitter, and so on. In each case, the history of the brewery or its processes, or even the physical brewery itself, helps tell the story of the style it follows. Beer is not just a product, it's a living tradition; these are the breweries that link the modern beverage to its history.

THE PACIFIC NORTHWEST

I live in Portland, Oregon, home to more breweries than any city on earth. The Pacific Northwest has the most developed beer culture in the United States, and has not only a ton of good beers and breweries, but local maltings, most of the country's hop fields and the USDA hop-breeding program, one of the two national yeast suppliers, and one of a small handful of degree-granting college brewing programs. In the nearly twenty years I've been writing about beer, you might imagine I've become just a little compromised by this bounty. You'd be correct. Every time I needed to ask a brewer a question, I had to stifle the instinct to pick up the phone and call one I knew. When thinking of the "Beers to Know," I had to stop and remind myself that there is wonderful beer in every corner of the country and the world. Nevertheless, if you detect the whiff of a West Coast orientation in these pages, my apologies. I come by it honestly.

PART ONE

Knowing

BEER

Finding Your BEARINGS

Imagine you and I weren't communicating through this book, but rather were sitting at the bar of a cozy, wood-paneled alehouse together. The taplist is extensive and well selected: Superb examples of almost every beer style are to be had by a simple gesture to the barman. In such a situation, you might use me as you'd be inclined to use this book and ask, "Which one is your favorite?" There's a common view that so-called experts know which among the multitudes is the best beer. In fact, "what's best?" is the wrong question. In our hypothetical bar, I'd answer with my own question: "What's *your* favorite beer?"

It's easy to overthink our choices when we are confronted by such bounty. Never in the long history of beer drinking—thousands of years!—have we had it so good: At our local pubs and grocery stores we can find beers from around the world brewed in dozens of different styles. Roasty stouts, floral English ales, zesty pilsners, and crisp witbiers—they're everywhere. These different species, products of specific places and cultures, can be mystifying. And now craft brewing, a worldwide phenomenon, has muddied things further by decoupling style and country—these days we find improbable mashups like Belgian stouts, American witbiers, English pilsners, and Czech IPAs. It *is* confusing.

I have good news. This isn't the world of haute cuisine. Beer isn't art or physics—you don't need to take a college course in theory to understand it. Beer is just malted grain, water, and yeast, usually spiced with hops. Though there's a huge amount you *can* learn about beer, the principal experience should be pleasure. You wouldn't say that there's a "best" dessert, though you might prefer peach cobbler to chocolate cake. Think of the different types of beer this way. If you're reading this book, you've probably found a brand you love. It may be light-bodied or syrupy black, hoppy or malty, sweet or bitter. That beer is a doorway into an amazing world of history, culture, and craft.

The best way to learn about beer isn't by trying every one out there; instead, pour your favorite and study it. It comes from a tradition of brewing that goes back decades or centuries and reflects the tastes of the culture that first brewed it. That Belgian witbier isn't an accidental ale; it dates back centuries to a small town called Hoegaarden. It has evolved and changed and even went extinct for awhile. Or pilsner—that beer came from a town called Pilsen in what is now the Czech Republic where the beer was so bad, townspeople decided to take action and start a new brewery. We know the name of the brewer who first brewed that pilsner and why it was a pale lager. The reasons witbier is made with coriander and pilsners are golden and hoppy have to do with their unique stories. You'll learn more about the nature of beer if you stop and study your favorite and see why you like it. That beer can be a reference point as you start poking around other

ABOVE: *"What's your favorite beer?"*

styles—and before long you'll be able to appreciate them for what they are. And that in turn will be a jumping-off point for other styles, which may no longer be so inscrutable.

So: What beer do you like? ■

Beer Wisdom. Charlie Papazian is one of the four or five people most responsible for starting the good beer movement in America. Before Charlie Papazian, there were just a few brands of beer in the country, all making the same type of pale lager. Now there are thousands of brands and dozens of types of beer. In the 1970s, he encouraged homebrewers to make the beer they couldn't find at bars and eventually, in 1978, went on to found the American Homebrewers Association, which now has 43,000 members. In Papazian's legendary how-to, *The Complete Joy of Home Brewing*, he coined the rallying cry for the age: "Relax, don't worry, have a homebrew." It still applies, even if you substitute the words "craft brew" for "homebrew."

EXPERIENCE THE BEER

HEN YOU SIT down with a glass of beer, you do a lot more than taste it. You will eventually put your papillae to the task, but they won't work alone. Your eyes take in its color, clarity, and vivacity. Your nostrils detect sharp or subtle aromas drifting off the surface. When you taste, you'll be smelling the beer while it's inside your mouth. Your tongue, meanwhile, will be noticing whether it's prickly with carbonation or smooth and still, whether it is thin or creamy or thick. You don't merely taste a beer, you experience it.

Of all the skills you might learn in tasting beer, attention is the most

RIGHT: *Experiencing a beer goes beyond merely tasting it.*

FACING PAGE: *To get a complete impression of a beer, first you must pour it into a glass.*

important. Your senses are important: They're like the hardware that delivers the raw data. But it's your mind and ability to observe— your software—that allow you to understand what you're drinking. Let's do a simple trial run. Go grab a beer from the fridge and a clear, clean glass from the cupboard. Open the

beer and slowly pour it into the glass. (For this exercise it's important that you can see the beer, that it's not in a bottle or can.) While pouring it out, make sure to bring your attention to the experience.

LOOK. Your eyes will tell you a lot about the beer. If you pour it from a bottle, notice whether it comes out syrupy or water-thin. Once it's in the glass, you can look to see the color and clarity of the beer, how vigorously the bubbles rise from the bottom of the glass, and what the head looks like. Does the head resemble a skiff of whipped cream, with bubbles so small you can't see them, or is it made of larger visible bubbles, stacked like tiny beads? What color is it? How fast does the head dissipate?

SMELL. A good beer will delight your nose. As you may know from eating when you have a head cold, much of what we taste is actually the alchemy between scent and flavor. Rouse the aromatic compounds by swirling the glass, then get your nose right down to the surface and inhale. Malt and hops contribute the most

obvious scents—bready, roasty, or nutty in the case of malt; floral, spicy, or citrusy from the hops. You might find other aromas that are less obvious, like pear, rose, or clove; these emerge from compounds created during fermentation.

SIP. You finally taste the beer once it washes over your tongue, but flavor isn't the only thing going on. Swish the beer around your mouth so the aromas warm and unfold—flavors will evolve as the beer enters your mouth and taste and aroma commingle, building as you swallow. Beyond flavors, you will pick up the texture of the beer, its viscosity, level of carbonation, and alcohol strength.

SWALLOW. The final experience comes after the beer is gone. As the beer travels down your throat, a final round of flavors and aromas emerges. Your nose will detect the vapors left behind and your tongue, still awash in a slight residue, will continue to taste. Only by swallowing do some of the most important characteristics emerge—crispness, roundness, hoppiness, and tartness, to name a few. And never, ever spit out a mouthful—leave that sin to the wine drinkers.

To the extent possible, just luxuriate in these sensations. Tune out the big guy yammering on the next bar stool, the game blaring on the TV. There are many virtues of beer, but none is greater than its simple pleasure. The appearance, flavors, and aromas are all clues to the ingredients, style, and brewing methods of the beer (ones we'll detail in "Tasting Beer Like a Brewer," starting on page 58).

Try a variety of different kinds of beers, pay attention to their characteristics, their principal qualities, and think what it is about them you like. One of beer's strengths is its variability, and the joy is finding which flavors you like the most. Once you become familiar with how these flavors line up with beer types, you'll begin to mentally map out the terrain of beer styles. These create a launching pad for further explorations. Take notes, observe, but enjoy. Life's too short and full of good beer to waste your time on beers that don't excite you. ■

HOW TO READ A BEER LABEL

OVER THE CENTURIES and across different languages, the lexicon for beer terms has changed a bit. Even today the terms aren't exactly settled, but "beer" is the word that encompasses the entire range of grain-based fermented beverages. Ales, lagers, lambics, bocks—they're all beer. Within this class of beverages are all manner of subcategories, styles, and designations, any of which might appear on a beer label. Beyond that, you'll find various bits of other information that may help you divine what's inside the bottle. These are the basics.

■ **Ale or Lager.** Except for a few oddballs, most beers can be divided into either the ale camp or the lager camp. In part this distinguishes the type of yeast used to

LEFT: *Many beer companies turn their labels into works of art.*

ANATOMY OF A BEER LABEL

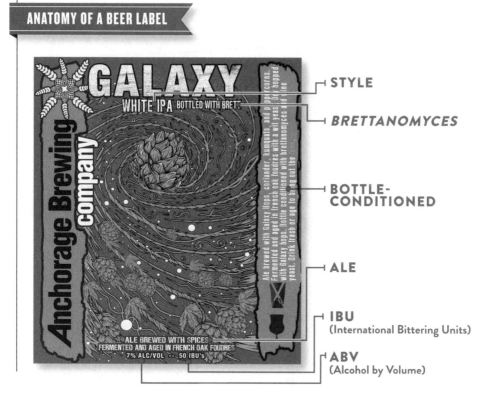

STYLE

BRETTANOMYCES

BOTTLE-
CONDITIONED

ALE

IBU
(International Bittering Units)

ABV
(Alcohol by Volume)

ferment the beer, and in part the manner of fermentation. Ales use a strain of yeast that prefers warmer temperatures and requires very little aging time. Ale strains produce other flavors in the beer, like fruit or spice notes. Lagers are fermented cooler and left in tanks for weeks or months to smooth out. This inhibits the production of fruity and spicy compounds, leaving purer notes of hop and malt.

■ **Style or type.** Most labels identify the style of beer inside the bottle—pilsner, stout, gueuze, and so on. This may actually reflect the beer that's inside the bottle, or may be an impressionistic or aspirational brewery description—or something the marketing team invented.

It may be a poetic rendering that *sounds* like a style ("rustic farmhouse ale"), but isn't, really. Styles are the subject of endless debates in taverns and chatrooms across the planet, and should be approached lightly.

■ **ABV (alcohol by volume).** This is the standard measure for alcohol in the United States, displacing the older measurement, alcohol by weight (a beer that's 5% alcohol by volume is about 4% by weight). Standard beer ranges from 4% to 8% ABV, though stronger (more alcoholic) beers can be as strong as wine—up to 17%.

■ **IBU (international bittering units).** This is the measure of how much hop acid is

the width of the glass, and the layperson's impressionistic sense of color ("straw," "amber," "chestnut") is at least as useful as a scaled measure.

■ **Unfiltered.** Beer clarity is a divisive subject. Beer that has been handled well and left to condition (a process of ripening) will settle into a more brilliant state—a good thing. But breweries may also filter beer, using technologies that scrub it of all solids including suspended yeast, microscopic hop particles, protein, and other rustic bits—bad things to people who see a little haze as evidence of the artisanal process. When a brewery describes its beer as "unfiltered," it's announcing its affiliation in the former camp (beers are never described as filtered). Many craft breweries and craft beer fans like a bit of fog in their beer, and some styles—Bavarian weizens in particular—actually demand it.

■ **Gravity/original gravity.** A number that expresses how much dissolved sugar is in the wort (beer before it is fermented)—a measure of the potential strength of beer. Although it's a bit arcane, gravity has the virtue of consistency; every beer has a starting gravity, and gravity doesn't vary under different circumstances. The usual units of measure are degrees Plato or specific gravity (indicated by "sp. gr."). Water is the baseline for both measures, expressed as either 0° Plato or 1.000 sp. gr. The range for normally fermented beers runs from about 8° Plato/1.032 sp. gr., which would result in a beer of about 3% ABV, to 26° Plato/1.110 sp. gr.,

dissolved in the beer—a rough measure of its bitterness. The perception of bitterness is mitigated by how strong and malty a beer is, so a 40 IBU pale ale may seem quite bitter while those same 40 IBU will translate to a sweetish strong ale. Worse, many breweries don't actually have labs to measure the acids chemically and instead predict them using mathematical formulas (to call this prediction "inexact" is kind). Finally, while hoppiness is a combination of flavor, aroma, and bitterness, IBU measure only the last. In Europe, the measure is sometimes labeled EBU (European bittering units)—but there's negligible difference between the two.

■ **Color (SRM/EBC).** The American Society of Brewing Chemists and European Brewery Convention have each created a numerical scale of scientific measures of the color of beer when viewed under certain controlled conditions. Since very few people have a chemistry set at home, the measure is of little use to the average beer drinker. Beer color is a function of the light and resulting in a towering monster of 12% ABV. For consistency, specific gravity is used throughout this book.

■ **Bottle-Conditioned.** Most beer is force-carbonated; that is, carbon dioxide (CO_2) is added to finished beer prior to bottling. In some cases, beer is dosed with sugar or yeast to produce a secondary fermentation in the bottle. Since the product of fermentation is carbon dioxide, bottle-conditioned beer naturally carbonates this way. Bottle-conditioned beer has a layer of yeast at the bottom of the bottle.

■ *Brettanomyces/tart or sour ale/wild ale.* Certain yeasts and bacteria, for centuries the joy and bane of brewers, have come back into style. With modern controls, brewers can more often get joyful results; these creatures add unexpected flavors to a beer that range from subtle dryness to eye-watering acidity. ■

THE BUILDING BLOCKS OF BEER

THE ESSENCE THAT animates a good beer—the way you recognize when a brewer has combined the elements perfectly—is known as "balance." At its most basic, the term describes the relationship between bitter hops and sweet malt, but balance also has a deeper meaning. It describes the harmony between contrasting elements, how that multitude of flavors and aromas come together like a choir. I discuss these constituents in detail in "Tasting Beer Like a Brewer" (page 58), but here are the four major taste- and aroma-producing agents.

■ **Malt.** Beer is made of grain that has been malted; this grain is responsible for the color of beer. The various hues come from the way the malt is kilned or roasted, which also contributes aromas and flavors. Malt is principally sweet, but roasted malt may be bitter like coffee. Malt gives beer the scent and flavor of bread, cracker, nuts, toffee, dark fruit, or chocolate—to name just a few.

■ **Hops.** The most versatile ingredient in beer is the hops. They may imperceptibly balance the sweetness of malt, as in light beer, or they may make a beer profoundly bitter, like some double IPAs. Hops can add intense aromatics and lush flavors as well, some good enough mimics to make you swear there's grapefruit, pine boughs, or mint in your glass.

■ **Yeast.** Yeast is an agent more than an ingredient, and you taste the chemical compounds it leaves behind. In some beers like lagers it leaves very little, but in others, like hefeweizens and saisons, it creates startlingly fruity or spicy notes that are the hallmarks of those styles. Generally speaking, the warmer the fermentation, the more flavor a yeast will give.

■ **Sugar, spice, and everything nice.** Beer must be made of water, malt, and yeast, but it may also be made of almost anything else. And it has been. In modern commercial brewing, the use of other ingredients is becoming more common: Breweries regularly add sugar to boost strength without adding body, but honey, maple syrup, or molasses give flavor as well. Spices like coriander are found in witbiers, and breweries may slyly use a pinch of spice in nearly any beer to suggest yeast character—or blast a beer to make it taste like Indian tea or pumpkin pie. And fruit, squash, and flavorings like coffee or chocolate are regulars in seasonal beers. ■

A MATTER OF STYLE

T'S IMPOSSIBLE TO approach beer without contending with the word "style." When people refer to style, they mean categories of beers like stouts, dunkel lagers, or witbier. The word is ubiquitous and spreads yearly like a fungus as new subcategories and sub-subcategories branch out from their root style. (The style guidelines for the Great American Beer Festival have gotten distinctly Dada: "pale American Belgo-style ale" and "German-style rye ale with or without yeast" are a couple of the high-water marks.) It's worth considering that the man who is more responsible for giving us the conceptual framework of "beer style," the late beer writer Michael Jackson, originally thought of beers as "types." In 1977 he wrote, "There are certain classical examples within each group, and some of them have given rise to generally accepted styles, whether regional or international. If a brewer specifically has the intention of reproducing a classical beer, then he is working within a style. If his beer merely bears a general similarity to others, then it may be regarded as being of their type."

Jackson lost the battle he helped start. What he called types we now call styles. Despite the ongoing style metastasis, though, it's not a terrible system. We need a common language to discuss the different types of beer, and although the way we talk about style now is overly fussy, it's not terrible. The one very important caveat to note is that *styles are constantly in flux.* The idea of style should be descriptive, not prescriptive. In the long history of beer, the beverages we've called, say, "porter" have morphed enormously. The porters of 1750 were brown, strong, and vat-aged to a vinous acidity. A century later they were still strong and acidic, but had gone from brown to black. Another century and they were no longer strong, were roasty instead of vinous, and still black.

And it doesn't take decades, either; in the thirty-odd years since craft brewing began in the United States, styles have shifted noticeably. This is why New Belgium's Peter Bouckaert provides perhaps the perfect working definition there is: "Style is the definition of a group of beers at a certain point in time." Use the term, but don't fix it in stasis. ■

GRUEL-BEER TO BLACK IPA
in 10,000 Years

In the beginning, there was gruel-beer. The epoch: sometime before the dawn of civilization, as hunter-gatherers in the Tigris and Euphrates valleys were just starting a flirtation with grain. These ancestors of the Sumerians had discovered that soaking grain in water softened it, forming a thin gruel. Over time they made refinements, learning to crush the grain and soak it in hot water—an innovation that released some of the grain's sugars and made a thicker, sweeter porridge. At some pivotal moment, humankind stumbled into one of those happy accidents that change the course of history. A bowl of gruel, perhaps secreted away in the cluttered cave of a teenager, sat out a night or two in the yeast-laden air. It fermented into a mildly intoxicating soup—what archaeologists call "gruel-beer"—and thus began the history of brewing.

There are three ways to think about what comes next. If we tell the story one way, it leads into the history of civilization, how humans decided to settle down, till the soil, found monotheism, and ultimately invent the iPhone. A more narrow telling of the story focuses on the history of brewing: how humans learned to malt the grains, mash them, add hops, and finally, thousands of years later, discover the existence of yeast. A third thread highlights the way in which peoples and beer evolved together, how beer styles reflected the people who brewed them.

Of course, we don't have to choose. All three are the story of beer, which has been a part of our history since the dawn of civilization. It has become tightly embroidered into our culture. When you start plucking up specific styles of beer, you haul up dozens of stories about the local agriculture, laws, wars, and technologies that shaped them. Why is a stout dark? Why are märzens named for a month (March)? Why is lambic sour? Just one question about one beer precipitates a story that, told fully, is the biography of the people who brewed it. ∎

EVERY BEER TELLS A STORY

TAKE THE 1936 vintage of Coronation Ale I have in my cellar. The English brewery Greene King brewed it specially to celebrate the ascension of Edward VIII to the throne. This was not unusual. For centuries, people had been making celebratory beer— the word "bridal," for example, derives from the Anglo-Saxon *brȳd-ealo* ("bride ale," which actually refers to the celebratory fest, not just the beer). If you recall your royal history, though, you know that the coronation of 1936 was unusual: It never happened. Edward, after a reign of just 325 days, decided he would rather marry the American divorcee Wallis Simpson than continue on as King of the United Kingdom of Great Britain and Northern Ireland and of the British Dominions and Emperor of India. The beer, a dark, relatively low-alcohol beer, sat in cellars in Bury St Edmunds for decades.

What does this beer tell us about Britain at the time? Quite a lot, actually. In centuries past, a batch of celebratory beer might have been rich and alcoholic. Breweries at English universities made "audit" ales for the feast celebrating the end of the annual exams. (Greene King made one of those, too.) In earlier times, the nobility competed to make the strongest beers, sometimes to celebrate

LEFT: *This bottle of Greene King Coronation Ale shows its age.*

FACING PAGE: *School's out for summer: Greene King's celebratory Audit Ale*

the birth of a child or a wedding. Why didn't Greene King make a beer like this for the future king? Beers had changed. Even thirty years earlier, 5%—the ABV of this beer—would have placed it among the weaker beers available in Britain. Standard strengths from Victorian times through the early twentieth century were around 6%, and a good many beers were stronger than 8% (standard Budweiser is 5% ABV).

So the question arises: Why was the 1936 Coronation Ale so weak? During the First World War, the British government put controls on the amount of grain breweries could use, and strengths collapsed.

All of a sudden, beers below 3% ABV were common. As the country climbed out of the postwar hole, strengths recovered a bit—which is the moment Greene King brewed Coronation Ale. Soon, the machines of war started grinding in Europe again, and strengths would again fail. The period of mandated low-strength beer lasted so long that the British developed a taste for it; even today, beers are nowhere near as hearty as they were before World War I. Celebration Ale is a fun example because it involves eloping monarchs, but every beer has its story.

Even conservative taxonomists will divide beer styles into dozens of distinct categories. Each one has a unique story. It's possible to draw a line from gruel-beer to Coronation Ale, but to connect gruel-beer and Pilsner Urquell requires an entirely different line. Climate, laws, war, technology, trade, and even religion have guided and shaped the way beers have morphed and changed. Styles evolved in increments, traveled and influenced other styles, and many times waned and flickered out. Yet all emerged because of certain conditions that were as specific and unique as the beer itself—and all are, even today, continuing to evolve. What follows is an overview of that process—a primer for understanding how civilization developed brewing, where styles came from, how they evolved, and why they persist. ■

ANCIENT HISTORY

NOW, back to that gruel-beer. Scholars suggest the first batches were enjoyed in roughly the years from 10,000 to 8000 BCE. In the Fertile Crescent, wild grain was abundant; people could release the seeds just by beating the grasses. Archaeologists suspect that ancient brewers were already developing the basic process of brewing by transferring batches of gruel-beer from clay pot to clay pot, unknowingly selecting and isolating yeast strains that lived in the pots' cracks and fissures. Gruel-beer was made from unmalted grain and would have been quite weak—one to two percent alcohol at most.

Eventually, beginning around 4500 BCE, the nomadic people we now call the Sumerians settled down. The impulse may have come from rapid population growth, or because people became increasingly tired of hauling around newly invented implements. Certain avid beer fans argue that agriculture began because the growing population couldn't rely on wild seeds and they just had to have a regular supply of beer.

(Archaeologists tend to favor bread making as the more likely motivation.)

There have been three revolutionary discoveries in brewing: malting grain, the use of hops, and the function of yeast. The first and biggest leap, malting grain, was taken so early it went unrecorded. At some point, humans discovered that germinated grain produced stronger beer than its raw counterpart. By the time of the first records of beer, people were already using advanced brewing techniques: malting and kilning grain and mashing it to make beer. In those oldest writings, Sumerians describe a beer recognizable to modern eyes as beer—much more rustic, but malted, kilned, mashed, and fermented.

As hunter-gatherers, small tribes were able to collect and hunt enough food to enjoy leisure time, which in turn led to relatively democratic societies. Diets were varied and healthy. By contrast, field work took huge effort, burning up to 5,000 calories a day. For their trouble, people made due with a less healthy, less varied diet. And the need for reliable, subservient labor brought societal stratification. To support this new life, the Sumerians had to consume more calories than they could get from bread alone. Beer—more energy-dense than bread—was consumed in huge quantities, and was drunk liberally by most Sumerians once they exited infancy. If beer wasn't the only reason people

Beer's Epic History.

"You are the one who waters the malt
set on the ground . . .
Ninkasi, you are the one who soaks the malt in a jar
The waves rise, the waves fall . . .
You are the one who spreads the cooked
mash on large reed mats,
Coolness overcomes . . .
Ninkasi, you are the one who holds with both hands
the great sweet wort."

—HYMN TO NINKASI, 1800 BCE, translated by Miguel Civil

"'Eat the food, Enkidu, it is the way one lives.
Drink the beer, as is the custom of the land.'
Enkidu ate the food until he was sated,
he drank the beer—seven jugs!—and
became expansive and sang with joy!"

— EPIC OF GILGAMESH,
circa 2500 BCE, translated by Maureen Gallery Kovacs

The First Beer Styles. From the very start, beer was made in different styles. One especially detailed list from Sumer lists beer by age, color, quality, and recipe. One type of beer had lots of spelt and no wheat, while another had lots of wheat and no spelt. Egyptians also had at least seventeen different beer types, including some evocative varieties like "joybringer," "heavenly," "beer of the protector," and "beer of truth" (though that one was just for the gods).

decided to take up agriculture in the first place, it was one of the main reasons they were able to continue once they had. No doubt beer's narcotic benefits helped loosen muscles and soothe minds after long days in the field—and probably helped quell rebellion.

FERTILE CRESCENT

Sumer wasn't the only civilization that developed beer; many early cultures across the world started brewing soon after they sowed their first fields. The Egyptians, who were just slightly later than the Sumerians, are the most famous early brewers. Evidence suggests preliterate brewing as early as 5000 BCE, and written records begin around 3100 BCE. Beer was a central part of Egyptian culture, from its ubiquity in daily diets to its use as an offering to the gods and the dead. Egypt was the first place to tax beer and likely the first place to export it.

Egyptians operated sophisticated breweries. They malted their wheat and barley and dried it in the sun, ground it, and used a two-phase system of mashing it. One of their early innovations was to add dates and pomegranates to flavor the beer. Brewing was integrated into life, where beer served as one form of payment, and—as the clay pots in tombs illustrate—important after death as well.

Elsewhere, brewing wasn't far behind. In Scotland people might have been brewing as early as the Egyptians. Recent archaeological evidence places both malting and brewing at some time between 4000 and 2000 BCE. These brewers may have been the most fanciful, fortifying their beer with honey and cranberries as well as a variety of wild herbs. Celts started brewing at least by 700 BCE; they not only learned to malt grains, but developed techniques to kiln-dry and roast it. They also added henbane, a toxic psychoactive herb that might have been used to flavor the beer—or make it more intoxicating. Scientists discovered an advanced brewery near present-day Berlin dating to 500 BCE.

ASIA, AFRICA, SOUTH AMERICA

Settlers near the Yellow River in China around 220 BCE also brewed, but they had to contend with less-nitrogen-rich soil. (The date is in dispute; some archaeologists argue brewing in China started as early as 9,000 years ago, or roughly the same period as the earliest Mesopotamian brewing.) Their grain of choice was millet, which tolerated the soil's conditions and also made a nutty brew. The Chinese spiced their beer with herbs, producing a product so popular that local leaders eventually had to pass laws to suppress drunkenness.

In Africa, people harvested millet as well—and sorghum, a grain still used in the production of local beer. The first use of sorghum, around 400 BCE, started south of Lake Victoria in what is now Tanzania and spread farther south as the Bantu speakers continued to look for new fields. Sorghum beer has been continuously brewed in sub-Saharan Africa ever since, in much the same traditional way. The more traditional variety is still brewed by hand using unrefined methods and is sold fresh in local bars, in addition to the large trade in commercial sorghum beer.

In what is now Mexico and Guatemala, the Mayans started making beer out of corn, probably around 150 BCE. Like the other early brewing societies, the Mayans first made a weak beer called *chicha* by adding cornmeal to warm water, but in one of the more remarkable (and perhaps unappetizing) developments, they also discovered that if they chewed the meal first, the resulting beer was stronger. The mouth contains salivary amylase, an enzyme that helps convert starches to sugar; the Mayans were performing a unique method of early malting. Like sorghum beer in Africa, *chicha* didn't die out with the Mayans, and continues to be made in Central and South America.

Those are just some of the main highlights. People across the planet, in what are now Russia, Scandinavia,

ABOVE: *Modern* utwala *beer, a traditional ale of South Africa, is made almost exactly the same as it was thousands of years ago. Unlicensed breweries malt their own grain (which may also include corn) and prepare the beer over the course of two days, adding infusions of flour and boiling the preparation periodically. After a short period of fermentation, the milk-colored, flour-silted beverage is ready to drink.*

Central Europe—pretty much wherever grain was a major staple—made beer. At the early stages of development, the kind of beer people made depended wholly on what grew locally. Wheat, barley, millet, sorghum, and corn defined the beers of the Egyptians, Sumerians, Chinese, Africans, and South Americans respectively. Russian and Scandinavian brewing came later than the first wave, but again, the beer they made was based on their local grain, rye.

The first few thousand years of brewing were fairly uneventful. After brewers figured out malting and mashing, they bumped along making traditional beer. They pretty quickly learned to add herbs and spices to make beer tastier and sometimes they used other sugar sources like fruit and honey to give their beers a bit of kick. But for the most part, brewing remained a domestic chore that people did on a small scale, following the same practices, one generation to the next. ■

BIGGER BREWERIES, SMALL INNOVATIONS

IN EUROPE, things advanced more slowly than they had in Egypt. It would take centuries for beer to reach Egypt's level of organization, and centuries more for beer to finally start to take a modern form. The biggest barrier was decentralization: Until the 700s CE, brewing was a domestic activity, not a commercial one. There were no specialized brewers, just farmers who made beer as one of the many tasks on the annual calendar.

Brewing continued like this from well before the time of Christ until things finally got going in the Middle Ages. In the eighth century, under Charlemagne, monasteries spread across Europe by the hundreds. The monastic life was shaped by a code, the Rule of Saint Benedict, drawn up around the year 529. It was a complete treatise on the spiritual conduct and operation of a monastery, running to seventy-three chapters. Among the

ABOVE: *Workers at the historic Brouwerij Rodenbach in Flanders*

practical effects were monastic self-sufficiency and industriousness (the code also exhorted monks to be cheery). As part of their spiritual practice, monks needed to support themselves, so monasteries managed large farms to grow food—and make wine and beer as well. Furthermore, the Rule encouraged an outward focus of welcoming guests. Monasteries made beer to slake the thirst of their members, but beer also made for a nice offering to visitors. Monks controlled all the stages of production, from maintaining the barley fields on their property to brewing, and consumption of the finished product.

Over time, monasteries became centers of considerable activity. Growing and malting grain and brewing beer met the standard for self-sufficiency, and the beer they made was an important feature of hospitality (particularly given the state of drinking water at the time). Based on blueprints that still survive for a Swiss brewery-monastery, some of these institutions produced more than a thousand barrels of beer a year—a substantial step up in scale from the farmhouse brewery. In order to make such a large volume of palatable beer, monasteries made technical improvements to their equipment and methods. Because of

Stages of Development.

In his book *Beer in the Middle Ages and the Renaissance*, University of British Columbia historian Richard Unger adapted a theory of development that is quite handy in understanding the various stages of European brewing. The first stage was domestic production, done in the home on provisional, seasonal equipment. It was the practice for hundreds of years, from the time of scattered brewing activity a few hundred years BCE until the eighth century CE. This evolved into a similar stage where brewing was still done in the home, but became a professional trade conducted on more permanent equipment by more skilled brewers, usually to supplement family income. During both of these stages, the brewers were women and the work was seen as domestic activity. Women continued to brew at home in a semicommercial arrangement until the nineteenth century—a kind of shadow to official commercial brewing later done by men.

The next stage began when brewers established full-time, stand-alone facilities. This stage was a function of urbanization, when skilled craftsmen gathered together to pool their resources and labor, and was the first wholly commercial stage. It's also when brewing began to gain some social status—which of course is the moment men decided to horn in and displace women. The final stage was manufacturing, when breweries became large-scale enterprises capable of producing a substantial amount of beer for distribution and even export.

One thing to note is that these stages weren't successive; they skipped forward and overlapped, and sometimes even regressed. There might have been major manufacturing happening in a town while a few kilometers out in the countryside, you saw farmhouse production taking place. It's also fascinating to note that with the huge popularity of homebrewing and the recent phenomenon of nanobrewing, all stages are once again active.

their size and regular production, monasteries could make better, more consistent beer than the average farmer. At their peak, six hundred monasteries were brewing beer across Europe. This was the first major advance in brewing in centuries.

There were a number of intersecting societal forces at work, and like so much else in this story, beer played an important role. Laws began to shape the way beer was made toward the end of the tenth century, as the government under the Holy Roman Emperor conceived an ingenious scheme to tax breweries. For millennia, brewers had added crushed herbs and spices—*gruit*—to their beers. According to the new plan, the government would retain the right to sell brewing spice to brewers—functionally, a way of taxing them. Emperor Otto II began to grant the right to collect the tax to loyal nobles or even to towns and this is the context in which the word "gruit" was introduced; the right to provide it was called the *gruit-recht*. Like water rights, once a recipient had gruitrecht, he could lease it out to others. *Gruiters* had their own recipes for gruit mixtures, and brewers were mandated by law to buy spices from these vendors. The law lasted for more than five centuries—well into the age of hops (which, inevitably, prompted the levy of *hoppegeld*, or hop tax). For centuries, then, control of the flavor of beer was dependent on agents who didn't even brew themselves—all as a scheme to support the activities of local government.

Gruit. From the juniper of Finnish *sahti* to the heather of Scottish ale, almost every imaginable flavoring found its way into beer. (One recipe for mum, an obsolete English beer, called for the inner rind of a fir tree. Tasty!) The gruit houses of medieval Europe relied on a more limited range of spices, though. Among those mentioned most often are wild rosemary, laurel leaves, sweet gale or bog myrtle, and yarrow, which is even to this day sometimes called "field hop." Beyond the main ingredients, gruit might have any number of other spices for flavor: ginger, cumin, star anise, marjoram, mint, and sage, to name a few. Other ingredients like laurel and alder bark were sometimes added as preservatives. The proportions were left to the gruiter, who carefully guarded his own personal recipe.

COMMERCIAL BREWING

Commercial brewing began in the eleventh century as people began moving off their farms and into towns. Even though it remained a domestic practice in the countryside, some brewers had begun to specialize and sell beer in communities. In towns, the process of specialization sped up, and independent breweries began to emerge. Much like monastic brewers, commercial breweries got more adept at making consistent beer (though they were also under the jurisdiction of the gruitrecht), grew larger, and began distributing beer around towns and local regions.

In the late seventh or early eighth century, people made the second transformational discovery that would change brewing: that hops could be used as a spice in beer. That is important, because people knew about hops long before anyone thought to put them in beer.

The Roman naturalist Pliny the Elder famously mentioned them in *Naturalis Historia* around the year 78, though he recommended them for their tasty shoots (he called them, charmingly, "Gallic asparagus"). The first definitive mention of their addition to beer comes from 822, in a text by Abbot Adalhard from Corbie, France. The reference was a bit convoluted, but Adalhard was clearly referring to their use in beer. There remains a curious gap in the historical record. After Adalhard wrote about hops, they seem to have vanished from all documentation for another 300 years. They made a triumphant return in the twelfth century, but the intervening period is a black hole. During that time, brewing edged forward on its sleepy pace of growth. Farmhouse breweries were still the rule, but commercial breweries were becoming more common in the cities.

The discovery of hops was significant beyond making beer more delicious. As the Benedictine abbess Hildegard of Bingen noted, they act as a preservative, and this had two important effects. Hops allowed breweries to do more with their recipes, like making stronger beer (without hops, strong beer would turn to vinegar before it was done conditioning). More important, beer that could survive for more than a few days had the capacity to travel. Until the discovery of hops, beer was rooted firmly to the region where it was brewed. After hops, beers were moving across the continent, influencing distant brewers and the beers they made. Not that the process happened overnight—it didn't. People didn't immediately take to the plant's unfamiliar, bitter flavor, and it took centuries for hops to become a standard ingredient. The use of hops was a revolutionary step in fighting infection and spoilage, though, and once hopped beer entered a region, it never left. In the eleventh century, almost no beer was made with hops; a thousand years later, almost no beer is made without them. ∎

Hildegard of Bingen, Hop Mama.

The two names commonly associated with hops are Pliny the Elder, credited with their discovery, and Hildegard of Bingen, credited as the first person to mention their use in beer. Pliny's status complicates the narrative. It's not even clear he was talking about hops when he identified the plant *lupus salictarius*—"wolf of the willows"—and if so, that he was really the first to mention them. Hildegard's status is more straightforward. The abbess of St. Rupertsberg, near Bingen, was a mystic famous enough to remain the subject of modern scholarly interest, and an unlikely candidate for brewing saint. Yet she did in fact write about hops in her classic text on the science of the natural world *Physica Sacra* (an English translation is still in print), both in reference to brewing and with the knowledge that they "keep some putrefaction" from drinks (presumably beer). Of course, while this is all well and good, she was scooped by Adalhard, who mentioned hops in his texts more than 300 years before Hildegard wrote her *Physica*.

THE AGE OF TRADE

HOPS WOULD ULTIMATELY PROVE to be the killer app that transformed beer into a commercial juggernaut. The first success came around 1200 CE from Bremen (located in what is now northwest Germany), a member of the Hanseatic League of trading cities. Just a short boat ride down the Weser River from the North Sea, Bremen was able to take advantage of the preservative quality of hops and begin export. Ideally situated to ship beer across northern Europe, Bremen's product went to Holland, the Baltic countries, and Scandinavia—and became the world's first international beer. Hamburg competed with and eventually surpassed its Hanseatic partner in the 1300s.

Once other brewers saw how well Bremen beer kept, it wasn't long before they began using hops, too. In relative terms, the transition was quick—though it still took decades. Government control of gruit and local tastes were part of the problem, but breweries also weren't sure how to use the new herb and the German breweries were very happy to keep the method to themselves. England was the last country to adopt hops and one of the most resistant (some local officials even banned its use in ale), but by the early 1700s hops had conquered Great Britain, too. Gruit 's day had passed.

Were Gruit Beers Boiled? Beer was not considered a subject worthy of much scholarship in the Dark Ages, and there's very little information about how it was made back then. One intriguing question is whether brewers even bothered to boil wort before the discovery of hops. Why would they? In order to release their bacteria-inhibiting goodness, hops need to be boiled, but boiling isn't necessary to make fermentable wort. So why would early breweries spend the time and money to secure the wood for an unnecessary period of boiling? Even if they did bring wort to a boil to extract more flavor from the gruit, there wouldn't have been any reason to leave it boiling very long.

Once hopped beer opened up distant markets, commercial brewing hit the big time. Larger German breweries were making more than a thousand barrels a year in the 1300s, twice that for the most successful producers. They made different styles of beer for different markets and sent out ships full of nothing but beer. Brewing had become big business, and brewers had become powerful men. With larger systems able to take advantage of efficiencies in production, bigger breweries could make beer more cheaply than smaller ones. These behemoths were able to influence the government, affect taxes (to their benefit), and with their size advantage, spark worries about consolidation. It might seem like a contemporary fear to worry about the power of huge breweries, but even then small brewers of the day were already raising warning flares. In time, beer's success had even pushed the line of traditional wine-drinking Europe south as it established itself in Flanders and Southern Germany, causing all the more worry and anxiety.

By the end of the Middle Ages, beer had become quite a different substance from the one brewed at the beginning. Before the discovery of hops, beer was weak and sweet, and spoiled quickly. Spices helped round the flavor, but they didn't exactly balance it in the way hops, with their unique spicy bitterness, could.

Once brewers mastered hops, they were making stronger, more consistent beer that lasted longer without spoiling. But it also had a totally different character; it was no longer defined by sweetness. There was still enormous variation in local styles from place to place, but the nature of beer had been changed forever. Hops had become an intrinsic flavor that defined beer. ■

INDUSTRIALIZATION

DESPITE THE RELATIVELY sprightly adoption of hops, the pace of evolution was pretty slow in absolute terms over the next few hundred years. There were the Dark Ages to slog through, the Crusades, endless wars, and plagues. But things were about to change. Between 1700 and the late 1800s, a great period of innovation occurred that transformed beer from a rustic, handmade beverage to a chemically stable, laboratory-pure industrial product. It took several hundred years

for the hop revolution to fully flower, but industrialization happened in a breathtaking period that was just eleven decades long.

Beginning in the early eighteenth century, the British picked up where the Hanseatic League had left off and became the world's great beer exporter. Breweries were making strong, heavily hopped beer called Burton that would survive years in casks and was well suited for long journeys across oceans. Porters followed—again, massive, heavy beers designed to last over long periods. The shipping network that sustained the British Empire transported beer all around the world—to Asia, Russia, Australia, and North America.

As the export market grew, so did the London and Burton

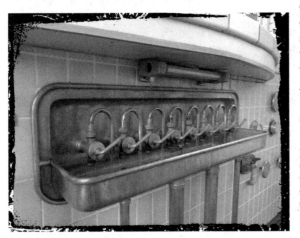

LEFT: *A copper grant at Rochefort. Grants allowed brewers to monitor wort clarity and control flow rate, and helped relieve vacuums from developing during lautering. Outside the Czech Republic, few modern breweries still use grants.*

The Technological Revolution.

The eleven decades between the adoption of the thermometer in the 1760s and refrigeration in the 1870s marked a period of staggering innovation in brewing technology—far surpassing all the advances made in the 8,000 years before. By the end of the period, brewing had become a modern industry, one improved upon in only small increments in the time since. Following is a list of the key inventions and discoveries and how they altered brewing.

■ **THERMOMETER**, circa 1760 (in breweries). Before the thermometer, breweries had no way of consistently reaching the same mash temperature batch after batch and could only gauge liquor temperatures with their bare hands or by assessing the amount of steam. The difference in a few degrees was the difference between a well-made beer and a failure.

■ **HYDROMETER**, circa 1780. The hydrometer allowed a brewer to determine the amount of dissolved sugar in solution, in both wort and finished beer. As a tool, it gave breweries a way of gauging their efficiency and improving their techniques. But it also changed the way breweries made beer. For example, the hydrometer revealed to London breweries how poor brown malt was in the porter-making process and led to the use of pale malts in the grist to improve mashing and fermentation.

■ **STEAM POWER**, circa 1785 (in breweries). Before the Industrial Revolution, breweries had to move water, grain, and barrels around with human- or horsepower alone. Brewers originally adopted steam power as a cost-saving measure, but soon realized that it also allowed them to produce far greater quantities of beer annually. For the first time, breweries were no longer limited to the beer they could sell locally. Industrial-scale breweries churned out porter that traveled around the world, creating an international market. Styles were no longer fixed in place.

■ **ATTEMPERATION**, circa 1800. Throughout brewing history, the summer heat was deadly to cooling and fermenting beer. In Britain, breweries learned that they could "attemperate" (lower the temperature of) wort with cool water. They ran hot wort through small pipes embedded inside larger pipes filled with cold water to bring it down to fermentation temperature in a matter of minutes and to pitch (or add) yeast quickly after boiling.

■ **SPARGING**, circa 1780s to 1850s. At the end of the mash, brewers sprinkle water on the grain bed to flush the wort and rinse the malt—the modern practice of sparging. Until the mid-nineteenth century, breweries conducted several mashes, drawing off successively weaker worts from the same grain bed. It was a laborious, time-consuming process, one much streamlined with the introduction of sparging.

■ **PASTEUR'S TREATISE ON YEAST**, 1857. Although brewers had for centuries understood the mechanism of yeast, prior to Pasteur's work they didn't understand why beer went sour. Not only did he clarify how beer was fermented, he pointed out why lagers typically had fewer problems with spoilage. The effect Pasteur had on brewing was stark and immediate. Lagers, a small minority of all beer prior to his publication, would come to dominate the global market within a few decades.

■ **REFRIGERATION**, 1870s. Heat has always been beer's biggest foe. Attemperation helped breweries master it, and Pasteur explained why controlling it mattered. With the introduction of refrigeration, breweries got yet more control over heat, no longer having to rely exclusively on chill weather, cellars, and blocks of ice.

breweries that supplied it. A big brewery in the 1300s made 2,000 barrels a year. By the mid-1700s, some breweries in London were making more than 50,000 barrels—and that was before the steam engine revolutionized the industry. The British enjoyed such success and renown because they were far ahead of other countries in technical innovation. They were the first to adopt thermometers, hydrometers, steam power, and refrigeration. In each case, these were innovations to the brewing method, and the result was more consistent, stable beer—and that, in turn, led to bigger breweries with greater reach. It gave the British a huge advantage in what was becoming a global market. Porter became an international

phenomenon and was the world's first truly modern beer. After porters, pale beers took hold and, like porters, they began to penetrate foreign markets and influence brewers elsewhere.

The next great international style, pilsner, was indeed a pale—but one brewed according to a different technological lineage. The method of lagering beer had been evolving in Bavaria since—well, no one seems to know for sure. Like the British effort to master temperature through attemperation, lagering—the process of fermenting beer cool and aging it in cool temperatures for weeks or months—gave Bavarian breweries a way to master souring organisms. It probably dates to the 1400s and developed only very slowly as breweries got more and more mastery over their fermentations. What brewers didn't realize at the time was that they were domesticating yeast strains that would perform well in cooler environments.

Every region had slightly different brewing techniques, and lagering was, until the mid-nineteenth century, a quirk of Bohemia and Bavaria. Their beers were dark and popular only regionally. In 1842, however, brewer Josef Groll (a Bavarian) took advantage of lager technology to produce a sparkling, pale beer at the city brewery in Pilsen in Bohemia. Within a few short decades, pilsner would make all previous international styles look like pretenders. The timing

FACING PAGE: *An early steam engine on display at the National Brewery Centre, Burton upon Trent, England*

BELOW: *Automobiles like this antique Palm Beer delivery truck were part of a wave of modernization in early 20th-century Belgian brewing.*

was perfect for one beer style to become a standard. Technological advancements made mass production and distribution possible (via ship and newfangled rail lines), and refrigeration protected beer from spoilage and even the violence of heat on more delicate qualities like hop flavor and aroma.

But most of all, pilsner was a lager. This was significant because fifteen years after Groll's first batch, Louis Pasteur published his studies on the science of fermentation, clarifying the role of yeast in the process. He explained how bad things happened to good beer, and he was a fan of lagering as a way of limiting the ravages of maleficent microorganisms.

This was the final of three groundbreaking discoveries that changed beer forever. Once breweries understood yeast, they quickly worked to produce pure strains. Around the turn of the twentieth century, N. Hjelte Claussen discovered a strain of wild yeast so common in British ales he named it for the country (*Brettanomyces*)—and yet within a very short time British breweries would eliminate wild bacteria and yeasts in their beers. Progress was slower in Belgium, where drinkers enjoyed tart beers, but by midcentury, soured ales would be a fading minority. Meanwhile, lager brewing spread worldwide, as Germans helped set up breweries across Asia and the Americas. Before breweries got a handle on pure yeast cultures, the character of beer had always been threatened by souring organisms—and most ales were at least tinged by acid sourness. Once breweries mastered wild fermentation, they eliminated it from all but a few precincts in northern Germany and Belgium. ∎

WAR, TEMPERANCE, AND CONSOLIDATION

WE HAVE COME 10,000 years or more from those lovely bowls of pre-Sumerian gruel-beer. Ninety-nine percent of history has been written. And yet, a survey of beer from the turn of the twentieth century would reveal a huge diversity of styles. Lager had begun its ascent, but it had barely touched Britain, Belgium, or France. Beer styles were still heavily conditioned by local traditions and preferences. That last one percent of history turned out to be eventful.

Consolidation began by the second half of the nineteenth century and never slowed down. London was home to the first industrial breweries in the eighteenth century, but steam power and technological advances allowed other countries to catch up. Once breweries became adept at producing large volumes of beer, they began snapping up market share. Big breweries could make beer more cheaply than inefficient village breweries, and their beer was usually better and more consistent. Even with population growth, there were only so many barrels of demand in the market, and it went increasingly to the more professional national breweries. Britain had more than 4,000 breweries at the turn of the century, a number reduced to 142 by the mid-1970s.

Had nothing else changed, the twentieth century would have been a time of continued consolidation as electrical grids came online and refrigerated trucks sailed along highways, giving ever bigger breweries the ability to make more and more beer. But things did change—and hugely.

The two events that changed modern history—the World Wars—also changed beer across Europe. The trenches of the First World War were cut across the heart of northern French and western Belgian brewing regions. The German war machine dismantled breweries, and most never recovered in France. During the Second World War, entire cities were turned to rubble—including their breweries. Physical destruction was only a part of the picture. To contend with years of war, European governments put

LEFT: *Cheap supermarket beers like this house-brand bitter from Sainsbury's in the U.K. have done pubs and real ale no favors.*

restrictions on the amount of grain brewers could use—so traditional beers were often destroyed, too. The world left in the late 1940s included far fewer small family breweries, and traditional beer styles vanished by the score. ■

BEER IN AMERICA

NORTH AMERICA FIRST made beer's acquaintance 400 years ago. It arrived in the bellies of British ships, a scurvy-fighting tonic for the long journey across the Atlantic. For the colonists fond of their lovely brown tipples from home, that would remain the revered source of beer for decades. As the new arrivals soon learned, barley didn't grow well in the Virginia or New England colonies. Virginians apparently made beer-ish beverages with corn, potatoes, persimmons, molasses, or whatever they could find that would ferment.

In between those two colonies, a different group had a bit better luck. Dutch immigrants settling in New Amsterdam (we now call it New York) built the first of many breweries on Manhattan in 1612. Breweries in Philadelphia and Baltimore followed later that century. Some of the breweries were successful, and the beer was apparently at least palatable—though everyone acknowledged that Britain's ales remained far superior.

In the early decades of European residence in North America, the best beer was the kind that arrived by boat. The British shipped massive amounts to the colonists there—far more than they ever sent to India or the Baltics. Imports weren't enough, though. Country brewers like George Washington made beer at home for the family and servants—a practice carried over from England. However, all of this was, pardon the pun, small beer: America was a rum and whiskey country.

The statistics are staggering. By 1763, New England alone housed 159 commercial distilleries; there were only 132 breweries in the entire country in 1810. By 1830, the U.S. had 14,000 distilleries; towns tolled a bell at 11:00 a.m. and 4:00 p.m. marking "grog time"; and the per capita rate of consumption was nearly two bottles of liquor a week for every drinking-age adult. Beer either wasn't very good or was an expensive import, and until later in the century it played only a minor role in the young nation's hard-drinking ways.

That changed, gradually, with the influx of German immigrants in the 1840s. They brought with them a knowledge of German lagering techniques, and began opening breweries by the hundreds across the country. For the first time, beer's role—and more specifically, lager's role—in American life started to grow. A few ale breweries managed to survive, but German immigration effectively ended ale's run in the U.S. Whatever vestiges did hang on were destroyed during the great social experiment of Prohibition. In Europe, brewing suffered in the early twentieth century thanks to wars; in the U.S., the suffering was self-inflicted. To get through Prohibition, breweries put out homebrew ingredients or made nonalcoholic malt-based products to compete with soft drinks. In 1900, there were nearly 2,000 breweries operating in the United States; in 1934, there were just 750. By then, lagers controlled the U.S. market and would eventually scrub all memory of ales from the American consciousness.

By the late 1960s, American brewing was no longer a craft—it was an industrial process conducted on a titanic scale. Breweries had learned efficiency, and the entire process was geared toward producing the largest quantity at the lowest price. Niche styles were inefficient. Small regional breweries were inefficient. The logic of industrial-scale brewing led to streamlining. Big companies bought up small breweries—many of which predated Prohibition—and converted their beers to the standard light lager.

The math was obvious: The remaining breweries were as big as battleships and turned out oceans of beer. Gigantism was the standard at every stage of production, from grain and hop deliveries to tun and tank size, from warehouse storage to fleets of delivery trucks. The bigger they got, the more efficient they got, all of which fueled consolidation in an ever-accelerating feedback loop. This efficiency was great on the production side. By the 1970s, consumption and sales were at an all-time high. In 1950, the largest five breweries controlled less than a quarter of the market; by 1980, they controlled three quarters and the total number of breweries had dwindled to fewer than a hundred.

For product offerings, the relentless homogenization was not so great. For one thing, beer drinkers had always been connected to their local breweries. They had always played up local imagery, local customs, even local pride. Resentment

George Washington's "Small Beer" Recipe.

As evidence that brewing was no easy task in colonial America, we have to look no further than the nation's father, who had a house recipe for a substance he generously called "beer." The text below; is taken verbatim; eccentric punctuation and capitalization are Washington's.

TO MAKE SMALL BEER

Take a large Sifter full of Bran Hops to your Taste.—Boil these 3 hours. Then strain out 30 Gallons into a Cooler, put in 3 Gallons Molasses while the Beer is scalding hot or rather drain the molasses into the Cooler & strain the Beer on it while boiling Hot. Let this stand till it is little more than Blood warm. Then put in a quart of Yeast if the weather is very cold, cover it over with a Blanket & let it work in the Cooler 24 hours. Then put it into the Cask—leave the Bung open till it is almost done working—Bottle it that day Week it was Brewed.

Even if we render bran as "malt," this looks like a bathtub version of beer—boozily fueled by lots of molasses. No wonder they liked the imported stuff better.

grew as the little guys got picked off, one after another. But more important, with each new acquisition the beer landscape got blander and more boring. Surveying the American scene at the time, writer Michael Jackson described the beery tableau this way: "They are pale lager beers vaguely of the pilsener style but lighter in body, notably lacking hop character, and generally bland in palate. They do not all taste exactly the same but the differences between them are often of minor consequence."

Fortunately, markets abhor a vacuum. The massive sales figures belied a growing discontent among a committed niche of beer drinkers. Over the course of the 1970s, a rebellion started to take shape. It included those who had traveled to Europe and tasted amazing, exotic beers and wished they were more available in the U.S. Many took up homebrewing. A few others wondered about trying to bring the tasty European beers back to the U.S. and sell them there. And a few especially romantic people tried to figure out how to start commercial breweries to make decent beers themselves.

In time, interest reached critical mass—enough to create an alternative market to the canned industrial product most Americans had come to know as beer. Homebrewers got organized and lobbied to have their hobby legalized. Fans of imported beer set up the first specialty importers or founded British-style pubs to stock those beers. Then, from 1976 to '78, three key events helped the disparate pieces coalesce: Jack McAuliffe founded America's first startup microbrewery, New Albion; Michael Jackson published his groundbreaking *World Guide to Beer*; and Jimmy Carter signed a law that legalized homebrewing. It was a tipping point that led to the first wave of new brewery openings since Prohibition.

It is difficult to imagine the situation those first craft brewers confronted. These days, if you want to start a brewery, the blueprint is easy enough to follow. Breweries are a relatively safe investment, and banks are willing to lend money. Metal fabricators make beautiful new equipment to brewery specs—and the growth in craft brewing means it's always possible to find a used system discarded by an expanding brewery. Educated, experienced brewers enter the market every year. Malt and hop companies work closely with craft breweries and will offer stock in tiny quantities. Most important, the market is substantial and growing, always thirsty for new beers. Small breweries are good business.

That was decidedly not the case in 1976. Craft breweries were tiny cogs trying to fit into the gears of a gigantic brewing industry. Banks wouldn't loan them money and manufacturers didn't make small-scale equipment. Malt companies dealt in volumes equal to train cars, not grain sacks. Distributors weren't prepared to mess with the odd keg or case of beer. Early brewers had to cobble together brewhouses out of scavenged equipment, borrow money from family members, and beg distributors to take them on. Very often, they had to appeal to state legislatures to change laws so they could even operate in the first place.

It took a long time for "microbrewing" to become a viable business model. The mortality rate for those first breweries was high. It had literally been generations since Americans had seen anything other than light lagers, so the craft brewers had to try to educate consumers as well as sell to them. By the mid-1990s, though, things finally started to change. Ales no longer seemed so alien to Americans, and millions were developing a taste for strong, flavorful beers. Craft brewing started growing, and has since posted annual growth every year for the past decade—even during the terrible economic downturn of 2008 to 2010. ∎

CRAFT BREWING RENAISSANCE

THE TRENDS THAT led to a monoculture of style and a bland, lowest-common-denominator product were not unique to beer. Cuisine suffered as we learned to buy vegetables in cans and meats in the freezer aisle. There was a whiz-bang element to industrialization that wowed us, and the convenience was nice, too. They are no substitute for taste, though, and eventually, there was a countertrend in brewing.

It started in the United States and Britain, two of the countries most ravaged by consolidation. By the mid-1980s, both countries had doubled their brewery counts as a small army of new brewers entered the market to counter the blandification of beer with stronger, more characterful "craft beer." The phenomenon spread to other brewing countries that were reaching their brewery diversity nadir in the 1990s. Those that fell the farthest rebounded the most impressively—Scandinavia and France boomed, and Italy, never known for its beer, has blossomed as a world leader in craft brewing. Established countries like Germany and Belgium have grown more slowly, but they have their own craft brewing movements. Canada, Spain, Brazil, New Zealand, and Japan are all getting in on the act. Added together, the number of breweries now has at least trebled from its lowest point.

Industrial-scale brewing is with us forever. Yet after just a few decades, some of those formerly small craft breweries have gotten quite big. The exciting prospect looking forward is that industrial beer may not always *taste* industrial. Large American breweries have been experimenting with "faux craft" beer for decades, and the Blue Moon and Shock Top lines are now among the biggest sellers in the craft segment. While this worries some discerning drinkers, they're still a massive step up from Bud Light, the nation's bestselling beer. This appears to be true across the globe, and some countries, like England, are hoping for an ale renaissance.

The market is not good at protecting monoculture. People like variety, and the long period of dominance by a single style was an aberration in beer's 10,000-year history. Tasty, complex beer will be around as long as there are people willing to buy it—and there are a surprising number of them. While it's true that craft beer makes up only a small segment of the total market, that doesn't correlate to a small number of drinkers. In 2010, a market research company surveyed consumers and found that 59 percent of American beer drinkers drink craft-brewed beer at least occasionally. More important, half of those surveyed said they would drink even more craft beer if they knew more about it. As the market grows and expands, they will.

As a coda to beer's history, let us finish where we started: evolution. Beer is never a settled matter, and beer styles never live forever. As craft brewing has revived interest in taste and variety, we're seeing preferences diverge country to country. Americans have developed a love affair with hops, so that nearly any style can be reinterpreted as an IPA, including, strangely, "black IPA." (Is there any other way to explain a black pale ale?) Britons, meanwhile, are still mad for a pint of session ale, though now that means more than just bitter. Germans are not about

to forsake their accomplished lagers, but they are changing them. Italians have engineered hybrid beers meant to be drunk with good food, while France leans toward elegant, refined ales (at the same time keeping their eyes on the dinner table). And of course, they're all influencing each other. Belgians are making hoppy beers, and Americans are making Belgian ales. The French are making cask ale, and the British are discovering craft lager. These trends get fed back into the cultural mill, shifting and mutating until they've created something yet again different and new. We can't know what beer will taste like in fifty years except to say this: It won't taste like it does now. ∎

The Effect of Laws on Brewing.

It would be difficult to say what affected the development of beer styles most, but local laws are surely in the conversation. The very first taxes involved the practice of government agents selling gruit, effectively a tax on ingredients—and this was a common category of law. The "German purity law" (*Reinheitsgebot*) is another, and the most famous. It was actually a Bavarian law—an important distinction because in the north, brewers made strange beers with spices, honey, and wheat. Indeed, it only applied to barley beers in Bavaria (the famous weizens were brewed under ducal exemption), and was also more a tax than a food-safety regulation.

Taxes have always been the main way government interacted with breweries, and how they levied their fees has had profound effects on what kinds of beer got made. In Britain, beer is taxed based on its alcohol content, resulting in various beers having appreciably different prices at the pub. It is little surprise that low-alcohol beers have long been favorites of both drinkers and brewers there. In Belgium, brewers were taxed on the size of their mash tuns—a bizarre system that resulted in small mash tuns no matter how much beer a brewery made. To get a lot of beer out a tiny tun requires ingenuity and elbow grease, and the old methods are still evident in the way lambics are made.

The absence of laws in an area was no less an influence on beers than their presence—especially when brewers were competing with their neighbors who had to adhere to more stringent regulations. Take the case of the small town of Hoegaarden, in Belgium. It fell outside the jurisdiction (or notice) of the taxmen of Liège, and as a consequence became a huge brewing center, exporting tens of thousands of barrels of tax-free beer in the sixteenth century.

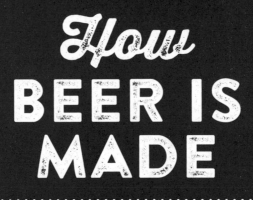

How
BEER IS
MADE

I f there's any lesson at all in the manufacture of gruel-beer, it's that beer must be easy to make. It is. Of course, as the long history of beer demonstrates, making good beer is a different matter entirely. Nevertheless, the process hasn't changed a great deal since it began. Modern commercial malting and brewing employs a lot of technology to ensure consistency and precision in the process, but brewers still go through the same basic steps. A medieval brewer visiting a twenty-first-century brewery might be confused by the computers and electronics, but the tuns, kettles, and vats would all be instantly recognizable.

Making beer always starts with the grain and hops and other adjuncts. A recipe may be made with as few as four ingredients or as many as a dozen or more. Employing these building blocks involves the same basic method whether the brewer is using a five-gallon home setup or working in thousand-barrel batches. Depending on the style, the beer will be handled differently, but in the end it's all just variations on a theme. Even with the use of computers and sophisticated mechanics, brewing beer remains an elegantly straightforward process. ∎

THE CRITICAL FOUR

NO MATTER HOW complex the recipe, beer is made up of four basic elements: a solution (**water**), a source of sugars (**grain**, either alone or with fruit or raw sugar), and **spice** (usually, but not always, hops). **Yeast**, the fourth, is the agent of fermentation.

In a nutshell, here's how everything works together: Malted grains are steeped in water to make them edible to the yeast that will be added later. This creates a sweet tea known as "wort" (rhymes with shirt) that's rich in simple sugars. Yeast would happily dive into the wort and make beer, but the result would be as sticky and sweet as honey. So brewers bring the wort to a boil and add spices to offset the sweetness of the malt. (Beer drinkers of the Dark Ages enjoyed good health not because beer was inherently wholesome—though that goes without saying—but because the process of boiling it killed all the deadly bacteria often found in the water.) Finally, brewers cool the beer down and add yeast, which does the rest, turning sugars into alcohol, and wort into beer. In most modern beers, the recipe employs barley, hops, water, and yeast; a sizable minority use other malts, sugars, fruits, and spices in addition to these basic ingredients. ■

HOW SWEET IT IS

SUGARS FERMENT EASILY. They are predisposed to fermentation, and yeasts crowd around, waiting for the opportunity to strike. The process is so natural that ripe fruit will ferment while still hanging on the tree. Monkeys know this, and look for "alcohol plumes" that alert them to boozy fruit. The result, even in its still-on-the-vine form, is considered a wine—though humans have refined the process considerably. When grains provide the fermentable sugars, we call the resulting beverage a beer.

RIGHT: *Sacks of grain patiently await the start of the brewing process.*

Grain is, beyond a source of sugar, the body of a beer, offering the flavor and aroma that characterize its nature. Beer

has been called "liquid bread," and anyone who has swirled it around her mouth knows exactly why. A beer may start with a whiff of wheat or barley and continue along with the homey, familiar flavors of cracker, biscuit, or cookie. Sometimes more exotic grains round out the flavor—the spice of rye, the creaminess of oats. Without grain, you don't have a recognizable beer.

Malt is the principal source of fermentable sugars in beer. It's a little different from grain, though the words are often used interchangeably. Unlike fruit, raw grains won't ferment well—their sugars, which start out as carbohydrates and proteins, are too rough and indigestible for yeast to eat. The grain must be malted first, a process of awakening the seeds so they begin to sprout. This creates chemical changes in the grain that convert the carbohydrates into simple sugars that make a tasty meal for yeast.

Beyond the flavors and aromas grains contribute, they offer these other essential elements.

■ **Fermentable sugars.** The sugars and carbohydrates that yeasts consider edible start out locked up inside the seed of the grain, stored there until they're called on to nurture the shoots of a new plant. Grain needs to be malted first—a process that converts proteins and carbohydrates into fermentable sugar.

■ **Color.** In preparation for brewing, malt is kilned and roasted. Unmalted grains may also be roasted. This imparts a color, ranging from straw to jet, and that color is in turn imparted to the beer.

■ **Body and mouthfeel.** Beer is thicker than water—sometimes much more so. This is known as "body," and it comes from unfermented proteins and caramelized sugars that the yeast couldn't convert to alcohol. The caramelized sugars, dextrines, are often intentionally left in—some malts are rich in them—and they increase a beer's viscosity.

Two-Row Versus Six-Row.

Barley comes in many varieties, but the two most common categories are two-row and six-row. Both are used in brewing. The number refers to the way the kernels cluster around the center stalk (not, as some people assume, how the grain is planted in the field). In two-row, the kernels grow on either side of the stalk; in six-row, they circle it like petals on a flower.

Two-row barley is generally favored for base malts because the kernels are plumper—the way they grow on the stalk gives them more room to spread out—and offer the greatest amount of carbohydrates for yeasts to work with during fermentation.

Because of its higher protein content, six-row barley browns more easily. This makes specialty malts taste slightly different when made with six-row barley—a flavor preferred by some breweries. Six-row is also used in darkly malted roasts where carbohydrate yield is irrelevant and where flavors and colors are the same for both types of barley.

RIGHT: *A mash tun at Brewery Dubuisson in Pipaix, Belgium*

■ **Protein.** In addition to adding body and mouthfeel, protein interacts with the natural carbonation in beer and is responsible for the head. Other alcoholic beverages—cider and Champagne, for example—also bubble up when they're poured, but lacking protein, they can't maintain the glamorous head that tops a fresh pint of beer.

Kilning (drying) and roasting are the final stages, and they play an important role in the flavor and aroma of a finished beer. Much as coffee can be roasted lightly or to an oily, midnight black to create different kinds of flavors, so malt can be roasted to different levels. As with coffee, roasting affects the flavor—but to an even greater degree. Some light roasts produce a warm toastiness, others a sweeter hint of dark fruit, and some a French roast–like bitterness. Some malts, known as "base malts," are kilned at relatively low temperatures and emerge a very pale color. Specialty malts are dried for longer periods of time and then roasted. When a brewer assembles a recipe, he uses a selection of malts in the "grain bill" that will provide color, aroma, and flavor specific to style.

THE GRAIN BILL

Designing a grain bill for a beer is like creating the recipe for a cake. Whether you're making a white cake or a chocolate cake, the main ingredient is flour. In a grain bill, base malts are the main ingredient. These pale malts are the foundation of any beer; they're loaded with simple sugars and enzymes that will convert easily to alcohol. Even in the darkest beers, the majority of malt will be base malt—just like flour forms the basis of even the darkest chocolate cake.

Another important category are the crystal or caramel malts. This class of malts is created by roasting still-moist grain *before* kiln-drying it. During the process, sugars caramelize. The resulting malt is brittle and crumbly; the sugars, which form longer chains during caramelization, can't be consumed by yeast and so are used to enhance body. True to its name, caramel malt contributes a pronounced toffee flavor; in larger amounts, it produces dark fruit notes; and in unbalanced proportions, it will lend the beer unwanted tannins. Once crystallized, these malts are roasted and may be quite light for use in pale ales, or very dark for use in darker ales.

Next are the dark malts used in schwarzbiers, stouts, and porters, and specialty malts that accent different styles. Dark malts add color, but their

THE MALTS AND THEIR CHARACTER

PILSNER	The lightest malt available. Imparts a slight flavor—sweet and gently grain-y. Despite the name, pilsner malt can be used in any style of beer.
PALE	Kilned slightly darker than pilsner, pale malt gives the beer a more bready flavor; typically used in ales.
VIENNA	Slightly darker than pale malt; used to produce light amber beers like bock and Oktoberfest.
MUNICH	Roughly twice as dark as Vienna, with an amber hue that heads toward red. It is prized for its rich, caramel flavor with hints of toast and nuts.
CARAMEL/ CRYSTAL	This category of malts includes examples that are quite light (for use in pale ales), medium, or almost brown (for use in darker ales).
CHOCOLATE	Used in porters and stouts; when combined with lighter, sweeter malts, its gentle bitterness can indeed closely resemble cacao.
BLACK MALT	Akin to espresso: intense bitter flavor, sometimes even charred. Adds depth and complexity to a beer as well as balancing sweeter malts in high-gravity recipes.
ROASTED BARLEY	Used primarily in stouts, it provides the deep, roasted flavor that characterizes Irish stouts like Guinness.
WHEAT	In some styles, the protein in wheat stays in suspension and clouds a beer, and works with certain yeasts to produce banana and clove flavors.
RYE	Rye thrives in poor soil, so its use in both bread and beer has been concentrated in colder, harsher regions. Finns and Russians used it to make their traditional beers, sahti and kvass.
OATS	Oats are used to enhance a beer's texture, creating a silky, creamy quality that works well in both stouts and pale ales.

effect on flavor varies. Some add roasti-ness, some sweetness, others coffee-like bitterness. Specialty malts contribute accent notes that fill out the flavor of a beer—a touch of honey, toast, or smoke.

Finally, malts from grains other than barley are occasionally used to give a beer different character. Wheat can be used as a base malt and adds a soft, bready flavor as in weizens and witbiers. Rye is a versatile grain that can add an earthy spiciness to darker beers or a spritzy, minty freshness to light beers. Unmalted roasted barley, used primarily in stouts, contributes less of the coffee-like sharpness of black malt; instead, the character is more rootlike and sour. Oats add body and mouthfeel, while corn and rice, used mainly in industrial lagers, lighten the body of a beer without adding much flavor.

OTHER SUGARS

Sugar in your beer? In Belgium and England, brewers regularly and proudly use it—many styles can't be made without added sugar. But in Germany, using sugar is absolutely verboten; this appears to be an almost moral issue with brewers there. Americans also hold a mild prejudice, associating the use of sugar with industrial lager production. Yet as people become more aware of the full range of beer styles, old biases are starting to die out. (Well, not in Germany.)

Sugar performs two roles in beer: It boosts alcohol, and adds flavor. Unlike malt, which never fully ferments out, sugar converts almost entirely to alcohol. This is useful for brewers who want to increase alcohol without adding body. Brewers use sugar to make tripels, for example, which rise to 8 to 9% alcohol but remain light-bodied. Compare these to all-malt barley wines of roughly the same strength; these beers are so dense and viscous their mouthfeel is as rich as a mocha's.

Brewers commonly use refined sugar (sucrose) to boost alcohol strength. In Belgium, brewers once used "candi" sugar, a form of sucrose crystallized into lumps like hard candy. Now almost all use sugar syrup, another form of sucrose. When Belgians use dark candy sugar, this is a caramelized form of sucrose that adds both color and a bit of caramel flavor. Caramel sugar is also a traditional ingredient in British ales, notably mild ales, used for the same reason. The British also use invert sugar, a variant of sucrose, wherein the constituent parts of glucose and fructose have been chemically split in two. Some breweries believe invert sugar is easier for yeast to ferment than straight sucrose.

Finally, brewers occasionally use less-refined sugars to add flavor as well as alcohol to their beer. Molasses, maple syrup, brown sugar, and honey all provide fermentables for yeast to munch on, but each also leaves traces of its distinctive flavor after fermentation. ■

A DASH OF SPICE

MAN CANNOT LIVE by bread alone, and neither can beer be made solely with malt. The very sugars that make grain the body of beer also make it overly sweet; a beer is not complete without spices to balance the malt, to scent it and bring it alive. Hops now perform this role in most beers, but it wasn't always so. Their regular use in beer is less than a millennium old; before that, brewers used a dazzling variety of other spices—as always, based on what was available locally.

Archaeologists have been most useful in documenting old recipes. By scraping residue from the inside of pots, they have been able to identify the grains and spices brewers used in the earliest beers. From these reports, we know that the Egyptians used coriander, the Chinese chrysanthemums, Scots favored heather and meadowsweet (a perennial herb in the rose family), and throughout Scandinavia brewers spiced their beer with juniper and sweet gale. It's safe to say that nearly every herb and root used in cooking has at one time or another been thrown into a brew kettle.

Spiced ales continued well after brewers began using hops, and this oft-quoted recipe from John Houghton in 1683 attests to the diversity of spices brewers once added to beer.

> To produce 42 gallons of mum start with seven bushels of wheat malt, one bushel of oat malt, and one bushel of beans. Once fermentation begins thirteen flavorings are added, including three pounds of the inner rind of a fir tree; one pound each of fir and birch tree tips; three handfuls of *'Carduus Benedictus,'* or blessed thistle; two handfuls of 'flowers of the *Rosa Solis'* or sundew; the insect eating bogplant, which has a bitter, caustic taste; elderflower; betony; wild thyme; cardamom; and pennyroyal.

Eventually, of course, hops were discovered. Much of the credit for hops goes to the Roman naturalist Pliny the Elder, said to have first named them—though this account is disputed. In any case, the first documented use of hops as a beer ingredient didn't come until 822, when an abbot in Northern France mentioned them in a manual of abbey rules. It took hundreds of years for hops to catch on—they tasted weird and were hard to use—but ultimately, recognition of their antibacterial properties led to their adoption. Other spices may have tasted good, but they couldn't match the preservative quality of *Humulus lupulus*.

HOPS

In common language, hops are the cones that form on female hop vines. (Technically, they're actually strobiles, not cones, which is their informal name, and bines, not vines—bines climb by encircling a vertical object, while vines send out tendrils to latch on.) They are remarkably energetic herbaceous perennials that can grow a foot a day and cover entire trees in the wild—but only in certain conditions. Hops require

European Skunks. Many people are familiar with the "skunky" aroma of many European beers—sometimes thinking this is the house character of those beers. It's not. Beer takes on a skunky flavor when exposed to light, a chemical reaction resulting from the decomposition of certain chemical compounds in the hop's isohumulones. The offending compounds are so strong humans can detect them in parts per billion. When it happens, a beer is said to be "lightstruck."

The main culprits are the green bottles many European breweries use, which are more light permeable. It is possible to purchase a hop distillate immune to becoming lightstruck—that's what American breweries use for their clear-bottle-packaged lagers—but the distillate lacks the character of fresh hops. For beer protection, brown bottles are better, and cans and kegs better still.

THE ANATOMY OF A HOP

BRACTEOLES: Leaves that protect the cone and provide additional oil and resin, as well as tannins and polyphenols.

LUPULIN GLANDS: Sticky yellow clusters that contain the essential oils and resins responsible for aroma and bitterness in beer.

STRIG: The cone-length stem from which bracteoles grow.

at least fifteen hours of daylight and therefore can only be grown between 35 and 55 degrees latitude. They do better in drier climates, but require a lot of water; hops are also subject to a number of diseases and infestations. As a consequence, commercial production is isolated in just a few regions—over 85 percent of the world's output is grown in Germany, the U.S., China, and the Czech Republic. In the United States, nearly all commercial hops are grown in the Northwest. The newest region to excite beer fans is the southern hop band in Australia and especially New Zealand.

In beer, hops are no ordinary spice. Through the alchemy of the brewing process, their acids are transmuted to what humans perceive as bitterness. Beyond bitterness, brewers can harness them to produce flavors of mango in one beer or black pepper in another; hops can scent a beer with the freshness of pine or the softness of jasmine. It is no wonder that they have replaced other spices, nor that they have beguiled so many beer drinkers; their character is so mutable that just by changing a single hop in a recipe—or by changing the moment the same hops are added to the boil—a beer's nature can be transformed.

HOP ELEMENTS

So what's in a hop that allows it to express such personality? The hop cone looks a bit like a papery, green pinecone, but under each petal are not seeds but globules of yellow resin called lupulin. The resin is where important acids and essential oils are located—those elements responsible for all the flavors and aromas hops contribute. The central function of the hop, bittering, comes from a group of five acids collectively called alpha acids or humulones. In their native form, alpha acids are insoluble. In order to unlock their bittering potential, they have to go through a chemical change.

TOP: *Core samples taken from the center of hop bales*

BOTTOM: *Brewers at Fuller's select hops for the coming year.*

"Noble" Hops.

Among the best-regarded hops are four that claim regal heritage: German Mittelfrüh from the Hallertau region; Spalt Spalter south of Nuremburg; Tettnanger, which take their name from the region around Tettnang; and Saaz or Žatec from Bohemia. Collectively, they came to be known as "noble" hops for that most ignoble of reasons: because that's what the salesmen started calling them in the 1980s.

They are widely considered outstanding hops, however, and their gentle, balanced qualities were thought to account for this. Other hops with similar qualities tried to join the club (Fuggle and East Kent Golding) with more or less success; partisans of the original nobles were reluctant to expand membership.

But over time, other excellent hybrids emerged that didn't have the same configuration of acids and oils. As time has gone on and research tells us more about hop chemistry, the "noble" designation seems like a relic of an earlier age. In the democratic scrum of the modern hop market, the old nobility hold on to their titles more out of ceremony than need. They are great hops, but now they have lots of company.

Hop Terroir. In winemaking, the concept of *terroir* is used to discuss the natural environment that produces the grape—the soil and climate of the vineyard. Brewers have less concern for terroir—they can make adjustments for water and grain variation, effectively removing environmental variables from the calculation.

Hops, on the other hand, seem very sensitive to terroir. Several famous varieties are associated with their small regions of origin, and in turn define certain styles or families of beers. Interestingly, when rhizomes of these very plants are moved to other regions, the hops they produce don't taste the same. Something about the soil, the quality of sun, the summer temperature, and the length of days makes an American-grown East Kent Golding taste different from one from East Kent. So for a truly authentic-tasting pilsner, brewers can't use locally grown Saaz; they must go to the source.

Boiling them causes this change (called isomerization), but it takes a long time. The longer the hops bob in boiling wort, the more bitterness they'll produce. Alpha acids are present in different levels in each hop type, ranging from 1 to 20 percent, so each variety has a different maximum potential for producing bitterness.

Another class of bittering agents in hops are beta acids. Unlike alpha acids, beta acids are immediately soluble in wort, but behave differently in finished beer. Isomerized alpha acids slowly lose their bittering capacity, but beta acids oxidize with time, growing in intensity and contributing a different quality of bitterness to aged beers.

Hops also contain essential oils, the compounds so important to the aroma and flavor of the beer. Of lupulin's entire makeup, just a tiny proportion—1 to 4 percent—is essential oils. Yet these oils exert a mighty influence on the way a hop smells and tastes. Brewers will often hand-select their hops from dealers, rubbing them together to burst the lupulin and expose the essential oils. What they glean from the scent comes primarily from a mixture of four oils: myrcene, farnesene, caryophyllene, and humulene, usually accounting

RIGHT: *After drying, hops are baled and stored at near-freezing temperatures to preserve their delicate oils and acids.*

RIGHT: *"Dwarf" or "hedgerow" hops only grow to eight feet, and can be harvested so the bines are left intact. The result, some researchers believe, are hardier, healthier plants.*

LEFT: *Dr. David Gent of the USDA stands in front of experimental fields of pesticide-free hops that employ varying techniques to control pests and blight.*

for 80 to 90 percent of the total. These four are also present in other botanicals, and it is tempting to make associations between those spices and the aromas we find in hops. Myrcene is found in bay leaves, thyme, and ylang-ylang; farnesene in gardenias; caryophyllene in cloves, rosemary, and black pepper; and humulene in *Cannabis sativa* (that is, marijuana), to which hops are closely related.

But here comes the mystery. These oils are volatile, and they are easily driven off. When hops are added early to the boil, very little of the oils survive. Even later additions, from which their characteristic flavor and aroma are drawn, are just as lethal. These oils remain only when a beer is dry-hopped, and yet their character is clearly present even when

they are added fairly early during the boil. The aroma that rises from the crushed hops in a brewer's hand is similar to the aroma that rises from a pint glass (sometimes: "rubbings" are not an exact science)—even after those volatile oils have been subjected to boiling wort and active yeasts. So how does the character survive when the oils do not? This is a mystery that scientists have yet to decode. Hops contain more than 400 aroma compounds, and some of them survive the boil and are unlocked during fermentation. There are even a few compounds that aren't released until they're worked on by the enzymes in the mouth. It's a very tricky matter, this hop aroma and flavor business, and we have lots more to learn about how it works.

HOP TYPES AND USES

Like any spice, hops contribute different qualities depending on variety and method of use. The earlier hops are added in the brewing process, the more bitterness they contribute; the later they are added, the more aroma. Somewhere in between they start adding interesting fruity-tasting compounds and other flavor elements, a process that continues along through fermentation. Because of their chemistry, hops are generally grouped by type: aroma or bittering. Hops useful for bittering should produce a clean, sharp flavor without harshness. Aroma hops provide distinctive scents full of floral, peppery, or citrus notes. Brewers tend to use high-alpha hops to bitter a beer (because of the alpha acid content, it means they don't have to use as many pounds of hops), and lower-alpha hops for aroma, but this isn't always true. Where hops are concerned, "bittering" and "aroma" are general categories.

Not all hops are used in whole form. Because whole hops have a great deal of surface area, they are the least stable form and most subject to degradation during storage. Many breweries use hop pellets instead; these are made by crushing whole hops into a powder and molding them into beads the size and shape of a pencil eraser. In most cases, pellets are more stable than whole hops, but some breweries believe the process of crushing changes the way they are converted during the boil. (Despite the ardor of their partisans, there's no evidence either form is superior.) Pellets and whole hops are used interchangeably in the brewing process, and many brewers use both depending on the situation. Among nonindustrial breweries, only a small minority use hop extract, a product that contributes a somewhat different quality; even more rare are hop oils, used to enhance aroma.

A recent list of hop types included more than 100 varieties from around the world, including several rare and new ones. Yet it surely understates the total, which expands by the year. Learning to recognize hop types isn't critical in beer appreciation, but it can help one isolate examples to pursue or avoid. The Appendix contains a list of major hop varieties with descriptions of their flavor and aroma.

FRESH HOPS

Immediately after harvest, hops are quickly dried before packaging. Drying and cooling stabilizes the hop components, but it also changes them. Because dried hops are the standard, all the information breweries use when creating recipes—oil amounts, acid levels—has been based on dried hops. When we talk about brewing hops, we're talking about dried hops.

About twenty years ago, English and American breweries began experimenting with hops fresh from the bine. In order to capture the most evanescent volatile elements, brewers collect hops from the fields and race them back to waiting kettles. The length of time between picking and brewing is never more than a few hours. The products of this process are known as "fresh-hop" or "wet-hop" beers, and they smell and taste quite a bit different from their regular hop cousins. The Pacific Northwest, where most of the nation's commercial hop fields are located, has a decided advantage in making these beers. Many are produced for draft sales, but a few, like Deschutes Hop Trip and

ABOVE: *A pantry's worth of spices—like this sampling from Brewery Ommegang—can be used in brewing.*

OTHER SPICES

Hops are not likely to be displaced anytime soon as the spice of choice in beer, but they weren't always the only option. Before hops came into widespread usage, brewers used local ingredients like juniper berries, heather, sweet gale, or yarrow. A few traditional beers are still made in the old way (Finland's Lammin Sahti with juniper is a good example). Revivals like Williams Brothers Fraoch Heather Ale from Scotland, Jopen Koyt [Gruit] beer from the Netherlands (a mixture of herbs), and France's Lancelot Bonnet Rouge, with elderberries, are some examples. American craft breweries have concocted New World unhopped ales with other spices, as well.

Far more common is the use of spice to enhance hopped beer. While the rest of the world catches up, Belgium's breweries continue to use spices even after they adopted hops hundreds of years ago. It is so common that Belgian breweries often don't mention it (did you know that Rochefort adds a dash of coriander?), leaving drinkers to wonder if that black pepper note comes from the spice or is a product of fermentation. Belgians regularly add orange peel, hibiscus, dandelion, paradise seeds, ginger, and cumin—to name just a few.

British brewers once had nearly the same affinity for adjuncts, putting everything from licorice and rosehips to oysters and spruce tips into their beer. The practice was very common until two or three hundred years ago when laws changed to regularize brewing

Rogue Wet Hop Ale, are sent farther afield in bottles.

Wet hops are unpredictable. They don't uniformly produce fresher, more vibrant versions of their dried selves. Some do, but the acids and oils exhibit their character capriciously. In others, the hop produces different flavors from those expected, and in some unfortunate examples, they result in very unpleasant flavors. (I've tried fresh-hopped Hallertauers—that famous "noble" hop— that tasted like sour beef. Sauerbraten is lovely with a nice amber lager; it is less so *in* an amber lager.)

So far, researchers haven't looked into how wet and dry hops affect beer differently. In research on other herbs like oregano and peppermint, scientists have found sharply differing levels of oils and acids. Interestingly, the differences weren't consistent across herbs, so it's not clear whether hops all behave the same way, either. Perhaps this is why some varieties lend themselves to wet hopping while others do not.

How Much Is Enough? The average brewery takes eight gallons of water to produce a single gallon of beer. For larger breweries, this can mean running through millions of gallons of water a year. Efficiencies can cut water use in half, but tuns, kettles, and tanks will always need to be cleaned out. As the planet warms, water availability—more than water quality—may one day dictate where breweries can be located. Craft breweries are on the leading edge of water and energy conservation, and some have cut that ratio down as far as 2:1.

ingredients, and trailed off substantially after the world wars.

With the rise of craft brewing, new breweries have taken up old practices, and now spiced ales are common. Many of the old spices have been rediscovered, including vanilla, elderberries, cinnamon, lavender, star anise, chamomile, sarsaparilla, cardamom, sweet gale, ginger, mugwort, and yarrow. Beyond tradition, modern breweries have experimented widely, adding things like tea, coffee, chocolate, chile peppers, and even exotica like cactus, persimmon, and palm nut. One of the more memorable beers I've tried came about when a brewer, inspired by a branch from an evergreen in his backyard, decided to cut it off, needles and all. He threw it into a porter, to surprisingly successful effect. If a brewer has been enchanted by an ingredient, he's probably tried to brew with it. ■

WATER'S THE SOLUTION

IN TWENTY-FIRST-CENTURY **BREWING,** the quality and composition of water is of little concern to breweries; they can easily adjust its pH and compensate for the presence of unwanted minerals. Water is now effectively just a blank canvas for the colorful play of malt and hops.

This wasn't always the case. Until they mastered chemistry in the twentieth century, brewers were at the mercy of their local water source. It was a definitive ingredient, and the most fixed. While hops and barley could travel a few miles, water was difficult to transport, so breweries were sited to take advantage of rivers, springs, or deep wells. Brewing consumes huge amounts of water, so the source had to be bountiful and reliable. But because it was fixed and immutable, local water exerted an unseen force on the beers made with it. Some water had lots of minerals, others had very little—and these conditions dictated that certain styles would be more successful than others. Stouts may have been a good fit for the chill, dreary rain of Dublin, but it was the water, not the

Discovering Yeast. For centuries, brewers regarded fermentation with wonder, attributing it variously to God or magic. The roiling tuns seemed to be enchanted—or perhaps imbued with the Holy Spirit. (Brewing has long been a monastic pursuit.) Amazingly, yeast wasn't actually identified until the 1800s. Before then, brewers had only the general sense that the dregs from the last batch, when dumped into a freshly brewed wort, made the resulting beer less harsh and vinegary. Brewers domesticated yeast without ever knowing exactly what it was.

It was Louis Pasteur who finally identified yeasts as living organisms in 1857, but yeast science really didn't get rolling until nearly the dawn of the twentieth century. For example, it was only in 1903 that Carlsberg Laboratory discovered that what made English beers funky at the time was the presence of a wild yeast strain, *Brettanomyces.* (Interestingly, it's now absent from English beers, and associated with Belgian ones instead.) This was surprisingly late in the game—by this time, breweries were already refrigerating and shipping their beer on rail lines.

weather, that made the style successful. Likewise, the pilsners of Pilsen, the pale ales of Burton, and the amber lagers of Vienna.

The reason is chemistry—and this also explains why water is now relatively unimportant in the brewing process. When a beer is in the mashing phase, the pH of the beer will dictate what elements are drawn from the malt. Dublin has a lot of bicarbonate in its water, making it hard and alkaline. This draws the tannins from the grain husks. When Irish breweries used a mash made solely of pale malts, the hard water produced a harsh beer. The addition of acidic roasted malts, however, balanced the mash, bringing it into more appropriate pH. Voilà!—fantastic Dublin stout.

On the opposite end of the spectrum, Pilsen, Czech Republic, has soft water with almost no dissolved minerals—and less than 1 percent the bicarbonate of Dublin. This water is especially suited to pale malts, needing none of the acidic dark malts to produce an appropriate pH. And so from this water, Czech brewers were able to brew the pale lagers that took the town's name. ■

YEAST, SECRET AGENT MEN

THE WORD "YEAST" comes from the Old English *gist*, which means "boil." To see a day-old vat of beer is to understand why: The wort turns milky and sends up a mighty cloud of froth that heaves and bubbles like a witch's cauldron. It sends off waves of carbon dioxide. Even the temperature rises—if left on their own, the trillions of active yeast cells would boost the temperature of the beer by ten to twenty degrees Fahrenheit. Boil indeed.

Yet yeast is a modest being—a ubiquitous single-celled fungus that floats through the air, coats surfaces of fruit, and lives on certain other organisms, notably insects. (There's even a variety that lives between human toes.) Yeasts have been enormously valuable to people, too, who've harnessed them to make bread, wine, and beer. All three of these products are made with the same broad category of yeast, *Saccharomyces cerevisiae*.

YEAST IN ACTION

By the end of the boiling process, lots of chemistry has already taken place in the wort. Malt starches have been converted to sugars, hop acids and oils have been put into solution and isomerized. It's during fermentation that the yeast cells perform the final acts of chemistry, turning sugars to alcohol, and it is here that beer is finally made.

Fermentation is fairly simple: Yeasts begin by consuming all the available oxygen suspended in the wort. If there is more oxygen than yeast (and in wort, there always is), the cells reproduce by budding, sending their children off to collect the remaining available oxygen. Once all the oxygen is gone, yeasts begin the chemical conversion that makes beer. They take in sugars, starting with the most digestible

kind first, and work their way along until they've consumed everything they can. The gobbled sugars go through the yeast cells and are excreted as alcohol and carbon dioxide. Within a day of the introduction of yeast, the beer will begin its transformation into bubbling cauldron, a process that peters out after a few days, as yeasts conclude their gorging frenzy and begin settling to the bottom of the tank, sated and still.

It's a mistake, however, to think that yeast's sole contribution to beer is alcohol production. Yeast cells are essentially miniature chemical plants, and in addition to alcohol and carbon dioxide, they produce other compounds like esters and phenols. For the brewer, these other by-products are nearly as important, for they make a profound contribution to the final character of the beer. Yeast can create flavors that mimic other ingredients like fruit and spice, they can make a beer taste drier, sweeter, or more alcoholic—all by the way they metabolize the malt.

Following are the four major categories of by-products that yeast may produce.

RIGHT: *"Double, double, toil and trouble"—yeast in action*

"Marmite: Love It or Hate It." In the early 1900s, a German scientist determined that spent brewing yeast was edible—and nutritious. An English company decided to monetize this information and Marmite was born. Spread on toast for more than 100 years, it remains a cherished product—albeit not by everyone. In the U.S., craft breweries feed their spent yeast to cows.

■ **Esters.** These compounds create the fruity aromas and flavors that characterize ales. Ester formation varies from strain to strain, so the effect on beers varies. Commonly, esters express themselves as apple, berry, pear, or banana, but may also be spicy.

■ **Phenols.** These compounds produce smoky aromas and flavors that may taste like cloves or plastic, or contribute an almost medicinal quality. Traditional German weizens and some Belgian beers have overtly phenolic qualities.

■ **Diacetyl.** All yeast produces diacetyl, a substance with a flavor so like butter that it is used to flavor candy and theater popcorn. Yeast eventually reabsorbs diacetyl, but sometimes breweries package their beer before the process is complete.

■ **Fusel alcohols.** In addition to ethyl alcohol, yeast can produce heavier alcohols that add sharp, hot notes. More common in stronger beers, they add complexity and warming sensations.

In addition to creating these flavor and aroma compounds, different yeasts metabolize sugars differently, too. Some are very efficient, consuming lots of sugars and drying a beer out. Some are less efficient and leave sugars floating in the beer, making it sweeter. And some are just weird; the yeast used by Moortgat to make Duvel, for example, generates an amazing amount of carbon dioxide, giving the beer dense, fluffy clouds of foam when it's poured from a bottle.

Conditions also exert a powerful effect on yeast. Some strains work best in temperatures just above freezing, while others like warmth. Even things that seem like they couldn't possibly affect yeast, do: In squat, wide tanks, yeasts produce different compounds than they do in taller, narrow ones. Breweries once regularly used open tanks to ferment their beer, which allowed yeast floating by in the air to drop in. Most modern breweries abandoned this as an anachronistic and unnecessarily dangerous method and prefer to keep their beer safely behind a sheet of steel, where no wild yeasts can find it. But research has shown that the numbers of phenols and esters produced in open fermenters, even using the same yeast, vary substantially. Indeed, when Orval switched from open fermenters to tall, closed cylindroconical fermenters, it took three years to re-create the Orval signature taste in the new tanks. Yeast is a living organism, and beer is its natural environment. Like any other ecosystem, the conditions affect yeast's behavior, and their behavior in turn affects the beer.

ALE AND LAGER YEASTS

The most important condition in determining how a yeast will behave is temperature—and temperature is what divides the two main categories of yeasts between ale and lager. Ale yeasts prefer temperatures above 60°F, and many do best at room temperature or higher. Lager yeasts thrive at cooler temperatures around 50°F or lower. Low temperatures inhibit the production of chemical by-products, so lager yeasts create a much "cleaner" beer with little in the way of esters, phenols, or diacetyl. Because ales are fermented warmer, they do produce these

by-products; the warmer the fermentation temperature, the more by-products they produce.

The differences in yeasts evolved only after centuries of domestication, as breweries repitched their house yeast over and over again, creating "house character." Eventually, the lines became distinct from each other as they adapted to their native environment—in this case, a particular brewhouse. (If a brewery borrows yeast from another and reuses that yeast, over time it will behave differently than it did in the brewery of origin.)

The technique of lagering dates back possibly as far as the 1400s in Bavaria, to a time when people had only a rudimentary understanding of yeast's nature. Bavarian brewers had isolated a yeast that didn't behave like the regular strains; it fell to the bottom of the fermenter and worked best at cooler temperatures. The same type of yeast didn't work well in warmer climates, but

Hefeners. Sometimes you read that the old brewers didn't know yeast existed. They didn't understand what it was, but they definitely knew it existed. Schlenkerla Brewery's Matthias Trum, who studied the history of brewing, explained how medieval Germans understood it:

The yeast is in fact not mentioned, that is correct. You have to put yourself in the mind of a medieval brewer. In the Middle Ages, they had a profession called the "hefener," so they knew exactly. [In German, hefe means "yeast."] The purity law lists ingredients, right? Yeast I put in the beer and I get more out of it. I harvest the yeast at the end and I put it into the next batch. And that was actually the job of the hefener. . . . The hefener's job was to harvest the yeast from the batches, to press out as much remaining beer as possible, which was sold at a low price to the poor, and then the yeast was added to the next batch. You started with a smaller amount of yeast and then you ended with a bigger amount of yeast.

Gravity Measurements. Expressing a beer's original and terminal gravities requires a scale, and unfortunately, breweries have adopted different versions. The Plato scale represents the measure as the amount of solids in suspension. On this scale, if wort is measured at 15° Plato, it has 15 percent sugars in suspension. Another compares the weight of water to wort. The scale assigns a value of 1 to water, so a wort of 1.050 specific gravity (sp. gr.) is 1.05 times as heavy as water. Low-gravity beer falls below 1.032 sp. gr./8° Plato, and high-gravity beer begins around 1.060 sp. gr./15° Plato and goes above 1.110 sp. gr./26° Plato.

Type of Beer	Original Gravity		Terminal Gravity		ABV
	Specific	Plato	Specific	Plato	
Berliner weisse	1.030	7.5° P	1.002	0.5° P	3.9%
Pale ale	1.050	12.5° P	1.012	3° P	5.0%
Barley wine	1.106	25° P	1.020	5° P	11.3%

Bavarian brewers were utilizing deep, cool caves and cellars so they could use this yeast during the cold months. In the nineteenth century, Louis Pasteur confirmed what those old Bavarians knew: Chill temperatures inhibited wild yeasts that could spoil beer. Within a few decades, these qualities would be so prized that the majority of breweries in continental Europe had switched to lager yeasts. With this strain's emergence, so evolved many of the famous beers that now define German and Czech brewing.

It is important to emphasize something here. For decades, otherwise well-informed scientists believed that ale and lager yeasts were taxonomically different; not only did they behave differently, but they were different *kinds* of yeasts. Cats and dogs. However, in the past decade, mycologists working with mitochondrial DNA have found that lager yeasts aren't pure. The lines cross and merge, and it appears that lager yeasts have ale as well as lager ancestors. The current thinking—and given how fast discoveries are being made, it should be considered a provisional finding— is that there are two separate hybrid lager yeasts, both with some ale parentage, but from different lines. It turns out they're more like different breeds of dogs.

Read a book on brewing written more than five years ago, and ale and lager yeasts will be described as genetically distinct. Now we know they're not, but this isn't a major mistake—lager and ale yeasts really do behave differently and belong in separate categories. Instead of distinguishing between yeasts based on type, though, it's more useful to distinguish them by *function*. They may not have a different genome, but ale and lager

Wild Yeasts and Bacteria.

The tart category is a small niche in the spectrum of beer—just a few examples from Germany and Belgium (and lately, the U.S.), with very little total barrelage to speak of. This is a recent development, though; until breweries began to domesticate yeast, soured ales were the norm. They were common in Britain into the twentieth century. A few traditional styles remain, and most beer drinkers regard them as anachronisms. But for some connoisseurs, they remain the pinnacle of the brewer's art.

Sourness may be tart and clean as in Berliner weisse, funky yet dry and austere as in lambics, or vinegary as in Flemish reds. These different qualities come principally from three major organisms— the wild yeast *Brettanomyces* and the bacteria *Lactobacillus* and *Pediococcus*. Other minor organisms, like *Acetobacter*, *Enterobacter*, and caproic acid also contribute to a sour or acid profile.

In some soured beers, bacteria are introduced and controlled, adding a tangy, sometimes sharp sourness. In some, like lambic, the experiment is wholly uncontrolled, and all the wild yeasts and bacteria jump into the beer and create a little ecosystem where they contribute different amounts and different types of souring compounds and flavors. Below is a list of the principal agents.

■ **BRETTANOMYCES.** This wild yeast inspires the most awe and fear among brewers. It will eat anything, including dextrins and sugars that other yeasts find unpalatable, achieving nearly 100 percent apparent attenuation—far more than regular yeast. (Brewers joke that it will start eating the bottle if you leave it long enough.) By contrast, standard ale and lager yeast strains attenuate at between 70 and 80 percent. *Brettanomyces* will produce both acetic and lactic acids, but the former only under certain circumstances. This extreme attenuation will eventually make a beer taste almost dusty in its dryness. There are many species of *Brettanomyces* and many strains within each. The most common is *Brettanomyces bruxellensis*, which is particularly funky, often described as having a "horse blanket" aroma.

■ **LACTOBACILLUS.** *Lactobacillus* gives tart Flanders ales their character, as it does some German ales like gose and Berliner weisse. As the name suggests, this bacteria produces lactic acid; it is far more finicky than *Brettanomyces*. It prefers warm temperatures, a low-oxygen environment, and low levels of hop acids. Brewers can control *Lactobacillus*, allowing it to turn a beer very sour or just tweak it only slightly. Lactic-soured beers are tart and refreshing—for those who appreciate this quality.

■ **PEDIOCOCCUS.** *Pediococcus* is the beastie that gives lambics their lactic tang, not *Lactobacillus*. This is mainly a function of the life cycle of a lambic. *Pediococcus* ferments in beer with little or no oxygen; likewise, it gives off no carbon dioxide. The *Pediococcus* gets active when the lambic warms up, creating long slimy strands on top of the wort. You can drink the beer at this stage, but it's oily and known as the "sick" stage. But from that unappetizing sickness comes the lactic acid, and eventually, the slime is reabsorbed as the *Brettanomyces* begins gobbling up everything that remains.

strains behave differently, and the beers they make taste different, too.

ATTENUATION AND GRAVITY

Two concepts related to the action of yeast are attenuation and gravity. Attenuation represents the degree to which yeasts have consumed fermentable sugars. Breweries measure this, based on a scale of gravity, by comparing the wort and the finished beer to pure water. Using water as a baseline, brewers can measure how much dissolved sugars are in solution. Sugars are more dense than water, but alcohol is less dense. So when yeast begins converting sugars to alcohol, the gravity drops. By measuring the difference between the readings taken before the yeast is added (the "original gravity") and after the yeast is done (the "final" or "terminal" gravity),

breweries are able to calculate the alcohol percentage.

When they make these calculations, brewers also see the attenuation, or how efficient the yeast was in consuming sugars. The lower the figure, the higher the attenuation, and the drier the beer will taste. This doesn't always correspond directly to a perception of sweetness, because esters may make a dry beer taste sweeter—but it's a useful guide to understanding how dry a beer is. In brewing jargon, the terms for high-/low-alcohol beers are often used synonymously with high-/low-gravity beers. Yet the two aren't identical, because if a yeast is poorly attenuated, a higher-gravity beer may not be as alcoholic as the original gravity suggested. So while it's useful to know the alcohol percentage of a beer, it's even more useful if you know both the alcohol percentage and the original gravity. ■

THE BREWING PROCESS

AT A CONCEPTUAL LEVEL, brewing beer is easy to grasp: Malted grain is soaked in water to extract fermentable sugars, boiled with hops, cooled, fermented with yeast, and packaged. More detailed descriptions, particularly accounting for the procedures practiced differently in Germany, Belgium, and the U.K., could fill volumes. Fortunately, unless one is interested in actually brewing, a simple description is more than adequate to understand the nuts and bolts of commercial brewing.

MALTING

Modern malthouses are wonders of technology where kernels of grain are subjected to constant analysis to ensure that they maintain optimal moisture and temperature levels and come out of the kiln plump and enzyme rich. They produce malt meeting the rigid specifications that brewers require to produce consistent batches of beer. Yet for all that, grain is still malted the same way it was thousands of years ago.

Essentially, grains (the seeds of the plant) are first steeped like tea in vats of water, a process that stimulates the kernel's embryo and begins the production of enzymes. Each grain needs to become sodden, and will be soaked and drained and soaked again over the course of a couple days. The seed is rousing itself to reproduce and begins important chemical changes, ultimately resulting in the first nubbin of a shoot, known as a "chit" in the trade. Next, the wet chitted grain is left out to germinate. This is the critical moment when those unfermentable proteins are broken down as the seed shifts into its growth cycle, a process known as "modification." The starches in each kernel exist to sustain this process, and the plant would quickly exhaust them if left to grow. Instead, after four or five days, the maltster dries the grain to stop germination and preserve the starches.

MILLING

Breweries store malted grain until they're ready to brew a beer. The first step is crushing (milling) the malt to prepare it for mashing. Much like grinding coffee, grain can be milled coarse or fine. Finely ground malt will release more sugars into the wort, but if it's ground into powder, the grain will clump and the husks will be too fine to create an adequate bed for running off. Brewery equipment dictates how fine the grist can be: Breweries with separate lauter tuns can use a finer grind than those using their mash tun as a filter; if a brewery uses a mash filter, the grind can be extremely fine.

MASHING

The mash process looks much like making breakfast porridge, but it functions more like making a huge kettle of tea. Malt and water are mixed together at temperatures designed to stimulate enzymes that will break down starches and proteins; liberated from the grain, starches and sugars will be rinsed off to make the barley-tea–like wort. There are essentially two ways to do this: either in a successive series of steps where the temperature of the wort starts lower and is raised and held; or with a single infusion of water (called "hot liquor") at a temperature that averages out the advantages of the step process.

(continued on page 56)

Homebrewing. Of all the ways to learn about beer, none recommends itself quite as well as homebrewing. The process of formulating a recipe, observing the brewing process, and tasting the results reveals levels of subtlety that are hard—though certainly not impossible—for the nonbrewer to apprehend. But homebrewing is also tricky and laborious and, like mastering the skills of car mechanics, not worth the trouble for many people—and far too detailed a process to cover comprehensively in this book. Take heart: There are several excellent books available (see the bibliography), and you can brew a one-gallon test batch in an afternoon and for as little as fifty dollars. I suggest you try it at least once; the more you brew, the more you understand what makes beer taste like it does.

THE BREWING PROCESS

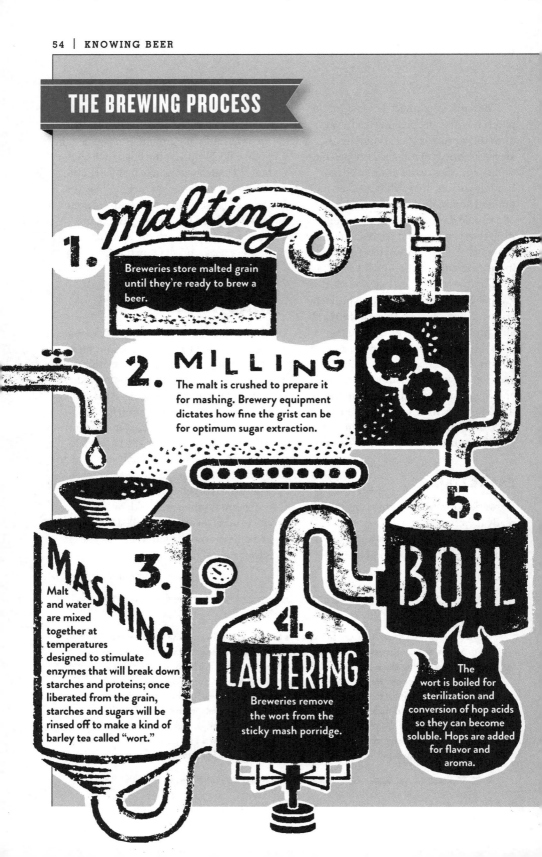

1. *Malting*

Breweries store malted grain until they're ready to brew a beer.

2. MILLING

The malt is crushed to prepare it for mashing. Brewery equipment dictates how fine the grist can be for optimum sugar extraction.

3. MASHING

Malt and water are mixed together at temperatures designed to stimulate enzymes that will break down starches and proteins; once liberated from the grain, starches and sugars will be rinsed off to make a kind of barley tea called "wort."

4. LAUTERING

Breweries remove the wort from the sticky mash porridge.

5. BOIL

The wort is boiled for sterilization and conversion of hop acids so they can become soluble. Hops are added for flavor and aroma.

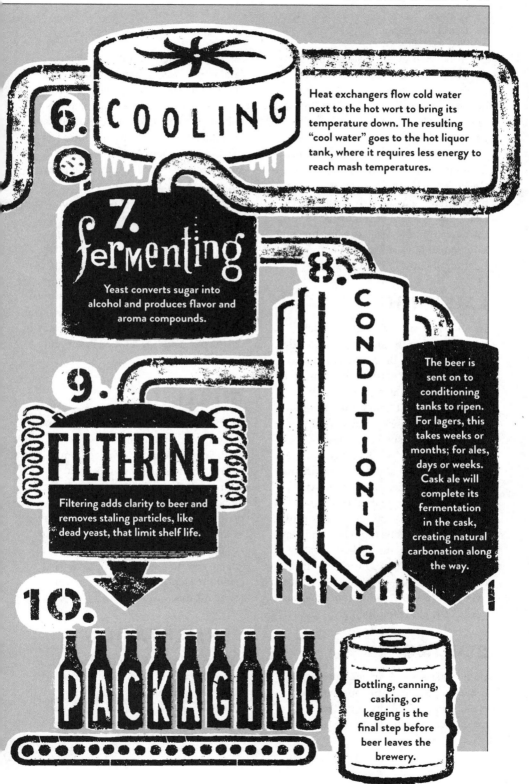

6. COOLING

Heat exchangers flow cold water next to the hot wort to bring its temperature down. The resulting "cool water" goes to the hot liquor tank, where it requires less energy to reach mash temperatures.

7. fermenting

Yeast converts sugar into alcohol and produces flavor and aroma compounds.

8. CONDITIONING

The beer is sent on to conditioning tanks to ripen. For lagers, this takes weeks or months; for ales, days or weeks. Cask ale will complete its fermentation in the cask, creating natural carbonation along the way.

9. FILTERING

Filtering adds clarity to beer and removes staling particles, like dead yeast, that limit shelf life.

10. PACKAGING

Bottling, canning, casking, or kegging is the final step before beer leaves the brewery.

(continued from page 53)

Modern breweries use the first process, called "temperature-programmed mashing." British and some American breweries use the second, called "infusion mashing." There's a third, much older practice called "decoction" that was a precursor to temperature-programmed mashing. Still regularly practiced in the Czech Republic and in some breweries in Germany—particularly Bavaria—it's a laborious process of removing some of the wort from the mash tun, heating and returning it to raise the temperature of the overall mash to the next step.

LAUTERING

In lautering, breweries remove their barley tea from the sticky mash porridge. In older systems, breweries have to lauter from their mash tuns, but modern systems avail themselves of a separate vessel known as a "lauter tun." In these systems, the entire contents of the mash tun are flushed to the lauter tun, a similar-looking vessel that contains a series of rakes and blades. The contents of the mash are heated to reduce viscosity, and the blades and rakes separate out the wort, which is collected underneath a mesh bottom. While they chop and plow, an arm inside the tun sprinkles water over the grain bed to continue to rinse the malt of sugar—the process known as "sparging." Finally, the accumulated wort goes to the kettle for boiling.

BOILING

Boiling has several virtues, but the most important is converting hop acids so they can become soluble in wort. The process takes a while, so breweries boil the wort for sixty to ninety minutes on average (and never for less than an hour). Hops also add flavor and aroma, but the compounds that contribute these qualities are delicate. To infuse flavor, additional hops are added twenty to thirty minutes from the end of the boil. Aroma compounds are especially fragile, so aroma hops are added in the last few minutes.

Beyond hop extraction, boiling sterilizes the wort, removes unwanted volatile compounds, and precipitates out chunky protein molecules to clarify the beer. Most brew kettles ("coppers" in Britain) are heated by steam jackets or heater tubes ("calandria"), but a few older breweries still use direct-fired kettles. The hot spots created by open flames caramelize the wort, adding a toffee flavor and darkening the beer.

CHILLING

Chilling beer quickly was an important innovation that allowed breweries to pitch yeast quickly to avoid contamination. In modern breweries, heat exchangers do the work—and save energy along the way. These devices work by using cold water to flow across plates next to the hot wort. The two liquids come to equilibrium, and the now-warmed "cool water" goes to the hot liquor tank where it requires less energy to reach mash temperatures.

FERMENTATION

The magic happens inside fermenters, where yeast converts sugar into alcohol, esters, and phenols. While most brewhouses look similar, fermentation systems vary substantially. The shape of

Floor Malting. In modern malthouses, germinating grains are carefully regulated and tended by machine. An older, more traditional method is known as "floor malting." This involves spreading the steeped grain out in the warehouse-like open spaces in the malthouse.

Germinating grain is fussy. The activity produces heat; maltsters regulate the temperature by both adjusting the depth of the grain bed and raking it. In earlier times, the master maltster monitored the process by hand and feel, and the job was regarded as a high art, equivalent in importance to the master brewer—critical if beer was to be palatable. Breweries themselves maintained their own maltings (a dangerous job that often led to fires). Because germination temperatures were so important, malting could only be done during the five or six coolest months of the year—which was true with brewing, as well.

As the brewing industry became more sophisticated, specialized companies took up malting and eventually most breweries abandoned the traditional method. It survives in Britain and the Czech Republic, where some brewers still prefer floor-malted grain for the rounded, malty flavor it gives their beer.

and temperature in the fermenter has a huge influence on the way yeast behaves. Primary fermentation takes just a few days for ales and up to ten days for lagers. Once it's complete, the beer will be sent on to conditioning tanks to ripen. In lager breweries, this may take weeks or months; in ale breweries, just days or weeks. The one exception is cask ale, which is transferred to casks before it has completely finished fermenting. It will complete its fermentation in the cask, creating natural carbonation along the way.

FILTERING AND PACKAGING

Not all beer is filtered—some breweries like their product served au naturel. Filtering has the advantage of adding clarity to beer; more important, it removes staling particles, like dead yeast, that limit shelf life. Some breweries take the additional step of pasteurizing their beer to prevent spoilage. The trade-off is that pasteurization requires beer to be heated—either for a short time at high temperatures, or a few minutes at lower temperatures—which accelerates the staling process. Most smaller traditional and craft breweries don't pasteurize.

Bottling, canning, casking, or kegging is the final step before beer leaves the brewery. The type of container is dictated somewhat by cost—bottling lines are very expensive, canning lines cheaper, keg fillers the cheapest of all—but also by beer style. Real ale must go into a specially designed cask. Many Belgian and French styles of beer require refermentation in the bottle and so they're not kegged. ■

Tasting Beer
LIKE A
BREWER

Every day at eleven o'clock, a sensory panel sits in a small, clean room next to the laboratory at the Widmer Brothers brewery. They conduct a "go/no-go" session, tasting every batch of beer that will leave the brewery. Each member of the panel pours out a measure of beer and rates it from one to five. They're using the power of their senses to detect any flaws or deviations from the intended beer that would make it unsuitable for sale.

Potential panelists are selected and invited to go through sensory training. It's a full forty-hour week of sniffing, sipping, and swallowing as palates slowly become attuned to characteristics like ethyl acetate, diacetyl, and isovaleric acid. Detection isn't enough—trained tasters need to be able to identify dozens of different flavor and aroma compounds that might compromise their beer, usually at levels of just a few parts per million. Those certified as trained or expert are routinely retested to make sure their palates remain acute.

On the day I visited, the panel clipped right through several bottles of lager and pale ale. Members set aside one batch for a compound I couldn't detect. Often, the offending flavors are rawer and more evident just after packaging but will harmonize within a few days—the panel would try it again the following week. Even in a brewery as modern and as carefully monitored as Widmer Brothers, batch-to-batch variation is inevitable. Members of the panel commented on the character and qualities of the beers as they went around, just noting their individual identities. These aren't the kind of differences the average drinker would notice unless she paid very close attention and knew the beer very well.

For the sensory panel, that subtle knowledge is critical. At one point, a growler of the Widmer Imperial Nelson IPA came around. The beer in the growler had been taken either from a keg in the brewery's pub or from a bright beer (or conditioning) tank. As I poured out a portion and sampled it, people started murmuring around the table. Someone flagged the beer as a "2"—problem—so the group went around one by one, explaining what they tasted. To a person, everyone identified the same issue: oxygen, a telltale sign of age. That would be a big problem for a beer needing to last three months on the shelf—but it turned out this was a different situation. The leader of the panel had given us a

ABOVE: *The Widmer Brothers pour out samples of a newly released gose.*

three-month-old sample from the pub; it was a test the group easily passed.

This is how brewers taste beer: They attune their senses to dozens of compounds so that they can easily recognize them in a sample of beer. A brewer can tell a great deal about the ingredients, the brewing methods, the state of freshness, and the faults of a beer just using his senses. The human body has sensitivities no machines can match and, properly trained, can detect enormous complexity in beer. No one has more riding on the quality of beer than the people who brew it, and they spend a lot of time mapping out the details of flavor. It's something beer drinkers can learn to do, as well. ∎

THE NATURE OF FLAVOR

WITH ANY GUSTATORY experience, our minds turn to *taste*. It seems self-evident why: Food and beverages go in the mouth where the taste buds await. Beyond this simple, apparently obvious axiom, we also think of taste as a fairly fixed measure: We know what our favorite beer tastes like, much as we know what our mother looks like. If we sit down to taste a beer, our senses will be able to give us a pretty clear—even *scientific*—read on what the beer tastes like.

It turns out this isn't how flavor works. In fact, what will go into the evaluation of a beer will be a wheelbarrow of random inputs that have very little to do with the beer: mood, opinion of the brewery, attraction to the label, what we just ate, previous experiences with the same beer, whether the Red Sox are beating the Yankees. Amazingly, even things we think we can trust, like taste, are likely to fool us.

Furthermore, we think we taste with our mouth, but in fact, the tongue is an incredibly crude instrument. When we "taste" something, we're actually synthesizing stimuli that come from the tongue, nose, and eyes, as well as memories of other tastes and fantasies about what we expect to taste. Scientists have found that the brain blends these experiences and thoughts together and what emerges is a mushy concept we call "flavor." Flavor is not like a sound or shape—things our senses can perceive directly and about which we can find wide agreement. Instead, it is a nested experience that is surprisingly susceptible to things happening outside our mouths.

This is not to say that assessment is beyond humans—trained palates, under the right conditions, can identify certain flavors with surprising accuracy. It is, rather, to say that we have to attend to what we're perceiving very carefully. We must understand the mechanisms of flavor and be discriminating in what our senses tell us.

FLAVOR, NOT TASTE

It's not going too far to say that our lives are ordered around eating and drinking. We devote hours of our day to preparing food and eating it, and over the course of

RIGHT: *A taster tray gives customers a chance to test the broad array of flavors in a brewery's beer range.*

our lifetime, we'll put food and drink into our mouths millions of times. Despite this, we have very little sense of what's really going on once we take a bite or sip.

Try this experiment. Take a bite of something, but before you do, inhale first and plug your nose. You probably know what happens next: Without the aid of your smeller, you have only a gross sense of flavor. The tongue can distinguish just five categories of taste: sweet, salty, savory (or umami), sour, and bitter. That bite of food will seem lifeless in your mouth—if you can taste it at all. As you let go of your nose, pay attention to what happens in your nostrils. The sense of flavor will come rushing into your mouth. And if you focus, you'll notice that you're exhaling through your nose at the precise moment that flavor bursts across your palate.

What's happening when we taste food (or beer) is a fusion of the gross sensation of the tongue and a constant sampling of aromas by a mechanism known as "retronasal smell." When we sniff something before putting it in our mouths, scents are taken to the olfactory bulb *ortho*nasally—from the front. Retronasal aroma comes after something enters the mouth. The substance is warmed, crushed if it's a food, swished if it's a sample of beer, and then the scent is taken to the back of our mouth and into the pharynx (the place inside the mouth where the nasal passages connect to the mouth and throat). Exhalation takes breath from the lungs past the food or drink, carrying the volatilized aromas past the olfactory bulb from the back—*retro*nasally. Interestingly, while orthonasal scents can be sampled on their own, retronasal scents are always detected in the presence of the tongue's taste; that fusion may be why we are so easily fooled to think "flavor" is something our taste buds sense. Yet in most cases, when we say "taste," we mean the overall flavor of something, and when we say "flavor," we largely mean retronasal smell.

The Importance of Smell.

The human sense of smell is routinely described as secondary to sight and less important than it is in other species like dogs. In fact, scent is enormously important, occupying the largest family of genes in our genome.

Our sense of smell grew out of an important adaptation that allowed us to identify beneficial and dangerous elements. Humans can detect a relatively limited number of scents (a few thousand), but the organic world has millions of different aromatic compounds. We evolved to be able to identify a few key scents from the cacophony of stimuli that guided us to food or away from toxins. As the brain evolved, the part that processed smells was located in the prefrontal cortex—the area associated with the highest cognitive functions. Humans have fewer receptors, but a gigantic processor. Combined with our capacity for retronasal smell, this gives us what neurobiologist Gordon Shepherd believes to be humans' unique ability to create and process a sense of flavor far richer than other animals'. We are born foodies.

Other senses are at work in constructing our sense of flavor, too. The mouth can feel food's texture—in fact, it's easier when your nose is plugged. A related sense is chemesthesis, which allows the tongue to distinguish chemical sensations like menthol, chile, or—important in beer drinking—the prickle of carbonation. Sight isn't necessary for flavor, but it does influence it. In a study of color and wine, oenology students were fooled by dyed white wine, mistaking it for red. People presented with two odorless substances in a different study said the colored one did have a scent, and in yet another study, people reported thinking brightly colored substances smelled stronger than dull ones. There are even senses we don't understand, like being able to detect the presence of essential amino acids.

Beyond what our senses tell us, other factors affect flavor. Whether we're hungry, full, or neither affects the way things taste. Mood exerts an influence, and even buried emotional memories from childhood tint our experience. Finally, perception of flavor is dependent on each person's own hardware. We don't detect the same aromas or experience taste (the sensations of the tongue) in equal intensity. Some people are indifferent to certain aromas that repel or attract other people. Women, for example, outperform men in scent tests. Breweries actually arrange their tasting panels to take advantage of this, making sure that someone is sensitive to each flavor—and that other people are insensitive to flavors as well. All of this gives them a fuller sense of how their beer will be perceived by their customers.

All of these sensations, feelings, and conditions affect the way we taste and shape our experience of flavor. When a sensory or judging panel sits down to taste beer, they're trying to control for as many of these factors as possible. Since many inputs confuse or augment beer flavors, they want to remove as many extraneous stimuli as possible. What they're left with are the flavors present in the beer. The human senses, despite their faults and variability, are still the most sensitive instruments we have for measuring flavor, and they can reveal an enormous amount about beer. ■

SENSORY OVERVIEW

TASTING BEER INVOLVES four of the five senses, and quirky tasters may put an ear next to the glass just to round things out. The process is iterative: Each sense will tell the taster a little bit about the process or ingredients, and as he goes along, he'll learn more with each new sense. Looking at a beer tells you something about the malts used to make it; you learn more with an orthonasal sniff and yet more with a sip, a swish, and a retronasal sniff. Together, all of these sensory samples help build a map of a beer's ingredients and how it was made.

COLOR AND CLARITY

Color, like any form of beauty, is deceptive. It's far from a fixed dimension. Because color is a form of light, the way a glass is shaped affects the way a beer looks. (Pour the same beer in a squat glass and a narrow one, and the color will be deeper in the squat one.) Beyond that, color must go through receptors in our eyes and be translated into mental images in the brain, allowing for individual variation. None of this stops breweries from using malts to paint their beer with color—indeed, a comely glass of beer is no small part of the pleasure.

In beer, color comes from the malts, sugars, or additives; the main source is the malt a brewer uses. The palest varieties have a light straw color and range upward to black. Of course, those malts also have flavors, so another way to achieve the right hue is with colored sugars, as the Belgian and British breweries sometimes use in dubbels and mild ales. Light sugars and adjuncts like corn and rice can also reduce color by diluting the grist. Finally, some beers use other ingredients like fruit or coffee, and these have their own distinctive colors.

Color by itself isn't always instructive. Breweries can achieve colors through limitless combinations of darker and lighter malts and it's not always easy to spot the difference between dark sugars and malts. Taken together with aromas and flavors, some of the malts may be identifiable.

Any color can be beautiful or dull, and clarity is important in making them pop. Beer is full of various molecules from protein, polyphenols, hop lipids, and yeast—among other things. All of these contribute to visual occlusion, all the way from a vague dullness to a dense, milky haze. The fewer particles a beer has in it, the "brighter" it will appear. The level of haziness can tell a taster a lot about a beer. A vibrantly aromatic pale ale that shimmers might be a clue to dry hopping. Some styles are intentionally hazy, like Belgian wits and Bavarian weizens, but sometimes haze is the sign of infection or age.

Beer is often filtered, and breweries have control over how much particulate they wish to remove. Extremely clear beer may be overfiltered, and have less character than a richer, less-filtered beer. The question of clarity isn't a matter of good or bad. Some craft beer fans love to see a little texture in their glass and regard it as a sign of handcraft. In purely aesthetic terms, clarity does enhance color, and most breweries like their beer to shine.

CARBONATION AND HEAD

A glass of beer is a lively thing. Bubbles sparkle like gems as the light catches them streaming up, destined to get lost in the fluffy head at the beer's surface. These two things, carbonation and head, are quintessentially beery. Soda and Champagne both dance with carbonation, but only beer, with its delicious surfeit of hydrophobic polypeptides, manages to sustain a head.

Carbonation occurs naturally in beer as a consequence of fermentation, though most breweries add carbon dioxide artificially just before packaging.

It seems almost an afterthought, an invisible and not very important characteristic of the beer—a bit of effervescence for good measure. In fact, carbonation is an essential part of beer. Those tiny bubbles add a bit of acidity to a beer that, when combined with the prickling sensation on the tongue, give it more of a crisp snap at the finish. This translates to a quenching sensation and is one of the main reasons highly carbonated, light-bodied beers are satisfying on a hot day. In contrast, beers that are lower in carbonation—such as cask ales—seem to have a heaviness on the tongue.

Carbonation affects aroma and taste as well. As carbon dioxide rises off the glass, it lifts volatile aromas up and out of the glass, too. It's the opposite with flavor; carbonation scrubs both malt and hop flavors, but especially bitterness. This is one of the reasons cask ale, which is roughly half as carbonated as a tin-can lager, has a full, rich flavor.

Carbonation is measured by the volume of carbon dioxide dissolved in beer. One volume is equivalent to the amount of space it would fill in a given container. If you filled up a beer glass with carbon dioxide at 32°F, that would be the amount of gas dissolved in a beer with one volume. For comparison, cask ale has around 1 to 1.5 volumes of CO_2, standard craft brewed ales 1.5 to 2.5, standard American lager 2.6, and certain effervescent Belgian styles and Bavarian weizens from 3 to 4 volumes. In the glass, carbonation may be visible by a cascade of bubbles (the "bead"). Certain glassware is even designed to produce this effect with an etched bottom called a "nucleation site" that allows bubbles to form.

The head of a beer is a more ornamental function of carbonation, not one that has much effect on flavor, and preferences for head size vary. The head can add a creaminess to beer's texture, though—especially in stouts like Guinness. (Guinness is served with a mixture of nitrogen and carbon dioxide, and the head is made of especially tiny creamy bubbles.) Even when a beer is served with a small head, the ability of beer to foam and retain its foam is an important clue to how well it has been made. A good beer will not only retain its head, but leave a lattice of residue on the inside of the glass. (One exception is among strong beers; alcohol can dissipate the head of even well-made beer.) Tasters look to see how structured the head is, whether the bubbles are tight and creamy, and how long they last—all clues to the quality of the beer.

AROMA

One of the most important steps in tasting is sampling the aroma. Aside from purely hedonic considerations—though we should never put them aside completely—the scents emanating from a glass of beer hold clues about the ingredients, brewing methods, yeast type, and any unexpected nuances that might be lurking within. Smelling the beer alone, before it enters the mouth and fuses with sensations of taste and texture, will give you a first sense of the beer. Aromas may have different intensities or valence when taken alone, and in any case, they help guide a taster toward certain flavors when she does finally take a sip.

Malts have their own character. They are the only element with a grain-y aroma, and the class of related flavors

A Dynamic Beverage. If the subject of beer flavor wasn't already complex enough, add this to the equation: Beer's properties aren't fixed. They change depending on how the beer is served. Two things in particular are important: temperature and glassware.

Beer behaves differently depending on its temperature. Aroma, flavor, and carbonation are all depressed at colder temperatures. This can be a serious problem in pubs, where pints of ale are routinely served 20°F below their optimum temperature. Allowing a beer to warm can be a revelation as the scents and flavors open up. Tart beers are an exception to the rule—when they're cold, they taste more intense, perhaps because sour isn't suppressed as well as other flavors. When a beer warms, the sense of sour decreases.

Glassware is important to both visual presentation and aroma. Stocky glasses darken beer and give a false sense of their color. More problematic are cylindrical or shaker-style glasses, which do a poor job of capturing aroma. Glasses with a bulb create a natural space for aromas to collect; heretical as it may sound, a wine glass is a better vessel than a standard shaker-style pub glass. Tulip pints, snifters, tulip glasses, and goblets all do a better job capturing aromas in serious tastings.

---

tells you something about the type of malts used—caramel, toast, biscuit, dark fruit, smoke, or roast (see the section on malts, pages 35–36, for more detail). Hops are even more distinctive—though with so many varieties, they're not as easy to distinguish. Over time, tasters become adept at matching flavors with specific hop types (see Hop Varieties at a Glance in the Appendixes). The intensity and type of aroma will tell a taster when hops were added in the boil and whether dry-hopping may have been used.

With practice, tasters learn how to spot fermentation-based aromas as well. They're even trickier than hops because they are similar to other scents. Esters smell sweet, like fruit—but malt and hops also have sweet-smelling notes. Phenols are another class of aromas generated during fermentation and may smell smoky, spicy, or medicinal.

Belgian yeast strains are responsible for a range of strange aromas like banana, anise, or rose, and certain yeasts, like *Brettanomyces*, have distinctive "barnyard" qualities. A related aroma is alcohol—though it's perceived more than it's smelled, like wasabi's sharp vapor plume. Beer may also produce higher (fusel) alcohols and these have their own smells, though confusingly, they're similar to sweet esters.

Some people spend too little time smelling their beer. Aromas require effort to distinguish. Even in balanced beers, hop or malt aromas tend to dominate, so the nose needs to acclimatize itself to pick out the minor scents. Locating esters or phenols, identifying specific hop or malt aromas—it takes more than a cursory sniff. All the effort is put to good effect, though, when you take your first sip of beer. ■

FLAVOR GLOSSARY

Following is a list of common flavors and aroma characteristics found in different beer styles.

■ **ACETIC ACID.** This is the acid that vinegar is made of, and it can be a wonderful component in tart beers like lambics, or ruinous in other beers, where it indicates spoilage.

■ **ALCOHOL.** Perceived more than tasted, the spirituous agent in beer is ethanol. Higher or "fusel" alcohols, which contain more carbon atoms, have flavors of rose, almond, or wine—and may also be noticeably "hot" or have the sensation of burning.

■ **ALMOND, WALNUT.** A characteristic of darker malts, nuttiness is prized in brown ales. Chemical almond aromas come from the fusel alcohol tryptophol.

■ **BALSAMIC VINEGAR.** A defining characteristic of the red/brown beers of Flanders.

■ **BANANA.** One of the most distinctive esters is isoamyl acetate, a dead ringer for banana. It's not appropriate in most beers but is desirable in Bavarian weizens.

■ **BARNYARD.** The wild yeast *Brettanomyces* is responsible for a number of strange flavors, including one that smells like goat's milk (caproic/hexanoic acid). Funky, barnyard animal aromas—sometimes described as "horse blanket"—also come from *Brettanomyces*.

■ **BITTER.** Many compounds can cause bitter flavors, but they are not all the same. Dark-roasted malts give a coffee-like bitterness, while hops provide a vegetal bitterness. Tannins from cherry pits, wood, or grain husks are other sources of bitterness.

■ **BREAD, CRACKER, BISCUIT.** Common flavors derived from pale malts.

■ **CARAMEL, TOFFEE.** These flavors come from crystal or caramel malts, commonly found in British and American ales.

■ **CITRUS.** The flavor and aroma of citrus is common in beer and has several causes. Hops, particularly American varieties, are the most common source, but wild yeasts, bacteria, and esters may also be responsible for citric notes.

■ **CLOVE.** Typical in Bavarian wheat beers, clove flavor comes from the phenol 4-vinyl guaiacol in the process of fermentation. Unless a brewery has included it as a spice, clove is usually considered a fault.

■ **COFFEE.** Aside from the increasingly common practice of brewing with actual coffee, coffee-like character comes from dark-roasted malt.

■ **DRY, CRISP.** The sensation of dryness on the palate is usually indicative of a highly attenuated beer—that is, a beer with little residual sugars. It may also come from high carbonation, tannins, or spices.

■ **ESTER.** Esters are compounds produced during warmer fermentation, and they're the main way ales are distinguished from lagers in character. Esters are typically described as "fruity," but they can read as sweet. Common esters include: ethyl acetate (fruity in low concentrations, solvent-like in higher), ethyl caproate (apple, anise), ethyl caprylate (apple), isoamyl acetate (banana or pear), isobutyl acetate (pineapple), and phenyl acetate (honey, rose).

■ **FUSEL ALCOHOL.** Fusel or higher alcohols are generally present only in more highly alcoholic beers. As many as forty-five are known to exist, and they can give beer fruity flavors or a sharp, burning sensation. Straight ethanol is usually not responsible for the "boozy" taste of some strong beers; those come from fusel alcohols.

■ **GERANIUM, GARDENIA.** A classically "floral" character that comes from American hops.

■ **GRAPEFRUIT.** Citrus flavors are common in American hops, but the most quintessential are the grapefruit notes that come from Cascade, Centennial, and Chinook.

■ **HONEY.** A sweetish honey note is most likely to come from honey malt, not actual honey, which is consumed in fermentation. It may also come from the ester phenyl acetate.

■ **LACTIC ACID.** Formed by the bacteria *Lactobacillus* and *Pediococcus*, lactic acid is a tangy compound that gives certain tart styles like Berliner weisse their zing. It is the same compound you find in sourdough bread and yogurt.

■ **LEATHER.** The flavor of leather may come from either *Brettanomyces*, where it is dry, or oxidation, where it is more plummy. Too much oxidation spoils a beer, but a little adds a refined sherry-like note.

■ **MINERAL.** Some historic brewing regions were famous for their hard, mineral-laden water. The styles they inspired are noted for a structured minerality that both sharpens hop bitterness and dries the beer.

■ **OAK.** The resinous, dry flavor of oak comes from beers aged in oak wine or bourbon barrels. Oakiness can also express itself as a slightly astringent or woody aroma.

■ **PEAR.** Usually indicative of the ester isoamyl acetate. Appropriate in some Belgian ales, but not lagers or British ales.

■ **PEPPER, SPICE.** Peppery notes can come from a variety of sources, from hops to phenolic compounds that arise in fermentation. Belgian breweries sometimes add pepper to accentuate these qualities.

■ **PHENOL.** Phenols are a class of compounds that may be derived from ingredients, fermentation, or infection. They are usually not appropriate, but phenols contribute smoky flavors in smoked beers, and a spicy, clove-like flavor in Bavarian weizens.

■ **PINE.** A flavor present in some hop varieties such as Simcoe. It may have elements of mint or spruce.

■ **RAISIN, PLUM.** Crystal or caramel malts create a "dark fruit" sweetness in beers. As darker beers age, they "stew" and take on a more pronounced raisin or plum flavor.

■ **ROAST.** In the process of browning (the Maillard reaction), simple sugars and amino acids are transformed into complex molecules that have rich, nuanced flavors (consider the difference between boiled or steamed foods and those that have been roasted or grilled). Malts that go through the Maillard reaction during roasting produce bitter, coffee-like flavors; the more intense the darker the roast.

■ **SMOKE.** Derived from smoked malt, which takes on the flavor of the wood used in the smoking process and can give a false sense of meatiness. (Hickory-smoked malts suggest ham; alder-smoked malts, salmon.) German rauchbier malts are smoked over beech and taste more neutrally "smoky" to American palates.

■ **SOUR, TART.** Sour flavors are characteristic of beer made with wild yeasts and bacteria. The character and intensity may range from a lightly acidic snap to a puckeringly sour wallop. In most styles, sourness is a sign of spoilage.

■ **SWEET.** Sweet flavors have a host of sources, starting with malt. Hop flavors, spices, fruit, and esters can all taste sweet as well.

■ **VANILLA, COCONUT.** A vanilla or coconut note is usually indicative of oak or bourbon aging in a beer, but may also indicate the presence of a particular phenol.

■ **WINE, SHERRY.** Vinous notes typically emerge from aging and take on a dry, refined character.

■ **WOOD.** Beer aged in oak barrels takes on certain tannins that can give it spice notes like nutmeg, cinnamon, and vanilla. Most beer is not aged in wood.

FLAVOR

The flavor of a beer comes from a synthesis of its taste, aroma, texture, and trigeminal stimulation (see Mouthfeel, below). Moreover, that flavor evolves in the mouth from the first contact through to the swallow—and even afterward. Agitating a mouthful volatizes warming aromas and washes beer over all the tongue's taste buds, giving a fuller sense of physical and chemical sensations. Finally, one of the most important elements of beer flavor emerges *after* swallowing. Known as "aftertaste," this final sensory echo combines the taste of residual liquid on the tongue and the aromas still wafting up to the olfactory bulb.

In the course of a single sip, then, the taster passes through three stages: the initial impression, when the most intense flavors dominate; the richer middle impression, when warmth and agitation allow lesser flavors to emerge; and finally, the aftertaste, which may vanish almost instantly or linger for a few minutes. Each one is different, each one critical to assessing flavor.

With all the sensations fused and happening at once, the sense of flavor becomes like a third dimension beyond mere aroma and flavor. The information a taster takes in by smelling the beer is elaborated during a sip, and she can identify more of the malt, hop, and fermentation characteristics. The sensations of the mouth and tongue add new information. We can detect viscosity, effervescence, and astringency. In addition, this is when a taster can synthesize information taken from texture and aroma to determine a beer's strength and level of attenuation. How heavy a beer feels on the palate, how dry it feels in the aftertaste, and how alcoholic it feels in the mouth—these qualities are a combination of multiple sensations. ∎

Mouthfeel. The concept of mouthfeel refers to the way the nerves of the tongue and walls of the mouth perceive the thickness, effervescence, and viscosity of a beer. The human mouth has a sophisticated matrix of nerves that make this possible. These include different receptors of temperature-, pain-, touch-, and pressure-sensitive nerves, all of which help create a mental image of the physical properties of the beer. It's how we can tell the difference between pilsner and imperial stout just by feel, or the difference between milk and water. One of the most important senses comes through the trigeminal nerve, which allows us to perceive sensations like the "cooling" of menthol or the "heat" of peppers.

These sensations of touch do more than tell us a beer's texture—they influence flavor as well. In the presence of pain (from, say, capsaicin), taste becomes less acute. Viscosity reduces the perception of retronasal smell. Warming temperatures release both taste and aroma. The process works in reverse, too: Sweet liquids feel more viscous, while sour ones feel less viscous.

BEER FLAVOR WHEEL

Some people respond to visual arrangements better than lists. Visual wheels are one way of illustrating the elements of flavor in all its tactile, aromatic complexity.

BUILDING A BLIND TASTING

HABIT AND ANTICIPATION are foes to careful tasting. So much information is available before that first sniff and sip come along: about the brewery, beer, beer style, price, our past experience, and the information taken from a label. We've already begun forming an impression of a beer, and that colors our experience when we finally do get around to trying the beer. One of the best ways to subvert this extraneous information and develop attention and curiosity is through the practice of blind tasting.

These need not be elaborate experiments. Start with your favorite beer and build a tasting around that style. It's good to have at least three beers but not more than perhaps a half dozen—too many and palate fatigue will dull the experience of the later pours. It's best if you have someone to proctor the tasting and pour out the samples, but it's easy enough to wrap the bottles in paper or tinfoil to conceal the label. Give everyone one glass for each beer, and make sure you number the bottles. Have water and saltines or plain bread handy as palate cleansers.

Then taste. You'll be amazed by what your senses can uncover. You may also be amazed to find that your old friend, that favorite beer, isn't as familiar as you think. I once did a blind tasting of four of my favorite IPAs and I was stunned to find that I had confused two of them. What was instructive in that tasting—aside from rediscovering my humility—was realizing that there were flavors and characteristics to those beers that I had managed to miss all along. ■

ALL BAD BEERS ARE ALIKE

ITH APOLOGIES TO Leo Tolstoy: All good beers are good in their own way; all bad beers are alike. Truly exceptional beer is always distinguished by an ineffable singularity. The pieces come together in a way that delights and surprises us. Bad beers are just the opposite: They bludgeon us either with banality or off-flavors. Some bad beers have objective flaws of process or infection while others fail because of sloppy execution or a faulty recipe. Unfortunately, bad beers are not rare. Perhaps a third of all commercially brewed beers qualify.

So what's a bad beer?

TECHNICAL FLAWS OR INFECTIONS

A lot can go wrong during or after the brewing process to ruin a beer. Once poor sanitation and infection were an unavoidable problem that breweries could only hope to mitigate. There's no reason for modern beers to be infected—but they can be. Poor sanitation or poor brewing methods can turn beer funky or sour. Some breweries have technical problems with their equipment that contribute to off-flavors. Old ingredients do a beer no favors and can lead to dull or stale flavors.

Not all bad flavors are a brewery's fault, though. Once a pallet of beer leaves a brewery, it may endure all kinds of violence; heat and sunlight, agitation, and age are no friends of beer. Not every pub takes care of its kegs, either. Some don't clean the hoses connecting the kegs and taps; some don't rotate the beer often enough. With cask-conditioned beer, vigilance is critical to ensure a fresh, tasty pint, and inattention leads to spoilage and souring.

The baseline for technical faults is not always absolute. A bug in one style of beer may be a feature in another—in the case of soured beer, literally. Indeed, most "faults" are acceptable in some styles of beer. We don't all have the same sensitivities to these faults, either. Some people have a hard time detecting one, where to others, they are intense (and usually offensive) even in very small doses. Below are some of the most common characteristics, their chemical sources, the cause, and the styles in which they're permitted.

■ **Astringency, huskiness, tannin.** Astringency is halfway between a flavor and a sensation, and can be confused with other elements in beer like bitterness and high attenuation. Think about the quality of black tea and you're in the ballpark. The sensation comes from the tannins of malt (though hops may also contribute), a dryness on the tongue that comes from a chemical reaction that causes proteins to coagulate in the saliva. It comes from oversparging and rinsing the tannins off the grain. Some breweries prefer low levels to enhance dryness.

■ **Butter, butterscotch.** This comes from the compound diacetyl, a substance with such a pronounced buttery flavor it's used to flavor margarine and theater popcorn. In low levels, it can be a pleasant, comforting nuance in British and American session ales. However, at higher levels, it tastes artificial and coats the tongue with an unpleasant slickness. Diacetyl is a natural by-product of fermentation, but yeast will reabsorb it if left long enough before packaging. Breweries rushing their beer out too soon may leave diacetyl in the beer, and it can also form from bacteria in dirty tap lines in pubs.

■ **Pungent cheese or stinky feet.** This unpalatable aroma comes from isovaleric acid, and is never appropriate. Isovaleric acid is found in some cheeses and the sweat of human feet (ew: again, *never appropriate*). It comes from poorly stored, oxidized hops.

■ **Cabbage, stewed vegetable, creamed corn, tomato juice.** The culprit here is the compound dimethyl sulfide (more commonly referred to as DMS). This is another aroma compound that is acceptable in low doses, particularly in German lagers, but in higher concentrations it is unpleasant. DMS comes from a molecule present in germinating barley that is usually driven off during kilning (that's why in light German malts, some remains), or from poor wort handling in the brewery.

■ **Green apple.** Another constituent of beer that grows in offense as it grows in strength is the compound acetaldehyde. Interestingly, acetaldehyde is a precursor in the process of sugars becoming alcohol—and it's also what our bodies immediately convert alcohol into in order to metabolize them. In beer it may be perceived as a fresh note (fine), or in larger concentration tastes worty, like green apples or cider (not fine).

■ **Metal.** This rare condition is partly a taste and partly a chemical/electric sensation. In any beer, it's unpleasant. It may come from poor water or old brewing equipment, or may be a function of oxidation. A keg may even be the culprit.

■ **Nail polish remover, solvent.** Yeast produces a lovely ester that forms the "fruity" character that beguiles us in ales. It can also produce a compound that has a piercing, volatile solvent note like nail polish remover. For breweries, the tricky part is this: Both flavors are caused by ethyl acetate. The solvent-y end of the continuum is a sign of poor handling and is more likely in stronger beers like abbey ales and barley wines. *Brettanomyces* also produces ethyl acetate in large quantities, and this characteristic sometimes overwhelms tart ales.

■ **Paper, wet cardboard.** These flavors come from oxidized beer—a process of staling. When beer ages, many of its chemical properties change. In a few types of beer, like old ales or strong stouts, a touch of oxidation produces a sherry-like note and can be welcome; in most beers it is not. As beer oxidizes, the flavors begin to get dull and indistinct and ultimately give a papery or wet-cardboard flavor.

■ **Skunk.** Drinkers of certain European lagers sold in green bottles may be familiar with a skunk-like flavor the beers sometimes vent. It used to be so common that skunkiness was considered a mark of authenticity. In fact, this is a serious flaw caused by light striking the iso alpha acids in hops. The reaction produces the offending aroma, which is a dead ringer for skunk spray. Clear and green bottles offer no protection against light; brown ones are better. Best are cans. If you have a choice, always skip beer in green or clear bottles.

■ **Soy sauce, meat.** Yeast cells contain certain lipids, amino acids, and nucleotides that are usually no bother to beer—they're safely contained within the yeast's cell walls. Under the influence of heat, age, or other conditions, the cells can rupture, causing autolysis. When the insides of yeast cells go outside, they give beer a meaty flavor. (Indeed, autolyzed yeast is used as an additive in foods to provide that meatiness.) In aged dark beers, yeast autolysis is one of the chemical reactions that may enhance flavor, but it usually is strange and off-putting.

The Science of Foam. When you pour Champagne or cider into a glass, they form a fleeting head. Beer's head stays firmly in place—the only beverage where that happens. Why? In a word: protein. Foam is normally unstable because the carbon dioxide gas usually passes from one bubble to a larger neighbor until it all evaporates in a rush. The proteins in beer form an electrostatic skin around the gas bubbles that prevent gas migration. When brewers want to increase head retention, they add a bit of protein-rich wheat or oats ("head grains") to the grist. Hop acids also help strengthen the walls of gas bubbles—which is why the foam may taste more bitter than the liquid beer.

■ **Stale.** The process that ultimately results in oxidation begins as a steady dulling of the clear, crisp flavors and aromas in fresh beer. Oxygen is a principal source, but other compounds like aldehydes also contribute. Staling begins within days after packaging, and at first merely occludes beer's most vivid flavors and aromas. Eventually beer becomes dull and inert. There's really no way to prevent this natural process, though breweries put a lot of effort into keeping oxygen out of their beer.

■ **Sulfur, burned matches, rotten eggs.** Sulfur compounds begin in the wort and may also be produced during fermentation, particularly in lagers. Another source, now quite rare, is untreated water of the kind made famous in Burton upon Trent. In those beers, the aroma of sulfur can be powerful. Sulfur dioxide is the brimstone aroma of a burned match—the sulfur found in lagers. Hydrogen sulfide is a rotten egg aroma, the one that is (amazingly!) prized by fans of Burton's pale ales; elsewhere it is considered an unwelcome guest.

This is by no means an exhaustive list. You may encounter any number of bizarre, unpleasant, or funky aromas or flavors in your travels. Rule of thumb: If it tastes bad, it probably is. The world of beer does admit a few oddball flavors and aromas to acceptable society, but those that are aggressively unpleasant are probably evidence of problems. Don't be afraid to send a beer back if it doesn't taste right.

FAULTS OF EXECUTION OR DESIGN

You might think Indian beer would be good—the British, who ruled the country for centuries, left behind artifacts like tea drinking and railroads. There's even a beer style with the word "India" in the title. But no. I had the great fortune of living in India for a time, and I never encountered a palatable beer. (Things have improved very slightly since.) People who drink beer there do so for a reason reflected in brand names like Knock Out and Hercules. Indian beers come in two varieties, regular and strong (something like malt liquor), and they're thin, harsh, and metallic.

Making exceptional beer is very hard. Coming up with a perfect recipe that can be brewed perfectly on a given system is hard enough that the birth rate for world classics is very low. Making excellent beer is easier—though not by much. Good or average beer, though, that is the obtainable objective to which all breweries should aspire. And yet still there is bad beer.

Keeping in mind that the measures of "good" and "bad" are subjective, aesthetic ones, what constitutes bad beer? The easiest examples are those, usually found in brewpubs or new breweries, where a batch didn't turn out like the brewer intended or expected. Not defective; just too much of something or too little of something else. Instead of writing it off as a costly mistake, the brewery decides to sell it, hoping the failure will appeal to someone.

The more difficult examples are those like the Indian beers that are clearly made the way the brewery intends—but where the beer just isn't good. In some cases it's driven by cheapness: A brewery makes a beer like Natural Light or St. Ides expressly to be purchased in bulk. No one expects it to be good, and it's not. Gimmick beers like Miller Genuine Draft Light 64 Lemonade are reliably bad—and usually evanescent; Miller killed that experiment after just three months. Attempts by big breweries to cash in on the craft beer phenomenon can also result in failed experiments, like Anheuser-Busch Shock Top Raspberry Wheat or MillerCoors Henry Weinhard's Belgian Style Wheat Ale (my nominee for worst beer ever).

But the industrial companies aren't the only ones making bad beer. One special category of bad is beer that has gotten too extreme for its own good. The current fetish for hops has led to some pretty terrible chemistry projects masquerading as beer. Acclaimed breweries like Stone and Mikkeller have been responsible for some of the worst offenses. Tart beers, among the hardest to master, are often badly made as well, with chemical or solvent notes, far too much acetic acid, or other off-flavors. Unfortunately, after a brewery has invested months or years making these, it is reluctant to dump them. And even innovative breweries like Dogfish Head sometimes let their creative juices take them too far.

Don't be afraid to call a beer bad. Some just are. Leave your mind open to the possibility that it is actually the beer, not your palate, where the problem resides. ■

PART TWO

Ales

LAGUNITAS

IPA

INDIA PALE ALE

THE
LAGUNITAS BREWING COMPANY
PETALUMA, CALIFORNIA

There are many ways to organize and taxonomize the great zoo of different beer styles. The English of Shakespeare's day used "ale" and "beer" to distinguish weaker, unhopped brews from the stronger concoctions incorporating that sexy new spice, hops, that was all the rage. This was, of course, long before brewers understood yeast and the differences among the strains; for them, beers came in more general categories. Further back, the Indo-European root, *alu*, connoted magic and intoxication, and suggested both beer's creation and its effects. No such subtlety was in play in the Baltic and Scandinavian countries, where the local equivalents (*öl*, *øl*, *alut*) were umbrella terms for all malt alcohols. And until recently in America, "ale" referred to a crude, old-timey drink; now it indicates a sophisticated artisanal product.

In the latter part of the nineteenth century, scientists began to understand yeast, and they realized it came in different strains. The common variety they named "sugar fungus" (*Saccharomyces*); they found it in bread as well as beer. Later, they isolated a dangerous stranger that took up residence in English ales; it was a wild yeast they called "British fungus" (*Brettanomyces*). They found other strains as well, and following their orderly scientific process, the discoverer of lager yeast named it after the brewery for which he worked (*S. carlsbergensis*). In the twentieth century, everything seemed very tidy: There were ales, and there were lagers, and the two were distinguished by the yeast used to brew them. Alas, more sophisticated genomic research has revealed a twisted lineage and commingling of gene lines. From imprecision to precision and back again.

If we haven't come to a final, definitive standard for sorting and organizing styles, we have at least come to general agreement. Ales are everything left over after you've culled the cooler-fermenting aged lagers from the group; those beers soured with wild yeasts and bacteria; or those whose most obvious quality is their wheaty body. Put these varieties in their own group and you're left with ales: a broad category of beers that includes everything from English mild ales to Belgian quadrupels.

LEFT: *Like the members of a family, these ales are related but distinct from one another.*

A few things do unite the ales: They're made with easygoing yeasts that require little fussiness from the brewer. Brewed at room temperatures, ales ferment quickly and can be ready to drink within less than two weeks. And during fermentation, ale strains produce chemicals that add fruitiness or spiciness to a beer's flavor.

The styles of beer we call ales have ancient lineages; it was an ale yeast strain that enlivened the first prehistoric bowl of gruel-beer. Because brewers quickly understood that adding a bit of one batch made the next one ferment, the process of domesticating yeast began thousands of years ago. This inadvertent yeast breeding led to particularity; "house character" varied from brewery to brewery, and national traditions and preferences led to schools of ales. When we survey the ale-producing world, what we see is the evolution of style on the microbial level.

That evolution is evident in the way ales taste country to country. Until a couple hundred years ago, the ales of modern-day northern Germany were strange and exotic. But thanks to the startling popularity of lagered Bavarian beer, ale producers in northern Germany began to exchange their flamboyant beers for more straitlaced ones. The ales of the Rhine eventually evolved to share the stripped-down elegance of the lagers that threatened them. Not so in neighboring Belgium, where the brewers favored exotic ales—like the German ale brewers used to make—that were packed with the flavors of fruit and spice. Belgians encouraged their yeasts to frolic at higher temperatures and throw off gaudy aromas and flavors.

British brewers, practitioners of moderation, split the difference. Their ales exhibited subtle fruity qualities— just enough to tease out the flavors of their hops and complement the mild sweetness of their malts. As American craft brewers developed a kinship to ales, they found they preferred to accentuate ingredients—hops, mostly. And so their ales were more neutral than Belgian and English ales: still lightly fruity, but not showy.

When you have an ale in front of you, there are many ways to detect the yeast's fingerprints. Fermentation produces a number of chemical compounds. Ales will have a quality that you might think is sweetness, but taste more closely. It's actually a fruitiness—pear or plum— rather than a sweetness. These are esters. You may notice spicy notes like clove or black pepper as well (phenols) or "hot" notes (fusel and higher alcohols). Study your ales, and then compare them to lagers. Soon you will begin to identify those markers that distinguish the beer, undeniably, as an ale. ■

BITTERS

In much of the world, beer names are good, solid nouns: bock, pilsner, lambic. Britons have a penchant for descriptors, like "mild," "stout," or "bitter." These terms aren't absolutes, though—they indicate relative qualities. The adjective "bitter" is used to distinguish this style from sweet, light milds. It's the bitterer of the two. But stripped of context, the name misleads. British bitters are characterized by a definite hop presence, but they have no violence in them. The hops ride atop a gentle biscuit sweetness and add marmalade and spice—but they aren't harsh or what we would, in other contexts, call "bitter."

Of all the beer styles, the most harmoniously

Bitters. An ideal place to enjoy a bitter is at a pub, preferably when the beer is drawn from a fresh cask. Although bitters come in a range of strengths, each is designed to showcase an elegant interplay between soft, caramely or bready malts and spritely hopping. The strongest bitters are forceful and bold, but unlike IPAs, they don't sacrifice malt flavor and aroma on the altar of hop intensity. The weaker versions, ordinary bitters, can exhibit surprisingly strong flavors, too, especially on cask. The world's best bitters come from Britain, where brewers treat them like artistic expressions. Their size and simplicity seem to be the point. It is no surprise that bitters make excellent partners with fish, either battered and fried or swimming in creamy soups.

STATISTICS

Ordinary ABV range: 3.5–4%; bitterness: 20–45 IBU

Best or special ABV range: 4–6%; bitterness 20–45 IBU

Serving temperature: 50°–60°F

Vessel: Pint glass

balanced might be bitters. They exhibit equal parts malt, hop, and yeast character, never favoring one over the other. Balance is one of the key factors in these beers, which are designed to be drunk in sessions of twos and threes. No single element wears out its welcome or tires the tongue. Instead, a drinker may stop to admire—even well into his third pint—the lively flavors that impressed him on his first sip. ■

ABOVE: *London Pride is a familiar cask bitter in the U.K. capital.*

ORIGINS

BITTER ALES WERE delayed until two discoveries made their birth possible: hops and modern kilning techniques. People knew about hops at least by the time of Christ, but they didn't first think to put them into beer until around the ninth century. Before the discovery of hops, beer was mild and sweet, balanced by herbs and spices. In France, the monks who first recorded their use took a long time to spread that particular gospel. (The intervention of war and plague probably didn't help move things along.) It wasn't until the early 1400s that hops finally made it to Britain—but only in the beers of immigrant brewers. It took the English another century to find religion and plant their own hops.

Straw-colored malts were also slow in coming. Before the 1640s, kilning was a crude process that left malt smoky and blackened. With the invention of coke—coal processed to drive off toxic chemicals—maltsters had more control over the kilning process and could produce relatively pale malts. The distant ancestors of bitter—heavier, stronger beers—were made with these malts. By the early decades of the 1700s, the great porter epoch was dawning, relegating other styles to niche status. Pale ales were brewed, but not in great quantities.

Pale beers began to find a larger audience around the time Queen Victoria ascended the throne in 1837. Several factors contributed to their rise. After decades in which London's porter breweries dominated the country, breweries in Burton upon Trent were finding success with two varieties of paler ales. Since the eighteenth century, brewers there had shipped a heavy brownish ale called "Burton ale" to the Baltics. In 1822, however, the Russian government placed a ban on imported beer (excluding porter), and the market for Burton ales dried up. With a little fine-tuning, making the beer lighter in color and more attenuative, breweries like Allsopp and Bass refashioned Burtons for the British market. They were still strong

ABOVE: *A "Burton Union system" typical of nineteenth-century breweries in the city—this one on view at the National Brewery Centre, Burton upon Trent*

BELOW: *Bass was once the largest-selling brewery in the world, and its pale ale was the standard bearer for the style.*

king and would remain so for decades to come, but pales gained popularity as they rode the new rails out of Burton to farther reaches of the kingdom. Another Industrial Age innovation helped raise their profile: machine-made clear glassware. People could see what they were drinking, and the bright-copper pale ales looked mighty nice in a tall, clear glass.

At the middle of the nineteenth century, bitters were not especially strong, but they were made with a great deal of hops. They were also aged, sometimes as long as a year. From at least the middle of the century onward, brewers also made pales with more delicate bitterness; these they called "light bitter." Although it had been legal to add sugar to grists for twenty years, it wasn't until the turn of the 20th century that it became more common in bitters.

Although bitters had been brewed for decades, they spent most of their long lives playing second fiddle to other styles. The porter era gave way to milds by the

like Burtons, but pale—a step closer to what we think of as modern bitter.

The breweries of Burton had a special advantage in producing paler ales: the water. London's water was highly carbonic; it brought out a harsh note from the hops, a key element in the new pale beers. Burton's water, which lay in gypsum beds below the city, was rich in calcium sulfate. This brought out hop bitterness without harshness and, as a bonus, worked to clarify the beer. The result was sparklingly vivid ales much of the rest of the country couldn't match.

Industrialization was one of the main drivers of the period. Porter was still

Kent Golding and Fuggle.

Hops got to Britain late, centuries after they had been spicing continental ales. Britain's beers would one day be famous for their hops, but the local brewers were slow to adopt them. The first fields were eventually planted in Kent, a county southeast of London, the region that would later become the hop heartland of the kingdom. Hops were a lucrative cash crop; the harvest was so massive that until World War II, as many as 80,000 Londoners would board trains and spend working vacations in Kent picking the bines in late summer. Growers bred a number of hop varieties over those centuries, but none so define modern British ales as Golding and Fuggle.

Golding emerged in the 1780s and brewers immediately recognized their quality. The classic variety is East Kent Golding, although a number of similar strains have been bred over the years. (Confusingly, Styrian Golding, a common modern variety, was bred from Fuggle stock.) East Kent Golding is complex but mutable. Always smooth, it sometimes tends toward the floral (lavender, lilac) or the citric (lemons), while at other times it can be sweet, with notes of apricot or marmalade. These different flavors emerge in the beer depending on when the hops are added to the boil and what notes they pick up from other hops, the malt, and as a result of fermentation.

Fuggle came ninety years after Golding and, like its precursor, was a quick hit: It would eventually become the staple hops grown in Britain, accounting for more than three-quarters of the harvest by 1950. A perfect dance partner for the light, top-noted Golding, Fuggle adds depth and gravitas with a woody, earthy, and sometimes peppery hopping. Unfortunately, the English Fuggle crop has struggled in recent years with blight and breweries have begun replacing it with modern strains.

Golding and Fuggle, which have been bred into dozens of other strains, are among the most famous and best-regarded hops in the world—deservedly so. Classic beers using them include Brakspear's Special, St Austell HSD, Young's Bitter, Wadworths 6X, Adnams Bitter, Brains SA, and Marston's Pedigree.

RIGHT: *The gentle climate of Kent, England, produces some of the world's most famous hops.*

Pale or Bitter? At their fringes, beer styles always fray. When does a porter become a stout? In the case of pale ales and bitters, it's not clear that there's any distinction at all—in the center no less than at the fringes. In the beginning, they were clearly not distinct. On bottle labels, where breweries controlled the message, the name was more often "pale ale," but in the era before pump clips (the signs attached to tap handles) identified beers, punters called the same beers "bitter" when they ordered a round. Same beer, different names.

Now even Britain's Campaign for Real Ale (CAMRA), the great defender of traditional styles, isn't sure. Bitter, they say, "grew out of Pale Ale but was generally deep bronze to copper in colour due to the use of slightly darker malts such as crystal that give the beer fullness of palate." Ah, so it's color that distinguishes them? Not so much. "Today," they write, "Pale Ale is usually a bottled version of Bitter."

One difference is that bitters are generally regarded as a range of beers, some as weak as 3.5% ABV, some as strong as 6%. Pale ales, by contrast, tend toward the middle of the range. Where pale ales truly become distinctive as a separate style is in the hands of Americans, but that's the subject of the next chapter.

turn of the twentieth century, and milds remained the ascendant tipple through the 1950s. When the world wars did come, rationing ravaged bitters as it did all styles, and their strengths plummeted. It wasn't until the Beatles were shaking the foundations at Wembley Stadium that bitter would finally become the country's bestseller. Among ale styles in Britain, it still reigns.

If we tend to think of bitter as the signature style of Britain, it's because it's been such a prominent part of pub culture over the past fifty years. Bitter was the dominant style from the 1960s through the 1990s (when, much as was the case everywhere, light lagers supplanted them), and is still the foundation of the cask ale movement in Britain. ∎

DESCRIPTION AND CHARACTERISTICS

F YOU HAD TO SUM UP British brewing with a single style, bitter would be it. Londoner Alastair Hook, the founder of Meantime Brewing, managed to reduce it to one sentence: "The only thing that's given in Britain is hand-pulled cask ale with a bitterness of thirty and an alcohol of four percent." To translate: The classic bitter ale is a coppery beer of 4% alcohol and 30 units of bitterness, and a version of this beer is available in every corner of Britain at the

LEFT: *The price list for the typical range of cask ales in an English pub*

BELOW: *Burton Bridge, making bitters in a city famous for them*

notes of fruit and caramel. Ordinary bitters are often made with sugar, leaving them thin of body but crisp.

STRONG BITTER

Some breweries offer two bitters, some three. If there's a middle bitter, it may be referred to by a variety of names, none precise: "best" or "special," while the strongest of the bunch might bear a name like "extra special," "strong," or "premium." (To add to the confusion, these names are sometimes swapped between the middle and strongest bitters.) Modern

local pub. This is the foundation for a range in the style that grows increasingly strong and hoppy at the upper ends.

What all bitters have in common is an easy drinkability and a careful relationship between the malt and hops. Some may be quite bitter, but these never lose sight (or taste or scent) of their malty foundation. Others may be less bitter— but never do these forget that the style is designed to showcase the flavor and aroma of their native hops. Where they principally deviate is in strength.

ORDINARY BITTER

The nomenclature of bitters is no more settled than their definition. Some have no name at all, some are called "ordinary bitter," some just "bitter." Whatever the name, the smaller of the two categories usually rings in at a specific gravity of 1.040 (10° Plato) or lower—usually 3.5 to 4% in final alcohol content. Bitters aren't golden; instead, they have a burnished cast and often an off-white head. The nose will be redolent of hops, usually light and spicy, and underneath this the milder

bitter is not a potent style, however, and even strong bitters stay south of 6%. Like ordinary bitters, stronger versions have deep, wood-toned colors. Also like ordinary bitters, the sensations of hop and malt are similar—but more intense. Many stronger bitters will be balanced more toward hops, and cask versions are often dry-hopped to produce especially heady noses.

CASK-CONDITIONED ALE

If you look closely at their labels, you'll notice that some of the classic bitters come in two strengths—one for cask and one for bottle or export keg. This is a clue to the proper habitat of a good bitter. No style benefits more from being served on cask; indeed, when many people try bottles of supposedly world-class bitters, they wonder what the fuss is about.

Cask-conditioning presents beer in its most essential, naked state. The flavors and aromas in bitters come with lots of elbow room, unstuffed and unadorned with the exotic or intense sensations found in some of the ales of other countries. They unfold and blossom in a way that further exposes the lovely marriage between their elements. Beer packaged by cask is pulled from the fermenting tanks just before the yeast has finished its work. (This can be one reason why a cask ale is listed at a lower alcohol percentage than its bottled—and fully fermented—counterpart.) Once in the cask (or "firkin"), the yeast will eat up the remaining sugars and naturally carbonate the cask. By tradition, carbonation levels are kept low—about half the amount of a standard American lager. This practice dates back to a time when casks were actually made of wood and could only tolerate low pressure. What comes from the swan neck at the pub is

Moreish. If you visit a pub in Britain, you might encounter the adjective "moreish" (that is, more-ish) applied to beer. The term has a straightforward meaning— the quality of being pleasant over the course of a few pints—and yet it says almost as much about the British as it does about their beer. In no place on Earth do people more enjoy pubgoing than in Britain. This dates back to the period before central heating, when a barroom was likely more cozy than a drafty sitting room. People spent not just an hour or two in a pub, but whole evenings. Patrons prized beer they could drink over several hours, one that remained lively and interesting but didn't lead quickly to drunkenness. Over time, the beers that evolved were low in alcohol but toothsome and balanced; none is more suited for an evening's session than bitter.

Sadly, the days when life orbited around the local pub now seem to be fading, and over the past decade Britain has seen the closure of thousands of pubs. For the first time in history, the amount of beer consumed on draft has fallen below 50 percent. In those pubs still peopled by real ale fans, however, the quality of moreishness is a necessity, not a luxury.

living beer, and it will continue to ripen in the pub cellar.

I had sampled many bitters in my life, but the first time I actually *tasted* one was when I found Coniston Bluebird Bitter on cask in the U.S. At just 3.6%, it is tiny by American standards, and yet on cask it is a seductive, spicy tour de force. I was left gasping. You don't find cask bitter too often in North America, but always be on the lookout: Your sleuthing will be rewarded with a revelatory pour. ■

BREWING NOTES

B ITTERS ACHIEVE excellence through a kind of Zen simplicity. I have tasted examples made with a single malt and a single hop that nevertheless exhibited enormous depth—anything more would have been an affectation. This is the hallmark of the style. The grist usually has more than one malt but the goal is always an uncomplicated foundation. A typical recipe starts with a broad base of pale malts (90 percent of the grist or more), and may include a touch of crystal malt for flavor and a very small amount of darker malt for color.

The reason the simplicity of grist works depends on the richness of source malts, particularly the famous British pale malt. The names of different barley strains from which they come have a poetry about them—Plumage Archer, Maris Otter, Halcyon, Pearl, and Pipkin—and new varieties are constantly in rotation. Each malt has different qualities and characteristics, and breweries make choices based on the quality they're looking for—more breadiness or nuttiness, or any number of subtle flavors. Americans tend to think of Maris Otter, one of the

ABOVE: *One of the many copper English mash tuns dating to the nineteenth century, Greene King, Bury St Edmunds, England*

most famous malts, which results in richly malty, bready beers, as the flavor of Britain. But for that same reason, other breweries eschew it. They prefer malts with different characteristics. When I visited Samuel Smith's, head brewer Steve Barrett said, "We've not used Maris Otter in the twenty-seven years I've been here." He uses Tipple and a bit of Optic.

Another important British process that adds even more flavor and character is floor malting. While modern industrial techniques allow maltsters to maximize malt's potential sugars—the chemical breakdown of starches and proteins into sugars and enzymes—floor malting is the

British Barley. In the U.S., brewers mainly speak of two- or six-row barley, not specific strains. In Britain, barleys are as important as hops in producing rich flavors in the country's low-gravity beer and, like hops, come in different, named varieties. New varieties are constantly being developed, and certain barleys come into popularity while others fall out. The churn is, if anything, more vigorous than it is among hop varieties. The king of British barley is Maris Otter, which for many people defines the flavor of England. A cross of two older strains bred in the 1960s, it is low in protein, producing a distinctive biscuit flavor. Maris Otter has had impressive lasting strength among malts, surviving long after others, like Pipkin, fell out of favor. Halcyon, Pearl, and Optic have emerged as alternate strains, and Golden Promise remains a Scottish favorite.

ABOVE: *The storage loft of an English malthouse built around 1834 serves as a maltings depository.*

to produce consistent beer speedily, and sugar helped the process. Now it's exceedingly common. Sugar, in contrast to malt, is completely converted to alcohol, which in turn thins the body and creates a crisper beer—key markers of the style. This gives brewers the best of both worlds: The malts can express their flavor and aroma without making the beer heavy or crowding out those all-important hops. Moreover, a crisp finish is ideal in a beer that drinkers will be enjoying pint after pint.

traditional practice, done manually in the cooler months. It results in a highly modified product, a more richly aromatic and flavorful malt—attributes that carry over into otherwise simple beers. They are the soul of a bitter.

It is also common for breweries to add a small amount of brewing sugar to their bitter recipes—not to sweeten the beer, though. Using nineteenth-century equipment and malt, it was much harder

Of course, the focal point of a bitter is the hops—and in this quintessentially British style, that usually means English hops. If terroir has any place in brewing, it's in the way hops adapt to the soil and environment. Czech varieties are tangy, German strains spicy, American hops wild and citrusy, and the British have fruity, earthy, and peppery types. Many breweries just start with the classic, Golding, then augment them with Fuggle, Target,

Challenger, Northdown, Progress, or First Gold. In order to accentuate the fresh, green character of the hops, many brewers tuck a sachet of whole hops into the cask at packaging (a form of dry-hopping)—another advantage to cask-conditioning beer. Even Americans tend to hew pretty closely to tradition when making bitters, and if they use local varieties, they choose the ones that were derived from English strains, like Willamette, which is a barely changed Fuggle.

The final element defining bitter ales is the water—or rather, the miner-als in the water. The modern style has its origins in the beers of Burton upon Trent, famous for the hard, sulfurous water that bubbles up through its wells. No other brewing city in the world had water with

Bitter remains a hugely popular style in Britain because it combines an assertive flavor profile with modest strength. Hops are a big part of the picture, but it's the balance and moderation that make it so beloved. No other style achieves this quality quite as well, but there are some close relatives. *American pale ales* are an obvious choice for bitter lovers. *American amber ales*, particularly modest-strength versions, are another first cousin. American examples, however, may drift away from the simplicity and balance of British bitter. Counterintuitively, the soft, balanced, eminently "moreish" *southern German pilsners* and *helles lager* may be closer relatives to this style.

IF YOU LIKE BITTERS

as much dissolved solids as Burton's, which exercised a strong influence in the development of style. The contribution of those solids—calcium, sulfates, carbonate, magnesium, and sodium—is to create a "stiff" sensation like carbonation on the tongue. They accentuate and draw out hopping. Other cities have less minerally water than Burton, but everywhere I trav-eled in Britain, from Brighton to York, brewers described the water as hard.

One of the ways to instantly recog-nize the difference between American and English ales comes from the water. When American brewer David Geary was making his pale ale, the first thing he did was amend the water. "We have what the Scots would call 'whisky water' here in Maine—totally devoid of minerals—so we add gypsum" to stiffen it up. If you see a beer described by a U.S. brewery as a "tra-ditional bitter" or find the word "Burton" anywhere in the description, it means the brewer treated the water with extra salts and minerals. ■

LEFT: *The grain mill in a traditional English brewery*

EVOLUTION

AS PALE BEERS began to enter the market as a rival to porters 150 years ago, they hadn't yet cohered into a style. Some were lightly hopped low-alcohol beers ("ales") designed to be drunk within a couple weeks of brewing. Others were stronger and more heavily hopped ("beers"). Eventually, the lineages would split and the former would become "milds," the latter "pales" and "bitters." Ah, but what of pales and bitter? Two names for the same style, or something separate?

The question is as much a matter of philosophy as taxonomy—is a tomato a fruit or a vegetable? Without taking sides in what has become an ancient battle, it is worth pointing out a few salient distinctions. Of the two, only pale ales migrated beyond Britain. They are brewed broadly and are perhaps the most commercially successful style of ale in the world. Bitters, on the other hand, mainly stayed on the island. Bitter, unlike pale ale, isn't just a style of beer—it's a cultural artifact. The proper consumption of bitter (on cask in a pub), the specificity of the hop character, and the slight salty wash—these things are as much a part of place as gumbo is of Louisiana.

As a consequence, they are at best a niche style elsewhere—and usually brewed in homage to the old country.

The Role of "Rationalization." Few industries are as sensitive to economies of scale as brewing. Because of complex regulations, taxes, and ingredient costs, much of the price of a pint of beer goes somewhere other than the brewer's pocket. If he can shave a few pence off his own costs, he can increase his margins. The result is consolidation—"rationalization" in the United Kingdom. And the rationalizing the British did, beginning in the 1950s, was no less impressive than consolidation that happened under Miller, Coors, and Budweiser in the U.S. In the early 1800s, when brewing was typically not a commercial enterprise in the way we think of it, Britain had 50,000 breweries. It still had more than 1,300 by the turn of the twentieth century. Stunningly, only 141 remained by 1976—and six companies collectively accounted for 75 percent of the beer brewed in the U.K.

As in the U.S., however, this was not the terminal state. The same kind of depressing decline in character and individuality accompanied consolidation and led, perhaps poetically, to an unexpected end. The big six too sold out to even larger concerns like Heineken and Interbrew (which through several mergers has become InBev). Two, Whitbread and Bass, decided to scrap their brewery operations to focus on pubs and hotels—it was no longer rational for their breweries to make beer. Meanwhile, the vacuum created an opportunity for smaller breweries to enter the market, and now the United Kingdom boasts more than 1,000 breweries.

That doesn't mean there aren't good examples elsewhere, particularly in the U.S. But since it is a style of tradition, bitter doesn't lend itself to tinkering. Brewers with a hankering for the taste of England brew them, but they usually stick close to the script. For innovation, they've got pales and IPAs instead.

Which is not to say that bitter is wholly static in its home country. A new crop of microbreweries have spruced up the old style and given it a few modern innovations. In Sussex, Dark Star offers a perfectly traditional Best Bitter, but for those who thrill to adventure, they have a fast little number called Hophead that is simultaneously lighter in body than most bitters but far stronger in hop flavor and aroma (and they use American Cascades, to boot). Still, it's served on cask and comes in at a very British 3.8% ABV.

In Derbyshire, Thornbridge Brewery's classic bitter, Lord Marples, is named for a noble who once lived in the house that gives the brewery its name. But Thornbridge's claim to fame is a range of nontraditional beers that are strange, strong, and vividly hopped. A notable example is Kipling, a robust 5.2% bitter made entirely with Nelson Sauvin hops from New Zealand. In London, Meantime has taken the style even further. Owner and brewer Alastair Hook had a long, slow epiphany. A German-trained brewer who spent time watching the American craft brewing industry take

ABOVE: *The historic Marston's Brewery in Burton upon Trent pioneered the Burton Union system.*

hold, he conceived a beer that looked very much like a standard bitter through most of its creation—the best British malts and hops, brewed at session strength. The one difference? He pitched it with lager yeast. Within its first six months of life, London Lager took up a quarter of Meantime's production.

Other breweries like Marble, Hardknott, Ilkley, and Moor are making the next generation of bitter. They don't always use traditional ingredients in their bitters, and some aren't even served on cask. A new generation of younger drinkers has taken to slightly edgier beers and they don't insist on tradition—"craft brewed" is to them a marker of quality and innovation. Whether these beers remain a niche or begin to loosen the definition of "classic bitter" is an open question. But change does seem to be afoot. ∎

THE BEERS TO KNOW

BITTER IS A style designed to be dispensed on cask from a beer engine, so it's not surprising that bottled examples are uncommon. Consequently, the best place to find bitter is on tap at your local brewpub. Failing that, a few bottled examples are available. Bottles shipped from England will certainly be worse for the wear—and the lighter the beer, the more it will have wandered from the brewer's original intent. Still, it's worth sampling imported bitters because while they may not be their freshest, they still exhibit the qualities that define the style.

FULLER'S LONDON PRIDE

LOCATION: London, England

MALT: Pale, caramel, chocolate

HOPS: Golding, Target, Challenger, Northdown; Golding, Target (bottle only)

4.1% ABV, 30 IBU (on cask);
4.7% ABV, 35 IBU (in bottle)

London Pride might be called a strong bitter at another brewery, but it's only Fuller's middle entry. A silky beer accented toward the caramel malt base, it has a fruity palate with apple. The hops are light and floral and keep the palate

engaged over a session. My favorite part is a slight mineral undercurrent—a taste of the city's famous water.

FULLER'S ESB

LOCATION: London, England

MALT: Pale, caramel, chocolate

HOPS: Golding, Target, Challenger, Northdown

5.5% ABV, 35 IBU (on cask);
5.9% ABV, 36 IBU (in bottle)

Fuller's Extra Special Bitter (ESB) is the big brother to London Pride and another bitter, Chiswick, all come from the same parti-gyled mash (see page 142)—an old technique abandoned by nearly every other brewery—each a bit weaker than the last. And big it is. For those who think of English beer as weak and malty, Fuller's ESB will be a shock. In terms of intensity, it's comparable to an American IPA, crackling with potency and hop zest. Yet it's illustrative of the difference between the American and British traditions: ESB has a wonderfully smooth, nutty malt base; the zesty hops have elements of pepper and marmalade in the palate; and the whole beer is tied together by a structured minerality. As a boon to American drinkers, bottles arrive in better shape and give a truer sense of its character than lighter, more delicate bitters. ESB has been named Champion Beer of Britain three different years and is one of the finest ales brewed in the world.

CONISTON BLUEBIRD BITTER

LOCATION: Coniston, England

MALT: Pale, caramel

HOPS: Challenger; Mt. Hood (bottle)

3.6% ABV (on cask); **4.2% ABV** (in bottle)

Many breweries make separate draft- and bottle-strength versions of their beers; Coniston actually has two recipes. The cask version is superior by some measure—though, sadly, firkins rarely reach America. The draft version is a symphony of flavor marked by a balance between the soft warmth of the malt (toast, cookie, and caramel) and the lively, zippy hopping that contains notes of lemongrass and currant. In the bottle, the flavors are much more muted.

FIRESTONE WALKER DOUBLE BARREL ALE

LOCATION: Paso Robles, CA

MALT: Two-row pale, pale, Munich, caramel, chocolate

HOPS: Magnum, Styrian Golding, East Kent Golding

5.0% ABV, 32 IBU

One of the best American bitters comes from one of the most interesting breweries: Firestone Walker, which employs a "Firestone union" system of oak fermentation (the brewery's riff on a Burton Union system). The base beer is classically British, with a toffee malt base and sprightly, earthy hops. A depth of flavor comes from the oak, which lends a toasted vanilla flavor and a woody dryness.

ADNAMS BITTER

LOCATION: Southwold, England

MALT: Pale

HOPS: Fuggle, Golding

3.7% ABV, 33 IBU (on cask); **4.1% ABV, 33 IBU** (in bottle)

Adnams amends its water to a Burton profile, and the effect is obvious—its Bitter has a stiff, mineral structure and a touch of burned match—sulfur—in the nose. Minerality draws out hop character, and this beer has loads of crisp, peppery bitterness. Many bitters are silky, but Adnams's is lively and bright, with a texture reminiscent of club soda. It is a refreshing, restorative bitter.

TIMOTHY TAYLOR'S LANDLORD

LOCATION: Keighley, England

MALT: Golden Promise

HOPS: Styrian Golding, Whitbread Golding, Kent Golding, Fuggle

4.1% ABV, 1.042 SP. GR. (on cask); **4.3% ABV, 1.042 SP. GR.** (in bottle)

One of the most decorated beers in the United Kingdom, Landlord is on the strongish side, which gives it a bit of room to flex its muscles. The brewery has long relied on Scottish Golden Promise malts, giving the beer a warmth and breadiness, and the Golding and Fuggle hops give it that classic marmalade spice. The yeast is a famous element of the beer, nurtured in open fermenting vessels, and adds fruit and an excellent crisp finish. A classic.

CALEDONIAN DEUCHARS IPA

LOCATION: Edinburgh, Scotland

MALT: Golden Promise pale, Optic pale

HOPS: Fuggle, Super Styrian Golding

3.8% ABV (on cask); **4.4% ABV** (in bottle)

Don't pay attention to the name IPA in the name—this beer is a classic bitter. Given the reputation of Scottish breweries for full, malty ales, Caledonian's are surprisingly dry; they also share a lemongrass note. Both of these qualities suit Deuchars, a zesty, spritzy bitter that very much leans into its hops. Two varieties of pale malt lend little in color—Deuchars is almost pilsner-light—but do hint at warm bread. It was named Champion Beer of Britain in 2002.

ELYSIAN THE WISE ESB

LOCATION: Seattle, WA

MALT: Pale, Munich, caramel, Belgian Special B

HOPS: Chinook, Cascade, Centennial

5.9% ABV, 60 IBU

Looking at the ingredients, it seems impossible that Elysian's very American take on the style will retain much Englishness, but remarkably, it does. Despite hearty hopping, the sweet honey and toffee malts are center stage. The hopping is American, but does have fruity hints that remind you of the British originals.

TADCASTER, ENGLAND

Samuel Smith

A TRADITIONAL TOWER BREWERY

THE TOWN OF YORK IN NORTHERN ENGLAND IS NOTABLE FOR BEING ONE OF THE COUNTRY'S MOST HISTORIC. AROUND THE OLD CITY RUNS A WALL ERECTED BY THE ROMAN EMPEROR SEVERUS IN THE EARLY 3RD CENTURY 210 CE. INSIDE THE WALLS, BUILDINGS SAG WITH THE WEIGHT OF CENTURIES. THESE VISIBLE SIGNS OF AGE HAVE AN INTERESTING EFFECT ON RESIDENTS—TIME COMPRESSES SO THAT EVENTS DECADES OR CENTURIES IN THE PAST SEEM ALIVE AND CURRENT. PEOPLE DON'T TOSS ASIDE OLD WAYS LIGHTLY—IF, INDEED, THEY EVEN SEEM LIKE OLD WAYS. SOMETHING AS RECENT AS A NINETEENTH- OR TWENTIETH-CENTURY INNOVATION MAY STILL BE ON ITS FIRST LEGS.

One example of the phenomenon can be found twelve miles away in another ancient town called Tadcaster. Built of pale limestone and also founded by the Romans, it's a brewery town—that limestone makes the water as mineral-rich as Burton upon Trent's. At one end of High Street, the immense John Smith Brewery greets people coming from either direction; but while John Smith may own a larger market share, it's a different spur of the Smith line, Samuel Smith, where the true family lineage resides.

The Smith family is intensely private, and they don't regularly give tours of the brewery, which is largely hidden behind a small, pleasant storefront. Nevertheless, everyone in Tadcaster understands the brewery's dedication to tradition. In the early morning, they hear the clomp-clomp of the horse-drawn dray as it wheels out onto the streets, burdened with oak casks. From the street, they can see a thin trickle of black smoke from the stack, and if they stop into the brewery pub, they smell the coal fire crackling in the back of the room.

This is only the camel's nose peeking from underneath the tent. Back behind High Street, the old brewery is almost an entirely intact Victorian structure, and the methods used by Sam

Smith's have for the most part remained unchanged for over a century. The original footprint dates to 1758, when the brewery was founded, but the current building was erected in the 1840s.

All breweries were once built at a water source, and Smith sits on two well heads. The water is heavy with calcium sulfate and calcium chloride and is very hard—somewhat less hard than Burton water, but "not dissimilar," according to head brewer Steve Barrett. Many older breweries still use well water, but most use a process of reverse osmosis to strip out the minerals. Not Smith; when making bitter, they use the water the way they find it (they do amend it for some recipes, however, most notably their lagers).

Near the wells is the boiler room, and near that is a storage room piled high with coal. Old breweries all used coal at one time and many Victorian English breweries still have their old coal chimneys. They give the buildings a romantic grandeur, but none vent smoke anymore. Again, not Smith; the brewery is still fired by coal—"actually quite an economic fuel supply," says Barrett—same as it has always been.

A state-of-the-art brewery in the mid-nineteenth century was built as a tower to harness the force of gravity, and that's the way Smith's still works. Malt is milled on the upper level, and it joins water in the mash tun a level down. The brew kettle is a level lower, and beneath that sit the chillers and fermenters. There's no elevator, so brewers hike up and down the steep Victorian stairs as they monitor each stage of the brew.

The most famous part of the brewery is near the bottom: the Yorkshire squares. It is still common for older English breweries to use square fermenters; the wide shape means the weight of the beer exerts no pressure on the yeasts, and the corners and edges stifle convection. In a square fermenter, yeasts produce more esters and give English beer the fruity character it's famous for. In the Smith brewery, the squares are made of Welsh slate, an enormously durable surface that has now outlasted the old steel beams that support them. The brewery is in a slow process of upgrading the supports to stainless—but has no plans to update the slate.

Like much in the brewery, the squares were devised as an ingenious way to solve a nineteenth-century problem. In the early hours of fermentation, yeast rises to a billowy cloud. If the brewery has a way to harvest that yeast, it can re-pitch it in subsequent batches. The Yorkshire squares were designed to maximize harvest. They are actually dual-chambered squares, stacked vertically and joined by a hole in the middle. The bottom chamber is filled nearly to the hole with wort; when the fluffy yeast rises, it spills out through the opening into the upper chamber where it is easily collected. The brewery now uses a vacuum to collect yeast from the top chamber, but this is the only concession to modernity.

The final stage is packaging, and here again, Smith sticks with tradition. Decades ago, breweries put their beer in wooden casks to send out to pubs. Everywhere else in England, stainless-steel kegs replaced wood: Steel is lighter, easier to clean, and requires no tending by a cooper. Not Sam Smith. Their Old Brewery Bitter only goes in wood and is distributed to all their pubs that way. Smith's is the last brewery to have a full-time

LEFT: *A brew kettle—known as a* copper *in England*

ABOVE: *Steam valves are used to regulate the temperature of the kettle.*

cooper on staff, and he not only makes new casks, but tends to the old ones. The barrels do have the virtue of longevity. "We see on some of our labels that some of the staves date back a hundred years," Barrett told me.

There is an interesting paradox to the whole enterprise in Tadcaster. The brewery is among the most forward thinking in terms of product development. Its reintroduction of stouts and porters was a major inspiration for American breweries, and foreshadowed the slow return of dark ales to England; its line also includes some of the first organic beers brewed in Britain. Moreover, the brewery has embraced certain technological advancements—key among them, the addition of a laboratory.

In fact, this lab is one of the main reasons the brewery can keep making beer the way it does. At one point during my tour of the brewery, we came across an old Baudelot wort chiller—another antiquated piece of technology. It works by dribbling hot wort from a trough over a vertical stack of coils running with cold water. The brewery only uses this for its India Ale, and does so for the sake of authenticity, not because it has any particular advantages. In fact, "it's a microbiological nightmare," Barrett concedes. (Exposing chilled wort to the air could easily introduce unwanted wild yeasts.)

But it's not a nightmare, really. Barrett told me something that he would repeat when I asked him about the wooden casks—another potential wild-yeast vector. "The lab are always monitoring the microbiology." Compared to modern equipment, brewing on Smith's is a high-wire act, but they *do* have a net. If anything shows up in the lab, they can make adjustments. The truth is, modern monitoring techniques and a greater awareness of microbiology are the very things that allow Smith to continue to make beer the way they want to, which is to say, the way they always have.

PALE ALES

ot everything that is popular is good, but some things are so good they can't help being popular. Such is the lot of pale ale, a beer so beguiling that it is loved equally by novices and connoisseurs. The attraction begins at first glance; pales, whatever their hue, are brewed to please the eye. Like so many descriptive styles, "pale" is relative. American versions tend to be honey-colored to amber, while British versions are often a deeper copper. Both are bright and clear, capped with snowy white or eggshell heads. The pleasures continue with the nose, where caramel malts and sunny, lively hops spring out of the glass, and the tongue, which is greeted by an explosion of flavor that always stops safely shy of challenging. Pales are buoyant and full of life; uncomplicated, for sure, but never boring.

Pale Ales. Pale ales are hop-forward, but they rely on a foundation of malt sweetness that tends toward biscuit or toffee. The hops are used more to scent and flavor the beer than add sharp bitterness (as they would in an IPA); the tongue will find bursts of citrus, pine, or flowers, not a lacerating, bitter cut. Effervescent, light, and appetizing, pales are among the most versatile beers at the dinner table, contrasting the acid of tomato paste and vinaigrette as well as they complement fresh fish or semisoft cheeses.

STATISTICS

ABV range: 4.5–6%

Bitterness: 25–50 IBU

Serving temperature: 50°–60°F

Vessel: English pint glass

ORIGINS

WHAT'S THE DIFFERENCE between bitter and pale ale? Cascade hops. The answer is actually more complicated, but as shorthand goes, you could do worse. Modern style guides generally do distinguish between bitter and pale, and for good measure, they add a third style for American-brewed pale ales. There's little historical precedent for distinguishing between them, though, and if all we had to compare were British bitters and British pales, there wouldn't be enough difference to remark upon. But when the pale ale left Britain, it changed. In North America, pales lost some color, gained some octane, and were infused with wild kinds of New World hops. Compare this beer with the English bitter (or pale ale, which is the same beer), and the gulf is too wide to call them the same style.

As discussed in the previous chapter, the British themselves didn't distinguish between pale ales and bitters a hundred years ago—pales were "bitter" when compared to milds. The overall pattern of paler ales did change: They started out as thick, sweet Burton-style ales in the early nineteenth century (see page 79) and became lighter (but not light), drier, and hoppier. Pale ales, to the extent they were distinguished from bitter, seemed to be lumped in with India pales (addressed in the next chapter). By the time they reached their modern incarnation in mid-twentieth-century Britain, pales were light-colored, weak to modest strength, and marked by a pleasing hop character.

Individuation came when Americans, led by the early California craft breweries in the 1970s, began using American hops.

Americans had been brewing beer and growing hops for more than two centuries, but it didn't occur to local brewers to seek out unique, indigenous strains to spice their beers. Instead, they used native hops only to offer a neutral bittering charge, and imported European hops to add flavor and aroma.

As early as the 1950s, though, hop researchers were testing out the new hybrid strains as cheaper, healthier stand-ins for expensive imports. European varieties, when grown in America, were disease prone, and produced anemic crops. Hop researchers were trying to find effective counterfeits that grew well in the Yakima and Willamette Valleys of Oregon and Washington. One strain called Willamette had done just that—a hearty grower, it approximated the clean earthiness of its parent, Fuggle. A second strain called Cascade, however, was proving to be a troublemaker.

The first hops from the USDA's hop research program at Oregon State University, Cascade was conceived as a replacement for German hops. Brewers were hoping to find a stable supply, provoked by depleted German stocks following a wave of disease. Optimistic researchers expected Cascade to provide the same refined, harmonizing note that the European strains did. Cascade was cheap, and companies like Coors invested heavily in large acreage of the stuff. Anyone familiar with the strain today will see immediately what went wrong: It doesn't taste anything like German hops. Consequently, Coors didn't like Cascade. The hops were exhibiting what

Sierra Nevada Pale. Ken Grossman has always been way ahead of his time. He was brewing his own beer in the late 1960s—well before Jimmy Carter made it legal to do so—and founded a homebrew supply shop a decade later. In those formative years, he experimented extensively with ingredients and recipes. When he decided to found Sierra Nevada in 1979, he planned to use locally sourced ingredients and produce a distinctive American beer. "I wanted to do something that was not British, that was American, and wanted to feature American ingredients wherever possible."

Sierra Nevada wasn't the country's first craft brewery. Fritz Maytag had purchased and rehabilitated the Anchor Brewery in San Francisco, and Jack McAuliffe and Tom DeBakker ran two short-lived California micros in Sonoma and Novato. In Colorado, two professors started Boulder Brewing. But no one had a clearer vision of what "American" beer might look like than Ken Grossman. His first beer was the famous Pale Ale—one that has used the same recipe for over thirty years.

As craft brewing expanded, the qualities Grossman produced in Sierra Nevada Pale became the hallmarks of American style. The beer's architecture was built roughly to the specifications of British style. Sierra Nevada Pale differed only in accents: It was lighter in color and more alcoholic. Grossman used a very clean yeast that allowed the caramel malts and hop flavors to pop. His pale was brighter and brassier than British examples. Everything was dialed up another quarter turn—the strength, the bitterness, and that surprising, citrusy hop flavor.

It was never inevitable that Americans would naturally migrate toward wild, intense hops or the wild, intense ales they produce. Cascade hops were on the verge of commercial failure, and were it not for craft brewing, growers may well have ripped them out of their fields. Until as recently as the 1990s, many in the European beer community derided American hops as harsh or unpleasant; they weren't subtle or delicate like European noble hops, and they produced beers of "rough" quality.

Fortunately, Americans blithely ignored the critique. Other craft breweries began to emulate this style, and today Cascade-hopped pales are as common in American taverns as Golding-hopped bitters are in British pubs. When Sierra Nevada introduced Pale, it created a template for American beers that has led to IPAs, imperial IPAs, reds, ambers, and even new styles like Cascadian dark ales. All share a similar quality that mark them as American—wild, zingy hopping, caramel malts, and lots of alcohol oomph. In a pretty straight line, they can all trace their lineage back to Grossman's Pale.

would become the hallmark of American cultivars—a wild, assertive citrus note, not the subdued elegance of the Hallertau they were designed to replace.

Of course, for American craft breweries looking to distinguish themselves from the big lager companies, wild and assertive was a perfect fit. Two early adopters were Fritz Maytag at Anchor, who put Cascade in Liberty Ale in 1975, and Ken Grossman, who launched Sierra Nevada five years later on the strength of his Cascade-hopped pale. Although Liberty Ale was the first, Sierra Nevada's was really the ur-pale—the first commercial hit in the American oeuvre. Saturated with Cascade hops, it was a refinement on Maytag's Liberty Ale and created the model for the style—fresh and crisp, slightly sweet, but long and citrusy in its

hoppy finish. More than three decades on, if you walk into any brewpub in the country, you're likely to find a pale ale much like Grossman's original. If anything can be called an American standard, a mid-alcohol, Cascade-hopped pale is it. ■

DESCRIPTION AND CHARACTERISTICS

ANY BEER EMERGING from the bitter tradition is likely to be hop-forward, and so it is with pales. Yet "bitter" is misleading; the essence of pales is hop flavor, not pure bitterness. What's the difference? When hops bitter a beer, they create a sensation more than a flavor—it's similar to the cutting quality you find in hardy greens like kale. When they provide flavor, hops function more like another ingredient—lemon zest or fir boughs. Beer can be generically bitter, but the flavors hops offer are particular and dazzling in their versatility. In a pale, those flavors—and their attendant aromas—should be immediate. A sampling of what you might find: lime, grapefruit, black pepper, lavender, bergamot, cedar, mango. Other elements are important too, like the soft, pleasing base of biscuity or caramelly malts and a crisp effervescence. Pales are a classic summer beer, and the hops function like the juice in a fresh lime soda, making it crisp, bright, and refreshing.

AMERICAN PALE ALES

When Americans brewed these ales in the 1980s, they took the name rather

more literally than it was meant to be used in Britain. As a consequence, most American pales are tow-headed beers, whereas British versions might be dirty blondes, ginger nuts, or even light brunettes. Cascade hops remain the tuning fork for pales, and brewers don't like to deviate wildly from them, though breweries use other similar American strains for variety—Amarillo, Centennial, Simcoe, and Citra are common. In any configuration, though, the goal is similar: a smooth blend of hop flavors balanced by a comforting caramel malt base. Breweries don't use pale ales to express their individuality; the style is comfort beer, and no one wants to see a classic fiddled with overmuch.

BRITISH PALE ALES

British and American pales share many similarities; look a little closer, and you find a number of differences, too. The most obvious are the hops: In British pales, the hops run the continuum from earthy to herbal to spicy. But British pales, occasionally brewed with lighteners like sugar or corn, are lighter-bodied and drier. They may also have a distinct mineral note that comes from the hard water—it might be prickly on the tongue or even salty. The effect, especially when combined with the use of sugar, is a crispness reminiscent of hard cider.

Some American breweries make British-style pales and these feature classic British hopping (that herbal-spicy note). In other ways, they reveal their Americanness: Almost all are made with 100 percent barley and are consequently rounder and less crisp. New England seems to be especially fond of British standards—perhaps because of Geary's in Maine, the first New England example, and one of the best British-style pales in America. ■

Pale Ales and Brettanomyces.

No country's beers have gone through as radical a change as those of the United Kingdom, which famously became much weaker thanks to the ravages of grain rations during the world wars. But this was only part of the change. Until the twentieth century, British beers were regularly inoculated with a wild strain of yeast known as *Brettanomyces* (*Brett* for short). *Brettanomyces* is a voracious yeast that ultimately transforms a beer, leaving it very dry, leathery, or sour. But it's also slow-acting, rousing itself to attention only after its more spirited cousin, *Saccharomyces*, has feasted. Beer a couple of weeks old remains untouched by this dawdler, and even after a few months its effects will be modest. Give *Brett* several months, however, and it will take over a beer.

One variety of these *Brett*-aged pale ales, known as "stock" ale, was regularly aged for a year or more in wooden casks. The character of stock ale is well documented in written accounts going back centuries; if it was aged, it expressed the character of the wild yeast that resided in the crooks and crannies of the barrels. This goes for regular pale ales, too, some of which were aged on wood for a few months. As late as the 1930s, a Dutch scientist isolated *Brett* cultures from the dregs of a Bass Pale Ale.

What would those beers have tasted like? One approximation might be a beer brewed a few hours away at the Abbaye Notre-Dame d'Orval. The beer named for the monastery, Orval, is not identical to one of those old British pales, but it's close. A golden beer, the hoppiest of the Trappists—and dry-hopped—it is pale ale strength when bottled. But among the mixture of yeast strains used to ferment Orval is *Brettanomyces*. The beer that starts out as a floral, brightly hoppy beer changes with time. The *Brett* comes on after six months or so and dries out the beer, boosting the alcohol to more than 7%—bottled, it's listed as 6.2%. Orval's hops and malts are different from those used in historic British pales, and not all of the historic pales were held long enough to be affected by the *Brett*. But those that were? They would have tasted *something* like year-old Orval.

BREWING NOTES

L IKE BITTERS, pales are uncomplicated beers. Their success depends not on intricate or innovative recipes, just care and balance. In the U.S., pales adhere to a similar recipe: pale malt and a touch of crystal. It's not uncommon for a brewer to sprinkle in a pinch of wheat to add softness and head retention. Some breweries use rye instead, which adds a peppery, crisp note, and still others tuck in oats for creaminess. All of these specialty malts are there to add subtle enhancements to the basic malt bill. The real focus is on hops, characterized by middle and late additions of the most aromatic and sunny varieties. While breweries on the West Coast usually deploy a larger bitter charge than those in other regions, the differences in IBU are not great. Dry-hopping, an additional measure designed to infuse aroma into beer, is also common.

Pale ales are designed to be interesting but modest enough for a session of drinking. It is no surprise that a close kin is another of the world's most popular beers, *pilsner*. These come in different versions, but for Americans used to energetic hopping in their pales, the Czech version is the closest match. For those who don't like lagers, *amber ales* are a close match to pales—though they are maltier and less hoppy. Similarly, *bitters* are very close—and in some cases just different names for identical beers. For the adventuresome, a hoppy *saison* (like Saison Dupont) might be a rewarding change of pace.

In Britain, pales are brewed like bitters (in many cases, they *are* bitters), often with sugar or adjuncts—though pales seem more likely than bitters to be all-malt. As an oft-broken rule, British pales are more substantial than ordinary or best bitters, and about as often feature slightly more hop kick. Although this seems to be changing, pales used to be bottled versions of bitter, and perhaps the need to compensate for staling led breweries to make them a bit stronger and hoppier. ■

EVOLUTION

P ALE ALES ARE THE OLDEST of the American craft styles, but paradoxically, one of the least changed. The style's early success has given it a stability rare in American brewing. Anchor Liberty, Sierra Nevada Pale, Deschutes Mirror Pond—all have been around decades without changing.

So while breweries may fiddle with the types of hops, the standard—a roughly 5%, pale-colored, hoppy ale—hasn't changed much.

The real change has happened in Europe and especially Britain, where the latest trend is American-style ales made with American hops. This is a remarkable reversal, because even at the turn of the twenty-first century, stalwarts in the Campaign for Real Ale (CAMRA) were arguing that American craft beer was out of balance and amateurish—the parents, telling the kids in America to turn down the damn volume. Yet Britain, led by the new craft breweries that have started there in the past decade or two, has discovered the pleasures of loud, free-spirited American-hopped ales. Thornbridge, The Kernel, Marble, BrewDog, and Dark Star are all newer breweries that look to the U.S. for inspiration. To cater to this demand, British hop growers have even begun planting classic U.S. varieties like Cascade and Willamette, sending craft brewing full circle: American growers first

ABOVE: *Dark Star is one of a group of new British craft breweries looking across the pond for inspiration.*

experimented with those strains as a way of reproducing the British Fuggle. Now Kentish growers nurture the parent hop's descendant. ∎

THE BEERS TO KNOW

PALE ALES ARE among the most reliable styles brewed in America, and rare is the actively unpleasant example. Most are brewed in the American tradition with caramel malt and citrusy American hopping, but pay attention if there's any hint of Britishness in the name or iconography of a pale. These will be more balanced and have less hop intensity, and the hopping will be more wood bough and earth than citrus.

SIERRA NEVADA PALE ALE

LOCATION: Chico, CA

MALT: Pale, caramel

HOPS: Magnum, Perle, Cascade

5.6% ABV, 1.052 SP. GR., 37 IBU

Sierra Nevada's pale is one of America's most familiar beers, and yet it never

fails to impress. It pours out the color of a California sunset and vents that famous perfumey, floral Cascade hop scent. A perfectly crisp, balanced palate of caramel malt and spritzy citrus hopping buoyed with lively carbonation. It's a bright, sunny pale and the standard for the style.

DESCHUTES MIRROR POND

LOCATION: Bend, OR

MALT: Pale, Northwest pale, caramel, carapils

HOPS: Cascade

5.0% ABV, 1.053 SP. GR., 40 IBU

Deschutes has built an empire on recognizably British beers that have been gently Americanized. In the case of Mirror Pond, the malt base is straight out of London—a fullness of scone malting with a touch of apple fruitiness. Here the Cascade hops are more lemony and mild than some examples, but Deschutes's less vigorous carbonation allows them to fully blossom.

NEW GLARUS MOON MAN

LOCATION: New Glarus, WI

MALT: Pale, caramel

HOPS: Five American, one New Zealand

5.0% ABV, 1.049 SP. GR.

The essence of a pale ale is a smooth approachability, and Moon Man is a charter member. It's not a show-off beer. Modest, grain-y malts and a spirited bitterness that is at once herbal and fruity—not citrusy like those from the West Coast. New Glarus brags that it's a "no coast" pale, a wink and an acknowledgment that not all beers have to be titanic to delight. This beer's legions of fans can happily attest to that.

GEARY'S PALE ALE

LOCATION: Portland, ME

MALT: English pale, caramel, chocolate

HOPS: Cascade, Mt. Hood, Tettnang, Fuggle

4.8% ABV, 1.047 SP. GR.

David Geary learned to brew in Britain and faithfully re-created his own brewery to make the beers he so admired there. The brewery's pale is an elegant, somewhat austere example—and very British. The beer is framed by bracing minerality; it stiffens the herbal, spicy hops and dries the cracker-like malts. Perhaps the best example of an English pale ale made by an American brewery.

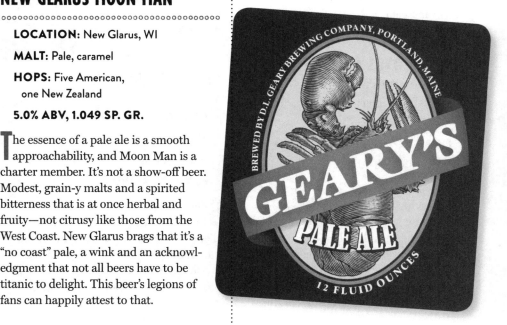

BOULDER HAZED AND INFUSED

ooooooooooooooooooooooooooooooooooooooooooo

LOCATION: Boulder, CO

MALT: Pale, caramel, roasted barley

HOPS: Nugget, Willamette, Crystal, Centennial

4.9% ABV, 1.050 SP. GR.

Pale is a relative term, not a dictate. Made with roasted barley, Hazed and Infused is a deep orange in the glass. Yet color isn't the emphasis here; hop flavor and aroma are. Dry-hopping produces rich grapefruit and orange aroma, and this is backed up by saturated flavors of citrus and cedar. The roasted barley comes in at the end, adding a snap of dryness that helps anchor the beer. If at all possible, try Hazed and Infused at the brewery; those dry-hop notes are delicate and evanescent.

THREE FLOYDS ALPHA KING

ooooooooooooooooooooooooooooooooooooooooooo

LOCATION: Munster, IN

MALT: Undisclosed

HOPS: Centennial, Cascade, Warrior

6.7% ABV, 66 IBU

There is a murky line separating American pale ales and IPAs, and Alpha King is sitting right on it. Three Floyds builds its muscular pale on a caramelly malt base, thick and sweet, which helps soothe the citrus assault of hops. It doesn't seem possible, but after a few swallows, Alpha King almost seems like a gentle beer.

SUMMIT EXTRA PALE ALE

ooooooooooooooooooooooooooooooooooooooooooo

LOCATION: St. Paul, MN

MALT: Pale, caramel

HOPS: Horizon, Fuggle, Cascade

5.3% ABV, 1.050 SP. GR., 45 IBU

This beer was first brewed back in 1986, but its flavors are as bright and full as anything made today. It's a fairly deep color for a pale, and those malts are rich and bready. They meld nicely with hops that are at turns citrusy and herbal. Spritzy on the palate, it's a great summer refresher.

ODELL ST. LUPULIN

ooooooooooooooooooooooooooooooooooooooooooo

LOCATION: Fort Collins, CO

MALT: Undisclosed

HOPS: Undisclosed

6.5% ABV, 46 IBU

Odell's St. Lupulin is a summer seasonal that offers the punch of an IPA at a slightly lower ABV. I don't know if it was intentional, but Odell seems to be evoking the summer in the fruity flavors the hops provide—peach, melon, and orangey-grapefruit citrus. The malts give a fairly thick, caramel body.

India
PALE ALES

espite its name, India pale ale (or the much more common "IPA") was never brewed in India. Nor was it consumed by Indians. Instead, it was brewed by the British for the British—first for those managing affairs in the colonies, and later for those enchanted by the idea of a beer with such an exotic provenance. In its first act, India pale ale was originally a strong, hoppy, elegant beer able to survive long-distance travel, as well as thrill English palates. But in the long decades of the twentieth century that constituted its second act, the style lived a degraded existence. It became just another bitter.

But that was not the last act.

India Pale Ales.

IPAs are brewed as a celebration of hops. Everything about these beers suggests vibrant hopping, from the lush nose to the sharp, green flavor—even the hazy golden color in some versions that comes from particles of hops floating in suspension. Try an IPA with spicy food and watch the hops dance with the chile—just as they did for British colonists dining on fiery vindaloo.

STATISTICS

ABV range: 5–7%

Bitterness: 40–75 IBU

Serving temperature: 50°–60°F

Vessel: Pint glass

In a final trick of export, IPAs came to America to be brewed by start-up craft breweries that found it offered a perfect template for local hops. Now it is one of the two most popular craft-brewed styles and nearly synonymous with craft brewing itself. The exporting continues; IPAs have spread to breweries across the globe in what has become the first international hit since pilsners managed the trick more than a century and a half ago. ■

ABOVE: *An authentic whiff of the past can be found in Worthington's English-style White Shield.*

ORIGINS

HE BRITISH BEGAN exporting beer almost as soon as they had colonies to which to export it. Shipments to North America and across the Baltic Sea went without a hitch—the cool waters ensured the beer made the journey in relatively good condition. But getting beer across the equator and around the horn of Africa to colonists living in India was a different matter. The first subcontinental shipments, which started arriving as early as 1711, included standard ales sold in London; none were specially brewed to endure the journey. Over the course of the century, records show that porter, pale ales, and table beer were all shipped to India.

Much of the beer that arrived was not fit to drink, and accounts describe some batches being dumped at arrival. There was just no way to mitigate the violence to which casks of live ale were subjected. As ships set out, the temperature of the North Atlantic was between 50° and 55°F—perfect cellaring temperature for beer down in the hull. But then sea temperatures rose to a tropical 80°F as ships passed the equator, dipped back to the upper sixties, and rose again to the mid-eighties by the time the boats reached India. All along that four-month ride, the ships rolled and bucked, keeping the beer at a constant froth. Of equal note: British beers of the era were all infected with *Brettanomyces*, a wild yeast resident in the wood of the casks. Wild yeasts can destroy a beer, effectively turning it to vinegar, and brewers compensated for its effects by keeping temperatures low or releasing beers fresh—neither of which was possible with ale shipped to India.

After decades of trial and error, breweries discovered that huge infusions of bacteria-inhibiting hops gave the beer at least a reasonable shot at potability

Burton Ale. Long before they became famous for sending pale ales to India, the breweries of Burton upon Trent were known for a thick brown beer they sent to the Baltics. The style took its name from its place of origin: Burton ale. The earliest versions, from the eighteenth century, were massive brews, heavy and viscous as honey. In 1822, however, the Russian government put a hefty tax on imported goods and the export Burton market suddenly died out. The breweries had to scramble to sell their signature product in Britain.

To appeal to locals, Burton ale brewers lightened their ale both in color and body and added hops. Even so, it was still a heavy beer and a hard sell. After a rocky start, the brewers realized that with a little age, Burton could become far more saleable; it was warming and comforting—and at more than 8% alcohol, quite strong, too. In the period of its popularity, Burton was strong but sweet and heavy with lots of unfermented sugars. Its tendency toward treacle was balanced by a stiff dose of hops, but this merely kept Burton from cloying. Thanks to wars and changing tastes, Burton gradually disappeared and now none are brewed under that name. A few beers matching its description are brewed, however—call them "disguised Burtons"—the best example of which is Fuller's 1845.

when it arrived in the East. By the 1760s, brewers were being advised it was "absolutely necessary" to use more hops for their Indian beers. Finally, by the 1790s, George Hodgson's Bow Brewery, east of London, began to find success with its heavily hopped pale ale; as a result, shipments to India grew tenfold. Yet for a beer with such renown, it's surprising to learn that the Indian market was never much more than a blip. Even at its height, India was receiving around 10,000 barrels of beer annually—just one-sixth the amount shipped to North America, and one-tenth the annual production of a single brewery at the time, England's Whitbread.

Based on those numbers, IPA should have merited no more than a footnote in the annals of brewing history before fading into obscurity—it was, after all, essentially just a strong, hoppy pale ale. But in 1820, English breweries started marketing a variety of beer back home of the same type that was "prepared for the India market." By the 1840s, breweries were calling it India pale ale and marketing it as a special treat. They played on the romance of the British Raj, elevating the style to one of elegance and adventure. One brewery even touted IPAs as the beer of "the gentry." It was a commercial hit, and this is when the style was truly born. India pale ales never sold well in India, but they became standards in England.

IPA has remained one of the most durable of styles, and versions have been brewed consistently in both Britain and North America since. Strength and hoppiness have waxed and waned, but the name—and the legend—have allowed the style to survive (and lately, flourish). ■

The Hodgson Dilemma. Among brewing historians (yes, there are such people) rages a debate: Did George Hodgson invent India pale ale to survive the four-month journey to India? In many books, he gets the credit. And indeed, Hodgson's Bow Brewery did come to dominate the Indian market in the early decades of the 1800s. But there are holes in the story: Beer, including pale ales, had been sent to India for decades before Hodgson. For a generation before him, brewers had known that high hop rates were critical to the survival of beers being shipped to warm climates. Unfortunately, the record is incomplete. What we know is that Hodgson *could* have invented IPA—though likely he was just the man who turned the information into gold—golden, hoppy ale.

DESCRIPTION AND CHARACTERISTICS

A S INDIA PALE ales have evolved, two branches have grown from the family tree—the British and the North American cousins. British IPAs, like Fuller's Bengal Lancer, are relatively modest beers—usually around 5% alcohol, with characterful if only moderate hopping. The American versions, like Bell's Two Hearted Ale, Sierra Nevada Torpedo, and New Belgium's Ranger, are stronger (6 to 7% ABV) and highlight intense hop aroma and bitterness. In England, India pale ale is a niche style; in the U.S., it is a mainstay.

AMERICAN IPAs

In America, India pale ales are a showcase for hops; all beers use them, of course, but in IPAs hops are the point. This quality is immediately evident in the nose, which will be fragrant with citrus, pine, or flowers, depending on the variety. Generous additions throughout the brewing process create beers with a saturated green character, extending from the nose through to the sharp, bitter finish. In IPAs, malts are designed only to add a touch of color and a bit of sweetness to draw out the flavor from the hops. Fruit notes are typical, such as grapefruit, tangerine, or apricot.

Twenty years ago, brewers inspired by the great journey the original IPAs took would occasionally add oak chips to fermenters to extract tannins like the original beers drew from English oak hogsheads. This affectation died out as IPAs became more established in the market, but some breweries have begun aging their beer in actual oak casks, thereby adding tannins and vanilla to the palate. Whether aged on oak or not—the great majority aren't— a good American IPA will be lively and invigorating, saturated in bright, hoppy flavors but not punishingly bitter or too heavy from either malt or alcohol. For many Americans, these qualities have come to define craft beer.

BRITISH IPAs

Whereas American IPAs focus on hop intensity, in Britain hopping does not come at the sacrifice of malt complexity. Typical British IPAs feature a more pronounced malt back-bone of caramel and toffee or toast and biscuit, and they are maltier, too, with darker hues of amber. Hopping is both lighter and of a different char-acter than in the American version, tending toward the earthy, spicy, or neutrally sharp hops of England. Although a couple of breweries have created revivals of the robust Victorian-era IPAs, most British examples come in just under or over 5% ABV. Finally, some British-style IPAs (whether actually British, or American) may vent a touch of sulfur—and in it drinkers will experience an authentic whiff of the past. The pale ale was perfected in Burton upon Trent, where water was drawn from wells deep in gypsum beds (see page 80). These were the breweries that came to dominate the Indian market, so a sulfurous nose is an appropriate nod to history (though not one people uniformly enjoy). A case in point—though sadly not available in America—is Worthington White Shield, a traditional IPA brewed in Burton upon Trent. ∎

People who like IPAs can pretty safely be called "hopheads." This style is all about the expression of hop aroma and flavor, combined with a touch of sweet malt. That last quality, though a minor note, is important—many fans of IPAs don't enjoy drier hoppy beers like German pilsners.

If you like a sweet ale note, go up or down the strength continuum—try an *imperial IPA* (up) or a *pale ale* (down). Another classic hoppy ale, though a maltier beer, is *extra special bitter (ESB)*. If you enjoy drier styles, consider hoppy *Bohemian pilsner* and *altbier*.

Burton Snatch. Burton water is famous not only for its hardness, but a distinct, infernal quality. A true Burton beer, one that has been pulled up through the gypsum-rich wells, should exhibit the "Burton snatch"—a whiff of unmuted sulfur. The scent comes in two varieties, one like a burned match (strange but broadly unobjectionable) and another like rotten eggs (objectionable).

I first encountered the Burton snatch in Burton upon Trent, when I lowered my nose over a pint of legendary Worthington White Shield, made locally. Worthington's is the rotten egg variety, and a whiff of it was enough to send me into involuntary recoil. How did this beer become so popular? Oddly, the nose attunes itself to this assault. The hard water gives a strong mineral scaffolding to the beer, one that works well with its fairly malty body. It's hoppy, but the hops work in tandem with the mineral salts. Together, the flavors make one of the most complex beers I've ever sampled. In fact, there's something almost Belgian about the way the aromas, texture, and flavors harmonize. Oh, and there's this, too—over time, the sulfur recedes, particularly in the bottle. Perhaps Burtonized pale ales succeeded in spite of the sulfur, not because of it.

BREWING NOTES

THE NATIONAL DISH of Thailand, pad thai, is so ubiquitous that there's no single quintessential preparation. Each chef makes it his or her own, and if you eat in a dozen restaurants around the country, you'll try twelve different versions. India pale ales are like that: Breweries try to craft versions that bear a personal stamp. In all cases, the key is the hops.

On both sides of the Atlantic, brewers start with similar grain bills composed largely of base malts. Some use 100 percent pale malt, though to add color and subtle flavor notes of caramel sweetness, they may include a small proportion of crystal, Vienna, or Munich malts. American brewers may use malts to add a touch of caramel, but otherwise they're looking for the hops to do all the talking. In the U.S., the intention in IPAs is to create a recognizable canvas: a pale to copper beer of 6 to 7% ABV. After that, it's all about the hops.

Breweries employ every combination of hops and method available. Some rely on early infusions to establish sharp bitterness, while others use hops throughout the boil for richer hop character. Two examples are instructive of the lengths breweries will go to in order to create a unique beer. Sierra Nevada was a pioneer in making IPAs, releasing their legendary Celebration in 1981. It's a classic American formulation—pale and caramel malts, and "three C" hops (Chinook, Centennial, and Cascades). The malt chassis is light, with a caramel-candy sweetness, and then it's all piney, grape-fruity hops. (The hop selection is the only thing that suggests it wasn't created just a few years ago; now the brewery would use hops like Citra or Equinox—two varieties the brewery helped develop.) It would take nearly thirty years before Sierra Nevada released another IPA in its regular rotation, but it made sure it was a good one—it even invented a device to brew it. The beer is Torpedo, an exuberant ale that showcases Citra hops. Sierra Nevada wanted to dry-hop the beer, but kept running into a problem with the volume of whole-cone hops they wanted to use. Sacks stuffed with hops came out dry in the middle, even

Equinox, Meridian, and El Dorado. Every IPA lives or dies by its hop character. To distinguish theirs from the scores of other IPAs on the market, some breweries have turned to new and experimental hops for exotic, novel flavors. Recent introductions include Equinox, a promising hop that by turns tastes herbal or tropical and can even produce the flavor of bell pepper; El Dorado, an intensely fruity hop that tends toward peach and apricot; and lemony Meridian, which can become minty in some beers. Hop growers give some breweries experimental hops to make test brews, and these just have numbers. Every year, new hop varieties come to market, so the variability of IPA is assured for the foreseeable future.

Ballantine IPA. In 1970, one brewery was still making India pale ales

the way the British brewed them in the 1830s. What's remarkable is where: Newark, New Jersey. Scottish brewer Peter Ballantine immigrated to the U.S. in 1830 and established his brewery in Albany, New York, in 1837. He moved it to Newark in 1840, where it stayed until 1971, when Falstaff bought it. The core brands survived until the late 1970s, and then vanished as the label was traded among brewing titans during consolidation. Falstaff no longer exists, and Pabst owns the Ballantine brand.

But for 130 years, Ballantine produced an amazing range of traditional English ales, including their IPA, a 7.5% ABV, 60 IBU monster that aged a full year in oak vats. Ballantine topped it off with hop oils made from Bullion—same as used in the boil—one of the early North American–European hybrids. The result was a sumptuous, woody beer with layers of flavor.

Ironies abound. Ballantine's was exactly the type of beer Americans strove to make when they started founding microbreweries in the 1980s. Had it survived a decade longer, Ballantine might well now be known as the beloved grandfather of the craft beer movement—and possibly a national treasure. Amazingly, it did survive through the rise of lagers in the mid-1800s, Prohibition, and the consolidation and homogenization of the beer market in the 1950s and 1960s—only to collapse just at the moment drinkers were poised to appreciate the kind of beers Ballantine made. It was a case of remarkable continuity; the brewery was a living link back to both early American brewing and to the tradition of the original India pale ales. It just couldn't survive that final decade.

In the final irony, craft beer may save Ballantine yet. In 2014, Pabst reintroduced Ballantine IPA, a 7.2%, 70 IBU bruiser, in small batches. Brewer Greg Deuhs researched the original recipe—it didn't survive the many changes in ownership—and includes an infusion of hop oil, just like the original.

---

after weeks of soaking in conditioning beer. Enter the "torpedo," a futuristic stainless-steel tube that might also have been called a "rocket"—but for liquids, torpedo is the better metaphor. The brewery fills it with hops and circulates fermenting beer through it. Not only does the torpedo make hopping more effective, but Sierra has discovered that it can control the levels and types of flavors and aromas the brewers put into the beer. It doesn't hurt that "torpedo" also makes a great name for an IPA.

Across the continent in Delaware, Dogfish Head took hopping even further,

developing a system of "continuous" hopping to dose their 60, 90, and 120 Minute IPAs. The system came to founder Sam Calagione while he was watching a cooking show that advised multiple additions of pepper to a soup. Soon he had jury-rigged a vibrating toy football game over his brew kettle. Loaded with hops, it slowly dribbled them like a misty rain into the beer throughout the length of the boil. (The brewery has since created a higher-tech pneumatic machine that adds hops every three to five seconds.) "It allows you to make a beer with higher

IBU that we find has more hoppiness but less bitterness," Calagione explains—though at 60 IBU, most drinkers find even the 60 Minute variety plenty bitter; the 90 Minute and 120 Minute IPAs are even stronger.

One of the more underrated differences comes in the yeasts. In the United States, breweries typically use neutral ale yeasts. In Britain, brewers compose recipes so that fruity flavors from the yeast add to the overall presentation. ∎

EVOLUTION

NDIA PALE ALES didn't change much through the nineteenth century, and in both Britain and North America breweries continued to brew them strong and hoppy. In Britain, things changed shortly after the dawn of the twentieth century as world events interceded. To save grain, all British beer was brewed at a lower strength during the world wars, causing a permanent change to IPAs. By the late 1940s, the style had become interchangeable with pale ale; in some cases, a brewery's IPA was weaker in strength than its pale (though usually more hoppy). Although breweries continued to make IPAs, the style never recovered its old strength. In North America, Prohibition and brewery consolidation ended almost all production of ales, largely ending IPA's run here.

India pales ales found their voice again in the 1990s on the American West Coast. Craft breweries discovered to their delight that they had a treasure trove of hops growing in their backyard, and they showcased them—and their unique, vibrantly green quality—in IPAs. It didn't take more than a decade for IPAs to become established as the local specialty, and now nearly every brewery and brewpub on the West Coast makes an IPA, and many brew more than one. IPA has

become the West Coast's signature style, but the rest of the country isn't far behind. Although consumers in other regions aren't uniformly devoted to hops, subcultures of hopheads thrive everywhere. As evidence of the style's popularity, for the past five years of the Great American Beer Festival, there have been more entries in the American IPA category than any other.

Breweries in the U.S. were the first to completely embrace IPAs and make them characteristically American, inspiring breweries in other countries. As their popularity spread, IPAs became something of a cultural prism. In Scandinavia, they became heartier, deeper beers. In Denmark, Mikkeller has released a series of IPAs based on single hop strains, most of them from the U.S. Norway's Nøgne Ø offers a classic American "three C" IPA, using Cascade, Centennial, and Chinook hops. They have the boldness of their American inspiration, and they have meat enough on their bones to weather a long, dark Nordic winter. New Zealand may have the most exuberant new market, powered by the new strains of local hops. Like American breweries, New Zealanders are crafting strong, saturated ales to fit their hops—in this case exotic tropical-fruit hops with names like Motueka, Pacific Gem, and Riwaka. Epic Brewing, 8 Wired, and

ABOVE: *Punk IPA helped introduce Britain to American-style brewing.*

Yeastie Boys breweries are leading the way with these intensely fruity beers.

Breweries in the U.K. seem a bit at a loss about which direction to turn. This most British of styles has been lost to the country of its birth and is now defined by New World breweries that appropriated the style. Walk into a pub and you might find Greene King's IPA (the country's bestseller), a wee slip of a beer at 3.6% ABV, or you might encounter a titan like Thornbridge's Jaipur IPA. Smaller, newer breweries like Marble, The Kernel, and Dark Star are following America's lead, but older breweries continue to make IPAs of the traditional weaker school.

The Belgians, too, have gotten in on the act—though in their usual oddball way. Following a visit to the American Northwest in 2005, the brewers at decade-old Urthel decided to try their hand at an IPA that predictably turned out less American and more Flemish by the time they were through with it. This is a trend, with Brasseries d'Achouffe, de la Senne, and de Proef, among others, following suit. And Italy, with a burgeoning craft beer market, has traced its own path, too. They borrow from America and New Zealand in terms of sourcing hops, from England in terms of malts and brewing techniques, and from Belgium in the way they re-ferment their beer in the bottle. Every country seems to use IPA as a blank canvas waiting for a new interpretation.

The style that began as an export to India has spent its life cycle circling the globe. Starting in England, it spread to North America, languished, revived, and now is moving back to Europe—all the while bearing the name of a country where it was never brewed. ■

THE BEERS TO KNOW

NDIA PALE ALES are among the most popular styles brewed in the U.S. There are literally hundreds of examples available. The British market is far more constrained, and most cask IPAs are not as accomplished as their American cousins—or even their European counterparts, where breweries have taken up the style with gusto. The beers in the following list demonstrate a range of types on both sides of the Atlantic. But keep in mind that the fresh IPA poured at your local brewpub may be the best in your area.

AMERICAN IPAs

BELL'S TWO HEARTED ALE

ooooooooooooooooooooooooooooooooooooooooo

LOCATION: Kalamazoo, MI

MALT: Undisclosed

HOPS: Centennial

7% ABV, 1.063 SP. GR., 55 IBU

One of the earliest and most important examples of American IPAs. Like West Coast versions, Two Hearted Ale has an effervescent citrus nose, one that softens to caramel sweetness as the beer warms. The flavor, however, is distinctive, with the hops offering an herbal, peppery kick. The malts are creamy and full of caramel, but also have the suggestions of mineral. This evokes British IPAs, placing Bell's halfway between California and London.

DOGFISH HEAD 60 MINUTE IPA

ooooooooooooooooooooooooooooooooooooo

LOCATION: Rehoboth Beach, DE

MALT: Undisclosed

HOPS: Warrior, Amarillo, a "mystery hop"

6% ABV, 60 IBU

A good example of the increasingly popular method of using multiple hop infusions—in this case, throughout the boil. The hopping quality is softer than in traditionally made IPAs, but more saturated; notes of grapefruit and pine have a slightly stewed quality. The process also produces a more balanced beer, and 60 Minute IPA has rounded toffee and brown-sugar malts to complement the hopping.

FAT HEAD'S HEAD HUNTER IPA

ooooooooooooooooooooooooooooooooooooooooo

LOCATION: Middleburg Heights, OH

MALT: Pale, crystal

HOPS: Columbus, Simcoe, Centennial

7.5% ABV, 1.070 SP. GR., 87 IBU

Brewed in the West Coast tradition, Head Hunter has a heavily "dank," sticky aroma redolent of marijuana. There are some lighter tropical fruit notes in the mix, but they are supporting characters. Crisp and well-attenuated to showcase the hopping.

NINKASI TOTAL DOMINATION

ooooooooooooooooooooooooooooooooooooooooo

LOCATION: Eugene, OR

MALT: Pale, Munich

HOPS: Summit, Amarillo, Crystal

6.7% ABV, 65 IBU

In its short life (it was founded in 2005), Ninkasi has gone from being the city brewery of Eugene to one of the state's largest, and it's thanks to beers like Total Domination, a confection of caramel malts and dense, layered hop flavor. Rarely are beers this hoppy described as "balanced," but the malt plays a prominent role in supporting the explosion of citrus.

BEAR REPUBLIC RACER 5

LOCATION: Healdsburg, CA

MALT: Pale, crystal

HOPS: Chinook, Cascade, Columbus, Centennial

7% ABV, 75 IBU

This classic "four C" IPA contains in its nose the familiar grapefruit of its West Coast brethren. But sniff deeper and you'll find something very close to marijuana. On the tongue, the ganja tastes more like pine tar. Don't be dissuaded by legal entanglements, though. This is dangerously approachable—its easy drinkability belies its hefty ABV—a layered, classically funky California ale.

SWEETWATER IPA

LOCATION: Atlanta, GA

MALT: Pale, Munich, caramel, wheat

HOPS: Chinook, Cascade, Columbus, Simcoe, American Golding

6.3% ABV

Like any style, American-style IPAs have shifted a bit since their inception, and SweetWater's recalls what the beers were like a decade or two ago. The trend in IPAs is for thinner malt profiles in order to accentuate hop flavor, but SweetWater's IPA is chewy with malt— more toasty than caramel—and zesty with citrus, like your father's craft ale.

BRITISH IPAs

BELHAVEN TWISTED THISTLE

LOCATION: Dunbar, Scotland

MALT: Pale, caramel

HOPS: Challenger, Cascade

6.1% ABV, 47 IBU

Among the milder British IPAs, Belhaven shows a bit of steel. A bit more robust than standard versions, it is characterized by a wonderful zip to its hopping. With its pale golden color and arctic head, you could mistake it for a pilsner; the touch of diacetyl and caramel flavor, not to mention the surprisingly creamy texture, set you straight. Some malt tannins add to the sharpness of the hops, making this an assertive example.

MEANTIME IPA

○○○○○○○○○○○○○○○○○○○○○○○○○○○○○○○○○

LOCATION: London, England

MALT: Maris Otter

HOPS: Fuggle, East Kent
Golding

7.5% ABV, 70 IBU

Meantime's IPA may stand
as the best example of
the difference between the
Old World (British style)
and the New (American).
Although it is a robust
beer, it is gentle and well
balanced. The body is
light and very dry,
the hops spicy but
not strident. It is an
elegant beer, not an
aggressive one.

THORNBRIDGE JAIPUR IPA

○○○○○○○○○○○○○○○○○○○○○○○○○○○○○○○○○

LOCATION: Bakewell, England

MALT: Extra light pale ale, Vienna

HOPS: Ahtanum, Centennial,
Chinook, Columbus

5.9% ABV, 50 IBU

Thornbridge evokes the
old empire IPAs with this
brew's name—a famous
city in India—but the beer
itself is purely American
in character. It looks
American, with its
haze of hop par-
ticles suspended in
a very pale, golden
beer, and it smells
American, with
a fresh-squeezed
grapefruit aroma.
But mainly, it tastes
American, with
a freight train of
screaming hops that
gathers strength the
further into the pint
you drink. A brash,
potent beer from one
of England's leading
craft breweries.

INTERNATIONAL IPAs

NØGNE Ø IPA

LOCATION: Grimstad, Norway

MALT: Maris Otter, Munich, wheat, caramel

HOPS: Cascade, Centennial, Chinook

7.5% ABV, 1.072 SP. GR., 60 IBU

Of the Scandinavian IPAs, Nøgne Ø's is the most similar to American versions. (The brewery's name, which means "naked island," is pronounced something like *Noog-ne Oo*.) A massive, burly beer that vents alcohol in waves, this is a beer fit for long winters. The body is syrupy and heavy with lees, but they can't disguise the strength of the hops, which border on the harsh (the Chinooks, which have a rough bitterness). Very strong, very bold—very American.

BRASSERIE D'ACHOUFFE HOUBLON CHOUFFE

LOCATION: Achouffe, Belgium

MALT: Pilsner, pale

HOPS: Tomahawk, Saaz, Amarillo

9% ABV

This may be a look into the future of the style—or represent a pleasant cul-de-sac. Brasserie d'Achouffe has taken elements of IPA and Belgianized them. Like a cubist painting, one can intuit the inspiration without pinpointing it. The result is a sparkling, hoppy, very strong beer with Belgian qualities— peppery yeastiness with massive, rocky carbonation. They even add coriander. *Très belge.*

Thornbridge

CRAFT BREWING IN BRITAIN

IF YOU WERE ASKED TO CONJURE AN IDEALIZED ENGLISH COUNTRY BREWERY IN YOUR MIND, SOMETHING A ROMANTIC MIGHT DESCRIBE IN A BAD NOVEL, WHAT YOU IMAGINE PROBABLY WOULDN'T BE FAR FROM THE ORIGINAL THORNBRIDGE BREWERY. IT GOT ITS START IN A TWELFTH-CENTURY ESTATE NAMED THORNBRIDGE HALL NEAR THE SILENT, MIST-VEILED FOREST OF DERBYSHIRE'S PEAK DISTRICT. ESTATE BREWERIES ARE AN ANCIENT TRADITION IN ENGLAND, SO FINDING A BREWING KIT IN ONE OF THE ESTATE'S OUTBUILDINGS IS NOT ENTIRELY RADICAL. THE CURIOUS THING ABOUT THE BREWHOUSE, HOWEVER, IS THAT IT IS A MODERN, TWENTY-FIRST-CENTURY ENTERPRISE. AND SINCE IT WAS FOUNDED IN 2004, IT HAS QUICKLY BECOME ONE OF THE MOST LAUDED AND IMPORTANT OF A NEW BREED—THE BRITISH CRAFT BREWERY.

The backstory is just about what you would expect. Jim and Emma Harrison bought Thornbridge Hall in 2002 and, like any new homeowners, started hosting social events there. As Jim brought in casks of ale for these soirées, he started thinking how nice it would be if he could serve his own beer. The homebrewery he installed was Thornbridge Brewery—bigger, perhaps, than the usual personal kit. In fact, it was a commercial-scale, ten-barrel system, and from the start, Jim was interested in producing beer for the local market, not solely for his houseguests.

Given how it started, Harrison's ambition for his brewery—both commercially and creatively—was breathtaking. Thornbridge produced a range of cask ales, but also experimented with historic revivals, more aggressive American-style beers, and even lagers. One of two inaugural beers was Jaipur IPA, a beer made with American hops at American levels of vivid intensity—the shot heard 'round Britain. Within no time Thornbridge began winning awards, gaining a national reputation, and growing so fast it had to

TOP LEFT: *The Packhorse Inn in nearby Little Longstone—one of four pubs the brewery owns*

TOP RIGHT: *Thornbridge Hall*

BOTTOM RIGHT: *Bottling in the main brewery*

install a new 50-hectoliter brewhouse in nearby Bakewell to handle its spiking volume.

For the first time in decades, there is a tangible sense of excitement in the industry. English ale fans have been waging a war against brewery consolidation and the spread of lagers that dates back decades. Consumers were the first to rush to ale's defense and helped save the local cask brewing tradition. But it has been these recent start-ups, which borrowed a page from American craft brewing, that have sparked a nationwide revival. Craft breweries have generated broad interest in beer, especially among younger drinkers and women—and breweries like Thornbridge are the reason.

The new brewery is a large plant near the Wye River on one of the world's first industrial sites—a cotton mill from the eighteenth century. It seems an unlikely industrial location—the region is wooded and sparsely populated, and tucked in among the trees. Yet past a bucolic bridge and around some charming buildings, the road emerges into a small clearing with light industrial properties, including Thornbridge. Built in 2009, it looks like a modern American craft brewery, and indeed, when the brewery's Alex Buchanan gave me a tour, he cited Victory and Odell as inspirations.

About the time we arrived at the brewery's massive hop back, Buchanan handed the tour off to brewers Caolan Vaughan and Rob Lovatt. Hops are a major part of Thornbridge's approach, and Vaughan confirmed how much of an influence American beer has had. The brewery had been using an old Yorkshire yeast, but shifted to the Chico strain (Sierra Nevada's) so common in America. Unlike the fruitier yeasts—or sulfurous ones, in the case of Thornbridge's old strain— Chico is mostly neutral. It allows hop aromas and flavors to pop, just like Thornbridge prefers.

But here's where Thornbridge departs from the path of American breweries. Even though hoppy beers are its central claim to fame, Thornbridge is at heart a British brewery. Well-balanced cask ales still make up more than half its

production. Lord Marples, named for industrialist George Marples who once owned Thornbridge Hall (and who was never an actual lord), is the classic 4% ABV bitter the brewery released when it opened. Kipling, made with hops from the South Pacific, is a slightly souped-up 5.2%, while Wild Swan is an absolutely lush wheat-softened ale of 3.5%.

And Thornbridge is heading in the other direction, too—back to traditional brewing from earlier centuries. The original ten-barrel Thornbridge Hall brewery seems to inspire these experiments in antiquity. When I visited, another brewer, Matt Clark, was working on a re-creation of

TOP: *Inside the low, raftered building that houses Thornbridge Hall Brewery*

BOTTOM: *The new, modern Thornbridge Brewery*

ABOVE: *What the new production brewery lacks in romance, it makes up for in technical precision.*

nineteenth-century imperial stouts. Not only did the conditioning include *Brettanomyces*, but brewers added salt to enhance mouthfeel, just like some old breweries had done. Another of the "Hall" range (the specialty beers brewed on the small system) is Bracia, a heavy, dark ale, made with chestnut honey, that was ripening in the barrel when I visited. As craft brewing gains more currency, beer geeks clamor for beers from the British archives—and breweries like Thornbridge are happy to oblige.

It is this intersection of past, present, and future that makes craft brewing different in Britain. National expectation exerts some limits on what breweries can do, but those expectations also create opportunity. For decades in Britain, the institution of cask ale has been defended by the Campaign for Real Ale (CAMRA), which has a rigid definition of what "British ale" means—one Thornbridge is gently pushing further and further away from milds and bitters. "We're moving away from just cask because we don't want to be seen or known as a cask brewery; we want to be known as a craft ale brewery," Vaughan told me.

The definition of "craft" is a moving target in Great Britain. Everyone agrees that it means "new," but beyond that, proponents are vague. Craft brewing means a departure from hidebound tradition but not a rebuke of it. It means a return to character and craft, but also experimentation. And it means a willingness to embrace strange and exotic flavors and styles, even when those styles are ones the British abandoned decades ago. To see where craft brewing is headed in England, keep an eye on Thornbridge.

Mild ALES

Britain has given the world a great many styles of beer. To revise a familiar boast: The sun never sets on the porter-producing empire. Pale ales and stouts, browns and bitters—all these the British sent throughout the commonwealth and beyond. Mild, however, is the one style Britain kept.

It suits its native land. Britain is a pubgoing country, and milds are built for drinking in triplicate. The word "mild" originally meant young or unaged, and the best milds are served that way still—preferably dispensed from a cask,

Mild Ales. Some people refer to milds as lunchtime beers, and it's easy to see why. Weighing in at just 3% ABV or a hair more, they are not brewed or drunk with intoxication in mind. Flavor, not strength, is the goal. Most milds are dark, ruddy to mahogany, but a few are pale. To compensate for the low alcohol, they're brewed sweet, with lots of body and a creamy texture. They have lower hopping rates than bitters, but dark malt flavors add some depth and contrast. They are nevertheless tasty companions to hearty beef dishes and that pub favorite, fish and chips.

Statistics

ABV range: 3–4%

Bitterness: 12–25 IBU

Serving temperature: 50°–60°F

Vessel: Pint glass or dimpled mug

where their understated flavors have a chance to express themselves. But the other sense of "mild"—gentle, moderate, unagressive—fits this little beer, too. Low in alcohol and hop flavor, it is mild to the palate as well. And mild ale, a beer so light and demure that it would be overlooked in other countries, is celebrated in Britain, where it has recently been picking up awards for Champion Beer of Britain with surprising regularity. ■

Milds in May. Milds are vanishingly rare in the U.S., usually appearing as seasonal or single-batch specialty releases when they appear at all. If you want to scratch that mild itch, Britain's the place to go. But even in Britain, milds are sometimes tough to locate. Every year, though, the British advocacy group CAMRA (the Campaign for Real Ale) has tried to address this problem by designating May as the month of milds and encouraging local pubs to stock at least one. You can find more information at its website, camra.org.uk.

ORIGINS

THE MODERN STYLE is indeed a mild-tasting beer, so the meaning of the name seems obvious enough. In fact, the original meaning was quite different, and it's only coincidence that the adjective still fits. Before the twentieth century, all British beer was packaged in wooden casks, and in the fissures and cracks of the wood lived microorganisms that soured beer. It took time for these creatures to work their tart magic, however. For the first couple weeks of a beer's life, it was fresh and sweet, completely untouched by wild yeast. From the 1700s through the early part of the twentieth century, this young beer was known as "mild," and that meant it was fresh or unaged. Any style or strength of beer could be called mild; what the term designated was age.

The general category of young ale is as ancient as beer itself. The beginning of what we would recognize as mild ale really picked up steam in the 1800s, as the popularity of porter finally started to wane. Although beer styles were modified by the adjective "mild"—"mild porter," for example—the word eventually transformed into a noun. It still didn't refer to a narrow style of beer, exactly—more a range. Milds were typically made with less hops, though not always. Perhaps as a contrast to roasty porters, they were mainly pale—though again, not always. Finally, they were brewed to a variety of strengths. Even the weakest of these (from 5% ABV up) was far stronger than modern milds, and they ranged to the truly titanic—up to 10% alcohol. Can you imagine a mild (that is, unaged) barley wine? Victorian brewers did.

Toward the end of the nineteenth century, certain related events helped milds cohere into a single type. In 1880, Britain passed a law allowing the use of sugar and adjuncts in beer, and almost immediately, brewers started using them in their milds. Modern brown ales were becoming popular, in part because of the use of darker sugars that turned the beers mahogany, which led to the second event in the development of mild ales: mild malt, which was slightly darker than the one used in pale ales. Milds were still being brewed at multiple strengths, but a steady inclination toward darker colors was underway. The final events were equally profound: World War I, which crashed into British brewing like a wrecking ball, and a massive tax hike on beer in 1931. The effect was the same in both cases: Beer strengths collapsed. Following the world wars, milds became the beers we know today.

The typical version was a chestnut-brown, about 3% ABV, and not especially hoppy. Pale milds were also available, but they were in the minority. After World War II, this modest little beer became the king of Britain; 70 percent of all draft pours were mild. Drinking a dimpled mug of mild in the local pub was a national rite. Yet like the porter it supplanted, its time at the top of the heap was finite.

Milds may have hung on as a popular pour longer but for the unfortunate habit some publicans had of returning the "slops" back to the cask. Most styles of cask-conditioned ales have a fine residue of yeast at the bottom of the cask. Publicans have to let cask ales rest gently so as not to rouse the yeast and produce a cloudy pint. But mild was packaged "bright"—it wasn't re-fermented in the keg and had no yeast to rouse. Tightwad barmen regarded the overflow beer in the drip trays as spilled pennies; pretty

Session Beers. The concept of a session beer comes from England, but it has been adopted by Americans wary of very strong beers. The idea is simple: A session beer is low enough in alcohol that a pubgoer might have a few pints in the course of an evening—a "session" of drinking. In Britain, about half the beer is consumed in pubs, and nearly all the beer on tap is below 5% ABV.

In the U.S., the *weakest* beers are often around 5% (light beer is less, but even lagers like Budweiser and Coors are 5%), and it is common to find draft beers at 7% or more. An American who downs two pints of strong IPA will have consumed as much alcohol as a British drinker who's had four milds—and the American will probably have drunk his beer twice as fast. Writer Lew Bryson established the Session Beer Project in the U.S. to promote beer under 4.5%, and brewpubs have embraced session beers to provide consumers with a good reason to buy another round. The movement seems to be gaining traction; breweries are starting to make more small beers, excited by the challenge of making them flavorful enough to lure IPA drinkers. More and more, you can find full-flavored, low-alcohol pilsners, so-called session IPAs, and low-alcohol saisons when you're out at the pub.

soon, those barmen were dumping the pennies back into the keg. There was even a machine that automated the process. This, unsurprisingly, did not charm mild drinkers. There was an element of fashion in the decline as well. The drinkers who helped make milds popular in the 1940s and '50s were becoming fathers and grandfathers by the '60s and '70s. Younger drinkers were moving on to a new style—hoppier, stronger, more assertive bitters.

Mild began losing ground at a precipitous rate. Total volume fell to 50 percent of all draft pours by the mid-1960s, and in 1968 milds were usurped by bitters, ending their reign as the country's most popular style. By the early 1970s, milds had dropped to just 20 percent of total draft volume; they bottomed out two decades later at barely 1 percent.

Interestingly, the rise of British craft brewers may give mild new life. The stigma against milds from the slops era is gone. Connoisseurs have rediscovered milds, and some, like Moorhouse's Black Cat, Rudgate Ruby Mild, and Hobsons Mild, are regarded as among Britain's finest beers. Mild ale isn't anywhere near as popular as it once was, but its pulse is getting stronger. ■

DESCRIPTION AND CHARACTERISTICS

MILD ALES ATTRACT delicious-sounding adjectives—"plummy," "toffee-like," "chocolatey"—and indeed the ales *are* delicious. But expectation is the biggest foe of the mild; outside Britain, people often find them woefully underpowered and tame. These are beers with the volume on low; you can't appreciate them by wishing someone would turn up the sound. Instead, you have to bring your attention to their quiet pleasures.

So, about those adjectives: Most milds are darker beers, and they look lovely in the glass. They're usually not black; tawny, mahogany, or russet are the norm, and under light's refraction, ruby highlights may twinkle back at you. Because milds are not stiffly hopped, the nose is given to malts—toffee, raisin, nuts, possibly a hint of roast or chocolate. Some even have the quality of burned sugar or a rumminess about their nose.

The palate is much the same, though the flavors can be quite subtle. Malt character inflects a sweet palate and a creamy, sometimes thick body. Because they're low in alcohol, brewers let them finish out with lots of residual sugars; this gives a mild a sense of substance even in the absence of stronger flavors. Balance is key, and not always the easiest thing for a brewery to achieve. A good mild is a little bit sweet, a little bit malty, and a little bit thick, but it should never be *too* malty, sweet, or thick.

Perversely, the bestselling mild in the world, Banks's, is a light mild, despite the style's reputation as a dark beer. Light-colored milds remain the minority, though, and they are distinguished from bitters mainly in their level of hopping. Bitters are drier and balanced toward hop character, while milds are sweeter and focus on malt flavors. Yet sometimes the line between a light mild and a bitter is so fuzzy that breweries switch back and forth between names, depending on which style is more in fashion. ■

BREWING NOTES

DURING THE GREAT mild heyday, breweries used a slightly darker base malt to make the style (called—no surprise—"mild ale malt"). Over time, the use of mild malt waned—most malt companies don't even make it—and now milds are made much the same as other beers, with grists consisting largely of pale malts, with darker malts added for flavor and color.

Since the style is more sweet than roasty, breweries gravitate toward crystal and brown malts to achieve color. Some add a dollop of chocolate malt or roast to give the beer some complexity and balance—two good examples are Brains Dark and Vale Black Swan Dark Mild. Also common is the use of dark invert sugar, which lends color without adding malt bitterness or roast character—as in Moorhouse's Black Cat. Batemans uses wheat to add softness and head retention.

Many of the most traditional bitters and milds include sugar in their grist—a fact that pains American craft beer fans. In America, the use of sugar once signaled the degradation of a beer and has left a permanent prejudice. But these maligned "adjuncts" (rice and corn are held in similar contempt) have certain virtues that can enhance a beer. Sugar is turned directly into alcohol. This in turn makes the beer lighter and crisper, all without adding body. Industrial American breweries have long afflicted

Invert Sugar. One brewing sugar used in British brewing is a converted form of sucrose—the kind of sugar that comes from sugarcane. Sucrose is a disaccharide—that is, it's a molecule made of two simple sugars. Inversion is the process of splitting that molecule into glucose and fructose, two simple monosaccharides. Invert sugar occurs naturally in honey and maple syrup, but when it's made for brewing, the process produces darker sugars ideal for brewing mild ale. Much like malt, invert sugar comes in a variety of colors, and brewers can use it to help darken milds and stouts or give bitters a toffee character without adding a lot of color. In milds, brewers substitute it for dark malts to get color without aggressive roasty notes.

their beers with adjuncts and sugars, but the cheapening of character was the breweries' doing, not the adjuncts'. In the hands of a careful artisan, they can make good beers better. In the hands of a mild ale brewer, sugars might just be necessary.

Mild ales reside in a forgotten little shed out behind the house of mainstream beers and they don't have many close peers. Light *brown ales* and *porters* approximate their sweet malt focus, and German *dunkel lager*— stronger, drier, but also malty—is not far from the mark. For fans of light milds, *bitters* are of course the closest cousins, particularly those balanced toward malt.

John Bexon, the head brewer at Britain's Greene King, pointed out to me how added brewing sugars work to accent native ones drawn from the malt. We had been studying a field of sugar beets from the roof of his brewery, and I wondered if he used those to make his beer. He crinkled his nose, but I pointed out that Belgian breweries use beet sugar in their beer. "I know, but it's *beet*. It's the wrong sugar profile. If you think about it, the sugars you're tasting in beer, they were originally starch in the grain. If you look at a starch molecule, it's"—and here he used his hands to sketch a molecule in the air—"glucose, glucose, glucose, glucose, glucose—and it goes in different directions. When you hydrate the enzymes, you chop off one glucose,

it's glucose. If it's two links, it's maltose. Three links, maltotriose. Where you get these branch chains that the yeast can't use, then they're complex sugars that leave body in the beer." This was a technical way of saying that in mild ales, the "right sugar profile" is obtained by the use of a peculiarly British (and old-timey) form called invert sugar.

With certain mashing techniques, it's possible to convert a great deal of malt's sugars into alcohol, producing a thin beer (a low mash temperature of around 144°F produces maximum fermentability). Traditional British methods, using a single-infusion mash, produce some residual sugars and give beer some heft— excellent for character and flavor. The use of sugar speeds the mash, thins the body back down, and adds a touch of alcohol. The idea is to brew a beer that is gentle of flavor and alcohol, but not so wispy it evaporates in the mouth. Milds have some body and residual sweetness more as a way of adding in substance. Hops are there to keep the sweetness in check, not to add a great deal in the way of flavor or bitterness. ■

LEFT: *Milds were once synonymous with England.*

EVOLUTION

MILD ALE IS one of the most endangered styles in commercial production. It is mainly brewed in the U.K., and appeared to be in jeopardy of vanishing even there until small craft breweries began offering more examples over the last decade or two. Mild will be an interesting style to watch as a bellwether for the direction of British brewing. Part of the market is headed in the American direction, with stronger, far more hoppy beers. In contrast, milds represent a return to an older tradition of British brewing.

Once craft breweries dusted off the old style and gave it a look, they saw rather impressive technique underneath its aged patina, and they've begun to make slightly bolder, more interesting milds in their slow rediscovery of the style. Where milds were once the after-work tipple of the factory worker, now they're becoming more and more the purview of the beer geek, someone pre-disposed to describe their beer in terms like "dark cherry" or "suggestion of forest fruits" (two adjectives used to laud recent award-winning milds, Moorhouse's Black Cat and Mighty Oak Oscar Wilde).

Milds are extremely rare in the U.S.; just a few breweries make one in their regular line. They're brewed occasion-ally by brewpubs interested in the odd revival, but rarely more than that. One champion is Dave McLean of the Magnolia Gastropub and Brewery in San Francisco. He acknowledges that it's "a little like swimming upstream against a massive current of hops and high ABVs," but he has nurtured a robust fan base. "I think we make it such a focal point of what we do and train our staff to spread the good word about them, too." It takes this kind of commitment to foster mild drinkers, and so far, McLean travels a lonely road. ∎

Champion Beers of Britain. Given that these days milds are quite rare in British pubs, it's hard to speak of a renaissance just yet—but "rehabilitation" is certainly justified. One marker of mild's new reputation is how well the style has performed in the annual judging held at the Great British Beer Festival. The contest involves several rounds of blind tasting that result in winners in ten categories; the winners are then judged against one another and one beer is crowned Champion Beer of Britain.

Bitters dominate the competition for Champion—it is Britain, after all. But in the last fifteen years or so, milds have made quite a showing. Moorhouse's Black Cat scored the win in 2000, Hobsons's Mild came along in 2007, Rudgate Ruby Mild followed two years later, and two years after that, Mighty Oak Oscar Wilde took the laurel. Once a scorned beer with a reputation just north of dishwater, milds are well on the way to a more august status.

THE BEERS TO KNOW

F YOU LIVE on the East Coast or in the Midwest of the United States, you might find a mild ale in a cask-friendly pub or brewery; West Coasters are often out of luck. The best place to find the beer is in its native environment: a British pub. There it will almost certainly be on cask, which is the way the style was meant to be served. Beware the bottled mild, though; these ales do not survive long or ship well, and any bottle you find may be substantially worse for the wear.

MOORHOUSE'S BLACK CAT

LOCATION: Burnley, England

MALT: Maris Otter

HOPS: Fuggle

OTHER: Brewing sugar

3.4% ABV

The black of this mild is actually, upon inspection, deep red. That's a nice metaphor for this beer: rewarding upon close inspection. Sweet malts evolve into licorice and dates if you give them a swish, and there is a slight earthiness underneath it all. Fair from the bottle, excellent on cask.

YARDS BRAWLER

LOCATION: Philadelphia, PA

MALT: Undisclosed

HOPS: Undisclosed

4.2% ABV

This is the closest most Americans will get to an English mild. It rides the line between dark and light—a dark amber. It's got quite a bit of complexity, with brown sugar and dates up front, and I detect both a hint of smoke and a lactose-like creaminess. The brewery's yeast adds a rich fruity note.

MAGNOLIA SARA'S RUBY MILD

°°°

LOCATION: San Francisco, CA

MALT: Maris Otter, specialty malts

HOPS: Fuggle

3.9% ABV, 1.042 SP. GR., 15 IBU

Magnolia's defense of small cask ales is so robust that they brew *two* milds (the other, nodding to the ghost of Jerry Garcia, is Dark Star Mild). Sara's Ruby is the standard, a lush little number with notes of caramel and figs, light and sweet. Sara's is ruddy and attractive, and those Fuggle hops give it the perfect pepper spiciness to balance the sweet English malts.

SURLY MILD

°°°

LOCATION: Brooklyn Center, MN

MALT: Pale, Golden Promise, brown, caramel, roast

HOPS: Columbus

3.8% ABV, 1.040 SP. GR., 21 IBU

A seasonal the brewery uses to welcome the depths of winter, Surly Mild has just a tiny bit of American heft to boost it up. The malts are toffee to cocoa, pleasantly dry—many milds are quite sweet—with a hint of roast. It's a richly thick beer for a mild; an excellent example that's worth seeking out if you happen to be in Minnesota in February.

JESTER KING COMMERCIAL SUICIDE

°°°

LOCATION: Austin, TX

MALT: Organic Munich, organic caramel, abbey, chocolate, wheat

HOPS: East Kent Golding

3.5% ABV, 1.028 SP. GR.

You won't find beers like this in England—it's not exactly a mild—but it's worth trying in order to get a sense of the power of small beers. Jester King specializes in using a Belgian yeast to make non-Belgian styles. Commercial Suicide, therefore, in addition to its dark, malty base malts, has a bit of phenolic character that gives it a smoky note.

Brown
ALES

The humble brown ale is not a beer that excites passions. How could anything called "brown" rouse excitement? In the eyes of most of the beer-drinking world, a brown is regarded—when anyone bothers to regard it at all—as an anonymous, workmanlike pour. But as any good spy knows, the virtues of anonymity are located beneath the surface. Browns are

Brown Ales. What qualities unite the various beers sold under the title "brown ale"? A quality of malt comfort. Much can be done with darker grain to create layered flavor, and browns express them with notes of toast, caramel, raisins, walnut, chocolate, or bread crust. Hops usually ride along as tour guides, helping direct the drinker to these malty depths. Depending on the type of brown, it might go perfectly with a chocolatey dessert or a spicy Mexican dish.

STATISTICS

ABV range: 3–8%	
Bitterness: 15–60 IBU	
Serving temperature: 50°–60°F	
Vessel: Pint glass	

RIGHT: *Brown ales are rare in the country of their birth, but you might find one in a pub in the old city of York.*

actually one of the most diverse styles. Freed from the scrutiny and national pride of many more famous styles, browns are a great place for a brewer to express himself. They can be burly or slight, thick or thin, sweet as treacle or dry as a cracker. What gives the style coherence is the emphasis on rich malt flavors and aromas, and these the brewer can achieve through a number of clever tricks. One brown may have notes of Kona coffee, another of roasted almonds, yet another the richness of hot chocolate. The result is a beer that is soothing, comforting, and far more interesting than most drinkers appreciate. ■

ORIGINS

B **ROWN ALES ARE** history's fly on the wall, peering in on civilizations as distant as ancient Sumer. The act of malting was until recent centuries difficult to control, and browned, smoked, or charred malts led inevitably to brown beer. Ancestors to current Belgian, German, and Czech browns were brewed around Europe throughout the Middle Ages. Any of the brown beers in history might have been part of the lineage leading to what we call "brown ale" now, but it was the English variety that won out. Here we have John Milton's famous "L'Allegro," written in 1645:

> And young and old com forth to play
> On a Sunshine Holyday,
> Till the live-long day-light fail,
> Then to the Spicy Nut-brown Ale

Milton's browns were remote in lineage from the modern version, however—Neanderthal ales doomed for extinction. The malting technique in Milton's time involved drying barley over roaring fires; what resulted was a smoky, roasty brown malt. The beer it produced was, by contemporary accounts, not good. When breweries began to change their malting techniques to produce porter after the turn of the eighteenth century, the musty old browns began to die out. They were effectively extinct by 1800.

The revival came 100 years later, from the London brewery Mann, Crossman & Paulin, amid the fascination with sweet, light beers like milds and milk stouts. Riding the trend, the brewery introduced a bottle-only product called Manns Brown Ale, a beer of just 2.7% alcohol. Even by later standards, that would have been notably low strength, but this was well before the "great gravity drop" of the world wars (see page 149). Manns was therefore at the far end of the spectrum and, unsurprisingly, didn't immediately set the world on fire. In fact, it took a couple decades and that gravity drop for the public to come around. In the 1920s, sales picked up sufficiently to spark a minor trend in brown ales.

During the same decade in England's North, Newcastle Breweries released a brown ale of nearly twice the strength of Manns (4.7%). To modern American tastes, Newcastle Brown is a sweet beer and relatively weak. Compared to Manns and its imitators in the Roaring Twenties, it was dry and strong, setting it apart.

In nearby Sunderland, England, Vaux produced a beer similar to Newcastle and later, Yorkshire's Samuel Smith made yet another similar product. As the decades rolled along, these hallmark beers began to stand for two schools of brown ales: northern and southern. The beer writer Michael Jackson solidified their standing as different styles, and you still see the separation observed in places like the American Homebrewers Association's style guidelines.

Although this distinction is common, it isn't without controversy. Lots of browns were brewed in the twentieth century, and they blurred the line between the two styles. Contravening rules, mild, sweet browns were sometimes brewed in the North, and stronger, drier examples in the south. From time to time breweries even blew the lid off their kettles with big, booming browns north of 5.5% alcohol (booming for post–World War II Britain, anyway).

In recent decades, browns have dwindled even more precipitously than milds. Newcastle, the country's biggest brown producer, now ships almost all of its product overseas. Samuel Smith makes a brown ale, as does Hook Norton, but these are the rare exceptions. Even CAMRA (the Campaign for Real Ale), the watchdog of British beer, doesn't list brown ale as a native style.

In the United States, one of the earliest success stories in craft brewing was a brown: Pete's Wicked Ale (see box, page 135). Founded in the mid-1980s, Pete's grew to become the second-largest craft beer company in the U.S., all on sales of its flagship, an assertive, malty brown. Like many beers of that era, Pete's Wicked began to lose market share as the market matured, leaving behind lighter or relatively sweeter beers. With the exception of Pete's, brown ales have never enjoyed much of a following stateside. ■

DESCRIPTION AND CHARACTERISTICS

Let US ASSEMBLE in our mind's eye a representative sample of the beers with "brown" in their title. They have two or three qualities in common: color, clearly, but also an emphasis on malt flavor and the gentle fruitiness of ale yeast. From there they range broadly in strength, hoppiness, and relative sweetness. Can we sort them into any meaningful categories? We can, and will, but first we have to deal with generations of earlier attempts. Some of these appear in style guidelines, others on the odd beer bottle. It's useful to know what they refer to.

ENGLISH BROWN ALES

The writer Michael Jackson was instrumental in popularizing this dichotomy between stronger, drier brown ales and less alcoholic, sweeter ones. The distinction seems to be giving way to a category of "English brown ales" within competitions. In either case, English browns are mild and malty, characteristic of the country that made soft malts and earthy hops famous.

AMERICAN AND TEXAS BROWN ALES

Like other British styles adopted by Americans, browns quickly acquired a Yankee accent. Rather than looking too closely at the English originals, Americans just slotted browns in between ambers (another Americanism) and porters. Standard American brown ales generally weigh in at about 5% ABV and are accented toward malt richness. Texas homebrewers launched a variant style that has few commercial incarnations now—hoppy, roasty browns. They are the bigger, tougher brother to standard American browns. The current trend seems to be typified by beers like Brooklyn Brown: hearty all-barley beers that use Britain as an inspiration, not a model.

STRONG BROWN ALES

Robust browns, made at IPA strengths, weren't invented in America—British brewers have made them periodically over the decades. But you're far more likely to find them in San Diego now than in London. Some are darker versions of IPAs (Dogfish Head Indian Brown Ale), or the inevitable imperialized versions like Tommyknocker. Scandinavians, too, seem partial to imperial browns (consider Nøgne Ø, Bryggeri, Mikkeller).

NUT BROWN ALES

As the Milton poem documents, "nut" has been used to describe brown ales for centuries. It appears that the term originally referred to the beers' color, though, not their taste. However, in the U.S., brewers were beguiled by the idea of nut-flavored ales. Some darker malts, particularly in combination with earthy hops, offer a suggestion of nuttiness. Many American brewers highlight this note, but some go even further. Rogue, for example, adds hazelnut extract to its Brown Nectar. A number of others use the phrase "nut brown" as a synonym for "English-style," which adds taxonomical confusion to the category of brown ales.

Despite the assorted categories and names, American breweries seem to have come to a broad agreement about what a brown should be. Although the British have more or less abandoned the style, Americans view brown ales as an artifact of English brewing. Most range between 4.5% and 5.5% ABV in strength, and their palates are tilted toward malts. Brewers favor English hops, which frame the malt notes with their earthiness. In fact, these American expressions are quite distinct from the ideal of a "traditional English brown" exemplified by Newcastle or Samuel Smith. As with "French" fries or "Canadian" bacon, brown ales seem to have become an American impression of what an "English" beer might be like. ■

The Rise and Fall of Pete's Wicked Ale.

The world of American brewing in 1980 was like a newly discovered, unpeopled continent. The first pioneers had landed, set up a beachhead, and were prepared to fan out and stake their claims. At that moment, none of them knew much about the continent, nor which places would later be considered prime real estate. Like little kings, they began planting flags: Fritz Maytag on the state called Steam Beer, Ken Grossman in Pale Aleland. In the Pacific Northwest, Pyramid and Widmer dueled over Weizenville.

One of the most successful companies was Pete's Brewing, founded in 1986. The founder, Pete Slosberg, decided to stake a claim on—of all things—brown ales. It was an unlikely style, but then, so was Vienna lager, and Boston Beer had built the country's first blockbuster craft beer around that style with Boston Lager. With Wicked Ale, Slosberg sketched the contours of the American version of the brown style: a russet, creamy ale of modest strength, a caramel-and-toast palate buttressed by a slight, earthy hop bitterness. It was not an aggressive beer even by the standards of the time, yet its color and body put it in sharp contrast to the longstanding American preference for thin, almost clear beer.

Remarkably, Pete's Wicked Ale was a hit. Within a decade, Pete's Brewing was the country's second-largest craft brewery, had national distribution, and was even exported to Canada, Australia, and Europe. In 1995 Slosberg offered an initial public offering, and Pete's appeared ready to solidify its position as a national company. It was a dangerous moment for craft brewing, though. Like Slosberg, many breweries expanded during the mid-to-late 1990s on the assumption that sales would continue to grow. They didn't, and huge capital expenses put Pete's in a tricky position. In 1998, Gambrinus, the parent company of Shiner, BridgePort, Trumer, and others, bought Pete's. Despite new product releases and renewed focus on consistency, the brand never recovered.

Like so many boom towns in the early American West, Pete's went bust. There were a number of structural flaws in the company's strategy, but one can't help thinking that the product itself was a major issue. Browns have never commanded huge audiences, and by 2000, the market had turned definitively toward hops. In early 2011, Gambrinus announced it would end production of the Pete's line, a dénouement that came a decade after the death of brown ale's brief American heyday.

BREWING NOTES

THERE AREN'T TOO many ways to get to a mahogany beer, and breweries use a predictable troika to achieve it: pale malt, chocolate malt (for nuttiness), and crystal malt (body, sweetness, and a note of caramel or toffee). In a survey of a half-dozen of the more popular American browns (Abita Turbodog, Avery Ellie's Brown, Brooklyn Brown, Sierra Nevada Tumbler, Smuttynose Old Brown Dog, Surly Bender), all used these three malts.

For its Turbodog (5.6% ABV, 28 IBU), Abita stops there. The others use small additions of specialty malts, and they all use different varieties. In Bender (5.5% ABV, 45 IBU), Surly uses two varieties of crystal malts and adds some oats for creaminess. Brooklyn's Brown (5.6% ABV, 36 IBU) uses a mixture of six malts including Belgian aromatic malts that impart a lush grain-y character. Smuttynose's Old Brown Dog (6.7% ABV, 18 IBU) is a stronger example than most and less hoppy. It achieves balance through roasted malt bitterness; the addition of Munich adds color and a soft, bready complexity. Similarly, Avery (5.5% ABV, 17 IBU) uses Munich. Finally, perhaps the most exotic addition comes from Sierra Nevada, which puts a bit of smoked malt into Tumbler (5.5% ABV, 37 IBU) that seems mainly to accentuate and lengthen the sense of roastiness.

Notice that only Smuttynose falls outside the 5.3 to 5.6% alcohol range. Similarly, five of the six use Willamette hops—essentially a U.S. version of Fuggle—and the final one uses Challenger, British hops. Some of these also use American hop strains, but all are using at least one strain to remind drinkers of brown ale's country of birth. ∎

Brown ales find themselves at the crossroads of other styles, equidistant from—yet similar to—*amber ales* and *porters*. Ambers have less malt and more hop character, and porters are roasty rather than nutty. In Germany, a very close relative (and one just as overlooked) is the *dunkel lager*. This is brown's closest kin, and brown ale fans should track down an example or two. Similarly, *Oktoberfest* and *märzen* beers are characterized by gentle malt character, and are toasty and warming. Slightly further afield, Belgian *dubbels* are a type of malty brown ale, though they're much more alcoholic and in possession of those classic fruity Belgian yeast qualities.

EVOLUTION

BROWN ALE'S PERIOD of evolution seems to have come to an end—or anyway, a plateau. Like an adult finally settling down after a vagabond youth, the style is moving away from the experimental. If there's one area to watch, though, it is the big browns. Americans are forever imperializing styles

(IPA, stout, pilsner), and it doesn't take much to imagine a subcategory emerging. Beers like Funky Buddha Doc Brown Ale (6.4% ABV), Short's Bellaire Brown (7% ABV), and Tommyknocker Imperial Nut Brown (9% ABV) are suggestive of the trend. As it stands, the brown remains almost a museum piece—a classic little beer to warm hearts and remind drinkers of English pubs. ∎

THE BEERS TO KNOW

LOVERS OF BROWN ales must be vigilant. The style is a minor one and, sadly, breweries often give their browns only minor attention. It's an easy enough style to brew passably, and passable browns are sadly more common than really good versions. The examples listed below made the cut because they were given the attention browns deserve, and they illustrate how much depth an ostensibly unassuming little style can possess.

AVERY ELLIE'S BROWN ALE

LOCATION: Boulder, CO

MALT: Pale, Munich, dark caramel, chocolate

HOPS: Cascade, Fuggle

5.5% ABV, 1.056 SP. GR., 17 IBU

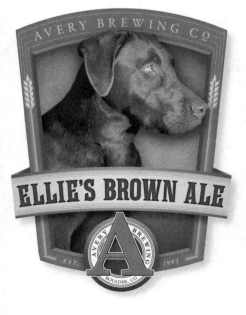

The first thing you notice about Ellie's is the malt aromatics in the nose—as fresh and appealing as oven-warm bread. The beer is a beautiful mahogany, with a thick body and creamy head. The malts have even more complexity in the mouth than on the nose, if that's possible, with notes of hazelnut, caramel, and a touch of roast. It's a beer that evokes a sense of wholesomeness and warmth. The perfect autumnal pint.

SIERRA NEVADA TUMBLER AUTUMN BROWN ALE

LOCATION: Chico, CA

MALT: Pale, caramel, chocolate, smoked malt

HOPS: Challenger, Yakima Golding

5.5% ABV, 1.055 SP. GR., 37 IBU

Like Ellie's, Tumbler is a richly aromatic brew; the notes are lighter, however— almond and toast. It is a fairer brown, more sienna than chestnut, and has a thick, sustained head. The malts are soft and bready and they are inflected by the spice of Challenger and Golding hops to create a sense of gingerbread. The hops also have a flowery quality that brightens the beer. If Ellie's is a brown for the chill of Colorado, Tumbler is geared for gentler Golden State evenings.

BROOKLYN BROWN ALE

LOCATION: Brooklyn, NY

MALT: British pale, Belgian aromatic malts, roasted malt

HOPS: Willamette, Cascade, U.S. Fuggle

5.6% ABV, 1.062 SP. GR.

Brooklyn's Brown Ale favors roast over nuts. At first contact, the tongue finds toffee sweetness, but that evolves into chocolate and, finally, medium-roast coffee. It's surprisingly hoppy as well, and the flavors are as mutable as the malts—first earthy and later something that invokes a forest floor.

SAMUEL SMITH NUT BROWN ALE

LOCATION: Tadcaster, England

MALT: Pale, roast malt, roasted barley

HOPS: Undisclosed

OTHER: Cane sugar

5.0% ABV, 1.048 SP. GR., 30 IBU

Samuel Smith was a huge influence on a generation of American craft breweries when it arrived in 1983, and styling their beer a "nut brown" has solidified the image. The color of dark maple syrup, it does have a nutty flavor—walnuts or pecans—but quite a bit of raisin and berry fruitiness as well. The hopping is distinctively English, an herbal, earthy note.

LAZY MAGNOLIA SOUTHERN PECAN NUT BROWN ALE

LOCATION: Kiln, MS

MALT: Maris Otter, caramel, wheat

HOPS: Nugget, Willamette

OTHER: Roasted pecans

4.4% ABV, 1.055 SP. GR., 19 IBU

In this literal nut brown ale, "brewster" Leslie Henderson (one of the growing number of women brewers) adds roasted pecans to help strike the nutty note. They also contribute an unorthodox sensation that is slightly tannic and sharp. With English base malts and Willamette hops, she is evoking England—and perhaps Samuel Smith—though despite the roasted nuts, Southern Pecan is pie-sweet.

ABITA TURBODOG

LOCATION: Abita Springs, LA

MALT: Pale, caramel, chocolate

HOPS: Willamette

5.6% ABV, 20 IBU

Turbodog isn't the best brown ale in America, yet its simplicity illustrates how well the style can make use of mild, pleasing ingredients. Turbodog is all mid-notes; a chocolate malted nose and milk chocolate malt center. There is a touch of cola in the first notes and, despite its heft, it seems like a light session ale. Perhaps most important, it is perfect with a plate of Louisiana red beans and rice.

SMUTTYNOSE OLD BROWN DOG

LOCATION: Portsmouth, NH

MALT: Pale, Munich, caramel, chocolate

HOPS: Cascade, Galena, Willamette

6.7% ABV, 1.060 SP. GR., 18 IBU

First brewed all the way back in 1988, this is a walk into American brewing's past, to when American ales were brewed on the sweeter side. Old Brown Dog has lots of malt depth, with showcase nuttiness getting support from toast, caramel, and cocoa flavors.

Porters and STOUTS

The word "beer" has meant different things to different generations. To ours, it generally suggests pilsner: a slender, elegant beverage as golden as the dawn sun. Pilsners are one of the world's two superstyles, brewed and sold across the planet. But to an earlier generation, "beer" would have meant just the opposite— a midnight ale, thick and lustrous as a ribbon of velvet. The first superstyle was porter, which was available almost as widely 200 years ago as pilsner is today.

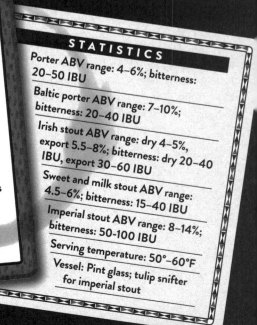

Porters and Stouts. The names were interchangeable for more than a century, but over time substyles have evolved. Regular or "brown" porters are ruby-black, brown-black, or most often, black-black beers of modest strength and medium body. Baltic porters, generally lagered, are silky smooth, creamy, and dangerously drinkable. Dry or Irish Stouts, typified by Guinness, are light-bodied ales with a pronounced roast note, and their big brother, export stout, is a beer of intense roastiness and tanginess. Sweet or oatmeal stouts are characterized by a thick, creamy mouthfeel. Finally, imperial stouts are the densest, most alcoholic of the family and among the most intensely flavored beers in the world.

STATISTICS

Porter ABV range: 4–6%; bitterness: 20–50 IBU

Baltic porter ABV range: 7–10%; bitterness: 20–40 IBU

Irish stout ABV range: dry 4–5%, export 5.5–8%; bitterness: dry 20–40 IBU, export 30–60 IBU

Sweet and milk stout ABV range: 4.5–6%; bitterness: 15–40 IBU

Imperial stout ABV range: 8–14%; bitterness: 50–100 IBU

Serving temperature: 50°–60°F

Vessel: Pint glass; tulip snifter for imperial stout

Porters and stouts run a continuum of flavors and strengths as broad as any style brewed, and yet something unites them in a single, easily identified family. Is it their appearance, the always fashionable black? Surely that's part of it. Who has not watched in fascination as the bubbles in a pint of Guinness do the moonwalk backward into the depths of the pint glass? More important are those elements that communicate richness: a creaminess on the tongue, a density on the palate, and spikes of flavor, variously intense, of coffee, vanilla, plum, chocolate, port, or licorice. Porters and stouts are the rare styles that are both immediately welcoming to the novice and eternally rewarding to the connoisseur. These dark ales are like liquid chocolate. No wonder they once conquered the world. ■

ABOVE: *Guinness has been brewed at St. James Gate Brewery in Dublin since 1759.*

ORIGINS

THE STORY OF porters and stouts is 300 years old and, like any multi-generational epic, stuffed with fascinating subplots, anecdotes, and apocrypha. Porters (and later, stouts) were the first international style, shipped to and then brewed in countries on five continents. But more importantly, they were the first industrial style, brewed on a scale inconceivable before steam power transformed brewing.

PORTERS

We begin the story in England around the turn of the eighteenth century. Brewing was still a rustic art, and the pubs of London poured as many as thirty different types of beer. One of the more common was a smoky, murky brown beer that endured despite its poor reputation ("heavy, thick, and foggy," in the words of one writer). Yet from this style emerged porter, a more flavorful variation on the old browns, but one that nevertheless relied on the same malt, which would characterize porters for a century and a half.

Maltsters of the day were able to make three basic varieties—pale, amber, and brown malts. Counterintuitively, they took progressively less time to kiln. Pale and amber malts baked slowly and expensively for many hours. Brown malt, the

Ralph Harwood and His Three Threads.

There's something narratively attractive in the idea of a single origin story. Alexander Graham Bell and the telephone, the Wright brothers and their airplane. For more than 200 years, an obscure, unsuccessful English brewer named Ralph Harwood has gotten all the credit for single-handedly inventing porter—but does he deserve it?

Here's how the Harwood story goes. The main beers in London in the 1730s were ale (low ABV, made with few hops), beer (robust and hoppy), and twopenny (a pale ale), and it was common for pubgoers to ask for a pint with all three blended together—a way of making a fourth beer on the spot. Harwood, based in Shoreditch, London, hit on the idea of brewing a beer that combined the character of the "three threads" that arrived whole, without the need to blend. The resulting beer, which he called "entire" because it contained all three, was the first porter.

It turns out most elements in the Harwood tale are false, despite their now prominent provenance in histories by some of the most careful writers. In researching the style, the historian Martyn Cornell began finding obvious inconsistencies with other accounts and eventually found the source of the famous three-threads story: a short piece by a writer named John Feltham in a London guidebook from 1802. Feltham got several things wrong. There was a drink called "three-threads" at the time, but according to contemporary observers, the beers were blended in the cask, not at the pub. Feltham compounded this error by conflating the three-threads blends with the practice of reblending parti-gyled batches to make porters. "Entire" didn't refer to the three threads, as he thought, but to blends of different strengths of the same porter.

Ralph Harwood *did* exist and he *did* brew beer in Shoreditch. Yet there's no evidence from any contemporary source that Harwood was particularly pivotal in the style's invention. In fact, Harwood went bankrupt in 1747, which would have taken real effort by the inventor of London's most popular style of beer. A more likely story is also more prosaic. Porters evolved slowly as breweries began to make incremental improvements over time. There's evidence of this, too. A writer from the mid-eighteenth century remembered that the early versions of porter weren't very good. (It wasn't until breweries began to age porter, shortly after his account, that it came into its own.) That writer made no mention of three threads, no mention of Harwood. But we like our single-origin stories, and so the legend of Ralph Harwood is likely to enjoy a long and robust life.

cheapest and worst, was subjected to intense heat for short periods, emerging hard, crusted, and scorched. It could be kilned over fires of straw, which produced fairly clean malt, or wood, which made it smoky; but in neither case was the finished product especially palatable.

Porter brewers, however, adopted methods of brewing that seemed to mitigate the faults imparted by brown malt. First, they employed a technique known as "parti-gyle brewing." This involved drawing several batches of beer off a single, massive mash. The first runnings were the most sugar-rich, and each successive beer grew weaker and weaker as the grains were washed of sugars. The brewers followed the same process, but instead of blending the batches to make different strengths of beers (the typical method), they mixed them all back together to make single batches of porter. The brewers called these beers "entire" (sometimes spelled "intire") because they contained all the mash runnings.

ABOVE: *Ticket porters unloading cargo from the Thames gave London's famous black ale its name.*

The second important discovery, and the practice that came to define the style, was aging. Porter makers learned that age helped soften the harsh edges of the beer. They stowed their beer in huge, 108-gallon casks known as "butts" to cure (porter was sometimes referred to as "entire butt," which is, sadly, less amusing when you understand the context). They left it there for at least several months and sometimes as long as two years. This had two practical effects. Freshly brewed porter expressed much of the harsh character of the cheap malt used to brew it. But age mellows beer, and the sharpness and smokiness softened over time. More important, it allowed the beer to be inoculated with wild yeasts living in the casks, which transmuted the beer into deep, complex liquids with the qualities of sherry.

The drink quickly became a hit among London's working classes, particularly the men who unloaded cargo on the river and distributed it around the city. These workers were known as "fellowship" or "ticket" porters, and before long, the beer they drank was known as porter, too. The early 1700s are not replete with accounts of the brewing market, but it appears that once porter brewers learned to age their product, it took just a couple decades to become the city's dominant style.

For the first time near the end of the 18th century, thanks to the steam engine, breweries were able to capitalize on a beer's popularity by brewing in larger and larger quantities. By harnessing the engine's power, they were able to mill massive quantities of grain quickly, reliably heat mash water, mix and stir the mash, and pump the beer throughout the brewing process. Breweries could produce ten times the amount of beer with steam power that they could before it—and mechanization meant more consistent batches, to boot.

Steam power didn't make porters any speedier to age, though, and finding space to let beer sit and ripen for months presented a challenge to London breweries producing hundreds of thousands of barrels annually. If a brewery owned 100

Ale vs. Beer. In modern usage, these two terms are roughly interchangeable. Beer is the larger category, made up of ales and lagers. However, until a hundred years or so ago, the words meant different things to Britons who distinguished brews low in alcohol and hops ("ales") from those that were robust and hoppy ("beers"). This vital information will serve you well should you happen across an English brewing manual from the eighteenth century or, say, discover time travel.

butts, they could produce, say, 200 butts of unaged beer a month—2,400 a year. But if they needed to let the beer cure six months, they could produce only 200 butts in a year. Less-wealthy breweries could do little to remedy the problem, but the rich ones seized their advantage. They began securing warehouse space all over London to store their beer. The large London brewery Whitbread leased a remarkable fifty-four locations. Thrale's, another major producer, owned 19,000 butts, or two million gallons of aging capacity.

The emergence of superbreweries fed another phenomenon: world shipping. London sent porter literally around the world. Major destinations included Russia and the Baltic region, India, Australia, and the New World. The British, with their world-traveling fleet, had already been shipping beer to the colonies when porter came on the scene, and rising volumes reflected porter's popularity. In 1750, Britain sent nearly 14,000 barrels around the world. By 1800, porter-fueled exports jumped to more than 90,000 barrels.

Porter wasn't the first beer to influence other styles, but it was an order of magnitude more popular than any the world had seen. Porter was such a hot style it was ripe for copying—another first in world brewing—and so copy it other countries did. First the style migrated to breweries in Ireland and Scotland in the 1760s and then it continued to spread. The U.S. was brewing porter by the 1780s, Sweden in the 1790s, Australia around 1800, Russia in the 1820s, South Africa in the 1830s, and Sri Lanka in the 1860s.

Toward the end of the 1700s, porter recipes were evolving. Brown malt was now made by slow-kilning for longer periods of time. When the malt was leeched of nearly all moisture, maltsters subjected it to a flash of very intense heat that caused it to "burst like popcorn." This was known as "blown" or "porter" malt, and it would be used in English porters for the next hundred years.

Malt prepared like this would have had none of the enzymes needed during fermentation, however. The change in brown malt techniques coincided with the invention in 1784 of the saccharometer, a device that measures fermentable sugars in beer. Brewers realized that pale malts were far more fermentable than darker malts—a fact that keenly interested them. The British government taxed beer based on ingredients; the more efficient the malt was, the less brewers needed, and therefore the less tax they paid. In short order, porter recipes started using a majority of pale malts; the blown malt was added to preserve porter's familiar flavor and color.

We're a hundred years into the story, yet porters were still strong, aged brown ales. It was around 1820 that porters finally turned black, thanks to a man named Daniel Wheeler, who in 1817 invented a technique for roasting malt at 400°F until it looked like espresso. (He patented the technique, giving the malt a name homebrewers will recognize to this day: "black patent.") Shortly after this innovation, breweries began darkening porters with a small amount of the potent black malt—and used less brown malt in the bargain.

During the early 1800s, porters remained essentially a single style, though "stout," a generic adjective affixed to high-alcohol versions, was creeping into use. The evolution of recipes led to an evolution—and splintering—of style. In England, breweries continued to employ brown malt, but Dublin's brewers embraced black malts and quit using brown altogether. As in London, Ireland's breweries made both porters and stouts, but the beers they fashioned were drier and more acidic. For the first time, there were two distinct varieties of porters and stouts—the brown-malt English ales, and those in Dublin that were made without it.

Back in England, porters continued to dominate the London market through

The Great Porter Flood of 1814.

Industrial-scale brewing led, inevitably, to industrial-scale accidents. Eventually, the ever-expanding porter breweries began to move away from butts and to larger wooden tanks. Over time, these grew, too, into vats containing hundreds of barrels of beer. The vats at one porter brewery, Meux's, were titanic in size. The largest were seventy feet in diameter and contained 18,000 barrels of porter valued at £40,000 (over £2 million in today's currency).

On the fateful afternoon of October 17, 1814, an iron hoop slipped off one of Meux's smaller vats (a mere 22-footer with a capacity of 3,555 barrels). This wasn't entirely unusual, and the storehouse clerk prepared a note to inform the owners. Unfortunately for the people of Tottenham Court Road, the vat was big enough, and the weight inside— 571 tons—heavy enough to overwhelm the remaining hoops and groaning staves. The vat exploded.

The gout of porter contained enough force to create a chain reaction; other vats gave way, and a torrent smashed through the brewery's brick walls and out into the neighborhood. The rushing porter destroyed homes and killed eight people as it swamped the neighborhood in a fifteen-foot wave of destruction. There was actually a tiny bit of luck in the disaster—if it had occurred an hour later, when people had returned home from the workday, the death count might have been even higher. But the victims surely didn't consider themselves lucky. One survivor wrote about the incident, "Whole dwellings were literally riddled by the flood; numbers were killed; and from among the crowds which filled the narrow passages in every direction came the groans of sufferers." Two centuries on, the thought of a wave of ale so powerful it could smash houses is almost hard to believe. But that's the volume of beer the London porter makers were aging around town.

the 1850s—they had now been king for over a century—but milds were beginning to cut into their popularity. At this point, different styles were beginning to emerge. Thanks to the increasing prevalence of "stout porters," regular porters were beginning to get weaker. Toward the end of the 1800s, the government ended a ban on brewing sugar and some English stouts went sweet, creating yet another line in a now-expanding family of dark ales. England now had beers called porter, stout porter, and sweet stout—all slightly different.

At about that same time, breweries began to treat porters badly. Some porters grew weaker to compete with milds, and most breweries, in an effort to save money, no longer aged them. Instead, unscrupulous brewers dumped in chemical coloring agents. In some cases, they were little more than stronger milds, and breweries were even borrowing the mild-brewing technique of using dark sugars to color their porters. As a result, by the 1890s, once-mighty porters occupied only a third of the London market. This was a precipitous fall for a style that had so long dominated other beers—and which had, as recently as thirty years earlier, controlled 75 percent of the market.

Still, porters hung on through the ravages of World War I and were still being brewed in the 1940s—but only just. They made it through World War II, but not for long after; by the 1950s, porters—once the style most identified with English brewing—were no longer brewed in England. They survived a bit longer in Ireland, but by the 1970s died out there, too. Porter had become an obscure style, brewed only in remote pockets of the world (including, surprisingly, a few examples in Canada and the U.S.) and was nearly a footnote in the annals of brewing—until microbreweries in the U.K. and North America revived the style in the 1980s.

STOUTS

The word "stout" is, like the names of so many British styles, an adjective. And as an adjective it was used to describe beers long before it became associated with any particular style. To pubgoers of the 1700s, the word meant "strong," and could be added as a descriptor to any style. Naturally, "stout" was used to describe strong porters, too—but as porter gained such a dominant hold over the London market, the word "stout" slowly became associated with porters. The London breweries helped the trend along, using it to describe their beer ("stout porter" or "brown stout"—both the same product). By the turn of the nineteenth century, the association started to stick, and within three or four decades, it would erase the idea that "stout" might have once been used to describe anything other than porter.

The stout porter of 1800 was, however, not a distinct style. Porters were brewed at different strengths, but the recipes were the same. In England, this was true even after the invention of black malt. Brewing logs of porter brewers Whitbread and Truman show that the grists for porters and stout were identical or nearly so—the stouts were just stronger.

Across the Irish Sea, changes were afoot. The invention of black malt didn't radically alter London porters and

Imperial Stout.

Imperial Stout. Certain beers have romantic histories, and none more so than the beers commissioned in the 1780s by Catherine the Great, empress of all Russia. This was during a period when London breweries were shipping porter around the world, and surely there were excellent examples arriving in Boston Harbor, too. Indeed, five times as much porter was shipped to North America as to the Baltic region. But Boston lacked a monarch, and whatever porters made it that far are long forgotten. The ones sent to the czarina's court have become legend.

The Baltic trade was very important to the brewers of England, one first exploited by makers of Burton ale (see page 22). London's porter breweries entered the market sometime in the second half of the eighteenth century, and the Russian connection was in place by the time Catherine came to power. Porters were brewed strong, and stout porters stronger still; the ones sent to Russia were purported to be the very strongest. Since the very start, writers have suggested that strength was needed for the journey, but that seems unlikely. The cool temperatures and relatively short distance would have been perfect conditions to ship beer. Rather, the Russians got strong beer because they liked their beer strong. The Burton ales sent before stout were strong, and the stouts were, too.

The word "imperial" was intended to signal the recipient of the stout, but it had an undisguised double meaning. These stouts—gorgeous, huge aged beers—were not only fit for royalty; they had become royalty. Long after the association with the czars lapsed, the word "imperial" came to denote the beer's status. Other beers have tried to co-opt this meaning. Imperial IPAs are in regular rotation, but I've seen everything from imperial pilsners to imperial hefeweizens (a stunning debacle). Yet in their power and authority, imperial stouts maintain their status as the kings of beers.

stouts—brewers just added in a pinch of the black stuff to their grists of pale and brown malt. Meanwhile, Dublin breweries abandoned the brown. Their beer was made largely of pale malt with around 8 percent black malt for color and taste. Combined with Dublin's soft water, the resulting beer was dry and sharp. Like their English counterparts, Irish brewers continued to make porter (called "plain" by locals) and stout, but stout grew in popularity. By the 1840s, more than 80 percent of Guinness's rapidly growing capacity was comprised of stout—though much was shipped to England, where it was regarded as a different product from local stouts. Ireland's thirst for porters and stouts was such that it could support three large breweries: Guinness in Dublin, and Beamish and Murphy's in Cork.

Back in England, a curious phenomenon was emerging. Toward the end of the century, stouts were developing an association with wholesomeness and healthfulness. Although breweries were happy to encourage this belief, they don't appear to have initiated it. In a stroke of luck for the breweries, doctors and scientists were the ones who believed stout was good for health. Stout had long been drunk with shellfish, for which it's a delicious partner, and was believed to aid in digestion. Perhaps that's why doctors started recommending stout as a way to restore lost appetite. In an effort to help the trend along, breweries began to bolster their claims by adding ingredients deemed especially salubrious. Two varieties thus created are familiar to today's drinkers: milk stout and oatmeal stout. Milk stouts were not actually made with milk, just lactose (milk sugar). Yeast can't consume lactose, so it gives beer a silky texture and adds a bit of sweetness. Oatmeal has a similar effect, adding texture—more creamy than silky—and a hint of flavor and sweetness. Breweries happily cited doctors as they claimed great powers for their milk and oatmeal stouts. They encouraged mothers to drink stout ("nursing stout"), recommended it for women in general ("ladies' stout"), and of course, prescribed it for the unwell ("invalids' stout").

Others are more obscure, like oyster stout, which sounds like a minor

RIGHT: *A hefty-looking bottle of McIntyre & Townsend Invalids Stout, brewed in New Brunswick, Canada.*

abomination. Londoners had already discovered the sublime pairing of the Thames's most famous bivalve with stout— brewers cut out the middleman and threw the oysters straight in the kettle. Oyster stouts have enjoyed a minor revival in the twenty-first century and, against all odds, they're actually pretty tasty. The oysters add salinity, but nothing fishy. Oyster stouts have a tinge of brine, but otherwise taste just like stout.

From the onset of this phenomenon to World War I, stouts may have taken a cue from P. T. Barnum in their sales pitch, but they were only waxing the apple. The brewery Vaux quoted from *The Lancet*, the prestigious British medical journal, which had observed, "As is well known, Stout appears to be easier of digestion than beer." Stout was served in hospitals and even prescribed to patients by doctors.

One company— Guinness—capitalized on this belief and rode it to

Mercer's Meat Stout.

Of all the stout brewers in Britain between 1880 and World War I, none took the notion of "nourishing" more literally than a small Lancashire outfit called Mercer's. Their stout recipe doesn't survive, but the label and a clipping from 1888 tell enough of the story. "NOURISHING STOUT," read the label, "brewed with the addition of specially prepared MEAT EXTRACT. *Highly recommended for invalids.* REFRESHING AND INVIGORATING." Mercer's even took out space in a newspaper advertisement to include medical documentation. Quoting a chemist's analysis, the brewery boasted that their stout contained "more dry solids than any other stout to be had." Dry solids—there's a phrase you don't see breweries using to tout their beers anymore. Especially *meat* solids.

Why Do the Bubbles Go Down?

A pint of Guinness is more than a beer—it's a ritual. As the publican slowly pulls a pint, the black of the beer and the tan of the head course into the glass in one frothy whole. Slowly, magically, the head begins to separate—but as the tiny, nitrogenated bubbles move toward the surface, they simultaneously appear to cascade down the inside of the glass. It's an amazing optical illusion. What gives?

Scientists have been no less fascinated by a pint of Guinness than we punters, but they have better explanations. Several things are happening. Most beer is carbonated naturally or force-carbonated with CO_2. Back in the 1950s, Guinness started experimenting with nitrogen carbonation. In regular beer, carbon dioxide bubbles continue to absorb more CO_2 as they float to the surface, becoming larger and more buoyant. Nitrogen doesn't dissolve as well in liquid, so the bubbles stay tiny—and less buoyant than carbon dioxide.

Inside a glass of Guinness, the liquid is circulating. At the edges, the bubbles touching the glass suffer drag; but at the center, where there is nothing to restrict them, the bubbles rush toward the surface. In doing so, they push liquid up in front of them; when that liquid nears the surface and has nowhere to go, it spreads out and begins to flow downward around the walls of the glass, pushing the not-so-buoyant nitrogen bubbles with it. Those bubbles touching the glass aren't able to resist the force of downward-rushing beer, and they get shoved along until the cycle carries them toward the center of the glass—and back upward. Of course, in a black pint of Guinness, you can only see the outside bubbles, which makes the illusion complete.

become the world's largest stout brewery. It had already enjoyed explosive growth at the end of the century, and World War I, which devastated both breweries and beer gravities in Britain, gored the Dublin brewery less lethally. In 1929, the brewery launched one of the most successful ad campaigns in history based on the catch phrase "Guinness is good for you." The tag appeared on iconic ads with colorful cartoon drawings for the next forty years. The ads featured different themes, but underscored the brand—in an age before people even understood the concept of branding: "Guinness for Strength," "My Goodness, My Guinness," and "A Lovely Day for a Guinness."

Back in the United Kingdom, the world wars crippled stouts, which were eventually brewed weaker than prewar porters. Yet stouts didn't just lose gravity; they began to change into something very different from what was shipped to St. Petersburg more than a century earlier. They were not only weak, but, thanks to the shift in the market toward women and sick people, they became overtly sweet. Although this helped them retain their popularity, it was a mixed blessing. Brewers continued to target women, trying to lure them with ever sweeter and milder stouts. Eventually stouts came to be associated with elderly women, which further hastened their decline.

Unlike porters, however, stouts never died out in Britain. This was no doubt helped by Guinness, which opened a brewery in England—among other countries around the world where it opened yet more breweries to serve the local markets. When the craft brewing revolution arrived in Europe and North America, stouts were one of the early success stories, and their popularity has remained intact. Stout is now one of the most admired styles among American connoisseurs. And, like their ancestors, the most admired stouts are the huge, wood-aged ales. After a long period of decline, stout has come full circle. ∎

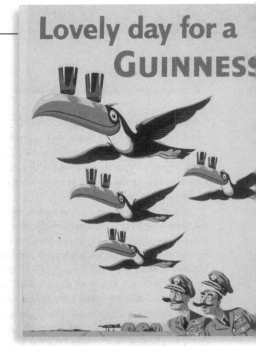

ABOVE: *One of many examples of Guinness's iconic advertising*

DESCRIPTION AND CHARACTERISTICS

T IS NOT UNREASONABLE for certain notions to afflict one's understanding about porters and stouts: Stouts are heartier than porters, more roasty, thicker. These observations, however true once, no longer match the existing spectrum. Irish stouts, though roasty, are weaker and thinner than most commercial examples of porter. Baltic porters, on the other hand, are stronger than most porters and stouts, and they, too, can be roasty. Sweet stouts are usually in the middle, and at the best only mildly roasty, while export and imperial stouts are big or bigger and have varying levels of roastiness. Beyond the general categories of porter and stout, you may find the names modified by any other number of adjectives as well: milk, oatmeal, maple, barrel-aged, coffee, molasses, cream, licorice, chocolate, sweet, dry, double, imperial. Are porters innately distinct from stouts? Are all these things separate styles?

Let's start with styles first. The difficulty is distinguishing between real and semantic differences on the one hand and, on the other, the brewing methods. Imagine Porter-Stout were not a continuum of beer styles, but a long-lived car company. Like that car company, over the years Porter-Stout has issued a long list of substyles, some no more enduring or loved than the Edsel. And yet, like those few Edsels still sighted on American roads, many of those funky old porters and stouts still get brewed from time to time. To make sense of things, people have collapsed the various permutations into smaller substyles numbering as many as ten or as few as three or four. To fully capture what are in fact fairly distinct styles, five is ideal: porter, Baltic porter, Irish stout (dry and export), sweet stout, and imperial stout. Each of these is distinct, and together they give a good sense of the full range.

As to the ingredients and flavors, this is trickier business. Breweries regularly modify the names of their porters and stouts, sometimes referring to an ingredient, sometimes to a quality. Chocolate stouts, for instance, often do not contain chocolate. Milk stouts usually contain the sugar of milk, lactose, but no actual milk. Other names may hint at ingredients with general adjectives—"sweet" stouts may include sugar, for example, and "dry" stouts probably include unmalted roasted barley. A word like licorice or molasses? Your guess is as good as mine. Unlike many other styles, though, at least the language of porters and stouts is direct. If a stout is called cream, it will taste creamy; if a porter is called dry, it will taste dry. Whether there's chocolate in a chocolate stout or not, it will taste chocolatey.

PORTERS

After pale ales and IPAs, porters may be the most abundant style in the U.S., with more than 1,000 commercial examples. There is something essential about these beers, an inherent "porterness," even when their flavors vary in striking ways. Take the example of two porters from opposite coasts: Deschutes Black Butte Porter from Oregon and Geary's London Porter from Maine.

Black Butte is so smooth and chocolatey that Deschutes founder Gary Fish quickly realized it was the perfect entry beer for novices. When people at his pub requested the lightest beer he had, he offered them a deal. "'I'll get you that beer, but taste this first.' We figured about 80 percent of them said, 'Oh, that's really good, I'll have one of those.'" The dark malts are martialed primarily for their caramel and chocolate elements, but a gentle roastiness rounds out the sweetness and adds balance.

For his porter, David Geary wanted to inspire the memory of the great porter heyday in London. He consulted a recipe from 1805 in creating his deep, roasty beer undergirded by caramel and molasses. It's long and roast-bitter, and Industrial Age words like "oil" and "creosote" spring to mind. (When I mentioned creosote to Geary, he shuddered, but I offer it as metaphor.) Amazingly, Geary's is the smaller of the two beers (4.2% ABV to Black Butte's 5.2%)—but the flavor rolls across the tongue like a freight train. If I owned a pub, I would definitely *not* offer this to the person requesting a light beer—yet it may be the best porter brewed in the world.

BALTIC PORTERS

Baltic porters—commonly brewed in the Baltic states, Scandinavia, Poland, and Russia—bear some similarity to imperial stouts: Made with black malts and, often, roasted barley, these porters are strong (up to 10% alcohol) and hearty. Yet most are brewed with lager yeasts and have a lighter, cleaner palate, with burnished flavors that tend more toward schwarzbiers than regular, ale-made porter.

Baltic porters have a bitter, roasty quality that can produce flavors of licorice and molasses, and sometimes even a rye-like sour. Because they're lagered, they have little in the way of esters, and the malt provides minimal sweetness—yet they're also very smooth and silky. In some you might find a sherry-like dry note; in others you find a plummier port note. They are purpose-built to address the long, dark, cold winters of the north. Many niche beer styles have lost market position because they're timid or a little boring. Baltic porters are neither—they're obscure because of the historical anomaly of the Cold War, and only now are they becoming better known to those who lost track of them while they remained on the other side of the Iron Curtain. They are one of the hidden treasures of the beer world—but perhaps not for much longer.

IRISH STOUTS— DRY AND EXPORT

For most people in the world, the word "stout" applies to one beer: Guinness. In the long period of decline among the porters and stouts of England, Irish companies established their product as *the* stout. Beamish and Murphy's, the two breweries of Cork, may not have achieved Guinness's fame, but for over a century and a half, they've helped Dublin's giant establish the dry stout (sometimes called Irish stout) as one of the world's most durable and popular beers.

The standard product of these breweries is a paradoxical brew. On the one hand, it's very thin and weak (about 4% ABV), no stronger than American light beer. On the other, it is brewed with acrid roasted barley and truckloads of hops, making it a sharp, bitter pour. And speaking of pour, the nitrogen that made Guinness famous livens most Irish stouts, abroad and in the U.S. (Trust Irish scientists to invent a nitrogenating "widget" that ensures each bottle and can results in a proper pint.)

An entirely different Irish stout is sometimes honored with its own category designation, yet the entire "style" is really defined by just a single brand. Few beers are as justifiably legendary as Guinness Foreign Extra

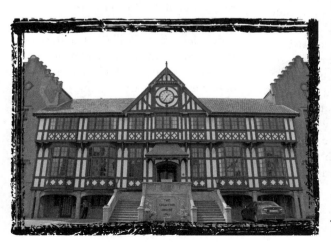

FACING PAGE: *The Counting House, a modern-day tourist attraction in the city of Cork, which used to serve as the face of the original Beamish and Crawford Brewery*

RIGHT: *Guinness's great vats*

Stout ("FES" to devotees), and few taste so vividly of the past. Guinness introduced this beer to the U.S. in 1817, though the recipe was different then. Typical of the era, the brewery aged some of its beer in large wooden vats and then blended a portion back into freshly made stout. Like London porters of old, that aged portion was inoculated with wild yeast and bacteria and grew acid over time. This was FES, and although the recipe has evolved thanks to the invention of black malts and the later inclusion of unmalted roast barley, it retained its character thanks to the huge vats still in use as late as the 1990s. The writer Michael Jackson visited then, reporting that aged, soured beer was still being blended in FES. The "lactic, winy" flavors came from "a blend of beers, one of which has been matured for up to three months in wooden tuns that are at least 100 years old."

Curiously, Guinness is now hugely secretive about its process. When I spoke to master brewer Fergal Murray, he wouldn't even acknowledge those lactic, winy flavors anymore. "Do you think it has those?" he asked coyly. He acknowledged that the pH was lower because of the roast barley, and "maybe these things are giving you, or the people out there in the world, that perception." Tours are no longer given, even to journalists, and the company speaks only in general terms about their process,

invoking the "unique mystery of Guinness." He elaborated on that mystery, sort of. "There is a special brew that is separated in the brewery and goes via a variation in process times in brewhouse and in fermentation—which we use to enhance the flavor characteristics of Guinness. More taste. Only known to a few."

Whatever the process, the result is one of the most intense beers on the market: a muscular 7.5% stout of great density and layered complexity. The black malts are charred and ashy, as bitter as French roast coffee but also tannic and dry. They would overwhelm the beer were it not for a latent acidity, which reins in the malt astringency and allows FES's quieter flavors to emerge—chocolate, dark bread, grassy hopping.

SWEET STOUTS

What qualifies as a sweet stout? The category is admittedly something of a catchall, encompassing all those low- to mid-strength, sweet-side stouts, including many of the "adjective stouts": milk, oatmeal, maple, cream, and chocolate. The "sweet" in the name is suggestive of more than just flavor; these beers often feature an elevated proportion of unfermented sugars and dextrins. Beyond the perception of sweetness, this lends a sense of creaminess and smoothness. Many sweet stouts have a mild roasted note for balance. In fact, despite their name, some may not even be particularly sweet. Rather, their mildness and smoothness are merely relative.

Thanks to the success of Samuel Smith Oatmeal Stout, a beer released for the first time in 1980, oaty stouts have become a familiar subtype. Oats have an oily, silky quality that provides body and flavor, perfect in this style. Until recently, milk stouts were a rarity, but they have found a voice in many of the examples produced throughout the U.S.—particularly in the South. Milk stouts have a richness that comes from unfermentable milk sugar (lactose). "Cream" stouts, a related variation, may or may not have lactose; the name often just refers to their quality, not ingredients. In the same way, "chocolate" may refer to an ingredient (Young's Double Chocolate Stout) or the blend of malts alone (Brooklyn Black Chocolate Stout). Whatever their source of smoothness and sugar, sweet stouts are toothsome, surprising alternatives to their bitter, roasty kindred.

IMPERIAL STOUTS

If beer were dessert, imperial stouts would be chocolate mousse. Strong beers are innately rich, but imperial stouts, with their heady combination of booze and dense, syrupy malts, are the kings of decadence. Breweries treat them like desserts, too: This is no beer for understatement, and brewers do everything they can to max out the flavor, density, thickness, and strength. Beer drinkers, much like chocoholics, return the love: Imperial stouts are regularly rated the highest among all beers by both fans and critics.

What makes them so beguiling is not just their strength. Barley wines and some Belgian styles are equally musclebound. But unlike those beers, imperial stouts have a secret weapon: dark malts. Pale malts by themselves are sweet, and in strong beers, this quality can cloy. The ways to offset that are few. Dark malts, on the other hand, contribute their own bitterness as well as a roasted or charred flavor. The very thing that makes some high-gravity beers sweet is what helps balance an imperial stout. The result is liquid dark chocolate—intense flavors stripped of excessive sweetness. Roastiness is the tentpole, but underneath the big top, an imperial stout may have an array of dark fruit, coffee, and port or sherry flavors. ∎

BREWING NOTES

THE ARCHITECTURE OF modern porters and stouts is similar, if counterintuitive. Both styles rely on pale malts (80 percent or more), which provide the convertible malt sugars and enzymes critical for fermentation. Everything that distinguishes porter and stouts—the color and flavors—comes from the remaining fifth of the grist. Yet that minority portion is where all the action is, and the possible variations mean that no two recipes will be exactly the same.

The key building blocks for black ales are crystal malt, chocolate malt, black malt, and roasted barley. Crystal malts add sweetness and a caramel note but will also inflect black malts, producing flavors of red fruit and cocoa. Chocolate and black malts are both roasted to varying degrees of color—think medium- and dark-roast coffee. Despite its name, chocolate malt can have a harsh, dry quality—it pairs well in grists with sweeter crystal malt. Black malt has a deeply roasted, burned bitter quality, and is so intense it's never used in more than a few percentage points of the total grist.

Finally, one of the key ingredients in Irish stout is roasted, unmalted barley, but it wasn't always so. It was only sometime in the late 1920s or '30s that Guinness started adding roasted barley to give its stout more flavor. The Guinness we know today is influenced heavily by that change; roasted barley imparts a dry, astringent, coffee-like bitterness. It's the taste of Irish stout—but not the ancient taste.

Porters and stouts are hearty wintertime beers and they share a number of close cousins. Porters are closely akin to a German style known as *schwarzbier* (sometimes identified on labels as "black lager"). Like porters, they are dark and rich; they are smoother, though, and sometimes less complex. In the Czech Republic, dark *tmavé* and black *černé* lagers have the porter-like sweet-to-roasty range.

Lovers of big stouts invariably appreciate another German style, *doppelbock*. Doppels aren't black, but they're dark, rich, and alcoholic. In a similar vein, but slightly further from the target, *old ales* offer strength and character, but they're lighter still.

To add depth and complexity, brewers may add small portions of specialty malts. Common ingredients include rye, for its earthy, spicy note; wheat, to improve head retention; oats, for body and silkiness; smoked malt, for flavor; and sugars (including brewing sugar, honey, molasses, and maple syrup), either to reduce body and add alcohol or to add color and flavor. Stouts and porters provide excellent foundations for flavored beers—they're hearty enough that fruits and spices add character without overwhelming. In recent years, coffee, vanilla, cocoa, fruit (cherries are a favorite), and chile peppers have become relatively common. ■

EVOLUTION

FOR A CATEGORY of styles as broad, historical, and occasionally weird as porters and stouts, "evolution" looks more like recycling. Many of the recent trends are a return to the old ways or variations on old themes. After decades of steel-conditioning, wood barrel–aging has returned to fashion in brewing, and imperial stouts are one of the most common barrel-aged beers. The

RIGHT: *The risks of barrel-aging: Some casks harbor wild yeasts or bacteria or allow in too much oxygen, spoiling the beer. One in every few dozen barrels may be lost.*

modern version of this process began in the 1990s in the U.S., where bourbon barrels are readily available (by law, distilleries can only use them for one batch of whiskey). Most breweries have great success with these limited-run stouts, and in some cases, as with Deschutes The Abyss, Three Floyds Dark Lord, Portsmouth Kate the Great, and Firestone Walker Parabola, they sell out as fast as Super Bowl tickets.

Americans didn't own the barrel-aged stout market for long. European breweries got in on the act—but of course, they used barrels from whisky distillers closer at hand. (Though it's worth noting that many Scottish distillers also use those cast-off American bourbon barrels, too.) This isn't limited to Scottish breweries—the Netherland's De Molen ages Hemel & Aarde ("Heaven and Earth") in barrels from Bruichladdich, on Islay, and breweries in Denmark and Norway also use Scotch barrels—but Scottish breweries seem to have made the most of it. Extreme beer king BrewDog ages its imperial stouts in a continuously rotating series of whisky barrels, while Harviestoun Brewery works solely with Highland Park for its Ola Dubh ("Black Oil")—a beer the brewery calls an old ale.

Beer aged in these barrels pulls not only vanilla oak tannins from the wood, but also the whisky, which is instantly evident on the nose. Bourbon adds a sweet, boozy note, while Scotch gives stouts an elegant, smoky touch.

Until about 2005, it was rare to find flavored stouts and porters, but now it is at least as common to find them flavored as not. Often this means subtle additives that blend in with the dark roasted malts, like coffee, cacao, or licorice (an ancient porter ingredient), but increasingly, fruit stouts, herb stouts, and other flavored stouts are easily available, especially at brewpubs. An especially interesting trend is the return of oyster stouts. Whole freshly shucked bivalves go into the kettle, and then brewers add the shells to the conditioning tank. Perhaps the first modern oyster stout was made in Dublin in the 1990s by the craft brewery Porterhouse. In the U.S., Harpoon and Flying Dog have offered recent examples, but the City by the Bay seems to have claimed the style for its own. Its Magnolia Gastropub and Brewery brewed a version in 2008 and 21st Amendment followed. Just up the road in Petaluma, HenHouse has also gotten a piece of the action. ∎

THE BEERS TO KNOW

PORTERS AND STOUTS are among the most varied styles available. It would exaggerate the point to say no two are alike, but not by much. The flavors that dark malts produce, which can range from milk chocolate sweet to charcoal bitter, offer breweries incredible range. The beers mentioned here are a representative sample of this diversity, but they could be matched by two or three times as many equally good sets of beers. If you like dark ales, you could make a life's work of trying them all—and what a nice life that would be.

Take note, also, that imperial stouts are among the best beers to age (and indeed, many *need* to be aged; some breweries are adopting "best after" dates). As their character evolves, harsh burnt or hop notes will soften and eventually vanish. In time, those port and sherry notes, along with fruit and chocolate, will begin to replace the rough edges. If the stout was sharp-elbowed in its youth, in maturity it will develop into a round, resonant beer.

PORTERS

DESCHUTES BLACK BUTTE

ooooooooooooooooooooooooooooooooooo

LOCATION: Bend, OR

MALT: Pale, caramel, chocolate, wheat

HOPS: Cascade, Bravo, Tettnang

5.2% ABV, 1.056 SP. GR., 30 IBU

A good way to get a sense of the range of this style is to compare Black Butte with either Geary's or Anchor porters. Black Butte is one of the most purely pleasurable beers on the market. It has a light-bodied but complex malt base of chocolate and caramel sweetness, with notes of nuts and a trace of roastiness. When people used to think of dark beer, they imagined heavy, aggressive, bitter beers; with Black Butte they get just the opposite.

ANCHOR PORTER

ooooooooooooooooooooooooooooooooooooooo

LOCATION: San Francisco, CA

MALT: Pale, caramel, chocolate, black

HOPS: Northern Brewer

5.6% ABV

Anchor Porter, dating to 1972, isn't America's oldest—that honor goes to the version Yuengling introduced in 1829. But it's certainly the oldest craft-brewed example, and remains one of the most characterful. Unlike Deschutes Black Butte, Anchor Porter is dense and rich, pouring into the glass like espresso with a long, sustained

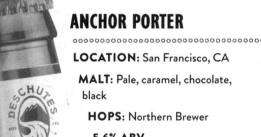

head. There's some coffee in the palate as well, but also a bitter roasted barley note that recalls Baltic porters. A perfect accompaniment for a bowl of chowder or plate of oysters.

GEARY'S LONDON PORTER

LOCATION: Portland, ME

MALT: Pale, crystal, chocolate, black

HOPS: Cascade, Willamette, Golding

4.2% ABV, 1.045 SP. GR.

David Geary has produced a beer that is not only a worthy homage to historic examples, but one that evokes Victorian Britain with its smoky, black palate. It is a lush, velvety beer with a long intensity that belies its modest strength. It is yet a step further away from Anchor and Black Butte—the Islay single malt of porters.

FULLER'S LONDON PORTER

LOCATION: London, England

MALT: Pale, crystal, chocolate, brown

HOPS: Fuggle

5.4% ABV, 37 IBU

It's wonderful that there's a traditional London brewery making porter again—even if porter has a ways to go before it can be considered rehabilitated. Fuller's is a great start, with an intensity of dark, roasted flavors that belie its strength. There's a bit of bready roundness underneath that softens the beer just a touch.

BALTIC PORTERS

ŻYWIEC PORTER

LOCATION: Żywiec, Poland

MALT: Undisclosed

HOPS: Undisclosed

9.5% ABV

Żywiec Porter vents an earthy and slightly sour aroma, one with a subtle molasses note. The vibrant flavor follows suit, with a cascade of bitter, roasted malts with the quality of coffee, molasses, and very dark chocolate. Some beers are so bitter that they start to come back around toward sour, and that's the case with Żywiec. Yet, amazingly, it's a smooth, silky beer that also lends itself to large, greedy swallows.

ALDARIS PORTERIS

LOCATION: Riga, Latvia

MALT: Undisclosed

HOPS: Undisclosed

6.8% ABV

The recipe for this Latvian porter goes back to the early twentieth century. Although it has roastiness that's characteristic of the Baltic porters, it is the one of the smoothest and sweetest examples available. The palate produces interesting

flavor notes: Beyond roastiness is a touch of licorice and a flavor that sometimes invokes beets, at other times cola.

OKOCIM PORTER

LOCATION: Brzesko, Poland

MALT: Pale, caramel, Munich, roast

HOPS: Undisclosed

8.3% ABV, 1.092 SP. GR., 38 IBU

Compared to Żywiec and Aldaris, Okocim is a meatier beer—though still smooth and elegant. Of all the Baltics, Okocim is the most balanced and approachable. It has a touch of roast but is largely characterized by a raisin-sweet body and silky texture.

IRISH STOUTS

PORTERHOUSE PLAIN PORTER

LOCATION: Dublin, Ireland

MALT: Pale, caramel, black, flaked barley, roasted barley

HOPS: Galena, Nugget, East Kent Golding

4.2% ABV

This 1990s vintage brewery is happy to claim the mantle of authenticity, and this beer is its calling card. It is heartily charred and if you hold your head one way you'll taste dark cocoa, but maduro cigar the other. A beer that's happy to invite comparisons with Dublin's more famous dark ale.

BEAMISH IRISH STOUT

LOCATION: Cork, Ireland

MALT: Pale, wheat, roasted barley

HOPS: Undisclosed

4.1% ABV

There are three traditional draft Irish stouts dating back to previous centuries—Murphy's, Guinness, and Beamish. All three have long since homogenized so that they appear identical in their graceful tulip pint glasses, topped by a luxurious meringue-like head. Each is different and has its bloc of fans, but of the three, Beamish has the most character. Wheat provides body the others lack, and the palate is deeper and more burnt. Beamish is the hardest of the three stouts to find, which only increases its allure.

GUINNESS FOREIGN EXTRA STOUT (FES)

LOCATION: Dublin, Ireland

MALT: Undisclosed

HOPS: Undisclosed

7.5% ABV

For those used to standard draft Guinness, FES is a shock. It is a huge beer, and rough and thick as a stevedore's neck. I find it ashy in its char, and the body does nothing to smooth things. Halfway through the bottle, subtleties emerge, like caramel and rye bread (or is it pumpernickel?). It will change the way you think about Guinness.

GUINNESS EXTRA STOUT

○○○

LOCATION: Dublin, Ireland

MALT: Undisclosed

HOPS: Undisclosed

6% ABV

M any people don't realize this beer exists, or if they do, mistake it for the Guinness they get on draft. Long before Foreign Extra came to the U.S., Extra could be found in squat bottles on grocery shelves. To my palate, this is the best of Guinness's offerings by far. It has a thick body, like FES, but is balanced more by a lactic tang than charcoal—vinous and complex. At 6%, one shouldn't drink it like a session ale, but I'll admit I have done so.

SWEET STOUTS

LEFT HAND MILK STOUT

○○○

LOCATION: Longmont, CO

MALT: Pale two-row, caramel, Munich, roasted barley, flaked oats, flaked barley, chocolate

HOPS: Magnum, U.S. Golding

6% ABV, 1.065 SP. GR., 25 IBU

S old in both regular and nitrogenated bottles, Left Hand is one of the only milk stouts produced in America. With tons of silky body and a rich mocha head, the beer starts sweet and creamy and evolves as licorice, coffee, and a hint of hop bitterness fill out the palate. It's decadent without being too heavy or saccharine.

LANCASTER MILK STOUT

○○○

LOCATION: Lancaster, PA

MALT: Pale, caramel, chocolate, black, roasted barley

HOPS: Cascade, Golding

OTHER: Lactose

5.3% ABV, 1.053 SP. GR., 22 IBU

M any milk stouts lack malt bitterness, but Lancaster has a nice foundation, with a thick lushness that belies its size. At the front end, it's all scorched stoutiness, but it softens toward the finish, turning from a dry to a sweet stout in the space of a swallow.

YOUNG'S DOUBLE CHOCOLATE STOUT

LOCATION: Bedford, England

MALT: Pale, caramel, chocolate

HOPS: Fuggle, Golding

OTHER: Dark chocolate, chocolate essence, sugar

5.2% ABV

Looking at the list of ingredients, you might think Young's is cheating by trotting out an alcoholic chocolate malted masquerading as a beer. It's a bit of a close call, for there are some deliciously treat-like qualities in the beer: a creamy, luscious head that may well be hiding a dollop of ice cream, and a bright ruby-black beer that is saturated in cocoa flavor. But then you notice the hints of roast, grain, and even a touch of those delicate English hops. It's a dessert-y beer, but it's a beer nonetheless.

ROGUE SHAKESPEARE STOUT

LOCATION: Newport, OR

MALT: Pale, caramel, chocolate, roasted barley, Dare malt (proprietary), oats

HOPS: Revolution, Rebel (proprietary)

6.1% ABV, 1.061 SP. GR., 69 IBU

Shakespeare Stout picks up some of its sweetness from the oats, which, when combined with the dark malts, give the beer a chocolate chip cookie wholesomeness. But there's also a density and bitterness at the beer's center that keeps it from being, strictly speaking, a sweet stout.

THE DUCK-RABBIT MILK STOUT

LOCATION: Farmville, NC

MALT: Undisclosed

HOPS: Undisclosed

5.7% ABV

In the best examples, the "milk" in milk stout inspires associations of farm-fresh wholesomeness. Duck-Rabbit's brew, frothy as latte foam, does this in spades. The flavor is latte-like as well, with perhaps a dash of mocha to round things out.

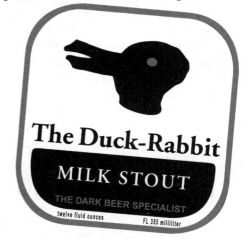

SAMUEL SMITH OATMEAL STOUT

LOCATION: Tadcaster, England

MALT: Pale, roast malt, roasted barley, oats

HOPS: Undisclosed

OTHER: Cane sugar

5.0% ABV, 1.052 SP. GR., 30 IBU

This venerable stout inspired many an American brewer, but it's not an easy trick to duplicate it. Smith's dessert-like stout has the velvet texture of oats but there's a stiff backbone that comes from the mineral-rich well water.

IMPERIAL STOUTS

SINEBRYCHOFF PORTER

LOCATION: Kerava, Finland

MALT: Pilsner, Munich, brown, caramel

HOPS: Saaz

7.2% ABV, 1.070 SP. GR., 45 IBU

The brewery produced porter as early as the 1860s, and this recipe has been in production since 1957. Brewed with an ale strain purportedly hustled out of England in a test tube, this ostensibly Baltic porter has much more in common with imperial stouts. It is as thick as maple syrup, and a curl of acrid bitterness rises from its surface. The burnt malt is intense and gives the beer a slightly acid quality reminiscent of Guinness Foreign Extra Stout. A lovely, chewy, dense beer that is surely a tonic to the long Finnish winters.

NORTH COAST OLD RASPUTIN

LOCATION: Fort Bragg, CA

MALT: Undisclosed

HOPS: Undisclosed

9% ABV, 75 IBU

Rasputin is a true titan, a beer in which each element is at the extreme of intensity, but remarkably, it holds together. The blackness of the beer swallows light and the body is stiff enough to float a quarter—that's how it seems, anyway. Rasputin is pure roast with just an ember of molasses sweetness in the middle and a core of alcohol warmth to balance things out. A beer for Siberian winters.

GREAT DIVIDE YETI

LOCATION: Fort Bragg, CA

MALT: Undisclosed

HOPS: Undisclosed

9.5% ABV, 75 IBU

If Rasputin is a beer to respect and perhaps fear, Yeti is a more cuddly giant. Black and roasted it is, but Yeti has a sweeter caramel filling than Rasputin—sometimes it even seems to have vanilla as well. Great Divide has expanded the line, which now includes oak-aged, chocolate, and espresso Yetis.

FIRESTONE WALKER PARABOLA

LOCATION: Paso Robles, CA

MALT: Maris Otter, Munich, caramel, chocolate, roasted barley, oats

HOPS: Zeus, Hallertauer

13% ABV, 82 IBU

The roast and liquor vapors hammer into your mouth like a fist, but if you pay attention, you can taste the breadiness of the base malts in this beer. Bourbon marries perfectly with roast in imperial stouts, especially here, when caramel malts help turn it from vanilla to praline. Ultimately, though, it's those base malts that make this a real standout.

Fuller's

TRADITION, INNOVATION, AND PARTI-GYLE BREWING

THE BREWERY IN CHISWICK, WEST LONDON, NOW HOME TO FULLER'S, IS SO OLD IT STILL BEARS THE NAME OF A PREVIOUS OWNER: GRIFFIN. CLIMBING UP ONE OF ITS WALLS IS THE OLDEST WISTERIA VINE IN ENGLAND, AND OUT FRONT IS A PUB THAT'S EVEN OLDER THAN THE BREWERY. RATTLING OFF A LIST OF SUPERLATIVES LIKE THIS IS NOT UNCOMMON WHEN CITING ONE BUILDING OR ANOTHER—INCLUDING, IT SEEMS, BREWERIES. BUT THOUGH VICTORIAN-ERA BREWERIES LIKE FULLER'S CAN STILL BE FOUND SCATTERED AROUND THE COUNTRY, THEY ARE INCREASINGLY RARE, LIKE SURVIVORS OF A NATURAL DISASTER.

In a sense, they are. Over the space of a generation, Britons abandoned hundreds of years of drinking habits, giving up their local cask ales for fizzy lager. Carnage resulted. From the 1970s onward, scores of England's famous old breweries vanished. Those that hung on were confronted by a very difficult decision. In order to appeal to changing tastes, should they continue brewing their well-known line of beers with the same traditional methods? Or should they overhaul their breweries and brands and risk extinguishing the very product they were trying to save?

Breweries didn't all make the same

ABOVE: *The Griffin Brewery name acknowledges the long history of brewing at this site—at least 350 years back, well before Fuller's acquired the land in 1845.*

ABOVE: *An interior view of the new brewhouse*

BELOW: *The brewery's wisteria vines are the oldest in the country, dating back two hundred years.*

distillery that Adnams installed in 2010. "When it came to work production," Jonathan Adnams, chairman of the family-run board, said, "we had a very different thesis, which was about going to the cutting edge of technology."

Fuller's (founded 1845) split the difference. In the 1960s and '70s, Fuller's was like other breweries: a traditional regional operation using a system that dated to 1883. "Fuller's was really a company not going anywhere—like a lot of regional breweries in the U.K.," head brewer John Keeling

decision. Greene King (founded 1799), the U.K.'s largest producer of traditional ale, went with tradition. The company invested millions of pounds into the old tower brewery, but not to modernize it. Instead, they refurbished their old equipment. "We could have gone mash-filter, we could have gone lauter, but no: We said we're staying with what we know," head brewer John Bexon told me. It has survived by purchasing the brands of smaller breweries on the edge of bankruptcy and brewing them at its plant at Bury St Edmunds. Adnams (founded 1872) instead tacked directly into the wind, completely replacing its current brewery with a state-of-the-art, eco-friendly German system. It turns itself on at four-thirty in the morning and can brew any style of beer to exacting specifications—including precise washes for the

Four Elements of Good Beer.

"On one side of the equation you have to have quality and consistency and that is balanced on the other side of the equation by flavor and character. There are breweries that specialize in producing high-quality, very consistent beer— companies like Budweiser and Carlsberg and Heineken. But maybe they forgot about the other side of the equation, which is to have some flavor and some character. Then there are some craft brewers who really go over the top on character and flavor. You can buy a pint of their beer and think, 'This is a wonderful pint.' But if you buy it again a week later, you might say, 'Well, it's not the same; I don't recognize it as that beer.'" —*JOHN KEELING*

explained. "The seventies come and it's still just really pottering along; not really thinking about the future." Two younger members of the family, Anthony Fuller and Michael Turner, joined the board at that time and set it on a new course. They invested heavily to replace the old brewery with a modern, stainless-steel system. Very slowly, they began expanding their line. They reintroduced London Porter, an evocation of a style once synonymous with the city. Over time they added a specialty line that included beers well outside the English mainstream—1845 (6.3% ABV), celebrating the brewery's 150th anniversary; Vintage Ale (8.5%), a bottle-conditioned old ale; and more recent experiments like Wild River (4.5%), which is brewed with American hops.

But front and center in Fuller's line are three beers—ESB, London Pride, and Chiswick Bitter—that are made by that most traditional, and now almost completely extinct, method: the parti-gyle. This system dates back hundreds of years and was a key feature in London porter brewing in the eighteenth and nineteenth centuries.

The way it works is this: Fuller's makes a mash of largely pale malt with a small portion of crystal malt. Then it begins running the wort into two coppers, first filling one, then the other. The first runnings from a mash are much richer in sugars, and as sparging continues, the wort becomes weaker and weaker. Brewers then collect two coppers of different-strength wort ("gyles"). They use the same hops, but in proportions equal to the strengths of each wort. Finally, brewers ferment the beer out and have two strengths of the same beer. With these

as building blocks, they blend the two in different proportions to arrive at four different beers—the three mentioned earlier as well as the burly 8.5% Golden Pride.

"Modern equipment makes the best beer," Keeling says. But old methods *also* make exceptional beers. Fuller's parti-gyle system has achieved something no other brewery in Britain has managed: Each of their three standard cask ales has won Champion Beer of Britain—

ABOVE: *The two masters of Fuller's beer: Derek Prentice (left) and John Keeling*

ESB three times, London Pride in 1978, and Chiswick Bitter in 1989. Those accomplishments followed Fuller's overhaul of the brewery. It's no coincidence that since Keeling arrived in 1981, the production at Fuller's has tripled, from 70,000 barrels to 220,000.

The brewery itself has become a metaphor for the Fuller's philosophy; when the company bought new equipment, it kept all the old coppers, tuns, and squares. Now both old and new stand side by side and a tour of Fuller's becomes a lesson in the lineage of English brewing.

American ALES

The existence of "American ales" has for decades been the subject of dispute. In broad outlines, the beers in this family conform to the styles of Britain. Take a random brewery (and especially a brewpub) in the U.S. and you're likely to find a golden ale, a pale, an IPA, a brown, a porter, and a stout; all are based on English styles. "Show me," say the proponents of one side of the argument, "any American ale: It's just an *American-brewed English ale.*"

· ·

American Ales are characterized by robust strengths and a saturation of hop flavor, aroma, and bitterness that comes from distinctive native hop strains. Golden ales were created to offer a close analogue to American light lagers: They are straw-colored, light-bodied, and lightly hopped. Amber ales feature a balance between malt and hop character and are generally fuller of body than either pales or browns. American red ales—which differ from the light reds of Ireland—offer a candyish sweetness as a foundation to a sharply hopped beer. Wheat ales, unlike Bavarian weizens, are brewed more in the vein of pales, with soft bodies and gentle, citrusy hopping. Most American fruit beers use a wheat ale as their foundation.

STATISTICS

Golden ale ABV range: 4–5%, bitterness: 10–20 IBU

Amber ale ABV range: 4.5–6%, bitterness: 20–40 IBU

Red ale ABV range: 5–10%, bitterness: 25–100 IBU

Wheat and fruit ales ABV range: 4–5.5%, bitterness: 10–30 IBU

Serving temperature: Golden and wheat: 45°–50°F; amber and red: 50°–55°F

Vessel: Pint glass; weissbier vase or pint for wheat

There's an appealing cleanliness to this argument, no doubt. In a Venn diagram of ales, the American and British circles intersect heavily. There remains a problem, though, and I will offer you London's The Kernel Brewery as an example. The Kernel currently offers several pale ales and IPAs—but no milds or bitters. The pale ales weigh in at over 5% ABV and the IPAs begin at 6.1% and range up toward double digits. All feature classic Pacific Northwest hop varieties; all are bracingly bitter. For good measure, The Kernel offers a massive 9% ABV Red Rye Ale, smoldering with hop heat. In London, no one considers these English beers—they're purely American.

Americans were certainly inspired by the ales of Britain, and for a time, even tried to brew them. Americans are not good about preserving cultural traditions, though; we inevitably begin changing things, adding a bit more of something here, a bit less of something there. It's how we ended up with Tex-Mex cuisine and American Chinese food. Within a few years of the first craft-brewed ales, American brewers started adding more caramel malts and hops to their beers, and three decades later, though they still borrow the British names, Americans have created their own tradition. ■

ORIGINS

AMERICAN ALES GO way back . . . to 1976. That is, ales with a character we could call uniquely American. The history of ales in America is a bit older: 400 years. Those older ones arrived with English and Dutch settlers in the seventeenth century, partly to stave off scurvy and dysentery on the long sea journeys, partly because the idea of leaving Europe without beer would have seemed as preposterous as leaving without food. The new colonists found that barley didn't grow well in their new home, and substitutes—potatoes, molasses—made only provisionally acceptable beer. The colonies were consequently a big target for English exports, which sustained the colonists until a few pockets of brewing finally did emerge. Pennsylvania, where locals felt their porter was a rival to London's, was one,

but an even more impressive hub was Albany, New York.

The town was not only home to dozens of breweries from colonial times through Prohibition, but also to a style of double or XX beer known as "Albany Ale." It was a huge, Burton-esque beer (see page 22) of more than 8% alcohol, heavily hopped but also sweet. Albany was able to bring in hops and barley from the western part of the state and ship beer out via the Erie Canal, giving it a monopoly on distribution as far west as Chicago and, following the Hudson south, to New York City. Riding the popularity of this giant, Albany became the center of American brewing. In the 1850s there were twenty breweries in town, including the nation's largest, John Taylor and Sons, which had a capacity of 200,000 barrels annually (enormous for the time).

Still, beer was a small market, and one firmly rooted in the British tradition. As the generations rolled along and the nostalgia for a proper English pint waned, American-born drinkers took to New World libations—rum and whiskey—which they guzzled by the gallon. By the time of the American Revolution, there were 100 distilleries for every brewery in the country. Ale had had nearly two centuries to beguile Americans, but whiskey was the beverage that won the nation's heart.

Beer reentered the national consciousness in the 1840s and '50s when German immigrants started arriving by the hundreds of thousands. They brought with them a sophisticated sense of brewing, an entrepreneurial zeal, and very tasty beer. At first, German brewers brewed their dark dunkel lagers for German immigrants, but soon they had learned of a kind of beer that was sweeping through Europe—light-colored, Champagne-beautiful pilsner. Even though there was a big enough market to support Albany's many brewers, Americans had never really fallen for heavy ales the way they did for liquor. But these effervescent lagers were something else. German brewers began to convert drinkers, and by the time of Prohibition they had largely turned the United States into lager country.

CONSOLIDATION

We could jump from the death of ales straight to the birth of craft brewing when ales reenter the picture, but it would deprive us of the heart of the story. The evolution of the beer market following Prohibition until the 1970s is the reason craft brewing happened in the first place—and also why ales were at its center.

After Prohibition, the remaining American beer companies went on a decades-long period of consolidation. They waged a constant war against each other to gobble up market share, all in the service of making and distributing beer more cheaply. With great size came more efficient breweries, more streamlined distribution networks, and bigger profits. Since the founding of the country, breweries had been regional businesses; with consolidation came the national brewery.

For the first time in history, the market seemed to favor consolidation over choice. Even as local breweries disappeared, along with local brands and sometimes quirky local products, consumption rose. By the end of the 1970s, breweries had largely been gobbled up and the U.S. had fewer than fifty brewing companies—the lowest number since before nationhood, and down from about 700 following Prohibition—all while sales rose.

By historical standards, this was bizarre. In beer-drinking cultures across the continents and millennia, it was far more common for multiple styles of beer to be brewed. Even if you go all the way back to Egypt and Sumer, you find a variety of styles. Yet here was the U.S. with one of the freest market systems in world history and for the most part it revolved around just a single style of beer.

CRAFT REVIVAL

Into this strange void stepped the first of the craft breweries in the 1970s. They were all tiny and woefully undercapitalized. Banks wouldn't touch them (when Redhook cofounder Gordon Bowker was looking for financial backing, one prospect told him, "Breweries don't start up,

An Indigenous American Style.

Until the 1980s, the U.S. was variously credited as having contributed very little to the world's brewing traditions or as having significantly harmed them. Neither is correct. In the nineteenth century, Americans were at the forefront of brewing innovation, and what emerged from the mash tuns in St. Louis and Milwaukee was both original and exceptional. Subsequent events harmed the beers' reputation and buried their memory—and left us with a false sense of America's place in brewing. Those early lagers deserve more credit than that.

When the first German brewers began setting up shop in the U.S., they made the beers they were trained to make back home—dark lagers that were easy enough to brew with American barley. The beers were heavy, though, and American drinkers found them overly rich. To accommodate local tastes, breweries began experimenting with corn, which lightened the body without reducing alcohol content. The experiments were qualified successes—breweries found they could reduce beer's body with lighter grains, but corn was oily and hard to work with, and more than a few batches ended up dumped into the rivers.

The use of corn might have died out were it not for the arrival of pilsner, which had begun spreading across Europe. Americans wanted to brew the style, too, but local six-row barley was a rough, high-protein strain incapable of producing the clarion golden beers of Bohemia. Barley couldn't produce them alone, anyway. But blended with white corn or, especially, rice, it could. It took years of development and tinkering, but in the end, led by St. Louis's Anheuser Brewing, American brewers figured out how to make beautiful, pale sparkling lagers. The beers were so good that Anheuser Brewing won the grand prize in a European competition in France in 1878 against German, Bohemian, Austrian, and Bavarian lagers.

Good beer fans sneeringly dismiss this so-called adjunct beer as an affront to the art of brewing. The term is meant to connote not just a type of beer but a moral failing. They think of adjuncts like corn and rice as fillers, used only to stretch a buck and dilute a beer. The use of adjuncts necessarily makes a beer worse, less beery.

But when breweries began using corn and rice in the mid-nineteenth century, the grains cost *more* than barley. They were hard to figure out and more complicated to work with. Breweries began using them not to cut corners or appeal to less sophisticated tastes, but because they yielded better beer. It was only much later that the use of adjuncts served the purpose of stretching a buck—and those ingredients were only one factor in the degradation of American beer. Originally, adjuncts were a triumph of brewing, and Budweiser really was the king of beers.

---

they shut down"). Metal fabricators didn't know how to make the tiny breweries they needed, and malt and hop wholesalers dealt on a scale an order of magnitude larger than the first "microbreweries"— as they were known then. The kind of people drawn to craft brewing weren't businesspeople and they didn't think of themselves as competitors with Budweiser. They were more like pirates launching periodic raids on the empire of bland beer, trying to spice things up. Their currency was hand-crafted brews, an artisanal product that had the quality

---

"Beer is proof that God loves us and wants us to be happy." Ben Franklin's famous (mis)quote is well known to beery types, and can be seen on about half the T-shirts at any given beer festival. It seems a satisfying verification of the things we know about Franklin and beer: Ben was a bit of a libertine, but a Founding Father whose love of beer seems to vouch for its patriotic purity. Unfortunately, it's also a crock: Franklin never said it. Worse, it's the misappropriation of a quote from a 1779 letter in which Franklin extols . . . brace yourself . . . *wine.*

"Behold the rain which descends from heaven upon our vineyards; there it enters the roots of the vines, to be changed into wine; a constant proof that God loves us, and loves to see us happy."

How French is that? (Franklin was, of course, a Francophile, one of the many reasons some red-blooded Americans hold him at some distance.) Turns out the fake quote was brewed up by the United States Brewing Association after Prohibition. As a part of their protracted campaign against liquor producers, they worked tirelessly to link beer to the Founding Fathers, patriotism, and, presumably, moms everywhere. Or possibly it came much later, when a clothes manufacturer put the quote on a T-shirt. Tinkering with the legacy of a Founding Father to make a buck? How American is that?

---

of a philosophical statement of purpose; they were the anti-industrialists.

Ales were the obvious choice for the insurrection. Many early craft brewers had visited Britain and were delighted by the rich, characterful beers they found there. Most had a background in home-brewing and knew it was possible to turn out a great ale in a couple weeks' time instead of the month or more it would take to make a lager. But mostly, they wanted to offer a sharp contrast to the impenetrable wall of impersonal, factory-made, pasteurized light lagers found at pubs and groceries.

Sierra Nevada founder Ken Grossman identified the two prongs of attack: "The craft brewers from early on wanted to do something different [that] also . . . really had some flavor impact." American industrial brewers aimed to produce exceptionally mild beers that evoked German lagers, with noble hops and a very light character. The early microbreweries raised the Jolly Roger and went for styles that not only offered a contrast, but tweaked the macros. They brewed ales; absolutely rejected corn, rice, and sugar—but not wheat; and proudly used the strongly tangy American hops the national brands eschewed. The first craft beers *were* different and, compared to every other available beer, packed a flavor punch.

TOWARD COHERENCE

It's a little bit hard to imagine, but by the 1980s most Americans had lost all sense of beer styles. They knew beer to be one thing—mild, light lager. For the first microbreweries, this presented an interesting challenge: simultaneously trying to educate *and* entice new customers. Yet since customers had no basis for judgment, they didn't know themselves what would be enticing. The first fifteen years of craft brewing was a period of testing as breweries cast about, trying to hit on the beers that would strike a chord.

For some breweries, this meant making beer that had at least *some* connection to light lagers. In San Francisco, Fritz Maytag had launched Anchor on its now-famous Steam beer—a close cousin to lager. Other West Coast breweries made pale ales (Sierra Nevada, Hale's) or golden ales (Full Sail). In regions with intact brewing traditions, like Wisconsin and Pennsylvania, early craft breweries like Capital, Sprecher, and Penn all started with lagers. Still others set out in different directions: Widmer Brothers thought German altbier would be a winner, so they brought a culture of yeast back from Düsseldorf to make the city's signature beer in Oregon. In Maine, David Geary built the first English-style brewery, complete with open fermenters and a traditional yeast strain.

Craft breweries launched many beers in the 1980s, and many were failures. The Widmers' altbier, a rich copper beer with a stiff dose of hops, was too aggressive for its time. Boulder Brewing Company (called Rockies Brewing for a while before settling, ultimately, on Boulder Beer) continued to tinker with its line from its founding in 1979 until it settled on its current crop in 2002. In Kansas City, Missouri, Boulevard Brewing was initially known for Bully! Porter and other English-style ales. Ultimately, the swaying Midwestern wheat fields suggested a different course and Unfiltered Wheat became not only Boulevard's flagship, but one of the bestselling beers in the Midwest. These were the lucky ones. Many breweries from the first fifteen years of the American craft movement didn't survive early failures and have vanished from memory.

By the early 1990s, a few trends had emerged. British-style ales were selling well in the U.S. and customers were becoming familiar with that manner of brewing. But in addition to standard British-style beers, Americans were also making things that seemed British—but weren't. Starting with golden ale (the lightest and the ale stand-in for Budweiser), a brewery would offer increasingly dark beers: pale, amber, red, brown, porter, stout. Americans jettisoned the mild ale—usually a dark, weak beer—and invented a range that went from light to dark and weak to strong. It wasn't the way British beer

LEFT: *Small-batch brewing started in places like Boulder, CO— Boulder Brewing (shown here) was one pioneer—and Chico, CA.*

worked, but it made sense to American consumers learning a whole new style of brewing.

This is an important deviation that set America on its journey to indigenous style. In Britain, each of the beer types had emerged from its own set of circumstances and entered a very mature market made up of preexisting beers; styles waxed and waned as trends and preferences swept through the market over the course of centuries. But in America, customers had no context for the ales microbreweries were offering. They had no more idea where a pale ale came from than a stout or a brown. The idea of a spectrum of beers, which ranged from lighter to darker, had an obvious logic—new drinkers could sample from the range and locate themselves on it. This meant two things. One, the whole range now had a relational quality. There was a coherence to the progression, a stylistic unity that ran through the beers. It was so pronounced that it produced a second phenomenon, the two middle colors—amber and red—that didn't exist in Britain. To fill out the line, American breweries essentially invented these styles.

AMERICAN WHEAT ALES

The standard ale range didn't represent the whole of early American craft brewing. A parallel development was happening with wheat ales. American breweries were loath to use adjunct grains like rice and corn in their lighter beers,

> "People didn't know anything about craft-brewed beers. Everybody had to be educated about what style it was—about what style *meant*—even what an ale was versus a lager. The distributors didn't know anything about it—they were just used to selling Rainier or Blitz or whatever else was on their truck. Customers knew even less than that."
>
> —*KARL OCKERT*, brewmaster of Bridgeport Brewing Company, founded in 1984

but wheat seemed as natural, wholesome, and artisanal as barley. It had the bonus of producing a soft, crisp beer that didn't shock those coming to craft brewing from regular beer.

Like many others, the trend got started on the West Coast. Anchor was the first brewery to make a wheat beer in 1983. It wasn't a big departure from the other ales American breweries were making—Anchor just used a sizable portion of wheat in the grist to make a light, golden wheat ale. After the Widmer Brothers Altbier got off to a slow start, they introduced an unfiltered wheat ale that became one of the first real hits in the Pacific Northwest. Across the Columbia River, Hart Brewing (now Pyramid) was having similar success with a straight wheat ale and one made with apricots. By the early 1990s, Midwestern breweries were offering similar examples, and it was there, in America's breadbasket, that the style really flourished. Over time, Bell's (Oberon), Three Floyds (Gumballhead), Goose Island (312 Urban Wheat), and Boulevard (Unfiltered Wheat) saw more and more of their production devoted to wheat ales. Taken together, they represent a substantial chunk of the American craft market.

CRAFT BREWING GROWS UP

Throughout the first decade of craft brewing, the industry grew at a steady, hopeful clip. Bit by bit, brewery by brewery, Americans were being introduced to new styles of beer. By 1990, there were more than 200 craft breweries, and they were turning out an impressive range of beers. Then came the gold rush—a massive explosion in the number of breweries—and with it, a period of serious style confusion.

The first generation of craft brewers had only wanted to brew good beer, but it was clear that microbreweries offered a real financial opportunity. A number of early breweries were flourishing, and some were getting quite large. Boston Beer Company led the way, passing a half-million barrels by 1994. Pete's Brewing and Sierra Nevada both crossed the 100,000-barrel mark by 1995.

Their success created a craft brewery bubble when speculators started flooding the market. The number of breweries more than doubled between 1990 and 1995 and then doubled again by 1997. Entrepreneurs rushed in without trying to understand either the craft of brewing or the market for beer. By the mid-1990s, grocery store coolers were awash with treacly fruit ales, insipid goldens, and light pale ales, as well as beers riddled with quality issues. For a time, customers were so excited about craft beer that they were willing

RIGHT: *Casualties of the revolution: Chicago Brewing, Indianapolis Brewing, and Jefferson State*

to try anything—including the bad ones. In a parallel development, some companies were catering to the nonbeer market, those who liked wine coolers and sugary flavored "alco-pops" like Zima. They were trying to cash in on the microbrewing trend, and their products further diluted the market. There were a shocking 1,376 breweries by 1998—a sevenfold increase in eight years—and many were making terrible beer.

Conversely, many breweries had entered the market determined not to condescend to their customers. Bert Grant, one of the pioneers, launched his brand in 1982 with a stunningly aggressive 45 IBU Scottish Ale (at just 4.7% ABV, it was surely the hoppiest beer in America). Sierra's Ken Grossman debuted with a beer that still sets the standard for American pales. Bell's, Summit, Pyramid, Redhook, Boston Beer, Catamount, Penn, and Stoudts all founded breweries making rich, flavorful beers. But by the late 1990s, these products competed against a confusing mess of knock-offs and wannabes. The interlopers used the same homey labels and professed the same level of devotion to artisanal brewing, but their beer was

watery or worse. Unlike the pioneers, many of these breweries were well capitalized and could afford to dump huge money into distribution and marketing—but often neglected the beer and breweries.

Then the inevitable happened: Customers started walking away from craft brewing, leading to the collapse of hundreds of breweries. In 1999, the number of craft breweries declined by 17 percent and sales stagnated. Consumers weren't tired of the fad, but they were souring on bad beers. Breweries changed their brands like designers changed the latest fashions. Buying a six-pack of beer became a roll of the dice. Breweries selling gimmicky beers watched their fickle customer base vanish —sometimes with devastating results.

SAVED BY HOPS

Although the future seemed gloomy at the time, this was a pivotal moment for American brewing. When the smoke cleared, what remained were the avid drinkers. They had been slowly developing their taste for the bold flavors of beer—working their way up the spectrum ladder—and by the early 2000s, the market turned decisively toward those types of beer: stronger and hoppier.

In California, Stone Brewing was a leader in superhopped beers, along with Lagunitas and Bear Republic. In the Pacific Northwest, BridgePort's 1996 launch of IPA fundamentally reoriented brewing toward beers made with saturated hop flavors and aromas. The Midwest featured maltier, more balanced versions that were also deeply influential, like Bell's Two Hearted

RIGHT: *Boulevard's Steven Pauwels (left) and Deschutes's Larry Sidor collaborate on a "White IPA."*

Ale and Three Floyds Alpha King. On the East Coast, IPAs that split the difference between English and American interpretations also had a large effect on the market—Harpoon IPA, Victory HopDevil, and Brooklyn East India Pale Ale.

The impact may not have been immediately evident in the sales figures (and in fact, it would take a decade for these examples to surface as top-selling beers). Yet the evidence was there. Entries into the annual Great American Beer Festival illustrate the waxing and waning of popular styles. In 1999, as craft breweries were just finding their voice, ninety-five breweries entered beers in the amber ale category—a favorite in craft brewing's first decade. By 2010, only eighty-three breweries entered amber ales. Conversely, in 1999, 118 beers were entered into the hoppy India Pale Ale category; by 2010, that number had jumped to 174.

This is finally being reflected in the marketplace as well. After years and years at the top of the bestseller list,

Contract Brewing.

Craft brewing began in part as a philosophical rebellion. To the scale and mechanization of industrial brewing, the first craft brewers offered handmade ripostes. They looked to an older tradition of brewing, where people hauled their own grain sacks and hand-tended cauldrons of bubbling wort. No computer screens, no push-button brewing. Of the few dozen breweries that started up in the first decade of craft brewing, nearly all began by building small-scale breweries to fulfill this vision.

Jim Koch took a different approach. When he founded Boston Beer in 1984, he saw no reason to build a brewery. There were plants all over the country with excess capacity, and his business plan called for a practice known as "contract brewing"—working with existing breweries to make his beer when they weren't making their own. He partnered with Pittsburgh Brewing Co. to produce Boston Lager and spent his energy selling, not manufacturing. It was a great move: Boston Beer quickly grew to be the largest seller of craft beers, and remains so to this day. As a practice, it took contract brewing a little longer than microbrewing to catch on, but when people realized there was money in good beer, it took off.

But the practice rankled the small brewers who'd spent precious money on steel. Microbrewing's one advantage was the sense that it was made locally, on a human scale by someone in the back room. Brewers saw themselves as craftsmen, not beer peddlers. Contract brewers—these guys were charlatans trading on the folksy image of microbrewing to reap huge rewards. Maureen Ogle documented this trend in her fantastic history of American brewing, *Ambition Brew*: To the other craft brewers, contract brewers were "more interested in making a buck" than brewing beer (Kurt Widmer), "a bunch of promoters" (Bert Grant), beer "brokers" (Ken Grossman), and salesmen "in three-piece suits" (David Geary).

In many cases, these criticisms were well deserved; in the early 1990s, contract breweries were turning out a lot of dreck, reflecting poorly on the entire industry. Boston Beer proved it was possible to compete directly with craft breweries, though, and has a roomful of awards and accolades to prove it.

Over time, the image of contract brewing changed. Jim Koch returned to his hometown of Cincinnati and bought the Hudepohl-Schoenling Brewery, one of the sites where Samuel Adams is now brewed. Breweries regularly take on contracts to fill their own production capacity, often for other craft breweries. This helps the contracted brewery's bottom line, and allows breweries to make beer in far-flung locations, rather than shipping it—which in the age of environmental consciousness has the virtue of being green, as well. It has become a regular practice in the brewing industry, perhaps still slightly stigmatized, but no longer so controversial.

Boston Lager, Sierra Nevada Pale Ale, and Widmer Hefeweizen are all having to share shelf space. The fastest-growing segment is IPAs, fueled by brands like Sierra Nevada Torpedo, Stone IPA, and Lagunitas IPA. In 2012, IPAs had captured 18 percent of the craft market—well ahead of the number two, pale ales, which claim just 11.5 percent of the market. By the end of the second fifteen years in craft brewing, big, hoppy, citrusy American ales are leading the way. ∎

The Ringwood Ales of New England.

Beyond a national character, regions within the U.S. have their own quirks and preferences. None has such a specific, single-source culture as Red Sox country. If you travel New England—especially Maine, Vermont, and New Hampshire—you'll find many ales brewed in the English tradition. Bitter is a standard, as are porters and stouts. Cask ale isn't obscure. Fuggle hops are as common as Cascade. Yet I was surprised, during one of my early visits, to notice a smooth, buttery character in the beers there—particularly the bitters. Not just one example, but one after another.

It turns out there's a very good reason for this. In the early 1980s, interested in starting his own micro, Mainer David Geary spent time working at breweries across Britain—Samuel Smith in Yorkshire, Belhaven in Scotland, and finally at an important early English craft brewery in Hampshire, called Ringwood. David Austin had brewed for decades at England's Hull Brewery, and when he started Ringwood in 1978, he brought Hull's ancient yeast along with him. The strain dates back possibly 150 years, and flourishes in open fermenters from which it produces dry, fruity ales with loads of character. Depending on how it's used, the yeast also produces diacetyl, that smooth, butter-flavored compound I noted in Maine.

This is how it got there. David Geary decided he liked Austin's system the best, so he hired Alan Pugsley from Ringwood to come set up the brewery and act as brewer. The system Geary's uses to this day is very much in the mold of Austin's brewery—round, open fermenters (Geary calls them "Yorkshire rounds"—a riff on the region's more famous Yorkshire squares) from which the brewery can skim fresh yeast for subsequent batches.

After helping Geary with his system, Pugsley continued on, the Johnny Appleseed of Ringwood brewing, setting up at least eight more New England–based breweries in less than a decade, including Magic Hat, Sea Dog, and Gritty McDuff's. David Geary has no tolerance for diacetyl, though, and his beers exhibit not a drop, but this is the exception. Unlike Geary, Pugsley likes a touch of butterscotch, and as a consequence, the later breweries weren't designed to minimize diacetyl. He established his final brewery in Portland, Maine—Geary's hometown—in 1994. That was Shipyard, now one of the twenty largest craft breweries in America. His legacy, though, is much more than Shipyard, and the next time you're north of Boston, stop in for a pint somewhere and see if you can't find his fingerprints.

DESCRIPTION AND CHARACTERISTICS

CONSERVATIVELY speaking, the roughly 3,000 American breweries produce 40,000 separate styles of beer each year. Every style of beer brewed commercially somewhere in the world is also brewed in the U.S., and American breweries even experiment with revival styles of long-extinct beers.

Because the American beer market was so wholly transformed by industrial-scale brewing, it lost a sense of a national tradition. Craft breweries have therefore felt unfettered freedom to brew any beer they have heard of or can imagine. It's safe to say that no country has ever produced the variety of beer currently available in the U.S.

That is not to say that there isn't a distinctive American tradition in brewing. There is. As American brewing evolved, it began to acquire the characteristics that now define it—and which can be seen across styles and traditions. Americans brew for intensity, a penchant reflected particularly in high hop rates and alcohol strength, but more broadly in ales that are just a bit *louder* than comparable ales brewed in other countries. This means tart ales are more puckery; roasty ales are a bit more acrid; strong beers are a bit more boozy; and almost all beers are a bit—usually quite a bit—more hoppy.

And hops are, of course, the key to American styles. Where German and British styles have seen a slow slide in terms of bitterness, Americans have been steadily amping up the volume. But this isn't *only* a matter of bitterness. Hops are the character around which American ales are built. It starts with American varieties—an ever-expanding landscape of dozens of strains—that boast wild, exotic flavors and aromas. Citrus is the word most associated with these hops, but many strains contribute strong elements of pine, mint, or tropical fruits. (There's a reference guide to hops and their character in the Appendix; see pages 606–613.) Some have an herbal character similar to oregano; others,

floral notes like lavender or gardenia. Some even suggest bizarre flavors like onion—which a minority of tasters locate in the Summit strain.

American breweries do everything they can to showcase hops. They may use complex and precise hopping schedules—including hopping the mash, adding hops in a hopback on the way to the chiller, or dry-hopping their beer (and sometimes all three)—or deploy baroque combinations of hops. Sometimes they use a single variety to draw out specific notes from the hops, like using a single wine grape. Whatever they do, though, the idea is to make vivid beers that glow with flavor and aroma. This is a general practice not limited to style.

One way of looking at hops' centrality in American brewing is to look at the styles of beers the thousands of breweries produce. By far the most common are pale ales and India pale ales—the styles most suited to being tricked out by hops. As a testament to how essential this style has become, forty-five of the largest fifty American breweries offer an IPA in their regular lineup. Most also offer a hoppy pale ale. Only two of those offer neither, and one is an all-lager brewery.

After mass-market lagers, pales had been king for two decades in American brewing, but they finally lost their title in 2011 when IPAs eclipsed them at the supermarket. Together, IPAs and pales now constitute nearly four in every ten craft beers sold at supermarkets while ambers, in a distant third place, continue to fall further behind in beer drinkers' favor.

As the country's brewers have become more and more associated with making ales like this, "American"

LEFT: *Mikkeller Single Hop is an American-style IPA brewed in Belgium.*

has become an adjective. And "American ales" are spreading elsewhere. Breweries in Britain, Belgium, Eastern Europe, and Scandinavia now explicitly produce "American-style" ales—as do, of course, hundreds of brewers closer to home.

GOLDEN ALES

When craft brewing was just finding its sea legs, breweries produced a category of light, inoffensive beers on the theory that they would act as a "gateway" or "crossover" to fuller-flavored beers. Golden ales were the early breweries' answer to standard light American lagers. Straw-hued and neutral, they had little in the way of character—just a light maltiness, fruity esters, and a kiss of citrusy hopping. Over time, the theory of gateway beers looked more and more dubious, and goldens have slowly been dropping out of beer lines across the country. As the market matures and new drinkers enter with no expectation about what "beer" should taste like, goldens will likely continue to migrate to the margins of craft brewing.

AMBER ALES

Amber ales almost certainly started life as beers designed in the mold of English bitters. Brewed for balance, early examples were maltier and sweeter than pale ales—an approachable yet robust style for the new craft drinker. James Emmerson, brewmaster for Full Sail, one of the first producers of American amber, acknowledged the source material "was English ESB, certainly." The word "amber" seemed a less confusing description for the American market, and it allowed breweries to soup up their interpretations. Full Sail Amber was designed with "more American hops, more alcohol, a bit more bitterness than was standard." Emmerson called it an "American ESB," and his version would become one of the benchmarks.

Amber ales haven't changed much since the 1980s. They still feature a balance point tilted toward sweetness. Made with a generous portion of caramel malt, they have a round, sweetish body that harmonizes naturally with citrusy American hopping. Ambers are not brewed for bitterness, but many have layered hop character that, like the architecture of an English bitter, rewards careful attention. Ambers are excellent session beers that seem to reveal more as one drinks—and many, because of their low-intensity flavors and excellent balance, are absolutely ideal for serving on cask.

Canned American Culture. When Americans started making ales, they went right to the British well for source material. Pretty soon, an American idiom developed, and like national traditions everywhere, it has emerged partly by brewer design and partly by customer demand. British drinking culture evolved around the pub. Central to pub drinking is the idea of session beer: low-alcohol beer of easy balance that drinkers can enjoy over the course of hours. Even with the success of packaged beer, British drinkers still consume over half their beer on draft. In the U.S., draft sales have been on a continuous decline for decades and now account for just 10 percent of the market. Instead, Americans drink their beer in front of TV sets, in backyards, at campsites—and mostly out of aluminum cans.

Almost as soon as cans were released, Americans adopted them, and by 1940, we were drinking over half our beer at home. Cans, prized for their portability, have been popular for decades but were for many years eschewed by craft breweries because of their association with mass-market lagers. Beginning in the early 2000s, though, more and more craft breweries bought canning lines—they are cheaper than bottling lines, preserve the beer as well, and have a smaller environmental footprint. Within a few years, consumers realized the virtues of cans, and the stigma of "cheapness" has largely evaporated. At last count, more than 400 breweries canned beer in America, and the number grows by the day.

RED ALES

Red ale is often lumped in with ambers, but it's an evolving style that has now wandered pretty far from its starting place—and away from ambers. Yet even at the beginning, reds were distinct. While ambers were essentially American interpretations of English bitters, reds were a kind of sui generis American ale.

As evidence, we need only to harken back to 1983 to the ur-red, Mendocino Brewing Red Tail Ale. The inspirations came partly from an old homebrew recipe from founders Michael Laybourn and Norman Franks and partly from the folk song "The Redtail Hawk"—singer-songwriter Kate Wolf's ode to California. An English bitter wasn't the touchstone, so there was no need to keep things in check: Red Tail was lighter in body, caramel flavor, and hopping than the early ambers,

but it was strong at 6.1% ABV. The beer, now more than thirty years old, seems tame by current standards, but it was a template for much of what would come to characterize American brewing.

The difference between Red Tail and modern reds is the difference in thirty years of craft brewing. As America began to fall in love with hops, reds got hoppier. As bigger beers became more popular, reds became bigger. Modern reds are in some ways the quintessential American beer. Some of the most popular examples are muscle-bound ales—examples north of 7% ABV are common. The color is there mainly to add visual interest, but the malt backbones are stripped bare—just a bit of neutral or candyish sweetness—to reveal the true essence of the style: hops, hops, hops. Because of their strength and focus on hopping, reds are similar to IPAs. Reds, however, are the hophead's hoppy beer. With no malt noise to interfere with the lupulin assault, they have the quality of hop distillates: pure tinctures of lupulin bitterness and flavor.

AMERICAN WHEAT ALES

Wheat ales were the beers that skipped the bouncers and came in through the back door. To drinkers, they seemed natural enough—light, soft, summery ales that offered a gentle counterpoint to heavier pales. But the traditionalists—the bouncers—fingered them as frauds. European wheat ales are full of quirky fermentation characteristics: Bavarian weizens are phenolic, Berliner weisses tart, and Belgian wits spiced. American wheats had none of this and a few were even adulterated with fruit. The decades have been kind to the style, though, and now they're welcome to the party.

As it happened, American wheats weren't failing at being other styles; they were exactly what the early brewers wanted them to be: uncomplicated, sessionable summer ales. Wheat is a grain far more familiar to Americans than barley, and wheat ales are comfortably recognizable. There is a quality of breakfast in a wheat ale—the wholesome grain-y flavor, a light spritz from American hopping, and a gentle, soothing finish. They offer other virtues as well. Wheat ales are a mutable accompaniment to a variety of cuisines. Contrasted with the sweetness of pork, they provide supportive crispness; yet they shift to add a sweetness that contrasts the tartness of a salad's vinaigrette. Wheat ales make fine bases to tinker with, too. Breweries regularly add fresh fruit, spices, or crisp lactic acids (through sour mashing or the addition of bacteria) in an ever-expanding portfolio of variations on the style. ∎

BREWING NOTES

THERE ARE NO hard-and-fast rules in American brewing—but there are a few rules of thumb. One is hopping, of course. (Rule of thumb: use lots.) The other is the use of crystal or caramel malt, a less-discussed but important marker of national character. These malts do two things: First, they create an obvious flavor note—caramel or toffee—that sweetens the beer and inflects the fruity tones of American hops. Second, they are kilned to produce complex sugars indigestible to yeast, which gives beer body and creaminess.

AMBERS AND REDS

American ambers and reds are similar, but one difference is this contribution of caramel or crystal malt. Ambers rely on crystal for both their color and flavor; they're heavier and sweeter with the residual sugars of that malt, and their color comes from it. Reds are lighter and drier and have a subdued caramel note—or none at all. Reds get their color from reddish Munich or Vienna malts, or sometimes from a touch of roast malt.

Take, for example, the classic ambers from Full Sail and Anderson Valley. Both have a light caramel aroma and distinctive toffee flavors. In Boont Amber, Anderson Valley uses crystal to combine with spicy hops for a gingerbread effect; Full Sail marries the caramel with the citrus from Cascade hops for a sweet, moreish middle. In contrast, the booming red Tröegs Nugget Nectar goes for the grist of an Oktoberfest—Munich, Vienna, and pilsner malts. These give the beer a bit of support, but mainly throw color; for Tröegs, Nugget Nectar is all about the intensely grapefruity hopping. Cigar City Tocobaga Red Ale does use a touch of caramel malt in the grist, but the predominant flavors are a hard candy base and a sustained, resinously woody hop note. One version of this beer is aged on cedar, imparting a nuance suggestive of some U.S. hop varieties—and the effect is a magical blending of flavors and expectations.

American ambers grew out of the British tradition, and a number of classic British styles have similarities to them: *strong bitters*, with their balance of caramel malt and zesty hoppiness, are the closest match, but *brown ales* and *sweet stouts* are also worth investigation. Reds hew closer to the American tradition, and bold, hoppy styles like *pale ales*, *IPAs*, and *imperial IPAs* are obvious choices. Further afield, they share some of the qualities of *Belgian strong ales* and *abbey ales*—particularly for drinkers who aren't wedded to huge blasts of hopping.

AMERICAN WHEAT ALES

These could be considered a class more than a style—variations on the theme are acceptable, even welcomed. The basic function is consistent, though: Wheats are light and quenching, softened by the presence of wheat without being oppressed by it. In some parts of the country, that means a very light ale, low in bitterness. Goose Island 312 Urban Wheat is a simple beer, made with standard two-row barley and torrified (puffed) wheat with Liberty and Cascade hops. It is quite light at 4.2% ABV and has just 20 IBU. Boulevard's Unfiltered Wheat is similar, a 4.4% beer made with a mixture of wheat types, two-row barley, Munich malts, and just 13 IBU of American hops.

Other wheat ales are less demure. Widmer Brothers helped introduce the style of American wheat, and their Hefeweizen, despite all the visual evidence to the contrary, has a lot more in common with pale ales than the Bavarian beer it was named for. The Hef is often served with a slice of lemon, and its yeast billows inside a grist of 43 percent wheat. But the flavor is crisp and spicy with 30 IBU of hopping—and the beer, at 4.9% ABV, is no lightweight. Bell's Oberon is even stronger, 5.8% ABV, with 26 IBU; Three Floyds Gumballhead is 5.5% ABV and 28 IBU.

FRUIT-FLAVORED WHEATS

Common variants of wheat ales, these are made with fruit. They are brewed in the American vein, a simple wheat ale base flavored with fresh fruit. They aren't soured or otherwise made more fussy—though their simplicity has a quality that might be considered "rustic" in another country. The style can be delicious, but a flood of overly sweet, soda-like examples in the 1990s nearly doomed it. Brewers learned to ratchet back on the fruit, let the beers dry out, and allow the wheat to emerge. The best examples, like 21st Amendment Hell or High Watermelon and Pyramid Apricot Ale, find that balance. In these beers, the fruit juice has fermented out, leaving behind a harvest-fresh aroma and fruit delicacy. On a balmy summer day, they're hard to beat. ■

EVOLUTION

AMERICAN CRAFT BREWING was born of a thirst for variety. Four decades later, the country boasts easily the greatest diversity of beer styles in the world. What the U.S. lacked at the dawn of craft brewing was a national heritage; the first decades were a process of exploration, and slowly the country began to find one. That trend suggests there will be a necessary narrowing of focus in the decades to come. In craft brewing, ales have the overwhelming advantage, and among them, this is especially true of those that are rich with American hop character. Other trends hint that some Belgian styles might be ripe for popularization, and drinkers' preference for strong flavors has given tart ales an opening. But in the second decade of the twenty-first century, America now has what it lacked in the 1970s: a national tradition, one copied across the globe.

Ambers and wheats are largely static styles. They achieved early success, and nothing freezes a style so well as popularity. Twenty years ago, wheat ales and

Mayflower Ale. Like so many important events in history, beer played a central role even in the fateful journey of the *Mayflower.* Settlers departed from England in the late summer of 1620 and by the time they sighted land, it was icy November. Despite the cold and storms, those dutiful English subjects didn't land there—they were observing their agreement to settle on land granted to them by the Virginia Company of London, located farther south. They battled poor weather and rough seas, and were starting to run low on beer. A worried passenger noted the danger in his diary: "We could not now take time for further search, our victuals being so much spent, especially our beer." After a few days of battling the weather, they decided to drop anchor at what would eventually be called Plymouth. English authorities had given them the right to settle in Virginia—which at the time extended to what is now New York. So to make things legal, the colonists drafted the famous Mayflower Compact to underscore their continued allegiance to God and King and disembarked.

ambers were session ales—wheats light and easygoing, ambers heartier and more filling. Both remain so today.

Red ales, on the other hand—never a wildly sought-after style—have been able to grow and change outside the scrutiny of mainstream tastes. Their development looks a great deal like the course of American brewing. In the mid-1990s, Jennifer Trainer Thompson published a book called *The Great American Microbrewery Beer Book* on the bottled beers of the U.S. (about 120 breweries in all). Only sixteen of the 500-plus beers were American reds (ambers numbered four times as many). They averaged 5.3% ABV, and three-quarters were less than 6%. This was typical for the time. I compared these with the sixteen most-rated red ales on the beer ratings website BeerAdvocate.com. These are the reds most broadly available, so they're typical for the era. They average 6.6%, range from 5.1 to 9.5%, and only a third are less than 6%. Trainer didn't track bitterness units, but looking at the IBU of the top few current reds—93, 67, 45, 90—we can assume those have spiked at least as dramatically.

Where American ales still have room to evolve—reds, pales, IPAs, and imperialized styles—they will continue to focus on hops. This doesn't necessarily mean more bitterness, though. In the past few years, breweries have focused more on hop varietals and hopping techniques designed to produce new, ever-more-distinctive flavors. Sierra Nevada and Widmer were active in bringing Citra hops to

American wheat ales have a number of qualities in common with other styles. Not all wheats are appropriate substitutes—Bavarian hefeweizens are loaded with clove and banana flavors most fans of American wheats find off-putting. *Belgian wits*, however, are an eccentric cousin that fit the bill with their approachability and soft wheatiness. American wheat ales are light and balanced in much the way of *Munich helles lagers* and a rare unfiltered lager called *kellerbier*. But perhaps the closest style is *kölsch*, which, with its springy yeast profile sometimes tastes of wheat—even though it's usually an all-barley beer.

market—giving them an early edge on "branding" their beers with the unique flavors they contribute. Other breweries are growing their own hops or supporting development of other strains.

Europeans, once scornful of rudimentary American offerings, are now brewing in the emerging American tradition. In Britain, where tradition is sacred and drinkers are hidebound in their preferences, American brewing has sent out shock waves. New, smaller breweries are popping up all across the country to brew American-type ales, and many, like Thornbridge, Dark Star, and The Kernel, are attracting big audiences for their huge, ultrahoppy ales. The phenomenon is so profound that British hop growers have planted famous American strains there.

Every style has its moment, and American ales will not always be on brewing's cutting edge; yet the fact that they have gotten there at all amazes anyone who was on the scene in the 1980s. The country has now joined the ranks of the traditions of Britain, Belgium, Germany, and the Czech Republic as a truly original brewing nation. ■

THE BEERS TO KNOW

WHILE THERE ARE a few styles unique to the United States, American brewing is more a state of mind. The most quintessentially American beers are the hoppy pales: pale ales, IPAs, and double IPAs, and these are the future of American brewing. But while America's love for wheat ales has waned somewhat, they remain among the most popular overall. And red ales in particular are a style to watch—they may one day challenge IPAs for America's heart.

AMBER ALES

FULL SAIL AMBER

○○○

LOCATION: Hood River, OR

MALT: Pale, crystal, chocolate

HOPS: Mt. Hood, Cascade

6.0% ABV, 31 IBU

I believe there's some dispute about which brewery gets to lay claim as the first amber, but Full Sail gets my vote. It has each of the hallmark qualities: a thick, caramel body with moderate sweetness; a creamy head; and a long, Cascade hops citrus finish. It's an American strong bitter, and predictably, is even better on cask.

ANDERSON VALLEY BOONT AMBER

○○○

LOCATION: Boonville, CA

MALT: Pale, caramel

HOPS: Columbus, Bravo, Northern Brewer, Mt. Hood

5.8% ABV, 16 IBU

Anderson Valley's amber is another classic, though it emphasizes malt where Full Sail tilts hopward. Like a nice bière de garde, Boont Amber is silky and rich, the malts communicating warmth through toffee, toast, and grain. The hops don't so much balance as adorn, adding an herbal delicacy to the malts.

STONE LEVITATION ALE

○○○

LOCATION: Escondido, CA

MALT: Pale, caramel, black

HOPS: Columbus, Simcoe, Crystal, Amarillo

4.4% ABV, 45 IBU

A number of breweries are known for hops, but few so well as Stone. Many of its beers are punishingly bitter, so I'd like to nominate wee Levitation, the little

sister in the family line. She is definitely a spitfire, with Stone's characteristic snap of bitterness, grapefruit to pine, but it is the rounded malts that suggest English softness, that carry the day—or beer, in this case.

RED ALES

MARBLE RED ALE

LOCATION: Albuquerque, NM

MALT: Pale, Vienna, caramel

HOPS: Chinook, Cascade, Centennial, Simcoe, Crystal

6.5% ABV

Even though Marble is a relatively new brewery, its Red, a 6.5% bruiser, is a little bit old-school, with a thick caramel malting like you find in ambers. Marble uses it to balance the gale-force hops that blow in with citrus and grapefruit gusts.

TRÖEGS NUGGET NECTAR

LOCATION: Harrisburg, PA

MALT: Pilsner, Vienna, Munich

HOPS: Nugget, Warrior, Tomahawk, Simcoe, Palisade

7.5% ABV, 93 IBU

Tröegs has a reputation for aggressive hopping, and Nugget Nectar is one of the reasons. The Simcoe hops seem to lead a piney, pineapple charge, but it's a mutable beer, and melon and lychee make appearances as well. The malts have a bit of caramel in them, but not enough to distract from the main event.

CIGAR CITY TOCOBAGA RED ALE

LOCATION: Tampa, FL

MALT: Pale, caramel, dark chocolate, Vienna, Munich

HOPS: Vanguard, Simcoe, Willamette, Cascade, Citra

7.2% ABV, 1.070 SP. GR., 68 IBU

Cigar City is another brewery with a reputation for hops, and their Jai Alai IPA has attracted the most attention. I prefer the Tocobaga, the color of a Miami sunset, hot and juicy with tropical guava and satsuma orange. The malts are a good example of a modern red—a bit of sweetness, a note of bread, but really, they're there for color and balance.

TERRAPIN BIG HOPPY MONSTER

LOCATION: Athens, GA

MALT: Pale, Munich, caramel

HOPS: Warrior, Centennial, Cascade, Ahtanum

8.8% ABV, 1.088 SP. GR., 73 IBU

In a contrast to Tocobaga, Big Hoppy Monster does have a fair amount of malt hoisting up the hops. It's more burnt sugar than caramel and is used to great effect to offset a powerful bittering addition of hops. The sugars fade to crispness in the swallow, the hops to pepper and pine (there are those Simcoe again), and it does not feel heavy going down.

WHEAT AND FRUITY ALES

BELL'S OBERON ALE

○○○

LOCATION: Kalamazoo, MI

MALT: Undisclosed

HOPS: Saaz

5.8% ABV, 1.057 SP. GR., 26 IBU

Oberon is a force of nature, greeted annually with its own day of celebration. A cloudily luminous light-orange color, it has a mildly citrusy, spicy top note to round out the crisp, cracker-like body. Released at the end of March, well before the summer has actually come to the Wolverine State, it has a bit more alcohol to help battle the lingering chill.

WIDMER HEFEWEIZEN

○○

LOCATION: Portland, OR

MALT: Pale, Munich, caramel, wheat

HOPS: Proprietary bittering blend; Willamette, Cascade

4.9% ABV, 1.047 SP. GR., 30 IBU

Appearance is critical to Widmer's wheat: something like cloudy lemonade

topped with a snowy head and—in some restaurants and pubs—a slice of lemon. There's a certain sleight of hand going on that prepares the mind for the citrus that follows, but the brain deceives. That note comes from the Northwest hops, not the lemon wedge (which, for the sake of the beer, you should toss aside). It has a bready body, but one kept refreshing by its lightness and sprightly carbonation.

THREE FLOYDS GUMBALLHEAD

○○

LOCATION: Munster, IN

MALT: Undisclosed

HOPS: Undisclosed

5.5% ABV, 28 IBU

To the unobservant drinker, wheat ales can seem to have a lot in common with mass-market lagers. It's easy enough to make a dent in a six-pack without realizing it. The best examples remain perfectly sessionable, but sneak in subtle character. Gumballhead has a light presentation, but it's a lively, bright beer. Instead of a bready wheatiness, it opts for lemon zest. The hopping is just present enough that you might mistake it for an extra pale ale in a blind tasting.

KONA WAILUA WHEAT

LOCATION: Kona, HI

MALT: Pale, wheat

HOPS: Hallertauer

OTHER: Passion fruit puree

5.4% ABV, 1.048 SP. GR., 15 IBU

Kona has developed a knack for using island ingredients to enhance its beers. Coconut dances with malt sweetness in its Koko Brown, and in Wailua Wheat, it's *lilikoi*—passion fruit to you mainlanders—that hulas with hops. On its own, *lilikoi* is an intensely tart citrus-y flavor, along the lines of a lemon. In Wailua Wheat, it adds the citrus character that is so often suggested by American hops. *Lilikoi* is a surprisingly good counterfeit, but better—hops are citrusy in the way atomized oil is in air freshener, but there's a juiciness and vividness in Wailua Wheat that lets the tongue know it's the real deal.

21st AMENDMENT HELL OR HIGH WATERMELON

LOCATION: San Francisco, CA

MALT: Pale, white wheat

HOPS: Columbus, Magnum

OTHER: Watermelon puree

4.9% ABV, 17 IBU

A hazy, lazy beer for a summer's day. There's no trick here—it's just soft wheatiness married to the light flavors of melon that roll nicely into a quenching acidity at the end. It's not complex or complicated, and that's just what you want out in the sunshine.

FOUR PEAKS ARIZONA PEACH

LOCATION: Tempe, AZ

MALT: Pale, pale caramel, white wheat

HOPS: Magnum

OTHER: Peaches

4.2% ABV, 9 IBU

In Arizona, Four Peaks is known for a Scottish ale and an IPA, but on one of those triple-digit midsummer scorchers, what I want is the superbly balanced Arizona Peach. It has an aroma of pure stone fruit and a flavor that actually has as much cracker-crisp malting as it does juicy sweetness. The best fruit ales are not cloying, taking just the essence of the peach and letting the beer carry the day. Four Peaks nails it.

Double Mountain

AMERICAN BREWING TAKES ROOT

FOR YEARS, I WAS SKEPTICAL THAT THE TERM "AMERICAN BEER" WAS ANYTHING MORE THAN A MARKETING GIMMICK. EVEN WITH THE ARRIVAL OF CRAFT BREWING, AMERICANS HADN'T DONE MUCH TO REINVENT BREWING. THEY MADE PALE ALES AND PILSNERS AND STOUTS—ALL BEERS THAT CAME FROM OTHER COUNTRIES. IT TOOK A TRIP TO EUROPE, PARADOXICALLY, TO CHANGE MY MIND. I WAS STARTLED TO HEAR BREWERS IN BRITAIN, FRANCE, BELGIUM, GERMANY, AND THE CZECH REPUBLIC MENTION HOW AMERICA'S STRONG, HOPPY, AND BARREL-AGED BEERS HAD INFLUENCED THEIR OWN APPROACH TO BREWING. ALL RIGHT THEN: WHAT *IS* AMERICAN BEER?

The more I thought about American beer, the more two memories sprang to mind—and they both involved the same brewery, Oregon's Double Mountain. In the first, the brewery's cofounder and brewer Matt Swihart was leading me on a stroll through undulating rows of cherry and peach trees on his land near the brewery in Hood River. Each year, Matt makes two types of aged sour cherry beers, and he always uses the harvest from his own land for the key ingredient. It's beautiful

ABOVE: *Matt Swihart (left) and Charlie Devereux, cofounders of Double Mountain*

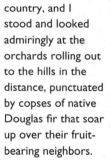

country, and I stood and looked admiringly at the orchards rolling out to the hills in the distance, punctuated by copses of native Douglas fir that soar up over their fruit-bearing neighbors.

Double Mountain, like many breweries in the Northwest, has access to locally grown barley and hops, locally malted grain, and even gets locally cultivated yeast. (Wyeast Labs, one of the two main yeast companies in the U.S., is about ten miles away.) It made sense that a brewer from the Hood River valley would use the region's fruit crops as well. Agriculture and beer have never been far separated, and it's hard to visualize a kind of local beer that doesn't depend on the expression of locally grown ingredients. (And of course, pungent, citrusy American hops are the one thing everyone agrees makes our beers distinctive.)

It's more than agriculture, though. In places where beer is something more

ABOVE LEFT: *The view from Matt Swihart's land*

ABOVE RIGHT: *The hop back*

LEFT: *Fermentation tanks*

than a commodity, it becomes an idiom understood to locals.

This brings me to my second recollection: of arriving at Double Mountain's pub perhaps a year after the brewery had opened. It was late autumn, already dark at five o'clock, and Hood River's tourists had long quit the place. Yet Double Mountain was packed. As I looked around, I saw workmen in dirty jeans and flannel shirts crowding around the bar. They were slugging back pints of Swihart's hazy, aromatic hop infusions. By that time, the brewery had already developed something of a reputation for its IPAs, and it was clear why. It's what the locals wanted, and they were drinking it by the gallon.

This development was organic, a communication between brewer and drinkers, and is the essence of how native beer comes to be. When Double Mountain opened, it offered a broad range of different beers on tap: pale ale, altbier, kölsch, and strong Belgian ale. Swihart shares my love of pale lagers, and I think he'd be happy making helles biers the rest of his life, but that's not what people drank. They gravitated to the IPA and the kölsch, which was electrified by generous doses of Perle hops.

Within a few months, Double Mountain added a second IPA called Hop Lava. This was pure West Coast—intensely green and citrusy, with a profound rind-like bitterness that scrapes the plaque right off your teeth. To brew it, Swihart added what he calls a hop back but what is in fact a massive side-tank he packs with whole-flower hops and steeps his beer in until it's literally green. Not long after, the brewery added another IPA to its regular lineup called Vaporizer, a lighter, less intense beer made with just pilsner malt and Challenger hops. Seven years later, those three IPAs constitute three-quarters of the year-round line (the hoppy kölsch is the fourth).

"Every decision we considered when building the pub or deciding on a yeast, or to filter or not to filter, was to make something that a drinker in Oregon would smile at," Swihart explained. There's a notion that skilled brewers, making exceptional, unique beers, drive demand, but it's exactly backward. When beer culture begins to develop, the drinkers have the final say. Their preferences guide the brewers. The very best, like Matt Swihart, take their direction and then make the exceptional beers that meet those preferences.

"If you can deliver a well-made beer, fresh with yeasty aroma and light texture, consistently day after day," he said, "then your brewery will likely succeed."

It's the process that led to cask ale in England and strong Belgian golden ales and dark lagers in Bavaria—very different beers the locals wanted to drink. As the process unfolds, regular drinkers are dictating what "American" means in other parts of the country, as well. Wisconsin's New Glarus sells lots of lagers and lager-like ales to the descendants of German immigrants. In New England, Shipyard, Portsmouth, and Cambridge make beer quite a bit like they do in old England—which is what locals expect. Fullsteam Brewery, in Durham, NC, is introducing the concept of Southern brewing. They use corn grits, sweet potatoes, persimmon, paw-paw, chestnuts, and more to bring the tradition of Southern cuisine to their beer.

When Europeans talk about American beer, they are pointing to one or more of these aspects that have developed to serve the preferences of different kinds of Americans. Double Mountain makes beer characteristic of the Pacific Northwest. It's cloudy and rustic, rich with saturated hop flavors and aromas, and generally a little less bitter and a little less strong than some of the California beers that made "West Coast" pale ales and IPAs famous. Double Mountain is often credited with having helped perfect this kind of Northwest beer, but actually, the brewers were only listening to their customers. Double Mountain makes exceptional beer, true. But the key is that it's Oregon—or *American*—beer, made the way drinkers want.

Barley Wines and OLD ALES

Modern marketing teams would never call their beer "old." Products should be vibrant and exciting, and whether the old in question was used as an antonym to "young" or "new" is of little concern—they're both bad. Barley wine isn't much better; wine, after all, suggests a rival product. But old ales and barley wines are not the products of modern marketers. If beer styles were people, barley wines and old ales would be the bald-headed, gray-whiskered men in the parlor, smoking pipes. They are styles that call to mind an earlier, more formal time.

Barley Wines and Old Ales. Intense, velvety beers of great heft and strength, barley wines are as robust as grape wines, and like dessert wines, some are rounded and sweet while others are aggressively bitter. All can handle additional time in the bottle, and cellared barley wines may improve for years. Old ales vary broadly by brewer, from light-bodied dark all the way to immense ales with the strength of barley wines. Indeed, there is great overlap between the two types. Historically, old ales were aged in barrels infected with wild yeasts, producing dry, sherry-like beers—a style returning with the recent rise of barrel-aging programs in the U.S. Barley wines and old ales are intense enough to overwhelm most foods, and serve as an ideal digestif or nightcap.

STATISTICS

Barley wines ABV range: 8–14%; bitterness: 50–100 IBU

Old ales ABV range: 5–9%; bitterness: 30–75 IBU

Serving temperature: 50°–60°F

Vessel: Snifter

As it happens, the "old" does refer to the beer's age, and it applies to both barley wines and old ales. The sheer amount of malt and hops it takes to make these styles means that at birth they are very green—all sharp elbows and spiky bits. To transform these beers into the dulcet elixirs they will become, breweries add one more ingredient: time. A few months will soften the edges and round the flavor of these burly giants, and in their maturity they will evolve into beers of density and complexity, like a fine tawny port. In the case of barley wines, many now rest in old whiskey casks, which accentuates the effect. The modern appellation "old ale" may refer to beers no stronger than a pale ale, and the amount of time they spend in tanks or casks varies widely. Yet the best examples of both continue to express the essence of the historical style—maturity and refinement. ■

ORIGINS

TO UNDERSTAND the origins of both old ales and barley wines—which even today are often conflated—we must begin with the history of strong beers. While there's no doubt that beer is a gastronomic triumph, we have to acknowledge the role of alcohol in its popularity. A tasty beer is one thing, a tasty beer with the booze to relax, lower inhibitions, and make one merry is a different, improved thing.

As a consequence, people started brewing strong beers as soon as it was possible. In Britain, that moment came more than 400 years ago with the arrival of hops. Until then, infection had been the main problem for medieval brewers. Stronger beer needed longer to ripen, but any beer that was not served quickly and rested in wood for any length of time was susceptible to unwanted microorganisms over which brewers had no control. Beer was drunk "mild"—that is, fresh, before it could turn to vinegar or pick up gnarly flavors from wild yeast and bacteria. The arrival of hops changed the balance of power, giving brewers just enough antibacterial might to mitigate the worst ravages of *Lactobacillus*, *Brettanomyces*, and their friends. The first strong ales must have been quite tart—but thanks to hops, they weren't vinegar.

Strong beers were then brewed for centuries in a wide variety of styles. The beers we now call barley wines and old ales were originally part of an undifferentiated collection of ales that went by many different names. An early example was "double" beer, made by pouring the first runnings of a mash back on the grain bed and mashing again—a practice that would result in gravities higher than 1.100. There was an even stronger version of this practice known as "double-double" (or "doble-doble" as rendered in period English), a beer considered so wasteful, strong, and dangerous that officials periodically banned it. Of course, the practice continued, as has ever been the case when authorities tried to get in between people and their buzz.

Beginning in the 1740s, recognizable styles emerged when the breweries of England's Burton upon Trent began making a similar strong beer for the Baltic market. Brewed at gravities over 1.100, Burton ale also needed time to age; eighteen months was considered a minimum. The Baltic-bound Burtons were intensely sweet and underattenuated; descriptions made them sound just this side of syrup. When Russian taxes put an end to the Baltic trade, Burton's breweries honed their recipes and the resulting beers, targeted at the domestic market—still called Burtons—were somewhat less sweet.

England's next great strong beer was porter, brewed in London. These were black ales aged until they became refined and acidic. London's breweries produced them in varying strengths but included huge, booming examples. The most famous market for these was—where else?—Russia and the Baltics (where porters were so beloved they were exempted from the tax), but hefty porters were also popular at home.

Finally, there was a more generic category of strong ales referred to as "old," "stock," or "stale" ales. Brewed strong with large doses of hops, these beers were put in casks to ripen. Their names hint at their nature: After a year aging in the cask, the beer would become "stale"—that is, lose its effervescence and take on a dry, tart character as the wood-borne microorganisms slowly turned the beer acidic. Old ales were also used as blending "stock"—they were poured into fresh beer to add a dash of depth and complexity. When we talk about old ales

Big Names. Over the years, breweries and drinkers have referred to big beers with all manner of endearing terms. Here are a few.

- Angel's Food
- Clamber-skull
- Crackskull
- Doble-Doble (Double-Double)
- Dragon's Milk
- Huffcap
- Mad Dog
- Merry-go-down
- Old Tom
- Stale ale
- Stingo
- Stock ale
- XXXXX

and barley wines, these are their distant ancestors.

Strength was the reason these beers were brewed, but their character was defined by their acidic palate. In a famous technical manual from 1901, scientists Robert Wahl and Max Henius describe analyses done on English stock ales that found large concentrations of lactic acid, varying from a quarter to over half a point of overall percentage. A time traveler to nineteenth-century London would find old ales that bore far closer resemblance to Belgium's tart beers than modern interpretations.

The origin of the term "barley wine" was really just the rebranding of old ale. Bass brought the name into vogue when it started calling its strongest beer, Number 1, a barley wine in 1903. Like many style "innovations," this was just marketing—Bass didn't invent a new style, just a new name. Elsewhere, other breweries went on calling their old ales "old ales." It would take a few more

---

Country Brewing. Imagine an advertisement for the modern British home circa 1600. The kitchen area, domain of the lady of the house and her team of servants, is a beautifully appointed space with all the necessities of modern life: the kitchen proper with attached larder, beer and wine cellar, herb and vegetable garden, and of course the hearth, flanked by the bakehouse and brewhouse. Yes, brewhouse. Such a facility was an indispensable feature of the Elizabethan home. Commercial sale of beer on a large scale is a relatively recent phenomenon; hundreds of years ago, brewing beer was just one of the many duties performed on country estates across England.

Pamela Sambrook, who wrote a wonderful history of the country brewery, *Country House Brewing in England, 1500–1900*, notes that "it is rare to find a country house of any size or age which had no record at all of the existence of a brewhouse." In the years before the British discovered coffee and tea, beer was the safe drink of choice (as opposed to water, which was not). Children were purported to have been weaned on it, and everyone in a country estate, family and servants alike, were given a daily measure.

Until the seventeenth century, home brewhouses were a domestic duty and the province of women. Over time, they became more elaborate affairs, often occupying professionally designed outbuildings, and men began to get in on the act—a period that coincided with the rise of male-dominated commercial brewing.

Yet commercial brewing didn't end the practice of estate brewing, and in fact, country ales had the highest reputation among all beers. One of the reasons was an expensive specialty known as "October beer." Until refrigeration, brewing was a seasonal activity, done only in the cool months. The best time to brew were the crisp days of October, after the harvests of grain and hop had come in. (A similar beer, called "March beer," was made in the spring, but was less prized because the ingredients weren't as fresh.) The expense associated with all the time and ingredients required for October beer made it a poor candidate for commercial production, but the gentry could afford to invest in these luscious, heady winter brews.

---

decades before the lineages split. For a while, Bass was the only one using the name. So how did barley wine come to be its own style?

Perhaps even more important to the evolution of strong ales were the ones produced not in commercial breweries like Bass but in the breweries of private estates. These were owned by the country gentlemen who made beer for personal and staff consumption. This practice was common (American colonials like George Washington practiced it, too), and most of the beer they made was ordinary-strength table beer. A small portion was very strong ale, though. This beer was massive—a 1703 brewing text suggests gravities around 1.130. Stowed away in the cellar, it would age for over a year at a minimum and sometimes would be left to refine for a decade or more. When it was finally deemed ripe, the gentlemen would sip it from small glasses like the cordials of heavily taxed French wine and brandy it had come to replace.

Barley wines became a fully distinct

style separate from old ales after the world wars. While most beers got weaker in Britain, a curious exception was barley wines, which continued to be quite strong until the 1970s. Many registered north of 8% ABV and a few made it to double digits. Perhaps the weakening of all the other styles made barley wines an important exception. Old ales, by contrast, followed the rest of Britain's beers down the gravity slide, and the style fractured. A few old ales continued to be brewed in the traditional manner—notably Benskin's Colne Spring Ale and Gale's Prize Old Ale, but weaker, unaged versions came along that used "old" nostalgically, not literally.

Eventually, even barley wines succumbed to gravity deflation too, and

Mind Your Xs and Ks. **If you spend any time looking at old price lists for British beer (as I'm sure you do), you'll see many listed by letter—principally X and K. The Ks stood for keeping, or aged, beers, and the Xs for mild or unaged beer. The number of letters lined up in a row corresponded to relative strength, so XXX was lighter than XXXX—but KKK and XXX were the same strength, just the first sold aged, the second sold fresh. (And the aged ones, because they needed to ward off the souring elements in the cask, were usually 50 percent hoppier as well.)**

became barely stronger than today's American IPAs. This happened as consolidation wracked the English ale market and left many formerly distinctive beers watery and flavorless. As with so many other styles, it took craft breweries to resurrect them, and now barley wines and old ales are no longer rare, niche beers. There are even a few examples aged in wood. ■

DESCRIPTION AND CHARACTERISTICS

BARLEY WINES are part of an old tradition of very strong ales, and modern examples would be generally familiar to Victorian pubgoers who enjoyed brawny, acidic "stock" ales. Thick and chewy, these rich beers are leavened by the warmth and energy of a mighty alcohol kick. Old ales are another matter. While a few examples are still brewed in the traditional manner—at great strength and with an extended rest in wooden casks—most are barely more than session ales, brewed like any other beer and released fresh and mild. We'll consider them separately.

BARLEY WINES

As we've seen, British strong ales were once brewed to a variety of different specifications—some light-colored, some dark, some sweeter, some drier. Over time, these variations were sorted out, with darker versions falling into the porter/stout camp and lighter versions landing under the heading barley wine.

Lighter is relative, however. Barley wines are never what you'd call light-colored—something similar to iced tea is more common. This is due to the sheer quantity of malt, with its dense, light-reflecting molecules of sugars and proteins, packed into every bottle. Barley wines often spend more time in the kettle than other beers—Sierra Nevada's Bigfoot enjoys a three-hour boil—which cara-melizes and darkens the wort. The truth is, among barley wines' many virtues, appearance doesn't top the list. There are more than a few murky, dingy examples that are perfectly delicious.

No matter. The real show happens in the darkness of one's nostrils and mouth. Barley wine is one of the rare styles from which much can be taken from the name. These beers are elixirs of malt; they pre-sent a dizzying alcohol plume that can fill a room with rich toffee and molasses aromas. Alcohol made from malt is dis-tinctive—worn leather, a whiff of tobacco. It's different from neutral alcohol—think vodka—in sugar-fortified beers, which the nose experiences as a tingling sensation as much as smells. Some breweries do aug-ment their grists with sugar, but this is a dicey business. Barley wines should exude the flavors and aromas of malt. If beer

were Scotch whisky, barley wines would be Islay single malts. Without peat you don't have an Islay; without the heaviness of barley, you don't have barley wine.

The palates of these beers are sur-prisingly varied. They begin with the malt base, always dense and thick, sometimes made with toasty, bready malts while at other times with more caramelly, rummy ones. Sweetness is a given, but whether it tends toward dark fruits or bread pud-ding is up to the brewery's whim—and choice of malts.

Some breweries—unsurprisingly concentrated in the American West—saturate their barley wines with hops in order to compete with the dense malt base. Examples like Great Divide's Old Ruffian or Rogue's Old Crustacean are so bitter consumers would be advised to put them on a shelf somewhere until the nuclear glow of hops subsides somewhat. In vertical tastings of Old Crusty, in fact, I've found three-year-old bottles that were still tongue-numbingly bitter.

British barley wines went through the gravity collapse that afflicted all English ales, but it's wrong to think of them as weak beers now. J. W. Lees produces Harvest Ale, a massive, 11.5% beer. Samuel Smith makes 9% Yorkshire

Barley Wine or Barleywine?

In Britain, the term is nearly uniform: "barley wine." In the United States, you're as likely to see "barleywine" as the two-word title. Why? Blame Fritz Maytag. In 1975, he was trying to get label approval for Anchor's Old Foghorn Barley Wine from the Bureau of Alcohol, Tobacco, and Firearms. They didn't like the word "wine" standing alone there—apparently they didn't trust drinkers to understand that it was a bottle of beer. Maytag resubmitted the label, this time for Old Foghorn Barleywine Style Ale. That version sailed through and now Americans use both versions interchangeably.

Stingo, and Traquair House in Scotland regularly releases specialty barley wines that rival the strength of their nineteenth-century predecessors. Many Americans consider these to be different interpretations of the style because they are less hoppy than the violent West Coast examples. This is probably sample bias. Those American versions were the first to the craft-era market and are the best known, but the style admits all comers who brew to strength and complexity with a keen focus on malt character.

OLD ALES

If the history of brewing illustrates anything, it's that beers evolve. What we think of as a given style is almost certainly different from a beer with the same name brewed decades or centuries ago. Inevitably, these changes lead to a little definitional fraying—though usually the confusion happens only with those marginal beers that have wandered some distance from the herd. The category we call "old ales," however, is like a living museum. A modern version has emerged, but there's still the ancient one, too, roaming the pubs like a ghost.

Now we have a collection of beers that includes the dark, sweetened 4.3% Harvey's Old Ale and the plummy, toffeeish 4.1% Adnams Old Ale as well as the deep cask-aged Gale's Prize Old Ale, weighing in at twice the strength of Harvey's. The famous, now sadly discontinued

RIGHT: The view from Greene King. The brewery's Strong Suffolk is the last of its kind and by law must be made in the county.

Thomas Hardy's Ale, a titan at 12%—nearly three times Harvey's strength!—was often considered a member of the club, too. So what in the hell is an old ale?

Let's begin with the true old ales, those beers brewed in the same way they have been made literally for centuries. The two signature examples of this among Britain's most celebrated beers are Gale's Prize Old Ale and Greene King's Strong Suffolk (Olde Suffolk in the U.S.). A story of remarkable continuity, these beers go back decades to the period when barrel-aging was the typical treatment for old ales. Gale's was brewed in Horndean, Hampshire, for more than 150 years until it was purchased by Fuller's in 2006. Prize Old Ale got its character from aging in old wood vats for up to a year; like old ales of earlier eras, it picked up the wild microorganisms resident in the wood, which slowly soured it. With the Fuller's acquisition, many worried this relic would vanish. Instead, brewer John Keeling continued to brew the beer in London after first inoculating his own barrels with the aged beer shipped from Hampshire.

Greene King's Strong Suffolk is made in a similar way. Brewer John

Bexon ages a 12% beer called XXXXX ("Five X") in wooden vats for two years. "There's a microflora embedded in the grain of the oak that inoculates and perpetuates maturation. It's very low pH and the resultant flavor is more or less like slightly sour sherry two years on," he says. To get Strong Suffolk, Bexon then blends that vatted beer back into a fresh, or mild, ale to create a beer of 6% ABV. It is winy and full of red fruit but stiffened by a stratum of flavor that has wood, tobacco, and nutmeg.

Breweries in the United States have been slow to take up old ales—a style wholly inscrutable to many Americans—but a few examples show fidelity to the throwback style. Most American examples are robust, like North Coast's Old Stock Ale (12% ABV) and Founders Curmudgeon (10% ABV). Some old ales were described as "glutinous," an adjective that serves Curmudgeon well; it is rummy and figgy, but balanced by a spine of oak. North Coast, by contrast, is drier and thinner yet full of boozy gravitas.

A few breweries have even taken to barrel-aging their old ales and dosing them with British strains of *Brettanomyces clausenii* for a truly authentic experience. The best of these is Billy the Mountain made by Upright, a small brewery in Portland, Oregon. It has a palate of berry jam and gingerbread, cut delightfully by a thin slice of balsamic.

Old ales—in Britain anyway—have about them a quality of poetry; breweries offer them as liquid meditations on the olden days. There, the designation "old ale" now refers to a beer shot through with nostalgia and affection, as when we recall a favorite grandparent or uncle. So to Harvey's and Adnams, nostalgia means mild ale, the style of choice to the men and women who defeated Hitler. Their versions are essentially strong milds—brewed to garnet with invert sugar, plummy with a suggestion of warmth. Darkness, in fact, is one of the key ways in which these ales now differ from lighter-colored barley wines—though, as always, it's a relative distinction. (This is a spectacular example of style creep. Recall that old ales descended from a line of beers that had been aged; recall further that the name "old" was used to distinguish them from fresh or unaged beer . . . known as "mild" ales. To see current examples self-consciously described as being "reminiscent of the mild ales"—to use Harvey's own language—is to witness the perfect inversion of meaning. But only to pedants; Harvey's and Adnams are using language at a higher level—the realm of metaphor.)

Working up the gravity ladder, we come to a class that includes Theakston's Old Peculier, often considered the standard of the style. It's brewed to a respectable gravity of 1.057 and 5.6% ABV (quite robust for a British beer), and has a cloudy rusticity about it. Fuller's makes three beers that could arguably be called old ales: Vintage Ale, Golden Pride, and a bottle-aged beer called 1845 that fits squarely in this category. Others include Burton Bridge's Old Expensive and Samuel Smith's Winter Welcome. These beers have more plum and raisin, a stouter middle, and a toothsome heartiness. They are still middleweights but have a vinous complexity that makes them seem bigger than they are. ■

The Peculiar Peculier.

If you're an obsessive speller, a bottle of Theakston's Old Peculier might cause you to snort. But that's no misspelling. Put on your reading glasses and look closely at the funny little seal on the bottle. In the two-point type, you'll find these words: "Seal of the Official of the Peculier of Masham." Strange. It turns out that a "peculier" is an ecclesiastical court established in the absence of a bishop to arbitrate church law on urgent issues like wearing a hat during communion or carrying a dead man's skull out of the churchyard. You know, common offenses. In this case, the peculierate was established in Masham (a town in Yorkshire) by the archbishop of York. The offices were terminated by a series of laws 150 years ago, but it's just like a brewery to keep this odd bit of historical trivia alive (if obscurely so).

ABOVE: *The Seal of the Official of the Peculier of Masham*

BREWING NOTES

BREWING HIGH-GRAVITY BEERS seems like relatively straightforward business: Just add more stuff. Yet the alchemy of beer is not linear, and it turns out to be more complicated than toting up gravity points. There are matters of biology and chemistry to consider that, in regular beers, largely take care of themselves. In barley wines and old ales, the sheer density of the wort is hard for yeast to fully ferment. The stress of trying can lead the little fungi to produce off-flavors and poop out before the sugars have been adequately digested. This is especially true with all-barley beers like barley wines. One way to boost alcohol strength cleanly is by adding simple sugars that ferment easily. Barley always leaves some unfermentables behind; in many ways, managing these is the trick to successful high-alcohol beers.

Remedies start with the mash. Brewers can adjust various elements to make their worts more or less fermentable. They do this by changing the amount of water they use and mashing at different temperatures, which will determine the amounts of simple or complex sugars. The more complex sugars in a wort, the less they will be fermented and the heavier the body will be. More simple sugars result in thinner beers with more alcohol. Since barley wines have such massive starting gravities, they will necessarily have lots of unfermented sugars left after fermentation—even when the brewer manages to get a relatively attenuated beer. So when brewing barley wines, brewers want to get mashes full of the maximum amount of fermentable simple sugars.

Darron Welch, master brewer at the Pelican Brewery on the Oregon coast, makes a renowned barley wine called Stormwatcher's Winterfest. It's a great example of a hard-to-brew beer for a couple reasons. First, he starts with a base of relatively low-enzyme Golden Promise malt from the U.K. Recall that enzymes are critical in converting the starches into simple sugars. Second, the beer is meant to reach 13% ABV—close to the maximum strength for an all-malt, naturally fermented beer. So he puts himself two strikes in the hole before he even crushes the grain. Welch addresses this by using a low mash temperature; he shoots for 142°F. "That low conversion temperature [drives] your enzymatic reaction toward favoring the more fermentable sugars," he explains.

Fermentation is the next stage—and one mainly in the hands of the yeasts, though Welch gives them every opportunity to thrive. Because the liquid is so dense, it will stress the yeast and make it difficult to reproduce quickly. To compensate, he begins by pitching five to six times the volume of yeast he would in a normal batch of beer. He doesn't use just any yeast, either; he wants cells that just finished fermenting a low-gravity beer.

These will be healthy and vigorous—not exhausted from a lot of heavy work.

Because barley wines are innately sweet, Welch tries to lower the amount of ester production—those fruity compounds that enhance the perception of sweetness. He does this by tinkering with fermentation temperature. He pitches at 66°F—the usual temperature for a Pelican beer—so that fermentation starts immediately. A day or two later, when the yeast is at its peak activity, Welch lowers the temperature by 2°F. Cold and pressure inhibit ester production, which is most active in those first days of fermentation.

Another major consideration is the hopping rate. Despite their immense strength, not all barley wines are highly hopped. Others practically glow green with hops. Every beer needs to achieve a harmony between the sweetness of malt and bitterness of hops, and barley wines are a study in differing approaches. Brewers have to contend with the density and intensity of the malt base and make a decision: Either try to match its strength with an equal blast of hops or allow the malt to express itself and dominate the palate. The two approaches produce markedly contrasting types of barley wines.

The perception of bitterness is relative; a beer will taste more or less bitter depending on the amount of sugars in it. To achieve a level of bitterness that will combat the sugars in it over 10%, breweries have to use staggering amounts of hops. Worse, the higher a beer's gravity, the less bittering agent gets absorbed, requiring even more hops. I once asked a West Coast brewer which hops he used in his barley wine and he joked, "all of them."

If amping up those IBU poses a technical challenge for hoppy barley wine brewers, achieving balance in malty barley wines creates an artistic one. It becomes a matter of recipe development and employing a malt bill that results in clean, distinctive—if necessarily sweet—flavors. Brewers need to pay special attention to finishing the beer out as neatly as possible and avoiding the production of heavy esters. The balance point in sweet barley wines will hinge on the clarity of malt flavor and the sharp, cutting blast of alcohol. ■

EVOLUTION

THE EVOLUTION of strong ales is one in which the current point looks much like the beginning. The twentieth century marked the triumph of mechanization as the bones and nerves of breweries turned to steel and electricity. In nearly every case, this resulted in the ability to make better beer, but barley wines and old ales were a notable exception. With new, modern breweries, both styles lost the two elements key to their nature: wood and time.

Fortunately, breweries have begun to address these erstwhile "improvements." Barrel-aging programs, vanishingly rare at the turn of the twenty-first century, are now common on both sides of the Atlantic. American craft breweries are leading the charge, but they're not alone; British breweries have rediscovered the old ways, too—often thanks to the arrival of new craft breweries.

The effect is not exactly the same; modern barrel-aged old ales and barley wines are rarely affected by the *Brett* resident in old casks. Instead, breweries secure cast-off barrels from distilleries and wineries, still wet with liquor and wine. In Manchester, for example, J. W. Lees uses port and sherry barrels for its popular barley wine, Harvest Ale, while American breweries like AleSmith (which makes Old Numbskull barley wine) and Central Waters (Bourbon Barrel Barleywine) use domestic bourbon barrels instead.

This lends its own character. Like the "crackskull" of old, barrel-aging gives these beers the rounded, refined quality that comes from a breathing, porous wooden cask. Instead of a secondary fermentation with wild yeast, modern barrel-aged barley wines and old ales take flavor notes from the liquors and wines that were previously aged there. Much as hops and malt are selected for flavor and aroma notes, the character of the barrel becomes a part of the recipe. ■

THE BEERS TO KNOW

THE RANGE OF old ales and barley wines forms a rather shaggy-dog assemblage—not inappropriate for a gangly style that goes back hundreds of years. Remember that these beers are great for aging, so buy a few bottles and put them in your cellar to ripen.

OLD ALES

HAIR OF THE DOG ADAM

LOCATION: Portland, OR

MALT: Organic pilsner, caramel, Munich, chocolate, black, peat

HOPS: Northwest-grown

10% ABV, 1.094 SP. GR., 65 IBU

Hair of the Dog is to beer what the Velvet Underground was to music. Brewer Alan Sprints crafts some of the beer most admired by his peers. Adam is purportedly based on the defunct German *adambier* style, but it's really a fantastic old ale. An almost black beer with an espresso's crema head, Adam is balanced by smoked malt and a fair dose of hops, all swaddled in layers of creamy malts.

GREENE KING STRONG SUFFOLK (OLDE SUFFOLK)

LOCATION: Bury St Edmunds, England

MALT: Pale, caramel

HOPS: Challenger, First Gold, Target

OTHER: Aged in a wooden vat

6% ABV, 32 EBU

Greene King wisely markets the beer as Olde Suffolk in the United States ("strong" would certainly confuse Americans who think of a 6% beer as normal strength), and it does taste like something from another time. It has a deep color but a relatively light body that's highlighted by a malbec-like complexity—a touch of tannin, plum, and acidity. The aged Five X beer—made exclusively for blending into Strong Suffolk—has a bit of iron in it as well as balsamic, but these are offset by the brighter, fruitier notes of the fresh ale that's added before bottling.

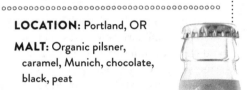

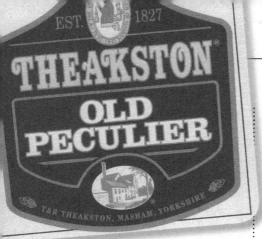

THEAKSTON OLD PECULIER

○○

LOCATION: Masham, England

MALT: Pale, crystal, torrified wheat

HOPS: Northern Brewer, Fuggle, other undisclosed hops

OTHER: Caramel sugar

5.6% ABV, 1.057 SP. GR., 29 IBU

O ld Peculier has been brewed in Masham since at least 1890, which gives it claim as "old" in both senses. It's a viscous old-style ale that froths up a lovely head and has the appearance of cloudy cola. The aroma is bready and hearty, much as the beer looks. Fruity notes waft up with raisin and plum, and the palate has a bit of earthiness that suggests rye or even sourdough.

UPRIGHT BILLY THE MOUNTAIN

○○

LOCATION: Portland, OR

MALT: Pale, mild, caramel, black barley (somewhat variable)

HOPS: Vary each year

OTHER: Molasses and *Brettanomyces claussenii*

9.1% ABV, 1.085 SP. GR., 40 IBU

B rewer Alex Ganum was inspired by the wood-aged and soured Gale's when he made Billy the Mountain (and by Frank Zappa, whose song is the basis for the name). Like Olde Suffolk, Billy is a product of blending, with a portion of mild ale mixed with year-old Billy, inoculated with wild yeast, and aged on wood. There's a tangy undercurrent that has—again, like Olde Suffolk—that balsamic tartness, but it is enclosed in a dense, sweet gingerbread beer with a touch of oak. Heavy and still, it would cloy if it were not brightened by the sprightly acidity. There's some spiciness in there as well, and a long, port-like finish.

NORTH COAST OLD STOCK ALE

○○

LOCATION: Fort Bragg, CA

MALT: Maris Otter

HOPS: Fuggle, East Kent Golding

12.5% ABV, 36 IBU

N orth Coast is particular about the name of this old ale—the brewery wasn't trying to make an American barley wine. Hugely alcoholic, it has none of the density of most similarly strong barley wines. It has more in common with Belgian quadrupels, with a sweet raisin nose and dark fruit palate balanced by a cutting alcohol note. But the deep amber color, so dark it almost becomes red, suggests an English-style ale. The malt has a bit of leather, too, and this references English old ales grown dry from *Brettanomyces*. There's no wild yeast here, but that dustiness hints at it.

BARLEY WINES

J. W. LEES HARVEST ALE

ooooooooooooooooooooooooooooooooooooooooooo

LOCATION: Manchester, England

MALT: Maris Otter

HOPS: East Kent Golding

11.5% ABV

Lees uses a triple yeast strain to produce Harvest Ale and ages some portion of the beer in port, whisky, and sherry casks; bottles indicate which barrels the beer came from. All versions of the beer are similar, though. A dark, murky beer that manages to rouse (if not sustain) a rich head. A sweet presentation and a very dense beer, but one that lacks "hot" alcohol notes—it's easy on the sipper. Of the barrel-aged versions, the whisky barrels provide the most contrast, adding a smoky, seductive center.

GOOSE ISLAND KING HENRY

ooooooooooooooooooooooooooooooooooooooooooo

LOCATION: Chicago, IL

MALT: Pale, caramel, crystal wheat, chocolate

HOPS: Pilgrim, Styrian Golding

13.4% ABV, 60 IBU

One of the rare dark barley wines, King Henry could pass for a porter (though light exposes it as a deep chestnut). One could call this a hybrid of an American and a British strong ale—the base beer has a round, full sweetness barely kissed by hops. (In a thundering barley wine twice as strong as an IPA, 60 IBU of

hopping is understated.) This is typical of the British style, but the bourbon character gives it an American touch. But perhaps that makes it all the more British—after all, Scotch producers have long used bourbon barrels for their whiskies. In any case, King Henry is a beautiful beer. It has a distinctly port-like nose, even grapey, and the bourbon is understated. It's more assertive on the palate, but in a warming, boozy fashion. It evokes a liquor-soaked fruitcake, and the body is almost that thick and cakey. At this strength, the beer might age indefinitely, though it is not bottle-conditioned.

PELICAN STORMWATCHER'S WINTERFEST

ooooooooooooooooooooooooooooooooooooooooooo

LOCATION: Pacific City, OR

MALT: Golden Promise, Munich, melanoidin, crystal, torrified wheat

HOPS: Hersbrucker, Golding, Fuggle, Glacier, Magnum

12.7% ABV, 1.140 SP. GR., 40 IBU

American breweries have a difficult time knowing how to balance a beer without using a bushel of hops. They should study Stormwatcher's Winterfest. Darron Welch gets a ton of complex flavors from his malts—everything from brown sugar and figs to sherry and pipe tobacco—but is able to keep the perception of sweetness in check. The malt itself, with able support from some potent alcohol, has enough complexity that all the hops can ride along and merely inflect flavors. This is a barley wine that evokes the old October beers.

American
STRONG ALES
DOUBLE OR TRIPLE IPAs

A merica is no place for restraint. If it can be made, it can be made bigger, better, stronger. It was inevitable that once Americans fell in love with strong, hoppy ales, we would naturally attempt to Texas-size them, as we have with cars, cinnamon rolls, and Super Bowl halftime shows. That inevitability has matured into a class of beers that collectively may be more American than any other styles going. Marking their strength by degrees with names like double (or imperial) or triple IPAs, these American strong ales are the twenty-foot-long finned V-8s of the beer world.

★ ★ ★

American Strong Ales

come by many names, usually preceded by "double," "triple," or "imperial." They feature an intense hop aroma and flavor that leave the tongue coated with hop acids. Lighter in body, color, and malt character than barley wines, they are intended as hop-delivery vehicles. American strong ales are too overpowering for most foods, but may find strange harmony with potent cheeses.

STATISTICS

ABV range: 7.5–12%

Bitterness: 65–100 IBU

Serving temperature: 50°–55°F

Vessel: Pint glass or snifter

The main feature in these beers is hops—nuclear, glowing lupulin intensity. The malt is useful to the extent that it allows the hop volume to crank to 11, but it doesn't actually contribute a lot of richness, flavor, or body—as in a barley wine—because that might slightly occlude the force of the hopping. With a good American strong ale, you should able to achieve a contact high just by sitting next to the person drinking one. ■

ORIGINS

T SHOULD NOW BE evident that strong ales are nothing new. Nor are strong, hoppy ales. Even in America, there is a long heritage going back through the Ballantine line, a tradition that Anchor tapped into when it made Old Foghorn in 1975. What distinguishes modern double or triple IPAs is their focus on saturated hoppiness. Breweries learned that by boosting the alcohol content, they could pack even more flavor and aroma into a beer—not to mention bitterness.

The first and most influential beer of this type was Sierra Nevada's Celebration. First introduced in 1981, it was envisioned as a way to take advantage of the first hops of the harvest. Sierra Nevada settled on the current recipe in 1983, a template for the broad category we now call IPAs: concentrated flavor and aroma of freshly plucked hops, wild with American character, layered over the top of a candy-sweet but largely insubstantial body. For decades, it was a cult beer among American hopheads who bought it by the case every fall. At just under 7% ABV, it was not the heavyweight of modern strong ales—but the contours were there.

Sierra Nevada was ahead of its time, though. American breweries and drinkers spent the next fifteen years timidly experimenting with light, inoffensive ales. Malcolm Gladwell didn't use craft beer as an illustration of his "tipping point" thesis, but what came next is a perfect example. A small group of hard-core fans—those guys who bought cases of Celebration—clamored for stronger, hoppier beer. In the late 1980s and early 1990s, breweries started to make hoppy pale ales and IPAs. Even though it was a small subculture in craft brewing, a passion for these kinds of beers took root.

The country reached the tipping point in the mid-1990s. IPAs had established enough popularity that breweries were escalating their intensity. Blind Pig and Rogue are credited with adding "double IPA" and "imperial IPA"—imprecise terms that signal strength—to the vernacular in 1994 and 1996, and breweries like Hair of the Dog and Stone Brewing released famous strong ales Fred and Arrogant Bastard, respectively, in 1997. These were rare examples, but they helped expand the definition of what a hoppy beer was, and the IBU continued to rise. These beers had become well enough established that the Great American Beer Festival added "imperial or double IPA" as a category in 2003. By 2012 (when the category was called "imperial IPA") it had the second-most entries at 128. ■

Extreme Beer. Somewhere in the mid-2000s, the arms race in beer strength and hoppiness got a name: extreme beer. There is no exact definition for the term, except the general definition of the word itself: "going to great or exaggerated lengths." Noting that these beers had many times as much malt and hops as the average light lager, *The New Yorker*'s Burkhard Bilger said they are "to Budweiser what a bouillabaisse is to fish stock." Boston Beer was one of the first extreme breweries, making Triple Bock, an 18% titan, in 1994. When Dogfish Head matched that strength with its 120 Minute IPA in 2003, the race was on. Voodoo's Black Magic (15%) joined the extreme club in 2009, but was no match for the competition: DuClaw's Colossus (17.3%) pushed the alcohol higher and finally Boston Beer took back the trophy with Utopias (27%).

The extreme philosophy is not unique to the United States, and indeed, reached further heights elsewhere. Once *Guinness World Records* listed Utopias as the world's strongest beer, it became a ripe target for German brewery Schorschbräu, who eventually toppled it with its Schorschbock (40%) in February 2009. For the next three years, the battle for most extreme beer was fought overseas as the title seesawed back and forth between Schorschbräu and Scotland's BrewDog, apparently concluding with a victory for the German brewer in 2012. At 57.5%, its amped-up Schorschbock was 115 proof, substantially stronger than most liquors. The competition actually sparked the founding of a third brewery named Brewmeister (another Scottish concern) devoted to breaking the record. It has, with a beer called Snake Venom, made to a staggering 68%. These breweries used a system of freezing, removing the water in the form of ice, and reducing the beer until the alcohol percentage of the remaining liquid reached these dizzying heights.

DESCRIPTION AND CHARACTERISTICS

S THERE ENOUGH difference between American strong ales and barley wines to justify a separate category? Or put another way: Isn't this style just an especially hoppy, lighter-bodied example of barley wine? Indeed, this is one of those cases where the distinction, perhaps small, makes a difference.

American strong ales are, for those who brew them and pursue them, a kind of ongoing quest to attain the platonic ideal of hop bliss. Unlike nearly every other beer style, where balance is prized, American strong ales are optimized to express one quality perfectly. Malt or yeast character and alcohol strength are useful only to the extent they heighten the sense of hop loveliness. The goal of an American strong ale is maximizing the vividness of hop aromas, flavors, and bitterness. The balance exists not between malt and hop, but rather among the various elements the hops themselves provide. The aromas, flavors, and bitterness should be in harmony.

Russian River Brewing Company makes two prototypical examples in their two Pliny varieties, the Younger and the Elder. In 1994, brewer Vinnie Cilurzo was on the vanguard of super hoppy beers when he made Inaugural Ale at his first brewery, the Blind Pig, in Temecula, California. In 2000, brewing at the other end of the state in Santa Rosa, Cilurzo created Pliny the Elder, a double IPA, which led to Pliny the Younger, a "triple IPA." In most styles, the "double" and "triple" refer to malt; to Cilurzo, they refer to the level of hopping. Both beers have light, golden bodies and shocking hop character. The elements come together best in Pliny the Elder, a dangerously light-bodied beer (8%) that has few rivals in the way it synthesizes the hoppiness.

Strength is an important part of the picture. The stronger a beer, the more it accommodates condensed, concentrated flavors. Alpha acids—the bittering agent in hops—dissolve more readily in alcohol than water, so the stronger a beer is, the more bitterness breweries can pack in. Alcohol also helps vent the aromas, which makes them particularly intense in the mouth as the volatile scents are taken to the nose.

The final pieces of the puzzle are the exotic flavors New World hops contribute. With their juicy citrus and tropical flavors, American hops are the old standbys, but New Zealand is the new kid on the block. Kiwi hops are even more exotic, with flavors that have elements of garlic, musk, and onion at high concentrations, and they are increasingly common in American strongs. Unlike many styles for which breweries try to achieve perfection of a traditional flavor, in American strong ales, breweries and drinkers are perpetually on the hunt for the latest, most exotic new flavors. ∎

Alimony Ale. The nation's first "extreme" beer may have been Alimony Ale, made in Hayward, California, by Buffalo Bill's—one of the nation's first brewpubs. Brewed by founder Bill Owens in 1987 to celebrate a customer's divorce, it carried the fitting tagline "Bitterest beer in America." It was purportedly 100 IBU, but has been scaled down over time. Buffalo Bill's still sells Alimony Ale, but at a more reasonable 70 IBU.

BREWING NOTES

T'S EASY ENOUGH to make a muddy, toxically hoppy strong ale—just add tons of hops. But American strong ales shouldn't become a heavy stew of alcohol and brute-force hopping. They're actually delicate beers that rely on several fragile elements. Hop flavor and aroma are at least as important as bitterness, but preserving them amid the onslaught of IBU is tricky. Similarly, the malt base has to provide enough sweetness to moderate the effects of those hops (indeed, it's important in inflecting them), but it can never intrude.

Breweries have several methods of addressing these issues. One trick is sugar, which reduces the influence of the malt while at the same time boosting octane. As an added plus, it lends a more crisp finish, critical in preserving those volatile hop elements. Russian River uses sugar in the Plinys to great effect, as does Surly in Abrasive Ale and Deschutes in Hop Henge. Bell's gets the same effect in Hopslam, its much-loved strong, by using honey instead. The use of sugar reveals the way in which American strong ales differ from their cousins, barley wines. Those latter beers are very thick of body and, even in the most hoppy American examples, have tons of malt character. American strong ales have a closer kinship with an unlikely beer: Belgian tripels. Both are pale and attenuated, both downplay caramel malts (American styles less so), and both highlight hops—though of course, American strongs more so. Odd as it may

> "If you want to know the difference between [Pliny] and a barley wine, it's got just 3.5 to 4 percent crystal malt in it. Having a low level of crystal malt, you really let the hops come through; they're not being muddled by the caramel character. Also, we're using a lot of sugars in the fermentables, so it's drying the beer out and giving the beer a nice light, dry body that's super crisp, yet really bitter. The malt lays the foundation and it's just there to keep the hops in check without being sweet, malty, or biscuity. It's a really simple malt bill and the hops are the shining star in that beer."
>
> —*VINNIE CILURZO,*
> Russian River Brewing, on Pliny the Elder

seem, Pliny the Elder may be closer to the slender, elegant Westmalle Tripel than it is to the syrupy and intense Rogue Old Crustacean.

Hopping is, of course, the key to the whole affair, and the best advice a brewer might give is: Try everything. Some breweries start with the mash, where the hops are exposed to water well below boiling temperature. This technique boosts flavor extraction, and Deschutes uses it for their annual Hop Henge. The sheer quantity of hops required for a bitter charge has led Cilurzo to use hop extract in the Plinys; in this concentrated form, he gets a pure, clarion bitterness without also picking up cooked, vegetal aromas from the hop cones. Hopping schedules vary brewery to brewery during the boil, but late-addition hopping is critical to pop flavor and especially aromas. Breweries use hopbacks and whirlpools for further additions, and dry-hopping is a nearly universal practice.

Breweries have different theories about whether to use many hop varieties

LEFT: *Released once a year, Bell's Hopslam is such a beloved beer that it has its own fan clubs.*

or just a couple, but this seems less critical than the method. Stone and Surly seem to do just fine extracting flavor from just two varieties. Most breweries do favor many varieties, though: Deschutes uses an astonishing eight, Bell's and Firestone Walker (DBA) six, and Avery (Maharaja) and Russian River four. ■

EVOLUTION

NVENTED JUST IN the mid-1990s, double IPAs are still babies. They are in many ways an invention of horticulture rather than brewing, enabled by the glut of new hop varieties that gushed into the market in the 1990s and 2000s. Newer hops have alpha acids and exotic flavors far in excess of earlier strains. Craft brewing sparked the interest in, and market for, strange and wonderful new varieties that headline beer flavors, and growers are happy to keep a new stream flowing into breweries every year.

Since strong, hoppy beers depend so much on the flavors and aromas of hops, their future is bound up with the development of newer strains with different flavors. This is happening on the international market as well, as hops from New Zealand—particularly Nelson Sauvin—have become popular in Europe. The American strong ale phenomenon is no longer limited to America—breweries like Denmark's Mikkeller, England's Thornbridge, and New Zealand's Epic are making some of the most accomplished examples in the genre. Americans were first on the scene, but the style has gone international. ■

New Zealand Hops. It wasn't too long ago that the Pacific Northwest was the lone international hop superstar. It still attracts the most attention, but an ingénue has marched onto the stage: New Zealand. The first big success came in the form of Nelson Sauvin, a hop with humid tropical fruit flavors and aromas (and, to some people, a little human musk). Motueka, another variety, is all lemons, limes, and pepper, while Green Bullet has a more refined, spicy character. Others include the exotic-sounding Riwaka (pine and bergamot), Pacific Gem (oak and blackberries), and Pacific Jade (citrus and black pepper).

New Zealand has a decided advantage over the much larger U.S. hop industry, too: The country lacks native pests or diseases that normally afflict hops; the plants are therefore not treated with chemicals. Dried using indirect radiators, the hops are kept further unfouled by oil or gas fumes. This makes it easy for New Zealand growers to produce organic hops, which has given them a nice platform to sell in foreign markets.

THE BEERS TO KNOW

DOUBLE AND TRIPLE IPAs are often released seasonally by breweries. Beyond highlighting their special status in a brewery's line, this emphasizes their evanescence. Unlike regular IPAs or barley wines, these beers will not last. Because so much of the hop character comes from late-boil and dry-hop additions, the aromas and flavors will begin to degrade within days of release. After a month the beers will have diminished—their flavors will be listless, the aromas faint—and after three they will have lost a great deal of what made them special. Buy and drink these immediately.

RUSSIAN RIVER PLINY THE ELDER

LOCATION: Santa Rosa, CA

MALT: Pale, crystal

HOPS: Amarillo, Centennial, CTZ, Simcoe

OTHER: Dextrose

8.0% ABV, 1.070 SP. GR., 100 IBU

Pliny the Elder is one of a handful of American beers that have altered the course of craft brewing, but more than that, it's one of America's best beers. By appearance and texture, you'd swear it was a 6% beer. It looks like a pale ale in the glass, topped with a dollop of whipped cream. The aroma is such an intense, distilled spritz of pine and grapefruit that you can almost taste the smell. That intensity carries over to the palate, but like a perfectly balanced fresh lemonade, it remains on the side of pleasure, never overwhelming the senses.

AVERY MAHARAJA

LOCATION: Boulder, CO

MALT: Pale, dark crystal, Victory

HOPS: Simcoe, Columbus, Centennial, Chinook

10.2% ABV, 1.090 SP. GR., 102 IBU

A deceivingly light apricot–colored beer with an innocent white head, Maharaja announces its identity to the nose—a blast of pineapple and mango. Like Pliny, Maharaja is piney, but the pine here has some eucalyptus. The hop matrix is rounded out by those fruity mango notes, and the malt provides just enough sweetness to keep the bitterness from scraping the taste buds off your tongue.

SURLY ABRASIVE ALE

○○○

LOCATION: Brooklyn Center, MN

MALT: Pale, Golden Promise, crystal, oats

HOPS: Warrior, Citra

8.8% ABV, 1.081 SP. GR., 120 IBU

Abrasive is a bit of a misnomer—the original name came from a grade of sandpaper—because this hazy golden offering has so much juicy hop flavor that it doesn't register as shocking. The malt base, though slight, has a honey sweetness that helps the hops pop. And pop they do, first with a citrusy bouquet, and later with spicier, darker, and slightly sativa-like "dankness."

DESCHUTES HOP HENGE

○○○

LOCATION: Bend, OR

MALT: Pale, Munich

HOPS: Millennium, Northern Brewer, Cascade, Centennial, Zeus, Simcoe, Brewer's Gold, Citra (vary by year)

OTHER: Sugar

8.5% ABV, 95 IBU

Released every January, Hop Henge takes advantage of a rotating selection of hops that strike the brewers' fancy after harvest. (The list here comes from the 2012 vintage.) Hops go in at every stage, from the mash through to the primary fermenter and conditioning tank. The flavors change yearly, but Hop Henge always manages to achieve the proper intensity: pleasure ratio.

ALCHEMIST HEADY TOPPER

○○○

LOCATION: Waterbury, VT

MALT: Undisclosed

HOPS: Undisclosed

8% ABV, UNDISCLOSED IBU*

Poured into a glass (against the advice on the can), Heady Topper doesn't look promising. It's a murky beer of indistinct color. Yet people don't give this beer raves for the appearance; they do so for the flavors and aromas, which are as concentrated and intense as in any beer made: almost pure grapefruit, juicy and sometimes even rindy, tailing off toward pine.

*"IBU—plenty" according to the can

LAGUNITAS HOP STOOPID

○○○

LOCATION: Petaluma, CA

MALT: Undisclosed

HOPS: Undisclosed

7.7% ABV, 1.085 SP. GR., 102 IBU

After Heady Topper, you might admire the clarity of Hop Stoopid, which is just a shade south of perfectly bright. Lagunitas has a famous connection with a certain herb—in the realm of metaphor, of course—and this hop extract beer is more than suggestive of it. Call it a pine-to-sativa "dankness," sticky, resinous, and enough to make a person light-headed. It has the characteristic double IPA lightness of body, which is lean and bereft of all but the tiniest hint of biscuit.

Scottish ALES

I n Britain's North lies a remote country where sinister crags watch over lonely rain-lashed moors, where the winter sun rises lazily and spends just seven short hours drifting across the southern horizon, where kilted William Wallace spilled English blood, and where Robert Burns spilled glorious ink. A country, in short, that inspires many romantic ideas.

Scottish Ales. As in England, the standard range of beers includes varying strengths of pale ales. Scotland abandoned cask ale and adopted lager sooner than England did, and local products bear the marks of this trend. These ales are far more likely to be poured from an artificially carbonated keg than a cask, and are usually colder and more effervescent. Scottish ales are on the whole less hoppy than English ales, but there are lots of exceptions.

Scottish session ales are closely related to English cask ale; they're balanced and smooth, designed to keep the palate interested over the course of three or four pints. Wee heavies are strong beers with rich malty bodies and a kiss of fruitiness. American Scotch ales are also strong but, owing to a misunderstanding by American breweries, are made with the smoky malts made famous in Scottish distilleries. Finally Scottish breweries have made a specialty of unique expressions that may be made with heather or aged in Scotch whisky barrels, or that harken back to earlier eras when breweries made stouts. In each case, local breweries are experimenting with new flavors and techniques as a way of rediscovering lost traditions.

Scottish ales are varied enough that they can't easily be summarized with statistics.

Romantic ideas swirl around the ales, too. People believe that the ales are made malty sweet because hops don't grow that far north; that the beers have become caramelized from long boils over an open flame; that strong Scottish ales are smoky from peat-roasted malt; and the most famous Scottish ale is a titanic brew burly and thick enough to hold a spoon upright and sweet enough to dribble on toast. Yet these are all more myth than fact. There are distant kernels of truth to such legends, but the real story of Scottish ale draws on the country's commercial and trade history—the part about Adam Smith, industry, and financial conquest.

In truth, Scottish beers don't differ so much from their cousins to the south, but they were and remain more worldly and responsive to trends. If you want a barrel-aged British beer, a potent stout or spiky IPA, you're more likely to find it in Scotland than down below the border. ■

ORIGINS

SCOTS HAVE BEEN brewing beer for a long time. Archaeologists have found what might be evidence of not only brewing but also malting in Fife and the Orkney Islands dating to 4,000 to 6,000 years ago. Those early brewers were well north of the nearest hop plant (which in any case wouldn't be discovered as a useful beer ingredient for thousands of years), so they spiced their beer with heather, meadowsweet, and other wildflowers. The case is not incontrovertible, but the weight of evidence suggests very early brewing—giving those ancient people bragging rights, along with the Sumerians, as the world's first brewers. The Scots have been making beer ever since.

The country's brewing history largely mirrors neighboring England's. Through the Middle Ages, beer was a rustic, mostly homemade beverage, only incorporating hops as a spice well after they had taken root in continental recipes. But after centuries of slow change, Scotland's brewing industry changed almost as rapidly as England's at the start of the 19th century. Although the country may appear remote to folks in London—or even those in Yorkshire—its port towns tied it to the world. As in England, Scottish breweries industrialized and innovated. In fact, sparging—the now-universal practice of sprinkling water on the grain bed—was developed in Scotland.

There's a persistent belief that Scottish beers were rough and rustic. For some reason, many Americans believe old Scottish ales would have been smoky because malting kilns must have been filled with clouds of peat smoke—as they were in the maltings of some distilleries. (It's why American brewers began making smoky "Scotch" ales.) But even as early as the seventeenth century, Scottish brewers were firing their kilns with coke to reduce smoky flavors. Smoke may be fine in an Islay single malt, but it has been 300 years since it was appropriate in a Scottish beer.

Scotland was one of the most modern brewing countries in the nineteenth century. As breweries grew to become more impressive commercial concerns toward the end of the eighteenth century, the cities of Edinburgh and Alloa became brewing centers. This seems largely due to the hard water, which was similar to the mineral wells found under England's Burton upon Trent. If there was ever a signature Scottish beer, it might have been Edinburgh Ale, a hearty beer tailored from that hard water. Made from 100 percent pale malt and served in tall, thin glasses like Champagne, it sounds much like Burton's famous namesake ales. One contemporary called it "glutinous and adhesive" in 1852. Another description, from 1833, described it this way: "It is as clear as amber, and of the same colour; soft and delicious in taste; so strong, that a few glasses produce a slight intoxication, or inclination to sleep; and has a thin creamy top."

Edinburgh was such a major center of brewing—by 1825 it had twenty-eight breweries—that it had earned the nickname "Auld Reekie." The city, swaddled in a layer of black smoke, may not have been fouled solely by breweries, but the industry was a major contributor. Not only did the city's breweries all have roaring fires powering their boilers, but many also malted and kilned their own grain, too, contributing further to the haze. Alloa, thirty miles west of Edinburgh on the banks of the Firth of Forth, was nearly as famous for its brewing industry. In the mid-nineteenth century, it was producing more barrels of beer every year than it had citizens. The beer from these towns was commanding premium prices in England, and production of beer doubled in Scotland between 1850 and 1870. Scottish ale was even famous beyond

ABOVE: *A pint of Belhaven Best settles.*

Britain. Writing in 1860, the French scientist Louis Figuier said it was "the strongest and best beer made in Great Britain. It is distinguished from all other domestic beers in its alcohol content, beautiful amber tint, and balsamic taste."

Scottish beer did feature a few idiosyncracies of method and ingredient. It was generally a bit less hoppy than English beer—but clearly by design. One of the long-held mistaken beliefs about Scottish ale suggests that the relatively less hoppy beers of Scotland got that way from want—hops just didn't grow nearby. This plausible line looks less so in light of the number of ships leaving with Scottish ale and returning with English barley (which was better than the rough native strain known as Bigg barley). If they were importing barley, surely they could have imported hops as well—had they wanted to. Indeed, Scottish breweries competed in the IPA trade and made plenty of well-hopped beers.

Shillings and Guineas. Like English ales, Scottish ales were long priced based on how alcoholic they were. Also as in England, Scottish ales used a scale to represent this range. Rather than Xs or Ks, though, Scots used the actual price for a hogshead of ale in the mid-19th century—hence the classic 60 and 80 shilling ales, which you still see even today. It was an obvious way to do things, but the legacy is confusion.

There were a couple problems. Prices varied depending on the cask size—regular barrels were cheaper than larger hogshead casks. Since all beers were priced in shillings, it didn't tell you much about what kind of beer was inside the cask—just its strength. A hogshead of 60 shilling might have contained a stout or a pale ale. Even more confusing was the occasional use of a different unit of currency, the guinea, to designate strength—for guineas went out of use in 1816 (and the fact that a guinea equaled a bizarre 21 shillings?—don't ask). Fowler's was still making 12 Guinea Ale 150 years after the coin's last use. Fortunately, 12 guinea ales were being renamed in the twentieth century to the far clearer "wee heavy." Clear, that is, once you know that "wee" referred to the small bottles they were sold in, and "heavy" to the strength of the beer, which was considerable.

OTHER DIFFERENCES

Scottish breweries used sugar less often and seemed to favor less attenuated beers than the English. One of the enduring myths about Scottish ales is that long boil times caramelized the wort, but historian Ron Pattinson, writing in *Scotland!*, found absolutely no evidence of this when he scoured brewing logs of the nineteenth and twentieth centuries. To the contrary, Scottish breweries used short boils—sometimes as little as an hour.

Scottish breweries made porters and stouts, not in great quantities, but consistently throughout the twentieth century. If there's any argument to be made about a unique Scottish beer, these versions of porter and stout may be it. The deviations from English styles began in the nineteenth century, when grists featured higher proportions of dark malts than English porters. The attenuations were consequently lower—in some cases lower than 60 percent. Scottish breweries followed the English trend of making sweeter stouts in the twentieth century, but they took the concept to new heights. Most were under 70 percent attenuated, and about a third were less than 50 percent attenuated—an amazing number for a modern beer.

A final characteristic of Scottish ales was low fermentation temperatures. There was a range, but most breweries pitched their beers below 60°F (lower for higher-gravity beers), giving Scottish ales a more lager-like character and far less fruitiness than English ales. This dates back at least to the early nineteenth century, and is the only real point of continuity in Scottish brewing. Belhaven's George Howell confirmed that yeast never used to be a significant factor in Scottish brewing. When he worked for Tennents in the 1970s and '80s, it functioned as a de facto yeast bank for area breweries. Whatever yeast was on hand was fine because the temperatures were low enough that character varied very little by strain.

The structure of the Scottish industry was unique in one important respect, and this turned out to be very bad for the country's breweries in the postwar period. Unlike England, where breweries were licensed to own their own pubs, in Scotland this was much harder. The effect was the inverse of England's, where breweries developed fiefdoms of pubs in their local region. In Scotland, independent pubs were common, so breweries competed for tap handles. To boost barrelage, breweries sold farther and farther afield, becoming quite adept at export trade. By the end of World War II, Scottish breweries—despite producing a fraction of Britain's beer— accounted for half of all British exports. Unfortunately, as the British empire collapsed, so did this lucrative market. With no local pub infrastructure to support them, many breweries watched their sales plummet.

The effect was massive consolidation (or "rationalization" to Brits). Breweries began buying each other out at fantastic rates. By the mid-1990s, there were only six breweries left making a total of twenty beer brands. Fortunately, that was the low-water mark. Craft breweries started opening up shortly thereafter, and there are now around 200 scattered across Scotland. ■

Bere, Bigg, or Bygg Barley.

Scotland is home to a particular traditional or "landrace" barley called "bere" (pronounced *bear*). Its original source is obscure, but the Norse word for barley, *bygg*, suggests some Viking parentage. Yet the substantial genetic variation among bere varieties and their difference from Scandinavian barley stocks suggest that it predates the Vikings—and archaeologists think that Neolithic people were making beer by at least 2000 BCE.

In any case, bere is a family of barleys particularly suited to long days, short growing seasons, and low-pH soils—all adaptations that make it particularly suited for Scottish agriculture. Bere was used by Scottish breweries until the nineteenth century, but it was considered a poorer grade and was less efficient in the mash (so much so that it was even taxed at a lower rate). However, scientists have begun reexamining bere as a possible hardy strain resistant to blight. They've discovered that it has loads of enzymes and actually ferments quite well, which poses an interesting mystery: Why was bere abandoned? Perhaps to help the revival, Valhalla, from the Shetland Islands, makes Island Bere exclusively from the barley.

DESCRIPTION AND CHARACTERISTICS

WALK INTO A PUB in Edinburgh and you'll find a range of offerings typical of most British pubs—an assortment of lagers and light ales. Based on a first glance, you may develop the superficial impression that there's not a lot of difference between the English and Scottish pub scenes. That's true to a point—but only a point. Although they can't always elbow their way into pubs, scores of Scottish breweries are making very interesting—and unusual—beers. The new guys have revived the tradition of strong ales by reintroducing wee heavies, the best versions of which are some of the world's finest beers. But they've also gotten experimental—though usually in a very Scottish way. Some have experimented with pre-hop ales; others are availing themselves of local whisky casks and making barrel-aged beers. Still others are dabbling in interesting throwback styles like stout.

No review of Scottish ales would be complete without a mention of New World interpretations. American breweries have gotten into the act by inadvertently inventing a peaty style based on a misunderstanding of Scottish malting. American Scotch ales may not be traditional, but they have developed a devoted (if small) stateside following and are, at least nominally, "Scottish."

SESSION ALES

Among the ale family, the most popular are those that are still recognizably "Scottish." These ales usually have characteristically Scottish names like 80 Shilling, St. Andrews Ale, or Flying

Heather Ale. Although archaeologists believe that the first heather ales may have been made six millennia ago, in Scotland it is the ancient Picts who are remembered for brewing them. So famous were their heather ales that they have entered folklore. In the stories, the heather ale is more a metaphor for things lost—not only the rare elixir, but the Picts themselves, who carried their secret recipe to their graves. What's fascinating is that, despite the legends, heather ale didn't die out. It continued to be brewed noncommercially through the end of the nineteenth century. The botanist John Lightfoot wrote about residents of Islay and Jura making heather beer in the 1770s. Writing in 1900, folklorist R. C. Maclagan interviewed people who remembered drinking or making heather ale in the 1800s. It is certain that all these beers were made differently, but the lineage is impressive—from the Neolithic through the Pictish era all the way to modern-day revivals such as Williams Brothers' Fraoch. Six thousand years of heather ale!

Scotsman; they're served in pint glasses and have a coppery hue; and they look like proper pints of bitter. So similar are they to the pub favorites of the country to the south that even the Scots don't entirely know how to distinguish them. When I was speaking with Belhaven brewer George Howell, I asked what made these beers "Scottish." It took him a long time to answer, and he hazarded that it might have to do with hops (less up north). But on the whole—not much difference.

They aren't the same as bitters, but you have to look closely if you want to locate that special Scottishness. Howell mentioned hops, but—if you'll allow an outsider's perspective—it's really the malt. Scottish session ales can be read as tiny treatises on the expressiveness of malt flavor. With reserved hopping, you can see the way soft, fruity esters play off a refined woodiness. You find all the classic malt adjectives in different brands—toffee, bread crust, walnut, biscuit—and yet they fail to capture the more evocative elements that spring to mind when you're pondering these unassuming little ales. Once, sitting in an airport lounge, I ordered a pint of Stewart's 80/- (their classic heavy) that brought to mind reeds swaying in springwater. Another romantic notion about Scotland? Possibly, but a pint or three of fine ale brings out poetic notions.

The most distinct element is the way they feel on the tongue. "Silky" is the only word that will do. Some of these beers aren't even 4 percent, and yet they have a soft viscosity that caresses the tongue. The quality isn't reserved for session ales—you find it in wee heavies, too—but it is illustrated best by them. Thin pub ales barely sustain you through one pint. A Scottish ale, with its quietly luxurious body, can easily sustain a night's session.

NEW EXPRESSIONS

The new crop of Scottish brewers bears some resemblance to American craft breweries: They are creative and improvisational, making aggressive, hoppy ales and strong, whisky barrel–aged beers on the one hand and re-creations of historic beers on the other. One of the most dynamic—and controversial—is Aberdeenshire's BrewDog, a brewery nearly as committed to provocation as it is to brewing. Its range of beers is illustrative, though: two New World–hopped IPAs, a Scotch whisky–aged imperial stout, and a series of experimental beers in a line they call Abstrakt.

Yet in the famous brewing city of Alloa, Scott and Bruce Williams have gone exactly the opposite direction at Williams Brothers Brewing, brewing beers based on what might have been crafted a thousand years ago. Their flagship Fraoch is a heather ale, and they added other strange creations over time: beers made with elderberry, pine, gooseberry, and seaweed. Of these beers, Fraoch is the most interesting—a sweet, flowery beer that has inspired many imitators, particularly in the United States.

Perhaps the most interesting of the new breweries is Harviestoun in Alva, just up the road from Alloa. Founded in 1984, Harviestoun has a typical range of beers—shilling bitters and seasonals. In 2005, however, it launched a line of beers named Ola Dubh. Called strong ales—but looking a whole lot like stouts—they are aged in Highland Park Scotch whisky barrels. Americans have been using American whiskey barrels for some time, but Harviestoun is the first to take advantage of Scotland's most famous beverage. Ola Dubh is thick and sweet, a perfect base for the smoky, peaty liquor infusion. Other breweries have followed suit, including BrewDog and Orkney. These are pure Scotland, and taste like they've been made for 200 years.

AMERICAN SCOTCH ALES

Many immigrants to the United States have received the same treatment: altered names, scrambled nationalities. A few generations down the line genomes wander some distance from their country of origin. This is the history of beer styles, of course. America melts more than national identity—it changes beers, too.

Scottish ales are a case in point. In their native land, they differ little from other British styles. In their Americanized form, they became peaty, often "perceived as earthy or smoky." That description is from the American Homebrewers Association, one of the early vectors of misinterpretation. The romantic ideas crept in, as did the influence of Scotland's other national beverage, whisky. Add the fact that American brewers were able to buy peat-smoked malt from companies like Simpsons that produce it for the country's distilleries—and you have all the makings for a little reinvention.

Strong, malty, often peaty or smoky

ales are now what Americans think of when they think of Scotland's beer. As a consequence, these are the kinds of Scotland-inspired ales you'll find in the United States. The nomenclature is a little blurry, but in the U.S., "Scottish ale" refers to cask-strength session beers, while "Scotch ale" refers to a fairly robust beer, seasoned with smoked malt. A couple popular smoky examples of Scotch ale are Pike Kilt Lifter, Odell 90 Shilling, and Samuel Adams Scotch Ale.

WEE HEAVIES

American and Scottish brewing intersect with wee heavies—or perhaps run in parallel. A wee heavy boasts a strength of between 7 and 9% ABV—not gigantic, but robust—perfect as an after-dinner ale. Many of the classic examples come from Scotland: Orkney Skull Splitter, Traquair House Ale, Belhaven Wee Heavy, and Broughton Old Jock. In truth, these beers don't deviate much from other British strong ales—they're malt-forward, rounded, fruity, warming, and very smooth.

American versions are—as always—more extreme. Not only are they more alcoholic, ranging from 8 to 10% ABV, but they are often heavier and more well-hopped. Of course, they also often have that smoke/peat note. Founders Dirty Bastard may be the country's best-known wee heavy, and it's made with a boggy underlay of smoked malt. At 50 IBU, however, it marks itself as definitively New World. Others of note are AleSmith's Wee Heavy, Great Divide's Claymore, Oskar Blues's Old Chub, and Silver City's Fat Scotch Ale. ∎

BREWING NOTES

THERE'S VERY LITTLE difference in the way Scottish and English breweries make beer— and even those differences are becoming less and less distinct. Historically, Scots fermented their beer at temperatures in the mid-fifties Fahrenheit, as much as 10°F lower than the English. Now the temperatures are closer to English fermentation temperatures, though still on the cool side. Unlike English ales, which are identified by soft fruitiness, Scottish beers don't have much of an ester profile. Scottish ales also have the reputation of packing less hop punch than English ales, but beers like Caledonian's Deuchars IPA make me doubt the claim.

Even though most now know better, many American breweries continue to use peat-smoked malt in their grists. This is what happens when customers get used to certain styles—for many American audiences, that smoky-peaty character has become a key marker of Scotch ale, even if it was invented in the States. Since the beers are relatively strong sellers for many breweries, it's likely that these American interpretations will remain the standard. Of course, there's a reason they've become a minor hit: They're tasty. Since their introduction, breweries have learned to include just modest amounts of peat-smoked malt—it doesn't overwhelm the beer. Instead, it offers drinkers just the suggestion of the Highlands. ■

> As we've established, Scotland has a wide range of styles of beer. The shilling-style session ales are very close to *English bitters*. Because Scottish beers are fermented cold, they have a lager-like clean palate. As such, *bocks* are closely related—they're malty, strong, and often amber to brown in color. *Doppelbocks*, with their rich, malty bodies and alcoholic heft have more than a passing resemblance to wee heavies. If it's the peat smoking you enjoy, Germany has a lager for you, too—*rauchbier*.

EVOLUTION

WE'VE ALREADY DISCUSSED the wave of change happening among craft breweries in Scotland. If other countries offer any example, some of the types of beers these breweries make will filter into the mainstream market. Perhaps more important, they will begin to nudge drinkers in the direction of more adventuresome flavors so that even standard shilling-type ales may begin to exhibit higher gravities and hop infusions.

Scottish ales have long animated the imagination of breweries far away. The Belgians took a particular shine to Scottish ales about a hundred years ago and continue to make their own interpretations (beer styles drift as much in Belgium as they do in the U.S.).

The next great wave of Scotch ales hit North America in the 1980s with their peaty reinterpretation. In the manner of an artist looking through his early juvenilia, though, there's now a sense of sheepishness in the United States about peaty Scotch ales. In fact, as a legacy to early mistakes, "authenticity"—beer made as close as possible to classic examples—has become an increasingly important marker of quality. The Great American Beer Festival has sequestered smoky Scotch ales in a separate category, perhaps trying to herd breweries back toward authenticity. Yet the peaty examples have a definite fan base—the world may have to reconcile itself to the idea of American Scotch ales for the time being. In terms of cultural imperialism, however, it's not the most egregious case. Have you ever tried Scottish curry? ■

THE BEERS TO KNOW

FINDING CHARACTERISTIC Scottish ales is something like taking a review course in English literature. There are so many different examples, the best one can do is dive in and start sampling. The following selection reflects four categories of Scottish ales: standard session ales of the type found in Scotland, unique expressions of Scottish brewing, wee heavies, and American Scotch ales.

SCOTTISH SESSIONS

BELHAVEN ST. ANDREWS ALE

ooooooooooooooooooooooooooooooooooooooooooo

LOCATION: Dunbar, Scotland

MALT: Pale, crystal, black

HOPS: Challenger, Golding

OTHER: Brewers sugar

4.6% ABV, 24 EBU

St. Andrews is a good place to start as a way of tuning your palate to Scottish brewing. It possesses the soft, gentle qualities that mark the tradition—almost like rainwater. A rounded, resonant ale perfectly characteristic of the Scottish impulse toward malt. In Belhaven's beers you'll find a very slight ester, which to my palate has the quality of rosewater. American breweries would do well to study St. Andrews, a beer focused entirely on malt; never, though, does it feel heavy or sweet. St. Andrews finishes with a satisfying crispness, luring you toward another sip.

STEWART BREWING 80/- (80 SHILLING)

ooooooooooooooooooooooooooooooooooooooooooo

LOCATION: Edinburgh, Scotland

MALT: Maris Otter, wheat, crystal, chocolate, carapils

HOPS: Challenger, Magnum, Tettnang, Styrian Golding

4.4% ABV, 18 IBU

This striking, deep amber beer is one of the finest Scottish ales on the market—though it is, unfortunately, only available on cask in Scotland. The nose is pure malt, at turns nutty and something like polished wood. Compared to the classics from older breweries, Stewart's Scottish ale is hearty and rich. The body is creamy, but the palate is never too sweet.

ODELL 90 SHILLING

LOCATION: Fort Collins, CO

MALT: Pale, caramel, chocolate

HOPS: Undisclosed

5.3% ABV, 23 IBU

Odell manages the nearly impossible by nailing every part of the equation. Its 90 Shilling is a lovely garnet-brown color, bright and scented with toffee, nuts, and an earthy spice. The beer's brewed to American strength and has the concomitant heft, but is as smooth and supple as an Edinburgh ale.

NATIVE SCOTTISH EXPRESSIONS

ORKNEY DARK ISLAND

LOCATION: Orkney, Scotland

MALT: Pale, chocolate, caramel, wheat

HOPS: First Gold, Golding

4.6% ABV

Somewhere between a mild and a porter, Dark Island is Orkney's effort to put some color in Scottish ales. There's a sweetness born of the darker malts, but esters, too—surprising for a Scottish ale—with the chocolate malts offering a bit of roasty balance. A creamy, supple beer with a hint of warmth for those long, cold winters.

HARVIESTOUN OLA DUBH (12-, 16-, 18-, 30-, and 40-year-old)

LOCATION: Alva, Scotland

MALT: Pale, roasted barley, oats

HOPS: East Kent Golding, Fuggle, Galena

8.0% ABV, 45 IBU

There are actually five versions of Ola Dubh, but the difference among them is the age of the Highland Park whisky barrels in which they've matured. The base beer that goes into the barrels is something between an old ale and an imperial stout, with an original strength of 10% ABV. Harviestoun then chooses among five vintages of Scotch barrels—12, 16, 18, 30, and 40 years old. The younger barrels seem to contribute fewer whisky notes. The 12-year-old has notes of wood, pipe tobacco, and vanilla along with the rich chocolate of the beer, while the 30-year-old is thin and intensely whisky accented, sending the beer to the background. In the middle vintages, you might find notes of umami, sea salt, and an earthiness like mushroom or truffle.

Ola Dubh is Gaelic for "black oil," and the name is apt; all five versions are extremely rich and creamy, attaining a viscosity rarely found in beers.

WILLIAMS BROTHERS FRAOCH HEATHER ALE

LOCATION: Alloa, Scotland

MALT: Pale, caramel, malted wheat

HOPS: None

OTHER: Heather, bog myrtle (sweet gale)

5.0% ABV, 1.050 SP. GR., 0 IBU

If you wanted to wax poetic, you could say this is the taste of ancient Scotland. Long before hops came to Great Britain, brewers were making beer with local herbs. Heather beer is a tradition as old as Scottish brewing. Does Fraoch taste like that ancient brew? Unlikely. Made with modern barley (not bere, the native precursor to domestic barley) and wheat, it has a smooth softness characteristic of modern Scottish beers. But it is easy to see how heather and sweet gale might have delighted ancient palates. They offer a sweet, herbal, and slightly minty counterpoint to the malt.

WEE HEAVIES

TRAQUAIR HOUSE ALE

LOCATION: Innerleithen, Scotland

MALT: Pale, roast barley

HOPS: East Kent Golding

7.2% ABV, 1.066 SP. GR.

Traquair House has been making strong, elegant beers for decades and is principally responsible for making strong ales popular once again; Traquair's ales are stronger and deeper than most. House Ale is a woody, dark amber color that has a perfumy nose made entirely of malt with notes of caramel, raisins, and brown sugar. The body is smooth and rounded, but also crisp. This is a lush, lovely beer.

ORKNEY SKULL SPLITTER

○○

LOCATION: Orkney, Scotland

MALT: Pale, caramel, chocolate

HOPS: East Kent Golding

8.5% ABV

A nod to the bloody nickname for the Viking seventh earl of Orkney, Thorfinn Einarsson, "Skull Splitter" doubles as a reference to the boozy "crackskulls" of old. This is a manly ale that announces its heft in the boozy, fruity nose, and keeps you thinking of it as you find rum and plenty of warmth. Lots of complex esters—dates and figs, principally—and rich caramel treacle round out the beer.

AMERICAN SCOTCH ALES

ALESMITH WEE HEAVY

○○

LOCATION: San Diego, CA

MALT: Undisclosed

HOPS: Undisclosed

10.0% ABV, 1.096 SP. GR.

A merican Scotch ales provide a real acid test for a person's palate—rare is the person who is indifferent toward them. AleSmith's offering may be the best peace-maker between the two camps. While it's very heavy and sweet, it doesn't quite taste like smoked porridge in the way some do. There is a fresh baked-bread nose, which picks up some notes that transmute it to something approaching gingerbread. Peaty more than smoky, with a stout-like color and even a touch of licorice. With its tobacco head and hot-chocolate body, it is a most comely beer.

PIKE KILT LIFTER

○○

LOCATION: Seattle, WA

MALT: Pale, caramel, Munich, carapils, peat-smoked

HOPS: Magnum, Golding

6.5% ABV, 1.064 SP. GR., 27 IBU

A beer notable for its reserve, Kilt Lifter is not a thumping peat bomb, nor is it overly treacly. Although there is a bit of peat underneath the malt, this beer does a good job of nodding toward Edinburgh. The nose is almost like rye bread—a spicy, earthy breadiness, and on the palate, the deep amber beer is nutty and sweet.

FOUNDERS DIRTY BASTARD

○○

LOCATION: Grand Rapids, MI

MALT: Undisclosed

HOPS: Undisclosed

8.5% ABV, 50 IBU

A rare American version that plays it mostly straight, this nearly-brown ale is a caramel confection balanced by a hint of nuts. It's far thicker and creamier than Scottish examples, but a recogniz-able descendant of ales like those made at Traquair House.

Belhaven

CONTINUITY AND CHANGE

IF YOU HAD TO CHOOSE ONE BREWERY TO REPRESENT THE HISTORY OF SCOTTISH BREWING, YOU COULD DO A LOT WORSE THAN DUNBAR'S BELHAVEN, THE OLDEST BREWERY IN THE COUNTRY. THE SITE IS LOCATED NEAR BARLEY FIELDS AND SITS ON TOP OF EXCEPTIONAL WATER—TWO INGREDIENTS THAT HAVE FUELED SCOTTISH BREWERS FOR MILLENNIA. BENEDICTINE MONKS SETTLED THERE IN THE TWELFTH CENTURY, LATER BREWING AND DISTILLING WHISKY. JOHN JOHNSTONE BUILT THE FIRST COMMERCIAL BREWERY THERE IN 1719—HIS ORIGINAL BUILDINGS ARE STILL A PART OF BELHAVEN—AND HIS FAMILY ADDED AN ONSITE MALTINGS IN 1814. AFTER A FIRE IN 1887, THE NEW OWNERS EXPANDED THE BREWERY. THESE STRATA OF CONSTRUCTION AND CHANGE MAKE UP THE MODERN BELHAVEN BREWERY, THOUGH THE CHARACTERISTIC OLD MALTINGS WERE CONVERTED TO OTHER PURPOSES IN THE EARLY 1970S.

ABOVE:
A seal marks the brewery's age.

By the time Belhaven discontinued malting, the Scottish brewing industry was in complete crisis. Scores of breweries had gone out of business, and the remaining few were hanging on by their fingernails. Belhaven passed from family control in 1972, but did manage to stay independent and had the good fortune to hire George Howell, who became head brewer in the 1990s. In

ABOVE LEFT: *The new brewhouse stands out at the old brewery.*

ABOVE RIGHT: *The beautiful old mash tun is still on site.*

the twenty years that Howell has been at the brewery, annual production has risen from 29,000 U.K. barrels (which translates to 40,000 of the smaller U.S. barrels) to 130,000 barrels (180,000 U.S.). During that time, Belhaven has modernized and evolved, a clear reflection of the trends in Scottish brewing.

The flagship is Belhaven Best, a 3.2% beer sold cold and sparkling from a keg (not on cask). Scotland took to lagers decades before England, and cask ale was all but abandoned. Belhaven Best, nutty with malt yet crisp and effervescent, is a fusion of the past and present. It's the bestselling kegged ale in Scotland and brewer Howell is unambiguous about what it means to the brewery: "Without Belhaven Best, we would not be here." Best is a Scottish beer for Scottish drinkers.

If this seems miles removed from the idea Americans have of Scottish ales, that's because it is. Yet there's another side of Belhaven consisting of sessionable

"Scottish-style" ales: 80 Shilling, St. Andrews, Robert Burns Ale, and Scottish Ale. These can be found in bottles or on cask and they conform more to foreign expectations with their silky maltiness. I find a rainwater freshness in them, and sometimes even a hint of rose blossom. They are also closely in keeping with the standard pub ales found throughout the rest of the island—British ales in the British tradition.

Scottish brewers have never been insular in the way English brewers are; they export a substantial amount of beer and are sensitive to foreign markets. Belhaven is no different. They offer plenty of beers for foreign palates, including a stout, a wee heavy, and an IPA. Scottish Stout is a booming 7% ABV beer that has a lush depth of malt character and is hearty and creamy (and, truth be told, would be perfect on a dark, cold Dunbar night—too bad it's only sold abroad). Their Wee Heavy, robust by Scottish standards at 6.5% ABV, is thick and sticky. And their Twisted Thistle stands as one of the most hop-forward IPAs in Great Britain. One of the reasons I was drawn to Belhaven was the Twisted

Thistle, but Howell concedes that he prefers less hoppy beers. It's a Scottish beer for American drinkers.

Although these three spheres are aimed at three different constituencies, the beers are all quintessentially Scottish. They have Scottish pale malt as their base. The hops are principally British-grown Challenger and Golding. Many of their beers have a dab of sugar to give them a crisp finish. And they are fermented cool with a strain of yeast that's only about twenty years old— "Nobody knows precisely where that yeast came from," Howell admits. This is typical—Scottish beers aren't brewed to pick up esters. They're almost as lean and clean as lagers.

In 2005, the large English brewery Greene King bought Belhaven. Unlike many of Greene King's other acquisitions, Belhaven was targeted both for its facility and its health. It made strategic sense by giving both breweries access to pubs in the others' countries. With the recent shuttering of many Scottish breweries, the partnership has been crucial to keeping Belhaven in business. "I think that the truth of the matter is that without Greene King coming in, we might not be here," Howell says.

Unusually, Greene King left brewing operations in Dunbar. It looks like a wise decision: If Scottish breweries learned anything from the massive consolidation of the twentieth century, it's that "brands" alone don't sell beer locally. "I think it's very important to have a brewery in Scotland.

ABOVE: *Head brewer George Howell in the new brewhouse*

Scottish people are . . . patriotic, as are most people, yeah? It would not work for Belhaven Scottish products to be brewed down south and sold in Scotland."

In 2011, Belhaven built a new brewhouse and replaced its old mash tun and whirlpool. Since the country's historic preservation agency, Historic Scotland, would not allow substantial alterations to the venerable old building, the brewery created a gorgeous steel-and-glass structure in the courtyard next to the former brewhouse. Immediately behind the new space is the old stack where smoke once billowed blackly into the gray skies. It's a nice metaphor for a successful Scottish brewery: Modernization and adaptation are critical, but breweries can never forget where they came from.

Ales of the RHINE

KÖLSCH AND ALTBIER

Cologne and Düsseldorf. They are described as rivals, these two cities of the Rhine, and they make much of their competition. "We don't say the name of that town here," a smiling brewer from Cologne said of Düsseldorf. But no two cities are more like each other, or more different from every other great brewing city in the world. As it is hard to imagine a Picasso without a Matisse, it is hard to think that either of these two cities' brewing traditions could have been born in isolation.

STATISTICS

Altbier ABV range: 4.5–5.5%; bitterness: 25–50 IBU

Kölsch ABV range: 4.5–5.5%; bitterness: 15–30 IBU

Serving temperature: Kölsch 38°–45°F; Altbier 45°–50°F

Vessel: Cylindrical stange glass

Kölsch and Altbier.

The cities may be twins, but the famous ales of the Rhine are more cousins than brothers. Kölsches are delicate and balanced, with spicy hop tracery etched into the smooth, cookie-like malts. They were invented to compete with pilsners, but they don't mimic them. Altbier suggests an older style (*alt* means "old"), with darker, woodier malts and more insistent bitterness. But both have a minerality that adds to their crispness, and both have a refined smoothness that comes from having spent weeks in lagering tanks. Like many medium-alcohol lagers, kölsch and altbier make fine dinner companions.

ABOVE: *Schlüssel Brewery in Düsseldorf is one of many in the altstadt that beckons to visitors.*

In the remarkable *altstadt* (old town) of Cologne, you can spend days popping in and out of breweries and pubs—perhaps also spending an hour or two to visit the cathedral, museums, or river—and find in each one a waiter with a tray of identical cylinders of golden kölsch. In Cologne, every pub serves this beer, every brewery makes it, and you will have to look hard to find anything else.

Düsseldorf is just a half-hour north by train, and it too has a remarkable altstadt. There you'll find breweries and pubs stacked on top of one another, and you can spend days visiting them, too (though you might visit the river, museums, or go shopping in the Königsallee neighborhood). In the breweries and pubs of Düsseldorf, you'll see waiters with trays of identical cylinders of deep copper altbier. Every pub serves this beer, every brewery makes it, and you will have to look hard to find anything else. These rivals may not be identical twins, but fraternal, surely. ■

ORIGINS

HOPPY ALES are nothing new in northern Germany. It was, in fact, where they were born. Until sometime probably in the twelfth century, beer was still made exclusively with a spice mixture called *gruit*. Spices may have helped balance beer, but they didn't preserve it—and it was brewers in the Hanseatic trading city of Bremen who first realized that hops would. "Bremen beer" made its way to other German towns (some, like Hamburg, appropriated it), where other brewers learned what those from Bremen knew: Hopped beer would last longer than gruit beer, which survived only days before souring. Because it lasted longer than local beer, even when shipped from leagues away, Bremen beer made its way out into the world—to Scandinavia, the eastern Baltic, the Low Countries, and Great Britain. It sailed around the region, too. One of the destinations for Bremen beer was the towns along the Rhine, the region that would come in future centuries to be most associated with hops.

As hopped beers spread across what is now northern Germany, brewers started hearing about a kind of cold-aged beer made in Bavaria. Northern breweries experimented with it, but the climate was milder there and beer spoiled more easily. The danger of making bad beer was strong enough that in 1603, the Cologne town council outlawed the use of bottom-fermenting yeasts, codifying ale brewing. So while Bavaria developed lagering techniques, breweries in the north continued to make a dazzling constellation of different top-fermenting beers.

Early writers catalogued all the beers brewed in different towns in the north—scores of them. They ranged from low-alcohol beers mostly free from sourness to low-alcohol lactic beers to heavy, sweet beers, some alcoholic, some not. The beers that would become kölsch and altbier appear to have come from different lineages. The kölsch line is the clearer of the two. One of the main types of northern ales was *bitterbier* brewed in Westphalia and along the Rhine River. By the turn of the twentieth century, descriptions sound an awful lot like kölsch.

Altbier's history is a little more obscure. Almost every writer on the subject points to the word *alt* and the fact that ales predate lagers, and leaves it at that. Well, true—but that could be said for any of the German ales. Is modern alt's ancestor a darker version of the bitterbier that was brewed more prominently twenty-five miles to the south? Or is it more closely related to a heavy, alcoholic brown beer from Dortmund fifty miles to the east, also called altbier? That beer, which was at other times called *adambier*, was sour and more like English porters of the day. Even Münster, another forty miles north of Dortmund, had a local altbier. (That beer is a less likely ancestral candidate—it was also sour, but golden, and lightly hopped to boot. Three strikes against Münster.) The most likely reading is that "old beer" doesn't refer to style, just the broad category of pre-lager beers made throughout the region.

Kölsch and altbier have been beset by trying circumstances for well over a century. The first barbarian at the gate was lager, riding the exceptional success of pilsner and sweeping up from Bavaria. Ale's heyday ended around 1870, as *lagerbier* overtook it in terms of overall production. By the end of the century, not only were top-fermenting beers losing market share, they were actively in decline. The second unfortunate event was war. In World War II, both cities were targets of massive Allied bombing raids and reduced to rubble. After the war, brewers rebuilt, but kölsch and altbier were isolated styles and production steadily shrunk. In 1980, the two controlled over 10 percent of the German market, but by 2008, they had a mere 3 percent.

ABOVE: *Brauhaus Früh, just steps from the famous Dom, in Cologne*

One Beer to Rule Them All. Superficially, the idea that in Düsseldorf they drink altbier and in Cologne, kölsch, seems like a reasonable one. But if you think about it for longer than three minutes, the concept is insane. We live in a market economy; new is exalted, variety demanded. Yet walk into one of the atmospheric pubs in Cologne—it's true in Düsseldorf, too, but especially so in Cologne—and you are offered a binary choice: yes or no. The drink is kölsch and your communication to the waiter only involves a welcoming nod or abjuring shake of the head.

This is remarkable. The breweries of Cologne sell almost their entire production to people living within fifty kilometers of their mash tuns. They have to: Outside that tiny range (except for the very small amounts exported by a couple of the companies), people don't drink it. Equally as amazing: Within the kölsch heartland there are no intense rivalries between breweries, no tub-thumping for the "true" or "original" kölsch. The city maintains a virtuous symbiosis, a gentleman's agreement, and the brewers brew, and the drinkers drink, just one beer. Kölsch is king, but only in Cologne.

Although alt and kölsch are still widely available in their hometowns, breweries fret as they watch annual production decline. And this points to a bleak irony in the fates of these two beers. By being lashed firmly to the identity of their home cities, they managed to create a native base in which they could thrive for decades while other styles petered out. But now, as locals fail to drink enough to keep production up, brewers in Düsseldorf and Cologne have nowhere else to turn. The decline hasn't been helped by a national trend away from draft beer sales; both alt and kölsch depend on pub consumption (about half of all the sales, twice the national average) to keep barrelage stable. For obvious reasons, these trends worry breweries. ■

DESCRIPTION AND CHARACTERISTICS

I**N CITIES FEATURING** single styles of beer, breweries distinguish themselves by making their beers a little differently from the place down the road. Drinkers from other cities may lack the discernment to appreciate these differences, but they're there. In fact, altbier and kölsch allow for fairly broad interpretation.

KÖLSCH

At first glance, kölsches seem to be doing a fine pilsner impersonation: They're pale, clarion gold, and topped by a snowy head. Light-bodied as well, they're very easy to drink and go down with a clean, crisp finish. All quite pilsnery. There are subtle differences, though. They do have a bit of yeast character if you look for it, a fruitiness so delicate it's difficult to specificy—pear? Honeydew? In Cologne, the kölsches have a noticeable mineral, club-soda quality that heightens hopping and gives it an herbal twist. Whereas pilsners tend to dryness, in kölsch you find a softer, creamier center.

These are the general characteristics. In the particular, the breweries of Cologne take the three main elements—light hopping, soft, gentle fruitiness, and a crisp finish—and find their emphasis. Gaffel is not only the hoppiest, but the hops are the most distinctive, herbal with oregano and black pepper. Reissdorf, by contrast, plays more to malt sweetness. Früh has a tangy yeast that is almost lemony, and boasts the most assertive malt flavor. Pfaffen uses grassier hops, plays down the yeast, and produces the beer closest to pilsner.

Outside Cologne, interpretations are more varied, especially in the U.S. Many are stronger and hoppier, but also less delicately complex. American breweries often add a touch of wheat to their kölsches and lack the fidelity to clarity you find in Cologne.

ALTBIER

Alt appears to be a simple enough beer. Two or three kinds of malt, two or three types of hops, all put together in the usual way in the brewhouse and aged for a month in conditioning tanks. And yet, it is extremely hard to reproduce outside Düsseldorf. American breweries, adept at re-creating nearly any beer in the world, almost never do justice to altbier—I've had good and tasty American alts, just none that fooled me into thinking they were from Düsseldorf.

Alts are said to be a bitter style, but that's misleading. Their most important quality is actually the downy softness of the malt. True, hops buttress the malt, but they're not purely bitter. They instead spice alts with a woody, peppery flavor. As with kölsches, altbiers also have a mineral spine, a quality rarely reproduced outside the city since it's tied to the area's water source. I also found a caramel flavor that suggested the malt had been scorched by an open flame in a couple of the Düsseldorf alts. There can be quite a bit of variation in these elements, but the essence of the style is lost without them.

Kölsch-Konvention. In the mid-1980s, the breweries of Cologne gathered to discuss how to protect their business and promote the city's signature beer. What emerged from the Kölsch-Konvention was a mission statement of sorts—and is the reason kölsch is such a fixture now in Cologne. At the time there were twenty-four signatories to the charter, and they strictly defined kölsch as a pale, top-fermented beer. It must be "hop-accented" and filtered, brewed within a gravity range of 11° to 14° Plato (1.044 sp. gr. to 1.053 sp. gr.), and served in a 20 cl stange glass. Additionally, Kölsch must by law be brewed within the Cologne metropolitan area. After Germany joined the EU, kölsch was given a Protected Geographical Indication—a legal designation for products coming from a particular defined region that are made in a particular defined way. North Americans don't pay a lot of attention to the rules of appellation, but within Germany the only kölsches you'll find will have been brewed in the city of Cologne.

Three local alts offer a survey course in how breweries can emphasize different qualities of their beers while retaining their essential alt-iness. Schlüssel is the least hoppy of the three, the softest, and the one in which the crisp, hard water is most evident. Uerige is at the other end, with the most assertive hopping, no caramel, and only a touch of hard water. In the middle is Füchschen, the most caramelly but also lively in hopping. In each case, the softness of the malt is a constant. When re-creating alts, Americans take the idea of hopping too far. It's true that Düsseldorfers don't use late-addition hops, but that doesn't mean they're trying to give the beer too much bite. If you start from the place that alts must buff the tongue in cottony malts, the constraints on hopping are clear.

There is also a tradition of brewing stronger, special occasion alts as well. The most famous is Uerige's Sticke,

ABOVE: *At the Füchschen Brewery in Düsseldorf, you will find not only a caramelly, lively alt, but a cozy pub buzzing with activity.*

released just twice a year. That beer is a slightly stronger version of the regular alt, but what makes it special is a dose of Spalt hops in the conditioning tank that produce a bouquet redolent of a forest floor. Füchschen makes a special alt called Weihnachtsbier released on Christmas Eve, and Schumacher produces Latzenbier for release on just one day in March, September, and November. ■

BREWING NOTES

T HERE IS AN OPEN, vigorous debate about whether kölsches and alts are ales or lagers. Kölsch and alt are foremost *obergärige* beers, that is, top-fermented. In other countries, people refer to beers of this type as "ale," but Germans relate to their beers differently. With *obergärige* beers, brewers skim yeast off fermenters—the top-fermenting part. Germans relate to the yeast's behavior

more than its effect on beer, which is much subtler than elsewhere, where esters add baskets of fruit flavors and shakers of spice. For this reason, it used to be common to see these beers called *obergärige lagerbier*—top-fermented ales that have been conditioned, or lagered, in tanks. In their Teutonic manner, Germans have given it a perfectly precise term—but one that mostly confuses people from elsewhere. But things may be changing. At Reissdorf, brewer Frank Hasenkrug emphasized the fruitiness of the beer and when I mentioned the concept of a lagered ale, he disagreed: "It's an ale."

German ale brewers are used to being misunderstood. They can't affiliate their beers with the much fruitier ales from abroad, but neither do they agree with foreigners who think their beers are "lager-like." They do not use foreign ales or local lagers as benchmarks. Their beers are just as they should be—a touch fruity, soft, full, and refined. They get their fruitiness from warm fermentation, anywhere from about 62°F (Gaffel, Schlüssel) to 70°F (Uerige). These

The closest kin to kölsch, and very close it is, is the less-fruity Bavarian-style *helles*; the beers could easily be confused in a blind tasting. If you like hoppier kölsches, *German pilsners* are probably up your alley, but if you like them maltier, *American wheat ales* and *golden ales* might be worth a look. *Steam beer*, which like kölsch sits on the fence between ale and lager, is another good choice.

Altbiers have fewer very close relatives. *Bavarian dark lagers* and *amber lagers* have the maltiness, but they lack the hop character. *Brown ales* might do in a pinch if they're on the hoppy side, but browns have a lot of fruit altbier lacks.

temperatures aren't warm enough to produce vivid esters, but they are noticeable. Lagering, usually three to four weeks at near-freezing temperatures, helps keep German ales in check and allows the beers to develop their characteristic smooth, refined lines.

The malt bills are simple and straightforward—a base of pilsner malt with a dash of Munich to enhance the golden color in kölsch, and darker Munich or cara malts for color (but never roastiness) in alts. Some breweries sprinkle a dash of wheat into their grists—perhaps 10 percent. The hop schedule is no more complex—peppery German hops are favored, though some breweries use high-alpha varieties like Herkules in the bitter charge, while others prefer aroma hops throughout.

Water in Cologne and Düsseldorf is hard, and every kölsch and altbier I sampled that was brewed in those cities had a mineral stiffness. In some cases it was slight, but it is a definite marker of place. The best alts and kölsches rely on this quality to assist in the overall sense of crispness that is a hallmark of Rhineland ales. ■

ABOVE: *In Cologne, waiters carry handled trays with glass-size recesses.*

EVOLUTION

NEITHER OF THESE types of beers, fixed so firmly to the banks of the Rhine, would seem to be a likely candidate for production beyond their cities. For altbier that has definitely been the case. Only a handful of breweries outside Düsseldorf feature an alt as a regular part of their lineup, and it is rare to find in stores or pubs. Uerige has maintained a regular U.S. importer, but other brands are less reliable. Where American breweries have dabbled in alts, they tend to be boozier and hoppier—often referencing *sticke* beers, a stronger version of altbier.

Kölsch is another matter. For some reason, foreign breweries dabble in this style more often. There aren't a huge number of all-season, American-brewed kölsches out there, but many breweries release a version for the summer months. Goose Island, Harpoon, Alaskan, and Saranac all make well-known summer kölsches. A few breweries, like Schlafly, Coast, and Chuckanut, do offer them year-round. With very few exceptions,

The Drinking Ritual. The *hausbrauereien* (brewpubs) of Düsseldorf and Cologne are, to an American's eyes, colossal affairs. Some, like Früh or Schlüssel, have ballroom-size halls, while others, like Uerige, are honeycombed into smaller rooms that create a cozier vibe. In the evenings they begin filling up, and you may find yourself sharing a table with strangers. No matter—everyone's there for the same thing: beer. Food, maybe, but definitely beer.

The waiters in both towns are known as *köbessen*, and in Cologne they carry trays with stange-size recesses—reminiscent of communion trays. (Some *hausbrauereien* have stained-glass windows, which enhances the ecclesiastical feel.) Düsseldorf *köbessen* carry regular trays, but they're often packed densely with groves of slender little becher glasses (the same kind of glass, but—possibly to tweak Kölners—they're a little larger). In both cities, the ritual is the same. Once you order a beer, your *köbe* will keep an eye on your glass. Periodically, he'll make a pass through the room with a fresh tray. If your glass is less than a quarter full, he'll drop a fresh one on the table and tick your beer mat (coaster) with a line.

In Düsseldorf, the glasses are a quarter-liter, but they're only a fifth of a liter in Cologne. Some new arrivals take umbrage at the small portions, but it's not accidental. Both altbier and kölsch are delicate drinks, at their best when they're chilled to the right temperature and sparkling fresh. Over a session of drinking, you'll never be long with a warming, flattening beer—very soon a fresh, chilled, bubbling beer will arrive at your table. When you're ready to leave, you can place your beer mat on top of your final glass—though this isn't strictly necessary. Uerige's Michael Schnitzler said, "You can do this, or you can *talk* to the server. It's also a good way." Maybe so, but the ritual is what makes the experience so much fun.

breweries make kölsches straight up, with standard ingredients and at standard strengths and bitterness. Many brewers, having visited Cologne, want to honor and protect the tradition, so experimentation is the exception. ■

THE BEERS TO KNOW

RECOMMEND tracking down kölsches and altbiers brewed in their home cities—despite the rarity of these beers—as a first step in understanding them. That ineffable character that makes them kölsches and altbiers is rarely found outside the Rhineland. But many foreign-made examples are worth trying for their own sake.

ALTBIER

UERIGE ALT

○○

LOCATION: Düsseldorf, Germany

MALT: Pilsner, Cara-Munich, Carafa roast

HOPS: Spalt, Hallertauer Hallertau, Perle

4.7% ABV, "ALMOST 50" IBU

A frothy, fresh dark amber beer that vents largely the aromas of malt—wood and bread. Those aromas carry through in the taste as well, even though the sprightly German hops add a current of herbal spice stiffened by water minerals. It is rich but light, one of the most flavorful beers you'll find under 5% alcohol.

UERIGE STICKE

○○

LOCATION: Düsseldorf, Germany

MALT: Pilsner, Cara-Munich, Carafa roast

HOPS: Spalt, Hallertauer Hallertau, Perle

6.0% ABV

Sticke is not a huge departure from Uerige's regular altbier, but the dry-hopping adds quite a bit of aroma and seems to heighten the sense of bitterness as well. This is a beer Americans can love, with caramel malt richness, strength, and layered spicy hopping, all wrapped up in a soft pillow of malts. One of the world's great beers.

FÜCHSCHEN ALT

ooooooooooooooooooooooooooooooooooooooooooo

LOCATION: Düsseldorf, Germany

MALT: Undisclosed

HOPS: Undisclosed

4.5% ABV

Füchschen's alt is slightly lighter in color than Uerige's, and perfectly bright. Although the hops are less bitter, they frame the beer prominently and have a clean, noble-hop spiciness. Underneath, the malts are lightly sweet with caramel and rounded.

KÖLSCH

GAFFEL KÖLSCH

ooooooooooooooooooooooooooooooooooooooooooo

LOCATION: Cologne,
Germany

MALT: Undisclosed

HOPS: Undisclosed

**4.8% ABV, 1.044 SP.
GR., 26 IBU**

Gaffel is known as Cologne's hoppy kölsch, and it is the most bitter. But more than that, it is complex, with an aroma reminiscent of green herbs. The flavors tend toward oregano and black pepper, and they gather around the soft malts to deliver a satisfying, crisp finish. Americans, fond of bold tastes, tend to gravitate toward Gaffel.

FRÜH KÖLSCH

ooooooooooooooooooooooooooooooooooooooooooo

LOCATION: Cologne, Germany

MALT: Undisclosed

HOPS: Hallertau, Tettnang

4.8% ABV, 1.046 SP. GR., 18–25 IBU

While Gaffel may be the hoppiest kölsch, Früh has the most yeast character. It is a delicate, complex beer, with crisp, tangy yeast character and a flavor that bends toward lemon. The malts are sweetly bready, and although Früh's is a low-key kölsch, it may be the most accomplished.

REISSDORF KÖLSCH

ooooooooooooooooooooooooooooooooooooooooooo

LOCATION: Cologne, Germany

MALT: Pilsner, Munich

HOPS: Herkules,
Perle

4.8% ABV

Reissdorf, the most readily available kölsch in the United States, is a mild (that is, less hoppy) version. Reissdorf finds balance among the elements of gently sweet malt notes, mineral crispness, and light hopping. The elements are best appreciated when you can enjoy

three or four stanges. Sadly, kölsches don't travel especially well, and their liveliness is often lost during shipment across the Atlantic.

DOUBLE MOUNTAIN KÖLSCH

LOCATION: Hood River, OR

MALT: Pilsner, Munich

HOPS: Perle

5.2% ABV, 40 IBU

Double Mountain more or less plays this beer straight—German malts and Perle hops—and many of the elements even create a kölsch-like balance. The crisp, grain-y malts support a subtle fruitiness and harmonize wonderfully with the black pepper spice of the hops. But there's no mistaking which country

it was brewed in—each one of these flavors is American-bold, especially the bitterness.

SAINT ARNOLD FANCY LAWNMOWER

LOCATION: Houston, TX

MALT: Pale, malted wheat

HOPS: Hallertau

4.9% ABV, 1.045 SP. GR., 20 IBU

One of the American brews that most closely resemble those from kölsch's home city, Fancy Lawnmower has a light graininess and dry crispness that reminds me of Cologne's minerally water. The hops are floral but have a hint of lemongrass. An excellent kölsch if you can't manage the trip to Germany.

German Cask Ale? In both Düsseldorf and Cologne you are liable to see kölsch and altbier served from a cask sitting on top of the bar. In some cases, the cask will even be wooden (especially in Düsseldorf). But don't be fooled—this is more a matter of presentation than preparation. Uerige's owner, Michael Schnitzler, described the practice: "It is just the traditional style of presenting the beers in a nice way. We tap it manually and then we put the barrel on the bar. . . . But there is no fermentation; there is nothing for the taste." The beer stays in the casks only a short time, and the wooden barrels are lined so the contents aren't exposed to either wood or oxygen.

Nevertheless, people take the barrels very seriously. All the wooden casks at Uerige are bound in metal bands painted red. This wasn't always the case; Uerige used to have some that had green and yellow bands. Over time, customers developed the idea that the beer from barrels with a red band was superior. "Nobody knows why," Schnitzler said, laughing. "The regular customers, they saw the barrels with the green ring on it and said, 'Oh no, we cannot drink this one.'" Uerige had to paint them all red.

Hausbrauerei Uerige

THE "ALT" IS FOR OLD

NAME A BREWERY THAT STILL USES A COOL SHIP, A BAUDELOT-STYLE DRIP CHILLER, AND OPEN FERMENTATION, AND SERVES ITS BEER FROM WOODEN CASKS AT THE BREWERY. NOW, NAME THE BREWERY IN GERMANY THAT DOES ALL THOSE THINGS. UNTIL MY EYES FEASTED ON THESE WONDERS, I WOULDN'T HAVE BELIEVED IT MYSELF, BUT THERE IS SUCH A PLACE AND YOU CAN VISIT IT THE NEXT TIME YOU'RE IN DÜSSELDORF. THE BREWERY IS ENTWINED IN A GORGEOUS, LABYRINTHINE PUB THAT WRAPS ITSELF INTO NOOKS AND POCKETS AROUND THE FERMENTERS, BREWHOUSE, AND OTHER EQUIPMENT. THERE ARE HOP WREATHES ON THE WALLS, STAINED GLASS OVER THE WINDOWS, WOODEN CASKS ON THE COUNTER, AND SCORES OF PEOPLE SITTING WITH SMALL GLASSES OF ALT IN FRONT OF THEM. EXCEPT FOR THE ODD CELL PHONE GLOWING IN THE SHADOWS, WITH A VISIT TO UERIGE YOU COULD BE STEPPING BACK IN TIME.

ABOVE: *The vessel used to cool wort at Uerige—the first step in their traditional brewing process*

It's surprising to learn that Uerige isn't all that old . . . for Germany. It dates only to 1862, when a brewmaster named

Wilhelm Cürten bought the property and converted it from a wine tavern into a brewery. Cürten was apparently not much of a people person, leaving the brewery only on Sundays for church. They called him "grumpy Wilhelm," and the name stuck—in the local dialect, the word for grumpy was *uerige*. (Pronunciations vary, but locals seem to start out with a sound halfway between *oor* and *err* that comes out in a long exclamation, followed by a half-voiced, short *i* as in *pick,* and a clipped *guh* to finish things off.) The brewery passed through four more owners until Christa and Josef Schnitzler bought the place in 1976. The Schnitzler family still runs Uerige, though it is Weihenstephan-trained son Michael who now guides activities.

The surprises continue when you learn that the brewery has recently been expanded and that Schnitzler added a distillery. Of course, the expansion only added capacity to the brewery, and the whiskies come from Uerige's own beer recipes. Schnitzler is not averse to changing his business, but the beer is sacrosanct. In Germany, "we lost the beer tradition," he told me. "We lost the typical way of brewing. Altbier—it means it is brewed in an old way, the traditional way."

Uerige takes tradition more seriously than nearly any brewery in the world. It still only brews one kind of beer, though it does have unfiltered and stronger variations. The process is uncomplicated but precise. The grist includes just three malt varieties, and the brewery adds two hop additions early in the boil, a blend of Hallertauer Hallertau, Spalt, and Perle hops. Only whole hops, of course—the traditional way. From the kettle, the wort goes on a strange journey back in time.

ABOVE: *The Schnitzler family has owned Uerige since Christa and Josef purchased it in 1976. Now their son Michael runs the show.*

The first stop is the wide, flat, cool ship where it will spend an hour to an hour and a half, depending on the ambient temperature. The boiling wort will cool to about 122°F in the winter and 150°F in the summer. Since that's far too warm for yeast, the wort spends another hour and a half dripping over undulating stacks of pipes running with cold water. When it finally collects in the fermenters, it is 68°F, perfect for fermentation.

The incredibly efficient Uerige yeast needs only a day in the open fermenters. I understand this has always been the case, but I wonder if the new fermentation room, lit like a nightclub with blue light to fascinate pubgoers, energizes the yeast. Perhaps because of its efficiency, the yeast produces little in the way of fruity esters even at moderately warm fermentation temperatures. But it is in the conditioning tanks, where the beer rests at icy temperatures for a month, that altbier achieves its elegance and smoothness.

ABOVE: *A visit to Uerige feels like traveling back in time.*

Uerige makes an unfiltered version of its regular alt; it is softer and seems to have even more flavor. The real rarity, though, is its Sticke, a beer wreathed in myth. The name, another word from the local dialect, means "secret." The brewery's Marie Tetzlaff explained it to me when we were sipping Sticke from the conditioning tank. "The word *sticke* means that the brewer in the tradition has made stronger beer—but secretly. It's kind of a verb that means to do something behind someone's back. Maybe he put more hops and more malt to make it stronger beer, but the people [weren't sure]. So they said, 'Ah, the brewer did something *sticke*, secret.'" There's a second meaning, which relates to the beer's release. It only comes around twice a year, and originally, the brewery didn't announce when it would be on tap. It was a way to thank regulars and give them something special. Now Uerige announces the dates (the third Tuesdays in January and October) and people flock from not only around Düsseldorf, but from all over the world.

Sticke and an even stronger beer called Doppelsticke are made the same way as the regular alt with two exceptions: They are lagered much longer—eight to ten weeks for Sticke, up to twenty weeks for Doppelsticke—and dry-hopped. This last feature makes Sticke even more rare because dry-hopping is not fully kosher according to the rules of *Reinheitsgebot*. But alt is an ale, a different beast— *Reinheitsgebot* was originally a Bavarian law regulating lagers—and dry-hopping Sticke makes it a spicily aromatic beer. After I had sampled the Sticke, brewer Sebastian Degen found some Doppelsticke in the tank that was nearly ready to bottle. It was a hugely creamy beer but more floral than the regular Sticke. At 8.5% ABV, it took the chill out of the cold conditioning room.

I had such a wonderful time visiting the pubs and breweries of Düsseldorf that I wondered how business was. Everywhere we went, pubs were bursting with patrons, even in the cold of October. Michael Schnitzler did not mince his words. "In general, the altbier is in bad condition. The former biggest Düsseldorf breweries, they started twenty or thirty years ago to quit brewing in the town. . . . [Real estate] prices are so high that everyone says, 'Come on, it's not [worth it] to sell beer. Let's put it out to rent.' So the breweries were sold to Warsteiner, Anheuser-Busch. So where is the *echte Düsseldorfer brauerei*, the real Düsseldorf brewery? That's the problem everywhere."

Well, not everywhere. Just off the Rhine River, on Burger Strasse in the altstadt is one *echte brauerei* that still keeps the tradition.

Belgian ALES

ny serious explorer into the world of beer
eventually has to contend with the complex world
of Belgian ales. They reside, like exotic creatures
in a dense rain forest, in their own realm, far from their
sedate, civilized cousins in nearby Germany and Britain.
No country has so many native beer styles, nor has been as
tenacious at holding on to them through the industrial age.

Centuries ago, breweries would make a beer typical
of their town, one different from those brewed at the next
town over. Modern Belgian
beers are visible inheritors
of that tradition and even
today, more indigenous
varieties manage to
persist in a country the
size of Maryland than
in any other. Some are
sour, some strong,

Belgian Ales. It is absolutely correct
to say that Belgian ales are so diverse as to defy easy
description. Some are light in color and alcohol while
others are black and boozy. Some are made with
spices, some with fruit; some are sour as lemons,
some sweet as candy. And yet, and yet . . . there's
something about Belgian ales that unites them. It
usually has to do with some combination of these
elements: light body, low bitterness, and a distinctive
yeastiness that may express itself as spicy, fruity,
or funky. "Belgian" can even be used as an adjective
to describe a beer that is just a little off center. If it
doesn't fit into any other national tradition, people
may assume it belongs to the Belgians.

Like Scottish ales (starting on page 213),
these beers are too varied to codify, hence the
absence of statistics here.

some dark; some are made by commercial brewers, some by Catholic monks. Some are made of wheat, many use spices. Most are defined by a quality that comes from the yeast—a spiciness, fruitiness, or funkiness—that has made the word "Belgian" an adjective of character as much as region. They are so varied that it takes some time to find your bearings, but explore Belgian ales long enough, and you may find other beers look a little monochromatic by comparison. ∎

ORIGINS

HOW DID A tiny country that didn't even gain independence until 1830 manage to avoid having its beer tradition subsumed by a dominant neighbor? How did Belgium become the one country with such quirky diversity and enduringly native styles? This is one of the central curiosities of a very curious beer country.

It started with a Belgian love for beer. The Greek historian Diodorus Siculus had written that they "make a drink out of barley which they call zythos or beer." Writing later, Athenaeus described it more precisely as a wheat beer made with honey. Even Julius Caesar encountered and admired the pastoral Belgae tribes, calling them the "bravest of the three peoples" of Gaul. (He was forced to admit that bravery may not have been associated solely with wine-drinking societies.)

The Romans were just the first foreign power to seize the cities of what would become Belgium as part of their empire. Many others followed, and the history of Europe is written fairly well on the land between Antwerp and the Ardennes. Belgium had the distinction of hosting armies from some of Europe's most famous conquerors: Following Caesar, it saw Napoleon and Hitler, not to mention dozens of minor lords and nobles across the centuries.

Through it all, a familiar pattern emerged: The cities of what would become Belgium flourished, empire after empire. Ghent was at one time the second-largest

RIGHT: *Belgian breweries often have wonderful steampunk gadgets like this.*

FACING PAGE: *The view of Bruges, possibly the world's prettiest good-beer city, from the iconic bell tower just south of the Grand Place*

city in Europe (after Paris), and Bruges, Leuven (or Louvain), and Brussels thrived at various times as well. Antwerp's port was and remains one of Europe's largest. When the region was under the control of the House of Burgundy in the fifteenth century, Philip III, Duke of Burgundy, chose to live in Brussels and Bruges rather than France. Mary of Burgundy, whose marriage to the Archduke Maximilian caused the Low Countries to fall under Hapsburg control, is buried in Bruges. (Mary is celebrated by Brouwerij Verhaeghe in their delightful Flanders tart ale, Duchesse de Bourgogne.) So while Belgium finally became an independent state in 1830, it was a relatively stable place for the rise and maintenance of certain cultural traditions—including brewing beer.

After those early Roman references, the historical record went silent about brewing until monks began to write about it again in the eighth and ninth centuries, as ecclesiastical power grew across Europe. Monasteries flourished during the period

and maintained lives of self-sufficiency. They grew their own barley (and later, hops) and made beer to serve themselves and visitors. Records show that some of their breweries were immense operations for the day, able to produce as much as a modern craft brewery.

Unfortunately for us, only scant references to Belgian beers describe their subsequent evolution between the ninth and nineteenth centuries. Stray observers did make oblique references, so we know that Belgians brewed with wheat, oats, and spelt in the late Middle Ages. This conforms well to an extensive survey of Belgian beer by a brewer named Georges Lacambre (sometimes rendered La Cambre) whose *Traité Complet de la Fabrication des Bières* was the first serious treatment of traditional Belgian brewing. Lacambre worked at a brewery in Leuven in the 1830s and his work expanded on writings done earlier in the century by two men, J. B. Vrancken and Auguste Dubrunfaut. What this book, first published in 1851, details is an absolutely extraordinary world of brewing—great diversity on the one hand, with village-by-village variation, and inconceivably baroque brewing methods on the other.

Lacambre catalogued around twenty different types of beer (he found many more, but only wrote about the "major" ones). Of these only three specifically called for all-barley recipes. Breweries used oats in more than half the styles, and wheat even a little more often. They used spelt more rarely, but it was the basis for at least one style of beer. The tax laws encouraged them to use strange mashing practices, but this was hardly the only methodological oddity. For *bière blanche de Louvain* (wheat beer of Leuven), Lacambre had to spend six paragraphs describing the mashing regime, which required five vessels, baskets and pans to strain and spoon out wort, and "eight to ten strong brewers" to manage the ordeal.

Boil length was just as shocking. The *average* boil was nine hours. Only four of the beers Lacambre mentioned had boils of three hours or less, and five were more than ten hours; the longest was twenty hours (!). In some cases, the long boils were intended to darken the wort; for dark beer styles, this was a mark of wholesomeness. But the breweries had a cheat—they added the mineral lime if they wanted to save some time and darken the wort artificially, a practice of which Lacambre rightly disapproved ("very detrimental to the interests and even the health of consumers").

Finally, a key to the character of all the beers was the way in which they were cooled. Instead of using cold water chillers, as was the practice in Britain, breweries left the beer overnight in wide, flat vessels known as "cool ships." This is still the way lambics are made, and we now know that wild yeasts inevitably infect wort cooling over the course of hours. In most cases, breweries would also pitch yeast into the cooled beer before racking it to casks. But it didn't matter—the beer was already inoculated. The consequence of this is implicit in Lacambre's description of beer that was aged any time at all—it was dry and sour from those yeasts.

Nineteenth-Century Belgian Taxes. One of the keys to understanding Belgium's ales is a bizarre nineteenth-century tax law. Rather than levy a fee based on the amount of beer produced or the strength of the beer, the government tax was assessed on the size of a brewery's mash tun. This is one of those cases in which a single law had a profound effect on the development of beer. The way breweries responded, of course, was to use tiny mash tuns—no matter how much beer they were brewing. To get some kind of efficiency out of their wee tuns, brewers used extremely thick mashes; after they had packed as much grain as they could inside, it left little room for water. As a consequence, breweries had to draw their mash water off and add new water to the grain bed several times for every batch. The legacy of this law is still evident in the turbid mashes lambic makers use.

Beers of Nineteenth-Century Belgium.

One wishes there were more historical tour guides like Georges Lacambre. A working brewer, he was not without prejudices and opinions. He discredited certain styles of beer—some he even admitted were renowned—and offered biting commentary about the methods of other brewers. But this lack of objectivity makes for lively and engaging reading. Following are a few of the old beers he described.

UYTZET (UITZET) One of the famous beers Lacambre derided, *uytzet* came in two strengths, ordinary (about 4% ABV) and double (6% ABV). "*Uytzet* is an amber beer, fairly dark yellow, and is very good quality when well-prepared, but ordinary *uytzet* usually has a characteristically dry and more or less sharp taste."

FLEMISH BROWN BEER This is the beer boiled up to twenty hours; it's similar to *uytzet* but darker. Locals loved it, and for this reason Lacambre begrudgingly admitted it might be an acquired taste. For his purposes, though, it was "far from being very pleasant indeed, for it is bitter, harsh, and astringent." Its descendants are still made in Flanders.

LEUVEN *BIÈRE DE MARS*, *ENKEL GERST*, AND *DOBBEL GERST* The beers Lacambre made himself, and it's no shock to learn that he thought they were the best. They were made from all-barley grists and divided into four runnings of the same mash. The first two made dobbel gerst, the final two *bière de Mars*, with *enkel gerst* being a blend of all four.

WHEAT BEER OF LEUVEN (*bière blanche de Louvain*) This beer went through an inordinately long and convoluted mash regime, but Lacambre seemed to like it. He described Leuven wheat beer as light and refreshing—something like a cross between lambic and witbier.

PEETERMAN This beer style survived into the 1960s, but based on Lacambre's description, one wonders how. It was similar to Leuven wheat beer, but brown and made with gelatin usually taken from fish skin. Tasty! Lacambre: "viscous, dark brown, and has a slightly penetrating and aromatic bouquet." Aromatic indeed.

BIÈRE DE DIEST This was a strong golden ale that, from Lacambre's description, sounds delicious: "Its creamy flavor is slightly sweet and has something honey-like that is highly sought after by connoisseurs, among which we must count the majority of women and especially wet nurses who [are looking to] find a drink that is comforting and nutritious."

MECHELEN BROWN BEER Another possible precursor to the tart ales of Flanders.

HOEGAARDEN BEER From Lacambre's description, this sounds very much like a lambic. Unlike lambic, though, it was served fresh, not aged, apparently to great effect. Lacambre: "This beer is very pale, refreshing and strongly sparkling when it is fresh; its raw taste has something wild that is similar to the Leuven beer it resembles in many ways."

LIÈGE SAISON A beer often made largely of spelt and aged from at least four months up to two years. Lacambre didn't like the brewing methods and seemed to regard this as a crude beer whipped up by bumpkins. He said that in the summer, the poor drinkers in Liège drank "more bad beer than good."

THE 20TH CENTURY

The world wars were difficult for Belgium—particularly the first. Belgium was ground zero for fighting, where some of the biggest battles took place, and where trenches scarred the countryside. The Germans systematically collected all the copper in the country for the war effort—to this day, no kettles date to before about 1920. Belgium rationed grain, and already-low gravities fell even further. After World War I, brewing rebounded and beers returned to form. Gravities recovered and beer quality improved. Things took another dive in the Second World War, when under German occupation, Belgians endured food and fuel rations. But after the war, the brewing industry again rebounded and brewers started making beer as they always had.

By the 1950s, many of the styles Lacambre described still had a presence. Writing a hundred years after Lacambre, Jean De Clerck, a brewing professor at the University of Louvain, made another extensive survey of the world of brewing in *A Textbook of Brewing* (1957). Among the styles he lists are many of those mentioned by Lacambre—*blanche de Louvain,*

Peeterman, Diest, *uytzet,* Antwerp barley beer, Hoegaerde, and Liège saison, to name a few. These "old-fashioned" beers were still made in shockingly old-fashioned, complex ways (it took seventeen hours to complete the mash for Peeterman). Sadly, he was recording the last days of many of these styles. Lagers and modern ales were making an assault on the market, and funny little country breweries could no longer stay in business by putting out rustic and wild nineteenth-century beer. They may have outlasted the wars, but they couldn't survive a modernized brewing market.

Frank Boon, maker of the eponymous lambic (see pages 510–513), came from a family of brewers and recalled this period from his youth:

In the 1950s and 1960s, breweries were closing and all the local styles were disappearing everywhere in Belgium. Leuven white disappeared, Peeterman disappeared, *uytzet* disappeared. I remember my uncles said that in the summer they could keep their beer for two weeks. Midsize breweries had beer that could keep one month or six weeks. In the 1960s, Stella Artois was the first to make beer that could keep for six months. Consumers switched to cheaper and technically better beer. In every village and small town, brewers said, "The only thing we can do is sell the brewery. There is no future for small breweries."

The Drinking Ritual.

The way a country consumes its beer offers subtle clues to the kind of beer it produces. In the United States, for example, the overwhelming majority of people buy their beer by the case and slug it back straight from the can. The overwhelming majority of beer is consequently made to enter the stomach by attracting as little of the tongue's attention as possible on its way down.

The way Belgians serve beer reflects the country's more refined approach: They savor each sip of their fine national beverage. When you order beer in a beer café, the waitress will bring you the bottle of beer along with a glass made specially for that beer. (Belgian ales are almost all bottle-conditioned, and therefore sold in bottles.) She will decant it for you into the glass, pouring it at a rate to ensure the perfect, pillowy head. She will stop pouring with a half inch of beer remaining (the portion that will have become clouded by roused yeast) and place the bottle next to the glass, rotating it so you may inspect the label. In Belgium, drinking a glass of beer is a sensual experience. The way the beer is made, the color and carbonation, the glassware—all these things are optimized to delight the eyes, nose, and tongue.

As was the case in every other country in the world, consolidation hit Belgium hard. The country had well over 3,000 breweries in 1900, a number that dwindled to less than a thousand by the middle of the century. Most countries hit their low points in the 1970s, but Belgium's came in the 1990s, when there were just 115 breweries left. In the end, Belgium was left with two titans and a scattering of small family breweries.

The largest of the titans was Interbrew, a company that started to dominate the Belgian market in 1987 when Artois merged with Piedboeuf (makers of Jupiler). Soon after, Interbrew acquired Labatt, Bass, Whitbread, and Beck's. Ultimately, it would merge with Brazil's AmBev and finally take over Anheuser Busch to become InBev, the world's largest brewing conglomerate.

RIGHT: *The Gauloise was the first beer brewed by du Bocq, in 1858.*

Hoegaarden, Leffe, Belle-Vue, Jupiler, and Stella Artois are all owned by InBev, and their pubs can be found everywhere from the Brussels airport and beyond. The

world headquarters are now located in Leuven.

At one point InBev (then Interbrew) controlled 70 percent of the Belgian market, but that figure has receded to below 60 percent due to the rise of a rival, Heineken. The Dutch giant entered the Belgian market forcefully in 2000 with acquisitions of Affligem and Alken-Maes, bringing a number of major brands under its portfolio: Grimbergen, Maes Pils, Ciney, and Hapkin. These compete for pub space with the InBev juggernaut, an arms race that smaller breweries simply can't begin to match.

The Belgian beer industry is now in a moment of transition. The international craft beer movement has pumped a little life into the market, but the number of Belgian breweries remains near historic lows. Meanwhile, InBev and Heineken have successfully concealed the provenance of many of their brands—making it harder for small ale brewers to compete locally. As a countervailing trend, the rest of the world has awakened to the genius of Belgian beers. The export market is keeping many small breweries afloat, but the erosion of the home market is troubling. InBev and Heineken will attempt to consolidate as much of the market as they can, but Belgian consumers are fond of their local brands. The next decade will be crucial for the future of Belgium's beers. ■

DESCRIPTION AND CHARACTERISTICS

BELGIAN BEERS COME in a spectrum of colors and strengths, though they're not fixed. There is constant churn and change, as trends drive producers in one direction for a time before they set off in a different direction a decade or three later. Old-timers lament the loss of traditional styles or what they claim is a dumbing-down of certain famous brands, and no doubt that happens—but they ignore how other old brands have spruced themselves up and how new breweries have helped usher in new styles. In Belgium, change is the constant.

Over the decades, Belgian ales have gotten more potent and lighter in color. Among the most popular styles now are blond or golden ales—a minority even a generation ago—and of these, there are silky, potent tipples that rival wine in strength. Hops are making a comeback, and many breweries have embraced organic brewing. But these are broad contours; Belgium is proud to tout a thousand different brands, and dozens of them are beyond the reach of style taxonomists.

What should you expect in a Belgian ale? Their reputation for quirkiness has scared off a good many beer fans, but this is largely misplaced. The sour ales are generally an acquired taste, but most Belgian ales are quite approachable. Here are four things to look for.

■ **Fermentation characteristics.** Belgian beers are fermented warm, a practice that produces interesting phenols (spicy) and esters (fruity and spicy). It is a nearly ubiquitous practice in Belgium to referment beers in the bottle, and this enhances those qualities.

■ **Light body.** Sugar is a very common ingredient. Breweries use it to thin the body, boost alcohol percentage, and balance low-hop beers with crispness.

■ **Strength.** Belgian ales run the full spectrum of strength, but no country has so many beers tipping the scale above 7% ABV.

■ **Spices.** Belgium's reputation for spicing is overblown; they are employed in a relatively small minority of beers. The nature of Belgian ale is one of fruitiness and spiciness; the addition of actual spices enhances this character. In some cases breweries don't even mention they've added them. The key to a Belgian ale depends less on whether actual spices are used than on how well the fruity, spicy notes express themselves.

AMBER AND BLOND ALES

Amber ales date back centuries in Belgium and were once a much larger part of the brewing scene than recent-arriving blonds. For centuries Belgians did not

Reading a Belgian Beer Label. Belgian beer labels may contain descriptions in English, French, or Flemish. Here's a handy reference of what they're telling you.

FLEMISH	ENGLISH	FRENCH
hergist in de fles	bottle-conditioned	*sur lies*
kruiden	spices	*épices*
gerst	barley	*orge*
mout	malt	*malt*
tarwe	wheat	*blé*
hop	hops	*houblon*
suiker	sugar	*sucre*
gist	yeast	*levure*
kriek/krieken	cherries	*cerises*
frambozen	raspberries	*framboises*

covet blond ales—even after breweries knew how to make pale malts. Deeper colors of amber and brown were the sign that a beer had been boiled a good long time and caramelized during the process—qualities prized in a beer. There are still several classic examples around, like De Koninck Amber, Dubuisson's venerable (and powerful) Ambrée, and Caracole's rustic flagship, also called Caracole. This group gives you a sense of how broadly this category can range, too. De Koninck's beer is a mere 5.2% ABV and has a lightly malty palate enlivened by gentle fruity esters. Caracole's more rustic version is a hearty 7.5% ABV, and has a spicy bouquet mixed with wild strawberry esters and a bit of dry tang from the yeast. Dubuisson's ale (sold as Scaldis Amber in the U.S.) is a booming 12% ABV with tons of nutty malt and alcohol warmth.

The lager wave was very late in hitting Belgium, arriving only in the 1960s, but when it did, very pale ales were the ale brewers' response. It's safe to say that the most important early pale ale was made by Moortgat. The brewery's flagship beer, Duvel (pronounced

DEW-vul), had for decades been a more traditional amber. In 1970, Moortgat decided to follow the market and lighten its beer. Working with Jean De Clerck, the scientist who consulted with Chimay, Rochefort, and Orval, the brewery transformed Duvel into a luminous golden ale. The name is derived from the Flemish word for "devil" and long predates the current incarnation; nevertheless, the beer's incredible silkiness, balance, and Champagne-like effervescence today make the name more apt than ever. The devil's power is his sneakiness, his ability to corrupt before the sinner knows he's sinned. At 8.5% ABV, Duvel drinks like it's half that, and more than a few people have been seduced to drink too much.

It is a huge credit to Moortgat that the blond they settled on is so rich in esters and hop character. Duvel illustrated to other breweries the possibilities in blond beers—and over the decades, they've had great fun reinventing the wheel. Blond beers are now legion, but some high-water marks include an amazing "session" blond by the monks of Westvleteren (it's 5.8%), which has a touch of handmade rusticity. Dupont's reputation within Belgium rests on their Moinette, one of the oldest pales in the country. A lighter blond that has zest and character is Brugse Zot from De Halve Maan. In the United States, Ommegang's Belgian Pale Ale is a spritzy, hoppy treat. These give a sense of the

LEFT: *The writing is on the wall—the Flemish translates to "Shhh, here ripens the Duvel." As Duvel is a reference to the devil, it has a darker sense as well.*

broad range of what a blond or amber can be in Belgium—weak to strong, sweet to hoppy, they're all part of the family.

BROWN ALES

Brown ales were once highly prized across Flemish-speaking Belgium. Decades ago, they all had something of the character that the tart ales of Flanders—Rodenbach, Liefmans, Verhaeghe—still have. But modernity allowed breweries to escape souring microorganisms, and browns evolved into hearty, often very strong beers not totally unlike British stouts and porters. Brown ales are not as popular as they once were, but they remain an important part of Belgium's heritage.

One of the touchstone browns is Du Bocq's Gauloise Brune, its evocation of "*la bière de nos ancêtres*"—the ancient beers of Belgium. Du Bocq has brewed the beer since 1858, but has changed the recipe. Some old hands criticize Du Bocq for bowdlerizing Brune, but it still has a lot of character, with bread, roastiness, and rummy burned sugar all working in harmony. Perhaps Du Bocq's critics aren't satisfied with a beer that's only 8.1%—maybe they cotton more to the likes of Caracole's Nostradamus, a 9.5% spicy

ABOVE: *Caracole's Nostradamus is a spicy 9.5% ABV.*

behemoth. You can't blame them—it's a wonderful warmer for the winter months.

A classic of the style is the flagship from Het Anker, Gouden Carolus, leaning much more toward sweetness than some examples. As a contrast, one of the best examples is a lightweight, Kerkom Bink Bruin (just 5.5% ABV). It has, nevertheless, a deep cacao character and a biscotti-dry finish. These beers share some qualities but show that disparate elements like spice (Caracole), roast (Gauloise Brune), and sweetness (Gouden Carolus) are all

Abbey Road. The monastic tradition is an important one in Belgium and has inspired a number of nonmonastic imitators. Two of the most important abbey ale styles are tripel, which is similar to Duvel, and dubbel, a type of brown ale. Those beers are not actually different from the blonds and browns discussed here, but they have a rich tradition all their own. As such, they are treated to a separate chapter (Abbey Ales, starting on page 297).

A Warning About Belgian Beer Styles. Belgian

beer is hard to classify. A few styles have extremely rigid definitions; these protect the traditional production methods of beers like gueuze and the tart ales of Flanders. A few other clusters of beer are tight enough to conform to style—beers like witbier, tripel, and saison (all of which are treated separately in this book). Far more fall into a netherworld of stylistic no-man's-land, and for these, it's best to abandon the framework of style altogether. The beers may have designations that suggest taxonomy—blond, brown, pale ale, and so on—but they're mirages. Breweries use them to distinguish their own beers, to give the customer a general sense of what to expect, or for reasons inscrutable to the casual observer. They aren't indicative of actual styles as the rest of the world understands them.

Indeed, Belgian breweries tend to think of their beers as singular creations, wholly original and uncategorizable—or at the very least they try to get you to think so. This impulse toward individuality makes it very hard to group them in meaningful ways, but it is possible to group them into broader categories.

---

part of the brown ale lineage. Bink Bruin shows they don't have to be boozy, either.

BIÈRES DE NOËL AND SPICED ALES

Europeans all share the tradition of making special beers for the dark months of winter, and especially festive ales for the holidays. In Belgium, these beers are among the most highly anticipated, and a recent tally put the number of offerings at close to a hundred—in a country with only 130 breweries. Belgians love their *bières de Noël.*

Although it's not uncommon for breweries to tuck spices into their regular ales, Christmas beers almost demand it. They're a good example of how adept Belgians are at using spices to accentuate the esters and phenols their yeasts produce. Fans of St. Feuillien wait every year for their Cuvée de Noël, a quintessential winter ale. Dark and warming (it's 9%), it

marries winter spices (the brewery guards its recipe, but my palate detects ginger and cinnamon) with a roasty, chocolaty body. The stiff dose of alcohol provides warmth. Huyghe's Delirium Noël uses seven spices in a beer bursting with zesty fermentation characteristics that combine to create a somewhat dizzying wall of flavor.

Not all winter ales are spiced, though—some just suggest spicing with their yeast complexity. One of the finest brewed anywhere is De Dolle Brouwers' Stille Nacht, a light-colored ale with a bouquet of esters and an intense, long finish. Dubuisson Bush de Noël, sold as Scaldis in the United States, is another tremendous unspiced ale. It's amber-hued but no less powerful (12% ABV).

On the other hand, not all spiced beers are Christmas ales, either. Some styles call for spices (witbier), or use them to accentuate spicy yeast character (rustic ales), or use them as unidentifiable accents (as Rochefort does). Breweries like St.

Feuillien use them so skillfully in their ales that it is difficult to tell which element of the spicy flavor comes from the yeast and which comes from actual spicing.

HOPPY ALES

It is not wrong to characterize Belgium's beers as "sweet" relative to the beers of other countries. Most exhibit modest hop character—not much bitterness and only subtle contributions to flavor and aroma. This proclivity toward sweetness is partly a matter of tradition, and partly a reaction to sodas, which have taken a sizable chunk out of beer's market. It's also partly because Belgium's ales are brewed light with sugars that ferment out completely. Since hops can easily turn vicious in a beer with a light body, fortified with only a small amount of residual malt sugars, Belgian ales typically use less hops than other ales. And, with the crispness and strength they get from sugar, these beers need less balancing hops, anyway.

Hops are grown locally, though, and some breweries have taken greater advantage of them. Located in Watou, a village within Belgium's hop-growing region, the Van Eecke Brewery is a perfect example. Made with local hops, their Poperings Hommelbier is halfway between an English strong ale and an older, more rustic kind of Belgian ale. It's a strangely delicate 7.5%, and the hops provide a lacy, spicy bitterness with wildflower aromas.

The trend to sweetness has provoked a small rebellion, and hops are starting to play a larger role in Belgian

RIGHT: *Local hops give Poperings Hommelbier a wildflower aroma.*

brewing. At the forefront are newer breweries that have no doubt been influenced by American craft breweries. Their interpretations are revealing, though. One of the best young breweries in Belgium is Brasserie de la Senne, makers of two hop-infused ales, Zinnebir and Taras Boulba. Yet both are distinctly Belgian. Unlike American and English hoppy beers, which have heavier, caramel-inflected palates, these are lighter, crisp, and effervescent. The brewery's yeast strain has the qualities of a saison—peppery and rustic—that are perfect for the spicy, grassy hops that power these beers.

Another craft brewery focused on hops is De Ranke, producers of the aptly named XX Bitter. Much like the beers of Senne, this one is light-bodied. The effect is an even more profound bitterness; although the brewery uses gentle Brewer's Gold and Hallertau hops, the bitter result is nevertheless nearly lacerating. There's nothing like these beers in the American or English tradition. (American hopheads love De Ranke.) Other breweries have tried their hand at hoppy beers, some with notable success, as in Gouden Carolus

Hopsinjoor, a beer gently garlanded by flavorful, peppery hopping. Other efforts have been less successful. In Triple Hop, for example, Duvel uses far too much kettle hops for such a light-bodied beer, and the result is punishing bitterness. ■

BREWING NOTES

B ELGIANS EMPLOY A lot of strange and wonderful methods in the brewhouse, but most of the real exotica is covered in the chapters on lambics and the tart ales of Flanders (starting on pages 494 and 514, respectively). When they set about making a straightforward ale, the process is—for Belgium—also pretty straightforward. Brewers typically use step mashes and a large percentage fortify their beer with sugar or cereal grains. The first time I encountered a cereal cooker, it was at the Palm Brewery in Steenhuffel. The technique isn't ubiquitous, but accepted—even very traditional breweries like Rodenbach use one, and the practice dates back to a time when grains were taxed at different rates. The effect of cereal grains is much the same as sugar—they fortify the beer, giving it a lighter body, more alcohol, and a crisper finish.

As Belgium's breweries modernize, more and more use the standard cylindro-conical fermenters employed throughout the world, but some still rely on square or open fermenters. Many artisanal brewers let their beer rise in temperature as it ferments and cap it at a level ideal for the house yeast strain. The temperature range is impressive and may go into the eighties or even nineties Fahrenheit. This is where the ales form their characteristic fruitiness and spiciness. Many breweries allow their beer to "lager" for days or weeks after primary fermentation to smooth out.

The final, nearly universal step is bottle-conditioning—this is, in many ways, what distinguishes Belgian ales from those elsewhere. Breweries store the beer for weeks—four seems typical—in a "warm room" (around 60°F) to ripen. This is the last stage of a Belgian ale's chemical evolution, and the beer won't be complete until the second batch of yeast has had a chance to add its character. It's an additional advantage for distant Americans; bottle-conditioning is the best way to preserve beer, so ales arrive in the United States in much the shape the brewers intended. British, Czech, and German beers do not always fare as well. ■

The Cereal Cooker. This contraption looks likes the mash tun's little brother. Indeed, it works like a mash tun, too, except that it's reserved for unmalted cereal grains like rice and corn. The grains are boiled in the cooker, a process that gelatinizes them and prepares them for conversion by enzymes they lack. Once they're ready, the cereal grains are added to the regular mash. Here, aided by the rich enzymes in barley, they are converted into fermentable sugars.

EVOLUTION

BELGIAN ALES have always been in flux, and that remains the case. With the increasing popularity of lagers, Belgian brewers have become a bit morose about the future of small, traditional, or family-owned companies, noting that the giants at InBev and Heineken, having taken 70 percent of the market already, are sneakily trying to seize the remainder with brands like Grimbergen and Leffe.

All true. But things aren't quite so bad in Belgium. There are still scores of family-run breweries many decades or even centuries old, and a modest crop of craft breweries that are devoted to traditional brewing methods. Meanwhile, the rest of the world has fallen in love with Belgian ales, and the export market is booming.

All of this has had two large effects. On the one hand, it has helped shore up sales for expensive, traditional ales, helping to preserve some of the most interesting breweries. It has also sparked a huge upsurge in the production of Belgian-style ales outside Belgium. The United States and Italy are leading the pack on the trend, and Scandinavia and the Netherlands are not far behind. Even some British breweries have tried their hands at Belgian ales.

Belgian breweries need not fear the competition. Far from challenging Belgian products, these foreign-brewed ales have introduced people to the joys of Belgium and helped expand the market. As more and more people learn about the wonderful world of Belgian ales, that market will continue to grow. ∎

St. Arnold and Gambrinus. Two figures stand tall in Belgium's history and hagiography: Arnold, a brewing saint, and Gambrinus, the king of beer.

Arnold, a brewer's son, was born near Oudenaarde in 1040. He began life as a knight, but "saw the light" (his words) in his thirties, converting to a life of God. In 1081 he became abbot at the Saint-Médard Abbey in Soissons, France. Among the miracles attributed to Arnold during his beatification was that he plunged his staff into a brew kettle, thus curing everyone who drank the beer of the sickness from water contamination that had been plaguing the area. In retrospect, this looks a lot more like the work of sterilizing heat, but no matter. Arnold was canonized and is now widely celebrated by brewers throughout Belgium.

Gambrinus's story is more prosaic. The duke of Brabant and Lorraine during the early thirteenth century, his principal accomplishment was allowing local mayors the right to grant brewing licenses. His fame seems to be built more on his avid love of and very public consumption of beer. Gambrinus was once declared the honorary head of the Belgian Brewers' Guild, and in his memory, the Guild now offers the *Chevalerie du Fourquet des Brasseurs* (knighthood to the brewer's fork) to beer-promoting honorees.

THE BEERS TO KNOW

I CAN THINK OF no more daunting task than producing a short list of excellent Belgian ales. A list of a hundred wouldn't have an average beer on it. Consider the following options a starting place. The best way to get to know these beers is by stocking up and sampling them. It could be a lengthy task, but one you'll enjoy the whole way.

BLOND AND AMBER ALES

MOORTGAT DUVEL

oooooooooooooooooooooooooooooooooooooooooooo

LOCATION: Breendonk, Belgium

MALT: Pilsner

HOPS: Saaz, Styrian Golding

OTHER: Dextrose

8.5% ABV, 1.069 SP. GR., 32 IBU

Duvel gets my vote as the world's most beautiful beer. The pilsner malts are harnessed so that they glow golden in a tulip glass; meanwhile, an amazing plume of bubbles flashes as they roil from the glass's bottom. Duvel's yeast is legend; it produces enormous carbonation and an impossibly tight snow-white head. The secret to Duvel is its balance—creamy and pinot gris–sweet at the front, but surprisingly peppery with layered hopping. Those 32 IBU go further in a sleek, unfettered glass of Duvel than they would a heavier pint of American pale ale.

OMMEGANG BPA (BELGIAN-STYLE PALE ALE)

oooooooooooooooooooooooooooooooooooooooooooo

LOCATION: Cooperstown, NY

MALT: Pilsner, pale, Munich, Belgian Aroma, caramel

HOPS: Columbus, Styrian Golding, Cascade

6.2% ABV, 1.056 SP. GR., 21 IBU

Since its founding in 1997, Ommegang has been committed to re-creating authentic Belgian-style ales (and the founders even re-created a Belgian-looking brewery). BPA *almost* plays it straight. The beer has the yeast character and

LEFT: *Is there a city more romantic than Bruges in which to enjoy a beer?*

complexity of the source beers, but it is slightly heavier in body (no sugar) and those peppery notes give way to the unmistakably floral aromas and flavors of the Cascade hops. Actually, Belgians would totally approve.

BRASSERIE DE LA SENNE
TARAS BOULBA

LOCATION: Brussels, Belgium

MALT: Undisclosed

HOPS: Undisclosed

4.5% ABV

If Duvel is deceptive by appearing lighter than it is, Taras Boulba misleads for the opposite reason: It's a tour de force for a beer so light in alcohol. It is no less violently carbonic than Duvel, and its white head is as thick and well-structured as whipped egg whites. But it's the aroma, thick with pepper and lavender, and the flavor, with an almond note to complement cracker and spice, where the beer astounds. It finishes bone dry, like a saison.

HALVE MAAN BRUGSE ZOT

LOCATION: Bruges, Belgium

MALT: Undisclosed

HOPS: Undisclosed

OTHER: Brewing sugar

6% ABV, 1.055 SP. GR., 26 IBU

Belgium is not known for sessionable beers, so Brugse Zot is a welcome outlier. It's a light, soft beer, hazily golden with a delicate floral nose and wildflower palate. The beer's finish has just a twist of citrus to make it crisp and refreshing.

BRASSERIE D'ACHOUFFE
LA CHOUFFE

LOCATION: Achouffe, Belgium

MALT: Undisclosed

HOPS: Undisclosed

OTHER: Coriander, brewing sugar

8% ABV, 1.065 SP. GR.

Known for its charming, silly garden-gnome mascot, La Chouffe gets respect among connoisseurs for its complexity. A perfect example of smoothness in strength, La Chouffe is all sweetness and spice—Meyer lemon and orange, coriander and lavender—and nothing to suggest its power.

VAN HONSEBROUCK KASTEEL BLOND

ooooooooooooooooooooooooooooooooooooooo

LOCATION: Ingelmunster, Belgium

MALT: Undisclosed

HOPS: Undisclosed

7% ABV, 1.057 SP. GR., 20 IBU

Amusingly, Van Honsebrouck styles this a "low-alcohol content" beer. It's a relative term (two other Kasteel beers are 11%), but also hints at what you'll find—a very delicate, light beer. This is a good ale to test-drive for esters, as well; it has tons. I find honey and apple, banana and bubble gum, and perhaps some sherbet for good measure.

BROWN ALES

KERKOM BINK BRUIN

ooooooooooooooooooooooooooooooooooooooo

LOCATION: Sint-Truiden, Belgium

MALT: Undisclosed

HOPS: Undisclosed

5.5% ABV, 1.048 SP. GR., 35 IBU

Brouwerij Kerkom has a knack for making revival beers that taste like rustic ghosts from the past. Bink Bruin is not one of those beers—it's a modern interpretation with filtered clarity and clean lines. The nose and palate have cocoa and plum notes made spicy and grassy by fairly stiff hopping. Despite its low gravity, the beer tastes rich and finishes with a refined, dry snap.

HET ANKER GOUDEN CAROLUS CLASSIC

ooooooooooooooooooooooooooooooooooooooo

LOCATION: Mechelen, Belgium

MALT: Undisclosed

HOPS: Belgian-grown

OTHER: Dark sugar

8.5% ABV, 1.074 SP. GR., 16 EBU

Het Anker casts its lineage back to the great tradition of its hometown, Mechelen. Even the name, Gouden Carolus, refers to long-lost local coinage. The historical Mechelen beers were brown, and so is Gouden Carolus. Fermented warm, it has a huge banana-bread nose and a very sweet, fruity palate. The alcohol is well concealed behind an ester-rich frontal assault. A very sweet beer that works best as an aperitif.

CARACOLE NOSTRADAMUS

ooooooooooooooooooooooooooooooooooooooo

LOCATION: Falmignoul, Belgium

MALT: Undisclosed

HOPS: Undisclosed

9.5% ABV

An enormously fluffy head tops this beer, and it manages to stay put until the final drop—remarkable in beer of this strength. Between pour and final sip are flavors of hazelnut and caramelized sugars. Caracole uses an open flame in their kettle to produce these flavors—one of the few breweries left in the world that does so—and amazingly, it's still wood-fired. A rich, satisfying beer that's ideal for colder months.

HOPPY ALES

VAN EECKE POPERINGS HOMMELBIER

LOCATION: Watou, Belgium

MALT: Undisclosed

HOPS: Undisclosed

7.5% ABV

Hommelbier has a rustic look about it—caramelized, orangey, and a little hazy. That first impression is accurate; Hommelbier could easily be called a saison. It has a cakey body and layered flavors of lemon, wildflowers, and honey. The strength is concealed completely, and you have to be careful not to slug it back in hearty, appreciative gulps.

DE RANKE XX BITTER

LOCATION: Wevelgem, Belgium

MALT: Pilsner

HOPS: Brewer's Gold, Hallertau

6.2% ABV

This is a beer that divides people, but everyone can find it instructive—it illustrates how Belgian hoppy ales deviate from the American tradition. In American brewing, hop bitterness is generally buttressed by rich hop flavor and aroma and at least some buffering malts. By contrast, in XX, De Ranke has a beer that is almost purely bitter, a tincture with very little residual sugar. Beyond its defining bitterness, XX is very dry and effervescent, qualities that add to the prickliness. Inspired by North American hop bombs, it is nevertheless rendered with a perfect Flemish accent.

BIÈRES DE NOËL AND SPICED ALES

ST-FEUILLIEN CUVÉE DE NOËL

LOCATION: Le Rœulx, Belgium

MALT: Pale, caramel, roasted malt

HOPS: Undisclosed

OTHER: Undisclosed spices, dextrose, maltose syrup

8.5% ABV

Cuvée de Noël is the most overtly spiced of St-Feuillien's spicy line, but even so, it's a blended, modest potpourri, helping to draw out roasted notes from the darker malts. The flavors conspire to create the impression of chocolate, but the dry finish keeps Cuvée de Noël from cloying.

DE DOLLE BROUWERS STILLE NACHT

LOCATION: Esen, Belgium

MALT: Pale

HOPS: Whitbread Golding

OTHER: Solid candi sugar

12% ABV, 1.092 SP. GR., 32 IBU

The name means "silent night," and De Dolle Brouwers releases this beer for the Christmas season. Stille Nacht goes through a very long boil, caramelizing the malt to produce a deep amber color and a beer of great effervescence. The yeast has a heyday with this massive beer, and there are lots of stone fruit and citrus notes. The brewery slightly acidifies the beer, which dries it out and preserves it. An ideal beer for aging.

DUBUISSON SCALDIS (BUSH DE NOËL)

LOCATION: Pipaix, Belgium

MALT: Undisclosed

HOPS: Undisclosed

OTHER: Brewing sugar

12% ABV, 1.101 SP. GR., 25 EBU

This was one of the first Belgian ales I ever tried; I was transfixed by the sparkly little bottle. Inside I discovered the world of Belgian brewing, and it took my breath away. It is a very dense beer, rich with the dried-fruit flavors of malt. The alcohol soaks the malts like a rum cake, and the finish is sweetish, like a ruby port.

CORSENDONK CHRISTMAS ALE

LOCATION: Brewed by Du Bocq in Purnode, Belgium

MALT: Undisclosed

HOPS: Undisclosed

8.5% ABV

Corsendonk has decided that at Christmas, everyone gets what they want. In this case that means a beer that satisfies all tastes: a bubbling, sweet, spicy, and strongly warming winter tipple. Pull out a bottle and people will nod sagely and say "Belgian." It has all the hallmarks—a thin and wildly effervescent body, very fruity and sweet, and a bit of spice for the season.

Saisons & Rustic
BELGIAN ALES

Beer is a product of agriculture, but it has long been removed from the daily operation of the farm. This wasn't always so. Centuries ago, farms across Europe regularly maintained their own small breweries. They could turn their grain—barley, of course, but also wheat, oats, spelt, and buckwheat—into beer. They might have also used spices, honey, or fruit—whatever was on hand. When beer became an industrial product, it lost that link between land and glass. In fact,

Saisons and Rustic Belgian Ales.

Rustic ales recall an earlier age in brewing, when beer had the character of fresh grain, spicy hops, and tart, wild yeasts. They were brewed to quench the thirsts of working men, not pacify them, and they needed to be light and refreshing. Those qualities still define these ales: They may be light or dark, weak or strong, hoppy or malty, but they're always farm-fresh and restorative. Because of their complexity and dryness, saisons and rustic ales are among the most versatile beers with food, able to make the sweetness pop in shellfish, to draw out the creaminess of soft cheese, or even to tame the fire of spice.

modern megabreweries have evolved into chemical plants where malt and hops are combined in a precise process that turns out vats of molecularly consistent beer (they're often run by chemists, too).

Rustic ales are throwbacks to that earlier time. They are to industrial lagers what farm-fresh raw milk is to pasteurized skim. Breweries are rarely still situated on farms, but when they want to make rustic ales, they use ingredients the way old farmer-brewers did. Saisons are the charter members of the club, but not the only rustic beers out there. With the rise of organic brewing, an emphasis on local ingredients, and a return to traditional brewing methods, rustic ales are one of the success stories of twenty-first–century brewing. ■

ORIGINS

THE STORY OF most beer styles is evolution. From an early period when brewers labored on primitive equipment, a style developed in fits and starts with each new technological breakthrough. Rustic ales are a study in preservation. The original saisons and country ales were rustic by necessity and they stayed that way by neglect or stubbornness until almost disappearing in the 1960s. Now breweries have to make an effort, with their precision-calibrated machines and refined ingredients, to recapture the essence that once defined all beer.

For most of its long history, brewing was a domestic chore. Breweries were extensions of the work of a farm, and beer was just one of the ways people converted their labor into sustenance. This changed very slowly, first with the rise of monastic breweries in the seventh or eighth century and then with the gradual commercialization of brewing in cities in the following centuries. As commercial trade increased and beer became more readily available, country brewing went into decline. The Industrial Revolution hastened this, and country brewing continued

When French and Belgian Farmhouse Ales Parted Ways.

If you happen to drive in Belgium from Watou, in West Flanders, to Pipaix, in Hainaut, you take a short jot south to the E42 and spend most of the drive in France. It's not obvious where the line is as you zip through the undifferentiated European Union. This is a return to the past, for the two regions on either side of the current Belgian border share a lot of culture and history.

Beer is one part of that shared heritage, and the greatest density of French breweries is in the Nord-Pas-de-Calais region, immediately next to its neighbor, the saison-brewing Belgian Hainaut. The French region is also famous for farmhouse brewing and its own farmhouse style—bière de garde. Yet as full of rustic charm as saisons are, bières de garde are refined and polished. What happened?

In a word: war. As recently as the early 1900s, bière de garde was being described in terms that sound a lot like Belgian saisons, as a vat-aged beer "purposely allowed to become acid, and at the same time acquiring a vinous flavour." (From an account by R. E. Evans in 1905.) The First World War however, decimated French brewing. Many of the buildings themselves were damaged in the fighting, brewing stalled, and due to the loss of life, the customer base shrank 25 percent. Few breweries returned after the war and they didn't brew the tart, rustic prewar bière de garde. Like so many other countries, France turned to lagers; surviving northern ale breweries made beers to compete with those lagers—soft, rounded, and easy-drinking. When bière de garde started to sell again in the 1970s, the style had more in common with bocks or Scottish ales than the saisons just across the border. Far from rustic, they had become satiny, smooth beers lagered for refinement (and sometimes made with lager yeast).

Bières de garde and saisons are routinely clumped together as "farmhouse ales," but it's misleading. While they share a common ancestor, they have become very different styles. Belgian farmhouse ales suffered from the wars, too, but the lineage was never completely broken. Belgium retained a taste for rustic ales.

on in only small pockets in northeastern France, Belgium's Wallonia, and Fraconia in Germany.

Brewing wasn't a well-documented profession, even where it was done professionally. Records of country brewing are almost nonexistent before the nineteenth century, so we know nothing about the types of beers farmers made, how they made them, or what they were made of beyond what we can infer from commercial breweries at the time. The first real records come from the mid-1800s.

Saisons and rustic ales of that era were brewed by farmers on primitive equipment—their own, in the case of big farms, or communal brewing facilities shared by smaller farms. Brewing in the fall and spring, farmers made beers that would nourish them through the winter and slake their thirsts in the summer. The spent grains were reused as food for their animals.

The beers themselves were made with ingredients a farmer could access, usually grists made out of multiple grains.

In addition to barley, wheat and oats were very common; spelt—a key ingredient of the saisons of Liège—was somewhat common; and buckwheat was an occasional ingredient. Farmers malted their own grain, producing inconsistent, poorly modified malt. Poor malting techniques resulted in that "rustic" character—in this case, a sometimes acrid, sharp, or even harsh beer. Beyond the malt, local hops were also described as "biting," and fermentation varied greatly as well. The addition of wheat and oats had the benefit of smoothing and softening those spikier elements.

It's easy to romanticize wholesome farmhouse ales, but these were amateur brewers making beer on wheezy, rusty, old equipment a few times a year—a lot of that beer would have been pretty gnarly stuff. Adding spices was another measure toward remediating harshness. Ginger was a mainstay, and nineteenth-century writers mention star anise, sage, peppercorn, coriander, and cumin as regular spices.

Yeast character was and remains the central element in these beers. Belgian brewers were the slowest to adopt modern wort-chilling techniques, and well into the twentieth century were still putting their hot wort in flat, panlike vats (cool ships) to cool overnight. As the wort cooled, wild airborne yeasts would settle on its surface. Although brewers pitched yeast in the morning, by then the damage was done—their beer had become inoculated with souring microorganisms that would quickly turn them tart. (This is still how lambics are made.) All old farmhouse ales were soured. The effect was less pronounced in the table beers, as they were served within a week or two of

brewing, but stronger stuff that had aged for months or years in the cellar had the wild, sour character of lambic.

In the decades following Louis Pasteur's identification of yeast in the 1850s, early microbiologists helped breweries manipulate their strains so they could produce more consistent, reliable beer that didn't spoil. Within a few decades, wild yeasts had largely been eliminated in Britain. Belgian brewers liked the character untamed yeast gave to their beers, however, and some breweries nurtured their old strains. They mostly abandoned cool ships (eventually), but continued to pitch house yeasts that were not fully domesticated.

Modernity caught up to the farmer-brewers in the twentieth century. After the world wars, there were almost none left. Some farmers abandoned brewing, and some abandoned farming, becoming brewers as the market landscape favored specialization. By the 1950s, most of the rustic styles were dead or dying.

Nineteenth-century farmhouse ales were all relatively weak, but after the Second World War, breweries started producing stronger bottled beers they labeled saisons (a term previously used for only one type of Wallonian beer). These were the descendants of the aged farmhouse ales, but their reputation was different. German lagers and British ales had come into the Belgian market, driving a trend toward quality and strength. Modern saisons were dry and complex—and popular in French-speaking Belgium. They were no longer associated with the farm but with quality—and were packaged in Champagne-style bottles as a signal to consumers.

Their moment didn't last long. By

the 1970s, all the old-time rustic Belgian ales had vanished—the Leuven wheat ales, the Peetermans, the *uytzets* (see page 247). The living lines of true rustic ales existed at just a few breweries like Dupont and Silly, and even there they had become small niche styles. Fortunately, they didn't die out. Foreign interest in Dupont brought new attention to the style in the 1970s and '80s, and revival breweries committed to old-school rustic ales started cropping up throughout Wallonia. Rustic ales still remain very much a niche species within the Belgian ecosystem, but one that has happily been taken off the endangered list. ■

DESCRIPTION AND CHARACTERISTICS

RUSTIC ALES WERE never brewed in a consistent style. They were made in ways that conformed to the very specific circumstances of a farmhouse brewery—which varied farm to farm. Modern rustic ales are much more coherent, and saisons in particular have fairly clear contours. How did this happen? Brasserie Dupont. There may be no other brewery more synonymous with a single style or more responsible for its existence.

As recently as the mid-1980s, it was a perfectly preserved brewery that might have been beamed in from the 1880s. Still a working farm dating to 1759, Dupont malted its own grain until 1986, used a mash tun that dated to before 1844 (when the brewery was added), fired its kettle with an open flame, and pitched yeast dating back to at least the 1920s. It must have been like stepping back in time.

The beer is, if anything, even more astounding. Belgian beer expert Tim Webb—a man generally given to understatement—said, "While there is no such thing as the best beer in the world, if there was, it might be Saison Dupont."

The beer is bottled joy, a buoyant orange that feeds a bubbling snowy head. The nose has deep herbal and earthy qualities but also summer fruits that lift off the fizzing surface. One wants to use the word "complex" carefully here, because the presentation is refreshing and effortless; however, a careful study reveals a spine of minerality (from both the carbonation and hard well water), the suggestion of caramel in the grain-y malt base, a surprising depth of spicy hopping, and a mile-long dry finish. Saisons were once made to quench thirsts, and few beers in the world can match a well-made saison in that regard.

Saisons have multiplied in Wallonia, where Blaugies, Fantôme, Vapeur, Lefebvre, Jandrain-Jandrenouille, Ecaussinnes, Ellezelloise, and tiny Cazeau have joined Silly and Dupont—though they remain hard to find, even in Belgium. Where rustic ales have really taken off is the United States, which now produces a number of exceptional examples.

Not surprisingly, Belgians and Americans have their own takes on the style. The word "rustic" comes almost

Rescuing Saison. The saison style had dwindled to near nonexistence by the 1970s. Brasserie de Silly made one and Dupont made one. Neither brewery depended on them. The saison had a tiny following and Dupont's future seemed to be with Moinette, a robust pale ale. When writer Michael Jackson began poking around Belgium in the 1970s looking for lost treasures, he discovered saisons and raved about them. For the first time, an English-speaking audience learned of their existence. He prevailed upon American importers to have a look at this obscure little style and, fortunately, Don Feinberg of Vanberg & Dewulf listened.

"When I did get to [Dupont], they told me that they wanted us to import Moinette," Feinberg recalls. "I told them that 'that's a great beer, but the beer that I really am interested in is Saison Dupont.' They proceeded to tell me that they were actually thinking of discontinuing Saison Dupont, which at that point was down to 2 percent of their sales." Feinberg encouraged Dupont to change the packaging, and then set off to sell it in the U.S. For those who love rustic ales, it was a pivotal moment.

Export to the United States (and later, other countries) not only saved Dupont's brand, but quite likely the style. Saisons remain a tiny niche in Belgium—and even at Dupont things haven't entirely changed. Olivier Dedeycker, one of the family owners and the brewer, told me that in Belgium, "when you speak of Brasserie Dupont, it's Moinette. A lot of people in Belgium don't know Saison Dupont." Saison Dupont is the flagship, sort of, but relies almost entirely on foreign export, which constitutes 40 percent of the brewery's output.

It's one of the more remarkable stories in brewing. Dupont has become a legendary brewery, easily one of the handful that most influenced American brewers. In the United States, saisons have moved from a weird fringe style to—well, to a less fringe, slightly more mainstream style. Lots more are brewed in America than in Belgium, though. Yet like the Pixies and Velvet Underground, who created revolutionary music that inspired far more successful bands like Nirvana and REM, few breweries have a greater status among their peers than tiny Brasserie Dupont.

unchanged from the Latin and it refers to the countryside. In Belgium, they take this literally, and many of the producers are located in historic farmhouses. With rare exceptions, Americans put the country in their saisons, rather than situating the breweries in the country. Belgian breweries are more inclined toward spices but less toward hops. Americans, of course, love them some hops. Breweries from both countries have experimented with wild yeasts, but Americans more so.

On both sides of the Atlantic, saisons have certain characteristics that distinguish them from other beers. Rare is the saison with all of these elements, but the goal is to use them as a way of signaling the beer's rustic heritage.

■ **Interesting grain character,** which could mean a wheaty softness, a silkiness from oats, or the nuttiness of spelt. Originally these beers were made with rougher grain not optimized for beer brewing. These beers shouldn't taste perfectly smooth and refined, like factory white bread; they should have some flavor and texture, like a handmade loaf of whole grain.

■ **A hazy appearance,** which might come from grains or starches, hop matter, or yeast. When breweries started to be able to make perfectly clear ("bright") beers, it was a signal to the customer that there were no infections or quality problems. A bit of haze suggests handmade ales of the age before filtering.

■ **A spiciness,** which may derive from actual spices or from hops and fermentation. If spices are used, they shouldn't dominate the beer. Rustic ales should be refreshing, not sweet, herbal stews.

■ **A crisp, refreshing dryness.** Rustic ales were originally the farmer's session beer, so they couldn't be very rich or heavy. Effervescence, minerality, hops, and/or yeast character may figure into the equation. Most saisons have a thin, vinous character that comes from their highly attenuative yeasts.

■ **Pronounced yeast character.** This is the most important quality in a rustic ale and it's really nonnegotiable. "Rustic" can almost be read as code for untamed yeasts and the wild, fruity, or spicy compounds they produce.

RIGHT: The evocative little building where Daniel Thiriez of the eponymous Brasserie Thiriez makes his rustic ales in Esquelbecq, France

OTHER RUSTIC ALES

Saisons aren't the only rustic ales in Belgium. It was the only style to survive the farmhouse era intact, but breweries haven't forgotten older traditions. Rusticity is a continuum, and it touches many beers not officially called saisons. A brewery may use an interesting grain, like Brasserie Silenrieux, located halfway between Charleroi and Chimay. Founder Eric Bedoret was fascinated with heritage grains like buckwheat and spelt and wondered if it was possible to brew with them. Working with professors at the University of Louvain, Bedoret came up with recipes for Sara, the buckwheat ale, and Joseph, a spiced spelt witbier. Sara has an unexpected combination of flavors—tobacco, currant, and light acidity—while Joseph is lemony and herbal. They hint at what beer might have tasted like when it came straight off the farm.

Brouwerij Kerkom ("Bink" on the bottles), just twenty-five miles from Maastricht in the east of Belgium, is another brewery that borrows heavily from old traditions. Its five beers are all made traditionally and have definite

farmhouse touches. Bink Bloesem is brewed in the summer with local honey and pear syrup; Adelardus, named for a local abbot, uses sweet gale. But the most interesting is Bink Blond, which has a pretty straightforward recipe (it lacks the honey, pear, or sweet gale). The character of this beer is pure farmhouse. With a cloudy amber body, herbal hopping, and a spicy, acidic yeast character, it reminds me of the nineteenth-century beers described in the history books.

If you start looking around, you'll see touches of rusticity in many goblets.

Orval, brewed the same way for more than eighty years, uses whole-leaf hops and a blend of yeasts including *Brettanomyces*. Bosteels's Tripel Karmeliet is a glitzy beer one would have a hard time calling rustic, yet the recipe is a throwback to a seventeenth-century ale made with wheat, oats, and spices. At Brasserie Caracole, they brew their rustic beers over an open wood-fired flame. Because rusticity can be accessed through so many different methods, the world of farmhouse ales extends beyond the group we call saisons. ■

BREWING NOTes

MORE THAN MOST styles, saisons and rustic ales get their character from process rather than ingredients. Not that ingredients aren't important—the use of multigrain grists and spices helps define them. But those old-timey flavors that breweries nurture emerge more from the way the beer is handled than what goes in it.

In Belgium, it is easier for breweries to have access to older equipment like kettles fired by an open flame. For Saison Dupont, the hot spots created by the flame caramelize the wort, producing the beer's characteristic orange color and contributing a light toffee flavor. Modern American breweries typically don't use open flames, so they compensate with darker grains. This may produce roughly similar colors, but the flavors taste

layered rather than integrated. Specialty malts have their own flavors, and they're not the same as those that come from direct fire. Similarly, Belgian water is

RIGHT: *As evinced by this gauge at Brasserie Dubuisson, in Belgium, breweries do not replace equipment just because it's old.*

hard, and this lends a stiffness to their beers. Brewers
elsewhere may prefer a softer
profile, but some, particularly when they're imitating
Dupont, amend their water.

Mashing techniques are
fairly standard, though breweries use low temperatures
to maximize fermentability
and reduce body—important
when using finicky farm-
house yeast strains. The hallmark of
this style of brewing is warm fermentation; indeed, when a Belgian brewery
describes its process as "high fermentation," they mean temperature—and are
signaling the use of rustic yeast strains.
Warm fermentation is critical to the
development of rustic beer's signature
ester and phenol compounds. American
breweries are often leery about letting
the temperatures rise too high during
fermentation, but this was the tradition before tanks were fitted with glycol
chillers. The yeasts can handle temperatures in the seventies and eighties (and
Dupont's is fine up to 100°F) and cool
fermentations will result in smooth beers
lacking character.

Other techniques help add rusticity. Old farm breweries didn't use tall
cylindro-conical fermenters. Those
vessels repress ester formation; wide
fermenters, especially open ones, allow
the yeasts to develop more character.
Another technique is the use of multiple
yeast strains, which also helps develop
esters and phenols. Bottled saisons
are bottle-conditioned (especially in
Belgium) and not filtered. This gives
the beer a level of haziness, sometimes
subtle, sometimes bordering on murky.

Saisons and rustic ales are characterized
mostly by yeast—a dry, sometimes
tart quality that is the definition of
refreshing. Nothing else is exactly like
them, but dry *witbiers* are not far off, and
German *kellerbier*, an unfiltered, hoppy beer
from the German farmhouse region of Franconia, is another
possibility. Trial and error may be the best way to explore
similar beers—rusticity is more a state of mind than a style.

All of these techniques influence the
flavor of beer. Even something as seemingly minor as laying bottles on their
side during bottle-conditioning can have
noticeable effects.

In terms of the recipe, there are no
rules except that they produce that rustic
je ne sais quoi. Spiciness may come from
the yeast, the grains, the hops, or actual
spices. Fantôme's Dany Prignon loves to
tuck herbs and spices into his saisons
(his use of black pepper is especially
clever), while other saison brewers eschew them. In Orange County,
California, The Bruery's Tyler King
adds a special ingredient to his saison—
one most people don't even realize is
there. "One cool little fact is that Saison
Rue has spearmint in it. If you take
Saison Rue when it's young, you can
taste the mint. But as the beer ages, the
mint goes away and the *Brettanomyces*
develops. We didn't design it this way,
but usually by the time you can stop
tasting the mint in the beer, it's ready to
be sold. It adds a layer of complexity; you
don't know it's there unless it's missing."
Hops, grains, spices, and yeasts are all
tools in the saison maker's tool kit. In no
case should any one element overwhelm
the others. ■

EVOLUTION

RUSTIC ALES ARE enjoying one of the least likely revivals in brewing history. Left for dead in the 1980s, by all logic they should have joined a breed of extinct beers that had already departed the Belgian scene. They are exactly the opposite of the kind of beers modern breweries like to brew: The best ones are made on the funkiest, oldest, or just strangest equipment with the trickiest ingredients and a process that begs for inconsistency. Yet here we are, not many decades later, in a world where saisons have become a regular offering by American breweries. Indeed, it's easier to find a Belgian saison than a German bock at the grocery store.

Grammarians warn of the mistake of "back formation," where writers take a word and shorten it, thinking they're taking it back to a more essential, spare root ("gruntle" from "disgruntled," for example). Americans have this tendency with beer styles, taking some half-understood sense and tweaking it for "greater" authenticity (see Scottish Ales, starting on page 213). But they may have redeemed themselves with saisons. Many American breweries have been deeply inspired by these beers, and they treat saison with loving respect. Not only are some of the best examples in the world being brewed by Americans, but some of the most historically authentic, as well.

"We're gonna come out with a saison." In 2011,

I wrote an article about the boom in American craft brewery openings. I found myself on the phone with Coby Lake of Avondale Brewing in Birmingham, Alabama. Avondale wasn't yet open, and the business depended on the state legislature loosening rules passed after Prohibition that made it very hard to start new breweries. The element that might have doomed Avondale was a part of the law that made tasting rooms illegal. Lake—who sounds almost *exactly* like the actor Walton Goggins (another Birmingham native)—has a gambler's attitude toward risk. In the background, I heard construction work on a new bar for the brewery—which wasn't yet legal. (The law passed.)

All of this was fascinating, and it took a while to get around to the beer. When I asked Lake what he planned to brew, I expected the owner of Alabama's fourth brewery—deep, deep in Bud country—to say a pale or maybe golden ale. Nope. Instead, Walton Goggins drawled over the phone, "We're gonna come out with a saison; we're gonna call it Spring Street." I was amazed.

He wasn't alone, either. I talked with Paul Nelson of Edwinton, North Dakota's second brewery, and they were also leading with a saison. Breweries in Texas, Nebraska, and Florida are all brewing them now. When breweries in remote parts of the beer world settle on saisons as their flagships, one has to conclude that the style is obscure no more.

Dave Logsdon, founder of Wyeast Labs, recently opened up his own farmhouse brewery in an actual farmhouse near Hood River, Oregon.

One of the best examples is New York–based, Moortgat-owned Ommegang and their spectacular Hennepin, a beer with yeast complexity rivaled only by Dupont. Or by Boulevard's Tank 7, another beer that has not only remarkable yeast character, but a malt rusticity provided by corn and wheat—an homage to the crops around the brewery in Kansas City, Missouri. Jolly Pumpkin, Goose Island, and Hill Farmstead all make world-class examples, too.

Where the Untied States really shines, though, is taking saisons back to their true, wild-yeast farmhouse roots. Two breweries stand out. The Bruery makes many Belgian-inflected beers, including two *Brettanomyces*-inoculated

examples, Saison Rue and Saison de Lente. Both use the wild yeast to add balancing elements of drying crispness; in Saison Rue, made with rye, the effect is spicier and more tart. In Corvallis, Oregon, brewery Block 15's Nick Arzner makes Ferme de la Ville Provision from a blend of young and aged saison, and the wild yeasts add only a drying, quinine-like note that accentuates the malt and primary yeast character.

Finally, as beer has begun to slowly insinuate itself onto the tables of some of America's better restaurants, saisons have been a natural fit. Their profile, dry and crisp, is recognizable to wine sommeliers; their native rusticity also plays nicely in restaurants where chefs relish fresh, farm-to-table simplicity. Saisons are so versatile because they pull out different flavors in different dishes. They highlight sweetness in shellfish, yet complement the bitterness of fresh greens. They are also one of the best beers to pair with cheese. ∎

THE BEERS TO KNOW

URVEYING BEERS WITHIN a style usually means looking for hallmarks that define it. With rustic ales and saisons, the process is a bit more elusive; one looks for the *spirit* of rusticity. Since these ales may be any color or strength, you're instead looking for qualities that come from pre-industrial methods, not ingredients or national tradition. But never fear, sample a few of these, and that spirit will present itself as mightily as hops in any IPA.

SAISON DUPONT

LOCATION: Tourpes, Belgium

MALT: Pilsner

HOPS: Undisclosed

6.5% ABV

Dupont is recognizable from the pop of the cork. It has a kind of vibrance that rouses both a roiling bead and a tall, snowy head. The color is somewhere between a hazy gold and orange, and it looks best in a tall glass or tumbler—something to show off the light and bubbles. Saison Dupont is an evolving beer, and a fresher bottle will have more hop character, particularly on the nose; as it ages, the hops fall back a bit, exposing the beer's fresh, mineral crispness. The yeast character grows and changes. I've had bottles that seemed full of citrus, while others were more peppery or herbal. It's a beer to befriend and take out to dinner as often as possible; you want to develop a relationship with this ale.

DUPONT AVRIL

LOCATION: Tourpes, Belgium

MALT: Undisclosed

HOPS: Undisclosed

3.5% ABV

Avril is one of the few examples of a farmhouse *bière de table* available (though it was only introduced a few years back). It is a masterpiece of beer haiku: Though it has fewer ingredients than its peers, it is remarkably flavorful. Cloudy and effervescent, zesty and well-hopped with earthy, spicy hops, it is as refreshing as a spring morning.

Product of Belgium 330 ml / 11.2 fl. oz.
6.5% alc. by vol.

Vieille Provision
SAISON DUPONT
Unfiltered Belgian Farmhouse Ale Bottle conditioned
Brewed by Brasserie Dupont, Tourpes, Belgium

Imported by Total Beverage Solution, Mt. Pleasant, SC

KERKOM BINK BLOND

LOCATION: Kerkom-Sint Truiden, Belgium

MALT: Two varieties, undisclosed

HOPS: Challenger, East Kent Golding, Saaz

5.5% ABV, 1.050 SP. GR., 55 EBU

This beautifully misnamed beer is not blond—it's a hazy amber. It must be shocking to consumers who expect a neutral, sparkling ale to instead find this rustic beer sending off waves of herbal, rosemary hopping. There is also a toffee note and bit of yeasty phenol—definitely not neutral. It's a highly carbonated beer that keeps aloft a skiff of head as you drink, which is ideal to feed the volatile hop aromas dancing under your nose.

JANDRAIN-JANDRENOUILLE IV

LOCATION: Jandrain-Jandrenouille, Belgium

MALT: Undisclosed

HOPS: Undisclosed

6.5% ABV

I was instantly taken with the first beer from a fairly new brewery to the southeast of Brussels—but it took me half a glass to place it. The key is lychee, which is evident both in the nose and on the tongue. Lots and lots and lots of lychee. It's a hazy, honey-colored beer with only modest effervescence. The aroma also has touches of floral hopping, and the palate is long and dry, with a touch of quinine and lemongrass. But that lychee lingers through that dry finish, and then even a little while longer.

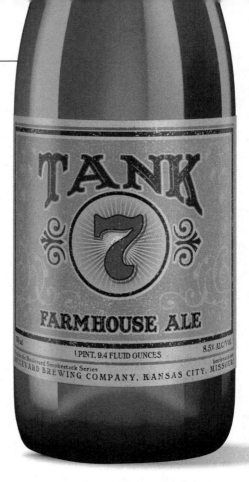

BOULEVARD BREWING TANK 7

LOCATION: Kansas City, MO

MALT: Pale, malted wheat, unmalted wheat, corn

HOPS: Amarillo, Simcoe, Tradition

8% ABV, 1.071 SP. GR., 38 IBU

Boulevard's brewer, Steven Pauwels, grew up in his father's brewery in Belgium. Before arriving at Boulevard, he made beer in the famous brewing city of Leuven and later in Bruges. Beer making is in his blood, and saison is his favorite style. His recipe is an acknowledgment of the farms around Boulevard in Kansas City, even if the brewery is no farmhouse. The wheat and corn provide a soft, lightly sweet malt base that's as comforting and familiar as a bowl of porridge. The aroma is pure saison, though, with a musty, slightly cellar-like yeast quality. Fermentation provides the white pepper and citrus notes, and they marry perfectly with the light, sweet grain. It's not as bone-dry as some saisons, but it finishes with a quenching snap.

OMMEGANG HENNEPIN

LOCATION: Cooperstown, NY

MALT: Pale, pilsner, corn

HOPS: Styrian Golding

OTHER: Coriander, sweet orange peel, ginger, grains of paradise, dextrose

7.7% ABV, 1.067 SP. GR., 24 IBU

Brewery Ommegang was one of the first American breweries to release a saison, and they didn't try to Americanize it. The spicing is subtle, and the ginger in particular works with the modest hopping to create the sensation of stiffer bitterness than the IBU would suggest.

It's difficult to tell where the spices end and the yeast character begins, but they harmonize beautifully.

BLOCK 15 FERME DE LA VILLE PROVISION

LOCATION: Corvallis, OR

MALT: Pilsner, wheat, oats, rye

HOPS: Golding, Sterling

OTHER: Honey

6.9% ABV, 1.049 SP. GR., 25 IBU

Ferme de la Ville is a blend of three vintages of the beer. Two of the portions are barrel-aged twelve and eighteen months, each constituting about 15 percent of the final beer. The remainder comes from fresh saison. The result is the definition of rustic: a beer full of grain-y complexity (at turns rye-spicy and oat-soft), with tart and refreshing stone fruit notes and a crisp, dry finish. Blending fresh and wild yeast–soured beer takes the edge off Ferme de la Ville; it's lightly tart and crisp, thirst-slaking like a tall glass of lemonade.

FANTÔME SAISON

LOCATION: Soy, Belgium

MALT: Undisclosed

HOPS: Undisclosed

OTHER: Undisclosed

8% ABV

Fantôme's saison, apropos for a rustic ale, has shifted and changed in the nearly two decades I've been drinking it. The first time I tried it, it was laced with black pepper and had a tangy phenolic finish. Later it was more cakey but citrusy, and later still more tart and herbal. It has never failed to communicate rustic, and the mutability makes it all the more enticing.

BLAUGIES LA MONEUSE

LOCATION: Blaugies, Belgium

MALT: Undisclosed

HOPS: Undisclosed

OTHER: Granulated sugar

8% ABV

Most twenty-first-century saisons tend toward the very pale to light orange—modern colors for farmhouse ales. La Moneuse is a rich amber, recalling the earlier tradition. It's a beer of amazing effervescence—the mousse-like head never has a chance to recede from the roiling bead. There's a touch of wild in the beer, almost balsamic, backed by a tannic chicory note. One of the driest saisons available—and that's saying something for one of the driest styles brewed.

GOOSE ISLAND SOFIE

LOCATION: Chicago, IL

MALT: Pale, pilsner, wheat

HOPS: Amarillo

OTHER: Aged in wine barrels with orange peel

6.5% ABV, 20 IBU

A vigorously effervescent, sunny golden beer, Sofie is a nice American take on the style. Hops are gentle but obvious—tropical and warm, picking up wonderful notes from the yeast. It has a bit of wild yeast in it, which elongates the fruits and draws them in a citric direction. The wild yeasts will continue to dry the beer out; the tropical notes give way to a beer that is very dry and vinous.

 Brasserie Dupont

CHANGING THE FARMHOUSE WITHOUT CHANGING THE BEER

ONE MAKES MANY REMARKABLE DISCOVERIES ON A TOUR OF BRASSERIE DUPONT: THE FLAME-FIRED KETTLE, THE EYE-POPPING FERMENTATION TEMPERATURES, THE RUSTIC PILSNER KNOWN ONLY TO LOCALS. BUT THE ONE THAT MOST AMAZED ME WAS SOMETHING OLIVIER DEDEYCKER TOLD ME AS I WAS ABOUT TO LEAVE: HIS FAMILY'S BREWERY MAKES ONLY ABOUT 13,000 U.S. BARRELS EACH YEAR (AS OF 2012). MORE THAN ANYTHING ELSE, THIS UNDERSCORED THE REALITY THAT DUPONT, EVEN AMID AN EXPANSION THAT WILL BRING TOTAL ANNUAL CAPACITY TO OVER 40,000 BARRELS, REMAINS A SMALL FARMHOUSE BREWERY.

Dupont is located in Tourpes, a tiny farming village nine miles from France in Hainaut province. That region looks like a crazy quilt of farm fields—none square—and Tourpes barely interrupts them. Dupont, itself a farm, is twenty years older than the United States, but the owners "only" took up brewing in 1844. In 1920, Louis Dupont bought the farm and it has remained in the family since. Dedeycker was born into the business. "My parents lived 500 meters from here

and my grandfather lived here, so we were always in the brewery. All of my holidays were spent here at the brewery." He started as brewing engineer in 1990 and took over as brewer from his uncle, the legendary brewer Marc Rosier, in 2002.

Remarkably, Dupont survived essentially unchanged through the mid-1980s, functioning very much as it did a century earlier. In the nineteenth century, farms incorporated brewing into their regular activities, which meant everything was done on-site. That remained true for Dupont, which continued to use its own well water, malted its own barley, and used nineteenth-century equipment to make the beer. (The one update: the kettle, which had to be replaced in 1920 after Germans took the original for the war effort.)

Over the past thirty years, Rosier and Dedeycker updated the brewery very slowly, deciding how to modernize the equipment without changing the beer. In 1986, Rosier discontinued the laborious and dangerous process of malting (fire is a constant problem, and Dupont, like many breweries, got burned), and in 2008 the old mash tun, which dated to before 1844, finally gave out and had to be replaced as well. While making the updates, Rosier and Dedeycker had great instincts about which methods they needed to retain to keep the spirit of the farm alive. There were places the brewery refused to modernize. Dupont still uses hard water straight from the brewery's well. The minerality contributes a stiffness

to the beer's profile, and Dedeycker has seen no reason to change. He is also a big believer in the direct-fired kettle, and during my visit, he flipped the switch so I could see and hear it roar to life. A flame concentrates heat on the bottom of the kettle and caramelizes the wort, giving Saison Dupont its trademark honey color despite the all-pilsner malt grist.

In the fermentation room, Dupont's remarkable yeast gobbles maltose in wide, square fermenters. This is the area where Dedeycker seems to take the most care; yeast is the heart of Dupont's character, and the brewery pays very close attention to how it's behaving. It may be the most famous yeast in the world, and many people have heard its reputation. During fermentation, yeast generates heat as it becomes active. Almost every brewery on the planet controls this temperature rise. Almost. Dedeycker lets his yeast free-rise as hot as it wants to go, way past where any other yeast would make something

BELOW LEFT: *The gas-fired flame roars to life; it is instrumental in caramelizing the wort.*

BELOW RIGHT: *Square fermenters are one more element in Dupont's yeast-based approach to beer.*

roughly as tasty as gasoline. Somehow, though, the Dupont yeast is adapted to blood-warm temperatures—and indeed, without them, the yeast fails to produce the beer's characteristic spicy, earthy flavors. When I visited, electronic monitors showed the fermenters in a range of stages, from the modest 22°C (70°F—a normal reading) to a robust 35.3°C (96°F). But fear not, on those rare occasions when the fevered yeasts go past 102°F, Dedeycker intervenes to prevent the bacchanal from getting out of hand.

The mystique of Dupont's yeast has captivated brewers for decades. When I asked whether it came from a red wine culture, as some have speculated, Dedeycker grinned and said, "Maybe." The secret and the yeast are both safe with Dedeycker's wife—a doctor of microbiology—who tends it in the lab. The brewery is able to re-pitch it for 150 to 200 generations before having to start a new culture (some breweries only reuse yeast for a few generations).

The bottling line, usually a point of only marginal interest, is yet another unexpectedly fascinating part of the brewery. Once bottled, the beers are laid on their side and stored for six to eight weeks in a warm room to finish bottle fermentation. The problem is the bottling line—it leaves the beers standing upright. This seems like it would be of scant consequence, but no. The beer changes depending on whether it conditions while standing up or lying down, a phenomenon Dupont has studied carefully. Standing up "we have a totally different beer. It seems to be only a small thing, but the impact on the taste is really big."

TOP: *The temperature inside the fermenters (left to right, 70°F, 93.4°F, 95.5°F)*

BOTTOM: *A sample is incomplete without Dupont's house cheese.*

For years, the solution had been for employees to collect the bottles and place them in a crate, lying down. But a month after I visited, Dupont installed a new piece of equipment—a robot that now completes the process in place of people. "We had to wait a long time to be able to buy it," Dedeycker said. This was a strange but perfectly apt metaphor for Dupont's evolution: using new equipment and techniques to preserve some of the oldest traditions in brewing.

French ALES

Pity the poor French brewer, toiling away in a country with legendary wine. Across two borders, his colleagues make beer known and loved throughout the world, yet in his own country his labors routinely go unnoticed. Even among connoisseurs, France is a footnote—home to *bière de garde*, a minor style, and not much else.

French Ales.

France's best-known style is bière de garde, an elegant ale lagered to accentuate its smooth malt textures. In the past decade or two, as a craft brewery movement has rolled through France, a homegrown philosophy informs a new crop of beers—sunny spring ales, hearty winter ales, and a whole range of rustic, sometimes spiced, country ales. Rooted firmly in the tradition of wholesome artisanal cuisine, these beers are subtle and complex—another example of the way local grains, herbs, and spices can be turned into something refined and decadent. And of course, they are exquisite with food.

STATISTICS

Bière de garde ABV range: 6–8%; bitterness: 20–35 IBU

Spiced country ale ABV range: 4.5–7%; bitterness: 15–25 IBU

Spring ale (March beer, *bière de printemps*) ABV range: 4–6%; bitterness: 15–25 IBU

Winter/Christmas ale (*bière d'hiver*, *bière de Noël*) ABV range: 7–9%; bitterness: 20–40 IBU

Serving temperature: 38°–45°F

Vessel: Tulip, goblet, or brewery-specific glassware

Pity the poor beer drinker, unwittingly cheating herself by overlooking France—currently home to one of the most exuberant beer scenes in the world. It boasts twice as many breweries as neighboring Belgium and has far more on offer than just those *bières de garde*—which are, with their rich history and French refinement, not just a minor style. Unfettered by local expectations, French breweries are quietly making some very interesting beers, many with spices, wheat, honey—whatever sparks the brewery's fancy. The spirit of French *gastronomie* seems to animate these toothsome beers, which deserve more than a footnote in the catalog of great beer styles. ■

ORIGINS

FRANCE AND BELGIUM shared a similar brewing heritage for much of their history. They had general similarities in brewing style, with very long boils, low attenuation, the regular use of wheat, and cooling in cool ships that made them part of one family, distinct from the traditions of Britain and Germany. Beyond the basics, though, brewing was a regional art, and the styles varied from town to town. If you were to travel west from Maastricht in the nineteenth century, you could zigzag your way through Leuven, Mechelen, and Belgian Flanders, finding a different style of beer in each city. Cross the current border and you'd continue finding different styles in Lille and Paris. In the 150 miles separating Holland and Lille, you'd bounce along the trail of dark spelt beer, aged barley beer, light-hued wheat beers, and kettle-scorched brown ales.

When Belgian brewer Georges Lacambre visited France in the 1840s, he was more impressed with the beer he found there than with many of his native beers. He praised the robustly effervescent French ales and compared them favorably to Champagne, which quickly loses its head. In Paris, they mainly brewed strong dark ales, though he noted an emerging style, *bière blanche de Paris*, that much impressed him. Made with coriander and elderflower, it was a perfect summer ale that "deserve[d] to be mentioned as one of the best known white beers."

Lacambre identified three major French brewing cities: Lille, Lyon, and

two years. Writing just a few years after Lacambre, the French scientist Louis Figuier agreed with the Belgian brewer's rankings of major brewing cities, but added Marseille and Tantonville, west of Strasbourg, to the list.

The popularity of French ales started to change in the twentieth century. Lagers were on the rise, already constituting a quarter of the market, and although Lille was still the center of French brewing, traditional ales were in collapse. British brewing scientist R. E. Evans visited in 1905 and reported back to the Institute of Brewing: "Five years ago, about 50 per cent of the beer consumed was of this nature, but now it probably does not exceed 20 per cent." Within a decade, the First World War would devastate local country breweries, particularly in the war-torn Nord-Pas-de-Calais region where the ales were most common.

By the time the Second World War ended, French brewing had been reduced by 90 percent from Evans's time and would ultimately drop to about two dozen breweries. The old styles were mostly vanquished. Where brewing continued, it

Strasbourg. Lille was France's most famous, where they made a family of styles he compared to the amber *uytzets* of Belgian Flanders. The vinous, tart beers were renowned throughout the region. Lyon made another amber, poorly attenuated and similar to Lille's stronger beers but "a bit richer." And Strasbourg, a city traded back and forth between the French and German empires, made a most intriguing beer that sounded very much like another defunct style, Polish-born Grodziskie. It was made of smoked malts, brewed strong, and "highly hopped and quite bitter" in order to age for up to

RIGHT: *The basilica at Notre Dame de Lorette in Ablain-Saint-Nazaire is one of the many World War I memorials in the region.*

Wait, What's the Name of the Brewery? Trying

to figure out who brewed a French beer isn't as obvious as you'd imagine. For reasons no one seems to know, local convention dictates that the beer will have its own brand name separate from the brewery's name. Ch'ti isn't the brewery, it's the beer line—Castelain is the brewery. You'll see Ch'ti Blonde, Brune, and Tripel, but you'll also find St. Amand, a non-Ch'ti Castelain product. Of course, to make it perfectly murky, not every brewery does this—La Choulette and Thiriez beers are made by La Choulette and Thiriez. Here's a cheat sheet for some of the prominent breweries and their labels.

BREWERY	BRAND
Castelain	Ch'ti, St. Amand
Duyck	Jenlain
Gayant	St. Landelin
Jeanne d'Arc	Grain d'Orge, Belzebuth
St. Germain	Page 24
St. Sylvestre	3 Monts, Gavroche
Theillier	La Bavaisienne

---

took the form of low-alcohol lager brewing, tailored to the tastes of industrial workers who wanted refreshing, drinkable beer. Ales were still being made, but they were a tiny, largely undocumented fraction of the market.

Ales started to make their comeback in the late 1970s, when the students in Lille adopted as their beverage of choice a strange throwback beer from the brewery Duyck called Jenlain Bière de Garde. It was one of those rare, oddball ales, first brewed around 1945, but it wasn't like any of the prewar bières de garde. Indeed, it bore a much closer resemblance to the bocks that started to replace ales before World War I. It was

strong, very smooth and malty, and was lagered. Hops played a minimal role, and unlike Belgian saisons, the yeast character was almost completely absent.

Jenlain's popularity in the late 1970s created the template for the modern bière de garde, and breweries like La Choulette, Castelain, and St. Sylvestre began making similar versions. Still, the success of these beers was modest and didn't immediately spark a brewing revival. By the 1990s, breweries were still closing down and the future of French beer was in jeopardy. But then the international wave of craft brewing finally arrived in France, and within a decade brewery openings exploded. There are currently more than 250 breweries, and they brew everything from traditional bières de garde and saisons to English cask ale. The market has reached an experimental phase; the breweries are out in front of their customers and it's not clear which experiments will find a following and which will fail. It's a time of transformation in France, and in a decade or two we'll have a better sense of what French beer really is. ■

DESCRIPTION AND CHARACTERISTICS

WHEN PEOPLE OUTSIDE the country consider French beers, they confine themselves exclusively to a single style brewed in a small region of the country by a handful of breweries that export their beers. Ah, the spoils of early entry. The breweries of Nord-Pas-de-Calais in the north were the first to find an ale style that could sell, and their success in establishing bière de garde put France back on the beer map. The style definitely deserves its reputation—it is an authentic expression of French brewing and one found nowhere else.

BIÈRE DE GARDE

The North Star in French brewing remains bière de garde. The country's biggest ale producers all make this style and it has become France's ambassador to the rest of the beer world. Because of its fame and commercial success, the style has become more and more well defined. Brewers even considered trying to establish a protected category (*appellation d'origine contrôlée*—much like those used for wine and cheese) for bières de garde, but couldn't bridge differences in production methods. Still, from a style perspective, there is substantial coherence.

The essence of the style is velvety refinement, a quality achieved more through method than ingredients. Bières de garde are all about malt and alcoholic strength; they tend to be on the sweet side, but never cloy, largely because of loving care in the conditioning tank. The idiomatic phrase *de garde* refers to the practice of keeping or aging the beer. Before the twentieth century, the souring yeasts and bacteria in these brews needed

ABOVE: *Steam wafts from the mash tun at Castelain.*

"My first influence, of course, comes from the local bière de garde. During the seventies, I was a teenager, and the 7% Jenlain amber ale appeared like a revelation, an eye-opener. It had so much more taste and more character than the Stella Artois lagers or other brands our parents used to drink when they were thirsty. Other similar beers, like La Choulette, Bavaisienne [Theillier], or later 3 Monts [St. Sylvestre], were also much appreciated. When I started professional brewing in 1996, I simply decided to brew the beer I wanted to drink (and to sell the rest of it)."

—DANIEL THIRIEZ, BRASSERIE THIRIEZ

time to mellow in the barrel. Even though the style has changed dramatically, the name still fits: Taking a cue from the lagers of the intervening decades, bières de garde are now fermented cool to minimize esters and then aged—in modern times, "lagered"—for weeks. The effect is consistent: a burnished, malt-scented beer of surpassing smoothness that is delicate despite its strength.

Bières de garde may be any color. A light amber (*ambrée* in French) was traditional, but both blonds and browns (*brune*) are also common. The aromas and flavors depend on the malt: blonds have the least, with just a hint of bread or cracker; ambers have more toastiness or caramel; and browns a bit of dark fruit, toffee, or bread. Hops may be so light that they are almost undetectable—this was the tradition for many years. While no one will mistake a bière de garde for an IPA, hops have lately been getting a bit more use. In beers like Page 24 Réserve Hildegarde and Thiriez Extra, they give a more floral nose and a lacy peppering on the palate.

Bières de garde are strong beers, usually from 6.5% to 8.5% ABV, but the alcohol is well integrated into the malt body. The watchword is smooth, and that also carries over to the body, which is usually lightened by a small amount of sugar. Despite all the elements that might lead to a cloying palate—high alcohol, sugar, and few hops—bières de garde are balanced by their low attenuation and dry finish.

Two variations on bière de garde are ubiquitous in France—lighter, sometimes wheat-based spring beers and darker, heartier, sometimes spiced winter ales.

RIGHT: *Daniel Thiriez pours out a glass of his rustic bière de garde.*

Releasing spring and winter beers is a tradition dating back to the time when brewing was by necessity a seasonal activity. Spring beers (*bières de printemps*) were made to cool and refresh during the hot working months while winter or Christmas beers (*bières d'hiver* or *bières de Noël*) were designed to warm and comfort during the cold season. The current examples follow this tradition, and a brewery's cold-weather brew is especially anticipated and celebrated. ■

BREWING NOTES

SINCE THERE ARE so many different styles of beer brewed in France under different conditions and on idiosyncratic equipment, we'll confine ourselves to a discussion of bière de garde, which has a few particular characteristics. For most of the Nord-Pas-de-Calais brewers, it's not enough to end up with a satin-smooth, malty strong ale at the end of the process. The process itself is a big part of the style.

The mash and boil are typical. Brewers don't employ exotic malts—usually just a pale base malt with small amounts of color malts like Munich for appearance. They don't use crystal malts, which would increase the body, and in fact, many add some sugar to reduce body and help attenuation. This is important in the versions where hops are used at a minimum. There is a growing sense that local ingredients are best (a matter of philosophy more than taste), but some breweries don't restrict themselves to only the limited number of French hop varieties. French malts, renowned worldwide, contribute a warm, grain-y character—though it is a subtle quality.

When breweries first started making bières de garde again in the 1970s, they were appealing to a public used to lagers. As a consequence, they quite closely resemble some German styles. *Helles bocks* are the closest fit, exhibiting the same soft maltiness and alcohol strength. *Scottish ales* are also fermented cold to produce lager-like clean maltiness.

IF YOU LIKE BIÈRE DE GARDE

A bière de garde's identity is born in the fermentation tanks. Yeast's role is to ferment the beer cleanly and then disappear, as in a lager or Scottish ale. Some breweries use lager strains, some use ale, but they all ferment at a temperature chilly enough to inhibit the production of esters and phenols. They lager or "garde" the beer to create the signature smoothness. This is not an optional process or even one breweries consider—it's just the way one brews. When I asked Brasserie St. Germain's Stéphane Bogaert about the reasons for garding the beer, he seemed mystified, as if the benefit were self-evident. At first, he didn't understand the question, and then he walked me through the process again, like I was just a slow learner. Breweries lager their beers for different lengths. Three weeks is the minimum, though a month to six weeks is usual. Castelain ages its beer for a minimum of six weeks and as long as twelve.

The final, mostly normalized process is filtration (another major way in which bière de garde differs from saison). Breweries do this partly because the final product—highly carbonated, cascading from a large bottle—sparkles with the clarity of lager, but some also believe it helps the beers age better, since most are not bottle-conditioned.

The brewers of the region have an almost patriotic sense about the lineage of their beers. Local ingredients are another part of the identity of bière de garde—not mandatory, but definitely part of the flavor. Alain Dhaussy, owner and brewer of La Choulette, believes this was an important part of the style's reinvention: "Using locally available resources—yeast, specialty malts, hops—small breweries in the Nord have made beers that represent a transition between top-fermented beers of the past and new classic lager beers." ■

EVOLUTION

N OTHER PARTS of France, bière de garde is not king. Most of the country's ale breweries are tiny enterprises. Most don't distribute much beyond their hometowns, never mind exporting. They are so small that about half don't even have websites. In the nineteenth century, brewing had distinctive regional differences, and that pattern seems to be emerging again. Away from the gravitational pull of the Nord, they are drawing influences from Britain, the United States, Germany, and Belgium. Collectively, the beers they brew coalesce into some general types—proto styles that may emerge in coming years as further examples of native French brewing.

As when any country experiences a mighty growth spurt, the current French beer scene is experimental, transitional, and unstable. Just as the United States sampled from other traditions during the 1980s and '90s until its brewers found their voice, France will probably follow suit. You can see signs of American influence in the hoppy ales of hip breweries, like Ninkasi's IPA (that's the Ninkasi from Lyon, not Eugene, Oregon) and La Franche's strangely named XXXYZ Bitter. The old German influence remains strong

RIGHT: *A café in Wormhout, France, in Nord Département— where bières de garde rule.*

Reading a French Label.

Most French-language beer labels (including Belgian ones) get a translation before coming to America. But since the vast majority of French beer is not exported, you have to pick up a few bottles when you visit. And on those bottles, everything's in French. Some words don't need translation—*blonde*, *ambrée*, *brune*, and *bière de Noël* are obvious enough. Others terms less so. Here's a quick reference.

avoine	oats
bière artisanale	hand-crafted beer
bière blanche	wheat beer (literally "white beer")
bio/biologique	organic
blé, froment	wheat
châtaigne	chestnut
coriandre	coriander
épeautre	spelt
gingembre	ginger
haute fermentation	fermented warm (i.e., ale)
houblon	hops
levure	yeast
maïs	corn
miel	honey
non-filtrée	unfiltered
non-pasteurisé	unpasteurized
orge	barley
refermentée en bouteille	bottle-conditioned
sur lie/sur levure	bottle-conditioned (literally "on the yeast")

in places like Strasbourg, where lagers are still king (think Kronenbourg, Meteor, and Fischer).

Other beers are influenced by the U.K., including British-style ales like those made at Merchien (bitter, porter, and IPA) and especially the Bastide Brewery, owned by Englishman William King, which makes only cask ale. In France, Scotland is still remembered fondly for the "Auld Alliance"—the commercial and military agreement between the two countries designed to impede English attacks on either. It may have ended more than 400 years ago, but that doesn't stop affectionate homages in the form of Scottish-style ales and even a Scottish pub in Paris called The Auld Alliance.

It's no surprise that the biggest influence is Belgium, as France is its largest export market. Tripels, wits, and rustic ales first entered the market as imports and were popular enough to inspire imitation. Tripels are often linked by name to some local monastic tradition like St. Landelin from Gayant, but that's not always the case (Castelain Maltesse has only a vaguely ecclesiastical connotation).

Witbiers seem less of an imitation than an inadvertent reproduction: Many breweries make a *blanche* (wheat beer) and the spicing seems to have occurred naturally to French brewers. Indeed, spicing is more important to French brewing than Belgian. Spices like coriander and orange peel are so common they find their way into not only blanches but bières de garde, spring beers, winter beers—just about any style may have a dash sprinkled in. The French can get far more creative, though. Brasserie du Chadron, inspired by local hemp fields, makes a hemp ale. Brasserie des Abers, makers of the Mutine line, also make a beer with hibiscus and another with seaweed. Rare Courtoise makes farmhouse-y beers with meadowsweet and dandelions. Brasserie du Sornin may have them all beat; their expansive range includes beers made with elderberry, lentils, anise, mushrooms, honey, and chestnut extract.

The latest development is the most interesting—the return of rustic, saison-style ales. Recall that originally, there was no difference between Belgian saisons and French bières de garde. They were both tart, spicy, and rich with whole-grain flavor. As Belgian saisons have become a worldwide phenomenon, they are once again being brewed in the Nord. Brasserie au Baron, literally on the border with Belgium—in fact, just feet away—makes one of the best-known saison-style beers, Cuvée des Jonquilles. Daniel Thiriez has also been sending his beers in a more rustic direction, especially with Extra and La Rouge Flamande.

Sadly, very few of these other beers are available outside France. In order to experience the full range of French brewing expression, you have to visit. (And there you were, just scheming for an excuse to go to France.) ∎

THE BEERS TO KNOW

THE FRENCH BREWING renaissance is in such an early stage of gestation that most of the country's diverse offerings are only accessible with a plane ticket. The beers prepared for export are largely bières de garde from the larger breweries of the Nord-Pas-de-Calais. That's not a terrible state of affairs; those beers offer a wonderful and unique world to explore.

ST. GERMAIN RÉSERVE HILDEGARDE BLONDE

LOCATION: Aix-Noulette, France

MALT: Pale, Munich

HOPS: Brewer's Gold, Strisselspalt

6.9% ABV, 1.076 SP. GR., 32 IBU

The beers of St. Germain's Page 24 line possess a deft softness that in another beer might come from wheat (only its Blanche uses it). The Blonde is smooth but not quite as polished as other bières de garde, perhaps owing to the delicate, herbal hopping. The IBUs belie what is actually a pronounced flavor somewhere halfway between lemon rind and wildflowers.

CASTELAIN CH'TI AMBRÉE

LOCATION: Bénifontaine, France

MALT: Pilsner, amber, crystal

HOPS: Magnum to bitter; undisclosed flavor hops

5.9% ABV, 18 EBU

First brewed in 1983, Ambrée is one of the oldest bières de garde available. Ambers are the most traditional, so

this is a taste of one of the first examples of the style. Ch'ti is highly carbonated and effervescent, but this somehow doesn't dampen its creamy richness. It is a pure malt experience, with no hops evident to the nose or on the tongue.

BRASSERIE AU BARON CUVÉE DES JONQUILLES

○○

LOCATION: Gussignies, France

MALT: Undisclosed

HOPS: Undisclosed

7% ABV

Brasserie au Baron is literally a stone's throw from Belgium, so it's not shocking that Cuvée des Jonquilles borrows heavily from the saison tradition across the border. Named for daffodils, the effervescent beer is fittingly a sunny blond and even a bit flowery in the nose. The flavor is marked by a crispness, a minerality, lemon, lavender, and some interesting phenolic notes.

LA CHOULETTE AMBRÉE & LA CHOULETTE BIÈRE DES SANS CULOTTES

○○

LOCATION: Hordain, France

MALT: Undisclosed

HOPS: Undisclosed (Ambrée); Magnum, Brewer's Gold, Golding (Sans Culottes)

8% ABV (Ambrée); **7% ABV, 22 EBU** (Sans Culottes)

These two beers are contrasts in style and appeal. Ambrée, the brewery's first beer, is made in the modern mode—dominated by malt, very smooth, and a little thick. It is robust enough to suggest a barley wine, though the brewer, Alain Dhaussy, is using caramel malts to evoke the "long boils at the beginning of the century." Sans Culottes (literally "beer without pants," a reference to the

1789 French peasant rebels who didn't wear upper-class *culottes*) was brewed two years after Ambrée, in 1983, but it is a revival of the old farmhouse tradition. The beer is much thinner, effervescent, spicy, and tart—akin to what we would now call a saison. To American palates, the Sans Culottes will delight, while the Ambrée may seem heavy and ponderous. In France, Ambrée is the much more common and expected style.

THIRIEZ EXTRA

○○

LOCATION: Esquelbecq, France

MALT: Pale, from French barley

HOPS: Brewer's Gold, Bramling Cross

5.5% ABV, 1.050 SP. GR., 50 EBU

By some margin, this is the most vividly hopped of export French bières de garde. Extra (Étoile du Nord in France) is a limpid honey-colored beer with an impressive white head, but the nose is pure earthy hopping. Like La Choulette, Thiriez makes a standard French ambrée, so Extra comes as a sharp contrast—more like the spicy, dry saisons made across the border. Daniel Thiriez credits the English Bramling Cross hops ("a lot of them") for the oily, peppery palate.

ST. SYLVESTRE 3 MONTS

LOCATION: Saint-Sylvestre-Cappel, France

MALT: Two- and six-row malts

HOPS: Nugget

8.5% ABV, 1.074 SP. GR., 20 EBU

St. Sylvestre's offering has an elegance that begins with a hugely effervescent pop at cork opening and a Champagne-like cascade of gold and bubbles. The beer is just as stylish. A bit more estery than other bières de garde, its smooth malt flavors are kissed by a bit of peach (or is it apricot?), which further reminds one of pale wines.

THEILLIER LA BAVAISIENNE

LOCATION: Bavay, France

MALT: Undisclosed

HOPS: Undisclosed

7% ABV

La Bavaisienne is a classic bière de garde, rich amber, ebulliently carbonated. It gets its color from wort caramelization, and leads with a brown sugar to toffee palate but, unexpectedly, not a sweet one. The finish is not exactly dry, but it is decisive, and helped along by a woody, herbal note that scrubs the palate for another sip.

SOUTHAMPTON BIERE DE MARS

LOCATION: Southampton, NY

MALT: Pale, wheat, Vienna, Munich, aromatic

HOPS: Magnum, Styrian Golding, Saaz

OTHER: Undisclosed spices

6.5% ABV, 22 IBU

If you're looking for the taste of France stateside, Southampton has an excellent offering. Brewer Phil Markowski has crafted a beer with classic French character—burnished malts with a touch of nectarine, reminiscent of riesling. Markowski gooses it with some spicing, but it's very subtle and just urges the flavors to pop.

Brasserie St. Germain

NATIVE FRENCH BREWING

THE NORD-PAS-DE-CALAIS, THE REGION BORDERING BELGIUM, IS THE TRADITIONAL AS WELL AS MODERN CENTER OF FRENCH BREWING. IT'S ONE OF THOSE PLACES WHERE HISTORY IS A CONSTANT PRESENCE, AND NOT ONE FILLED WITH THE GLOSSY IMAGES FROM A TOURIST BROCHURE. THIS IS COAL-MINING COUNTRY, AND SCATTERED ALONG THE UNDULATING LANDSCAPE ARE WHAT LOOK LIKE CONICAL HILLS BUT ARE IN FACT IMMENSE SLAG HEAPS. FOR DECADES, COAL FUELED THE LOCAL INDUSTRY, AND THE NORD HAS AN UNGLAMOROUS, WORKING-CLASS PAST. IT WAS ALSO ON THE FRONT LINES IN THE FIRST WORLD WAR, A MEMORY THAT PERSISTS VISIBLY IN THE BATTLEFIELD MEMORIALS AND CEMETERIES THAT CROP UP EVERY FEW MILES.

This sense of history carries over to brewing, too. While much of the rest of France enjoys a freewheeling exploration of beer styles, in Nord-Pas-de-Calais they still cherish traditional brewing. When you enter Brasserie St. Germain, tucked into a recessed building on Route d'Arras in Aix-Noulette, you are immediately greeted by that history. In a beautiful, hop-draped room not currently licensed as a pub, the walls are lined, curiously, with signs for Bières Brasme. When co-owner Stéphane Bogaert tells the story of St. Germain, he doesn't begin when he, his brother Vincent, and Hervé Descamps founded the brewery in 2003. He goes back much further, recounting the history of brewing in Nord-Pas-de-Calais, the rise of modern bière de garde in the 1970s, and the importance of Brasme, which at one time brewed 215,000 barrels of beer in Aix-Noulette.

Most breweries start their history with their own founding, but at St. Germain, they trace their lineage through that earlier brewery.

Indeed, all of that history is critical, because the men of St. Germain have thought deeply about what it means to run a French brewery. To the Bogaerts and Descamps, the future will be a return to local brewing, artisanal brewing, and a style of brewing that is peculiarly French:

> Our philosophy is to respect the bière de garde tradition. The major activity of the brewery must stay with this kind of beer. That's why I say to my colleagues that they should write 'bière de garde' on their labels; it's profitable for everybody. We want to be different from Belgium and we want the people, especially in America, to talk about French beer. Bière de garde is something you can say, "Okay, it's a French style."
>
> —STÉPHANE BOGAERT,
> BRASSERIE ST. GERMAIN

There are really two traditions in French brewing. The most recent are the bières de garde that developed a following in the 1970s—strong, malty, "garded" (lagered) beers. But there's an older tradition that is more rustic and relies more on local agriculture. St. Germain decided to make bières de garde that were respectful of those made by the older breweries in the region. Their beer follows the general model laid down by Jenlain, Ch'ti, and others. They brew a blond, an amber, a *printemps*, and a hugely successful *Noël*. But they also wanted to make beers that were a part of the earlier tradition, when farmhouse breweries used more hops and local ingredients.

The Nord-Pas-de-Calais is one of the few places in the world where it's possible to get all local ingredients, and St. Germain decided to make its beer entirely out of local crops. Hops are grown just down the road, and the barley, which now goes to Belgium to be malted, is also local (the nearby malt producer, Soufflet, provides them with specialty malts). The brewery even uses sugar from local beets to fortify its beers. Specialty beers include a piquant rhubarb-infused beer (*Rhubarbe*) that evokes old-time fountain sodas, and a roasty, copper-colored beer (*Chicorée*) made with chicory—an ingredient common in French beer a century and a half ago. Of course, the rhubarb and chicory are local products, too.

Hops became the centerpiece of the St. Germain line—not muscular American-strength hopping, but flavorful, aromatic hopping. That's where the name Page 24 comes in. It is a reference to Hildegard of Bingen, one of the first documenters of the use of hops in beer (see page 20). Page 24 is the apocryphal location of these comments in her writing. Of course, working with only local ingredients has a couple of major disadvantages when it comes to hops. Local growers produce only a few types, limiting St. Germain's recipes. Local farmers grow crops conventionally, too, so the brewery had to abandon organic beer. On the other hand, St. Germain is working with the farmers to cultivate a wider variety of hops; the English variety Challenger should be available soon. There are only eight growers left, and the patronage of St. Germain may well ensure

they're in business to supply local hops for years to come.

The central hurdle for French brewing is establishing an identity. Even in France, Belgian beers are far better known. "Everybody thinks Belgium when you say beer," Bogaert acknowledges. "In this region, we are not so famous compared to Belgian breweries." A generation ago, makers of bière de garde got the ball rolling and put France on the map. St. Germain hopes to continue its work and make bières de garde that are even more characterful and flavorful—and more French.

Abbey and TRAPPIST ALES

The ale brewed at the Abbey of Sint Sixtus near Westvleteren is easily the most coveted regular-production beer in the world. It's not because of the beer—well, not entirely. To acquire a bottle, you must visit the abbey, which happens to be seventy miles from the nearest Belgian city. The last part of the journey sends you zigzagging through fields of Brussels sprouts on one-lane roads. The abbey itself is hard to miss, but no signs direct you to the restaurant where travelers are welcome.

Abbey and Trappist Ales.

These ales are a class rather than a style, though in recent decades they have come to greater coherence. They are brewed in the Belgian tradition (even when not brewed in Belgium) and feature qualities often associated with wine—strength, complexity, and smoothness. They are made with sugar for a lighter body, greater strength, and a dry finish. The three most common styles range in strength from darker dubbel (Flemish for "double") to lighter tripel ("triple") to very strong beers that might be light or dark. Yet there are others, from spiced beers to lighter, sessionable beers to the inimitable, legendary Orval that wanders far from the pack.

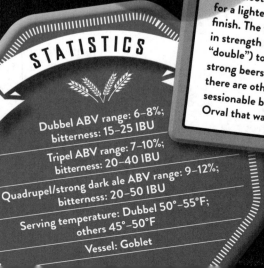

STATISTICS

Dubbel ABV range: 6–8%; bitterness: 15–25 IBU

Tripel ABV range: 7–10%; bitterness: 20–40 IBU

Quadrupel/strong dark ale ABV range: 9–12%; bitterness: 20–50 IBU

Serving temperature: Dubbel 50°–55°F; others 45°–50°F

Vessel: Goblet

When you do finally arrive at the one building on the planet where bottles of Westvleteren beer are sold, you have a final test: Will the gift shop be open? If everything goes according to plan (a plan that must include a meal with a creamy, mild slab of abbey-made cheese and a goblet of draft beer), you will leave the building with no more than one case of beer—the monks disallow hoarding.

Not all abbey ales are this hard to find, nor are all made in monasteries; yet they seem to possess the spirit of reverence, sanctity, and stillness that cloaks Sint Sixtus. In fact, there are only a handful of brewing monasteries, though secular, commercial makers do their best to invest their products with ecclesiastical essence. The beers in the abbey range are fit for chalices: deep, resonant, and alcoholic. There's no one type—some are light, some are dark, some strong, some, well, not quite so strong—except that they should be special and rare, deserving of all the mystique. ∎

ORIGINS

MONASTIC BREWING may seem somewhat contradictory—devil's water and godly monks—but it has a long history. Since its advent, brewing had been a solely domestic chore. Monasteries changed that when they took up brewing around the seventh or eighth century. The practice grew out of Cistercian rules that charged monks to be self-reliant and welcoming. Beer, safer than water, was a nutritious avenue to both ends. Monks grew their own barley (and, later, hops), made and drank their own beer, and offered a wholesome mug to pilgrims passing through.

Monks advanced the state of the brewing art by elevating it in scale and scope. Under Charlemagne, monasteries proliferated across Europe. At their height, 600 monasteries were making beer. In order to serve their growing consumer base, monks developed techniques of mass production that commercial breweries later adopted in the twelfth and thirteenth centuries: larger kettles and tuns, and better systems for managing the mash, boil, and fermentation. Monks were also the first to incorporate hops—or at least the first to write about their use—hundreds of years before they became a standard ingredient.

Commercial brewing eventually ended the monasteries' preeminence, but they continued to make beer on a small scale. It took the French

RIGHT: *The saint in this mosaic is holding a mashing fork.*

Meet the Trappists. Only one Catholic order currently brews beer

(though that may change soon), the Trappists, a reform branch of the Cistercian order. Armand Jean de Rancé led the reforms in the 1660s, which called for stricter fidelity to St. Benedict's rules; the order takes its name from the monastery at which he was abbot, La Trappe (the official name remains Order of Cistercians of the Strict Observance).

Until 1962, however, the Trappists were not the only brewers using the word "Trappist" on their labels—commercial breweries regularly appropriated the name. Chimay and Orval pushed for legal protection and managed to get the law changed then, but commercial breweries continued to exploit loopholes.

In 1985, the Trappists won improvements to the law, and now only cheese, beer, and other goods made at a monastery can use the words "Authentic Trappist Product." In this iteration, monks tightened the law so that to win the designation, beer has to be brewed inside monastery walls. Sounds clear enough, right? When you buy a beer with the hexagram seal and "Authentic Trappist" seal, you can be assured it was brewed at a monastery.

The trouble comes with a second designation. When the 1962 law was passed, breweries that had been making monastic-inspired beers had to scramble. Not all of these breweries were merely trading on the name—some had arrangements with local monasteries to sell beer under their name, with some proceeds directed back to the monks. Others used monastic names to evoke the history of their town or brewery. The nonmonastic breweries came up with the word "abbey" to describe their beers. All well and good until 1999, when the Union of Belgian Brewers gave sixteen breweries a special designation to indicate some vague monastic connection: "Recognized Belgian Abbey Beers."

These relationships all vary, and they are in many cases no different from similar relationships in other countries. The language gives them a confused status and has led titans like Stella Artois/InBev (Leffe), Heineken (Affligem), and Alken-Maes (Grimbergen) to rub robed elbows with Orval and Westvleteren. Charity may encourage us to look at this as something other than a con job, but suffice it to say that the big producers are in no hurry to correct people who think their beers were monastery brewed just like "authentic Trappist products."

Revolution to end production completely at the close of the eighteenth century. The revolutionary government seized monastery holdings and scattered fleeing monks as far as Russia. However, with the fall of Napolean, and particularly with the birth of Belgium in 1830, monks had the opportunity to rebuild old monasteries or start new ones. Since Westmalle and Westvleteren began brewing in the nineteenth century, monastic brewing has slowly been adding new members to its small fraternity. There's even a new kid on the block: Austria's Engelszell installed a brewery in 2011. In its typical deliberative manner, the International Trappist Association (the body that oversees Trappist economic interests) took its time considering the monastery's bid before adding it to the official list in 2012.

The romance of the abbey was not lost on commercial breweries, which by the nineteenth century had begun to trade on the Trappist mystique to sell their own beer. Laws now protect the Trappist brand, but the romance has proved potent—Trappist and abbey ales have enjoyed a rapidly growing market in Belgium. Abbey-themed brands are among the most popular and have shouldered aside many older, more traditional brands. It is a strange irony that in a country where church attendance is at record lows, beer brewed at monasteries or associated with them are more popular than ever. ■

DESCRIPTION AND CHARACTERISTICS

WHEN MONKS RETURNED to their ancient practice of brewing in the nineteenth century, they couldn't turn to a distinct tradition. Monasteries had always been fixtures of local regions, brewing beer according to local, rather than Trappist, tastes. If you look closely at the extant Trappist breweries, you see traces of those older traditions. Like its region around Antwerp, Westmalle is famous for its strong blond ales. Westvleteren makes hearty, dark beers in the style of West Flanders. (Stan Hieronymus writes in *Brew Like a Monk* that Westvleteren's beers used to be tart as well, situating them even more firmly in the regional tradition.) Finally, there is Orval, the oddball with wild yeast and fragrant dry-hopping, which seems to bear no resemblance to the other abbey ales. Yet it does taste a great deal like saisons, which were common in the south of Belgium where Orval is located. Trappist ales have grown stylistically closer together in recent decades, but they emerged from separate traditions—ones still faintly visible in their lineups.

That we can speak of them as a group at all is thanks to the constant pressure of a market that bends the arc of change toward customer expectation. Commercial breweries entered the market with their own versions of preexisting beers, replicating features of the originals. Styles like dubbels and tripels were made double and triple strength, further solidifying these beers as hallmarks. As a result, abbey ales now constitute a range of ales that bear consistent similarities. They are strong beers fermented warm to produce an interesting yeast character, but are dry and crisp. Some are dark, some are light, but they are all brewed with sugar to produce a lean body, help add strength, and dry the beers out. They are rich, effervescent, and luxurious.

Yet "abbey ales" are not a well-kempt style. There are stragglers like Bosteels Tripel Karmeliet, made with oats, wheat, and spices. Orval is a style unto itself, the one abbey ale made with wild yeast. Monasteries occasionally offer lighter beers like Westvleteren's fresh, hoppy Blond, Chimay Dorée, and Westmalle Extra. Some of the commercial abbey-style ales like Leffe, Affligem, and Grimbergen are closer to pale ales.

DUBBELS AND TRIPELS

There are two curiosities about the beers we now know as dubbels and tripels. The first is that they are associated with monastic brewing. Historically, breweries regularly made double-strength beer (dobbel gerst, double Diest, and double *uytzet*, to name three, were standard styles in the nineteenth century). I know of no reference to triple-strength beer prior to the twentieth century, but the idea of a range of beers, each stronger than the original, can be charted back to the distant past. Yet now dubbels and tripels are recognized solely as monastic-style beers.

The second curiosity is that the dubbel is now exclusively a darker beer while a tripel is golden. There's no reason a brewery couldn't make a dark tripel or a golden dubbel—except that convention now dictates the reverse. Such is the caprice of style evolution.

Whatever their original source (accounts vary), no one disputes that Westmalle popularized golden tripels— nor that every other tripel will ultimately be compared to Westmalle's. The hallmarks of that beer are strength (9.5% ABV)), dryness, and assertive hopping. The abbey is near Antwerp, a region where strong hoppy beers gained early popularity. As the style has evolved and spread, it has retained its strength but not always its hoppiness. St. Feuillien, Gouden Carolus, and St. Bernardus are all excellent, but sweeter, examples.

Tripels are now among Belgium's bestselling styles, but it wasn't always so. As recently as 1980, Westmalle's style-defining Tripel constituted less than 30 percent of production. Dubbel, accounting for the rest, was the flagship. Three decades later, again owing to the vagaries of the market, the products had nearly reversed position.

As a consequence, dubbels are now less common, though they have a longer lineage. These brown beers were once the norm in Belgium, and a rich color was the sign of quality. Even now, all the Trappists, with the exception of Orval, produce brown beers, and many emphasize them. Brewed to almost the strength of tripels, they are a homier style, with a comforting toasty or cocoa character wrapped in a warming blanket of malt. Rochefort 8 might be the

LEFT: *With its gracious space, polished copper equipment, and stained glass windows, it's not uncommon to hear Rochefort's brewhouse described as the world's most beautiful.*

exemplar of style, but St. Bernardus 8 is the most characterful and interesting, with a rich cocoa base, a touch of roastiness, and a dry biscotti finish.

STRONG DARK ALES AND QUADRUPELS

As if 8 to 9% ABV tripels weren't strong enough, the Trappists have located a higher rung on the ladder. Most of these very strong ales are dark—Westvleteren 12, St. Bernardus Abt 12, Achel Extra, and Rochefort 10. Very strong beers aren't new, but the name "quadrupel" is; La Trappe coined the term to describe a beer that has some of the darkness of those other dark abbey ales, but enough amber-orange luminosity to connect it to popular tripels. Fortunately, no brewery has yet tried to pioneer a quintupel. Yet.

In terms of enjoyment, few beers age as well as dark, strong abbey ales. Artisanal Belgian breweries typically

re-ferment their beer in the bottle (as all the monastic breweries do), further preparing them to age well. Stored at a cool temperature, these beers will mature for years, continuing to evolve like Port wine.

THE FAMOUS TRAPPIST BREWERIES

You might not think Catholic monks would brew exceptional beer and yet of the products produced by the Trappist monasteries of Belgium and the Netherlands, three are regarded as world standards, one is arguably the best beer in the world, and none is less than excellent. When you stop to consider their business model, though, it makes sense that the monks would brew very well. They have the long view, not regarding beer as a commodity so much as another extension of God's work. They are in no rush to turn a buck and have no intention of becoming multinational

The Belgian Degree System.

Monastic institutions are dedicated to preservation, and it's little wonder that their beers could serve as exhibits in the museum of brewing history. Achel and Rochefort, for example, still use the old Belgian degree system of measuring gravity. It's a simple system where specific gravity is converted to degrees by subtracting one from the number and multiplying by 100. The system is visually intuitive: a beer of 1.060 becomes 6°, 1.080 becomes 8°, and so on. Rochefort's line of beers include 6, 8, and 10, and they correspond to gravities of 1.063, 1.078, and 1.096 respectively.

For people familiar with the Plato system (see page 50), Belgian degrees can be confusing. In the Plato system, a degree works out to about 0.004 on the specific gravity scale; a beer of 8° Plato is therefore a puny 1.032. Conversely, a beer of 8° on the old Belgian system works out to about 1.079, or 19° Plato.

giants. The monks bring care and attention to their beers, and they have been perfecting them for decades. Considering these facts, it isn't surprising in the slightest that they would produce uniformly wonderful beer.

Following is a description of each Trappist brewery, beginning with the oldest.

WESTMALLE

(Abdij der Trappisten van Westmalle)

The monastery was founded in 1794, just northeast of Antwerp. The monks started brewing in the 1830s for their own use, and started selling beer to locals in the 1870s. In 1921, Westmalle decided to sell its beer more widely. The famous lineup evolved until settling to the current three in the 1950s. Since that time, Westmalle hasn't fiddled with them, though the recipes do change to adjust for malt variations.

Everyone knows that tripels are golden-colored, but until recent decades, strong ales were largely brown. How did tripels lose their color? Westmalle is one possible candidate. Certainly no brewer is more associated with the long tradition of golden tripels than Westmalle, which popularized the strong golden style even if it didn't invent it. The abbey's Dubbel is slightly less famous, but its impact just as strong. It remains a ruddy brown—one of Belgium's classic hues.

The beers form a nice counterpoint to one another. Both express a fair amount of spicy, estery yeast character, but the beers take these qualities in different directions. The gorgeous Tripel is known for its amazing head stability. A beer of 9.5% alcohol should burn off its foam, but if you look in your goblet following your final swallow, you may well find a final skiff, coating the bottom of the glass like a dusting of snow. Tripel is hoppy at 39 IBU, something that is not evident in the aroma (those hops help the foam stick around). Instead, the sweet, rich, alcoholic notes subtly hint at their presence on the first impression. The spicy hops come later and rescue the beer from becoming overly rich. The body is full and creamy, effervescent, but not heavy. In Tripel, yeast accentuates spice. Dubbel is more gentle and homey. The aromas and flavors are toffee sweet, leavened with figs and banana. The malts are dry, though, scone-like, and the finish is crisp. Here, the yeast has more fruit and the spice becomes a balancing note.

LEFT: *Brewery or house of worship? The Trappists view beer-making as an extension of the Lord's work.*

WESTVLETEREN
(Sint-Sixtus Abdij van Westvleteren)

The Sint Sixtus monastery was founded in 1831 when monks from Sainte Marie du Mont des Cats abbey (which would, fifty years later, send monks to found La Trappe) joined a hermit living in the woods. These woods just happened to be outside Poperinge in Belgium's hop-growing region. The small community grew slowly, and monks added the brewery seven years later. In a rare exception to the historical rule, the brewery went undisturbed in World War I, and in 1928 it started selling to the public to fund an expansion. In World War II, however, the monastery wasn't so fortunate and had to suspend brewing. In 1946, Westvleteren licensed nearby St. Bernardus to brew its products under the Sint Sixtus name, an arrangement that lasted until 1992. (St. Bernardus continued to brew the erstwhile Westvleteren line under its own name; see box on page 305.)

Westvleteren's beers are undoubtedly the most coveted in the world—at least for regular, year-round beers. The reason is because the monks refuse to ramp up production. Beer is sold only in the monastery café, In de Vrede, and by the crate (one only, please!) at the brewery dock. The monks believe the brewery serves the monastery, not vice versa, and the restricted production is a matter of practice for the monks who spend six hours of their day in prayer.

Until 1999, the brewery made a range of beers from a

RIGHT: Scourmont Abbey, where the illustrious Chimay brewery is located

4% ABV light table beer to the signature 10% strong dark ale that is now known as 12. That year, the brewery replaced the two weakest beers with a hoppy blond ale—a nod to both changing convention as well as local hop fields. The most famous is the aforementioned 12, a beer that regularly fetches twenty dollars or more on after-market sales. It is a warming, bready beer with banana and hazelnut notes. It ages well for years and acquires the character of an English barley wine. The 8 is roastier, with touches of smoke and caramelized sugar. The real treat is the least famous of the beers, the Blond. Far more complex than the others, it has the hazy, rustic quality of a saison. The nose and palate have the floral scent of blossom and the sweetness of honey, yet it is a crisp, dry beer with rich hop character. An irony, but true—hidden among the most famous beers is an overlooked wonder that is the true classic.

CHIMAY
(Notre-Dame de Scourmont Abbey)

Chimay is the best known of the Trappist breweries, and most beer fans will

St. Bernardus.

When wandering wild forest land, you will from time to time come across two trees growing so closely together that they share a single bole near the ground and only start to be two trees when you look upward; such is the case with St. Bernardus and Westvleteren. Following World War II, when the monks at Westvleteren decided to locate their brewing activities outside the monastery, they looked to a cheese maker in the village of Watou. The little operation was already called St. Bernardus, a vestige of its origins as a monastic community that had fled there from France.

The monks from Westvleteren relocated the brewing equipment to Watou and the brewmaster taught St. Bernardus how to make the beer according to their specifications and methods. The first three beers brewed there will be familiar to modern fans of the brewery: Abt 12, Prior 8, and Pater 6, all dark ales in the tradition of Flanders. At St. Bernardus, they used the same yeast and ingredients to make these beers as they had at Westvleteren, and have now been making them for nearly seven decades. In an interesting twist, one could argue that these three beers carry the Westvleteren legacy the closest. They (and all the brewery's beers; the line expanded to eight offerings) use Westvleteren's original yeast strain, which the monks no longer use. In addition to the original three beers, St. Bernardus brews a well-regarded tripel, witbier, and Christmas ale.

have had a glass—it's available at many grocery stores and you even see it on tap sometimes (it's the only Trappist beer sold that way). One shouldn't construe this availability as evidence that it's a mass-market beer, though; Chimay is one of the most highly regarded brands in the world.

Monks built the Notre-Dame de Scourmont Abbey near the village of Chimay in 1850 and equipped it with a brewery. Like most of the Trappist monasteries, the monks cast about with different recipes and multiple iterations before finding their voice. The current beers sprang from a collaboration between Father Théodore and the famous scientist Jean de Clerck. Between the late 1940s and 1966, the monastery introduced the familiar chromatic series—Red, White, and Blue. Still, the recipes change slightly. In addition to changes in fermentation, the hops also shift. Chimay surprisingly prefers American hops, using Galena, Nugget, and Cluster at various times to bitter, changing varieties for optimum flavor. (Hallertau is used to flavor.) Interestingly, it doesn't use whole hops, but extract, a quirk since picked up by Orval and Westvleteren but rare elsewhere.

Although most people know them by their colors, the beers actually have names. Première (Red) is the lightest in the range at 7.1%, and is roughly dubbel-like in style. Cinq Cents (White) is a tripel weighing in at 8.2%, and Grande Réserve

(Blue), at 9%, can be slotted with stronger dark abbeys like Westvleteren's. The line shares a strong family resemblance: The beers are elegant, sporting heady, refined aromas and rich tones, but they're delicate, light, and quite dry. Of the three, Grande Réserve is the standout. It has a spicy, complex nose and a deep chestnut body topped by a silky latte head. The flavor is dessert-rich: creamy and soft with vanilla notes and plum, and then the long finish, a little sharp with alcohol, just to remind you that this is an adult's beverage.

LA TRAPPE (Abdij Koningshoeven)
In 1880, the abbot of Sainte Marie du Mont des Cats, concerned about the French government's attitude toward religious institutions, sent Brother Wyart to the Netherlands to look for a potential site in friendlier lands. The envoy found a lovely farming area near Tilburg that the locals called Koningshoeven—the Royal Farms—and the brothers decided to establish a second monastery there. They renovated a sheep barn and, to help support a growing population, built a brewery four years later.

There are several ways in which La Trappe is unlike the other Trappist breweries, and it has little to do with location. Notably, the monastery started brewing lagers and continued to do so for a hundred years. In 1969, Koningshoeven (a name used not only for the land but also the monastery itself) licensed its brewery to Stella Artois, an arrangement that lasted over a decade. When the monks resumed control of the brewery in 1980, they made the momentous decision to abandon lagers and produce beers typical of the Trappist family. The

licensing experiment didn't sour the abbey on commercial partners, though, and in 1999, Koningshoeven set up a partnership with Bavaria Brewery (a Dutch company, despite the name). Now Bavaria rents the equipment and buildings from the abbey and operates the brewery for the monks. The partnership caused a dispute over La Trappe's status as a Trappist brewery, but in 2005 the International Trappist Association affirmed the affiliation—the beer is officially Trappist.

Despite the abbey's historical roots, the beers of La Trappe are now in the familiar range of strong ales—a Dubbel, a Tripel, and the first beer ever called a Quadrupel. Of all the Trappists, La Trappe's beers are the sweetest and least complex. Hop character is absent or nearly so, and the yeast character enhances the sense of sweetness. The beers find their balance through alcohol heat—in the Quadrupel, it's legendary—yet the relatively low levels of attenuation leave the beers on the sweet side.

ROCHEFORT
(Abbaye Notre-Dame de Saint Rémy)
The Abbaye Notre-Dame de Saint Rémy began life in 1230 as a convent; it didn't become a monastery until 1464. Brewing started in 1595, and monks cultivated hops and barley on the grounds. After plagues, schisms, and wars ravaged the property in the coming centuries (it was sacked by Calvinists in 1568), the entire monastery began restoration in 1887. They completed the brewery in 1899—sans hop and barley fields.

Rochefort's early beers weren't very good. By 1950, it was in danger of being put out of business by Chimay, sixty miles away. Instead, Chimay sent Jean de Clerck to help it make better beer. Over the next five years, Rochefort introduced the beers it still produces, though two of the names have changed.

The beers of Rochefort are simply made. They use two principal base malts as well as sugar and wheat starch to boost alcohol. The water is much prized for its purity and hardness, and the brewers believe it's the key to Rochefort's complexity. They use two hop varieties, Hallertau and Styrian Golding, and finish with a blend of two yeast strains. And just to mix things up, they tuck in a tiny dash of coriander.

The brewery produces just three beers: 6, 8, and 10. They are all brown ales and have a similar raisiny, earthy, bready nose. The flavors tend toward sweetness, and as the beer rests on the tongue, is something like a liquid fruitcake: lots of winter fruits, a healthy warmth from rummy alcohol, and you can even find bread and nuts if you let your tongue soak long enough. A vigorous effervescence and those hard water notes balance the beers and keep them from cloying.

ORVAL (Abbaye Notre-Dame d'Orval)

A full description of the brewery and beer appears on pages 314–317.

ACHEL (Sint Benedictus Abdij)

When most people think of Trappist breweries, they count six Belgian and one Dutch. But it's really one and a half Dutch. The Abbey of St. Benedict started life in 1686 as a hermitage (that's what its informal name, Achelse Kluis, means) in Achel, Belgium, near Valkenswaard, Netherlands, with part of the property located across the border in the Netherlands. The monks were expelled from the monastery in 1789, but a priory was reestablished by monks from Westmalle in 1844, complete with a brewery and maltery. In a familiar story, the Germans destroyed the brewery during World War I and despite plans to rebuild it, Achel went brewery-less until the late 1990s.

When the abbey decided to reinstall a brewery, the monks relied heavily on the Westmalle influence. Brother Thomas, a retired monk from Westmalle, created the initial formulations and conducted the first test batches. The recipes for Achel's line came into focus over the course of the first few years (with later help from Brother Antoine, a monk from Rochefort) and have remained constant since the mid-2000s. The link between the abbeys continues through use of the same yeast strain.

Achel's three main beers are a blond and a brown called 8° (both are 8%) and a strong dark beer of 9.5%. At the brewery, they also offer a 5° beer, but only sell it onsite. Like most of the Trappist ales, the recipes for Achel's are elegantly simple: pilsner malt, sugars (light or dark, depending on the beer), a bit of darker malt where necessary, and Saaz hops. Extra, the dark beer and Achel's strongest, is the most complex. It's actually a dark amber more than fully brown, and the foam is no match for all that alcohol. Rum notes come through the nose and palate, with burnt sugar, prunes, sarsaparilla, and a dash of banana ester. The alcohol, though deadly to the beer's head, is gentle and soothing in the drink. Perhaps because Achel has not had decades to refine its palate into something unique and unmistakable, the brewery's beers, while lovely, seem to echo some of their inspirations at Westmalle and Rochefort.

STIFT ENGELSZELL

The Abbey of Stift Engelszell is located in far northern Austria on the Danube River, just one mile south of the German border, and fewer than twenty southeast of the Czech Republic. Founded in 1293, it spent 500 years as a Cistercian monastery until it was dissolved and placed in secular hands in 1786. Trappists took it over again in 1925, lost it during World War II (when Hitler dispatched five of the brothers to a concentration camp), and started anew after the war.

The monastery is more famous for liqueurs and cheese, but it also added the world's newest small Trappist brewery in 2012. The International Trappist Association accepted its application a year later and it now offers two products: a strong saison, Benno (which the brewery calls a tripel), and a strong dark ale named Gregorius. Of the two, the Benno is the more interesting beer, with spicy farmhouse notes and a dollop of honey that adds to a cakey, sweet palate. Early bottles were not quite in focus, but the beer is unique and like nothing in the Trappist range—given years to evolve, it might become a standout in its own right. ∎

BREWING NOTES

WHAT DISTINGUISHES ABBEY ales is not their methods—which are typical for Belgium—but their execution. The breweries making the hallmark beers have been doing so for a very long time: Chimay's most recent recipes date to the 1960s, Orval's to the 1930s, Rochefort's and Westmalle's to the 1950s. St. Bernardus and Westvleteren, breweries with entwined histories, have recent recipes originating just after the Second World War. Any alterations in method, equipment, and ingredients were made only after careful consideration and have been implemented incrementally. The beers are so good because they've been fine-tuned for decades.

The beers begin with a base of European pilsner malt and a sizable

portion of sugar—this is key to their profile. Even the heftiest abbey ales are light bodied, and that comes from grists of up to 20 percent sugar. Invariably referred to as "candi sugar," Belgian grists actually employ various types of sugars and sometimes a mixture within one grist. The basic sugar is sucrose (the same table sugar used in baking), usually in liquid form, and often it comes from locally grown beets. In dark beers, breweries use a caramelized amber syrup that adds both color and a fruity, rummy flavor. Dextrose is a slightly different form, also common.

Abbey ales are not fundamentally different from many Belgian ales. Strong, hoppy ales like Duvel are a close match for *tripels*, as are, counterintuitively, *double IPAs*. These latter beers require an appreciation for intense hopping, but they share the tripels' light, crisp body and robust strength. Dubbels are essentially stronger versions of *Belgian brown* ales and have some qualities in common with *sweet stouts*, which are admittedly lighter. Some of the lighter Trappist beers, like Achel 5° and Westvleteren Blond, are actually *Belgian pale ales*, and the very strong, dark abbey ales are cousins to *English barley wines* and *old ales*.

Hops, often a neglected element in Belgian brewing, are sometimes used to great effect in monastic beers. Because the beers are so strong, even where they're not marked by hop character they must be balanced. Spiciness plays an important role in many abbey ales, and hops work with yeast to create the flavor. By American standards, Westmalle and Orval aren't aggressively bitter, but they are green and lively, hoppier than most Belgian ales. This inclination has opened the door to other hoppy interpretations such as those by De Ranke (Guldenberg). A minority of breweries add spice, usually as a subtle accent note.

As with so many Belgian styles, yeast takes center stage. Belgian strains are famous for producing more esters and phenols than ale strains in the United States and Britain. That's true of the Trappist yeasts, too, though the effect is not uniform. Wyeast Labs ran experiments on the strains they isolated from the breweries and found that some (Chimay and Westmalle) were predisposed to produce clove notes. The yeast from Rochefort produces a particular ester that tastes like roses or honey. The yeasts are all alcohol tolerant and don't produce some of the harsh fusel alcohols other strains do in similar circumstances.

One of the biggest factors in the way these yeasts behave is temperature. The higher the temperature, the more esters and phenols a yeast will produce. Belgian brewers pitch at different temperatures and let the activity of the yeast raise the temperature to different levels. Rochefort pitches at 68°F and lets the temperature rise just to 73°F. Chimay is pitched at the same temperature but is allowed to rise to 82°F. Orval is pitched at a cool 58°F and allowed to rise to 72°F; however, in Orval's case the brewers have found that time is more important than temperature within that range. Orval always takes five days to ferment, and the brewers adjust the temperature to speed it up or slow it down. All of these decisions affect the way the final beer tastes, giving them their unique character.

We have a lovely real-time experiment of how the same yeast strain behaves differently in different circumstances. Westmalle provides fresh cultures of its strain to Achel and Westvleteren (that is, there's no "house effect" of later-generation mutations) and all make a similar dubbel ale. Westmalle begins fermentation at 64°F and lets it rise to just 68°F; Achel also starts at 64°F but allows it to rise to 73°F; Westvleteren goes warm, from 68°F all the way to 84°F. The effect is pronounced. Westmalle's dubbel is smooth and dry, characterized more by the malts and sugars than yeast.

Achel 8° picks up a bit more fruit from the esters. Westvleteren 8, by contrast, has an assertively phenolic smoky note. None could be confused for the other.

Abbey-style ales have become popular enough that they are now brewed around the world. In deference to their august origin, most breweries tend to follow the spirit of the Trappist ales, though American breweries are less likely to use sugar (or use less when they do), more likely to use color malts, and tend to ferment cooler. There are now hundreds of examples of these beers, and many made by secular breweries are exceptional. ∎

EVOLUTION

ABBEY ALES HAVE gone mainstream. If we consider the Trappists the starting point, then there has been a bit of creep away from their boozy standards. Three of Belgium's bestselling brands are sold with an ecclesiastical gloss (Affligem, Grimbergen, and Leffe), but they're all in the 6% ABV range—a mass-market concession well below the strengths of the Trappists.

In the United States, abbey ales have gone the other direction, toward strength. They often skip the dubbel and go straight for robust tripels. Americans have also championed the quadrupel, inevitably called "quad." American consumers are understandably confused by why a dubbel would be brown, a tripel blond, and a quadrupel brown again, and perhaps for this reason, there seems to

be a trend toward golden quads as well. Avery's The Reverend, Victory's V-12, and Schlafly Quadrupel are all on the copper-orange continuum.

There may be a relationship between tripels and a very American-style beer: the double IPA. When American breweries were looking to make lean, golden-base beers to act as hop tinctures, they discovered techniques the Trappists have long used. Both styles are made with pale malts, use sugar for lightness and attenuation, and are brewed to great strength. In a hoppy tripel like Westmalle you can even see a direct link. It's odd to think of such an American style as the offspring of such a Belgian one, but the links are more than cosmetic. ∎

THE BEERS TO KNOW

T HE ROMANCE and mystique of the abbey and Trappist ales make them the standard-bearers for this category of beer, and this is why they were all treated and described separately in this chapter. Their products do, however, have secular equals. It's hard to corral them all into a cohesive group—there's no abbey "style," after all—but many make their identities known through allusions to the ecclesiastical. Here is a selection of good commercial imitations to try.

DUBBELS

ST. BERNARDUS PATER 6

LOCATION: Watou, Belgium

MALT: Alexis, Prisma, roasted

HOPS: Target, Styrian Golding

6.7% ABV

O ften overlooked is Pater 6, one of the finest abbey ales made. Amazingly creamy and fluffy, it has a deep, nutty palate with a touch of roast and dark fruit, and a surprisingly dry finish. In Belgium, 6.7% ABV may be considered a "moreish" strength—if so, this is its avatar.

NEW BELGIUM ABBEY

LOCATION: Fort Collins, CO

MALT: Pale, chocolate, Carapils, caramel, Munich

HOPS: Willamette, Target, Liberty

7% ABV, 1.066 SP. GR., 20 IBU

N ew Belgium's offering has the telltales of "high fermentation," namely banana, bubble gum, and clove, those esters and phenols that come from warm fermentation. The heart of the beer is cocoa, with a caramel and bread edging. It's sweet, warming, and inviting.

CHOC DUBBEL

ooooooooooooooooooooooooooooooooooooooooooo

LOCATION: Krebs, OK

MALT: Belgian pilsner, Special B, aromatic

HOPS: Perle

8% ABV, 20 IBU

Choc's dubbel is on the far side of sweetness, and the brewery helps keep it from cloying with volcanic effervescence. The flavors will remind you of dark foods—brown sugar, raisins, and chocolate. The sugars begin to gather with warmth, giving it a wassail-like quality.

TRIPELS

UNIBROUE LA FIN DU MONDE

ooooooooooooooooooooooooooooooooooooooooooo

LOCATION: Chambly, Québec, Canada

MALT: Undisclosed

HOPS: Undisclosed

OTHER: Coriander

9% ABV, 19 IBU

Unibroue was way ahead of its time, providing North America with Belgian-style ales that were accomplished enough to rival the originals. La Fin du Monde was an early triumph: a huge, buoyant ale that froths into a tulip glass with energy and life. A sweet beer further sweetened by coriander, it has complex esters and phenols that open up in the mouth. The swallow brings a surprisingly crisp finish.

ABOVE: Grimbergen is brewed by Alken-Maes, not monks, but the large beer company is happy to capitalize on the confusion.

LA RULLES TRIPEL

ooooooooooooooooooooooooooooooooooooooooooo

LOCATION: Rulles, Belgium

MALT: Pilsner, pale

HOPS: Amarillo, Cascade, Warrior

OTHER: Dark sugar

8.4% ABV, 1.074 SP. GR., 38 EBU

La Rulles is a fascinating example of modern Belgian brewing. Gregory Verhelst founded the brewery in 2000 and borrowed Orval's yeast. But in putting together his tripel, Verhelst looked to Yakima, Washington, for hops that would give it a tropical flair. It is a rustic beer, though, with peppery yeast character, a grain-y, honeyed malt base, and wildflower aromatics.

ST. FEUILLIEN TRIPEL

○○

LOCATION: Le Rœulx, Belgium

MALT: Undisclosed

HOPS: Undisclosed

OTHER: Undisclosed spices;
dextrose and maltose syrup

8.5% ABV

When St. Feuillien reclaimed its brewing tradition from Du Bocq Brewery, to whom it had entrusted it for a decade, it launched Tripel, now its flagship. A distinctive take on the style that depends on hard, mineral-rich water and a very dry palate. Malt aromatics blend with unidentifiable spices (which the brewery, protective of its formulation, keeps a secret) that are at turns herbal, grassy, and tingly with eucalyptus. The yeast contributes more spiciness, which accentuates the dry palate and minerality.

DARK STRONG ALES AND QUADRUPELS

ST. BERNARDUS ABT 12

○○

LOCATION: Watou, Belgium

MALT: Pilsner, black

HOPS: Target, Saaz

OTHER: Sucrose, dark caramel syrup

10.5% ABV, 1.090 SP. GR., 22 IBU

Despite its nearly ebony color, Abt 12's only roasty notes come across as dry cocoa; the rest of the nose and palate are dominated by fruit. Lots of plum and raisin marry a refined, vinous palate. Like the Pater 6, it is a creamy beer, but—thanks to a large dose of sugar in the grist (just below 20 percent)—it's thinner and more sharply alcoholic, like brandy. Dessert in a glass.

OMMEGANG THREE PHILOSOPHERS

○○

LOCATION: Cooperstown, NY

MALT: Pilsner, pale, caramel, extra special, Munich, Belgian aromatic

HOPS: Styrian Golding, Hallertauer, Spalter Select

OTHER: Dextrose, Liefmans Kriek

9.2% ABV, 1.090 SP. GR., 21 IBU

Three Philosophers came from Ommegang's collaboration with homebrewer Noel Blake and is a slight departure from classic Belgian examples. The base beer is brown-sugar sweet with a raisiny, chocolatey quality. This is then blended with 2 percent Liefmans Kriek (Ommegang and Liefmans are part of the Moortgat family) for a cherry finish. It's a decadent treat.

Abbaye Notre-Dame d'Orval

MORE THAN A TRAPPIST BREWERY

IF A COUNTRY THE SIZE OF MARYLAND CAN BE SAID TO HAVE REMOTE AREAS, THE MONKS OF THE ABBAYE NOTRE-DAME D'ORVAL FOUND ONE. THE GENTLE UNDULATIONS OF CENTRAL BELGIUM TURN TURBULENT IN THE ARDENNES OF THE SOUTH, WHERE OPEN FIELDS GIVE WAY TO FOREST LAND AND RIVER VALLEYS LACED IN MIST. THE MOUNTAINS AREN'T HUGE, BUT THEY OFFER DRAMATIC VIEWS AND, FOR PEOPLE SEEKING SOLACE, QUIET POCKETS PROTECTED BY TREES AND PEAKS. FOR NEARLY A THOUSAND YEARS, PEOPLE HAVE USED THE LAND AROUND ORVAL ABBEY FOR JUST THIS PURPOSE.

The first monks arrived from Italy in 1070, but abandoned the site shortly after. Monks returned and completed the abbey in 1124. In the following centuries, the monastery bore the suffering that scarred Europe: Orval was destroyed by fire and war (and dutifully rebuilt) in the thirteenth and sixteenth centuries. At the end of the seventeenth century, the abbot Charles de Bentzeradt established Orval as a member of the Order of the Strict Observance (the Trappists). But the monastery's grace period didn't last. Once again, the monastery was razed in 1793 during the French Revolution. Although the current monastery looks hundreds of years old (and there are ruins that stand as testament to its history), Orval was rebuilt for the last time beginning in the 1920s—once more of the ochre-colored sandstone known locally as *pierre de France*.

The brewery was completed in 1931, well before the monastery—and indeed, the brewery was conceived in order to fund construction. Every abbey has its own method of managing its brewery. Sometimes monks are still involved (Westvleteren), while in other cases the brewing has mostly shifted to lay brewers. At Orval, monks never brewed. Instead, they set up the brewery as a private business that operates under their direction inside the monastery. Currently, 45 percent of the proceeds are adequate to maintain Orval; the monks use the remaining 55 percent for their charitable activities. As François de Harenne, administrative and commercial director of the brewery, put it: "It is their company within their walls, but it is not really their activity."

Unlike the other Trappist breweries, Orval has only ever produced a single

ABOVE: *The lovely Abbaye Notre-Dame d'Orval*

BELOW: *Although the mash/lauter tuns and kettles are made to look like old coppers, the glass floor reveals just how modern the brewery is.*

beer. It is a curious blend of influences. The first brewer was a German named Martin Pappenheimer, who was in turn assisted by John Vanhuele, a Belgian who had spent much time brewing in England. In Orval's telling, the vibrant hopping came from Pappenheimer and Vanhuele was the source of infusion mashing and dry-hopping.

The beer is little changed from the original recipe, crafted during a time when British beer was popular in Belgium. Orval uses two types of caramel malts, typical of English ales, but rarer in Belgian ones. The brewery uses hard water and mashes at a low temperature, then adds a stiff dose of hops (Hallertauer, American hops, and Strisselspalt, which have come to replace Styrian Golding) during the boil. At this point, it bears a strong resemblance to English pale ales, and that effect is

LEFT: *Horizontal fermenters, where Orval is dosed with wild yeast and dry-hopped. The fermenters extend back 15 to 20 feet.*

BELOW: *One of the specially prepared sachets of hops for use in the horizontal fermenters. Ten bags will go in each fermenter.*

enhanced by dry-hopping. But then Orval shifts gears. After a five-day fermentation, the beer goes to horizontal tanks where it is dosed with a second yeast infusion that includes *Brettanomyces.*

There's no reason to doubt the story of Pappenheimer and Vanhuele, but what about the wild yeast? If anyone knows who inspired that, they're not talking. The yeasts begin to dry out the beer and work with the carbonate water—straight from the "Matilde spring" (see "The Legend" on the facing page)— to stiffen it. It spends three weeks in the horizontal tanks and another month in the bottle, ripening. At release, it is a beer of just over 6% alcohol—hoppy, dry, and rustic. And here's the most curious thing of all: Despite the influence of two foreign brewing traditions and the creep of decades, Orval would be very familiar to nineteenth-century saison producers

of the region. It is justifiably called one of the country's most traditional beers and is firmly in the saison family.

Orval went through a major renovation in 2007 that nearly doubled the brewery's capacity to 67,000 hectoliters (about 57,000 U.S. barrels). The abbey upgraded the brewhouse for greater efficiency; a week's brewing on the old system can now be done in a day. To ferment the increased capacity, Orval had to switch from open primary fermenters to more space-efficient cylindro-conical fermenters. The brewers were worried that it would compromise the flavor profile, so they spent three years in transition. De Harenne described the process: "We had part of the beer fermented in open vessels and part of it in cylindro-conical tanks. And when we were completely sure there was no difference in the taste of the beer coming from one side and the other side, we mounted the other five cylindro-conical tanks."

Unusual for a Belgian brewery, almost all the production stays in Belgium. Just 14 percent is parceled out to the rest of the world, and demand far outstrips supply. There's no more room to grow on the monastery premises, and the monks want to keep production entirely within the walls at Orval. The world is getting as much Orval as it ever will.

THE BEER

It is true that Orval makes only one product (a second product sold only at the monastery, Petit Orval, is just a diluted version of the original), but it's a shape shifter, becoming very different beers as it ages. One is vibrant and spirited, marked by hops that are as resinous and green as any in Belgian beer. As Orval ages, the hops fall back and the *Brettanomyces* comes on, providing a lemon-zest note. The beer gets drier the longer it ages, and will become an austere, sherry-like ale of enormous complexity. Although there's a loss of liveliness, Orval becomes more soulful, like an older singer whose range has been replaced by life and character. Wild yeasts constantly change the beer, making mutability its nature.

It is bottled at a strength of 6.2%, but can pick up another full point of alcohol as the *Brettanomyces* continue to

work. It is one of the few beers regularly cited as the best by other Belgian brewers, all of whom have preferences about at what age Orval achieves perfection. Put a few bottles in your cellar and get them aging so you can determine your preference as well.

THE LEGEND

On Orval's label you will find a picture of a fish with what turns out to be, on closer inspection, a golden ring in its mouth. There's a legend behind the image, and it starts with the Tuscan Countess Matilde, a widow and one of the first arrivals to the region in the eleventh century. Before the monastery was built, she was sitting near a spring to rest and restore herself. When she reached into the spring, her wedding band slipped off. Distraught, she immediately started praying and before long a trout rose to the surface of the water, her golden ring in its mouth. "Truly this place is a Val d'Or [valley of gold]," she exclaimed. To this day, the pool of legend enjoys a prominent place at the monastery—and the spring remains the source for the beer.

RIGHT: *Fields just outside the abbey, a reminder of the self-sufficiency of the Trappist monks*

The Beers of
ITALY

Across the world, little breweries have popped up like mushroom caps after a spring rain. Craft brewing has become an international phenomenon, and rare is the nation where some homebrewer hasn't welded together a mash tun and kettle big enough to start selling on a commercial scale. Brazil, New Zealand, and Spain are among the leading formerly beer-poor countries to catch the craft brewing bug, but even places like India and Ukraine have nascent scenes.

But none has shown the originality and expressiveness of Italy, which has gone from no craft breweries in 1995 to more than 450 today. Bereft of a beer tradition, Italians felt free to pick and choose from the styles and techniques of the world, and have appropriated methods from Belgium, Germany, England, and the U.S.—but employ more than a little Italian originality as well. Many Italian beers are made from hybrid techniques—some even borrowed from winemakers—and most are crafted with an eye toward the dinner table. Many have local products tucked into the recipe, and they have launched at least one new local ingredient, chestnuts, into regular use. The beers of Italy remind you of beers elsewhere, but only in melody; the arrangement and tempos are different, and they are works of strikingly indigenous, original art. ∎

ORIGINS

F YOU DRIVE from Milan toward Turin with the serrated tips of the Alps rising to your right, the landscape won't *appear* to be beer country. The green hills roll toward the mountains, vineyards basking on their sunny sides. You won't see hop or barley farms here; historically, Italy lies below the "beer belt," in the steamier lands of grape and olive. Yet this is beer country now, or at least new beer country, and little breweries are tucked into the villages that lie in the valleys across this gorgeous region.

The figures are still quite modest. At 13 million hectoliters (11 million barrels), Italy produces far less beer than countries like Spain and Poland (never mind Germany and the U.K.), and looks up to even France and Romania. The vast majority of Italy's output is still made by companies like Peroni and Moretti, who make typical, mass-market lagers. Yet beer has a long history in Italy—archaeological discoveries place its arrival well before the time of Christ—and there's no reason the beer belt needs to be tethered only to countries producing grain. That must have occurred to Italian beer fans twenty years ago, because without coordination or significant knowledge of each other, they started founding little breweries in an effort to bring beer back to wine country.

In that early vanguard were two leaders whose influence came to define Italian brewing, Baladin's Teo Musso and Birrificio Italiano's Agostino Arioli, two men whose passion for beer goes back to the 1980s. Arioli got started first, taking up homebrewing as a college student in 1985. At the time, it was impossible to buy ingredients or equipment locally—no one homebrewed in Italy—but Arioli's father found him a source in the brewing industry who helped him get started. His interest in brewing led him to Germany, where he found guidance from "new-style" brewpubs that were very delicately experimenting with old traditions. (In manner, Arioli shares something of the

ABOVE: *Italian brewing pioneer Teo Musso tasting vintage beer with translator Fabio Mozzone in Piozzo*

Germans he first studied with—he is ordered and precise in the way he thinks about beer.) After that, Arioli started shifting his coursework toward technical classes like biochemistry and refrigeration that might help him as a brewer, and after graduation he worked for brief periods at two brewpubs in Germany before finally founding his own brewery, Birrificio Italiano, in the Lombardy region in 1996.

Musso wasn't far behind, establishing a pub in his tiny Piedmontese hometown of Piozzo in 1986. Unlike Arioli, who carries himself like a scientist, Musso looks and acts like a rock star. When I first arrived in Piozzo, he was surrounded by fans from Spain who raved about his beer like groupies. Musso has tousled hair, a rakish beard, and speaks low, so that you are forced to lean into his orbit. He began his brewing journey as an avid beer fan, gradually assembling a bottle list that would ultimately grow to 200, almost all European imports. Having sampled his way through a buffet of the world's beer, it was those from Belgium that captivated him, so in 1991, he started traveling to the homeland to "discover the secret of the production of beer." By 1995 Musso was ready to start his own brewery and, with the help of Jean-Louis Dits of the Belgian farmhouse producer La Brasserie à Vapeur, he welded together a five-hectoliter brewery and hung out a shingle for Baladin.

These weren't the only Italian breweries to open in the mid-1990s (others, like the collective that formed Lambrate, had similar quixotic aspirations), but Musso and Arioli introduced two styles that would come to define Italian brewing: the German lager school and the Belgian bottle-conditioned school. (The third, American-influenced, school would come later.) Like the United States in the

"In Italy we have three schools. The first two were, one, the Belgian school (the most important producer is Teo Musso), and then we had Agostino Arioli of Birrificio Italiano (that is, of the German school). These were the first two schools or inspirations. Then we had Birra del Borgo, which was more English in the beginning but then became American. This is the third school. More creativity, more extreme."

—BRUNO CARILLI OF TOCCALMATTO (A BREWERY OF THE THIRD SCHOOL)

What's a Craft Brewery? The phrase "craft brewery" has its

origins in the United States. It evolved from "microbreweries," the first name given to
the tiny breweries founded in the 1970s and '80s. In the American context, it has at
least a little utility. By the time microbreweries arrived, the entire market consisted
of mass-market lager, a bland style of beer made by huge national companies. It was
easy to see how the micros differed: They were independent and small, and they made
artisanal beer to "gourmet" standards. The word "craft," echoing "hand-crafted," was a
way to draw attention to the emphasis on quality, not just the breweries' small size. Time
has eroded the clarity of the term—not all beer made by craft breweries is exceptional
in quality, and not all craft breweries are small or independent anymore—but it still has
some meaning. As craft brewing begins in countries like Italy—which has large national
beer companies and nothing else—the term is similarly useful.

In other countries, it's far more problematic. The dichotomies between large/small,
independent/corporate, and mass market/artisanal don't make any sense. Many of the
most accomplished breweries in Britain, Belgium, Germany, the Czech Republic, and
France throw these definitions on their head. They may be independent, large, and
artisanal—and *old*. In those countries, the younger and smaller breweries may compete
against august establishments just down the street that have walls full of medals—
rightfully so—and have been brewing for decades.

1970s, Italy in the '90s had no particular
brewing tradition; customers had no
expectations about what craft-brewed
beer should taste like. With Baladin and
Birrificio Italiano as models, they began
to form them.

Musso and Arioli saw success,
and their approaches came to define
Italian craft brewing. Soon customers
started expecting either rich, elegant
lagers like Italiano's or complex, food-
friendly ales in the Baladin mode. For
the first decade, you could slot Italian
breweries into these two traditions. As
time went on, a third tradition emerged,
inspired by the vibrantly hoppy beers
of the United States. Sometimes these
brewers call themselves "second-gen-
eration" brewers because while they

look to the brash flavors of the U.S.,
they continue to use Musso and Arioli
as touchstones. They lager some beers,
bottle-condition others, and always
stay connected to the importance of the
dinner table.

Just as Italian brewers were feeling
the American influence, they also started
experimenting with barrel-aging and the
production of tart beers. Italian breweries may have taken some inspiration
from Americans for this, too, but more
important was an influence at home:
wine. Not only did Italian breweries
begin using Italian wine casks to age
their beers, they began to take cues
from wine itself, making beer that was
more tart, elegant, and balanced than
American barrel-aged beers. ■

DESCRIPTION AND BREWING NOTES

WHETHER MAKING LAGER or ale, Italians brew for the dinner table. This is an innate instinct; after getting confused looks, I quit asking Italian brewers whether it was important that their beer complement local cuisine. I might as well have been asking if air was important to breathe. "We are the sons and daughters of our food and beverage culture in Italy," said Arioli. "We are automatically looking for something tasty, but at the same time elegant or balanced. And that's why I was looking for something a bit more complex."

This has a few practical effects. Italian brewers prize balance. Even when they make "extreme" styles of beer—hoppy ales, barrel-aged tart beers, strong ales—they eschew ostentation. Hoppy beers burst with flavor but aren't painfully bitter. Barrel-aged beers may be tart, but they don't go to the sour frontier of some American wild ales. It also means that Italian brewers treat beer like it's a part of the cuisine. They add herbs and spices the way you'd flavor a soup; they use local fruits and vegetables as if making a salad. The use of very local ingredients like wine must, chestnuts, or herbs round out the typical portfolio.

COOL CELLARS

To understand Italian lagers, we have to return to Birrificio Italiano in Lurago Marinone, north of Milan. This is where Agostino Arioli first brewed his "German" lagers and created the mold that breweries have followed since. The thing is, they're not entirely German. Arioli did indeed study brewing in Germany, but he didn't return to Italy with the idea of replicating their beers. He was much more a brewing polymath, and his German connection was at least partly one of necessity. "The only chance I had to find good yeast was lager yeast. That's why I started mainly with German-style beers."

Even with the first batches, he started reinterpreting traditional beers. For the most part, he used the classic German method of decoction mashing to brew them (traditional), but he fermented them on the warm side for lagers, from 52° to 55°F (unusual). In Germany,

RIGHT: *Wine barrels are a common sight in Italian breweries.*

brewers are almost allergic to ester formation, but Arioli encouraged it with these temperatures. Rather than stripping his beers down, he adorned them with fruitiness and fullness.

His flagship, a full, fruity, and hoppy pilsner called Tipopils, is a perfect example of adaptation. He uses a step-infusion mash rather than decoction—which doesn't amount to full apostasy—but then he goes a bit further. When he visited English brewers and studied English cask beer, he made one key observation: "I knew that they were using dry-hop in the cask. I thought, why don't I do this with my Tipopils?" So now he dry-hops the beer, both during primary fermentation and maturation, leaving it faintly shimmery with hoppy particulates. Warm fermentation, step-infusion, and dry hopping. We're not in Munich anymore.

Whether Arioli created the mold others followed or tapped into a collective unconscious, his style of fuller, hoppier, fruitier lagers is what became popular in Italy. Where Germans prefer light, clean lagers, Italians like the burlier examples that come from warmer fermentation. Brewers like Arioli don't scrimp on lager times, either—they let them age for a month or more, so the final product, while round, is smooth and elegant.

Arioli and the early lager breweries created a market for their style of beers that came with attendant expectations, but they're not immune to change. Lambrate, an early lager practitioner, has also begun migrating toward hops. One of its workhorses, a helles called Montestella, is sharply bitter. So is Toccalmatto Uber Pils, and as a bonus, it is bottle-conditioned in the Belgian mode. And Arioli, whose line now includes

ABOVE: *In the brewpub at Birrificio di Como, diners have a window into the lagering tanks.*

standard ales, fruit ales, and tart ales, also makes a pilsner with undried fresh hops. In Italy, style is a beginning point, not a final destination.

WARM ROOMS

At the same time Arioli was visiting German breweries and becoming steeped in the language of lagers, Teo Musso was traveling to Belgium. He had already done a survey course in international beer styles at his Piozzo pub, and it was the fruity ales of Belgium that captured his imagination. Musso had no greater access to brewing knowledge than Arioli, so he went to the source.

Even in the age of molecular biology and computer-operated brewing, countries hold on to native practices. German

---

Chestnut Beer. Italian brewers have been plying their trade for less than twenty years, but they already have an indigenous type. The idea came when Italian breweries began incorporating local ingredients into their beer. Chestnuts, one of Italy's most important agricultural products, were an obvious choice. For centuries, Italians have ground chestnuts into flour and used them in baking—so why not try them in liquid bread?

Andrea Bravi at Birrificio di Como makes one of the best-known chestnut beers, Birolla (profiled on pages 328–329). The flour he uses comes from chestnuts roasted over beech, and is tinged with smoke. "First I mash the chestnuts at 75°C [167°F] because the starch has to become gelatinized. Then we add the malt and water to get a good saccharification. In Italy people all have individual [preferences], so I do milled chestnut, but someone else will use roasted chestnut, some others boiled chestnuts, some raw chestnuts—so, a lot of different beers." Como is in the lager tradition, while Birolla is brewed with bottom-fermenting yeast and lagered. (Andrea Bravi, steeped in the German tradition, is reluctant to call his chestnut and chestnut-honey beer a lager, though.) Other breweries make ales, some lighter, some darker, some spiced, some not.

Chestnut trees are in the same family as oaks, and the nuts themselves are starchy like acorns. Their effect on beer is subtle, but is most apparent in its texture, which will be thick and silky—almost oily—a bit like oats. The flavor can be roasty or smoky depending on the way the chestnut was prepared, and I sometimes detect the earthy flavor of root vegetables underneath the more obvious notes.

---

brewers would no more dream of adding rice to their grists than English brewers would forsake floor malts. In a broad portfolio of idiosyncrasies, the feature that most distinguishes Belgian brewing is not particularities of style, but the use of a warm room. Here, bottle-conditioning beer goes through a second fermentation, further developing the fruity, spicy notes created during the first round. It hardly matters whether the brewery is making saisons, pale ales, or oud bruin; this is an important step in the process. Few breweries outside Belgium have adopted the practice, even those that regularly make Belgian-style ales. In Italy, Musso built a warm room. It would prove to be a fateful decision.

The Baladin line includes beers recognizable as Belgian: a saison (Wayan), a witbier (Isaac), an abbey (Super), and a kriek (Mama Kriek). But it also has a flavor of Belgium even in beers brewed out of style. Nora, made with Egyptian wheat and spiced with myrrh, is no one's example of typical, but the balsamic tartness, the rich fruitiness, and the effervescence all point to Belgium. Re-fermentation in the bottle delivers the country's distinct flavor like no other technique, so even when Musso is making a beer he calls "Italian ale," as he does Nazionale, it tastes Belgian. So many breweries have followed suit that this has become a feature of Italian brewing.

Over time, breweries have pushed further, incorporating unusual ingredients and different production methods. The Belgian base beers provide a perfect platform for fruit or spice additions. These beers are so common—most breweries make at least one—that they've become a defining niche in Italian brewing. It is here that the influence of food is most pronounced, and where the line between beer and food blurs. Piccolo Birrificio brews some familiar Belgian styles, but has a wormwood blond (Chiostro). Birrificio Troll's fanciful Shangrila is made to resemble a tandoori dish with ten Indian spices.

If food could influence breweries, it was inevitable that wine would make an appearance, too. Barrel-aging is now at least as common in Italy as it is in the U.S., but of course Italians make use of wine casks. Many have begun to incorporate wine must into their recipes, and this works perfectly with Belgian methods. Indeed, while Italians do not regularly use sugar in their grists—as Belgians do—the use of grapes has a similar effect on the body and crispness of beer. Grapes also add a bright fruitiness to the beer, and breweries have had success in allowing particular varietals to express their character. The leader in this is Valter Loverier at LoverBeer who uses grapes to inoculate his wort, but the technique has been used by Birra del Borgo (L'Equilibrista, brewed with 50 percent sangiovese grape must) and Birrificio Montegioco (Tibir, brewed with timorasso grapes), among others.

HOP BACKS

The most recent development in Italian brewing follows international trends: a love affair with the hop. Superficially, this looks like the least overtly "Italian" direction brewers have gone, but it turns out that the beers are quite different from their superhopped American inspirations. The biggest difference is that most brewers working with hops use the typical Italian/Belgian systems geared

ABOVE: *A peek into the warm room at LoverBeer*

LEFT: *"This door must remain closed," says the writing on the wall of Birrificio Baladin. "Re-fermentation in the bottle."*

Italian Malt and Hops? Teo Musso

is the renaissance man of Italian brewing. Not only did he found one of the first craft breweries, but he designed his own labels and bottles, later created a chain of craft beer pubs, and has a sound engineer experimenting with the effect of music on fermenting beer. Perhaps his most interesting project is an effort to grow grain and hops in Italy. His grain acreage—mostly barley but also farro, a native grass related to spelt—has grown to 230 acres and produced 318 tons of malt in 2012. He has two different hop fields, one of German Mittelfrüh and Hersbrucker, another of a mixture of New World hops, that produced 1,300 pounds the same year. Baladin Nazionale, a delicate Belgian-style pale ale, is the first beer made from these all-Italian ingredients.

toward bottle-conditioning in a warm room. Hoppy American beers have little yeast character; they achieve balance through sweet malts, particularly caramel malts—just enough to serve as a platform for the hoppy maelstrom. This isn't the Italian approach.

Rather than maximize recipes to produce bitterness, Italian breweries think of balance. (Food pairings are always on

their mind.) Bruno Carilli, who worked for Carlsberg for seven years, developed a love of hops. When he founded Toccalmatto in Fidenza, Parma, he wasn't shooting just for intensity, though. He wanted "a beer with American flavors but European drinkability." To Carilli, that meant tinkering with the formula. "Some American IPAs have too much caramel and body. We like the aromas of the American hops, but the idea was to produce an American pale ale using Cascade hops but more dry and less full."

He uses pilsner malt instead of pale ale malt—common among Italian brewers—and rarely uses caramel malts. Repurposing his filter as a hop back, Carilli infuses his beers with tons of aroma hops, many from New Zealand and Australia. The beers emerge with intense aromas and flavors but are only modestly bitter. The hop acids and oils interact with different yeasts during fermentation and bottle-conditioning, and from this marriage emerge unexpected flavors. Toccalmatto Re Hop ("King Hop") has a distinctive lemony-mint flavor, while from Oceana, a hoppy saision, you get the bergamot of Earl Grey.

In this vein is one of the most interesting beers in Italy: Gaina, from Birrificio Lambrate.

LEFT: *The Lambrate Five (from left to right): Davide Sangiorgi, Paolo Maran, Fabio Brocca, Alessandra Brocca, and Giampaolo Sangiorgi*

Lambrate is a vibrant brewery run by five still-young owners who founded the operation in 1997. It has a large portfolio of beers that run the gamut from weizen and bock to smoked imperial stout, but the beers shine brightest when packed with hops. Gaina is a fruit basket of a beer, with explosive apricot and strawberry flavors. Lambrate Ortiga is called a golden but is nearly American in its sharpness, and its Montestella, a lager, is nearly as bitter. ■

EVOLUTION

TALIAN BEER IS not yet two decades old, and already it is well ahead of where the United States was at a similar stage in the late 1990s. It is now possible to talk about the features of "Italian brewing" that differ from any place else in the world. Italian drinkers are slowly switching over to this new kind of beer and the market is still quite small. Even the largest craft breweries produce only 10,000 to 12,000 barrels and most are a fraction of that size. The assurance and confidence of the new Italian brewers and their real contribution to technical evolution belie the market's small size, though. In less than twenty years, Italy has already stepped forward as a leader in brewing. ■

THE BEERS TO KNOW

SHUDDER EVEN TO TRY to give a representative sample of an entire country's output—especially when most of these beers are so hard to find. There are a number of excellent breweries making beers in each of Italy's three traditions. Consider them a starting place, excellent beers that only hint at the riches that lie beyond.

BALADIN NAZIONALE

ooooooooooooooooooooooooooooooooooooooooooo

LOCATION: Piozzo, Italy

MALT: Italian-grown

HOPS: Italian-grown

6.5% ABV, 1.056 SP. GR., 27 IBU

Baladin founder Teo Musso made his bones selling exotica, but I wonder if it won't be Nazionale, with Teo's own Italian-grown grain and hops, that will ultimately be the most significant. I like it because it's not adorned; rather, the richness of the hops, herbal and lemony, marries so well with the rustic malts and esters in the yeast. A beer of simplicity sometimes shows more than one bedecked with baubles.

on the skins of the barbera d'Alba grapes, is no different. The satsuma and strawberry notes from the grapes add hints of wine, but it's the crisp tartness, not the fruit notes, that makes it more like a wine than a tart ale. An amazing, unusual beer.

BIRRIFICIO ITALIANO TIPOPILS

LOCATION: Lurago Marinone, Italy

MALT: Pilsner

HOPS: Northern Brewer, Perle, Spalter Select

5.2% ABV

Tipopils was the beer that launched Italiano, and it's an excellent example of Italian borrowing. Fermented 8°F warmer than Czech pils and dry-hopped during both fermentation and lagering, it takes on a bit of fruitiness and hop vibrancy. The grain flavor really shines as well, wholesome and fresh, and the beer has more creaminess than most pilsners. The aroma is, as you'd guess, full and spicy.

LOVERBEER BEERBERA

LOCATION: Marentino, Italy

MALT: Maris Otter, three specialty

HOPS: East Kent Golding

OTHER: Barbera d'Alba grapes

8% ABV

All of Valter Loverier's tart ales have a vinous—which is to say, relatively restrained—tartness. BeerBera, made exclusively with the wild yeasts collected

LAMBRATE GAINA

LOCATION: Milan, Italy

MALT: Maris Otter, caramel, Carapils

HOPS: Chinook, Centennial, Boadicea, Simcoe

6% ABV

My first stop in Italy led me to understand that the country's beer would surprise me. After a breathtaking smack of hops in Montesella, purportedly brewed in the mild helles style, I approached this American-style pale with caution. The hops here were as surprising, but for entirely different reasons. They were so fruity I was literally fooled into asking what was added. I guessed strawberries and apricots. The bitterness is restrained, so you find yourself wondering what new kind of beer you've encountered.

COMO BIROLLA

LOCATION: Marentino, Italy

MALT: Pilsner, Munich, Caramunich

HOPS: East Kent Golding, Cascade

OTHER: Beechwood-smoked chestnuts, chestnut honey

8% ABV, 1.066 SP. GR., 22 IBU

f you want to detect chestnut in a beer, try identifying it by mouthfeel, not flavor. Chestnut flour adds a creamy density. Birolla has the color of a chestnut and the creaminess of a milkshake. A touch of roast coupled with some light esters and a gentle honeyed aroma make it a wonderful autumnal warmer.

TOCCALMATTO RE HOP

LOCATION: Fidenza, Italy

MALT: Pilsner, special

HOPS: Perle, Cascade, Tradition

5% ABV

n Italian, the word for king is *re*, an association that's easier to make when you see the label, with a hop-headed robed monarch. This is a beer in the Gaina mode—cleanly articulated hop flavors, but unexpected ones. Some of Toccalmatto's beers have a note of mint in them, and here it melds nicely with the perfumey, lemony hop flavors.

MONTEGIOCO QUARTA RUNA

LOCATION: Montegioco, Italy

MALT: Undisclosed

HOPS: Undisclosed

OTHER: Fresh Volpedo peaches

7% ABV

nother brewery that takes cues from the wine industry in its barrel-aging practices, Montegioco makes a range of fascinating beers. Quarta Runa uses whole peaches, taking from them not only the sunny brightness of the fruit, but also an almond flavor from the pits. It's a bubbly beer and very slightly tart—elegant and seductive.

DUCATO LA LUNA ROSSA

LOCATION: Roncole Verdi di Busseto, Italy

MALT: Undisclosed

HOPS: Undisclosed

OTHER: Morello and sour amarena cherries

8% ABV

iovanni Campari is one of the most respected of the young new brewers in Italy, and his specialty is barrel-aged beers. La Luna Rossa ("the red moon") is a blend of different vintages of wild ales, aged on Morello and amarena sour cherries. It is an aggressive beer, dry and very tart, with just the essence of cherries in the background.

LoverBeer

BORROWING WINE TECHNIQUES

ACCORDING TO THE ITALIAN WAY OF THINKING, LOVERBEER'S VALTER LOVERIER IS COUNTED AS A "SECOND GENERATION" BREWER—NEVER MIND THAT THE FIRST GENERATION PRECEDED HIM BY ONLY A DOZEN YEARS. IN HIS CASE, IT MAY MAKE SENSE; MORE THAN ANY OTHER BREWER, LOVERIER HAS BEGUN TO REFINE WHAT "ITALIAN BEER" MEANS IN WAYS THAT ARE BOTH NOVEL IN THE WORLD OF BREWING AND YET PERFECTLY ITALIAN.

Loverier made a slow, careful study of brewing techniques before starting his brewery in 2009. He consulted old hands like Teo Musso (see pages 319–321), but also looked further afield, to the United States and Belgium: "Italians have free minds that are not anchored to the old tradition like Germany or England." He began picking and choosing elements from different countries. Where he departed from most Italian brewers is stepping across the aisle—or field—to speak with winemakers and experts in viticulture. "We needed to create a new product, and Italy is different and has a cultural connection to wine and food," he said.

From these influences came an idea about how beer could be brewed. "This is the philosophy of the brewery: to join, to have a fusion of the old recipes of the Flemish area, sometimes forgotten, with Piedmont winemakers', and so we use wood, fruit, grapes."

The brewery he ultimately founded, LoverBeer (a play on his surname), is located on a beautiful hillside in the residential part of Marentino—a hamlet twelve miles from Turin in Piedmont. The Alps cup the region, a rustic stretch draped with some of the best grapevines in Italy. Loverier built the brewery to his own specifications and it is like no other in the world. The main brewery roughly follows English design, with a combined mash tun/lauter vessel and kettle. He also borrows the grist tradition from England, using Maris Otter malt as the basis for all but one of his beers. The back end of the brewery is more Belgian, with a warm room where he bottle-conditions his finished beer. The middle, however, is less like a brewery and more like a winery.

In the beer world, spontaneous fermentation is a vanishingly rare practice. Wine is different; it has always had a spontaneous tradition. But whereas lambic breweries depend on airborne yeast—a difficult practice that can lead to spoiled beer—winemakers have it easier. Grapes are coated with wild yeast, so wine naturally inoculates itself. In thinking about these two traditions, Loverier had what now seems like an obvious insight: Why not combine them? This is how BeerBera came to be (yes, the pun suggests what you think it does). Instead of pitching yeast, Loverier pitches the must of barbera d'Alba grapes into his wort instead. He then ages the beer in 17-hectoliter French oak vats normally used by wineries, later moving it to ripen in wine barrels. The result is an orange-to-crimson beer—the color depends on the grape vintage—that has the light acidity of wine and a rich, fruity flavor of strawberry and mandarin.

Those vats are critical in most of the beers in Loverier's line. Although BeerBera is the only spontaneously fermented of his beers, most spend time in the large vats where the wild yeasts and bacteria have taken up residence.

Other beers in the family include my favorite, BeerBrugna, made from very small, local plums called ramassin. They have a tiny window of ripeness, and are best when plucked, freshly fallen, from the ground. I've never had a ramassin plum, but the fruit flavor is so well-preserved and bright that drinking the beer is like eating the fruit fresh and warm from the tree. Another grape-must version called D'uvaBeer is made with freisa grapes, but pitched with regular yeast and aged in the inoculated vats. The character is similar to BeerBera, but more clearly grapey and a touch sweeter—though all Loverier's beers are very dry. Dama Brun-a is a Flanders brown ale brewed to the traditional specifications of the region—four months in the large vats and another year in wine barrels. Madamin, an amber, spends four months on oak and has a woody, spicy quality.

Because those yeasts come from Piedmont grapes, the character of the beer, its sour wildness, is unique to LoverBeer. Unlike American wild ales and even Belgian tart ales, Loverier's ales are only mildly acidic. True to the Italian way, they feature balance and depth. But where other breweries have crept up to the line separating beer and wine, Loverier has erased it. It's not that the beers are vamping as wines; rather, Loverier has found a way to use the native tradition of fermentation and harness it in his beer-making. This is exactly in accord with the millennia-long traditions of brewing, and how native styles have always emerged. Italians have a flair for improvisation that seems to harmonize with older traditions, and Loverier has taken that impulse a step beyond, creating that rarest treasure in the beer world—a truly novel kind of beer.

Fresh-Hop
ALES

Toward the end of August, hop growers begin to caress their crops. Like fruit, hops ripen, and a farmer can tell from the springiness and stickiness of the cone whether the hop is ready. They have sophisticated techniques to measure water content, but an experienced farmer can tell just by squeezing a hop and splitting it in half to inspect the yellow lupulin particles inside. On the day the cones are judged to be perfectly ripe, growers give brewers the call: They're ready. Within just a few hours of harvest,

Fresh-Hop Ales. Any style of beer can be made with fresh-picked hops, but in the two decades breweries have been making them, they've settled on a standard pale ale as the typical base. Lagers age too slowly and darker beers obscure hop flavors. Here you want the focus to be on the hop character, which differs markedly from conventionally hopped beers. They aren't as concentrated or sharp but rather delicate, lissome, and vegetal. And this isn't just a difference in degree, but kind; sometimes undried hops produce flavor completely absent in their dried form, and vice versa. They are a wild, joyful expression of the growing hop plant and a delight to the hopheads of the world.

STATISTICS

ABV range: 4.5–7%

Bitterness: 25–60 IBU

Serving temperature: 50°–55°F

Vessel: Pint glass

RIGHT: *Hop cultivation is such a specialized trade that there are no manufacturers for hop-picking equipment. Each grower must adapt existing equipment to remove the bines.*

while the heat of the summer sun still warms them, the hops will go into a boiling kettle of beer and become a fresh-hop ale.

We call it "lupulin nouveau"—a style of beer that blossoms once a year at harvest time. Fresh-hop ales capture the essence of the green, living vegetable. Their flavors are by turns softer and wetter, more earthy and wild, than beer made using dried hops. They taste their best just days after they're kegged, while that living essence is still at its freshest. By Thanksgiving, they're all gone. Fresh-hop ales are the ultimate harvest beers, ones to be savored in the moment of ripeness, not hoarded and saved. ■

ORIGINS

BREWERIES LEARNED millennia ago to brew in cool weather, and the most prized ales were made just after harvest. No reference has explicitly distinguished fresh and dried hops, but it's safe to guess that the use of fresh hops dates back to the beginning of the hop era. If brewers did make their October beers with fresh hops in the distant past, the practice had ended by the industrial age and wasn't rediscovered until around 1992.

American breweries may have made the first attempts—there is at least one reference to an effort by an unnamed brewery in the early 1990s—but the Wadworth Brewery in Devizes, England, was the first to make a batch we can document now. The brewer at the time, Trevor Holmes, got the inspiration while watching the autumn harvest, wondering what green hops would taste like in a batch of beer. The beer's conceit came to him fully formed and is now the standard practice in making these beers. An employee is dispatched, predawn, to get to the farm by six to collect hops both freshly dried on the previous day and green hops freshly picked on that morning. He returns by nine-thirty so that the first of two coppers can receive the hops. This timing is critical. The current brewer, Brian Yorston, describes the process:

In 2008 I decided personally to do the hop run; I made the mistake of stopping for a coffee on the way back, only to find a posse of brewery operators standing by the gate waiting impatiently for my arrival. Such is the important timing of getting the hops on time to meet the brew.

Brewers in the United States next made fresh-hop beers around 1996. Sierra Nevada and Bert Grant both made versions, but Grant had the decided advantage: His brewery in Yakima was just a few miles from the hop fields. By the end of the decade, more breweries were making them—largely in areas around Yakima and the Willamette Valley—but it was still a rare practice.

The explosion came about five years later, propelled by festivals celebrating the harvest in Oregon and Washington. (These two states account for around 90 percent of the commercial hop acreage.) Breweries began to develop relationships with hop growers, and the number of fresh-hop ales grew exponentially. Scores of breweries now make fresh-hop ales, and they make around 200 different variations—a number that grows annually.

While the style had been focused in the Pacific Northwest, more and more breweries across the country have started to get in on the act. Initially, far-flung breweries had hops flown in from Yakima or the Willamette Valley, but this was hugely expensive and the hops spent a long time between field and kettle (sometimes overnight)—a less than ideal arrangement. A few breweries in other parts of the country started planting small plots of hops for their own use. Then, in an even bigger development, breweries became interested enough in local hops—both fresh and dried—that farmers in New York, Wisconsin, and Colorado put in hop fields. Already those fields have provided local craft breweries with fresh hops for harvest ales. Crops in other states are now in the planning stages. ■

DESCRIPTION AND CHARACTERISTICS

FRESH-HOP ALES are regularly compared to Beaujolais Nouveau, but the analogy is only partially apt. Both are products of the harvest, drunk fresh lest the life seep out of them. They have about them the joy of the harvest. But there's a big difference. Karen MacNeil, writing in *The Wine Bible*, said of the wine: "Top-quality Nouveau has a kind of exuberant berryness. Its charm is its innocent, not-quite-wine character. Drinking it gives you the same kind of silly pleasure as eating cookie dough."

Fresh-hop ales are simple and lean, but they are fully evolved beers. The hops that give them their exuberance aren't in the process of becoming—they've arrived, and the flavors they give are expressive and vivid, less cookie dough, more freshly baked cookies. Top-quality fresh-hop ales are revelatory; their flavors are fecund and green in a way that seems *more* complete. Flavors become concentrated in dried hops, and the resulting beers are more intense. But fresh-hop ales have the very delicate flavors and aromas of living things—notes as gentle as spring blossoms and as sweet as fresh berries.

They are not, however, truly predictable. Regular hops are lab tested and analyzed, and breweries know how they'll behave in beer. (Even when breweries don't change a recipe, they have to make adjustments to seasonal variations in malt and hops in order to keep the flavors consistent.) The flavors and aromas that come from fresh hops are unlike their dried hop counterparts. They don't produce the same aromas and flavors, nor at the same intensities.

In the ten years breweries have made fresh-hop ales in substantial numbers, they've discovered that some hop strains lend themselves to the practice, while others really don't. When they don't work, they can give off gassy, grassy, or even compost-like vegetal flavors. Over time, brewers have settled on a relatively small group of old reliables. For instance, Cascade, Centennial, and Crystal hops have found their way into between one-third and one-half of all fresh-hop ales in recent years. Amarillo, Willamette, and Nugget are only slightly less common. All other varieties make up between one-quarter and one-third of the rest. ■

BREWING NOTES

WHEN HOPS ARE HANGING on the bine, a great deal of their weight comes from water. In most cases, that moisture will be removed before the hop is packaged for storage. The plant is harvested whole: After being severed near the root, a specially outfitted truck comes by, clips off the plant from the top of the trellis, and loads it in the bed. From the field, they're taken directly inside to a processing plant where the cones (or if you're feeling pedantic, strobiles) are separated from the stems and leaves. If the hops are being dried, the final stage is putting them in a kiln—which actually looks like a massive warehouse with a swimming pool of hops—set to 140°F. After nine hours,

RIGHT: *In kilns like this one in the Willamette Valley, hops piled three feet deep scent the air with an intensely green aroma.*

the hops' moisture will have dropped to 8 percent, and they'll be ready for baling.

In fresh-hop brewing, strapping young gents from the brewery show up before the hops go into the kiln and hustle them back to the brewhouse where a boiling kettle stands ready to accept them. That's the ideal, anyway—and when hop fields are nearby, breweries can pull it off. Timing isn't just about the poetry of the occasion—the longer a truckload of wet hops sits, the more their most delicate qualities erode in the hot air. That's why if the hops are not being made into fresh-hop ale, growers like to get them into the kiln immediately.

The actual brewing is straightforward, and the only real question is the hopping schedule. When breweries use wet hops for bittering, it takes at least five times more wet hops to achieve the same level of bitterness as with dry hops. Instead, many breweries use a bitter charge of dry hops at the beginning and then use wet hops throughout the boil. Both methods produce beers with distinctively green, fresh-hop goodness, but beers with initial dry-hop charges have a cleaner bitter note. All-fresh–hop beers, because they have so much hop material in the boil, are much softer and more vegetal; these beers may also be more susceptible to the strange and unpleasant flavors that sometimes come from green hops. Can you dry-hop (add the hops to the conditioning tank) with wet hops? Yes. Mark Tranter, who brews a fresh-hop beer at Dark Star in Sussex, England, bitters with conventional Simcoe hops (piney to grapefruit when dried) and then uses freshly picked Targets (fruity marmalade to light citrus when dried). "We get them picked and down here the next day, put them in the hop tank we use for dry-hopping and let that circulate for a few days. It tastes like some kind of tropical fruit thing. For some bizarre reason, Simcoes and Targets work well together." ■

EVOLUTION

THE FRESH HOP phenomenon coincided with a change in the relationship between farmers and brewers. Even ten years ago, craft breweries didn't have close relationships with hop farmers. In earlier decades, growers did all their business with the huge lager companies, which purchased hops purely for their bittering potential. Their substantial hop purchases made growers a de facto branch of their business, and they grew the high–alpha acid varieties the big companies wanted.

When fresh-hop ales came on the scene, craft breweries began forging their own special relationships with farmers—relationships that have had mutual benefits beyond the small fresh-hop purchases. This is particularly true in the Willamette Valley, where growers have less connection to the multinational companies than those in the Yakima Valley. Fresh-hop ales built a bridge, but now farmers and brewers are working together to plant other crops used in craft brewing. Knowing that craft breweries are willing to buy aroma and flavor varieties (especially Cascade and Centennial) has encouraged farmers to plant more of them, and growers and brewers occasionally even collaborate on developing new strains.

Fresh-hop ales are for the moment celebrated more enthusiastically in the United States than anywhere, but New Zealand isn't far behind. English breweries are also beginning to follow Wadworth's lead, and around a dozen now make fresh-hop beers. Because lagers aren't an ideal fit for fresh hops, Germany hasn't shown signs of taking advantage of its own bounty, but you never know. Unlike many innovations, fresh hops are *Reinheitsgebot*-compliant. ■

Fresh Versus First. When is a fresh-hop ale not a fresh-hop ale? When it uses freshly dried hops instead of freshly picked ones—a distinction some breweries are happy to blur. Fresh hops are hard to work with, their character is fleeting, and they can produce unpredictable flavors. So instead of messing with them, some breweries use the first hops of the year, but ones that have already been dried. The difference is not incidental; consider the difference between fresh and dried herbs. To clarify what they mean, some breweries label their beer "wet hop"—an unambiguous term. But there should be no confusion—fresh basil is not served dried, and fresh-hop ale should only ever be made with freshly picked, undried hops.

THE BEERS TO KNOW

AN EVER-GROWING NUMBER of breweries make fresh-hop ales—Sierra Nevada, Great Divide, BridgePort, and Deschutes are some of the more established brands. I would caution against buying bottled fresh-hop ales, though. When fresh-hop ales are very fresh—less than a month old is critical; two weeks or younger is ideal—they retain their essential liveliness. But they are the most evanescent of beer styles, and after a few weeks they tend to become dull and lifeless. I've never encountered a bottle of fresh-hop ale that did real justice to the hops. On one occasion I sampled a draft pour of fresh-hop ale at a brewery, but when I tried the bottled version of the same beer—no more than a week in the bottle—at home later that day, I found it lifeless. The draft was miles better. The best way to sample these beers is fresh from the brewery, ideally at their source in the Pacific Northwest, which becomes a fresh-hop bacchanal every October. There are websites that track the pub locations of fresh-hop ales as they become available in Seattle and Portland, and Yakima and Hood River have annual festivals celebrating these rare seasonals. Like the turning fall leaves of New England, they have their moment for just two or three weeks before they fade away into the winter darkness. ■

Lesser-Known & EMERGING STYLES

• •

eer styles are never static. This is not a perfect analogy, but imagine beer styles as animal species. Some, like pale lagers, are common and successful; others—lambics, say—are highly specialized within small niches. As circumstances change, like technical innovation and consumer preferences, adaptable styles flourish while others find themselves in irreversible decline. The churn leads to the constant birth of new styles and, inevitably, the extinction of others. In this chapter, we'll look to the margins of the beer world, where styles are coming and going (and sometimes coming back), or clinging, tenuously, to their ever-shrinking habitat.

• •

BEERS WITH HERBS, SPICES, FRUITS, AND VEGETABLES

UNTIL VERY RECENTLY it was, in the polite world of professional American brewing, a vulgarity to mention adding fruit, vegetables, or other ingredients to beer. These were known as "adjuncts" or adulterants—the purview of homebrewers or Belgians, not serious brewers. As a visit to a gastropub or food-focused brewpub will quickly show, this is no longer the case. Brewers now regularly add novel ingredients like a chef adds spices to a soup: to enhance certain characteristics already latent in the beer. The trend has already become so prevalent that it may, in the next decade or two, change the way we think about beer.

Our current rigid definition—water, malt, hops, and yeast—is actually the anomaly. The use of hops is only a thousand years old or so, and before that all beers were spiced. Many brewers also regularly used available fruits, vegetables, and honey to boost strength and add flavor. The list of additives in medieval beer corresponded roughly to what you'd find at the local market, and some concoctions like braggot—a blend of honey mead and ale—were common enough to have their own names. And long after hops entered the scene, breweries continued using natural flavors. Vestiges of the tradition survived well into the twentieth century in Germany, Britain, France, and of course Belgium, where it never died out. When craft breweries began making fruit ales and spiced pumpkin beers, among others,

they weren't inventing new styles; they were reclaiming them.

The current trend is partly an expression of enthusiasm among craft breweries clamoring to experiment. Indeed, they began using oddball ingredients almost as soon as they started brewing. Craft brewing emerged in part as a rejection of large-scale brewing with its use of chemicals and stabilizers, and the idea of using wholesome, traditional ingredients made sense. Unfortunately, those early brewers hadn't yet mastered their craft when they first started using fruit and spices, and the effect was often to mask the flavor of beer.

In the 2000s, brewers came back to spice with a different philosophy: revealing the flavors, rather than concealing. This was partly driven by the increased sophistication of brewing techniques and a better understanding of historical styles. But inspiration also came from the food world, which was relying more on local, seasonal fresh produce. Spicing a beer is a way of adding layered depth, in most cases accentuating flavors already present in beer, while the use of local fruits and vegetables is a return to more traditional, place-based brewing. (So, for example, a beer with peppercorns may not taste like a pepper beer, just something spicy; but a cherry beer will taste like cherry.) New Englanders have a fondness for local blueberries (several breweries have used them), while Wisconsin's New Glarus looks to the famous Door County cherries. In

Italy, chestnuts are so popular they've formed an entire genre.

Kona Brewing has been especially adept at this, borrowing local island flavors that accentuate traditional beer recipes: coconut to round and scent the nutty flavors in a brown ale; passion fruit to play on the citrusy character of hops in a summery pale ale; and the smooth, roasty flavor of Kona coffee in a porter. But the flavors don't have to be purely local. New Belgium delivers one of the most accomplished mar-riages of flavors in Tart Lychee, which gets tropical essence from fruit and cinnamon and a snap of acidity from barrel-aging.

It's no surprise that the use of herbs and spices in beer also coincides with a trend in brewing beer specifically to complement dishes—or that France and Italy have joined the United States on the vanguard of the trend. Rich Higgins, one of the most avid exponents of culinary beer, created lagers and ales to specifically partner with the menu when he opened San Francisco's Social Kitchen brewpub. Spices migrated from the kitchen to the brewery, and Higgins tossed everything from ginger and lemongrass to mustard seeds into his brews. In one case, he added beets to a dubbel. "You get a nice earthy sweetness from the beets that melds very well with the roasted malts and the fruity yeast. The yeast has really high elements—I call them 'spiky'—the flavors of bubble gum, figs, plums, and cherry. And then with the lower-down flavors that form the foundation of the beer you get some vegetal earthiness from those beets." By smoothing the roast notes, it "increases the number of foods the beer will go with."

Adding extra flavors doesn't define a new style of beer; rather, it's a way of expanding the range of existing styles—and nearly any beer could be tricked out with a dash of spice. (Though practitioners of some styles like very traditional German lagers might be appalled by such an adulteration.) Belgian ales, with their more assertive esters and phenols, are obvious can-didates, but brewers don't stop there. American brewers regularly heighten the citrusy and spicy flavors of hops with citrus zest and spices. Porters and stouts are common targets for choco-late, coffee, and chile peppers. Light wheat ales are made slightly sweet, aromatic, and sometimes tart by fruit additions. Even Christmastime lagers are sometimes treated with a bit of spicy garnish. ■

SEASONAL ALES

THERE IS A certain seasonal rhythm to beer drinking—darker, stronger beers in the cold winter months and paler, lighter beers for the hot days of summer. Some are so suited for a certain season that we mainly think of drinking them only during that time: heavy stouts, barley wines, and doppelbocks in winter; kölsch, weizen, and pilsner in the summer. But a few beers have emerged as purely one-season specialties—much like matzoh, fresh corn on the cob, and gingerbread.

Why do we have so many winter drinking rituals? Perhaps to survive the season. In the days before central heating, getting through winters was a trial, and not everyone made it. Those who did endured months of icy fingers and frozen windowpanes. People have been whipping up potions to withstand that nasty chill and dark for . . . ever? Well, a long time. In England, they called it "wassailing," which is a precursor to our tradition of caroling, and it goes back at least a thousand years. The word comes from the Old Norse *ves heill*, a toast meaning, "to be of good health" or fortune. The English were wassailing before the Norman Conquest, and the tradition carried on until the nineteenth century.

Properly speaking, a wassail is a bowl of hot, spiced ale. Preparations varied, but it was typical for the beery concoction to include liquor as well as sugar and spices, fruit, and sometimes eggs. Sometimes toast was floated atop the bowl—the origin of our practice of offering toasts. The mixture was heated but never boiled (the hops become unpleasantly bitter if it reaches a boil). One recipe from 1835 gave these instructions: "Pour a pint of strong, hoppy beer over a half-pound of brown sugar and grate nutmeg and ginger into the mixture. Add three slices of lemon and two sugar cubes rubbed over lemon peel." Next you'd actually put the whole thing through another fermentation, with—oddly enough—toasted bread added to the mix. After a few days, it could be served (presumably warmed) with hot roasted apples floating in it. That recipe is notable for lacking booze, but another, from Scotland, deploys a half-pint of whisky to a quart of beer—plus two eggs—and was said to "get a man's boots off on a cold night."

For some reason, spiced and warmed egg-beer has fallen out of fashion. In its place an indistinct category known as "winter warmers" has emerged. Like amber and red ales, these are sort of an American invention. British brewers will sometimes label a beer as a winter warmer, but in the sense of a category, not a style. In the United States, breweries have honed the concept. From deep amber to mahogany, and brewed strong (7% seems typical), American winter warmers feature candy or dark fruit malts with spicy hop garlands. Breweries started brewing these in the 1980s, and perhaps because brewers of the day avoided adjuncts, most are not spiced. Like so many craft styles, this one was pioneered on the West Coast, and many of the originals are still standards: Pyramid Snow Cap, Deschutes Jubelale, and Anderson Valley Winter Solstice.

Another seasonal concoction has roots entirely in the United States:

pumpkin ale, a harvest style made in time for Thanksgiving feasting. The humble pumpkin, totem of Halloween (the poor Irish, who apparently invented jack-o'-lanterns, had to make due with turnips), was used by American colonists to make rough beer for those who could not afford the good imported stuff. The Virginia historian Robert Beverly, writing three score and twelve before the nation's independence, said it was a kind of beer the "poor sort" brewed "with molasses, bran, Indian corn malt, and pompions [pumpkins]." Finding suitable sugars for yeast to digest into beer was always a chore for those early colonists. (No wonder that America was therefore principally a cider and rum country.)

Craft breweries revived pumpkin beers as a novelty in the 1980s. Instead of making olden "pompion" beers, though, they made orange-tinted ales seasoned with pumpkin pie spices. We can probably blame Bill Owens for this. The founder of Buffalo Bill's Brewery had been reading about these colonial brews and decided to try one in the mid-1980s. He actually

grew the pumpkin himself and added it to an amber ale, but alas, "there was no pumpkin in the flavor." It occurred to him that he might evoke a squashy flavor if he added pumpkin pie spice to the conditioning tank just prior to carbonation. The beer was a hit and in the three decades since, Buffalo Bill's Pumpkin Ale has had many, many imitators.

There is actually no reason pumpkin beers need to be spiced, Halloween-orange ales, but most of them are—enough that they have evolved into their own style. Buffalo Bill's original is a modest beer (5.2%), but some are quite boozy; Southern Tier Pumking, maybe the current standard-bearer for the type, is 8.6%. Schlafly Pumpkin Ale is 8%. A few breweries chart different courses, but they stand out as the exceptions. Seattle's Elysian Brewing gets more excited about pumpkins than just about any brewery. They have made a multitudeof pumpkin beers, including a stout and IPA. Lakefront makes Pumpkin Lager. And Trinity Brewing, from Colorado Springs, makes Emma's Pumpkin Saison. ■

THE LOST SMOKED ALES

THE GERMANS suffer under the weight of the stereotype that they are overly rigorous and precise, even officious—that there is a right way to do things and that way is the German way. The stereotype extends to beer: It is made to exacting standards and improvisation is verboten. There is something to this, especially in the realm of the famous lagers. But Germany is not all pilsner and bock. Consider styles like

altbier and Berliner weisse—or even the banana-and-clove weizens of Bavaria. Poke around a bit more and you'll find references to the names of obscure beers that eventually died out—Lichtenhainer, Grodziskie, and gose. (Though fortunately, all are enjoying a tiny revival in Germany, Poland, and the U.S.) They are smoky or sour (sometimes both), salty, spiced; they're the kinds of beers we associate with unruly Belgium, not Germany.

These obscure ales point to a wonderfully rich history, one that brewers are beginning to reclaim as they make beers once thought lost for good.

We don't have to delve into the mists of time to find a very different landscape—going back just 150 years will do. The Germany of the mid-nineteenth century had far more in common with neighboring Belgium than with its modern self. As in Belgium, German beer styles were hyperlocal; names of the beers were more often than not the name of the local town with an "er" suffixed on: Cottbuser, Crossener, Kulmbacher, Cöpenicker, Lebuser, Bernauer, and so on. Over the centuries, there are references to scores of these kinds of beers, representing a range every bit as diverse as those of Flanders and Wallonia. Some were popular enough to transcend local tastes—very old styles called *Mumme*, *broyhan*, *adambier*, and *jopenbier* were examples—but they were highly individual, even bizarre beers.

Take *jopenbier*. Made in the Prussian city of Danzig (now Gdańsk, Poland), it was popular enough in its day to be shipped as far as Britain. It was brewed at a staggering original gravity well north of most barley wines, and made in the fashion of Belgian ales with a twenty-hour boil and spontaneous fermentation. It was aged up to a year "covered with a thick blanket of greenish-white mould" and even then finished out with a gravity of a strong beer (1.080 or above). By all accounts, the extremely rich beer was tasty—but not something one could drink a lot of. It was often used as a mixer.

We could go through the list, gesturing like a carnival barker at the strange and freakish expressions of ancient German brewing. (It would make its own compelling book.) Yet there was a thread running through these old ales. Most of them were quite weak, below 3% ABV, and some were as weak as 1%. They were fermented incompletely, with typical attenuations of 30 to 60 percent (modern beers are around 75 percent attenuated). They were sour, as infected with bacteria and wild yeast as the beers of Lembeek. The historian Ron Pattinson, writing in *Decoction!*, put it this way:

> What are the common characteristics of many traditional German top-fermenting styles? Low ABV and high level of acidity. That about sums them up. A beer like Berliner Weisse, nowadays at the extreme low end of ABV and extreme high end of acidity, was a fairly run-of-the-mill beer 150 years ago.

Four of these kinds of beers survived well into the twentieth century: Berliner weisse, Lichtenhainer, gose, and Grodziskie. The latter three appeared to go extinct by 1993, but as mentioned, all have been rediscovered in the last five years like a lost bird found deep in the rainforest. In addition to being low in alcohol and largely acidic, nineteenth-century German ales were often made with wheat and some had a smoky element. A flavor diagram of the four styles might look like the Venn diagram on the next page.

You can see that there's a lot of intersection. (Lichtenhainer is the only beer that finds itself in three groups, but that was only true intermittently;

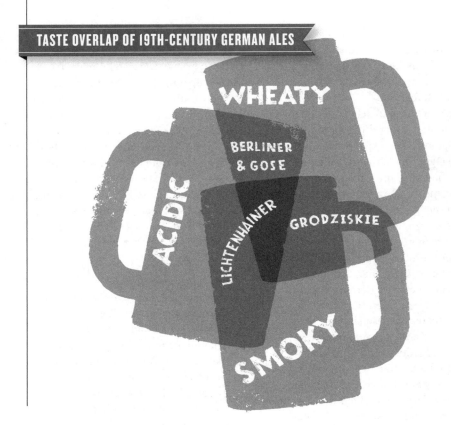

TASTE OVERLAP OF 19TH-CENTURY GERMAN ALES

WHEATY

BERLINER & GOSE

ACIDIC

LICHTENHAINER

GRODZISKIE

SMOKY

some versions were made with all-barley grists and some included wheat.) These characteristics were common among what were at the time called "weisse" beers: white, not necessarily wheat. They were distinct from the brown beers that were more typical in the period before pilsner swept through the countryside. What's especially fascinating is that you could plug Belgian and French *bières blanches* of the era into this diagram and they would populate those intersections. And Belgian, French, and German breweries also had separate traditions of brewing brown ales.

Berliner weisses are the sole living link to this family of ales, but the others were not long separated from the family. Of the dozens of gose breweries in business before the world wars, only one survived into the 1960s, closing mid-decade. Yet in the 1980s, breweries began experimenting with the style, and in 1999, Gosebrauerei Bayerischer Bahnhof committed to brew it full time. (The two styles are treated to their own chapter starting on page 389.)

Of the smoked ales, Grodziskie has shown a bit more life than the other. The beer outlasted Prussia, but was defeated by the attack of lagers. Brewed for generations in the Polish town of Grodzisk, the style was still made until the mid-1990s. The fascinating difference between Grodziskie and its cousin, the never-endangered German rauchbier, is wheat. Rauchbier used smoked barley, Grodziskie smoked wheat—an ingredient that perished with the style, making its revival much more difficult. However, in 2012, Weyermann Malting reintroduced oak-smoked wheat malt, and a number of breweries immediately brewed their own versions of Grodziskie. Lichtenhainer, the other smoked ale, remains the most obscure. The beer, something of a cross between Grodziskie and Berliner weisse, was last brewed in 1983. A few examples have made brief reappearances since Lichtenhainer's death, though interestingly, none are smoked. Brauerei Talschänke brews a beer called Wöllnitz Weissbier in that mode. Predictably (and perhaps correctly), many classify it as a Berliner weisse. A touch of smoke would help clarify the distinction.

Grodziskie and Lichtenhainer were related beers. Both used smoked malt, and both were light bodied. We know from recipes mentioned at different points from the 1860s until just before World War I that Grodziskies changed. By the end of that period, they were made with 100 percent wheat malt and very heavily hopped. One source calls them a "rough, bitter beer." But earlier recipes were different. In one, Grodziskie sounds a lot more like its acidic cousins. Brewers added willow bark to the mash tun, left the beer to cool overnight, then transferred the willow to the fermentation vessel to assist the process. That beer had only a "slight taste" of smoke.

Unlike the later version, which didn't sour after even two years in the bottle, the earlier one was probably more acidic—and therefore more closely related to Lichtenhainer. Like Grodziskie, Lichtenhainer was brewed differently in different eras. One source said it used only barley malt, while others said it might contain as much as 50 percent wheat. In Lichtenhainers, though, it was the barley that contributed the smoke—as in rauchbiers, made farther south in and around Bamberg. The beer sounds most beguiling: "They are highly-attenuated, highly carbonated and wholesome and are regarded as special beers."

Because we associate smokiness with meat, the type of wood used to smoke malt is important to its presentation. Hickory suggests ham; alder, salmon. Weyermann smokes its wheat with oak—a clean, neutral smokiness that doesn't overwhelm recipes made with as much as 100 percent of the malt. Weyermann's beech-smoked barley rauchmalt, on the other hand, does begin to get meaty after proportions of 40 to 50 percent.

In a similar vein, the beers should be fermented with a neutral ale strain, not a weizen yeast. The clovey phenols and banana esters clash with smoky flavors. Lichtenhainers may begin with a lactic fermentation or regular alcohol fermentation (there are historical examples of both methods), but the beer was not as acidic as Berliner weisses. Grodziskies are generally not described as tart beers, but there is evidence that they were 150 years ago. Some brewers have helped balance their Grodziskie with acidulated malt or sour mashes. I've found this helps modulate the native intensity of the style, which can easily lapse into "rough bitterness" if left undefended against the forces of malt and hop. ∎

A Recipe for Braggot. In the Bickerdyke text, the Victorian authors quote a recipe from 1584 not likely to be reproduced by your corner brewpub.

"Take three or four galons of good ale or more as you please, two dayes or three after it is cleansed, and put it into a pot by itselfe, then draw forth a pottle thereof and put to it a quart of good English hony, and sett them over the fire in a vessell, and let them boyle faire and softly, and always as any froth ariseth skumme it away, and so clarifie it, and when it is well clarified, take it off the fire and let it coole, and put thereto a peper of pennyworth, cloves, mace, ginger, nutmegs, cinnamon, of each two pepperworth, stir them well together and sett them over the fire to boyle againe awhile, then being milk-warme put it to the rest and stirre all together, and let it stand two or three daies, and put barme upon it and drinke it at your pleasure."

BRAGGOT

I F THE WORD *braggot* conjures any mental image at all, it may be something along the lines of a medieval woodcut of men in tunics and long socks drinking from foaming tankards. Or perhaps the famous couplet from the story of the miller in *Canterbury Tales*: "Hir mouth was sweete as bragot or the meeth, /Or hoord of apples leyd in hey or heeth." Nothing lodges in the mind so firmly as a Middle English love poem, does it?

Braggot, as these references suggest, is ancient. There is no strict definition beyond honeyed beer, and by that description, braggot goes all the way back to the Sumerians. Archaeologists have discovered honeyed beer in pottery from Phrygia from 700 BCE (that's where legendary King Midas ruled; the beer inspired a Dogfish Head brew called Midas Touch) and in Gaul during roughly the same time period. But braggot is most often associated with the medieval period, particularly in Britain and Ireland, where it was called variously *bracket, bragotte,* and *bragawd* (among others). It was usually spiced, and there were famous versions brewed around London and in Wales.

As Chaucer told us, braggot was a sweet drink. The British were the last of the Europeans to adopt hops, and braggot flourished while preferences still ran toward the sugary. As tastes eventually turned toward hopped beer, braggot waned, eventually dying out by the mid-nineteenth century. As with so many lost styles, braggot has captured the fancy of craft breweries, and they have revived it from time to time.

Writing under the pseudonym John Bickerdyke in 1889, Charles Henry Cook, John Greville Fennell, and J. M. Dixon made this observation, which should be taken as axiomatic when discussing braggot: "To define Bragot with any degree of preciseness would be as difficult as to give an accurate definition of 'soup.'" It is commonly described as a mixture of mead—honey wine—and ale, but this wasn't always the case. Sometimes it referred to beer made with honey as an ingredient, or beer sweetened with honey and spices. Or, as you can see in the recipe on page 346, it can be a drink made by boiling finished beer with honey and spices and then fermenting it again. No doubt there were dozens of other permutations over the centuries.

The old medieval braggot would shock modern palates with its sweet heaviness, a porridge likely tinged with sour (the more so as it aged). Breweries making braggots in the twenty-first century update it to accommodate the evolution of our palates. Modern interpretations are left a little sweet by beer standards to accentuate the contribution of honey (though nothing in comparison to medieval brews)—which actually gets consumed during fermentation. These beers tend to be quite strong, and some split the difference between mead and beer—with tripel-like results. It remains a very obscure style, however, and the field is wide open for experimentation and exploration. ■

GLUTEN-FREE BEER

CELIAC DISEASE and its slightly less-evil stepsister, gluten sensitivity, are serious conditions that can cause real pain and suffering. As more and more people are diagnosed, there is an increasingly large demand for gluten-free products—including beer. Glutens—the proteins in cereal grains such as wheat, barley, and rye—long seemed inescapable in drinks brewed from those very ingredients. But as gluten-free diets have taken hold, so have enterprising brewers developed beers that eschew barley, wheat, or rye in an attempt to satisfy the demand.

Gluten-free beers started appearing on market shelves in the mid-2000s, and all of the early products were made with sorghum. This makes sense: Sorghum has been used for millennia as the basis for African beers. The problem, at least for markets where people expect beer to taste a certain way, has been that these have an entirely different taste and texture from barley beer. This also makes

Gluten-Free Standards. The definition of "gluten-free" seems self-evident, doesn't it?— no gluten. With government regulation, however, it depends on which self you ask. The World Health Organization sets its gluten-free standard a bit higher—twenty parts per million or less. This is also the European standard. In the United States, the Food and Drug Administration is currently leaning toward a definition that would exclude any food (or beer) "derived from a prohibited grain," irrespective of tested gluten levels. (The FDA doesn't believe it's possible to accurately test for the presence of gluten.) This decision will affect the fortunes of the nascent industry, and breweries using sorghum-based recipes are cheering the FDA's current thinking.

Gluten-Free Beers and Their Grists.

SORGHUM-BASED
Bard's Tale (Buffalo, NY)
Green's (Stockport, England), includes buckwheat, rice, and millet
Ground Breaker (Portland, OR), includes chestnuts and lentils
Mbege (Sprecher, Milwaukee, WI), includes millet and bananas
New Grist (Milwaukee, WI), includes rice
New Planet (Boulder, CO)
O'Brien (Bakery Hill, Australia), includes millet and rice
Redbridge (Anheuser-Busch , St. Louis, MO)
St. Peter's (Bungay, England)

ENZYME-TREATED BARLEY–BASED
Brunehaut (Brunehaut, Belgium)
Daura (Estrella Damm, Barcelona, Spain)
Omission (Widmer Brothers, Portland, OR)

sense: African sorghum beer is unhopped, soured, and served fizzy with active fermentation—not exactly like your average pilsner or pale ale. Breweries have continued to experiment with other grains and even legumes to achieve a more beery-tasting beer. Green's, an English brewery, uses buckwheat, rice, and millet. Ground Breaker, an Oregon gluten-free brewery, uses chestnuts and lentils.

Producing a decent facsimile of regular beer remains the holy grail for gluten-free breweries. The first efforts just weren't very good. Sorghum doesn't taste like barley or wheat; it's thin and can produce sour or metallic flavors. Thick, fluffy heads are formed by protein, so sorghum beers had head-retention problems. To combat the differences, breweries added fruit, gave the beers extra fizz, tried to sweeten them—but they have never been able to really complete the alchemical magic of making them match customer expectation.

The most promising recent innovation, and a controversial one in the celiac community, involves using regular malted barley. In the brewing process, enzymes denature the protein molecule, leaving the finished beer with gluten levels below international standards. The technique was a happy accident, discovered while trying to reduce chill haze in regular beer, but because these beers do contain some gluten, they may cause reactions in celiac sufferers. The upside is that while these beers taste a bit thinner than regular, gluten-rich beers, they are in other ways identical. If research confirms them to be safe for the gluten-intolerant, the market will surely move in this direction.

Breweries that add other grains to the grist have had more success. Not only do they add more richness to the body and more flavor complexity, but they help offset the cider-like flavors that come from sorghum. The experiments have only begun, so further discoveries are bound to pop up. ∎

THE BEERS TO KNOW

WHAT FOLLOWS IS a starter course, not a full meal. You'll have to explore in your area, as most of these types of beers come along as specials and one-offs. Concoctions like braggot and Lichtenhainer are rare indeed and even the adept beer watcher will search in vain for months before sighting such a creature in the wild.

FLAVORED ALES

DOGFISH HEAD MIDAS TOUCH

LOCATION: Milton, DE

MALT: Undisclosed

HOPS: Undisclosed

OTHER: Honey, grapes, saffron

9% ABV, 12 IBU

An experiment that started with an archaeologist ended in a beer that is intended to evoke the beer of ancient Phrygia (now in Turkey). It's a bit braggot, a bit wine, and a bit spiced ale—all in a beautifully sparkling golden ale that has a cooling, refreshing quality. It's actually quite clean, with a peachy, gewürztraminer palate.

DIEU DU CIEL ROSÉE D'HIBISCUS

LOCATION: Montreal, Quebec, Canada

MALT: Pale, malted and unmalted wheat

HOPS: Undisclosed

OTHER: Hibiscus flower, coriander, orange peel

5.9% ABV

Dieu du Ciel ("God in heaven") calls Rosée d'Hibiscus a witbier, but that's misleading. Hibiscus is no shrinking violet, and adds both color and tons of flavor. The beer is wheaty and crisp—almost tart—but the hibiscus is perfumey and lends a piquant note. It has no hop character, so the effect is a bit like that of a *gruit*. It's one of those beers you need to drink down to the bottom to really appreciate—and perhaps even to the end of your second bottle.

Handcrafted Ancient Ale
with barley, honey,
white muscat grapes & saffron

12 fl. oz.
9% Alc. by Vol.

SEASONAL ALES

SOUTHERN TIER PUMPKING

LOCATION: Lakewood, NY

MALT: Pale, caramel

HOPS: Magnum, Sterling

OTHER: Pureed pumpkin

9.6% ABV, 1.079 SP. GR., 40 IBU

The aspirational "king" in the title has turned prophetic, as Pumpking has become one of the favored pumpkin ales. The idea is simple: more. It is everything the traditional pumpkin ale was, but compressed into a pie filling of satisfying density. Lots of spice and sweetness, which both conceal the alcohol cleverly.

HIGHLAND COLD MOUNTAIN WINTER ALE

LOCATION: Asheville, NC

MALT: Pale, pilsner, Vienna, caramel, chocolate, wheat

HOPS: Cascade, Mount Hood

OTHER: Spices (vary by year)

5.2% ABV, 28 IBU

Highland's winter seasonal has no fixed spices (much like Anchor's Christmas Ale), so the character changes with the calendar. The base beer is a deep amber (look closely and you can see holiday red) and warming malt notes of dark fruit and toffee. Sometimes the brewery uses vanilla, which makes it a sweet treat indeed.

UINTA OAK JACKED IMPERIAL PUMPKIN

LOCATION: Salt Lake City, UT

MALT: Undisclosed

HOPS: Undisclosed

OTHER: Undisclosed

10.3% ABV, 39 IBU

It is nearly impossible to discern the flavor of pumpkin in beer, a fact Uinta has turned to its advantage. Instead of coddling the squash, it squashes it instead with alcohol, bourbon, and vanilla. The pie spices inflect the wood-and-liquor more than the beer and draw it out, giving it a curious flavor not unlike crème brûlée.

PYRAMID SNOW CAP

LOCATION: Seattle, WA

MALT: Pale, caramel, chocolate

HOPS: Nugget, Willamette, East Kent Golding

7% ABV, 1.071 SP. GR., 47 IBU

In the 1980s, there swept through the Pacific Northwest a wave of sturdy, dark ales hopped stiffly and often with sylvan scents of cedar and fir. An enduring favorite is Snow Cap, which is warmed not only by alcohol but also by malt sweetness. It's made seasonal by its woody hops of English descent.

ST. PETER'S WINTER ALE

LOCATION: Bungay, England

MALT: Pale, caramel, chocolate, wheat

HOPS: Challenger, Golding

6.5% ABV, 1.065 SP. GR., 34–38 IBU

A winter ale should warm, and it's partly the malts that accomplish that. Hops are steely and sharp, but malts, especially the toffee-rich ones that infuse St. Peter's beer, soothe. There's a bit of chocolate here as well, and the malts are garlanded with a touch of spruce-like hops. Leave the figgy pudding, take the Winter Ale.

SMOKED ALES

CHOC GRÄTZER

LOCATION: Krebs, OK

MALT: Undisclosed, but includes smoked wheat malt

HOPS: Lublin

4% ABV

If the Grodziskie style emerges in the U.S., Choc gets all the credit. Krebs's finest went above and beyond by not only tracking down an original Grodziskie yeast strain from Poland, but also convincing Germany's Weyermann Malts to introduce oak-smoked wheat malt. Add Polish Lublin hops and you have the closest thing to the last historical Grodziskies.

Because it harkens back to the most recent Grodziskies, Choc's is lightly hopped, with just a touch of hay and herb behind the main melody—a smoky wheat sonata that is by turns crisp, fluffy, and smoky. It doesn't seem like smoke would be thirst-slaking, but in a light wheat ale, it really is.

BRAGGOT

ATLANTIC BROTHER ADAMS BRAGGET HONEY ALE

LOCATION: Bar Harbor, ME

MALT: Pale, black, Munich

HOPS: Pilgrim, Wye Golding

OTHER: Honey

10.5% ABV

The brewery ages this beer for six months and encourages you to continue aging it as long as you like. Fresh, it is honey scented and sweet, but undergirded with syrupy caramel maltiness and a spine of boozy heat. The alcohol is subsumed in folds of sweetness as the beer ages and the dark fruits and caramel increase.

GLUTEN-FREE BEERS

OMISSION GLUTEN-FREE LAGER

LOCATION: Portland, OR

MALT: Pale, caramel

HOPS: Citra, Sterling, Mount Hood

4.6% ABV, 20 IBU

Gluten-free beers usually thwart the expectations of beer drinkers. Not Omission, though, which would pass among a passel of gluten-rich beers. Employing the denatured barley process, it has a bright straw color and a lively bead. I'd call it a helles, with the delicacy of hop and malt working in harmony. Of the three Omission beers (all gluten-free), the lager works better than the ales, which have a thinness of body that hints at what's been removed—though hop-heads will enjoy the IPA.

BRUNEHAUT AMBRÉE

LOCATION: Brunehaut, Belgium

MALT: Undisclosed

HOPS: Undisclosed

6.5% ABV

Like Omission, Brunehaut uses an enzyme-extraction method that begins with barley. But Brunhaut's beer is Belgian, with all the fruity esters and yeast character you want. A bit of fig, rum, and a dry finish. It's a beer good enough that you could serve it without mentioning the gluten-free part; people will be so distracted by the characteristic Belgian flavors that they won't even miss the gluten.

GROUND BREAKER IPA

LOCATION: Portland, OR

MALT: Pale roasted chestnuts, lentils, and organic tapioca maltodextrin

HOPS: Horizon, Willamette, Cascade, Meridian

5.8% ABV, 60 IBU

I will confess that most gluten-free beers not made with the enzyme process leave me cold. They lack the body and depth of regular beers. But Ground Breaker uses both chestnuts and lentils to add texture and the result is closer to "regular" beer than other efforts. It's still thin, but it's incredibly silky. The lack of body means the hops are electrical and alive, but they add mostly vivid flavor and not unbearable bitterness.

Traditional
REGIONAL
ALES

The word "traditional" has a somewhat fraught status in the technologically sophisticated world of commercial brewing; it's usually just marketing gloss to evoke nostalgic images of rustic brewing. The word comes from the Latin *traditio*, "the act of handing over," and this pretty well defines true traditional brewing, where knowledge is passed on from generation to generation. Before the twentieth century, most beer was made this way: brewed with locally available ingredients using methods handed down from brewer to apprentice from generation to generation. This kind of brewing was conducted on, at most, a semiprofessional level and evolution was slow and incremental.

Fortunately, commercial beer hasn't destroyed all vestiges of traditional methods. Africans still brew sorghum beer, Finns strain rye beer wort through juniper, and

Southern Indians brew coconut toddy. These beers have been made in similar fashion for generations, and they are sipped in villages where refrigeration is a rarity. Ancestral beer survives even in Europe, sometimes competing in the marketplace with modern lagers and ales.

Traditionally made beers have certain features in common, and others that make each one a distinctive product of place. These ancient beers can be found scattered around the world, often outlasting a region's reputation for having a brewing tradition. ■

AFRICA

THE RICHEST VEIN of traditional brewing runs through Africa, where beer goes by many names—*umqombothi, utwala, malwa*; it is much the same from Ghana to Ethiopia to South Africa. Indigenous African beer is made the same way it was 2,500 years ago, with sorghum, a grain that flourishes in both temperate and tropical climates. It can survive harsh conditions—salty soil; hot, dry temperatures; even floods—which makes it versatile enough to grow in the continent's diverse regions.

Sorghum is now malted commercially (and because it's gluten-free, sorghum has gained popularity in the U.S.; see pages 347–349), but traditional African brewers typically malt their own grain on grass mats. Once it has germinated, they dry it rather than kilning it; down the line, this gives the beer a milky white color. Brewers may make all-sorghum beer or add corn, millet, or cassava root to the grist. The mash is more of a soak—it is left to sit overnight in warm water, where it develops a lactic zing in much the way sour mashes do.

The next day, brewers boil the entire mixture and let it cool. Depending on their habit, they may put the sludgy wort into a fermentation vessel then, or instead add more sorghum and let it sit another day (inoculating it with fresh bacteria) and repeat the boil. Finally, brewers put the wort in a covered fermenter and let it ferment spontaneously for a few days. (The brewer judges when it is ready.) The beer is served before fermentation finishes, usually when the beer is around 3 to 4% in strength. It's cloudy, yeasty, and tart, contains flour residue, and arrives still foaming in the glass.

LEFT: *West African* Umqombothi *beer*

There are some variations on the method and ingredients. In West Africa, brewers skip the lactic souring stage, so the beer is less tart. In Namibia and Nigeria, millet is the principal grain, though brewers sometimes add sorghum. In different regional variations, brewers flavor their beer with hibiscus, gesho (a shrub used as a bittering agent), banana, and other local fruits and spices. ■

ASIA

TRY TO CALL TO MIND an Asian style of beer. It's not easy until you think of the right grain—rice—and then a Japanese sake should materialize in your mind's eye. Indeed, Asia's brewing tradition is as old as Europe's and in some places, equally important.

RICE BEER

Where is the world's oldest ale still produced? Not Belgium or Germany, but China, where a product called *huangjiu* can trace its lineage back at least 2,500 years. Archaeologists disagree on when this multigrain beer was first made, but the modern beverage, made with rice, millet, and sorghum, is a recognizable descendant. The methods of production and the rituals of consumption attest to the beer's rich heritage.

For centuries, beer has been celebrated throughout China. In the Tang and Song dynasties, it inspired poetry, music, and painting. Even today, huangjiu remains a part of ritual and tradition. At the birth of a daughter, families bury a strong red variety of huangjiu called *nu'er hong* and let it ripen for years until her wedding feast. The name is translated as "red daughter" or sometimes "virgin red." (Boys might get the same treatment, though the beer,

ABOVE: *Jugs of Chinese* huangjiu *rice beer*

known as "scholar red," is associated with studies, not love.)

To prepare the rice, brewers steam it to gelatinize it, then acidify it. They steep the grains in warm water and pitch specialized starter cakes (*jiuqu*) made of yeasts, molds, and bacteria into the porridge. Over the course of a week, the mixture becomes acidic and alcoholic (up to 16% ABV). The final product is filtered, aged, and (usually) pasteurized.

Thanks to the varied yeast and bacteria, the flavors of different beers vary widely, from lightly sweet to sharp, musty, and pungent to rich and vinous—some are even salty.

Japanese sake is a closely related beer made entirely from rice. Once a traditional beverage (it dates to somewhere between the third and eighth centuries), it is now fully commercial and refined. The brewing process—similar to the one used to make huangjiu, yet more complex—results in very subtle, flowery beers that are so wine-like that they tend to be grouped more with California whites than German pilsners. At least one company, Japan's Kiuchi, has done its part to meld the Japanese and European tradition: The sake and beer maker has combined both products to make Red Rice Ale.

In eastern India, *handiya* (sometimes *hadiya*) is the local rice beer, and it bears at least a superficial resemblance to sake and huangjiu. Handiya brewers—as in most traditional cultures, almost always women—boil rice (either whole or ground) and add a yeast cake to spark a fermentation that lasts two to five days. The difference between handiya and the rice beers

RIGHT: *Kiuchi's Red Rice Ale*

of China and Japan lies in the yeast cake. Indian brewers make the cake, or *ranu*, from a special preparation of up to two dozen local roots, barks, and plants. The ingredients are ground and held together with previously ground, soaked, and dried rice; in fact, the only yeast in the ball is incidental and environmental. Not only does the ranu add flavor to the finished beer, but some of the ingredients—always a secret mixture designed by the brewer—are added to increase intoxication.

PALM BEER

Fermented grain is usually called beer, while fermented juice is wine. If you chance to encounter some local indigenous fermented beverage, though, you can't always trust the translation—Chinese beer, made from rice, is known as wine. In much of Southern Asia, you might encounter something called "beer" that's made from tree sap. Taxonomically, that's not precisely correct (it's more like a mead), but let's describe it anyway.

Collected from palm and coconut trees, the sap is highly fermentable and will begin active fermentation within hours, when seeded by the fecund air and the yeasts resident in the collecting vessel. Unlike most indigenous ales, the twin processes of acidification and fermentation happen very quickly and sap beer must be consumed the same day it is made; otherwise the souring bacteria will overwhelm the beer and spoil it.

In India, the palm tree

gives the drink its name, *tadi*, and also gave us the word "toddy." In Indonesia it's called *tuak*, in the Philippines *tuba*. People make palm beer across South Asia and Southeast Asia as well as in Africa—and for a time it was made in South America, too. While Anderson Valley's Fal Allen was living and brewing in Singapore, he came across a bubbling mug of *tuak*, which he described this way: "The aroma was of fermented fruit and fresh bread with a hint of decay, and the taste was sharp and citrusy." ■

RIGHT: *In Japan, sake-making is considered an art and the brewmaster (tōji) a fine craftsman.*

THE AMERICAS

NORTH AND SOUTH America have a comparatively thin lineage of indigenous beer styles. The cereal grains associated with beer—barley, wheat, rye, and oats—aren't native to these continents. The Americas did have corn, and by at least 150 BCE people were making beer from it, but beyond that, Native Americans were compelled to look to saps for fermentable sugars. Of the many versions that were once commonplace, only three varieties of ancient corn and sap beers are still in production.

CHICHA

Save for the fact that it's made from corn, the native beer of the New World is closely related to those brewed in Africa and Asia. *Chicha* is a cloudy, sourish beverage served young and made largely in domestic or semicommercial volumes. It has been made for over two millennia in much the same way throughout Central and South America.

What distinguishes chicha—and what has given it minor fame among American beer geeks—is its production method. Chicha is made from unmalted corn, and although the old practice has declined sharply, brewers used to chew the kernels in order to produce the enzymes that convert corn starch to sugars. This bizarre and somewhat unappetizing step was taken because human saliva contains the enzymes that would normally be produced in a mash of malted grain, so mashing wasn't necessary. Instead, brewers—women, overwhelmingly—left little balls of chewed corn to dry in the sun; they boiled these into a loose porridge (which sanitized the saliva), and then left them to spontaneously ferment in earthenware jugs. In three to six days, the chicha became mildly alcoholic (1 to 3% ABV), and they served it fresh and still fizzy with active fermentation.

Now brewers use malted corn called *jora* and most of the resulting *chicha de jora* is produced delightfully spit-free. The modern production method, however, stems more from the greater ease of manufacture (and potential volume) than customer squeamishness. Chicha can also be made with yucca root (cassava) or as a nonalcoholic drink (*chicha morada*).

AGAVE AND MAPLE SAP BEERS

The paucity of American grains didn't stop people from conducting experiments in fermentation. They just had to be creative and forage for different kinds of sugars. In the case of pre-Columbian Mexico, the favored source was agave and the resulting drink, *pulque*. Agave is also the source of mezcal and tequila, but in contrast to those beverages, which use the cooked pulp of the plant, pulque is made with the sap.

Most traditional beers have simple recipes and can be made at home on the stovetop, but pulque is anything but simple. Agave plants must mature for years before they can be tapped, and pulque producers must cultivate fields to feed their production. Once a plant is tapped, it will survive only a few months, having given all the sap it will ever give. In further contrast to most traditional beers, pulque isn't fermented with wild yeasts, but rather with a bacterium specific to the beverage. Makers seed their sap with finished pulque to begin fresh fermentation and monitor the progress for a week or two until it is at an ideal state of ripeness. Unlike yeasts, the bacteria will continue to eat away at the pulque, eventually ruining it. Modern Mexicans still make pulque, but a number of factors limit it from large-scale production. Waiting a decade for plants to grow to maturity is one bottleneck; but even if there were an unlimited amount of sap, the short window of freshness makes it very hard to package or distribute. It's also a bit of an acquired taste—if you can get past the viscous, somewhat slimy texture. Good pulque is a bit musty and funky, with a hint of agave—but travelers report finding *pulquerias* serving mugs of liquid tasting and smelling like rotting fruit. Perhaps for this reason, pulque is often served blended with fresh fruit juice.

Sap beers were not confined just to Central and South America; New England had a version made from maple trees. It was made from the last runnings of sap that were boiled down halfway to syrup, often with hops and sugar or raisins. Brewers fermented it with regular (probably bread) yeast. The style survived through the Depression but is now effectively extinct—though a brewery in Vermont, Lawson's Finest Liquids, has revived the tradition with periodic small batches. ■

EUROPE

GIVEN THE EXTRAORDINARY technological and commercial advances brewers have made over the past 200 years, it isn't surprising that traditional brewing has mostly died out in Europe. Yet there are a few surprises to be found at the periphery—namely, in Scandinavia, the Baltics, and Russia. There, brewers have managed to keep techniques alive that would have been common before the introduction of hops (and possibly long before that). Renewed interest in traditional, hand-crafted beer styles has even given them new life in the marketplace.

SAHTI

Thanks to revivals by breweries like Dogfish Head and New Belgium, the secret of Finland's native beer style is no longer so well kept. *Sahti* is made of rye and juniper and is known for its odd flavors. But far more odd—and rare and wonderful—are the ancient practices that bring the beer into the world.

Brewers start with a grist of malted barley and 10 to 40 percent malted rye, mashing in wood-fired cauldrons of the kind used in saunas. The brewer brings the temperature up through a series of rough rests or strikes at a single temperature of around 140°F. Then things get interesting. The brewer may bring the whole mash up to the point of boiling here, adding hops and juniper, and sometimes dropping heated stones right into the kettle (creating *kivisahti*—"stone sahti"). Or the brewer may choose not to boil the beer, skipping directly to the straining phase. This may help answer an old question: Did brewers bother to boil beer before they started using hops? It appears that sahti brewers didn't—and why would they? Boiling was slow and arduous, and unhopped sahti tasted just as good without it.

Modern breweries use a vessel called a lauter tun to separate wort and spent grain; in sahti-making, this vessel is known as a *kuurna* and looks quite a bit different. In the past, sahti brewers hollowed out the bole of an aspen tree and lined it with juniper boughs. Now it is more typical to use a similarly shaped stainless-steel trough with steel mesh.

RIGHT: *Sah'tea, Dogfish Head's take on Sahti, the traditional Finnish brew, incorporates black tea as well as juniper berries foraged from the Finnish countryside.*

The brewer controls the gravity of the beer by sparging—a lot for a lighter beer, less for a heavier one. In the past, brewers collected the first runnings and then sparged to produce a lighter small beer from the second runnings.

In one of its only nods to modernity, today's sahti is no longer spontaneously fermented—brewers use bread yeast now. Sahti is typically strong—6% ABV and above—and may be a range of pale to brown in color. The flavor is characterized by an unusual blend of banana esters, rye, and juniper, and can taste bready or minty.

KVASS

An even more ancient—and strikingly simple—method of brewing begins with bread: Add water, let stand, strain, and drink. In a variation, the mixture starts with flour rather than baked bread. This is essentially the method used to make Russian *kvass*, one of the only traditional beers in the world that is still a widely consumed drink.

Kvass is a handy way to use up stale bread, which may have been how it first gained popularity. The process couldn't be easier: Makers start by crumbling the bread, then pour boiling water over it. Other ingredients like peppermint or lemon slices may be added for flavor, while raisins or sugar help boost the alcohol content. After the mixture sits for a day, brewers add a packet of baking yeast or use sourdough starter to make it ferment. (Originally, it would have been a spontaneous ferment.) The result—a fizzy, low-alcohol drink—is bottled and sold on street corners. ■

PART THREE

Wheat Beers

Wheat and barley have an ancient and entwined history. Seeds from the two wild grasses were originally harvested in Mesopotamia and both have been used to make bread and beer for millennia. The grains are packed with the nutrients and carbohydrates that fueled the rise of civilization, both in liquid and baked forms. Sumerians brewed with ancient varieties of wheat and barley, and the Egyptians were also famous for their wheat beer. As beer spread to Europe, wheat became more refined, eventually evolving into the variety we know today. All the while, brewers were adding it to their mashes. Even as late as the seventeenth century, it was rare to find a beer made exclusively of barley; wheat regularly composed a quarter to two-thirds of the grist in many recipes.

But wheat and barley are not exactly the same. Wheat has more protein than barley, and 80 percent is sticky, elastic gluten—perfect for making dough that will rise into pillowy loaves of bread. Gluten is, however, less prized in brewing, where "sticky" is not a favored quality. For the brewer, there's an important anatomical difference as well. Barley has husks that act as a natural filter in the grain bed. Wheat doesn't; when ground and soaked in water, the result looks something like paste.

Barley's advantages and deficits are inverted. Its lower levels of gluten

produce brighter beer, and because barley is richer in enzymes, its starches more easily convert to sugar. But when it comes to baking, having less gluten means barley dough doesn't rise. Barley flour can be turned into tasty flatbreads, but they are harder and less elegant than their wheaten cousins.

Both bread makers and brewers used blends to combine the strengths of the two grains. Over time, though, users of wheat and barley started specializing. Wheat started being reserved for the oven; barley, for the brew kettle. Governments helped the process along by banning the use of wheat in beer during times of famine. In Britain, wheat was banned for almost 200 years, from 1697 to 1880. Bavaria enacted the most famous of these restrictions with *Reinheitsgebot*, a law actually designed to keep brewers out of the bakers' wheat supply. (Except, of course, in the manufacture of the region's famous weizens—but we'll deal with that confusing story later.)

Wheat didn't completely leave the brewing scene, however. The popularity of Bavaria's famous ale was only briefly in jeopardy, and in the north, tart wheat ales slaked Berliners' thirst. Meanwhile, in a large swath of Belgium, breweries continued to use wheat throughout the first half of the twentieth century. The wheat beers that survived to see the world wars were members of an older brewing tradition, though: lambics, Peeterman, and Hoegaarden beer in Belgium; gose, Lichtenhainer, Berliner weisse in Germany; Grodziskie in Poland. They were holdovers of the kinds of beers that were brewed centuries before—sour, smoky, cloudy concoctions that would have been familiar to Handel or Bruegel. A few even survived the wars to live on a little while longer, and some—Bavarian weizens, Berliner weisse, and Belgian lambics—continue on in an unbroken line.

Fortunately, interest in wheat beers has picked up again. In Germany, weizens have continued to increase in popularity and are now popular outside their home of Bavaria. Pierre Celis initiated a Belgian revival when he rebooted witbier in the 1960s. And lately, the tart beers of northern Germany have been making a comeback of their own—even as far away as the United States. ■

FACING PAGE: *Bottles of Schneider Aventinus Weizenbock age in a cool cellar.*

German WEIZEN

··

The family of German beers is dominated by very proper, respectable lagers. They are the bank managers and museum directors of the beer world—crisp lines, subtle refinement. But if you dig very far back into the family tree, you begin to find oddballs and black sheep. The signature example is a shockingly flamboyant Bavarian wheat ale. Known variously as weissbiers, weizens, or hefeweizens, these bubbly potions are characterized by their strange notes of fruit (particularly banana) and peppery spice (especially clove). Fermented in open vats, they are an old, rustic form of beer closer in flavor and temperament to the saisons of Belgium than refined bocks or

German Weizen.

The wheat ales of Bavaria are one of the rare survivors of an earlier, more rustic style of brewing. Many are served cloudily unfiltered, and vigorous carbonation feeds a billowing, white head. With unusual flavors like bubble gum, banana, and clove, they are perfect summertime beers and are fantastic at the dinner table, pairing well with everything from pizza to pork, salad to seafood.

STATISTICS

Weissbier ABV range: 4.5–5.5%; bitterness: 10–18 IBU

Weizenbock ABV range: 7–9%; bitterness: 20–35 IBU

Serving temperature: 45°F

Vessel: Weizen vase

pilsners—the country farmers of German beer.

Weizens (also called "weizenbier" and "weissbier") have been brewed for centuries, and in that time their fortunes have waxed and waned. At one point during the nineteenth century, they almost went extinct. But their vitality and ability to revive and refresh, particularly on a warm afternoon, have given them new life. They have recently departed their homeland of Bavaria for parts north in Germany and indeed can now be found across Europe. Americans have been more slow to adopt them, but thanks to

ABOVE: *Franz Inselkammer Jr. of Brauerei Aying with a glass of his family's hefeweizen*

offerings by Sierra Nevada, Live Oak, and others, they are finding a following here as well. ∎

ORIGINS

WORKING UP A FAMILY TREE for a style as old as Bavarian weizen requires a bit of guesswork. The current style isn't exactly modern; it features old-fashioned elements like open fermentation, character-laden "heirloom" ale yeast strains, and of course, wheat. That last element is our strongest clue. Wheat beers have been around as long as beer has, but the use of wheat has been inconsistent. Sometimes breweries ruled it out because of cost—or sometimes that was why they ruled it *in*. Regulations had the same effect. Wheat, the choicest grain for bread making, always had other suitors, and in times of scarcity, governments sometimes restricted its use. As a result, we can trace the comings and goings of wheaty beers over the centuries and look for likely starting points.

Historians believe that weizen's great, great, great grandfather came from Bohemia. It was there, in the 1400s, that a new beer came into vogue among the nobility. While the peasants were drinking rough brown beer, aristocrats sipped a newfangled wheat beer. The flashy upstart entered Bavaria around 1500, but tentatively. In the town of Schwarzach near the modern Czech border, Hans VI, Duke of Degensberg, set up the first and only weizen brewery. Because the right to brew wheat ales was restricted by the rulers of Bavaria, the Wittelsbach family, the Degensbergs held a monopoly for a century. In 1602, the Degensberg line died out, and Maximilian I, Duke of Bavaria

Weiss ≠ Wheat, At Least Not Always.

The word *weissbier* for all practical purposes now means "wheat beer." But *weiss* actually means "white." Centuries ago, the term referred to the beer's color, not its grain bill. How did "white" come to be taken for "wheat"? Wheat was either unmalted (raw) or dried at a low heat. It gave beers a whitish look, especially in comparison to "red" or "brown" beers made with fire-roasted barley malts. White beers were therefore usually wheat; as it was with weissbier, so it was with *wit* and *bière blanche*. But one variety of barley malt was air-dried, leaving it as pale as wheat, and the beer made from it was also called "weissbier." Today you are in no danger of getting an all-barley beer if you order weiss in a German pub—though if you happen to be digging through old historical manuals (as surely you have found yourself doing on the odd afternoon), you might keep this in the back of your mind.

(not to be confused with the ruler of the Holy Roman Empire from a century earlier), decided to expand the ducal right to a few other specially designated breweries.

Now, the obvious question arises: Why would a duke need to grant breweries the right to make wheat beer? The answer: *Reinheitsgebot*, the famous Bavarian "purity" law. Like so many laws, the question of what it actually protected is the subject of some spin. In the most charitable reading, the law ensured the purity of beer by restricting the ingredients—no adulterants like willow bark allowed. But it also protected bread making by ensuring bakers had enough tasty wheat to work with. Then there was the political dimension of meting out rights to a restricted number of breweries, and after Maximilian expanded the privilege to other breweries, it became a lucrative state revenue source to boot.

Weizen beer steamed along through the seventeenth and eighteenth centuries until it hit a brick wall around 1800. As lagers started becoming dominant, the popularity of wheat beer plummeted.

By the year 1812, the tide of fashion had turned and there were just two full-time weizenbier breweries left. By midcentury, lagers were king—and next door in weizenbier's Bohemian birthplace, a Bavarian brewer had perfected the recipe for pilsner. If you were a betting person, you wouldn't have put a lot of money on the survival of weizen in the years after 1850.

Fortunately, a brewer named Georg Schneider decided to take a gamble. In 1855 he acquired the lease on a weizen brewery in Munich while scheming to end the royal control over who could brew that beer. He succeeded in 1872, not just for himself, but for all wheat beer breweries. The Schneider business expanded to a town north of Munich called Kelheim in 1927, and after the original brewery was destroyed in World War II, all operations moved there. Amazingly, through most of the first century of Schneider's operation, the future of weizen was never assured. Had it not been for the patronage of the Schneider family, weizen might only be a footnote today like so many other forgotten nineteenth-century

RIGHT: *At Weihenstephan, the brewery doubles as a classroom for the next generation of German brewers.*

German beers. Even as late as 1960, it amounted to only 3 percent of Bavaria's annual production. For a beer as popular as the weizen has become—it's now the most popular style in Bavaria and one of the most popular in Germany—it took a long time to make a comeback.

But it *has* come back—with a bang. Production doubled in the 1960s, tripled in the '70s, and doubled again in the '80s. When I visited Reissdorf in Cologne, Jens Stecken mentioned that although kölsch's hegemony is hardly in doubt in that city, he has started to see weizens pop up. "In the 1970s, the beginning of the 1980s, weizenbier was only known in Bavaria," he told me. "In the last ten, twenty years, maybe because of advertising, maybe because people came back and remembered sitting outside in the sun on holidays in Bavaria, they started wanting a weizenbier."

Total weizen barrelage passed 10 million in 2008, and weizens continue to be one of the bright lights in a stagnant German market. In 1980, weizens controlled less than 2 percent of the market; thirty years later, they have nosed above 10 percent. Wheat beer is spreading north from Bavaria, and in Bavaria, breweries that previously relied on lagers now see wheat beers making up a bigger proportion of their sales. Perhaps most encouraging for Americans, weizens are among the most actively exported styles, with a brand or two available in most good-beer grocery or liquor stores. ■

DESCRIPTION AND CHARACTERISTICS

MAGINE YOURSELF SITTING outside in a Bavarian biergarten under the dappled sunlight of a summer day. On the table are a bowl of pretzels, a pot of brown mustard, and a plate of sausages. In front of you—and dotting the sea of tables that scatter out under the shade trees—are tall, curvy glasses of cloudy wheat beer. This is the native environment of the weizen, and it tells you a lot about the nature of this venerable rustic ale.

Bavaria, Germany's largest state, is the keeper of traditions. This is the land of lederhosen and dirndls, where *schweinshaxe* is on the table and deer antlers are on the walls. It is the country's agricultural heartland, and the place where barley and the most famous hops grow. Once an independent state, it has its own personality, dialects, and culture. In terms of beer, it's also where many of the traditional little breweries have managed to survive, some making unfiltered or "unbunged" beer, often on old equipment that wouldn't be out of place in a Belgian farmhouse brewery. All of these elements—agriculture, tradition, and place—are what contribute to that glass of weizen.

Weizens are optimized to be refreshers. This begins with carbonation levels that far exceed those in most beers, creating a very lively glass of beer with a thick, mousse-like head. Most beer styles are engineered to be clarion, "bright" liquids that refract color and light. Not weizens. These are opaque, hazy with wheat proteins and ale yeast. With their yellow to orange colors, they bear a closer resemblance to a fruit smoothie than beer. As striking as they appear to the eye, though, that's nothing compared to what greets the nose and tongue. An unusual combination of brewing techniques and ingredients produces amazing fruity esters and spicy phenols in weizens. The most famous are banana and clove, but

these are just two among a multitude. Depending on the yeast strain and brewing equipment, brewers may instead conjure apple, lemon, vanilla, bubble gum, white pepper, or anise. These aromas waft gently off the glass, and in the mouth blossom into flavors that persist through to the swallow. Though they are gentle, they're not subtle. What makes weissbiers so refreshing is the bubbling carbonation, their light body, and dry finish. The grain-y character of wheat softens the palate, and along with the fluffy body, makes the beer smooth and quaffable.

Weissbiers come in several variants, and in the German system are identified by adjectival suffixes or prefixes:

■ **Hefeweizen.** Sometimes *hefe-weizen* or *hefe-weissbier*, this is the cloudy, orange-colored original. The "hefe" refers to yeast, which is part of what causes the cloudy haze.

■ **Kristallweizen.** Filtered weissbier, this is more popular in northern Germany than Bavaria.

■ **Dunkelweizen.** A dark weissbier. The term is relative, and dunkelweizens are usually amber to light brown. Brewers add darker malts to a hefeweizen recipe, producing a beer that is a bit thicker in body and nuttier or more toasty than regular hefeweizens.

■ **Weizenbock.** A generally dark weissbier brewed to doppelbock strength (7% ABV and higher). These

> "For me, wheat beer is terrible to produce. There are so many screws you have to turn, and these open fermenters are very hard to control. It's crazy. But the result is amazing if everything works perfectly."
>
> —BREWMASTER HANS-PETER DREXLER, SCHNEIDER AND SOHN

beers still have the same fruit-and-spice flavors but also have stronger malt flavors and a noticeable, warming alcohol sensation.

■ **Rauchweizen.** A quite rare style of weissbier made with smoked malt. Like other weizens, these beers have the fruity and spicy yeast character, but a portion of smoked malt adds nuance.

BREWING NOTES

EXPERT pie makers know there's no secret recipe for making a soft, flaky crust. The trick is being able to recognize the precise moment when the dough is thoroughly mixed but not yet overworked. It's all about the way it feels. Pie making and weizen brewing have something in common. On paper, brewing wheat ales doesn't look so hard; it follows fairly predictable steps, and doesn't include any offbeat ingredients. But brewing weizen relies a lot on biological processes (some that need to happen, some that never should), and managing them is the real trick.

Let's start with an overview of the process. By convention, weizens are made with at least 50 percent malted wheat (to be *Reinheitsgebot*-compliant, the wheat must be malted), though grists may contain up to 70 percent. Pilsner malt usually rounds out the balance, though a brewery might add a dash of darker malt for color. The mashing process, which may or may not include decoction, involves a weizen-specific rest at around 105° to 113°F to release ferulic acid. The boil is relatively short and unremarkable.

If you've managed to stumble onto just one of the family, go introduce yourself to the rest of the relatives—*hefeweizen*, *dunkelweizen*, *weizenbock*, and *kristallweizen* are their own closest kin. Another good option is *witbier*, a Belgian wheat beer that gets its spiciness from actual spices. A less obvious direction is *saison*, a type of beer that, like weissbier, gets its character from fermentation. One style that would seem to be related is American wheat beer, but it is actually more similar to golden ale than weissbier.

Weissbier next goes to the fermenters, which is where the real action happens. In traditional breweries, they are wide, shallow, and open—three conditions that play an important role in the way the yeast behaves. Finally, when the beer is ready to bottle, breweries dose it with some fresh wort called *speise* (literally "food") so that the beer will continue to develop in the bottle, and also become highly carbonated.

Weizens are primarily products of fermentation. The grist and mashing regime are important, but except for the ferulic rest, breweries get fine results from many different processes. At Ayinger, John Forster shocked me when he said, "It's more effective now to do infusion. We say decoction is for old breweries. We can do it, but it's not necessary." But when it comes to fermentation, Ayinger

Bananas, Cloves, and Open Fermenters.

Bavarian wheat beers are defined by the tropical fruit basket of flavors they showcase, which come from chemical compounds created by the yeast during fermentation. These compounds can either add toothsome complexity to a beer or ruin it; in many styles, they're considered faults. Weizen brewers must try to coax the flavors out of the yeast, but only those that are tasty, and only in the right proportion.

The science behind these compounds is fascinating. Both barley and wheat contain an organic compound known as ferulic acid. This phenolic phytochemical contains the potential to produce the clovey flavors in weizens, but it must be released from the wheat and barley and also interact with the right kind of yeast. The grain releases ferulic acid at somewhere between 105° and 113°F, which is why it's crucial to have a step at that temperature during the mashing process. Weizen yeasts also have a special ability to turn ferulic acid into a phenol that gives the beer its spice. They are more able to produce this phenol in the presence of oxygen, which is why open fermenters are so vital.

Open fermenters help in other ways, too. Esters, the other important flavor constituents, are also formed during fermentation. In studies measuring phenols and esters, researchers found that fermenter shape has a pronounced effect on both, but especially on esters. In open fermenters, beers developed about 50 percent more phenols than they did in tall, enclosed cylindro-conical tanks. But amazingly, the ester responsible for the banana flavor in beer (isoamyl acetate) was produced at more than double the amount when an open fermenter was used.

In creating the palate she wants in a beer, a brewer can tinker with the temperature of the ferulic acid rest, the type and amount of yeast pitched, and the fermentation temperature. These decisions are what Hans-Peter Drexler is talking about when he says there are so many "screws to turn" (page 368). It may be maddening to try to keep track of all these variables, but it all leads to a satisfying end product—the best of which are among the world's most complex and interesting beers.

sticks to the old ways. It recently installed a high-efficiency ultramodern brewery, but in the middle of rows of gorgeous steel tanks is a two-story glass cube. Inside are the brewery's open fermenters, protected from wayward yeasts.

The competing German inclinations toward tradition and sanitation are tested in the weissbier brewery. On the day we entered Schneider's fermentation room, Hans-Peter Drexler literally flinched. "The biggest challenge in the brewery is to keep the biological balance in the right way," he said. Drexler has been brewing at Schneider since 1982, and he seems to be able to see the rogue yeasts, unauthorized germs, and wild bacteria floating around the room, endangering his beer. But this is also where Schneider Weisse becomes one of the world's great beers. "For me, there are three different styles of aroma in a Bavarian wheat beer. Most of them are very fruity. One is more neutral. And

RIGHT: *Open fermenters at Schneider roil and bubble like cauldrons.*

there are some that are more like the Schneider yeast. Spicy tasting like clove and nutmeg. It is these we are very interested in."

After primary fermentation, weissbier goes quickly to the bottle—in some cases without stopping over in a conditioning tank at all. From here on, Bavarian weizens use the same bottle-conditioning techniques Belgians do. Germans feed their beer fresh wort—*speise*—at this point. With an ample dose of wort, the weizens will go through a secondary fermentation inside the bottle, continue to ripen, and carbonate. Weizens are the most lively of beers, reaching levels of carbonation double that of regular ales. ∎

EVOLUTION

WEIZENS ARE NOT, as a category, the kind of beer brewers race to tinker with, to say the least. Many beers are part of a long tradition of brewing in a particular way; few are so important in larger cultural traditions. That sunny biergarten just wouldn't be the same without a tall, voluptuous glass of weissbier at your side. But the beer style itself is a wonderful platform for tinkering, and a few brave experiments have shown that tradition can be sweetened by a bit of innovation.

The only brewery that seems willing to tempt change is the one with unimpeachable weissbier cred—Schneider. There, Hans-Peter Drexler has slowly begun experimenting with the practices of foreign lands. On one track, he's using exotic hops to add even more flavor to his wheat ales—a recent trial deployed Nelson Sauvin hops to produce a more tropical weizen, with notes of papaya and tamarind. He is also currently coordinating with growers in the nearby Hallertau region to make a minty spring beer with an as-yet unnamed new hop variety.

On the second track, Drexler has begun a barrel-aging program. Schneider makes both a doppelbock and an eisbock, and has experimented with long-term bottle aging. In the last few years, he decided to try putting those beers in merlot and pinot noir barrels. He started out filling only four wine barrels and blending the results together, and the finished

Thick as a Milkshake. The first thing anyone notices about a weissbier is the cloudiness. There's something natural and organic about this, and next to a perfectly filtered pilsner, they do look less handled. But in fact, it's not so easy to make a beer that remains evenly hazy—those solids want to drop out of suspension. The murk in a weizen is composed of both wheat proteins and yeast. Yeast has a propensity to flocculate (clump together). When many cells form larger aggregates, they fall out of suspension. But some yeasts are less flocculant than others and will stay in suspension. People who particularly like yeasty weizens may rouse whatever yeast has settled by rolling or swirling the bottle.

Wheat proteins behave in much the same way. They are able to stay in suspension at certain concentrations, but if they get too high, the proteins fall out. Brewers can help optimize the chemistry by including a protein rest during the mash. Weizen yeasts— it seems to always come down to the yeast with weissbiers—are another factor. Polyphenols created during fermentation interact with proteins to increase haze. So again, more screws to turn—yeast's behavior, its products, and the proteins in the grain—to create that beautiful cloudiness.

product, Mein Cuvée Barrique, was startling. It had a blackberry fruitiness and the depth of a sherry, but it was also kissed by *Brettanomyces*—unthinkable even a few years ago. Drexler is quick to point out, however, that nothing he did violated Reinheitsgebot. That would be going too far. Other breweries haven't yet followed Schneider, but weizens offer such a colorful palette that they may one day be tempted.

Outside Germany, weizens are becoming ever more popular, spreading with vigor east to neighboring Czech Republic and beyond to Ukraine and Poland, as well as south to Italy. In North America they remain a niche style, competing in some ways with indigenous wheat beers. Where it has spread, weizen has largely been brewed to reproduce the qualities of the Bavarian originals. ∎

THE BEERS TO KNOW

HERE ARE a few different siblings in the family—hefeweizen, kristallweizen, dunkelweizen, weizenbock—but get to know them and you'll find that their differences are small compared to their similarities. Look for spicy phenolic flavors and fruity esters, see how the beers appear in the glass, and notice how they go down with a crisp, refreshing finish. Whether the weizen in question is a light hefe or a burly bock, you will find these family traits.

SCHNEIDER WEISSE

°°°

LOCATION: Kelheim, Germany

MALT: Pilsner, malted wheat, chocolate

HOPS: Magnum, Tradition

5.4% ABV, 1.052 SP. GR., 14 IBU

If you've had a few hefeweizens before you sample this one, you'll be surprised by its deep amber color. A taste will make it clear why so few people have dared to follow Schneider's example: This really is the best weissbier in the world. The body is quite rich and smooth, slightly nutty with malt. The spice is pure clove, but the esters have little banana—they're more tropical fruit and citrus.

LIVE OAK HEFEWEIZEN

°°

LOCATION: Austin, TX

MALT: Undisclosed

HOPS: Undisclosed

5.3% ABV

Brewer Chip McElroy made the rather quixotic decision to use *both* decoction and open fermentation to create his Hefeweizen—but you can't argue with the results. Live Oak has an impressively even haziness and a dense mousse of head, fueled by cascading effervescence. The aromas and flavors are vibrant, balanced between banana

and spice with a twist of lemongrass. The best New World weizen I've encountered.

SIERRA NEVADA KELLERWEIS

°°

LOCATION: Chico, CA

MALT: Pale, wheat, Munich

HOPS: Perle or Sterling

4.8% ABV, 1.050 SP. GR., 15 IBU

Sierra Nevada is happy to brew traditional styles traditionally, but it doesn't like to plainly imitate. Its Kellerweis is brewed with open fermentation and a Bavarian yeast strain—traditionally, in other words—but unlike its German cousins, this beer has an unusual smoky flavor. The characteristic weizen clove comes from a phenol, but phenols can also suggest fire, as this one does. It is appropriately light and wheaty, but the smokiness makes it unique.

WEIHENSTEPHAN KRISTALLWEISSBIER

°°

LOCATION: Freising, Germany

MALT: Pilsner, malted wheat

HOPS: Undisclosed

5.4% ABV, 1.050 SP. GR., 16 IBU

This beer is so clear and pale in the glass it makes a fine pilsner imposter—until you get a whiff of its perfumey spice. Kristall-weissbier is a delicate creation that is nevertheless complex; it's rich with nutmeg, bubble gum, stone fruit, and a crisp, crackery wheat.

AYINGER UR-WEISSE

LOCATION: Aying, Germany

MALT: Undisclosed

HOPS: Undisclosed

5.8% ABV

Although Ayinger styles Ur-Weisse a dunkelweizen, you might be skeptical—amber is as dark as it gets. Perhaps the brewery is trying to hint at the extra body and richness in this weizen, which is far heartier and bread-like than some. It leads with spicy clove but has banana and a hint of coconut underneath.

WEIHENSTEPHAN HEFEWEISSBIER DUNKEL

LOCATION: Freising, Germany

MALT: Undisclosed

HOPS: Undisclosed

5.3% ABV, 1.050 SP. GR., 14 IBU

Dark weizens are really more weizen than they are dark, and that's certainly true with Weihenstephan's. It is not a lot darker than Schneider's regular weissbier, and the malts give it a hint of toast and peanut. Clove is more prominent than nutmeg, and the fruit falls back a bit. For all that, it would be hard to say, with your eyes closed, what color the beer is.

SCHNEIDER AVENTINUS

LOCATION: Kelheim, Germany

MALT: Pilsner, wheat, chocolate

HOPS: Magnum, Tradition

8.2% ABV, 1.076 SP. GR., 16 IBU

Aventinus is evidence of how long Schneider has been tinkering with tradition. It was first brewed in 1907 when owner Georg III's widow, Mathilda, thought to create a weizen at bock strength. The rest is history. Aventinus is a rich, figgy wheat that seems sweet on first sip but dries all the way down. The alcohol is almost completely hidden behind the skein of spice and fruit.

AYINGER WEIZEN-BOCK

LOCATION: Aying, Germany

MALT: Undisclosed

HOPS: Undisclosed

7.1% ABV

Ayinger's weizenbock is a pale-colored version; a hazy, rich golden beer that seems to capture light. The aroma has a touch of clove and breadiness, but the palate is much richer. That breadiness turns into scone on the tongue, and the fruitiness is distinctly vinous, like a pinot gris. An exceptional beer.

G. Schneider and Sohn

HOLDER OF THE WEISSBIER TRADITION

THE TOWN OF KELHEIM IS THE MOST IMPORTANT BREWING CITY NO ONE HAS EVER HEARD OF. IT'S NOT EXACTLY HIDING—IT'S LOCATED AT THE CONFLUENCE OF THE ALTMÜHL AND DANUBE RIVERS IN A BARLEY-GROWING REGION, AND IT IS JUST DOWN THE ROAD FROM THE HOPS OF HALLERTAU, ONLY AN HOUR FROM MUNICH. THE LOCAL BREWERY IS ONE OF THE COUNTRY'S MOST FAMOUS, BUT THE TOWN'S LONG HISTORY OF WEISSBIER BREWING ISN'T WIDELY KNOWN, AND SCHNEIDER, ORIGINALLY A MUNICH BREWERY, IS A LATECOMER—AT LEAST ACCORDING TO THE SCALE BY WHICH GERMANS MEASURE TIME. OF ALL THE PLACES IN BAVARIA AND BOHEMIA, THOUGH, THIS IS WHERE THE SPIRIT OF WEISSBIER RESIDES.

Kelheim got its first weissbier brewery in 1607, and wheat beers have been brewed in that building ever since. Nowhere else can claim this kind of unbroken lineage. The most important family in the preservation of Bavarian weizens didn't enter the picture for another 250 years, when Georg Schneider decided to buy a Munich weissbier brewery. The Schneiders (all the sons have been named Georg; Georg VI now heads the company) championed a fading style, one that might have died out completely were it not for the family's fierce commitment to the style. In 1927, the company purchased the old Weisses Brauhaus in Kelheim, linking together the early and modern histories of wheat beer brewing.

Schneider takes this history seriously. Brewer Hans-Peter Drexler has been with Schneider since 1982 and has been its master brewer since 1990. He puts it this way, "We have the traditional wheat beer brewing system. It is

LEFT: *Hans-Peter Drexler*

BELOW: *The Schneider and Sohn brewery is situated in the center of Kelheim.*

FACING PAGE: *As in many small Bavarian villages, the two most prominent buildings are the local brewery and church.*

very important to have the right equipment. It's the same system as a hundred years before—the only difference is one hundred years ago they had wooden vessels and we have stainless steel." He means this literally. All Schneider makes is wheat beer—a rarity among Bavarian breweries. The equipment used in a weissbier brewery is particular; until the mid-2000s, the brewery couldn't have made anything else.

The brewhouse proper isn't configured differently from other German kits, but as soon as boiling wort leaves the kettle, everything is designed for making weizens. From the kettle it moves to an open fermenter, which Drexler believes is critical to developing the proper flavors in weizen. It spends five or six days in primary fermentation before going straight into the bottle. Schneider Weisse has never been filtered and never spends a minute in a conditioning tank. After primary fermentation, it gets dosed with *speise* (a special wort the brewery uses

to feed the yeast) and finishes developing its character in the bottle. "We didn't have any filtration in the brewery. We had no cylindro-conicals, nothing." That changed when Schneider decided to brew a filtered weizen. The krystallweizen required conditioning tanks and a filter, so it now looks more like a typical brewery, but most of the beer still goes through the older, traditional process.

These features of weizen brewing—open fermentation, *speise*, bottle-conditioning—are not universal at weissbier breweries. Many have abandoned open fermentation, some no longer bottle-condition their beer, and a few weizens are even pasteurized. But Schneider is not about to modernize the way it makes wheat beer. This is why it's so surprising to find that in other ways, Schneider is on the leading edge of innovation.

It's almost unthinkable, but this most traditional of German breweries was inspired by . . . America. In 1998, Drexler was invited to the U.S. to judge beer. "I saw all these American beers. It was a new beer world for me. When I started in the brewing industry, people used to say, 'Oh, the Americans are just like chemists and pharmacists.' That's when I found Cascade hops, and I thought it should be easy to match the American citrusy Cascade hops with Bavarian-style weissbier." It led to Drexler's first experiment with new flavors, a Cascade-hopped wheat called Wiesen Edel-Weisse. Since then, Schneider has been among the vanguard of German breweries willing to try crafting American-strength hoppy beers. In 2007, Drexler collaborated with American brewer Garrett Oliver to make Hopfen-Weisse, a strong, hoppy weissbier halfway between a weizenbock and an IPA. A string of hop-centered weisses followed, all experimenting with the way the fermentation flavors of weizen could interact with the oils and acids in hops.

Schneider has also begun aging its beer. This project began when Drexler decided to reclaim some old cellars that had been gathering cobwebs and age bottled Aventinus, Schneider's weizenbock. Later, he wondered about aging beer in wine barrels. The brewery is far from the first to think of this, but it seems so unlikely in Germany. The first trials—eisbock and weizenbock split into four wine barrels—produced a beer slightly soured by *Brettanomyces*. I had the chance to try this beer, Mein Cuvée Barrique, in 2012 and it was a surreal experience. The flavor of wild yeast was the kind of thing a German brewer might once have recoiled from. How odd, then, to find a brewery willingly courting it—it tasted like the flavor of a new era.

Or maybe not. Drexler was quick to point out that hops and the use of wooden barrels are perfectly German. "For me it's interesting to play with old tradition," he said. Schneider proudly displays a copy of the *Reinheitsgebot* in the brewery, and Drexler doesn't see anything transgressive about the beers he's making. "It means we have three raw materials to work with: hops, malt, and water. If you take different varieties of hops or malt, you can do so many different things." In a strange way, it's the restrictions that seem to free up Schneider. The brewery will always brew weissbier the proper—which is to say, the traditional—way. But with 400 years of tradition to work with, there are a lot of other fun old things to try as well. Schneider has only begun to scratch the surface.

Belgian WITBIER

There are few stories in the long history of beer as surprising as the revival of Belgian white (*wit or witte* in Flemish, *bière blanche* in French), a style that was all but left for dead sixty years ago. This acidic, milky-white beer was brewed for centuries in the towns between Brussels and Hoegaarden (pronounced *Hoo-gar-den*), but world wars, lagers, and industrialization took their toll, and the last of the witbier breweries, Tomsin, shut down in 1957. Eight years later, a milkman decided to revive the style. He drew on his experience of having worked at Tomsin years before and consulted with a retired brewer to create a new recipe. In 1966, he started selling a revival witbier.

Witbier. A hot day demands a cool beer, but more than that, a cooling one. Soft and delicate witbier (also known as white ale, white beer, or simply wit or witte), laced with the zest of citrus and spice, has few peers in this capacity. A blend of pale barley, unmalted wheat, and oats produces a straw-colored beer tinged with white haze. Coriander, orange rind, and other spices lightly scent and flavor the beer, making it an excellent partner with shellfish, sushi, or goat cheese.

STATISTICS

ABV range: 4–5.5%

Bitterness: 10–20 IBU

Serving temperature: 40°–55°F

Vessel: Tumbler (traditional); tulip (better for aromas)

It substituted spices for the lactic acidity of the old witbiers, and was a crisp, refreshing ale that would gradually win hearts far beyond the town lines of Hoegaarden. Remarkably, the obscure beer would one day be picked up by brewing giants in the United States and become the bestselling ale style. Now most beer-producing countries from France to Ukraine, Argentina to Japan have their own local examples. ∎

ORIGINS

N THE ROUGHLY rectangular area running from the valleys south of Brussels north to Mechelen, as far east as Maastricht and Liège, is a famous stretch of towns that have produced some of the most renowned wheat beers in the world. We now associate witbier with the village of Hoegaarden, whose fame actually stretches back centuries. In the early sixteenth century, tiny Hoegaarden fell between the regions ruled by Liège and Brabant, placing it in a tax-free seam that gave it an exporting advantage lasting through the end of the eighteenth century. During that period, beer exports buoyed an energetic collection of hometown breweries—as many as thirty-eight in the mid-1700s.

But Hoegaarden wasn't the only famous town brewing wheaty beers in the region. The town of Diest produced a creamy, golden wheat beer that was "highly sought after by afficianados," according to the nineteenth-century brewing scientist Georges Lacambre. To Brussels's north, the town of Mechelen was famous for a brown beer that might be a second cousin to the tart brown ales made in Flanders. Closer to Hoegaarden,

> "When fresh, this beer is very pale, very refreshing, and strongly sparkling. Its raw taste has something wild that is similar to the Leuven beer it resembles in many respects—but it is not as sweet as the latter, no doubt because it contains more oats and less wheat, and because the boil of the sweet beer is shorter than the equivalent wort used to prepare Leuven white beer."
>
> —GEORGES LACAMBRE, 1851

Leuven was a famous brewing center and produced a "refreshing, frothy" *bière blanche* and a darker wheat beer called Peeterman. And in Brussels and the river valleys of Pajottenland, the wheat ale of choice was lambic.

Lambics and the beers produced in Leuven and Hoegaarden had much in common. They were made with grists of unmalted wheat (20 to 60 percent) and often oats. Those known as *blanche* employed "wind-malted" barley—that is, unkilned grain, left simply to dry in the breeze. The Leuven and Hoegaarden beers were cloudy and very pale.

All Belgian breweries used flat cooling vessels known as "cool ships" before the twentieth century, so tart acidity from wild yeast and bacteria was a given. How the breweries encouraged or discouraged

was the length of time they were allowed to age. Brewers put lambics away for months or years, allowing all of the wild yeasts to exert their influence. The beers of Leuven and Hoegaarden were served fresh. In the case of Leuven's beers, aging took just four or five days, and never longer than two weeks in the summer. In Hoegaarden, because of somewhat slower-acting wild yeasts, aging took

this characteristic depended on the way they brewed the beer. Lambic brewers never added yeast, letting the beers ferment spontaneously—or from wild yeasts only. In some of the methods of Leuven, brewers boiled their worts; in others, they set aside a portion of several unboiled mashes, where a coating of wild organisms on the yeast would continue to thrive. Hoegaarden's brewers used a mixture of these techniques. Lacambre reported that brewers in Hoegaarden spontaneously fermented their beer after blending mixtures of three strengths of wort, one unboiled. (A similar method that allowed the beer to retain its spontaneous fermentation was used until the 1930s.)

Collectively, these beers formed an extended family, but what made them distinctive

eight to fifteen days, and continued to ferment in the serving casks. Hoegaarden's beer was effectively a variation on a green lambic; because many of its microorganisms didn't have a chance to get active, the beer was characterized mainly by lactic tartness.

Following the Second World War, Belgium suffered an enormous loss of indigenous beer types. Once renowned, ancient styles like Peeterman, *uytzet*, and

ABOVE: *Hoegaarden is well known as the birthplace of wheat beer.*

RIGHT: *An old copper kettle greets visitors as they enter the city.*

Antwerp's indigenous barley beer were all dying as people turned to industrial lagers. Up to a dozen major styles would be lost by the 1960s; among the old ales from the wheat belt, lambics were the survivors.

AN UNEXPECTED REVIVAL

On one hand, the 1960s were a terrible time to try to resuscitate a lost style; consumers were moving away from tradition and looking for more consistent, modern beer that would last longer than a few days. On the other hand, there might have been some genius in the timing. One virtue of extinction is nostalgia, and the lost white beers of Hoegaarden were still very much in the memory of people like Pierre Celis, the milkman who had earlier worked in the last brewery in town.

Hoegaarden. When he founded his witbier brewery in the mid-1960s, Pierre Celis named it after the town of Hoegaarden. Later, in the late 1970s, he changed it to the monastic-sounding De Kluis in a well-played attempt to boost sales. After a fire gutted the brewery in 1985, Celis sold a majority share to the local giant, Stella Artois, and moved to Texas to start over. In the three decades since it acquired the brand, Artois and its various parent companies (currently Anheuser-Busch InBev) have called the beer Hoegaarden.

What was once a small Belgian brewery has become a giant, but its iconic beer is still brewed in the village from which it takes its name. InBev takes pains to associate Hoegaarden with the town's rich heritage—the label touts the date it was founded—but the beer has gotten less interesting over the years. In the early 1990s, Michael Jackson wrote that "its fruity sourness gives way to a honeyish sweetness." Whatever you can say about its honeyishness, there's certainly nothing sour left for drinkers in the new millennium. The exigencies of being an international brand have nudged it in a blander direction. Yet Celis's legacy is clear: After only an eight-year gap between batches of witbier, the town of Hoegaarden is once again synonymous with its local beer.

Instead of picking up where the old breweries left off, Celis had a different idea. He reformulated the recipe and adopted modern brewing methods. The grist for his Oud Hoegaards Bier followed tradition, with pale barley, unmalted wheat, and oats. But instead of wild fermentation, Celis pitched a characterful strain of yeast. To evoke the crispness and tang of lactic acid, he used the peels from bitter oranges and coriander. Much as is common in Belgium today, Celis also bottle-conditioned the beer for a month before releasing it.

That beer sparked a (slow) revolution. Celis labored for years, selling around 1,300 barrels annually until he changed the name of his brewery to De Kluis ("the cloister") in 1978. Associating one's beer with the monastics was a tried-and-true gambit in Belgium, and it worked for Celis. His beer took off, and soon the style had spread to the Netherlands. By 1985, Celis's business had grown nearly fifty-fold. He sold a portion of the company to Stella Artois, precipitating the chain of events that eventually led to the formation of InBev. In another radical move, Celis decided to sell the company and relocate in Texas in 1992, bringing witbier to North America.

The style had surprising legs. Witbiers would eventually pop up in unlikely places like Japan and Eastern Europe. In France and North America, witbier became a staple for craft breweries. Although Celis found success in the United States, it was actually Coors that made the style a huge American success with its Blue Moon label. For years this appeared to be only an interesting experiment, but by the mid-2000s, it was clearly bound for success. Anheuser-Busch responded with Shock Top Belgian White and now the two beers account for millions of barrels of production, making witbier America's bestselling ale. ∎

"For every brew of 2,500 liters (one thousand bottles) use 625 kilos raw material such as unroasted malt, oat, and wheat. Oat and wheat are then ground and undergo three processes with boiling spring waters, successively at [113°F, 131°F, and 163°F]. The mixture remains two hours in a boiler. Then seven kilos Czech hop is added. This wort chills to [63°F] and ferments in the yeast tub for seven days. Then follows a secondary fermentation for about a month in beer tanks. This beer is not filtered."

—*PIERRE CELIS: MY LIFE*, BY RAYMOND BILLEN

DESCRIPTION AND CHARACTERISTICS

A MUG OF WIT is a curious thing. It looks like a pilsner blended with coconut milk, and vents a tropical aroma. Yet swish it around and you will detect a soft breadiness and a refreshingly crisp finish—all infused by a citric acidity. White ale is the vanishingly rare style that is at once familiar and approachable while still seeming exotic.

For thirty years, whites were made using a recipe as specific as a Martini's: unmalted wheat and oats in the grist and coriander and bitter curaçao orange peel. This was Pierre Celis's prescription, and to international brewers dabbling in Belgian brewing, it might as well have been written on a stone tablet. Wheat and coriander remain the gin and vermouth in the cocktail: inviolable. Thanks to the style's slow, slight evolution, though, brewers have begun to fiddle cautiously at the margins—using, say, ginger along with coriander. Some have experimented with chamomile, lemongrass, black pepper—anything that puts a twist on the balance between gentle, summery comfort and snappy, crisp refreshment. People know too much about whites for complete reinvention, but brewers can alter the arrangement so long as drinkers still hear the melody.

An oddball recipe is not all that makes white beer unusual: By far the majority of the best examples are now brewed outside Belgium. Indeed, in Belgium, the witbeer style isn't particularly widespread. Two of the finest versions come from opposite sides of the planet, Maine's Allagash and Japan's Hitachino Nest White, and they do a nice job of illustrating the style's range.

When Rob Tod founded Allagash in 1995, he wanted to highlight Belgian beer styles, and the first product out of the kettle was White—still the brewery's flagship two decades on. It was inspired

Another Low-Tax White Beer.

There's a strange echo of the law that helped popularize wheat beer in Belgium—a very similar law, centuries later, in Japan. When Kiuchi decided to brew beer in the mid-1990s, they didn't choose witbier at random. The Japanese brewing laws had just changed, allowing small producers to enter the market. One of the new rules discounted the tax on beer made with 50 percent adjuncts. Hitachino Nest White Ale, made with a grist of flaked (unmalted) barley and wheat and the addition of orange juice, met the criterion.

by Celis white, one of Tod's early craft beer encounters. At first, he says, "I thought there was something wrong with it." That changed as witbier became one of his favorite styles. Tod doesn't think of white beer as a summer confection, though, and he strives for a refinement eschewed by most other wit makers. Using unmalted wheat, he brews one of the palest whites; it looks a bit like unfiltered pear juice. Tod's use of a highly attenuative yeast strain is the hallmark of the beer, which ends on a crisp, very dry note. Coriander and orange accentuate the effect, and White evokes the character of the best dry rieslings.

Unlike relative newbie Allagash, the Kiuchi sake brewery dates back to 1823. But it only started making beer in 1996. It has an eclectic mix of brands and has begun introducing Japanese specialties such as an ale made with rice—similar to sake—and another brewed entirely from Japanese malt and hops. Their witbier, Hitachino Nest White Ale, heads in a different direction from Allagash's. In addition to unmalted wheat, Kiuchi also uses unmalted barley, which gives the beer a thicker, almost buckwheat-like body. White Ale is spiced not only with coriander and orange peel, but also nutmeg and orange juice. Like Allagash, the elements are light and complimentary, but where Allagash is refined, Hitachino Nest is more rustic.

Within Belgium, the two current pace setters include Caracole, which makes a spirited little darling called Troublette that relies, as does Allagash's, on a dry, vinous acidity. The other example, and one often cited as the best brewed, is another of Pierre Celis's many progeny: St. Bernardus Wit. Celis didn't craft the recipe, but the brewery did call on him to tune it up. St. Bernardus Wit has a massive dose of coriander that infuses the nose and palate, but is balanced by a tangy, tart finish. ■

BREWING NOTES

WHEN HE ADAPTED the recipe for the first modern white, Pierre Celis produced a bottle-conditioned beer that looked in many respects like other Belgian ales. With spices and a grist of oats and unmalted wheat it was slightly unusual—but these were all familiar ingredients in the Belgian canon. Celis fermented his wit cooler than most modern versions, but this was only a modest deviation. As a result, the style has changed little in the fifty years since Celis first introduced his new recipe.

The grists of old Hoegaarden beers routinely employed unmalted wheat—originally as a way to minimize taxes and later by tradition. Oats were also commonly used, not just in *bières blanches*, but throughout Belgian brewing. Celis returned to these grains for his recipe, but not all brewers do. Some use malted wheat (Blue Moon); some don't use oats (Allagash). Brewers use the grist to emphasize different aspects of their beers. Since the style is so lean and delicate, the grist plays a substantial role in the overall character, so these decisions lead to noticeably different interpretations. Some incline toward a fuller, breadier quality, others toward light crispness.

The real distinctiveness of witbier comes from its citric spiciness—which may come from actual spices or from the action of the yeast. The role of yeast should not be overlooked. Although

Curaçao Orange. The peel of any orange—or any citrus fruit, for that matter—may be used to spice a white beer, but the variety you'll see most often is curaçao. The fruit is more accurately called a Lahara, the descendant of oranges that Spaniards planted on the Caribbean island of Curaçao in the sixteenth century. The island's nutrient-poor volcanic soil and dry climate forced the trees to adapt, and the fruit changed in the process. It shrank and became bitter and inedible, but distillers realized the aromatic peel could be used to make curaçao liquor.

And, of course, beer.

Celis originally fermented his white cool, it is more common to follow the Belgian practice and let the temperature nose up into the mid- or upper seventies where the beer will form fruit and spice notes—as wits from Hoegaarden, New Belgium, and Ommegang do. The spices then accentuate this yeast character. Phil Leinhart, at Brewery Ommegang, says, "It's supposed to be a delicate, refreshing beer and the approach should be a very light touch. It should create a very well-blended beer, and you should think, 'What is that?'"

Coriander is the style's workhorse. It's a versatile spice that can lend sweetness, a lemony snap, or a gentle floral note. Celis used bitter orange peel in his recipe, but brewers sometimes use the peels of sweet oranges, or orange zest— or different citrus altogether. The use of some citrus peel is still a standard practice, though this is a more negotiable element than coriander. More negotiable still are other spices, and many find their way into white ales—though not always explicitly. Even Celis was cagey when asked whether he used additional undisclosed spice. In witbier, it is a brewer's prerogative to add a dash of mystery. ■

Thanks to Blue Moon, many people enter the world of beer through the witbier door and wonder how to expand their horizons. If what attracts you is the gentle, easy-drinking quality, you might consider *American wheat ales* like Bell's Oberon or Goose Island 312 Urban Wheat. *Golden ales* and *kölsch* are other possibilities. However, if you're an Allagash fan or like the witbiers that have a dry or complex palate, try an *abbey ale*, *saison*, or *Bavarian weissbier*.

EVOLUTION

NOTHING STOPS innovation as fast as commercial success, so it's not suprising that white ales continue to be made using only slight variations on the wheat-and-oats, coriander-and-orange-peel template. Yet their success also makes them attractive to brewers hoping to exploit their popularity. One of the more interesting developments is "white IPA," a style that combines the soft spice of wits with the natural citrus of American hops. The debut was a collaboration between Boulevard and Deschutes, but Saranac, Blue Point, and others have followed.

Some hybrids sound better on paper than when they appear in a pint glass, but white IPAs show real promise. Breweries deemphasize hop bitterness in favor of flavor, and the citrusy continuum—from coriander to Cascade—harmonizes beautifully.

The second variation is a return to the traditional, wild ales of Hoegaarden. The pioneer was Jolly Pumpkin, the Michigan brewery that introduced Calabaza Blanca when it opened in 2004. The beer is a light, 4.8% ABV interpretation, brewed with the standard coriander and orange peel but barrel-aged with

Blue Moon Belgian White.

In 1995, Keith Villa kicked off a unit within Coors Brewing Company (now MillerCoors) to make ales that would compete in the craft beer market. Ultimately called Blue Moon, it was housed in the Sandlot Brewery at Coors Field and immediately earned plaudits from craft beer fans. One of the initial products was a witbier called Bellyslide Belgian White, a beer made with malted wheat, coriander, the peels from sweet Valencia oranges, and an English ale yeast.

At a time when breweries were trying to figure out how to appeal to mass-market lager fans, Villa signaled his beer's approachability by garnishing it with a wheel of orange. Of the initial offerings, it was the Belgian white that took off, ultimately becoming synonymous with the name Blue Moon. Although its success chafes fans of small-batch imperial stouts, it followed the blueprint drafted by craft breweries—though having national distribution was an enormous asset as the brand stretched from coast to coast.

With sales reportedly approaching 2 million barrels, Belgian White now outsells all other American ales, and its production is larger than all but one craft brewery. Blue Moon is the king of mass-market ales, but it's also a fine beer that invites the question about what it means to be a "craft beer." It has an oaty, wheaty base and a hearty coriander wash that takes it within sight of cloying—but stops just short. Blue Moon might not be regarded as the nation's best white beer, but it is better than a number of mediocre craft-brewed attempts. And it has demonstrated that there's no reason ales can't become big sellers. All of this signals a change in the American beer market, which should be considered very good news by anyone tired of mass-market lagers.

RIGHT: *An advertisement for Blue Moon emphasizes its "craft" appeal—and its now-signature orange wheel garnish.*

wild yeast. Boulevard has done a different version, a strong wit called Two Jokers, additionally spiced with cardamom, lavender, and grains of paradise. These are hybrid wits, combining the wild yeast of previous decades with the novel spices Celis introduced (none was mentioned in old texts). As soured ales become more popular, we may see more examples of old-style *bière blanche*. Who knows, one day a brewery may even forgo the spice in favor of spontaneous fermentation. ■

THE BEERS TO KNOW

WITBIER CONSTITUTES a narrow band of flavors—at least among the finest examples. There are more out there, but these six will give you a good sense of the style.

ALLAGASH WHITE

∘∘

LOCATION: Portland, ME

MALT: Pale, red wheat, unmalted white wheat

HOPS: Saaz, Styrian Golding

OTHER: Coriander, orange peel

5.0% ABV, 1.048 SP. GR., 21 IBU

In Allagash's very pale example, you can see why people originally started calling these "white" beers. The aroma has a suggestion of coriander, pepper, and lemons that carries through to the palate, which is light and crisp. This is the driest of the witbiers, and the most suggestive of white wine. Allagash is complex and sere, a contrast to some crowd-pleasing versions out there.

KIUCHI HITACHINO NEST WHITE ALE

∘∘

LOCATION: Naka-shi, Japan

MALT: Pale, malted wheat, flaked wheat, flaked barley

HOPS: Perle, Styrian Golding

OTHER: Coriander, nutmeg, orange peel, orange juice

5.5% ABV, 1.055 SP. GR., 13 IBU

The nose of lemon meringue pie is surprising, given the various parts of Japanese oranges included in the beer, but it's unmistakable. Hitachino Nest turns herbal on the palate, with a touch of *hojicha* tea and white pepper—and the requisite coriander. Heavier than most examples, and its grains taste of buckwheat.

ST. BERNARDUS WIT

oooooooooooooooooooooooooooooooooooooooo

LOCATION: Watou, Belgium

MALT: Pilsner, wheat

HOPS: Target, Styrian Golding

5.5% ABV

Vivacious and heavily carbonated, St. Bernardus comes out of the bottle as opaque as a vanilla milkshake. It's saturated in coriander but saved by a zingy tartness that's suggestive of lemonade. Refreshing and uncomplicated.

OMMEGANG WITTE

oooooooooooooooooooooooooooooooooooooooo

LOCATION: Cooperstown, NY

MALT: Pilsner, wheat, unmalted wheat, oat flakes

HOPS: Spalter Select

OTHER: Coriander, orange peel

5.2% ABV, 1.046 SP. GR., 11 IBU

Witte follows the standard recipe, but the result is a more rustic beer, like a spiced saison. Tangy, light, and very refreshing, it has a strongly spiced layer, but doesn't cloy. The spices and yeast conspire to create a wine-skin acidity that veers into zesty rather than sweet.

CARACOLE TROUBLETTE

oooooooooooooooooooooooooooooooooooooooo

LOCATION: Falmignoul, Belgium

MALT: Pilsner, unmalted wheat

HOPS: Saaz, Styrian Golding

OTHER: Undisclosed spices

5.0% ABV

A lively, lovely rustic wheat ale, Troublette has a zesty, white-grape palate long on acidity and short on coriander. Light and refreshing, it compares with a pinot gris, but is sharper and more citrusy. The tartness and full wheat flavor hint at what the older Hoegaarden wits might have tasted like.

JOLLY PUMPKIN CALABAZA BLANCA

oooooooooooooooooooooooooooooooooooooooo

LOCATION: Dexter, MI

MALT: Pilsner, wheat malt, raw wheat

HOPS: Tettnang

OTHER: Coriander, sweet and bitter orange peel

4.9% ABV, 1.039 SP. GR., 15 IBU

If you want to take the Troublette thought experiment a step further, try Calabaza Blanca, a barrel-aged witbier that is even more acidic. In this beer, the tartness is a bright, lactic piquancy that has lots of lemon in it. "Yellow" springs to mind more than white when you're drinking this beer, as the citrusy coriander and orange peels add more zing. The beer doesn't bite, but it refreshes like the best fresh lemonade.

Tart German Wheat Ales
BERLINER WEISSE AND GOSE

. . . .

The world used to be full of bizarre fermented beverages. Some were impossibly thick porridges packed with honey, fruit, and spice that sounded more like food than beer. Others were very light on alcohol but heavy on ingredients we don't normally see in beer these days, like ashes, tree bark, and beans. They had wonderful names like Mumme, jopenbier, and

Tart German Wheat Ales.

If any beer illustrates that flavor and strength are not correlated, Berliner weisse, with its bright, sharp tartness, is it. During their occupation of Berlin, Napoleon's troops called Berlin's weissbier "Champagne," and with its roiling effervescence and wine-like appearance, it's easy to see why. Gose is a stranger, more complex tipple. It's a wheatier beer, salty, and less tart than Berliner weisse, with a soft, delicate palate elongated by coriander. What surprises is how well the addition of salt frames the beer and makes it an extraordinary hot-weather quencher.

STATISTICS

Berliner weisse ABV range: 3–4%; bitterness: around 5 IBU

Gose ABV range: 4–6%; bitterness: 5–10 IBU

Serving temperature: 40°–45°F

Vessel: Goblet (Berliner weisse); stange (gose)

Cöpenicker Moll. Most have been replaced by more sedate, reasonable beers made with boring barley and hops.

Most.

Fortunately for connoisseurs of the unusual, a few oddities remain. One is Berliner weisse, a sparkling low-alcohol beer so sharp with lactic acid that Berliners took to dosing it with sugar syrups. It has the kind of bracing finish that will snap you awake faster than a cup of French roast. And that is normal compared with gose (which is pronounced *Goze-uh*), another tart wheat ale spiced with coriander . . . and salt. Imagine salted yogurt. Goses, which originally hailed from Goslar before emigrating to Leipzig, did actually go extinct for a time, but Berliner weisses never did. Fortunately, the same interest that led beer fans to pursue the unusual new flavors found in craft beers also led them to investigate unusual *old* flavors. Gose and Berliner weisse are still fairly obscure beers, but they are starting to win fans on both sides of the Atlantic. ■

ORIGINS

GERMANY'S BREWING history is far weirder than most people realize. The lager tradition was, until the twentieth century, isolated in the south; *Reinheitsgebot* was a Bavarian-only rule until 1906 with no currency in the north. There, beers were as funky and variable as those in neighboring Belgium, where wheat beers were also a popular specialty. As in Belgium, many North German ales were specific to single towns or villages. Heinrich Knaust, writing one of the earliest compendiums on beer in the late 1500s, catalogued 150 different kinds. Another writer of the period described some of the ingredients of the day, and they give you a sense of how strange the beers really were. Laurel and ivy were kosher as preservatives, he wrote, but henbane could lead to insanity while chimney soot (!) would damage the lungs and kidneys. (You don't say . . .) If soot was thought to be a suitable ingredient, it's difficult to imagine what the sixteenth-century brewer would have ruled out.

As odd as they sound to us today, a lot of these old styles survived through

Bottled Gose. It was common in the case of both gose and Berliner weisse for the brewery to deliver fermenting wort to pubs, where it was stored in cellars. Once the beer was nearly fermented, the pub workers bottled the beer. Gose bottles are oddly shaped—fat and round at the bottom, with a long, slender, tapering neck. The reason? As the beer finished fermenting, the yeasty foam rose up and crusted, forming a plug in the neck—and so the bottles required no additional cork or crown.

Cobbler's Glue. Old accounts of brewing techniques often leave you scratching your head. Take, for example, this passage from the 1773 *Oekonomische Encyklopädie*, which historian Ron Pattinson translates:

> *After five or six hours, when the fermentation goes well, a white spot appears in the middle of the beer, and the Weissbier brewer then usually puts his beer immediately into [barrels], without waiting for a full fermentation in the mash tun. The beer is taken into the cellar and here it must ferment or, as they say, belch. First sticky and pitch-like yeast appears, which consequently in Berlin is called pitch or pitch barm. Cobblers use this yeast as glue.*

Yeast that's as sticky as pitch? Life was indeed hard in the olden days.

to the twentieth century, or modern times. They started dying off, though, and names like Lichtenhainer and *adambier* have mostly been lost to history books. Others, like Grodziskie, failed late enough to remain in memory. Gose and Berliner weisse are the last remnants of the funky wheat ales of North Germany and are important links to a brewing tradition that lasted until just a few decades ago.

As broad as the range of beers was between the 1500s and 1900s, there were some notable similarities among a certain band of light-bodied wheat ales. Although the recipes and methods varied considerably over the ages, both goses and Berliner weisses, in general, were low-alcohol beers made to be served fresh and marked by a lactic zing. Berliner weisse dates to at least the late 1600s, but may have been around well before that. Gose may have been a contemporary of Berliner weisse, or it could be a much older style—at least one source mentions imports to Hamburg of Goslar's *gosa* from the late 1300s.

Accounts of both beers show that they changed over time and that they were made in different ways. Some Berliner weisses made before 1860 used smoked wheat malt, like Grodziskie. In one description from the 1700s, brewers boiled most of the batch, but kept an unboiled portion back, which they pitched with the yeast. (The wheat grains, coated with *Lactobacillus*, would have inoculated the wort with souring microorganisms.) A century later, an observer reported that brewers didn't boil the wort at all. That was still the process in some breweries at the start of the twentieth century, but other breweries split their batches, fermenting half with regular ale yeast and half with *Lactobacillus*. This innovation was helped by technology that let brewers control their process; after the lactic half had reached the right level of pH, brewers boiled the beer and mixed it with the other half to finish fermenting out.

Goses were just as variable. They were once spontaneously fermented (one of the links that make historians wonder

"Berlin is the city of all others where the *kühle blonde* ['cool fair maiden'] is obtained in the greatest perfection, and where *bier-stuben* offering no other beverage to their frequenters abound. The beer is drunk by preference when it is of a certain age, and in perfection it should be largely impregnated with carbonic acid gas and have acquired a peculiar sharp, dry, and by no means disagreeable flavour."

—HENRY VIZETELLY,
Berlin Under the New Empire, 1879

if gose and lambic aren't somehow related), but by the nineteenth century, they were merely unboiled. Again, this would have been quite useful in sparking a lactic fermentation. Gose was popular enough that by 1740, Leipzig taverns, 100 miles to the southeast, began selling it. Before long, Leipzig breweries were making it themselves, and eventually their town would be more known for gose than Goslar was.

Both styles were threatened and abused in the twentieth century. Gose got the worst of it, blinking in and out of existence as wars and lagers battered German ales. It looked to be well and fully dead by 1966. The last gose brewery, Wurzler, had closed, and Wurzler's brewing book containing the gose recipes was accidently destroyed. Revivals depend on champions, and it was a publican named Lothar Goldhahn who stepped forward and saved the style. He managed to track down a Wurzler employee who miraculously had some old notes on the beer; Goldhahn then arranged for it to be brewed at a Berliner weisse brewery in Berlin. Once an assemblage of old gose drinkers deemed it authentic, gose was back in business—exactly twenty years

after it went extinct. (You can still visit Ohne Bedenken, Goldhahn's *gosenschenke*— gose tavern—if you happen to be in Leipzig.)

Berliner weisse enjoyed a larger market than gose, and after the Cold War made it an East German specialty, multiple breweries made versions. Each brewery did things a little differently, though it was common to brew stronger beers and add water to bring them down to traditionally weak strengths. Beyond that, the methods remained essentially unchanged from earlier decades. By the 1970s, however, the beer had become somewhat debased. Somewhere along the way it became too tart for modern tastes, and publicans started serving weissbiers with sweet green or red syrups. Michael Jackson, writing in 1977, described what had become of the style: "'White' is a particular misnomer for a beer which is usually drunk either red or green. However delightful they may find the beer itself, visitors from other countries are apt to be shocked by these colors, but Germans are frequently surprised at the thought of drinking a Berliner weisse without a *schuss* (a dash of raspberry juice) or *Waldmeister* (essence of woodruff)."

Gose and Berliner weisse remain obscure specialty beers, but now that may be what keeps them alive. American craft beer fans, ever on the lookout for something different, have rediscovered these beers (rarely served flavored stateside) and become fans. In Germany, they are slower to find the favor of locals, but even there, gose and Berliner weisse are gaining new supporters. ∎

DESCRIPTION AND CHARACTERISTICS

DESCRIBING ENDANGERED **BEER** styles, particularly those hanging precariously on the fortunes of a single extant example or two, is dicey business. There's the question of sample size—is it really reasonable to discuss style on the basis of so few beers? But more important, just the act of staying around often leaves a beer reduced in character and distinctiveness. Is it enough to look at existing examples? Of course, one can instead turn to history and its spotty descriptive record, or look to the revivals and one-offs as liquid thought experiments in what the style might have been. Or triangulate from all of the above. Yes, let's do that.

There's every reason to believe goses and Berliner weisses are in the midst of a renaissance. Breweries have spent the last decade mining the archives for interesting beers to make, and tart ales command a passionate—if small—following.

Berliner weisse, in particular, seems ripe for reclamation. The final Berlin-brewed weisse is a sad shadow of those erstwhile "Champagnes"—it is fizzy but listless, tart but strangely sweet, a beer that isn't what it once was nor what modern Berliners want a beer to be. But new examples, particularly from The Bruery, Dogfish Head, and Bear Republic are anything but tired.

If I had to guess, I would say The Bruery's Hottenroth is as close to "authentic" as Berliner weisses get. In the hands of American breweries, beers tend to succumb to gigantism—a special risk for beers that historically hovered around 3%. Hottenroth, a modest 3.1% beer, is a tiny powerhouse. Although The Bruery lets a little *Brettanomyces* into the wort, the palate is dominated by a sharp, quenching lactic tartness. Henry Vizetelly would have admired how the "carbonic gas impregnation" helps lighten and

Is There Brett in the Berliner? Berliner weisses are not

funky. They have the clear, "clean" tartness that comes from wholesome *Lactobacillus*. For this reason they were assumed to be free of wilder things like *Brettanomyces*, producer of flavors reminiscent of goat and horse. It turns out tastes can be deceiving. *Brettanomyces* is not only resident in beers from fifty years ago and more, but its contribution actually seems important to making a "typical" Berliner weisse sour. While *Brettanomyces* doesn't have a chance here to get all the way to full goat, what it can produce are two key esters, ethyl acetate (the ester that tastes like pear or apple) and ethyl lactate (like wine or coconut). A number of modern interpretations, like those by The Bruery and Bear Republic, include *Brettanomyces*, hoping to reproduce that "typical" flavor.

What About the Syrups? If you order a Berliner weisse in a pub (though it's far more likely in Berlin than the U.S.), you might be asked whether you'd like it green or red. That is, would you like a very sweet raspberry (red) or woodruff (green) syrup with which to dose your beer? The choice is yours, but be forewarned: These syrups will transform your beer into something you'd expect Fanta to make. The woodruff, incidentally, tastes something like an herbal marshmallow—and it's quite a vibrant shade of green.

balance the beer. Dogfish Head makes a version fermented with peaches that gives the beer a hint of fruit without much sugar. Fruit and acidity in a dry beer—it never hurt a sauvignon blanc. Bear Republic, using spontaneous fermentation, is easily the sharpest of the bunch. It's enough to make you consider a dose of *schuss*.

Goses are more obscure, but they have better indigenous champions. The first and best-known is Gosebrauerei Bayerischer Bahnhof, which debuted in Leipzig in 2000. Their signature beer is light and gentle, but suitably gose-y . . . by which I mean confusing. Although it looks and smells like a wheat beer (the coriander lends a whiff of witbier), the sour and salt in tandem evoke something entirely different: Indian lassi. Lassi is a popular yogurt-based drink served either sweet or salted, and the latter is a dead ringer for the salty tang of Bahnhof Leipziger Gose.

Döllnitzer Ritterguts is the other well-known German gose. Brewed under contract by Hartmannsdorf for the descendants of nineteenth-century gosebrauerei owners, it is a more aggressive beer. All the dials are turned up on Döllnitzer—the sour, the salt, and the coriander. It also has quite a bit more clove, like the southern weissbiers from Bavaria.

Is either one more authentic? At one time, Leipzig was home to scores of gose breweries, and no doubt there was a range of differences. Authenticity is a moving target. A few American breweries have tried their hands at goses—some are trying to meld the unusual flavors of coriander, salt, and lactic acid (Boston Beer Verloren), others have taken the idea and hustled off in a different direction (Widmer Marionberry Hibiscus Gose). Beer styles only attract loyal defenders of tradition once they've been around awhile, so we'll have to check back in a few decades. ■

BREWING NOTES

WITH SO MANY different interpretations of these old styles, you might imagine there are many ways to brew them—and you'd be right. Let's start with what they have in common. Wheat is obviously central to both gose and Berliner weisse. Because *Reinheitsgebot* takes a dim view on unmalted wheat, breweries use malted—even when they're making beers that are far outside the purity law's guidelines. At least one-third and up to half the grist should be wheat for both styles:

The farther off the grid you go, the harder it is to match beers. Gose is essentially *sui generis*, a class of its own. Perhaps *gueuze* could be called a related beer, but it doesn't quite match the sour-and-salt flavors of gose. *Lambics* (and gueuze) are closer to Berliner weisse. Other sour beers, like *tart Flanders ales* and *American wild ales* are only distantly related, but nevertheless worth exploring.

Kindl only uses one-quarter, but this is low. Pilsner malt, with possibly a small portion of color or head grains, rounds out the bill.

The other key element in both styles is lactic acid, and breweries get it in

Lactic Acid Versus Lactobacillus.

Unlike beers made from wild yeasts, which may have funky animal-like or musty flavors, Berliner weisses and goses usually get their clean, bright tart flavor from a bacterium called *Lactobacillus*. Like regular brewers yeast, *Lactobacillus* gobbles sugars, but it produces lactic acid instead of alcohol. Sometimes breweries describe processes that lead to "lactic fermentation," and this is what they mean. Lactic acid is commonly found in sour milk products like yogurt, which is what gives them their similarly tart flavor.

In the wild, *Lactobacillus* clambers onto the husks of grain. The sturdy little fellow can survive hot, subboiling temperatures; one method of starting lactic fermentation is leaving some or all the wort unboiled and letting the wild bacterium run its course. (Other breweries pitch the *Lactobacillus*.) When it does its thing, though, *Lactobacillus* creates more than just one compound—as is the case with regular yeast as well. It produces other acids, enzymes, and substances called bacteriocins. This is important because beers made with lactic fermentation taste fuller, rounder, and more complex than those to which a brewer has simply added food-grade lactic acid. Lactic acid by itself is more cutting—sometimes even with a "chemical" edge—sometimes slick, and sometimes salty. A good brewer can conceal the off-flavors, but he won't be able to replace the more subtle flavors that come from fermentation.

myriad ways. The easiest path—and generally the poorest—is to add lactic acid straight to the beer. Brewers do this to eliminate the need to mess with live bacteria and also because it gives them precise control over the amount that goes in. Other breweries turn to wild yeast and bacteria. Fritz Briem doesn't bring his Berliner weisse to boil, relying instead on natural *Lactobacillus*. To ensure healthy lactic fermentation, when he pitches regular ale yeast, he also pitches a *Lactobacillus* culture taken from the malt. At Bahnhof, Matthias Richter cultures *Lactobacillus* in his basement and then adds it to the boil when he makes Leipziger Gose. This is the same process the brewery uses for its Berliner weisse, but Richter now also makes a version of the Berliner with *Brettanomyces* added to secondary fermentation. The most radical is Bear Republic: To make Tartare, they use spontaneous fermentation—yet they still get quite a clean (if pronounced) lactic tartness.

These beers never had a perfectly "traditional" method of production. That is still the rule. At The Bruery, Tyler King uses a totally idiosyncratic method. He employs a single, twenty-minute-hopped mash at 168°F. The beer is boiled for only twenty minutes and then goes to the fermenter for a two-week primary fermentation with only *Lactobacillus* and *Brettanomyces bruxellensis*. "We knew what flavors we wanted," King says. "We knew we wanted a sour beer, but we also wanted the beer to have body to it—we didn't want a thin, light beer. That's why we do such a high rest on it, to try to keep some of its body."

With these beers, hops are almost beside the point. They are there only to provide antimicrobial support, not flavor or bitterness. In making his 1809 Berliner weisse, Fritz Briem puts hops into the mash where decoction will isomerize them—but otherwise allows them to leave a small footprint. At Bahnhof, brewer Matthias Richter dips a single addition of hops in his gose. Of course, gose's flavor comes in large part from salt and coriander, both added near the end of the boil. The final step is the bottle-conditioning that, particularly in the case of Berliner weisse, leads to that Champagne-like carbonation. ∎

EVOLUTION

BOTH BERLINER WEISSE and gose are effectively revival styles. Berliners no longer seem interested in their hometown beer, which means breweries in other places, particularly the U.S., are picking up the baton. So far, these breweries have tried to hew to at least the spirit of tradition. They make smallish wheat beers with big, tart flavors. It's very hard for American breweries to sell a 3% ABV beer, however, and one obvious deviation they've made is in strength: Most are north of 4%, and a few, like Southampton and White Birch, are more than 6%. (Even Munich-based Fritz Briem makes his 1809 at an awfully burly 5%.)

A different trend is being pioneered by Dogfish Head and Canada's Brasserie

Dieu du Ciel, which are venturing into the fruit frontier. Dieu du Ciel was the first brewery to use fruit during fermentation—raspberries, as in a Belgian framboise—in Solstice d'Été in 1999. Meanwhile, Dogfish Head's use of peach was a brilliant inspiration, as the flavors in the stone fruit marry those in the beer perfectly. Others have tried fruit versions as well, like Florida's Funky Buddha, which has experimented with a number of tropical fruits, and Flying Dog, where the brewers add cherry.

Gose is more unpredictable. It's such an odd beer to begin with that just brewing it straight is a flight of fancy. Beyond that, it's still extremely rare, and most brewers haven't even discovered it. Beginning in about 2010, though, the style unexpectedly swept through Portland, Oregon, where at least four breweries started making it—working up a dozen different variations in all. At Cascade Brewing, Ron Gansberg decided to make a seasonal selection. The Summer Gose was traditional, while the other seasons got different spices and lighter or darker malts. Widmer started with two straightforward recipes, then began adding fruit and flowers. And at Breakside, brewer Ben Edmunds used cucumber in one recipe, and in another offered syrups, à la Berliner weisse, on the side. Are these the future of gose? Is Portland to become the new Leipzig? We'll just have to wait and see. ∎

THE BEERS TO KNOW

WHEN I FIRST stumbled onto the gose style, it had the feel of spotting an ivory-billed woodpecker flapping through the Florida cypress swamps: What wondrous, lost creature is this? Shortly after I sampled a bottle of Bahnhof's—my first gose—I happened to stop in at Portsmouth Brewery for lunch on my way from Boston to Maine. By some miraculous coincidence, they had a gose on tap. This is probably the way you'll encounter Berliner weisse and gose: by chance, unexpectedly. If you have a very good beer store nearby, you may get lucky and find one or two of the following options I've listed. But otherwise, just keep your eyes open: You never know when one might flap by.

THE BRUERY HOTTENROTH

ooooooooooooooooooooooooooooooooooooooooooooooo

LOCATION: Placentia, CA

MALT: Vienna, 60 percent unmalted wheat

HOPS: Stisselspalt

3.1% ABV, 1.026 SP. GR., 2 IBU

An attractive, honey-colored Berliner weisse with a lovely white head and the scent of lemons. For anyone who doesn't believe that bigger is better, I give you this luxurious beer with its soft breadiness, full mouthfeel, and citrus acidity. It thrums with flavor but ends so crisply you immediately want another sip.

BEAR REPUBLIC TARTARE

LOCATION: Healdsburg, CA

MALT: Undisclosed

HOPS: Undisclosed

4% ABV, 8 IBU

Tartare is the kind of Berliner weisse that might convince you to try woodruff: It is *tart*. Although the brewery uses spontaneous fermentation, the flavor is almost purely lactic sour—screaming, face-puckering—though in one vintage I thought I detected the telltale leather of *Brettanomyces*. Once you adjust, Tartare becomes a lemony treat, with some esters that suggest apple or perhaps apple blossom.

DOGFISH HEAD FESTINA PECHE

LOCATION: Milton, DE

MALT: Undisclosed

HOPS: Undisclosed

4.5% ABV

Festina Peche has a little bit to love for everyone. It has a gentle, wheaty body but a bracing tartness. The two are lashed together by the fresh essence of ripe summer peaches. This sunny weisse intoxicates the senses, if not the brain.

BAYERISCHER BAHNHOF LEIPZIGER GOSE

LOCATION: Leipzig, Germany

MALT: Wheat, pilsner

HOPS: Northern Brewer

OTHER: Coriander, salt

4.5% ABV, 1.044 SP. GR., 10 IBU

For those with fixed attitudes about how beer should taste, gose will offer you a real challenge. It *looks* regular enough, cloudy orange and sudsy and redolent of coriandered witbier. The tartness is of a tangy variety and arrives first, supplemented by cakey wheat. It's with the swallow, when the salt and coriander barge in, that things get wild. The effect is something like salted yogurt.

DÖLLNITZER RITTERGUTS GOSE

LOCATION: Hartmannsdorf, Germany

MALT: Undisclosed

HOPS: Undisclosed

OTHER: Undisclosed

4.2% ABV

If you start with Bahnhof, you'll find Döllnitzer even more bizarre. It is saltier, has a sweeter, more orangey coriander note, and finishes with a sharper tart pop. And that's more or less how the flavors unfold—plus a sense of crisp wheat and a pronounced clove note in the center. The clove may be one ingredient too many—but Döllnitzer believes it's authentic.

Der 84 Jährige nach 50 jährigem Gosentrunk

1 PT .9 FL OZ

~ Original ~ Ritterguts Gose

PART FOUR

Lagers

What exactly is a lager beer? This question is, at its heart, an existential one: Is lager a final, objective state, or the process of becoming? By one definition, lagers are known by the type of yeast they use—one that enjoys cool temperatures and that tends to sink rather than rise. The other definition demands that the beer be conditioned or aged after primary fermentation. The German word *lager*, in fact, comes from the sense of "storing."

In most cases, the distinction is purely academic; "lagers" are understood both to use a particular type of yeast *and* to have gone through a period of conditioning. Yet some ales are "lagered," that is, brewed with ale yeast and then put down for a period of time. Around Cologne and Düsseldorf, brewers may refer to their beer as top-fermented lagers (*obergäriges lagerbier*). French *bières de garde* are routinely called "ales," yet are conditioned for weeks or months—and in some cases even brewed with lager yeast strains. On the other hand, America's most famous indigenous style swings the other way. "Steam beer" is brewed like an ale but with lager yeast. For the purposes of discussion, let's ignore the oddballs. As they are broadly understood, lagers meet both definitions: They are made with a yeast strain that prefers cold temperatures and they are conditioned for a period of weeks or months.

What distinguishes lagers is less the way they're manufactured than the way they taste

RIGHT: *The biggest breweries in the world, like Munich's Paulaner, have lager running through their veins.*

(though of course one begets the other). Yeasts laboring in cool temperatures are less flamboyant than those found in warmer-temperature ales. The chill inhibits the production of esters and phenols, those compounds that taste like fruit and spice, leaving the beer's basic ingredients to carry the day. When you sip lager, you're experiencing the soft, wholesome flavor of the malts and the delicate spice of the hops without any filter or film. Cold fermentation leaves beers coarse and unfinished, but the period of conditioning sands away rough edges and exposes the rich grain of malt and hops. Lagers are refined, clean, and polished beers. Isn't it wonderfully symmetrical that Germany would become the greatest champion of this new way of brewing? Absence of ornamentation, harmony between design and function—these describe Bauhaus architecture as well as lager brewing.

The remarkable story of lager begins around the late thirteenth century, as brewers began to intuit the presence of yeast. Until that time they fermented their beers spontaneously, but eventually they learned to skim yeast from actively fermenting beer to seed the next batch

of wort—a practice mentioned first in a logbook from the mid-fourteenth century. Over the decades, brewers refined their process so that they later maintained stores of yeast. Even though it would be centuries before anyone discovered what the tiny cells were, brewers understood how to use them. By collecting the barm (yeast cake) and repitching it, they were, over time, very slowly domesticating brewers yeast.

In Bavaria (or possibly neighboring Bohemia) in the early 1500s, some of those yeasts started behaving strangely. Most of the yeasts preferred warmer temperatures, but one variety emerged that liked it cold. In fact, this strain settled out of suspension and refused to work well in the warmer months—when brewers had to return to the older, warm-weather yeast. These beers were the first lagers, and they were prized in the region. By 1539, the Bavarian government actually mandated that brewing only happen in the cool months when the favored yeast could work its magic. By the turn of the seventeenth century, brewers elsewhere had become aware of the two different strains. Outside of cooler Bavaria and Bohemia, though, lagers were hard to brew. In fact, the results were so bad that lager yeast was banned by the Cologne city council in 1603; England and Flanders were likewise too mild. So for hundreds of years, lager remained a local specialty limited in production to the cellaring caves of a small, southern region of the beer world.

It wasn't until the nineteenth century that the golden age of lagers dawned. In the early 1840s, three brewers working in three different countries began experimenting with pale malts to produce sparkling golden-to-amber lagers: Anton Dreher in Vienna, Gabriel Sedlmayr in Munich, and Josef Groll (another Bavarian) in Pilsen (Plzeň), Bohemia. Two decades later, Louis Pasteur finally revealed the science behind yeast. (He strongly recommended lagering to improve purity). And finally, by the 1870s, refrigeration made it possible to start brewing lagers in warmer climates.

The effect was profound—if slow to develop. Two decades after Groll started brewing pilsner, there were still more than twice as many Bohemian breweries making ale as lager. But by 1875, almost the entire country had flipped—of 849 breweries there, 831 were making lagers. In Germany, the change took a bit longer. By 1870, the vast majority of breweries were still making ales, but the lager breweries were growing and had already eclipsed ale production. By the turn of the century, lagers had seized more than 80 percent of the market and were still growing. That proved to be a harbinger of trends across the globe. Although there are still more styles of ales than lagers, the battle for hegemony is long over—lagers make up more than 95 percent of the world's beer production (and the vast majority of those are pale lagers). A hundred and fifty years ago, the percentages were just the opposite. ■

Dark Lagers
DUNKEL, SCHWARZBIER, AND CZECH TMAVÉ

I n Bavaria, they're known as "dark" (*dunkel*), in Thuringia they call them "black" (*schwarz*), and in the Czech Republic they're both (*tmavé* or *černé*): These stolid, dark lagers are as straightforward

STATISTICS

Dunkel ABV range: 4.7–5.5%; bitterness: 15–25 IBU

Schwarzbier ABV range: 4.7–5.2%; bitterness: 20–30 IBU

Tmavé/černé ABV range: 4.0–5.5%; bitterness: 15–35 IBU

Serving temperature: 45°–50°F

Vessel: Mug or pint glass

Dunkel, Schwarzbier, & Czech Tmavé.

Bavarian dunkel lager may be anything from amber to black, but it is always smooth and malty, with only hints of roastiness. Schwarzbier, a rarer style, is reliably dark in color and marked by a gliding smoothness, but the flavors range from cocoa and vanilla to licorice and coffee. In the Czech Republic, dark lagers wear the interchangeable name tmavé ("dark") or černé ("black"), and may come in any strength, though most are brewed around the strength of their German cousins. They differ, however, in the quality of the malt, which is fuller and tends more toward caramel. These beers come from meat-loving countries, and pair nicely with roasts—but they work equally well with American barbecue.

and direct as their names, and they remain workhorses in much of the lager-drinking world, as they have been for centuries. Indeed, when we gaze into a frothy mug of chestnut beer, it's as if we're looking back in time to the very first lagers. Made from rough, smoky malt and smoothed by a long nap in a cool cellar, the beers turned smooth and Bohemians and Bavarians drank them by the gallons.

Over time, the homey pleasures of a smooth dunkel gave way to the shimmering glitz of pilsner. But even as they were elbowed aside by the new, trendier golden beers, dark lagers got ever smoother. Brewed with new Munich malts that lacked smoke, they remained a humble pleasure, but a more refined one, eminently smooth and round. There is something in their story that reminds one of the fortunes of English mild ale, except that—happily—finding a half-liter of dunkel in Munich now is nowhere near as hard as finding a mild in London. And in the Czech Republic, there's enough enthusiasm for tmavés that they're still quite easy to locate. ■

ORIGINS

YOU APPROACH the brewery at Weihenstephan by passing through the charming town of Freising, which has the feel of the college town it has become. Monks once occupied the hill outside Freising, but now instead of quiet reflection, it buzzes with the activity of students zipping back and forth to classes. The monastic grounds were eventually converted into a university campus, which is draped like a cape across the shoulders of the hill. Monks first started making beer there in 1040, and the presence of a brewhouse has been the one constant through the centuries. To find it, keep climbing up. Its current location takes advantage of a feature common to early Bavarian lager breweries—hillsides, where it was convenient to bore deep caves and cellars to store cold-fermented beer. There was no refrigeration in the late Middle Ages and brewers learned that underground cellars kept beer at a consistently cool temperature. This was the secret to early lagers.

DUNKEL

The first lagers were brewed in either Bohemia or Bavaria, and at least by the end of the 1300s and the early 1400s, cities like Nuremburg and Munich had started to regulate them. The science of malting was primitive, and beers made from kilned malts were dark, smoky, and probably a bit harsh. They were definitionally "dunkel," but they weren't really like the modern-day versions. As brewers developed the techniques of making lager beer, they learned how to contain the sourness that spoiled top-fermented ales. Surely another benefit was how the harsh burnt compounds smoothed and mellowed as the lagers ripened in those caves.

Dunkel lagers enjoyed dominance in Bavaria and Franconia (a former duchy north of Bavaria) for centuries (they seemed to wane in Bohemia in favor of ales), until malting techniques changed in the 1800s. The pioneers of this new method were actually the British, who were obviously far from the lager lands in the south. They discovered how to lightly kiln malt so that it didn't scorch, but it took the son of a Munich brewer to bring the knowledge back to Bavaria. That brewer, Gabriel Sedlmayr II, took over the Spaten Brewery from his father and developed an amber malt that completely changed the character of dunkel from a roasted, smoky beer to a smooth, rich one. That was the birth of the modern incarnation of the dunkel lager, one that still relies heavily on Sedlmayr's Munich malt.

SCHWARZBIER

The similarities between dunkel lager and schwarzbier might suggest a common ancestor, but evidence points to parallel evolution rather than a forking line from a single ancestor. The center of dunkel production was Munich, but schwarzbiers had two hometowns farther north: the famous Franconian brewing city of Kulmbach and a tiny hamlet farther north in Thuringia known as Bad Köstritz. In Kulmbach, brewing dated back all the way to pre-Christian times, where archaeologists found residue from a black bread–based beer. This was about as close to contemporary schwarzbier as the Model A is to a hybrid, but it does show the long tradition of brewing in the town. The more modern history—one documented in the written as opposed to

London Calling? **Schwarzbiers have been brewed in Bad Köstritz for nearly 500 years, but they were perhaps not always the schwarzbiers we know today. In the mid-nineteenth century, when London's famous porters were reaching their peak as an international style, Germans developed their own version. They were akin to the porters shipped to the Baltics, strong and hearty, and sometimes even soured by *Brettanomyces*. They only registered a blip on the radar of German styles, but could their legacy reside in the roastiness of modern schwarzbiers? Braver souls than I have suggested so, but we lack proof to declare it with certainty.**

LEFT: *Once a monastery, Weihenstephan is now a college campus and brewery.*

archaeological record—dates to twelfth-century monastic brewing, and creates a link with the town's current standard of schwarzbier, the one brewed by Kulmbach, once a monastic cloister.

Similarly, monks founded a monastery at Bad Köstritz in 1543 and began brewing a dark beer there. The town, not far south of Leipzig, was in ale country—and indeed, the monks were then brewing top-fermented schwarzbier. The Köstritzer brewery didn't convert the beer to lager until 1878, nearly 100 years after it was secularized. In an interesting twist on the usual story, though, the aftermath of the Second World War may actually have helped preserve the style; Bad Köstritz, located in East Germany where innovations and trends were far slower to develop, continued to make the obscure roasty beer until reunification.

CZECH TMAVÉ AND ČERNÉ

As for Czech dark lagers, we know even less about them. Although Bohemia was a sister to Bavaria in early lager brewing, top-fermented beers were still the most common when Josef Groll brewed his famous pale lager in 1842. Northwestern Bohemia is snuggled into the crescent of dark-beer brewing from Bad Köstritz down to Munich, so surely they were brewing černés and tmavés, though perhaps not in huge numbers. Whatever the case, once word of Groll's lager spread, golden beers quickly supplanted them.

The usual story arc for ancient styles involves near-extinction at the hands of wars and pale lagers. That describes the general contours of the story of dunkel, but with a happy asterisk. Just before the Second World War, dunkel controlled nearly two-thirds of the Bavarian market. By the 1960s, that was down to a bare 10 percent. So, like every beer style, they were forced to take a supporting role after pale lagers took center stage. (In Bavaria, though, they were helles lagers, not pilsners.) Yet production percentages are a bit misleading; even today, they are a standard in pubs across Bavaria, and most breweries make a version. Schwarzbiers are far rarer in Germany, but apparently stable. As for the Czech Republic, black lagers are enjoying a renaissance there. Although still small by percentage, they are one of the fastest growing types of beer and easily found in most pubs and restaurants. ∎

DESCRIPTION AND CHARACTERISTICS

DARK LAGERS HAVE a fair amount in common, but a handy tool for distinguishing them is to look at the level of roastiness. Bavarian dunkels have none or very close to it. Schwarzbiers have a touch, but nothing dangerous. Czech dark lagers can have very little, but they may also have a lot. Some are roasty enough to pass for a dry Irish stout. Since there are two terms to describe them—*tmavé* ("dark") and *černé* ("black")—and these align identically with the German terms, it is easy enough to think of them as Czech versions of German dark lagers. Czechs don't actually follow that logic, though—darks may be heavily roasted, blacks less so or vice versa.

DUNKEL

How dark is "dunkel"? The answer, judging from the range offered in the hundreds of Bavarian house breweries, is variable. A brewery may make a beer just past amber—barely brown—and call it dunkel; conversely some may call their mahogany beer, purportedly lighter amber, a märzen. Red highlights are typical.

The flavors are more consistent, though. Dunkel lagers are a showcase for Munich malts, and they create rounded, sweet flavors. Brewers are able to draw out different flavors, from nut and bread crust to coffee and chocolate. There's an underlying sweetness to the malts, though, so whatever bitterness or

ABOVE: *Kreuzberg Kloster (Monastery) is one of a handful that still maintain a brewery. The house beer is a light, refreshing dunkel lager.*

roastiness that might normally be associated with these flavors is glazed in malt syrup. If they have much hop character, it's delicate and usually the pepper of German strains—but normally they don't have much. These are perfect pub beers and psychic brothers of the session milds of England.

SCHWARZBIER

Okay, then, how black is "schwarz"? More varied than the name suggests; they range from dark chestnut to ruby-black, never going, ironically, to complete jet black. Indeed, schwarzbiers have a vitreous clarity when held up to light—you can get lost in their deep hues if you're not careful. They are more complex than dunkel lagers, as well. Schwarzbiers balance sweetish cola-like malt notes with more bitter licorice and roast notes. These darker qualities are never strong; they're just hinted at, and schwarzbiers have a smooth, dry finish. It's a delightful balancing act, and when done properly is a marvel to experience.

CZECH TMAVÉ AND ČERNÉ

Czech dark lagers are still comparatively rare, but they're growing fast. They are not brewed particularly to imitate other styles, and vary from the very sweet to the almost acrid. The most common strength is the standard *ležák* range— around 4.5% to 5% ABV—and they tend to have roasty, coffee, and dark chocolate flavors. Unlike Czech pilsners, they're generally not heavily hopped, though some have a slight bitterness underneath the dark roast. James Emmerson, who brews a range of Czech-inspired lagers at Full Sail in Oregon, distinguishes them from their German counterparts this way: "Maybe it's a different brewing philosophy. The Czech beers in general have a really nice creaminess that is different than the kind of malt character that came from a Munich beer." Recently, though, some breweries have begun to make a more hoppy form as well—probably part of the craft beer trend that has influenced newer Czech breweries. There is also a more obscure dark lager called a porter, which by legal definition is a big beer—with an original gravity above 18° Plato or 1.074. These Czech porters are essentially Baltic porters. (For more on that style, see Porters and Stouts, starting on page 140). ∎

BREWING NOTES

THE DESIGN of a brewery is often a dead giveaway as to the nature of the beer made there. Cask fillers tell you you're on the island of Great Britain; a warm room filled with crated bottles means you're in Belgium. So where are you if you find a four-vessel brewhouse? In Lagerland: Germany and the Czech Republic. A standard ale kit includes a mash tun, lauter tun, and

Dark lagers run a continuum from malty to roasty. On the malt side are *amber lagers* and *bocks*. The roast heads into *porter* and *stout* territory. For those who like a little alcohol with their roast, *Baltic porters* are a great choice—they're sort of like imperial schwarzbiers.

brew kettle. Three vessels. In many lager brewhouses—and nearly all of the Czech breweries—there's one more: a device called a mash cooker used in decoction.

"In Germany, it could be rainy and cold for like **ten years.** Then you have barley with protein levels that are atrocious, with glucan [glucose polymers that can cause haze or clog filters] levels you can barely live with. So that's why the Germans invented those complicated mashing methods, because [that way] you can achieve consistency of beer by technology."

—JÜRGEN KNÖLLER,
BAYERN BREWING IN MISSOULA, MT

In most mashing systems, it's possible to raise the temperature of the mash using a course of steps to produce the right types of sugars and amino acids. Decoction is an older, pre-thermometer technique: Brewers remove a portion of the mash, bring it to a boil, and put it back in the mash tun. When the boiling portion is returned, it raises the temperature of the whole mash. Breweries may go through this process from one to three times. Back when malts contained fewer enzymes, brewers commonly conducted triple-decoction mashes. With modern, well-modified malts, too much boiling actually degrades the malted grain and produces worse beer. Most traditionalist German breweries now use double decoction, and that process is also standard in the Czech Republic.

For the breweries that use it, decoction has a nice effect on dunkels and Czech dark lagers. Few styles depend so overwhelmingly on one element as dunkel lagers do on malt, and this is exactly what

decoction accentuates. Take two examples that I think are especially good—Penn Dark from America and U Fleků *tmavý ležák* (dark lager) from Prague. Many visitors to Prague have sampled U Fleků's amazing dark lager (for decades, it was the city's signature brew), the only beer the brewery makes. As creamy as a mug of cocoa—and nearly as chocolatey—the malts seem to shift between a light char and a blackened sugar, caramel note. Penn's dunkel is more delicate, which has the effect of enhancing the malt roundness. Here those malts suggest cola and brown bread, with possibly a hint of molasses. Do these full, rich malty flavors come from decoction? Penn's Nick Rosich thinks so: "It gives you that extra flavor," he says. "Like the steak over the wood fire." (Speaking of fire, he adds another log in the debate by saying infusion mashing is "a shorter process; i.e., the microwave." Let the arguments rage!) Of course, there are really exceptional examples that aren't made with decoction.

RIGHT: *The four-vessel system at Weihenstephan*

The Great Decoction Debate.

In the distant past, decoction was a clever way to both maintain consistency in brewing methods and get added oomph from more rugged, unrefined barley. Now its benefits are more elusive. Proponents believe decoction imparts a richer, rounder texture with better head retention to beer, while critics say it's mainly a great way to waste time, energy, and money.

There are two relevant questions in the debate: Can a normal person detect a decoction-brewed beer? If so, is decoction worth the trouble? The answer to the first question is a qualified yes. Travel through Bavaria and try the traditional lagers made in village house breweries, and you will begin to notice how full and rounded all the beers are. Adam Brož, brewmaster at Budvar in the Czech Republic, says: "Decoction is very important. We compared decoction versus infusion on a small-scale brewery. The beer brewed by the infusion process was emptier in its taste—the body was not correct for the lagers. Also the color changed. If you boil during the decoction, you prepare the compounds which cause golden color. The infusion lagers were yellowish, and not so full in their taste."

Is it worth the trouble? Each brewery has its own answer. There are countervailing forces that buffet breweries: tradition on the one hand, efficiency and ecological friendliness on the other. For some, tradition demands that the old ways continue—the evidence of their superiority lies in decoction's subtle character. For others, because decoction adds hours to the brew day and euros to the energy bill, there's really no justification for such a large process that adds so little—and anyway, say these breweries, there are other ways to achieve that richness and color. As someone who has put a fair amount of study into the question, I will go this far: No matter where you land, the research is a lot of fun.

Ayinger Altbairisch [Old Bavarian] Dunkel is a model case—nutty, slightly roasty, with a note of black tea: excellent but different.

In the Czech Republic, decoction provides an additional advantage. Although many Czech breweries still rely on traditional floor-malted barley for their base malts, they stick to decoction as much out of tradition as anything. If there's a difference, it probably has more to do with barley variety than malting method. The process is both less efficient and less precise than modern malting methods, and the malt is not as well modified as similar malts made in modern facilities. Full Sail's Emmerson, who labored to give Session Black the creaminess of Czech lagers, fingers malt as the key: "Certainly when you're using the kind of malt they're using, it lends itself more to decoction than the kind of malt we're using. The degree of modification here does a lot of the work for you, but it takes away some of the opportunities as well. The challenge for us is to use American malts and specialty malts to try to re-create those flavors." Decoction brewing is so central to the Czech brewing tradition that the Ministry of Agriculture only allows beer made that way to be called Česke pivo (Czech beer).

Beyond the question of mashing, dark lagers are simple affairs. Dunkel relies on Munich malt—the source of the red tinge—but may use pilsner malt and a tiny portion of dark malt for color. Schwarzbiers take a higher proportion of dark malts, including roasted malts. Czech dark lagers follow this prescription as well. Czechs may also use caramel malt. The beers are typically hopped lightly, making hop flavor and bitterness faint to absent, depending on the beer. ■

EVOLUTION

THE DIFFERENCES in flavor among schwarzbiers, Bavarian dunkel lagers, and Czech dark lagers are small enough that even distinguishing them is sometimes a challenge. A few handfuls of hops and some roasted malt one way or the other and a dark becomes a black. Interestingly, their currency outside Germany and the Czech Republic is quite a bit different. Schwarzbiers seem to travel well. A number are made in Japan, Xingu sells well in Brazil, and in the U.S., Sprecher, Dixie, and Saranac have found success with this style. Foreign versions are faithful to the originals, however—you'll see no wild hopping or alcoholic gigantism in the New World schwarzbiers.

Bavarian dunkel lagers, not so much. There is something about their very soft palates that doesn't translate well. A few breweries do make them—notably Penn and Harpoon—but they are far more common inside Bavaria than out.

The final member of the triumvirate is the most interesting. Even within the Czech Republic, styles are evolving—a craft beer movement has brought ales and dark lagers back in recent years. You can even find IPAs now around the

ABOVE: *The Augustiner Brewery should be the first stop for any dunkel lovers traveling to Munich—and helles lovers, too.*

country, especially in Prague. Dark lagers are almost wholly unknown outside the Czech Republic, but this too may change. In addition to Full Sail, Virginia's Devils Backbone has begun to champion them and of all the dark lagers the brewery makes, Morana Tmavé is the most popular. Keep your eyes peeled for more. ■

THE BEERS TO KNOW

DARK LAGERS ARE sometimes given less attention by brewers than they deserve. They are simple beers, unspectacular and unassuming. But that doesn't mean they need to be ordinary. A good dunkel will have depth of flavor and a richness to complement its easy comfort. Good schwarzbiers balance roast, sweetness, and crispness on a razor's edge, never letting one destabilize the others. And Czech darks, if you should ever find one, are a bit more wintry and hearty.

AUGUSTINER DUNKEL

LOCATION: Munich, Germany

MALT: Undisclosed

HOPS: Undisclosed

5.6% ABV

Augustiner makes one of the world's best dunkels, a beer that alternates between being rich and burnished, and crisp and light-bodied. It falls somewhere between brown and amber, but has a creamy latte head and a yeasty-fresh aroma. There's a bit of tang in the finish.

CAPITAL DARK

LOCATION: Madison, WI

MALT: Munich, black, caramel

HOPS: Mt. Hood

5.4% ABV, 1.055 SP. GR., 28 IBU

Capital's version of a dunkel lager features toasty malts. It has a bit of roast—perhaps more than a Bavarian would enjoy—but the body is rounded and soft. The beer has a satisfyingly dry finish that leaves the remnants of oven-warm bread on the tongue.

MOTHER EARTH DARK CLOUD

LOCATION: Kinston, NC

MALT: Undisclosed

HOPS: Undisclosed

5.1% ABV

A meatier interpretation than most, this dark amber has an ale-like fruitiness to its rounded, nutty palate. It's the roasted malts, more than the hops, that keep the beer in balance. They add some chocolate and toast, and make Dark Cloud a more-ish pour. A dry palate and minerality add depth.

KÖSTRITZER SCHWARZBIER

ooooooooooooooooooooooooooooooooooooooooooooo

LOCATION: Bad Köstritz, Germany

MALT: Undisclosed

HOPS: Undisclosed

4.8% ABV, 1.046 SP. GR., 26 IBU

One of the world's truly spectacular beers, Köstritzer manages to be at once assertively roasty while still maintaining a delicate caramel sweetness. The color of cola, it has a top layer of coffee-like roasting quite similar to an Irish stout; the palate is remarkably complex, however, and licorice, chocolate, and port all add distinctive notes. Perhaps most impressively, the beer finishes dryly, leaving no lingering flavors; the finish is so complete you almost immediately raise the glass for another taste.

MÖNCHSHOF SCHWARZBIER

ooooooooooooooooooooooooooooooooooooooooooooo

LOCATION: Kulmbach, Germany

MALT: Undisclosed

HOPS: Undisclosed

4.9% ABV, 1.050 SP. GR.

In a contrast to Köstritzer, Mönchshof's schwarz is softer and only hints at roastiness. The dark malts come across more as chocolate and caramel. It has wonderful balance and more character than some dunkels, though, and is a standard of the style.

FULL SAIL SESSION BLACK

ooooooooooooooooooooooooooooooooooooooooooooo

LOCATION: Hood River, OR

MALT: Undisclosed

HOPS: Undisclosed

5.4% ABV, 18 IBU

Full Sail followed up the success of their all-malt Session light lager with a dark version ("the yin to Session's yang," brewmaster James Emmerson calls it). Based on a tmavé, it is light but smooth, with just the slightest suggestion of roastiness. Although a bit strong at 5.4%, it does drink like a session beer.

XINGU BLACK BEER

LOCATION: Santa Maria, Brazil

MALT: Undisclosed

HOPS: Undisclosed

OTHER: Brewing sugar

4.6% ABV, 1.048 SP. GR., 20 IBU

Brazil's Xingu is not brewed precisely to a style (the sugar isn't textbook German), but schwarzbier isn't too far in the distance. It has a wonderful combination of caramel and roast that gives the beer depth and complexity, though it's a light enough beer to drink in a rain forest. The effect is actually quite a bit like a petit Baltic porter—lots of flavor, but only half the alcohol.

DEVILS BACKBONE MORANA TMAVÉ

LOCATION: Roseland, VA

MALT: Bohemian floor malt, Munich, Cara-Bohemian, Carafa Special

HOPS: Saaz

5.8% ABV, 1.056 SP. GR., 22 IBU

Devils Backbone makes the best New World effort to make an Old World beer. Using a double-decoction mash and traditional ingredients, they've crafted a strong beer with soft, bready malts and nothing in the way of roast. The substantial alcohol content is hidden dangerously in the gentle folds of malt.

Czech Lagers

THE WORLD OF CZECH LAGERS IS MOSTLY HIDDEN TO THOSE OUTSIDE EUROPE. WE KNOW OF "BOHEMIAN PILSNERS" AND ASSUME THAT'S ALL THERE IS TO THE COUNTRY THAT INVENTED THE WORLD'S MOST FAMOUS STYLE. BUT THE CZECH REPUBLIC HAS A LAGER TRADITION NEARLY AS RICH AS GERMANY'S AND IF YOU HAVE THE GOOD FORTUNE TO VISIT, YOU WILL FIND MORE THAN GOLDEN LAGERS THERE. THE THING WE KNOW AS PILSNER IS CALLED "LIGHT LAGER" (SVĚTLY LEŽÁK) IN THE CZECH REPUBLIC—"PILSNER" IS RESERVED FOR THE BEER MADE AT THE URQUELL BREWERY. BUT YOU'LL ALSO FIND THINGS CALLED TMAVÉ, ČERNÉ, AND POLOTMAVÉ IN HUES RANGING FROM LIGHT AMBER TO BLACK.

The Czech system for producing beer runs along two axes: strength and color. On the one side you have beers of different strength categories based on the Plato scale. These are actually legal regulations, and they changed slightly in 2011. They are:

■ **Stolní pivo**, table beer up to 6° Plato. The pronunciation is roughly **Stole-nyee Pee-voh.**

■ **Výčepní pivo**, from 7° to 10° Plato. Strangely, *výčepní* comes from the word for taproom, and the term literally means "draft beer." It is applied to all beer in this range, irrespective of package. Pronounced **Vee-chep-nyee Pee-voh.**

■ **Ležák**, from 11° to 12° Plato. Again, to add to the confusion, *ležák* literally means "lager"—and again, it applies to all beer in this range whether lager or ale. Pronounced **Leh-zhak.**

■ **Speciál**, strong beers above 13° Plato. Pronounced **Spet-zee-al.**

Colors are slightly more straightforward, although if they're arranged out of order, it becomes even clearer.

■ **Světlé**, or pale-colored. Pronounced **Svet-leh.**

■ **Tmavé**, or dark. Pronounced **T'ma-veh.**

■ **Polotmavé**, which literally means "semidark" or "half-dark," refers to a color in the amber band. Pronounced **Poh-loh-t'ma-veh.**

■ **Černé**, or black. Pronounced **Cher-neh.**

If you imagine a grid, with strength running across the top and color running down the side, you'll have a clear sense of how this works. It won't always track exactly; strong beers may not be described by color, and černé and tmavé don't have precise ranges (sometimes černé will look lighter than tmavés and vice versa).

But that's just the overview. When you get into a pub, you'll find even more terms. In *Good Beer Guide Prague*, Evan Rail warns ominously: "The most difficult thing to get your head around is that there might be two words for the same beer, or two very different beers with the same name, and the terms can stack up like VWs in an ice storm: Primator's hefeweizen can also be called "upper-fermented, light, wheat yeast beer." Actually, it's probably not that hard. Armed with these designations, you need know only a few other key words:

■ *Kvasnicové pivo.* Literally "yeast beer." It is a specific preparation that involves adding yeast or fermenting wort to fully lagered beer—called *kräusening* in Germany—right before kegging. It brings a liveliness to the beer that has Czech beer geeks in a swoon. Pronounced *Kvass-nit-so-veh Pee-voh.*

■ *Nefiltrované pivo.* Unfiltered beer. Slightly confusing because both *kvasnicové* and *nefiltrované* will appear less than perfectly clear, and both may enjoy the benefits of richer, brighter flavors. Unfiltered beer does not have fresh yeast added. Pronounced *Neh-fil-tro-va-nay Pee-voh.*

■ *Pšeničné pivo.* Wheat beer. Weizen-style beers are becoming popular, and you'll see these words with fair regularity in the pubs. Pronounced *P'shay-neech-na Pee-voh.*

■ *Tanková.* Tank beer. This is a relatively new way of serving a brewery's regular product. The beer is pumped into large tanks at a pub. The beer is unpasteurized and carbonates naturally in the tank, resulting in sharper, more vivid flavors. Pronounced *Tank-oh-vah.*

Czechs have also come to the craft brewing party, so in addition to lagers, you may find ales, including IPAs (often called "eepah" by locals)—though probably mainly in Prague. And if you go to Prague, skip the eepahs—it's those amazing *kvasnicové* lagers you'll want to try. Outside the Czech Republic, there's nothing like them.

Pale Lagers
PILSNER, HELLES, AND DORTMUND EXPORT

T he enigmatic pale lager—at once the most prized and revered of beers and the most reviled. The first one was brewed in 1842 by a Bavarian brewer who had been recruited to come to Bohemia and make newfangled lagers for the people of Pilsen. His creation was a revelation for its time—sparkling, clarion gold, and elegant. It had flavors of bready malt and peppery hops but none of the sour staleness of local ales. It was the

Pilsner, Helles, and Dortmund Export.

Pilsners are sometimes divided between the Czech originals and those later made in Germany. The difference is mainly in the approach to hopping. Czech versions tend to be a bit deeper in color and more vivid with tangy Bohemian hops, while German pilsners are malt forward and have more peppery hopping. In both cases, the beers balance gentle grain-y malt bodies with enlivening—but never overwhelming—hop spice. They are crisp, effervescent, and refreshing. Helles lagers have much in common but emphasize soft maltiness even more. Their hopping, though subdued, takes its delicacy from German aroma hops. Dortmund exports were once burly,

brassy beers full enough of alcohol, malt, and to satisfy the considerable thirst of coal and ste workers. But they have since become a lighter, assertive beer—one now in search of an identity While the classic pale lagers all have their streng pilsner is the most versatile with food, easily cutt fried foods and spice but also framing the sweetr of pork (especially those Bavarian sausages!).

STATISTICS

Pilsner ABV range: 4.4–5.5%; bitterness: 20–45 IBU	
Helles ABV range: 4.5–5.5%; bitterness: 15–25 IBU	
Dortmund export ABV range: 5.0–6.0%; bitterness: 25–35 IBU	
Serving temperature: 38°–45°F	
Vessel: Pilsner glass (pilsner, export); stein (helles)	

most important beer ever brewed, and it changed the course of brewing history.

Descendants of the original pale lagers—sometimes called pilsner or, in the Czech Republic, *svetlý ležák*—are the ones that still captivate drinkers. Brewers have always admired them because they are the hardest beers to make and the most satisfying when made successfully. For centuries, drinkers have marveled at their balance of flavors, their visual spectacle, their ability to quench. The first pilsners and their earliest imitators—helles lagers from Bavaria, "export" lagers from Dortmund—are the reason pale lagers would one day speed around the globe, gobbling up other beer styles as they spread. They are not easy to make, are regularly sapped of

ABOVE: *The iconic Jubilee Gate outside Pilsner Urquell, erected fifty years after the brewery's founding*

their character, and can be insipid or even unpleasant. (Those are the reviled ones.) But in the right hands, a pilsner or helles becomes the pinnacle of the art—a delicate powerhouse, a beer capable of conquering the world. ■

ORIGINS

THE LEGENDARY ODYSSEY of the great pilsner style began much more modestly, as a minor municipal dispute. Bohemia may well have been the birthplace of lagers, but by the nineteenth century, ale brewing—and especially wheat ale brewing—was by far the most common. In the small western Bohemian town of Pilsen, all the local beer was ale. It wasn't particularly good ale, either. Local publicans were therefore importing better and cheaper lager from nearby. Its popularity with their customers made things even worse for the hometown brewers, since their ales sat

around too long and spoiled. The situation came to a head in 1838, when local authorities dumped 36 barrels of spoiled beer in the town square.

Local burghers—citizens with special rights to brew beer—decided to take action. They wanted a market for new, bottom-fermenting "Bavarian" beer for themselves. So, like something out of an episode of *Parks and Recreation*, the burghers rallied the town and won the mayor over to their idea. They called on a prominent local architect, Martin Stelzer, who went off to study in Munich and elsewhere in Bavaria before drawing up

ABOVE: *The burghers' brewery today is a wonderful facility, both beautiful and technologically advanced.*

plans for the new brewery. It was a state-of-the-art facility, including a malt house and a kiln "equipped in the English manner." This last part was critical, because the kiln allowed the burghers' brewery to produce light-colored malt like the kind that was being used in Britain at the time to make its famous pale ale.

The last piece of the puzzle was the brewer, Josef Groll, whom Stelzer found in Bavaria. The man they hired was apparently arrogant and rude, and he only lasted three years at the burghers' brewery. (His own father called him "the rudest man in Bavaria.") But he managed, in that time, to do what no other lager brewer had: create a sparkling lager the color of English pale ales. He brewed his "pilsner" on October 5, 1842, and it debuted at St. Martin's fair on November 11. Groll was out by 1845.

His beer, by contrast, was decidedly in. Pilsner Urquell—as the brewery came to be known—sold about 3,000 barrels its first year, and instantly began following the kind of growth curve we see in craft breweries today. Production was up to nearly 5,000 barrels three years later, and by 1847 the burghers' brewery was beginning its first major expansion. Pilsner's success was abetted by a coincidental innovation in machined glassware that made clear vessels commonplace—they were perfect for viewing the new clarion beer. In 1873, the brewery went through an enormous expansion that replaced the original buildings and sprawled across (and under, since the brewery kept tunneling out more cellar space) an astounding eighty-nine acres.

Although it was a successful local beer, pilsner was a slow juggernaut. At the time of its birth, ale breweries were still overwhelmingly dominant in Bohemia—according to one source, they outnumbered lager breweries ten to one. It took a bit more than twenty years for lagers to catch up. There were still 281 ale breweries left in 1865—remarkable for a region as small as Bohemia—but that number soon plunged, dropping to 137 five years later and to just two (!) by 1876.

The success of pale lager spread, first to the south, where it was sold in Vienna in the 1850s. The Pilsen burghers sensed that they were onto something and in 1859 tried to register a trademark on the name (unsuccessfully). Pilsners jumped the Bavarian border in the 1890s when Munich breweries started dabbling in pale lagers. There were a few precursors, but by tradition the first true Bavarian pale is credited to the Spaten Brewery for the beer they first crafted in 1894.

Smuggler Monks and Other Myths.

The decades have wreathed pilsner, like any great beer style, in an assortment of myths and legends. Some are true, but two of the most common are decidedly not. The first one claims that the yeast used at the burghers' brewery was hustled out of Bavaria on the down-low. One version has Groll conducting the espionage, and in another, it was a rogue monk. The idea of monkly misconduct is so alluring that I'd love to leave it in the record, but alas, neither tale is true. Lager brewing was already well underway in Bohemia, and so lager yeast was not a Bavarian state secret. The boring truth is that the brewery just bought the yeast.

The second often-repeated myth involves the pale malt used to make the famous golden lager. In older tellings, the malt was delivered to Groll mistakenly. This is clearly false; the burghers built their brewery with its own malthouse, so no one delivered it at all. Evan Rail, who has written extensively about the beers of the Czech Republic, adds an important note: "In Czech, the main word for 'brewer' is *sládek*, meaning 'the man who prepares the malt,' or 'maltster,' as for centuries here, the task of many brewers—like Mr. Groll—was, in large part, to make malt." So we know that Groll used the brewery's own barley, and malted it to his own specifications.

Spaten didn't call it pilsner, but "helles." The word not only meant *light* or *pale*, but also *bright*—which this translucent golden beer certainly must have seemed to Bavarian eyes used to dunkel (dark) lagers. Thomasbräu, a Munich competitor, followed quickly with their own version the next year—though it was labeled a pilsner.

As a testament to how seriously local brewers took their native dunkel lagers, these new pale beers created a scandal. Outraged Munich breweries called a meeting to protest this abomination and even threatened to form a dunkel coalition committed to blackballing helles. There was a temporary schism as some Munich breweries boycotted the new style, but eventually the helles won out. There is no mistaking helles for pilsners, though. Bavarians were used to drinking soft, rounded dark lagers, and in the transition to light lagers some of those same characteristics were carried over. Helles was, and remains, sweeter and less hoppy than Bohemia's pilsners.

The last decades of the nineteenth century concluded a 200-year burst of technical innovation with two events that changed the fortunes of lagers forever. The first was Louis Pasteur's treatise on yeast, which not only revealed the biochemistry of fermentation but also explained why bottom-fermenting and lagering reduced spoilage. The second event was the introduction of refrigeration, which made it possible for breweries to make lager year-round in any climate. What was once only possible in the colder areas around Bavaria and Bohemia could now be practiced anywhere.

So lagers spread, and the lagers people wanted to drink were those glorious pales from Bohemia. From Bavaria,

pale lagers spread north, notably to Dortmund, forty-five miles northeast of Düsseldorf. The town had blossomed in the nineteenth century as the industrial revolution brought it the coal and steel industries. By midcentury, it was beginning to take up lager brewing. Dortmunder Union brewed the first pale lager in 1887. The brewery made their beer at two strengths, and the stronger version, called "export" was a hit. By that time, Dortmund had swelled with hardworking, beer-drinking men, and the breweries grew to industrial sizes, too. Export was a sturdy beer that ranged from 5.5% alcohol on up. It had some of the malt sweetness of helles, but added the hopping of pilsner and the whiff of

sulfur that came from the local water. It was a robust beer for thirsty workers.

In Germany, pale lagers took the form of these indigenous twists on pilsner. Even ale-producing Cologne started brewing beers that were golden and snappy—slightly fruity from ale yeast, but smooth and clean from cold-aging. For the first half of the twentieth century, local beers won out—especially export lagers. Dortmund's business in export would eventually come to dominate German brewing, capturing two-thirds of the market after World War II and commanding more than half of all sales through the 1960s. Bavarians continued to drink their helles lagers— they still have 25 percent of the Bavarian market, roughly equal to pilsner—and pilsner was slow to ascend.

Elsewhere it had a more direct route, but not an immediate one. Scandinavia began to adopt lagers, and Denmark, home to Tuborg and Carlsberg, became a majority pale lager country by 1907. In the United States, German

ABOVE: *Lager has always been aged in larger vessels; before steel, they were made of wood.*

RIGHT: *The original Únětický Brewery dates to the early eighteenth century but was one of the casualties of World War II. In 2011, enterprising entrepreneurs brought it back, making two exceptional* světlý pivos, *a* výčepní, *and a* ležák.

German versus Czech. We sometimes forget how much the world has changed. In 1842, there was no Czech Republic—or Germany, for that matter. The map of the region was dominated by two powers, the Austrian empire to the south and Prussia in the north. Bohemia, which was at various times the center of power during the Holy Roman Empire, had for centuries seen its language and culture erode as German became the language of dominance under the Habsburgs. This eventually led to a revival known as the Czech National Movement—an attempt to reclaim their language. Language and nationality are not identical, and there were also a substantial number of Germans living in Bohemia by the time of the Czech National Movement, an era coinciding with the rise of pale lagers. And interestingly, two of the towns most associated with that beer, Plzeň and České Budějovice, both had large German populations, and alternate, German names—Pilsen and Budweis.

This history became the focal point of Czech–German conflict in the early part of the twentieth century and was later a central issue in both world wars. In a span of less than three decades, Bohemia and Moravia were variously engulfed by the Austrian empire, the Germans under Hitler, and the Soviet Union—and for a time were also independent. The effect on the relations between German speakers (a quarter of the population after World War I) and Czechs was poisonous, and after the Second World War, 2.6 million German speakers were expelled to Austria and Germany. The legacy of this troubled history lives on awkwardly in the names of the most famous beers, Pilsner Urquell (a German rendering of the translation of "original pilsner," known as Plzeňský Prazdroj in Czech) and Budweiser Budvar (Budějovický Budvar). Or maybe it's not awkward. The names, though they may confuse distant fans, do serve as a living testament to the country's long history.

immigrants initially brought their experience in brewing dark lagers, but by the 1870s they were hoping to try the new light-colored lager. Brewers working with coarse six-row barley had to figure out a way to lighten it and get the chunky proteins to drop out of suspension, a trick they eventually accomplished with the addition of rice and corn.

Aided by industrialization, the spread of pale lagers really accelerated in the twentieth century. Not only did large-scale brewing drop the price of beer, it improved quality, and small local breweries began to fail at alarming rates. Ale-producing countries (including Germany) saw massive extinction of traditional styles—and wars, various efforts at prohibition, and globalization all played a role. Refrigeration and industrial production made it possible to set up breweries in formerly beer-free countries, and in the space of a few decades in the first half of the twentieth century, beer became an international product. The beers new breweries wanted to make were the popular pale lagers, which eventually covered the globe. Now whether you walk into a pub in São Paulo, Sydney, Schenectady, or Stockholm, you'll find a frosty glass of golden lager. We take this for granted today, but in the ninety-odd centuries before, no one beer style held more than a marginal proportion of international production. Do you think Josef Groll could have imagined this when he decided to use pale malt in his first batch of pilsner back in 1842? ■

DESCRIPTION AND CHARACTERISTICS

CONCEPTUALLY speaking, people agree on the definitions attached to the categories of pale lager: Czech pilsner, German pilsner, helles, and Dortmund export. Czech pilsners are hoppier than German, and both are hoppier than helles. Dortmund exports are like slightly hoppier, bigger helleses. In the wild, however, these beasts are not always so easy to distinguish. The lines overlap and brewers incorrigibly refuse to hew to expectations. So on the one hand you can say that Czech lagers are generally hoppier than their German counterparts, but you have to allow for Budvar (sold in the U.S. as Czechvar), one of the two standards of the style, which has a mere 22 bitterness units—below the level of many German pilsners and on par with a number of helles lagers. In other words, the distinctions aren't ironclad.

So we'll run through the major identifiers of each type of pale lager, recognizing that it's a continuum and any given beer may be called one thing but seem more like another.

PILSNER

How many different types of pilsner are there? One, two, four? Any answer is defensible, depending on how close to the ground you're prepared to go. Two is usual. No matter what number you land on, you have to start in the Czech Republic. The *světlý ležáks* there are golden colored, somewhat full bodied, and scented and flavored with Saaz (or Žatec in Czech) hops. Each one is particular to Bohemia. The color and body come from both the rustic floor-malted barley typical in Czech brewing and the use of decoction to convert those less-modified malts. The deeper color comes from boiling the mash, slightly caramelizing the malt, and the fullness from those malts. The buttery flavor of diacetyl isn't uncommon in Czech pilsners—Pilsner Urquell is a famous case—and this increases the fuller mouthfeel. Saaz hops are also unmistakable; they are usually described as spicy, but to my palate they have a unique tanginess, with equal parts cedar and lavender. Czechs often use more hops to balance the sweeter, fuller palates, so everything is a bit bigger and richer in their versions. Czech pilsners, especially those made by smaller, less-automated breweries, have an echo of British cask ales—somewhat more organic and mutable, unrefined, but full of life and wholesomeness. They are like living things.

Beer taxonomies usually include at least one other pilsner category—those

Only One Pilsner. In the Czech Republic, no one refers to the "pilsner" style. There they call it *světlý ležák*—light lager. When you say pilsner, you are referring to a single beer—the one brewed at Pilsner Urquell. When I visited Budvar, the brewmaster Adam Brož put it this way: "Always there is a discussion of the definition of pilsner lager. It's really difficult to compete with Pilsner [Urquell] because it became the style of the pilsner type. We are a bit different in this category because bitterness is really fine, the alcohol is a bit higher than the Pilsner has." He paused before adding: "The Budvar beer is really different." It's a strange irony, but it's true: The Czech Republic, birthplace of pilsner, is the one country where you won't find a style that's actually called "pilsner."

from Germany. To the untrained eye, pilsners from both sides of the border share the same broad outlines. Look closer, though, and the differences appear. Germans have access to very fine, well-modified malts, their water is harder, and their hops more delicate and spicy. Their pilsners are therefore thinner, lighter in color, more refined— "clean"—and spiced by the hops of Hallertau and Hersbruck. None of these characteristics shouts at you on its own, but taken together, they amount to a different take on the style, a very German take: pilsners that are always polished, balanced, and consistent, but that may in some cases seem a bit tame or even fussy. Hard water can put an edge on the hops in German pilsners and, because the malts are kilned at low temperatures, you may encounter a touch of cabbage from dimethyl sulfide.

Now, if you're feeling very, very particular, you can actually break the German branch into three parts: the Austrian and southern German type, the central German type, and the northern German type. They break down along a balance point between malt and hops—with malt predominating in the south, hops in the north, and the two Goldilocks-ing in the central region. This is maybe a bit much for the nonnative to absorb, but among Germans, where pilsners are the dominant style and are taken very seriously, the differences are large enough to map out. ■

HELLES LAGER

Outside Bavaria, the king of pale lagers is undisputedly pilsner, which dominates the national market. Inside Bavaria, however, pilsners share top billing with another blond—Germany's original pale lager, the helles. If there's a reason helles continues to sell so well in Bavaria, it's because unlike pilsners, which come tastily packaged in bottle or keg, helles is a beer for drinking on tap. Walk into one of the cavernous bierhalls of Munich and you will find mugs of shimmering helles, served by the liter (or, for the modest, half-liter). It is, for Bavarians, the equivalent of cask bitter—the session tipple that will keep mouths wet and happy for hours on end. A person of dull senses might call helles merely a less-hoppy pilsner. A poet, on the other hand, would notice the depth of the malt, pillowy soft and scone-sweet, and the way the sprinkle of hops brightens the beer with herbal zest.

Munich's Famous, Infamous Hofbräuhaus.

One of the most recognizable pubs in the world is in the center of Munich, and it has been a destination for every tourist in the city for centuries. Wilhelm V, Duke of Bavaria, directed construction of the Hofbräuhaus in 1589, but the pub everyone knows today was actually the site of the second brewery, built to make wheat beer in 1607. It was expanded into a sprawling tavern in 1828 under the direction of King Ludwig I, and thereafter was the watering hole for a number of famous figures: Vladimir Lenin, Mozart, Empress Elisabeth of Austria, Josephine Baker, and Louis Armstrong.

But by far the most famous patron—one mentioned nowhere in the official material of the Hofbräuhaus, not surprisingly—was Adolf Hitler. In the chaotic months following the end of the First World War, political groups were meeting regularly in Munich beer halls to debate politics. Hitler, head of publicity for the German Workers' Party, organized an event at the Hofbräuhaus in February 1920 that was attended by nearly two thousand people. Although he wasn't the keynote speaker, Hitler was the one to outline a twenty-five-point program establishing the newly renamed National Socialist German Workers (Nazi) Party. Hitler would go on to speak regularly at the Hofbräuhaus through 1944 when he made his last speech there. His comrades, celebrating the twenty-fifth anniversary of the event the following year, had to do so without Hitler, who could no longer travel safely to Munich. He sent a telegram instead.

DORTMUND EXPORT

The sad tale of Dortmund's famous style is one of diminishment. First as a matter of market share, then later in terms of heft and distinctiveness. It was not so many decades ago that you could say this about export lagers: They were stronger and drier than helles, more full-bodied than a pilsner, with hopping levels somewhere in between the two. In Germany, though, the style has shrunk and flattened. The export breweries that once lined Dortmund's streets consolidated, leaving only one, DAB, and its beer is no stronger nor more hoppy than a helles (4.8% ABV, 22 IBU). It is still a firm lager, hardened by calcium-rich local water, but not a beer of enormous character. Other breweries have taken turns brewing exports, notably Great Lakes with their flagship Dortmunder Gold, but it seems that unless the city of Dortmund works to reclaim its eponymous beer, the style's future is uncertain. ■

> "If you can make a good pilsner, you can make any beer. It is *hard* to make good pilsner. That's the German philosophy: If you can make this beer—in which you can't hide anything— if you can make that beer with all the technological tools we give you in your tool kit, you can make anything. You can make a hefeweizen; it's slightly different, but it's the same principles. You use different ingredients, you use a different mill setting for the wheat, you use different mash schedules, you use different yeasts, you use an open fermenter, but you know all about that because you learned how to make a pilsner beer."
>
> **—ALAN TAYLOR, ZOIGLHAUS BREWING**

BREWING NOTES

BREWERS LOVE the challenge of brewing a good pilsner. Why? When asked, they always give a nearly identical answer: Because there's nothing to hide in a pilsner. Pilsners—and the same can be said of helles lagers and Dortmund exports—are shockingly basic beers: one kind of malt, one kind of hops, balanced on the slender, lithe chassis of an 11° to 12° Plato beer. Any off flavors (diacetyl

Pale lagers form a family of beers, and they each recommend one another. Similar but slightly less pale lagers include *Oktoberfest/märzen* and *Vienna lagers* as well as more rustic versions like *kellerbier* and *ungespundet*. If hops don't thrill you, *cream ales* might, but if you want a bit of bitterness, *kölsch* and *steam beer* might be better choices.

and DMS—dimethyl sulfide—are so common in pilsners they're acceptable in small amounts) have no fig leaves to stand strategically behind. But even more than that, any flavors that are there have been placed by the brewer, as carefully as the flowers in a formal Japanese arrangement. The challenge in brewing a pilsner is placing the flavors where you want them with the knowledge that mistakes won't go unnoticed.

There are two important moments in brewing a pilsner, the mash and the first addition of hops—they help distinguish German and Czech brewing. In German systems, brewers now mostly use a simplified step-infusion mash rather than the more time-consuming decoction procedure. It may begin with a protein rest at around 119° to 122°F if the malt is poorly modified, but it more commonly begins with a twenty- to thirty-five-minute step beginning at 144°F for saccharification, then to 154°F and 162°F, and finally finishing at 172°F. The whole mash will take around an hour and a half. These numbers aren't critically important to the layperson, but because pilsner is the keystone beer in the brewer's manual—all others use pilsner as a reference point—it's worth noting them.

Of course, this is not how the Czechs do it. Decoction is still king there, typically with two periods of removing and boiling the mash—though Pilsner Urquell and others use the traditional, very laborious triple-decoction system. Czech brewers hew to tradition more stubbornly than brewers in many countries, but there's another reason they prefer decoction. Pilsners are made entirely from pale malt (though brewers may add a tiny bit of Munich for color), and in the Czech Republic, that means malt undermodified by modern standards. During decoction, Czech brewers begin with a protein rest stage to finish converting proteins to starches. The effect of both the Czech malt and decoction process is not subtle and makes these full-bodied pilsners distinctive.

In the Czech Republic, the pale lager is the bedrock style, the beer all breweries make. But that doesn't mean they're all made the same way. To use an analogy craft beer fans will immediately understand, think of American IPAs. From a distance, they may appear similar. But each brewery uses different methods to distinguish their IPA from others. It's the same in the Czech Republic. While decoction is nearly mandatory, breweries (often secretly) employ different techniques to imprint their own stamp on the beer. Únětický Pivovar intentionally lagers for less time than other breweries in order to create a more rustic quality—hops a bit more unruly, malts a bit more raw and doughy.

The most interesting example may be Kout na Šumavě, a brewery in the far southeast, near the German border. It's a relatively new concern, but one that has reinhabited an eighteenth-century building—so tumble-down it now resembles a ruin—that formerly housed a brewery. Brewer Bohuslav Hlavsa does three very interesting things when he makes his *světlý ležák*. After putting it through a traditional triple-decoction mash, it heads for a two-hour boil, the longest I encountered. Then he makes three hop additions, with equal amounts of Saaz hops going in at the start of the boil, forty-five minutes later, and again forty-five minutes after that. The last addition goes in with thirty minutes left in the boil. As you might expect, there is not a lot of hop aroma in Kout's beer, but a very stiff hop bitterness from the long boil.

But the most remarkable thing is

Bohemian Floor Malting.

If you want to understand why Czech *světlé* lagers taste different from those elsewhere, go to a place like Pivovar Ferdinand in Benešov, just south of Prague. The brewery was established in 1897 and included on-site maltings dating to 1872—typical for nineteenth-century breweries across the world, but far less so among those in the twenty-first century. Indeed, floor maltings in general are common only in two countries, and the only breweries to make lagers from this kind of malt are those in the Czech Republic. This old system cannot produce malt to perfectly uniform standards; floor malts therefore produce more characterful beers.

The process begins in a vented loft on the top floor of the building, where piles of raw spring barley remain cool and dry. Each pile comes from a different farmer. They will be malted separately and blended to maximize the best qualities of each. When it's time to malt the barley, a machine weighs out 50-kilogram measures (about 110 pounds) from one of the assorted piles and sends them to a large vessel two floors below to soak in a bath of cold water. After one measure is fully soaked, another goes in, and so on until the vessel is full. They will spend the next three days cycling between soaking and drying in the steeping vessel. The idea is to let the grain absorb an adequate amount of water. It needs "air pauses," says *sladmistr* (malt master) David Mareš, "to let it breathe."

Once the barley has drawn in enough water, it is deposited through the bottom of the vessel to the malting floor below. There the maltsters will spread the wet grain out to a depth of between six and twelve inches and let it germinate for four days. During the germination period, the grain is beginning the process of reproduction; cell walls and protein convert into starch and enzymes begin forming. The conversion requires a temperature of not more than 54°F, meaning traditional facilities like Ferdinand's can only malt during the winter. In its one gesture to modernity, though, Ferdinand now has a temperature gauge that automatically turns electric fans on and off. The germinating grain generates heat, and at intervals of roughly twelve hours, the brewery uses a funny little machine the size of a Zamboni to turn over the grain and release the heat that's built up. The malt master judges the readiness of the malt by crushing it and assessing the smudge of doughy starch left on his fingers; fingers are a big part of the technical equipment Mareš uses.

Finally, the malt goes back up two floors to be dried in the two-chamber kiln. The malt then needs to cool and mature for three to four weeks, after which Mareš runs tests to assess the technical specifications for each lot. To get a consistent product, he blends batches until he hits his standards. Because Mareš produces more malt than Ferdinand can use, he sells the remainder to Weyermann, which packages and sells it as "Bohemian Floor Malt."

LEFT: *Taking a drive to turn the barley*

this: He uses caramel malt. This may actually seem obvious, because it's what any American brewer would do—but for a Czech brewery it seemed wholly transgressive. Everyone "knows" pilsners are made exclusively with pilsner malt. The golden color and caramel flavor come from process, not ingredient, right? Not necessarily. Through a translator, Hlavsa seemed to be reading my mind when he added, "This is perfectly legitimate in terms of Czech brewing."

The Czechs have a concept they use to describe beer called *říz*, or "cut." It's the way a good beer strikes you, and it can mean "character" or the sharp, full flavor of a good beer. Unlike German brewers, who often make a helles that tastes fairly similar to the helles in the next town over, Czech breweries aim for distinction. They want *říz*, and in such simple beers, they need to be creative to achieve it.

Interestingly, the Germans are not without their own idiosyncrasies. One way to tinker with the beer is to adjust a mash's pH. A more acid mash produces a "smoother" bitterness, speeds up lautering and fermentation time, lowers beer color, and improves hot and cold breaks. In the United States, a brewer might just add phosphoric or lactic acid. Germans, however, are bound by the *Reinheitsgebot*, which forbids the addition of foreign substances. *Lactobacillus* bacteria, naturally present on the malt husk, are not considered foreign, though, and brewers can use them to make their own acids. Essentially a sour mash they use to culture acids, "biological acidification" is a laborious process that adds a lot of time and risks contamination—but it qualifies as an all-natural, *Reinheitsgebot*-compliant way to lower pH.

Hops play an important role in defining pilsners. Low-alpha European hops, with their very restrained, clean, spicy or herbal flavors, are critical to maintaining the delicate balance in a pilsner. A typical way of achieving this character is a process called "first-wort hopping," wherein the hops are placed in the kettle and allowed to steep as the wort arrives during runoff. Hops are added again when the wort starts boiling and once more about a half hour before the end of the ninety-minute boil. Counterintuitively, the process of first-wort hopping somehow infuses the beer with the kind of character usually found in later additions. Scientists are not yet clear on why this would be the case, but you can test the theory out with both Budvar and Pilsner Urquell. It is especially evident to my senses in Budvar, which has about

LEFT: *An antique cooling system shows that brewing equipment has greatly evolved over the decades.*

RIGHT: *Horizontal tanks are preferred for lagering in the Czech Republic because of their low hydrostatic pressure.*

50 percent less bitterness than Urquell. Brewmaster Adam Brož agrees. "You will find in Budvar that the bitterness is very mild—not so low—but *mild*."

The fermentation and aging process is fairly standard, though again, Czechs do it a little differently. Budvar subscribes to the old system of allowing primary fermentation to continue one day for every point of Plato—so twelve days. That's not typical, though, and most breweries go through faster primary fermentation. Budvar also lagers their beer for a shockingly long three months.

Visitors in the 1980s reported that Pilsner Urquell also lagered their beer that long, but now the brewery lets it rest for a more standard four weeks. Long maturation is what Brož calls "the most important thing"—and indeed, Budvar must be very committed to any practice that requires three times the number of lagering tanks. ■

EVOLUTION

N **O BEER HAS** been subjected to more "innovation" than Josef Groll's original pale lager. Some of the changes were unobjectionable—witness the creation of helles and export—but as pilsners became the international standard in brewing, many of the other changes have been disastrous. As pale lagers thinned out and lost their hops, they went through terrible fits of adulteration and weird gimmickry as they tried to lure a larger and larger audience. Strange as it is to imagine, beers like Olde English 800 and Natural Light—regularly rated worst in the world—are distant descendants of Groll's original work.

Fortunately, there has lately been a return to lagers with character. The Czech Republic is enjoying a brewing renaissance, and traditional lagers are leading the way. Beer fans there are especially interested in the properties that make their lagers distinctively Czech. Current trends include *nefiltrované pivo* (unfiltered beer) and *kvasnicové pivo* (yeast beer—a treatment in which fermenting wort or pure yeast is added to finished beer), two ways of serving beer aimed at preserving character and freshness. These hazy presentations are so popular that when I visited the Únětický Pivovar, they told me they couldn't sell their exceptional 12° Plato beer if it wasn't cloudy. "If the [beer] lagers for longer than a month, it will get too clear and in the pubs they will complain that it is too clear. They want more yeast."

There are similar trends developing outside the Czech Republic as newer, smaller breweries try to reclaim lagers from the industrial giants. In North America, a number of breweries make well-regarded examples of Czech and German lagers—Victory, Moonlight, Sixpoint, and Berkshire—and some breweries, like Washington State's Chuckanut, are devoted almost exclusively to lagers. A minor trend of so-called pre-Prohibition lagers is in its second decade and gaining steam; these beers harken back to a period in American brewing when lagers included corn or rice in the grist to soften the harsher American barley, but were still robust and full of hops.

As small breweries explore lager techniques, they mine their own traditions for inspiration. In London,

Alastair Hook has had enormous success with London Lager, a beer made with English ingredients but in the Bavarian manner (where Hook studied brewing). American breweries periodically run similar experiments with their native hops. In Italy, they borrow from multiple traditions—bottle-conditioning like the Belgians, dry-hopping like the English, lagering like the Germans—for sumptuous, rich beers.

In one of the most interesting developments, large multinational beer companies, after decades of thinning beer down, may be reversing course. With sales of its flagship brand dropping, in 2012 Anheuser-Busch launched an initiative called Project 12 to experiment with different pale lager recipes. Brewmasters from each of Budweiser's plants worked up their own recipes and the company ran extensive tastings before unveiling Black Crown in 2013. The release coincided with the debut of Beck's Sapphire— both companies are owned by A-B InBev—another beer that is stronger and hoppier than the regular company flagship. Two beers don't make a movement, but they do offer the prospect of intriguing shifts in the market. ∎

The Budweiser Conundrum.

You may have noticed: There are two Budweisers. The story of how this came to be and how a global economy reconciles the two is the subject of more than a century of rancor and lawsuits. Which is to say: It's a really good tale, full of drama and irony.

The town of Česke Budějovice is located in the southern lobe of Bohemia, a place long controlled by the German-speaking population who called it Budweis. Beer brewed there, as it has been since the thirteenth century, was therefore either Budějovický or Budweiser—literally, beer of the town of Budějovice or Budweis. Fast-forward to the period following the success of Josef Groll's 1842 pale lager in Pilsen. Other Czech breweries began making pale lagers, too. The Civic Brewery in the town then called Budweis was one of them. As a supplier to the court of King Wilhelm II, it earned the lager the nickname "the beer of kings." Ring a bell?

By the 1860s, an enterprising American brewer, enchanted by the idea of Bohemian beer, decided Budweis's were the best. It was no easy task to make those kinds of beers in the United States, but Adolphus Busch of the Anheuser Brewery managed to do it and in 1876 debuted his own Budweiser beer. Busch was selling beer for twenty years under the Budweiser name before a new brewery opened back in Budweis as a rival to the older German-owned company. This new brewery, the Joint Stock Brewery, was one of a wave of new Czech-owned businesses to spring up as a part of the Czech National Movement of the late nineteenth century. Eventually that brewery became Budějovický Budvar.

The fascinating part of the history is that the claims and counterclaims the two companies hurl at each other are generally founded in fact. As it happens, Adolphus Busch did find inspiration for his beers in Budweis and did spirit away both the type of beer and the name. But it's also true that he brewed his beer before Budweiser Budvar even existed. He did also apparently appropriate "the beer of kings" and turn it into "the king of beers"—one of the most valuable corporate slogans in the world. (Budvar disputes the history of "beer of kings.") But the brewery that inspired Busch is no longer in existence. And in the most wry of ironies, neither company has a clear historical claim to the name Budweiser. Busch obviously borrowed and rebranded it with absolutely no connection to the town or people; on the other hand, except as a valuable trademark, why would the people of Česke Budějovice want the name? "Budweis" is the name the city has abandoned. Budvar remains state-owned and is an artifact of the Czech National Movement.

In the long years since the conflict became an international incident, the two companies started by splitting up the globe and tried to protect certain markets before deciding the world was too small for that. They finally agreed to sell in the same markets, but under different names. You'll find Budvar sold as Czechvar in the United States. The legal feud continues. Don't bet against Budvar, though. Despite Anheuser-Busch's efforts to take over the relatively small, state-owned company, it remains independent. Indeed, it has outlasted the biggest brewery in the world, the very one it was fighting, which was gobbled up by brewing conglomerate InBev in 2008.

THE BEERS TO KNOW

PALE LAGERS MAY line grocery store shelves, but quantity doesn't equal quality. Czech breweries rarely export, so only a couple native pilsners are widely available, though two are the very definition of the style. There are more German pilsners on offer, but many of the most famous—Beck's, St. Pauli Girl, Warsteiner— lack character. Fortunately, even though a number of below-average pale lagers are ubiquitous, above-average ones are easy enough to find, too. That is particularly the case as a number of craft breweries make excellent examples.

PILSNER URQUELL

LOCATION: Pilsen, Czech Republic

MALT: Pilsner

HOPS: Saaz

4.4% ABV, 1.047 SP. GR., 35 IBU

One of the greatest crimes in brewing is the use of green bottles, the effect of which is to convince Americans that "skunk" is the flavor of European beers like Pilsner Urquell. It most decidedly is not. Buy a can of this beer instead, and you will discover a full-bodied lager bursting with rich, grain-y malting and an insistent snap of tangy Czech hops. You may find a touch of butterscotch, too—that's diacetyl, which the Urquell yeast produces in abundance.

BUDĚJOVICKÝ CZECHVAR

LOCATION: České Budějovice, Czech Republic

MALT: Moravian pale

HOPS: Saaz

5.0% ABV, 1.047 SP. GR., 22 IBU

Czechvar (or Budvar, as it is sold elsewhere) starts out with the same gravity as Urquell does, but it finishes out more fully. It is drier and more alcoholic, but more lightly hopped. Of the two beers, Czechvar's is better for tasting those wonderful, aromatic malts. The bitterness is lower as well, but the hops are actually more aromatic than in Urquell.

JEVER PILSENER

LOCATION: Jever, Germany

MALT: Undisclosed

HOPS: Undisclosed

4.9% ABV, 1.045 SP. GR., 40 IBU

Jever's reputation is for hops, but it's relative. Americans are generally pleasantly surprised by their insistence—a touch of lemon zest with the usual herbal spiciness of German hops—but not bowled over by them. The body is lean and elegant, the finish crisp and dry.

VICTORY PRIMA PILS

LOCATION: Downington, PA

MALT: German pilsner

HOPS: Saaz, Northern Brewer

5.3% ABV

Prima has long been one of America's most celebrated pilsners, and the reputation is well earned. A delicate blend of hops and malt that produces flavors like clover and honey, wildflowers and black pepper. You're supposed to drink pilsners cold, but Prima is so well made that the scone-like malts and floral hops open up if you linger over a glass.

SLY FOX PIKELAND PILS

LOCATION: Pottstown, PA

MALT: Pilsner

HOPS: Saaz

4.9% ABV, 1.047 SP. GR., 44 IBU

Brewer Brian O'Reilly makes excellent lagers, and Pikeland has the medals to prove it. Although Sly Fox calls it a Northern German pils, it's actually a hybrid—very crisp and dry in the German mode, but hopped to Czech levels. The malts are expressive and grain-y, and the hops are zesty but also a touch floral. Sold in cans so you'll never end up with a skunky pour.

CHUCKANUT PILSNER

LOCATION: Bellingham, WA

MALT: Pilsner

HOPS: Tettnanger, Spalt

5.0% ABV, 1.050 SP. GR., 38 IBU

Industry veteran Will Kemper has founded or helped found a number of breweries over the decades. His latest, Chuckanut, opened in 2008 with a focus on German and lager beers. The pilsner, with vivid, crisp hopping built on an unobtrusively grain-y base, takes some of its inspiration from local tastes, but keeps true to the continental style.

AUGUSTINER LAGERBIER HELL

LOCATION: Munich, Germany

MALT: Undisclosed

HOPS: Undisclosed

5.2% ABV

Augustiner's helles is full and creamy, with a frothy head and a brilliant golden body. The malts have the gentle softness that typify Bavarian hellesbiers—with just a hint of sugar cookie. But where it differs is a tangy yeast quality that adds a rustic twist that's unusual for German lagers.

STOUDTS GOLD LAGER

LOCATION: Adamstown, PA

MALT: Undisclosed

HOPS: Undisclosed

4.7% ABV, 25 IBU

There are ways in which this golden helles recalls the lagers of Munich, but it has some American touches, too. The malt is light but crisp and cracker-like, limned with honey, and the hops are grassy and (more than in most Bavarian hellesbiers) insistent. The extra hops may make it more American, but they take nothing from the sessionability of the beer.

GREAT LAKES DORTMUNDER GOLD

LOCATION: Cleveland, OH

MALT: Pale, caramel

HOPS: Cascade, Mt. Hood

5.8% ABV, 1.057 SP. GR., 30 IBU

An American take on the export style, Great Lakes restores Dortmund's lost strength and produces a round, slightly sweet beer with citrus highlights. It lacks some of the hallmarks of the original style (exchanging them for American touches), but still manages to capture export's spirit.

Budějovický Budvar (Czechvar)

DECOCTION MASHING AND DEEP MATURATION

ON THE OCTOBER DAY I VISITED BUDĚJOVICKÝ BUDVAR (PRONOUNCED ROUGHLY *BOOD-YE-OH-VITS-KEE BOOD-VAR*), THE FIRST SNOW OF THE SEASON WAS JUST BEGINNING TO DROP FAT, WET FLAKES ON BOHEMIA. DESPITE THE WEATHER, BREWMASTER ADAM BROŽ GUIDED ME TO ONE OF TWO WELL HEADS OUTSIDE THE BREWERY. THERE ARE A NUMBER OF FEATURES THAT MAKE CZECH BREWING DISTINCTIVE, AND THERE WE WERE STANDING IN FRONT OF ONE OF THEM. THE WELL GOES DOWN NEARLY 1,000 FEET TO A BASIN OF PURE, SOFT WATER—ONE OF THE KEYS TO UNLOCKING THE SECRET OF PALE LAGERS. IT'S EASY ENOUGH TO MANIPULATE WATER NOW, BUT BUDVAR MAINTAINS THE TRADITION OF USING ONLY UNTREATED WATER FROM THEIR SOURCE DEEP BENEATH THE BREWERY.

We ducked inside to the warmth of the brewhouse, where Brož told me about the ingredients Budvar uses. To most people, that discussion begins and ends with the

RIGHT: *An old postcard depicts the brewery hard at work.*

spicy Žatec (Saaz) hops for which pilsners are famous—that Budvar does use, in whole-flower form. But in fact, Czech beers are more dependent on their lush, aromatic malts. The barley grows in both Moravia and Bohemia, and as in Britain, farmers are continually experimenting with new varieties. "The breeders are making new varieties every three to five years," Brož explains. Each brewery chooses barley from the region they prefer—Budvar uses only Moravian malt—and then must maintain strict controls to keep flavor and quality consistent as barleys change year by year. "In spite of the fact that the analyticals are very similar or the same, both variety and origin could change the taste profile of the beer."

The brewhouse features the classic four-vessel system of decoction I'd come to expect there. What I didn't anticipate was finding a grant in between the lauter and kettle. An old piece of equipment to which Czechs seem absolutely faithful (Pilsner Urquell's ultramodern 2006 brewery also uses one), the grant resides underneath the lauter tun in a recessed pocket, with a long array of swan-neck faucets with attached valves. They are designed to control the flow out of the lauter tun, though now computers, not hand valves, do the work. Wort aeration is always a danger, and Brož noticed my surprise that he willingly risked it. He acknowledged the research but said he believed it was valuable in the case of his beer and cited contradictory research. The oxygen pickup, he said "influences the reaction of polyphenols and proteins. It influences this

reaction. So if the sweet wort runs through these valves, a small amount of oxygen is taken in and the reaction between proteins and polyphenols ends well."

Time and again, I had similar discussions with Brož, a brewer who is keenly aware of all the current scientific research. Yet he wasn't using it, as so many breweries do, to guide him through technological change. Quite the opposite; he uses it to prove why Budvar's old ways remain superior. At one point he described how a small part of the inside of the kettle was copper—another oxygenating risk. He grinned and called it a "homeopathic" amount. He said they'd studied it, but

BELOW: *The wellhead, which leads nearly a thousand feet down to Budvar's famously soft water*

ABOVE LEFT: *Adam Brož*

ABOVE RIGHT: *With an entire wall made of windows, Budvar's brewhouse is as well lit as any airport terminal.*

assured me they couldn't find any effect. "We tried, but it's impossible to measure it." So the copper stayed.

The last part of our tour took us down into fermentation and then farther down, to the vast cellars where torpedo-shaped lagering tanks were stacked on their sides, massive as whales.

Brož fetched an old tin-lined copper mug that brewers at Budvar have used for decades and we sampled beer from different tanks—the flagship pale lager, the roasty tmavé, the incredibly smooth *speciál*. Each one, though not ready to package, had already spent far longer in the lagering tank than most beers ever would. Budějovický Budvar produces around a million barrels a year and could save money by streamlining its production. Those whales we sampled from could easily swallow two or three times more beer if Budvar

went to a lesser standard for aging time—as nearly every other brewery in the world has done. Yet again, Brož cited research on why the beer needed to stay in the tanks so long. "Deep maturation," he called it, a process that not only smooths the beer, but develops the hop character. (There were other points about hydrostatic pressure and other chemical effects too technical for me to follow.)

I don't doubt Brož's research in the least, nor do I doubt that Budvar would change its practices if their studies told them they could make better beer some other way. But standing shivering in those icy cellars, sipping that raw, living beer, I knew exactly what was most convincing to Brož and his team. "Our tasting panel here in the brewery is the most important analytical instrument," he said. "You can have expensive equipment and devices, but the taste—that's the best." And so Budvar stays with its decoction, its copper grant, and its long maturation times.

Amber Lagers
MÄRZEN AND VIENNA LAGER

T he purpose of some beers is to cool, as on a midsummer's day; of others, to warm in the dark of winter. Amber lagers, the color of autumn leaves, have glowing within them the ember of warmth left over from the August sun—halfway beers of the equinox. Before refrigeration, they were brewed in the spring so they could ride out the heat in cool, dark caves and be drunk when the first frosts came. They

Amber Lagers. Strictly speaking, märzen points to strength, not color; in practice, it has come to mean an amber-colored beer. In the glass, märzens (also called Oktoberfest) and Vienna lagers may look more golden or reddish than amber, and indeed, beauty is one of their central characteristics. They lead with their malts, rich and round, with perhaps a dollop of caramel flavor or a hint of toast. Of the extended lager family, no beers are as well suited to food as amber lagers. They are regulars in both pizzerias and taquerias, and they work so well with roasted chicken that Bavarian fest goers abandon their prized sausages to enjoy the perfect pairing.

STATISTICS

ABV range: 4.5–6%

Märzen ABV range: 5–6.5%; bitterness: 18–30 IBU

Vienna lager ABV range: 4.5–5.5%; bitterness: 15–30 IBU

Serving temperature: 38°–45°F

Vessel: Stein

became the centerpiece of the world's most famous harvest festival, a beer of celebration.

In Munich, märzen lagers are still the toast of the town for three weeks in September and October, but Vienna has lost her famous namesake beers. They have jumped the ocean and are now more commonplace in North America. From Mexico City to Boston, they're among the easiest beers to find on tap—and most people have no idea they originally hailed from Austria. ■

ORIGINS

F ANY STORY in the beer canon was going to be optioned by Hollywood, it would be the one starring two brewing scions from Vienna and Munich. The tale would start as a buddy movie and morph into a classic capitalist tale à la *Citizen Kane*. Call them *Citizens Märzen*. Our story begins in the 1830s when two young brewers are learning their craft: Anton Dreher in Vienna, and Gabriel Sedlmayr in Munich. As part of their training, both men decide to go on an epic tour to learn the ways of brewers in other countries. Dreher travels to Munich, Sedlmayr to Vienna, and then they set off for points north.

The men are both ambitious and curious, and they go to great lengths to prize secrets from foreign breweries. In 1833, they arrive in Britain together, the most advanced brewing country in the world— something like landing in Silicon Valley to rub elbows with the technical elite. This is where things get interesting. While in Burton upon Trent, they take a page from Ian Fleming and use a hollowed-out walking stick to steal wort and yeast for analysis. In our movie version, I imagine Dreher draped over the edge of a fermenter, stick in hand plunging into foaming wort, while Sedlmayr keeps the lookout.

In the nonmovie version, however, yeast and wort weren't especially valuable to these young lager-brewers. What they took from Britain was far more valuable than biological samples: They took the knowledge of the "English method" of making pale malts. Both returned home, Dreher to his father's Klein-Schwechat Brewery, Sedlmayr to his father's Spaten.

RIGHT: *Munich Oktoberfest, a celebration fueled by amber lagers*

Dreher took over his brewery in 1836, Sedlmayr in 1839. Putting their knowledge to good use, the two men came out with the first amber lagers in 1841—and Sedlmayr used that year's Munich Oktoberfest for his debut. The malts they developed to brew these beers took the names of their home cities and became standards in brewing—still used by the ton in breweries across the world.

After their release, the beers followed different paths. Dreher's beer was a huge success almost immediately. It was a reddish-blond beer, at the time one of the palest in the world and the fairest-colored lager—at least for a year, until Josef Groll introduced Pilsner in Bohemia. It spread across the Austrian Empire, and Dreher became a very rich man. At the Paris World Exposition in 1867, the Viennese beer hall was a big hit, and by the 1870s, drinkers could buy a glass of "Vienna beer" in London and Paris. By that time, the Schwechat Brewery was the biggest in continental Europe.

Dreher's lager transcended its brewery—it made Vienna famous for its beer. Visitors to the city seemed to fall mesmerized under its spell. This is from an Englishman who visited in 1866:

> Above all, that, when poured into a glass fresh from a cask just brought up from the ice-cellar, it glows like fluid amber, and is crowned with a delicate beading of bubbles, which are true bubbles of the air, and not like the soapy foam of Scotch ale, bubbles of the earth. To sip from a glass of Läger, puffing wreaths from a cigarette of choice Latakia, while you gaze vaguely to a sky flaming with the gold and crimson of a Danubian sunset, and catch the rhythm of waltzes and mazurkas—this is the perfection of ignorant and mechanical bliss. And nowhere else is such blessedness so surely to be found.
>
> —*CORNHILL MAGAZINE,*
> VOLUME 14, 1866

The tremors in Munich registered much more lightly on the Richter scale when Sedlmayr's amber lagers arrived. Munich was already one of the two or three most important brewing cities in the world, and beer drinkers there were plenty satisfied with their chestnut dunkel lagers. Bavarians had so little interest in pale beers that it would be decades before they'd get around to making a helles. Instead, Spaten's märzen became a favorite at Oktoberfest. Made with darker

LEFT: *How dark can a märzen be? Matthias Trum sits in front of one of his family's smoked märzens at Schlenkerla—dark as many dunkel lagers. Although märzenbiers are now largely amber-colored, the term once referred to beers of a certain gravity, not their color.*

March Beer. The origins of March beer (*märzenbier*) go back to a Bavarian ducal decree in 1553 that made it illegal to brew beer from April 23 to September 29. Those were the months when wild yeasts and bacteria were especially adept at ruining beer. To prepare for the long summer, brewers went into a frenzy to make enough beer to last until fall. The original märzenbiers weren't amber, of course—they were darker lagers typical of the time. When Spaten released its amber lager in 1841, Sedlmayr called it a märzen, and in Vienna, Dreher called his lager märzen as well. From then to now, märzen means amber beer.

Munich malts, märzens were halfway between dunkel and Bohemia's new pale lager. They were not so light as to spark controversy—as helles later did in the 1890s—and other brewers began imitating Spaten.

In the second half of our buddy movie, Dreher and Sedlmayr move into their *Kane* phase, bestriding empires like kings. Dreher actually did get into politics—winning a seat in parliament in 1861. Sedlmayr continued to innovate, bringing steam power to the brewery in 1844 and introducing refrigeration in 1873 (it's widely believed that Spaten was the first brewery to do so). Even though he was the coinventor of amber lager, Sedlmayr's brewery grew to be Munich's largest thanks mostly to his success with dunkel. Sedlmayr retired shortly after installing refrigeration, cementing his run as one of the most important brewers of that or any century.

We'd probably have to take some artistic license with the story to make that last bit more dramatic, since there is no record of either man's descent into loneliness or failure. Dreher did die young, in 1863, but Sedlmayr watched his sons carry on at Spaten, innovating as he did. (They were the ones to introduce helles lager to Munich.) Sedlmayr received the rare honor of being cited a meritorious citizen by the City of Munich. Spaten continued on as one of Munich's most successful breweries, and remains so to this day. Well, Rosebud or no, it's a good story. ■

DESCRIPTION AND CHARACTERISTICS

THE CATEGORY OF amber lagers is not perfectly precise. Oktoberfest or märzen beers (hereafter, märzen) were once probably the darker expression of the style, drawing more color from their Munich malts than the Vienna lagers drew from their lighter-roasted Vienna malts. There's a curious historical twist that makes their colors relative, however. When märzens were first introduced, Munich was a dark-beer town. The rest of the world might have been falling in love with faddish pale beers, but not the earnest Bavarians. So märzen was quite likely a darker light beer (or even a dark beer). Things have changed, however. A century and a half on, pale beers have finally crept slowly to ascendency. Märzens are still compared to the dominant style, helles, but now that means light beer. Over the last two or three decades, the color of märzen has done a reverse, and is now a lighter amber beer—a lot like Vienna lager. (Though dark märzens are still brewed by a few smaller Bavarian breweries.) It can now be hard to tell them apart by color alone.

MÄRZEN

There is a concept in some Asian aesthetic traditions that refers to the essence of expression. In India the term is *rasa* ("juice") and it points to the mood or emotional state that accompanies art. Music in particular may be composed to capture the mood of late afternoon or romance or wonder. March beers have a *rasa* about them, too—celebration. Märzens are infused with the spirit of fest-going. Brewed a bit stronger than standard lagers, but made to cascade down the throat with abandon, they're both the result and cause of merriment. They're more harvest beers than autumn beers, more sunny warmth than crisp chill, and they're drunk at the time when people are still hanging on to the relaxed mood of summer.

Brewers help encourage this fusion of spirit and drink by making a beer built on a solid, smooth base of caramelly Munich malts. They are sweet enough to encourage hearty swallows, but crisp enough so they quench and encourage further gulps. Hops are an important part of the composition; in the best märzens, they add further harmony to the balance. The classic hop profile contains the delicate spiciness of German strains and may bring to mind gingerbread when situated amid the pillowy malts. Over time, German märzens have lost some of their color and tend more toward golden than amber, but in the U.S., Oktoberfests (as they are usually called) have the color of the harvest—deep, rich amber.

VIENNA LAGER

The funny thing about Vienna lager is that it's mostly not brewed in Vienna anymore. By far the most famous versions—especially to North Americans—now hail from the New World. During the long period of style collapse in the U.S., Vienna lagers were a mainstay south of the border—think Victoria and Dos Equis Amber, for years some of the most interesting beers left in American grocery stores. When Jim Koch (pronounced Cook) decided to abandon law and take up the old family business, he dug up his great-great-grandfather's recipe and brewed a Vienna lager that he called Sam Adams Boston Lager.

Historically, märzens were darker and more caramelly, while Vienna malts gave Vienna lagers a crisp toastiness. The distinction—if it was ever very large—is collapsing. Now that the style has jumped the ocean, breweries rely on more American hop bills; heavy on pale malts with caramel to color and taste. Take two of the most well known, Great Lakes and Sam Adams. Both follow the

Munich Oktoberfest.

The kickoff to the first Oktoberfest, a five-day celebration that included feasting, parades, and horse racing, was a wedding. The betrothed were not ordinary Münchners, but Ludwig, the future king of Bavaria, and Princess Therese of Sachsen-Hildburghausen. Of course, at the time the citizens of Munich didn't think of it as a recurring event, though the ceremony that accompanied the wedding had a certain force. The horse race, in particular, seemed to galvanize the people, so Munich decided to host another fest the next year, featuring an agricultural exhibition instead of vows. There was an element of politics and local pride to the whole affair, which came on the heels of the Napoleonic wars. They called the site of the festival Theresienwiese, in honor of the bride, and Oktoberfest has been with us ever since.

Beer became the central focus of the festival almost immediately. The märzenbier we know today wasn't at the first celebration—Munich was still a dark lager country then. Spaten debuted their amber märzen at the 1841 Oktoberfest, and in 1872 was the first brewery to call it Oktoberfestbier. Beginning in 1896, the big Munich breweries erected huge "castles" to serve their beer and established a monopoly that continues to the present. Only six breweries can sell their beer there—Augustiner, Hacker-Pschorr, Löwenbrau, Paulaner, Spaten, and the Hofbräuhaus—and they have the exclusive right to call it Oktoberfestbier.

Oktoberfest is not only the world's largest beer fest, it is a staggering force of nature. Running the final two weeks of September and the first of October, it is host to up to seven million people. They drink eight million liters of beer, eat half a million chickens and 125,000 sausages. All of this pumps over a billion euros into the local economy. But while Oktoberfest has a reputation of being a tourist draw, it remains a largely local celebration. Sixty percent of the attendees are from Munich; three quarters are from Bavaria. The dirndls and lederhosen aren't just for foreign cameras.

TOP AND BOTTOM: *Dirndls, lederhosen, beer, and sausage—no wonder seven million people march into the tents in Munich's Theresienwiese every year.*

pale-and-caramel prescription. In Eliot Ness, Great Lakes also adds Munich malt, but neither uses the malt that once defined the style. Eliot Ness tips the scale at 6.2% ABV, while Sam Adams is a lithe 4.9%. Is one more märzen-like than the other? Are they anything like the beers once brewed in Austria? It's clearly hard to say, beer to beer. In the U.S. and Mexico, Vienna-style lagers typically have a lightly malty body characterized by caramel. American malts are a bit stiffer than German malts, so the presentation is crisp and clean, not soft. Beyond that—well, it's really the brewery's decision. ∎

BREWING NOTES

A**N EXISTENTIAL QUESTION:** If we relocate a type of beer 4,000 miles from its point of origin and dismiss a key ingredient that arguably defined the beer, is it still the same kind of beer? The question is relevant because when we think of Vienna lagers now, we think of Boston Lager, not the beer Anton Dreher first brewed in 1841. The question is also essentially moot— styles change, and if the tradition of brewing amber lagers had persisted in Vienna, the style would have morphed on its own anyway, as happened with märzen.

But a glance at Boston Lager is interesting because it shows how the beer evolved. When Jim Koch used his family's heirloom recipe—it was once called Louis Koch Lager when it was brewed in St. Louis—to re-create an amber lager, he was looking at an American beer already a step removed from Austria. According to Koch, his Boston Lager "is exactly the same recipe." Allowing a little poetic license—malts change, techniques improve—it's a revealing recipe. Louis Koch used a decoction mash, and Jim says he uses a "traditional four-vessel process" as well. American hops were not particularly prized, so Louis used German hops. "The Hallertau and Tettnang hops are still grown on the same farms and often by the same families," Koch said.

Those elements at least are little changed from Dreher's day. But Louis used American malts, coloring his amber lager not with Vienna malts, but caramel. Koch acknowledged this difference. "We used the same two-row barley but varieties have changed. I don't know whether there is any taste difference from nineteenth century malt." The beer was brewed again in the 1950s when, according to Koch's father, it was dry-hopped (as is Boston Lager). This is surely a more modern, and American, change. Continental brewers don't dry-hop their lagers, and immigrant brewers probably wouldn't have, either. To recap: It's a beer made with American barley, caramel malt, and it's dry-hopped—and it's a standard for the style. If a brewery submitted a beer like the one Dreher brewed to the Great American Beer Festival, it would lose points for not tasting like a Vienna lager.

American brewers are fairly cavalier about their malt bill; they're happy to use pale American two-row and augment with color malts to approximate German styles. Try a German and an American beer side by side and you'll notice that the American beer probably has more caramel and is stiffer; a German amber lager will be softer and breadier. I asked two German-trained brewers working in America how they handle the differences in malt. Dan Carey, who founded New Glarus Brewing in 1993, agreed that there's a big difference. "We use mainly American malt by far, but when it comes to some of our German-inspired beers like Staghorn, that's nearly all German malt. I personally feel very strongly that there is a difference in flavor."

In Montana, Jürgen Knöller uses Canadian grain, but malted to his specifications by a German maltster. "I have a

Both märzens and Vienna lagers have close relations among the lager family: *Helles* and *dunkel lagers* are less alcoholic, but equidistant in hue; *bocks* are less hoppy, but similar in strength and impact; Czech *polotmavés* are another version of an amber lager. *Amber ales* share some similarities, but are fuller, heavier, and fruitier (and sometimes hoppier).

degree in brewing and malting, so when I talk to a maltster, I can tell him, this is exactly what I want. Still, 75 percent of the profile of your beer is happening in the malthouse. The influence you have as a brewer—I mean give or take—you have maybe 25 percent chance to influence it in the brewhouse and 75 percent of the character is already preset at the malthouse." It is possible to make an amber lager with American pale and specialty malts that *looks* like a German märzen, but the taste won't be identical. ■

Mexican-Viennese Lagers.

Have you ever noticed how Mexican mariachi bands have a funny echo of German oom-pah music? Maybe you even noticed that connection while drinking a pitcher of Dos Equis Amber. Well, interesting story: Back in the 1860s, Mexico was actually ruled briefly by France, odd as that sounds. In 1864, the French installed an Austrian archduke, Ferdinand Maximilian, as Mexican emperor. He was captured and executed in 1867, but during his brief reign, he managed to bring over a number of Austrian brewers who stayed on in Mexico and continued to brew the lager they knew: Vienna lager. This wasn't the moment when the great flood of German immigrants swept into the country, bringing polka with them—that came later. But I like to think that they were encouraged to come by all the good beer that had already arrived.

EVOLUTION

AMBER LAGERS HAVEN'T been subject to a lot of recent changes. Mexican companies kept Vienna lagers alive in the long, dark period of American brewing consolidation, and they didn't change much. Samuel Adams didn't help the cause of innovation much when it made a juggernaut out of Boston Lager; other breweries pretty much ceded that slice of the craft-beer pie to Jim Koch, and you see very few other examples. German märzens have lost a bit of their color, and probably a bit of hops, too. New Glarus's Dan Carey calls them "basically 13.5° Plato helles biers." But the beers served at the Spaten tent in today's Oktoberfest would seem largely familiar to drinkers beamed in from fifty years ago. A bit of color loss, but otherwise recognizable. In North America, local Oktoberfests are staged from Ontario to Arizona and proud German descendants

ABOVE: *Boston Lager as it appeared in 1985.*

want the same, frothy amber stuff they drink in Bavaria. Thus when you think of amber lagers, you really don't think of a style on the move. ■

What's in a Name? We have these names: Oktoberfest, märzen, and Oktoberfest-märzen. Do they refer to one beer? If so, how do we account for the confusion in months—October in one name, March (märzen) in the second, and most perplexing of all, both in the third? What's going on here?

They do refer to one beer. March indicated the month they were originally brewed, October to when they were removed from cellars and drunk. In the United States, where umlauts are verboten, we call the beers Oktoberfest. In Germany, though, that term carries the weight of law: Only the six breweries that serve their beer at Munich's legendary Oktoberfest may use that term; other beers in the style are called märzen. Either is acceptable stateside. If you do use the German, that umlaut renders the first syllable something like the vowels in "heir," like *Meirt-zen.*

THE BEERS TO KNOW

THE RANGE OF flavors in the amber lager family is one of the tightest of any style. You'll only need to try a few and the beers reveal themselves. Paradoxically, the difference between a mediocre amber lager and an exceptional one is immediately apparent. Here you'll find a few of the really good ones.

MÄRZEN AND OKTOBERFEST

PAULANER OKTOBERFEST

LOCATION: Munich, Germany

MALT: Pale, Munich, caramel

HOPS: Mt. Hood

6.0% ABV, 1.055 SP. GR., 20 IBU

The classic images of dirndl-clad women holding mugs of Oktoberfest beer wouldn't be the same without the thick, fluffy heads you see on the beer. Paulaner obliges here, with a *festbier* that billows with clouds of the stuff. The beer itself is toasty, almost a little plummy, and sprinkled with palate-cleansing cedary hops.

NEW GLARUS STAGHORN OCTOBERFEST

LOCATION: New Glarus, WI

MALT: Pale, Munich, caramel

HOPS: Cascade, Saaz

5.5% ABV, 1.053 SP. GR.

Wisconsin is lousy with Oktoberfests, and a handful of them are excellent examples of the genre. My favorite comes from New Glarus, which started out making its bones by selling lagers to German-American cheeseheads. This is a Halloween-colored beer spiced with peppery hopping and a creamy, pecan-like body.

SLY FOX OKTOBERFEST

LOCATION: Pottstown, PA

MALT: Pilsner, Vienna

HOPS: German varieties

5.8% ABV, 1.056 SP. GR., 25 IBU

For those who can't afford a trip to Munich, this is a pretty good way to try the beer. Brewed to the lighter hue now popular in Germany and lagered five weeks, this festbier is wonderfully smooth. It ends with a light snap of herbal hopping that encourages further sips.

FREE STATE OKTOBERFEST

LOCATION: Lawrence, KS

MALT: Pilsner, Munich, CaraMunich, Carahell

HOPS: Nugget, Hersbrucker

5.4% ABV, 1.054 SP. GR., 25 IBU

I imagine that the märzenbiers of the nineteenth century looked like Free State's—deep amber, like a medium-grade maple syrup. The beer has the complex body that has a more overt caramel flavor buttressed by lighter grain-y and biscuit notes. The hops have a touch of cinnamon in them that carry home the image of autumn.

VIENNA LAGER

GREAT LAKES ELIOT NESS

LOCATION: Cleveland, OH

MALT: Pale, Munich, caramel

HOPS: Mt. Hood

6.2% ABV, 1.061 SP. GR., 27 IBU

Breweries too often add color to otherwise indifferent lagers to make "Vienna lager." Great Lakes has done an able job of giving their Vienna some of the luxury of malt flavor and aroma. The malts are round and gentle, honey-sweet, and the whole beer is balanced nicely by spicy hopping.

SAMUEL ADAMS BOSTON LAGER

LOCATION: Boston, MA

MALT: Pale, caramel

HOPS: Hallertauer Mittelfrüh, Tettnanger

4.9% ABV, 1.053 SP. GR., 30 IBU

By contrast, Boston Lager is a crisper interpretation of a Vienna lager. The malts have a touch of caramel, but they defer to the hops, which steal the show. Boston Lager is dry-hopped with Hallertauer Mittelfrüh, completing the final layer of spicy, aromatic hopping. Effervescent, light, and crisp, this much-decorated beer remains one of the best available in the United States.

Bocks

ost people have seen beery images involving wooden barrels and goats, those old-fashioned pictures that don't quite make sense but seem familiar. That is bock. It's an old style of beer, but not excessively so. Mainly it has endured, especially rare in places like the U.S. where so few styles did. What remains of bock in the cultural imagination is a strong beer and perhaps a vague prejudice against the old , as one might maintain against horehound candy.

Bocks. Bocks are Germany's sipping beers. They are not only strong, but refined and elegant, with plush maltiness that melds luxuriously with alcoholic warmth. Pale bocks depend most strongly on the polished malt flavors, while dunkel bocks and doppelbocks feature dark fruit and leather as well. Eisbocks, the strongest of them all, are actually distilled beers, and they taste it, with concentrated flavors that give the impression of port wine. The heartiness of bocks tempers spicy dishes, but the beers also complement chocolatey desserts—better yet, try them with both in a chicken mole.

Helles or maibock ABV range: 6–8%; bitterness: 15–30 IBU

Dunkel bock ABV range: 6–8%; bitterness: 15–30 IBU

STATISTICS

Doppelbock ABV range: 6.5–10%; bitterness: 15–35 IBU

Eisbock ABV range: 9–13%; bitterness: 20–40 IBU

Serving temperature: 45°–50°F

Vessel: Stemmed pokal (goblet)

The strong part is right. Even the relatively light May bocks are sturdily built, and darker doppelbocks and eisbocks are among the strongest beers in the world. Any prejudice against them, however, is misplaced. Like so many beers of German origin, *bockbiers* are malt-centered and brewed for refinement. Like märzens, bocks are often made for special occasions—to usher in the cold, the warmth, or to fortify during the Lenten season. ■

ORIGINS

WHEN ANYONE STARTS telling the family history of bock beer, they haul out an old scrapbook and point to a photo of great-great-grandpa Bock, who lived in the northern German town of Einbeck. There's no doubt that a Mr. Bock lived there, and he was a famous resident indeed. An important shipping town, Einbeck sent its beer far from home. We know that as far back as the 1570s, Munich had imported beer from Einbeck, which according to a 1612 source was a "thin, subtle, clear . . . bitter" beer that had "a pleasant acidity on the tongue, and many other good qualities." You can see from that description that the ancient Einbecker beers were very different from the lagers we know today. They were ales and, like other northern beers, soured by wild yeasts.

The bock scrapbook ought properly begin with a picture of Elias Pichler. He was an Einbecker trained in the ways of the town's beers, but in 1614 he took a job in Munich running the newly opened production facility of the Hofbräuhaus. The royal household that owned the Hofbräuhaus wanted something potent like the Einbecker beers and charged Pichler with the task of crafting a Bavarian facsimile. The beer he brewed was an entirely different beast. Working in the lager tradition, Pichler did a lot of experimenting before he came up with a beer he called "maibock." That was the first true *bockbier*, and while it may have taken inspiration from beers brewed in Einbeck, it was Bavarian through and through.

DOPPELBOCKS

Doppelbocks were another Bavarian invention, and their connection to Einbeck is all the more tenuous. They were originally brewed by Franciscan monks near (and what is now in) Munich. They brewed a special extrastrong bock, and later began selling it during the Feast of the Holy Father. The beer was known

RIGHT: *Salvator is still made in a beautiful, Old World copper brewhouse.*

as Sankt Vater Bier ("holy father beer"), later shortened to Salvator. The eight-day festival that accompanied the beer's release was widely attended and it became customary to toast the duke of Bavaria with Salvator. Salvator beer was a style of its own—a very heavy, sweet, underfermented concoction. This may help explain why monks used it to ease them through their days of fasting during Lent. Unlike today's much more alcoholic doppelbocks, old Salvators were heavy but modest in their alcohol content—"liquid bread" indeed.

In 1799, the monks sold their brewery to the state. A few years later, a brewer named Zacherl purchased it—and still later, the brewery changed its name to Paulaner. As the decades rolled by, "salvator" became a generic name, like helles or märzen, that referred to doppelbocks. Dozens of Bavarian breweries already offered their own salvators when Paulaner

The Einbeck Bocks.

Einbeck joined the Hanseatic League in 1368, when member towns Bremen and Hamburg had already been shipping beer as far as Scandinavia and Britain. Though late to the party, Einbeck made up for lost time with quality. The town maintained its own brewing equipment and employed professional brewers. Town burghers could malt their own grain and brew their own beer—but they had to use the city equipment to do it. The equipment was small enough to haul around from house to house, and the wide gateways built to accommodate the kettles and tuns are still visible in some of the older buildings in Einbeck. The brewmaster was responsible for monitoring malt quality and overseeing the brewing process. Everyone had to use the same recipe and adhere to the same standards of brewing quality. Finally, all beer brewed in Einbeck had to be certified by the town brewmaster before it could be sold or exported, ensuring the name "Einbecker bier" was always associated with quality.

Towns all across northern Germany made beer, and some achieved minor levels of renown. But Einbeck's status knew few peers. No less than Martin Luther, defending himself in front of the Assembly of the Holy Roman Empire, had a jug filled with Einbecker beer. He said it was the "best beer known to man." Perhaps even more telling, it was famous enough that a duke in distant Munich would hire an Einbeck brewer to reproduce it closer to home.

applied for and was granted a trademark on the beer around the turn of the twentieth century. To retaliate, brewers appropriated that -ator suffix, so now there are countless variations on that theme: Celebrator, Animator, Optimator, Maximator, and so on. One senses the memory of this transgression remains a faint irritant, at least to the other breweries. Paulaner, however, celebrates this history by reprising the festival every year around Lent and tapping a barrel of Salvator.

EISBOCKS

The one bock developed outside Munich is the oddest: eisbock, or ice-bock. The history of this style is claimed by the brewery that makes one of the most famous versions, Kulmbacher. There's no reason necessarily to dispute it, except that independent documentation is hard to find. (Brewery histories aren't always the most scholarly works, particularly when the PR department sees a benefit in certain claims.) But Kulmbacher's story is this: Back in the fall of 1890, a brewer at the Reichelbräu brewery (now owned by Kulmbacher) forgot to move two barrels of bock into the cellar. They spent the winter out in the harsh Franconian weather getting buried under ice and snow. When they were discovered the following spring, the barrel staves had burst, but inside a bit of bock remained trapped in ice. The beer's water had frozen, leaving behind a concentrated elixir—the world's first eisbock. ∎

Bock's Strange Name.
Bottles of bock regularly feature a goat on the label—a visual pun. One of the meanings of *bock* in German is "goat." But how did the beer come to be called bock in the first place? Well, let's step back. Germany is a land of many dialects. In the 1880s, an imperial linguist named Georg Wenker found that there were nine separate dialects across Germany. Even today, Bavarians are ribbed by northerners for their funny accents. So imagine the late sixteenth century, when Einbeckers (Wenker called their dialect "west low German") were shipping their beer to Munich. What started out as *Ainpöckisch bier* in Einbeck eventually ended up as *bockbier* in Munich. Neither city's pronunciation had anything to do with goats.

DESCRIPTION AND CHARACTERISTICS

EVERY OCTOBER, AS the chill begins to blanket the Franconian countryside, breweries schedule special barrel tappings for their bockbier. In Bamberg, the streets outside breweries—Mahr's, Schlenkerla, Fässla, Ambräusianum, Spezial, and more—fill up with revelers holding half-liter mugs of the strong stuff. Before the night is over, there will be dancing, kissing, toasts galore. If märzenbier is the most purely celebratory of the German styles, then bock is the style used for transitions. They welcome the cold in Franconia, but in Munich doppelbocks are associated with the Lenten season. And when the spring has finally cracked the winter ice—but before the first summer heat wave—that's the time for May bocks.

PALE BOCKS
(aka Maibocks or Helles Bocks)

Bock is not only a type of beer, but according to German law, also a category—*stark* or "stout" beer—which is to say, strong. (That ought to serve you well in beer trivia, too. The German stout? Why bock, of course.) Pale bocks, however, are brewed to usher in the warmth, the first days in the biergarten. They must therefore have a delicate touch—robust but light. It's one of the hardest tricks to pull off and too many end up sweet and gluey. Done right, a maibock will have a delicacy of malts, soft and creamy but crisp, and a tracery of hops to stiffen and enliven the presentation. There's

no reason a maibock has to be light-colored—those first lagers made by Pichler surely were not—but even the darkest are still only a dark honey hue.

Imports from Germany are rare, and American examples, usually seasonal, aren't thick on the shelves, either. There are some excellent ones, though, from Sprecher's slightly underweight but sumptuous Mai Bock, which picks up a bit of crispness from a wheat addition, to Smuttynose's super-heavyweight Maibock, a malty boomer that surprises with its light, lavender-hop finish.

DOPPELBOCKS

In the last decade, ale brewers have been pumping their beers with steroids to come up with imperial-this and triple-that. Long before those came along, doppelbocks reigned supreme as the kings of the beer world. It's not just their strength—everything about doppelbocks impresses. They are dark, sometimes with sparkling ruby highlights, as clarion as a mountain lake, and as rich and smooth as mousse. It's like driving a very powerful sports car; you sense the power coiled inside, but all you can hear is a low, purring rumble. In some ways, doppelbocks are the best examples of a lager. In strong ales you find not only malt sweetness but also ester fruitiness—they must be balanced with roast or hops. Well-made doppelbocks have only the pure flavors of malts—and usually not a lot in the way of hops. They may have toast and bread or darker flavors—chocolate, licorice, treacle—and they're the style most likely to nod in the direction of roastiness. All of those flavors bathe the tongue in cultured sophistication, but the drinker, feeling a warming rush, can sense that underneath it all is a well-concealed alcohol charge.

One of the most-lauded dopplebocks is Ayinger's Celebrator, which attracts praise for its balanced complexity. It is also an unusual one, just 6.7% strong, but rich enough that no one would dare exclude it from the pantheon of stronger versions. It is more common that these beers rise to around 8% ABV, though, as is the case with the classic from Paulaner and Weihenstephan. In Madison, Wisconsin (a state with a strong German heritage), Capital Brewery has something of a cottage industry in doppelbocks. Autumnal Fire is, as brewmaster Kirby Nelson calls it, "Capital's most notorious product," and a wonderful American doppel. Just a shade under 8%,

ABOVE: *The old Ayinger brewery, where Celebrator was born*

it has bread and caramel in the malts, a hint of hoppy spicing, and an instantly warming wash of alcohol.

Bockbieranstiche. The small Franconian town of Bamberg is off the beaten path. It was remote enough to be spared the bombs of World War II, and as a result, the entire old town was listed as a UNESCO World Heritage site in 1993. The cobblestone roads, medieval half-timbered buildings, and ancient churches are enough to draw tourists aplenty, but Bamberg also has a special place in the heart of beer lovers. Home to nine breweries (in a town of just 70,000 residents) and the famous Weyermann maltings, it is touted by the tourist council as "the beer city." No time is better to experience the city than the fall, when breweries take turns hosting *bockbieranstiche*—"bock beer tapping." Much of what happens in Bamberg feels as though it's been happening there a long time, and being handed a krug of beer poured straight from the barrel before joining the townspeople filling the streets makes it easy to imagine you're in a scene from centuries past. For a list of the barrel-tapping dates, visit bamberg-guide.de/bamberg/bierundbierkultur/bockbieranstiche.php.

Samichlaus. One of the strongest beers in the world was first released in 1980, long before anyone expected that such a thing would be a fad. The beer was called Samichlaus, brewed by the Hürlimann Brauerei in Zurich. A titanic beer at 14%, it had the distinction of being fermented naturally—still an impressive feat. Hürlimann brewed it only one day a year, on December 6, then put it in conditioning tanks for most of the rest of the year. It was a celebrated and beloved beer, but that was not enough to save Hürlimann, which closed in 1997. But that was not the end of the story. With the help of some of the Hürlimann brewers and the original recipe, the beer was revived, but this time in Austria by Schloss Eggenberg. This particular brewery was an apt savior, having already been a longtime maker of another titan called Urbock 23. (The number refers to the gravity.) Most everything remains the same for Samichlaus: the stunning strength, the single day of brewing, even the label. It has remained, for over thirty years, in the upper reaches of doppelbock muscularity.

EISBOCKS

There's something vaguely disreputable about eisbocks—though it's not their fault. When they are brewed for flavor, they can astonish. But beginning in the mid-1990s, breweries began to use the technique of freeze-distillation to create beers at liqueur strengths. Samuel Adams was on the forefront, introducing a beer called Utopias that reached 27% in 2007 and sparked a strength war that led to a Scottish brewery making a 65% (130 proof) "beer" in 2012. It hasn't helped that national companies have used freeze-distillation to make down-market beers like Icehouse, Busch Ice, and Natural Ice. The distillation process doesn't add a lot of oomph (these beers usually run 5.5% to 6% ABV), but it does tend to concentrate some of the less appealing mealy qualities that light lagers conceal predistillation.

True eisbocks, which weigh in at a much more modest 10% to 15%, should not be relegated to beer's sideshow. Indeed, they can be quite impressive. Distillation concentrates flavors, which means balance is everything to these beers. Hops can quickly become jagged knives; malt can easily turn into plum preserves. Good eisbocks, like Kulmbacher Eisbock, push the richness right up to the edge without going over.

DARK BOCKS AND AMERICAN BOCKS

While most dark bocks are doppelbocks and most maibocks are light-colored, there is a rarer dark bock brewed below doppel strength. Like dunkel lagers, dark bocks take a bit of flavor from the added malts, but they are rounder, sweeter, and more on the cocoa-chocolate continuum than the roasty-coffee one.

In the United States, there remain a few examples of beers called "bock" from

from previous generations—Shiner, Genessee, and Huber. They're a strange kind of hybrid beer, refugees from an early, benighted time in American history. As beer got progressively weaker and less interesting, American bock beers lost their strength. The ones that remain are no stronger than standard American lagers—4.4% to 5.5% ABV. But Americans, who associated color with strength, nevertheless thought of these beers—dark amber to brown—as "strong." They could constitute their own style, except they have been fading from the scene for decades. They were brewed for drinkers of a different time and don't seem to have any natural place left in the beer landscape. ■

BREWING NOTES

THE METHODS AND techniques of brewing bocks don't differ appreciably from any other type of German lager, save for recipe formulation. What is different, however, are industry standards and expectations. A perfect example of this is the doppelbock made by Jürgen Knöller at Missoula's Bayern Brewery. Knöller, a Bavarian, trained and began his brewing career around Munich. "I worked for four different breweries in Germany; of those four three are no longer," he said, warming up to the story of how Bayern Doppel Bock came to be. "The first one was Brauerei Schiff—'Ship'—and we had a *very* traditional brewery. We are talking a four-vessel brewhouse with a falloff tank—whatever that is in English—it's a fifth vessel. It had a cool ship, it was *beautiful*. We did beers there that I have never really seen being brewed anywhere else."

It was such an old brewery that it used a device something like a hop back that both extracted fresh hop aromas as it went through

IF YOU LIKE BOCKS

In one way, bocks are not terribly unlike less-alcoholic German beers—*helles* and *dunkel lager, märzen.* They share those beers' clean lines and malty center. Their power separates them, though, and beers like *Baltic porters* and *imperial stouts* seem more like doppelbocks than dunkel lagers. Another unlikely location to find similar beers is in France's northeast, where strong, smooth *bières de garde* are brewed. Perhaps it's not surprising; French brewers were heavily influenced by bocks.

and also filtered the hot break. Then the beer went to a cool ship where it would go through the cold break. "They were just terrific beers," Knöller said. "The doppelbock they brewed—they left it in the tank for almost a year. In Germany [we won a number of awards]." Of course, breweries have become much more modernized since the 1970s. The owner of the Schiff brewery died and eventually the brewery was lost through the mismanagement of subsequent owners.

But the Bavaria Knöller brewed in was a different one, too. "Now, when we were brewing in those days back in Germany—well, put it this way: I'm still brewing the German lager beers from 1985. What's different between our beers here in general is that they're all probably a little bit stronger,

a little bit darker, whereas in Germany they have gotten a lot lighter." Even in Bavaria, where there are practices dating back to guild law and rules that date to *Reinheitsgebot*, change is a constant. The 1970s, when Jürgen Knöller was running hot wort into a cool ship, were not that far removed from today, yet the production methods have changed dramatically and the beers have changed a bit, too. Sometimes, it's easier to see the shift through the eyes of an expat. ∎

EVOLUTION

ALTHOUGH THEY ARE considered a special brew, only one in a hundred beers brewed in Germany is a bock. The style never had a moment, like dunkel lager and export, when it was a national leader. That element of specialness seems to both preserve and limit it in its home country. When German immigrants began populating foreign lands, they took their bocks with them. That was certainly true of the United States. Bocks have been brewed continuously since Germans arrived, and they were one of

the few styles to survive Prohibition and consolidation. That familiarity seems to have limited their currency in the new wave of craft brewing.

If there is a bit of new movement, it's happening where breweries are attempting freeze-distillation in search of superstrong beer. The absolute numbers of these kinds of beers are quite small, but the attention they receive is inversely proportional. Samuel Adams kicked off the trend and has been releasing a beer called Utopias every two years for more than a decade. Breweries in Scotland, Belgium, Italy, and Germany have tried their hands, making perhaps three dozen beers north of 20% ABV over the years. Breweries begin with all manner of base beers before they distill, so it's difficult to think of this as a style. Moreover, the effort required to freeze and refreeze and refreeze the beers means they'll never be much of a commercial venture. But as publicity goes, they seem to have a fair amount of life left. ■

THE BEERS TO KNOW

BOCKS ARE ONE of the most famous styles, especially to the layman, but they are brewed at best sporadically in the United States. Places rich with German heritage, like Wisconsin and Pennsylvania, have the most reliable offerings. Doppelbocks, with cross-genre appeal, are slightly easier to find.

SPRECHER MAI BOCK

ooooooooooooooooooooooooooooooooooooooooo

LOCATION: Milwaukee, WI

MALT: Pale, caramel, wheat

HOPS: Mt. Hood, Tettnanger, Willamette

6% ABV, 1.061 SP. GR., 24 IBU

A honey-colored beer that also has a touch of honey in the nose, along with fresh-baked bread and caramel. The brewery dry-hops the beer. That, combined with the slightly low gravity, takes it outside the strict guidelines for the style—but it's an inspired choice, giving the beer a freshly floral scent that accentuates the otherwise herbal character that comes from kettle hops.

EINBECKER MAI-UR-BOCK

ooooooooooooooooooooooooooooooooooooooooo

LOCATION: Einbeck, Germany

MALT: Munich

HOPS: Hallertauer, Hersbrucker, Perle

6.5% ABV, 1.065 SP. GR., 32 IBU

Distilling a Stronger Beer. As I write this, the current record holder for strongest distilled beer is a small brewery in Scotland called Brewmeister, which made 65% ABV Armageddon in 2012. The trouble is that a single freeze only adds a few points of alcohol. To get to these extraordinary heights, a brewery has to refreeze the beer over and over again. For a time, the German brewery Schorschbräu held the record. Brewer Georg Tscheuschner explained why it is so hard: "To create the 43% beer, I had to filter around fifteen times. I actually lost count, but I think it was fifteen times. You end up with only fifty liters from the 800 to 1,000 liters that you started with." Since he broke the record in 2010, it has been broken a couple more times since, and some brewery will no doubt pass Armageddon. There is a physical limit, though (70%? 75%?), and once breweries reach it, the fad ought to lose steam.

Einbecker dates back to 1749, when the city combined brewing rights to create a single brewery. Mai-Ur-Bock, released each March, isn't actually the first mai-bock—"bocks" may have originally come from Einbeck, but not lovely, toffee-rich confections like this lager. It's a reimport from Munich, but a worthy member of the canon.

PENNSYLVANIA ST. NIKOLAUS BOCK

LOCATION: Pittsburgh, PA

MALT: Pale, Munich, chocolate, dextrin, caramel, black

HOPS: Perle

6.5% ABV, 1.061 SP. GR., 25 IBU

One of the rarer dunkel bocks, Penn's is brewed in the Bamberg tradition of warming up cold fall evenings. The malts create a wonderful play of blackened toast, nuts, and cinnamon, and it finishes with a dollop of toffee.

VICTORY ST. BOISTEROUS

LOCATION: Downington, PA

MALT: Pale

HOPS: Tettnanger, Saphir

7.5% ABV

Perhaps the name's ironic—there's nothing boisterous about Victory's quietly powerful pale bock. The flavors are all turned to "subtle"—silky malts that have touches of bread and a gentle, floral scent that has a note of citrus. The alcohol warms but does not impose.

AYINGER CELEBRATOR DOPPELBOCK

LOCATION: Aying, Germany

MALT: Undisclosed

HOPS: Undisclosed

6.0% ABV, 1.055 SP. GR., 24 IBU

Celebrator impresses even before bringing a nose or tongue into play. Pellucid despite its dark color, Celebrator has a scent of raisin and molasses—warming, comforting smells. They open up in the mouth so that the darker flavors, molasses and roast, are center stage, yet are limned in sweet toffee. I find the plumminess of aged beer in Celebrator, which makes it seem rare and special.

BAYERN DOPPELBOCK

LOCATION: Missoula, MT

MALT: Undisclosed

HOPS: Saaz, Hallertauer, Perle

8.1% ABV, 1.080 SP. GR., 23 IBU

Bayern hides the alcohol as well in this beer as in any brewed, and it does it in satiny folds of malt. The flavors begin sweetly, something like chocolate fig, and then deepen through toast and nut to something almost like rye. Rich but refined, and dangerously drinkable.

CAPITAL AUTUMNAL FIRE

LOCATION: Madison, WI

MALT: Pale, Munich, honey

HOPS: Hallertauer Mittelfrüh

7.8% ABV, 1.081 SP. GR., 30 IBU

The name must have been inspired by the color, which smolders sunset-orange—lighter than most doppelbocks. The overall presentation actually recalls a märzen—lovely bready flavors balanced by very fresh, peppery hops. (I can't imagine how many pounds of Mittelfrüh, a low-alpha strain, would be necessary.) With warmth, honey notes emerge.

SCHLOSS EGGENBERG SAMICHLAUS

LOCATION: Eggenberg, Austria

MALT: Undisclosed

HOPS: Undisclosed

14% ABV

Samichlaus is something of an acquired taste. At first contact, you might mistake it for pancake syrup. Too strong to have much in the way of effervescence, it is a viscous, sweet beer that gets most of its balance from the warmth of alcohol. A veritable catalog of malt flavors if you can brace yourself and withstand the intensity.

Ayinger

A BAVARIAN BREWERY EVOLVES

THE VILLAGE OF AYING IS JUST FAR ENOUGH SOUTH OF MUNICH TO BE NESTLED AMID A GREEN CARPET OF FARMLAND. IF YOU'RE NOT PAYING ATTENTION, YOU CAN SAIL RIGHT PAST THE NEW AYINGER FACILITY AND DROP INTO THE TOWN PROPER, AS I DID ON A MISTY AFTERNOON IN OCTOBER. THE OLD BREWERY IS STILL IN ITS ORIGINAL LOCATION—OR THE SHELL OF IT IS, ANYWAY—AND STANDING IN FRONT OF IT IS THE 350-YEAR-OLD ONION-DOMED ST. ANDREAS CHURCH MADE FAMOUS ON AYINGER'S LABELS. THE SCENE ON THE LABEL IS BUCOLIC AND NOSTALGIC, BUT THE REAL THING, ESPECIALLY SEEING IT SHROUDED IN FOG, SEEMED WEIGHTIER, MORE HISTORIC.

This was where they began brewing in 1878 and continued for 120 years. The brewery managed to weather two wars, changes in family leadership, and competition from the big breweries up the road in Munich. Following German reunification, the Inselkammer family looked at their aging brewery and realized they had to make a decision—reinvest in new equipment or close up shop. It was no small financial commitment; once the family voted to spend the money, they ultimately put up 21 million marks to

LEFT: *The iconic spire of Saint Andreas, which also adorns Ayinger's labels*

LEFT: *Ayinger flourished under Johann Liebhard's leadership in the late nineteenth century.*

BELOW: *The new brewery, built like a lodge, was designed with hospitality in mind.*

FACING PAGE: *The traditional Weissbier open fermenters are separated from the rest of the brewery.*

build the new facility just west of the old brewery. I finally found the new place after a local Ayinger told me that I passed it coming into town.

By Bavarian standards, where age is measured in centuries, Ayinger is only entering a feisty adolescence. With an annual production of just 85,000 barrels of beer, it's also a lot smaller than titans like Spaten and Paulaner. But youth, small size, and family owner-ship—combined with a recent near-death experience—infuse Ayinger with a kind of daring that is rare in German breweries. Still, Ayinger also has a streak of tradi-tionalism that can seem almost quaint. So on the one hand, the Inselkammers have built one of the most modern brewer-ies in the world, outfitted with advanced energy-conserving green technology. On the other hand, they have erected a special glassed-in cube to protect the process of traditional open fermenta-tion for their wheat beers. It's unusual

for German breweries to sell so many different brands, but Ayinger has twelve regular-rotation beers. All of them are in the lineage of Bavarian styles, and the Inselkammers only use local ingredients: hops from Hallertau and a source near Nuremberg, malt from Regensburg and Bamberg. They even dug a 577-foot well to tap into pure mineral water below the brewery.

The most striking change was their decision to abandon decoction brew-ing. Decoction is no longer the standard in German brewing, though it's not

uncommon in Bavaria. But more to the point—the brewery made the decision *after* it had already installed the new brewhouse. There's the mash cooker, big as day, but the brewery decided it wasn't adding anything to the beer except time and BTUs, so they switched to temperature-controlled mashing.

By skipping the slow decoction process, Ayinger manages to speed six 150-hectoliter batches through the brewery each day at the height of the summer season. The system is fairly typical, although the wort is boiled under pressure. Afterward, the deep-well water cools the wort, warming in the process before being used in the next batch. The wheat beers go to the glass cube, where they're pitched with an ale strain so hardy Ayinger can harvest and repitch for up to three years. The lager yeast is a strain new to the brewery, and they reuse that, too, but only up to seven or eight generations (typical for lagers). No beer spends less than a month lagering, and some spend four in the conditioning tanks—though Ayinger conditions their beer warmer than some breweries, at around 45°F.

It suggests a company that is committed to the traditional flavors of Bavarian beer, but using only those methods the Inselkammers believe are necessary to produce them. You can't argue with the results. From top to bottom, there is no brewery that produces better and more consistent beer than Ayinger—including a märzen, dunkel, export lager, hefeweizen, dunkelweizen, maibock, and doppelbock that are all considered standards for their style.

If you look at the ratings sites or read beer reviews, you know that Ayinger's weizen line—hefe, dunkel, and bock—are beloved, as is their maibock. But the brewery's crown jewel is the doppelbock, Celebrator. It goes back far enough that the family isn't sure when it was first brewed. Franz Inselkammer Jr. assumes it goes back to the brewery's founding. "The recipe has never been changed, at least as long as we know, but the name changed in the early 1980s from 'St. Andreas Bock' to 'Celebrator.'" An American importer helped with the name change, but the formulation and process—which Inselkammer is reluctant to divulge—are wonderfully Bavarian. Celebrator serves as a good metaphor for the brewery as well. It's on the low edge for strength, different from most others. Ayinger was happy to change the name (though for those who have seen the namesake church, "St. Andreas" might have had special meaning) but not touch the recipe. It may be different from beers made elsewhere, but that doesn't bother anyone, either. You don't have to be the same to be traditional.

Mass-Market LAGERS

Nearly every beer made in the world today is a pale, effervescent lager. All of the other styles together amount to barely more than a rounding error in terms of total volume. Among connoisseurs of beer, an icy can of lager is the ultimate object of contempt, and there is some justification for this. In the past century, beer companies have been happy to debase the pilsner style by stripping away flavor, replacing quality malt with cheap sources of fermentable sugar, even stuffing them with additives, flavorings, and colorings. Breweries should be ashamed of some of the products they've put out to market.

Mass-Market Lagers.

Some people like to divide the categories of mass-market lagers into separate camps, usually placing American versions in a style ghetto called "adjunct lagers," but they all have a great deal in common. The focus is on quenching thirst, and whether it's a dry Japanese beer, a sweeter American beer, or a firmer European beer, the divergence isn't enough for the average drinker to debate. These beers are best served icy cold to protect the crispness, and they are more than serviceable when called to quiet the fires of hot wings or chile peppers.

STATISTICS

ABV range: 4–5%

Bitterness: 5–20 IBU

Serving temperature: 35°–38°F

Vessel: Pilsner glass

But there is another side. The people can't be wrong all the time; there's a reason people drink gallons of this sparkling liquid. It refreshes and it quenches. Mass-market lagers— the Budweisers, Heinekens, Pacificos, and Sapporos of the world—are simple beers with lots of effervescence and a kiss of sweetness. Even drinkers who love IPAs may hanker for a cold one on a hot day. These mainstream brews have less flavor than most styles, but that's by design, not mistake. Breweries like Anheuser-Busch care as much about the consistent quality of their beer as any brewery on earth because they have millions of fans who want their Bud to taste exactly like a Bud. ■

ORIGINS

THE STORY OF how mass-market beer came to be is much like the stories of mass-market everything: The industrial revolution made it possible to produce beer on a giant scale, and this led to mass marketing and mass distribution and the practices of standardization and preservation. In this way, beer isn't much different from meat or bread or cheese. The development of mass markets make it possible to manufacture and distribute a product cheaply, putting it in front of the largest number of people possible. Tailoring products for huge populations, in beer as much as in other product categories, necessarily means appealing to the center of the bell curve, where most people's tastes congregate. When made to serve the median palate, a product loses its thorns and idiosyncrasies and becomes a more generic, blander version of itself. More or less, that was the story of twentieth-century beer.

The numbers tell a part of the story. Thanks in part to Prohibition, the U.S. offers the starkest example. In 1950, after breweries had had 17 years to recover, the four largest American brewing companies (Schlitz, Anheuser-Busch, Ballantine, and Pabst) produced a hair more than 20 percent of the country's beer. By 2000, the four largest (Anheuser-Busch, Miller, Coors, and Pabst) made 95 percent of it—and all of that production comprised mass-market lagers.

But it's perhaps even more telling to see what happened in Germany over the same period. Germany is considered a diversity success story in which the total number of breweries never declined below 1,234. Yet production shifted dramatically to serve mass markets there, too. In 1958, the four largest German breweries made just 12 percent of the beer. By 2000, it was half, a number that jumps to two-thirds if you expand the group to include the top eight producers. In Germany, these are very different markets, and Germany's largest beer company makes Jever and Radeberger, classic pilsners. The point is, even in the most diverse country, mass-market beers are the norm.

This phenomenon repeats itself in country after country. It's fun to play a game where you think of a country and try to name the big national beer brand. The Netherlands? A softball: Heineken.

Skunk Alert. **Although it's been mentioned elsewhere, here's a reminder: Beer should *never* smell or taste like skunk. It is an article of faith among European brewers that people will only buy beer from green bottles, but these are vulnerable to a chemical change that happens when light interacts with a hop compound. At least half the green-bottle imports I've purchased have been skunked, and I now have a hard rule against buying them. Perhaps an educated populace unwilling to buy the beer will compel companies to switch to brown bottles or cans.**

Denmark? Seems tougher, but give it a second and you remember Carlsberg. Australia? That famous television ad springs to mind—Foster's. It's true even in countries where you might not expect national brands, like Turkey (Efes), Thailand (Singha), or Kenya (Tusker). Labatt, Tsingtao, Stella Artois, Panama, Brahma, Kingfisher—the list goes on and on.

The process of consolidation doesn't always lead to identical beers across all nations. In the nineteenth century, American brewers softened the roughness of local six-row barley with corn and rice in their grists, an indigenous twist that led to national brands using corn and rice—even when they'd long abandoned six-row barley. In a similar story, Indian beer was for a long period made from inferior barley—high-moisture, variable kernel size, coarse—largely grown as livestock feed. It was also cut with rice, but since it still wasn't very good, breweries made it strong to get the job done more quickly. Japanese beer developed in a different set of circumstances that included cultural expectation. People appreciated a more austere product with the quality of *kire*—literally "cutting," meaning sharp and refreshing. So Asahi developed a very dry beer made crisp by rice that transformed the market. Japanese beers are consequently extremely crisp.

But while Coors, Beck's, and Foster's aren't identical, they have a great deal in common. This is another effect of the mass market—the beer is made to travel well. As the twentieth century rolled along, traditional styles vanished or became marginalized, supplanted by a ubiquitous yellow lager that can be found in every country where beer is legal. ∎

DESCRIPTION AND CHARACTERISTICS

MASS-MARKET LAGERS descended from pilsners, which they still resemble. Both are translucent golden and sparkling, topped with frosty white heads. Very often, people don't even know enough to distinguish them. Yet the distance between Pilsner Urquell and Budweiser is not incidental. Pilsners are full-bodied and hoppy (if not always bitter). They may be rich but are not sweet, and the malts have articulation and definition: grain-y, bready, toasty. Mass-market lagers aren't as intense and are rarely anywhere near as hoppy. One could leap to the conclusion that they're more like helles lagers then. Well, no, that's not quite right, either.

It's not that mass-market lagers have less flavor than other styles. Rather, it's that the flavors are more processed and harder to distinguish. Sugary sweetness is a hallmark of mass-market food—manufacturers load products full of the stuff to make it more beguiling. The public embrace of sodas increased their expectations of sweetness, and now products like tomato sauce, salad dressing, and coffee drinks have teaspoons upon teaspoons of sugar. Over the twentieth century, beers also got sweeter while at the same time bitterness units slowly eroded. The standard supermarket beer bears the mark of that decline in the form of a generic dulcitude of a kind that is so common in foods. It doesn't have the specificity of the malt flavors found in pilsners, in which you can taste the type of grain used and the way it was kilned. Beyond their sugary flavor, mass-market lagers are heavily carbonated (which has led to a popular view that beer is "gassy") and lack much hop character. It is usually very difficult to get a bead on the nature of the hop type, beyond a sense of its minor contribution to bitterness. Finally, these beers are built on a lean chassis to make them both less filling and less caloric.

Not every mass-market lager is the same, of course, and in a lineup one begins to notice certain differences. Some are fuller, others more watery; some are sweeter, others drier; some have a discernible corn flavor, and some have little more flavor than a glass of club soda. Following are three different types of mass-market lagers and their characteristics.

CORN- AND RICE-ADDED BEERS

Back in the 1870s, Americans led by Adolphus Busch began to cut their beers with rice and corn in an effort to temper the huskiness of native six-row barley. American barley left unsightly proteins floating in the beer, making it unsuitable for golden lagers. That evolution led to an indigenous variety of beer that has long outlasted the constraints of American barley: Most American lagers have, for more than a century, used corn or rice as a part of the grist. Their ability to lighten beer's body without adding a lot of flavor have made them popular worldwide. Rice

"Cheap" Adjuncts. To many drinkers, corn and rice are "cheap fillers" that breweries use to slice precious pennies off the cost of a barrel of beer. We have to score that claim "mostly false." When breweries first started using them, these grains were more expensive than barley. Even now, commodity prices bounce up and down, and rice is more expensive than barley; corn, which might have been cheaper a decade ago, has trebled in price since 2000. The flavors of these grains help define a beer's taste, and breweries are more interested in maintaining a consistent flavor profile than using the cheapest grains at a given time.

is converted cleanly into alcohol and dries a beer—critical for the palate of Japanese beers. Corn also lightens the beer, but adds its own flavor that helps define American lagers like Miller and Coors.

ALL-MALT BEERS

Some mass-market lagers are made exclusively with barley malt. This is especially true of German lagers, which follow *Reinheitsgebot* and use only barley. All-malt beers are a bit fuller and may have more distinctive malt flavor—though not always. In the realm of mass-market lagers, this is a fairly rare type.

LIGHT BEERS

In this category of beers, the "light" refers to body and indicates a low-calorie beer. In the 1960s, Joseph Owades, working at the Rheingold Breweries in Brooklyn, discovered an enzyme that helped yeast consume starch. The resulting beer, which had fewer carbohydrates, was lower in calories. Rheingold released a product called Gablinger's Diet Beer in the late 1960s based on Owades's research. In 1975, Miller released its own light beer, and that was the one—propelled by the memorable "tastes great, less filling" ads—that launched the trend. It was slow to develop, but light beer eventually took over the American market and now three of the four bestselling beers are Bud Light, Coors Light, and Miller Lite. In 2013, regular Budweiser nipped in front of Miller Lite to retake third place.

With almost no body and a tiny wash of malt flavor, light beers have even less flavor than regular mass-market lagers. Hopping is generally below the threshold of flavor. The beers are low alcohol (the big three are all 4.2%), highly carbonated, and inevitably described as "crisp," an accurate enough description; there's little else to say. Light beer is made to be drunk ice-cold, fast, and with as little attention as possible. ■

What about "Dry," "Ice" & "Triple Hops Brewed"?

Beer companies have always polished the apple. They boast of "finest ingredients" or "Rocky Mountain spring water." Sometimes these are more than slogans. "Ice" refers to the process of freezing the beer and removing water to make slightly stronger beer like Icehouse and Molson Ice. Other times the claim is a hazy blend of marketing gloss and real technique, like "dry" beer, which can refer to highly attenuated beer or to nothing at all. Then there are the completely meaningless slogans like "triple hops brewed" in which standard brewing practices are hyped as something extraordinary.

My lovely and insightful wife, while watching a commercial for Miller Lite in a "vortex bottle," coined an extremely handy axiom I've come to think of as Sally's Rule: Never buy it if the brewery is trying to sell you packaging instead of beer. Cans in the shape of bow ties, cans that tell you the temperature of your beer, cans shaped like kegs—it's amazing how often I have to invoke her rule.

BREWING NOTES

WASN'T really sure what to expect when I arrived at the Anheuser-Busch brewery in St. Louis. This is a company that sells so much beer it needs twelve breweries across the country to fill the orders. The St. Louis flagship is the country's second-largest brewery and produces more beer in a year than all the craft breweries in the country combined. My mind conjured images of mash tuns as big as warehouses, fermenters the size of oil tankers, all in industrial tones of cement and steel.

ABOVE: *Brewmaster Jim Bicklein at Anheuser-Busch brewery, St. Louis*

I was being naïve. In fact, the St. Louis facility is probably the most beautiful brewery I've ever seen. Built right around the turn of the twentieth century, it was originally a classic gravity-fed system, five stories tall, lit by a soaring atrium and a central column of open space that reaches from top to bottom (an early communications system). Chandeliers crafted for the 1904 St. Louis World's Fair curl and twine down long chains in the shape of hop vines. Column finials are detailed with golden leaves and fleur-de-lis, and wrought iron railings, painted crisp white, protect you from stepping out into the open shaft of light.

The operation is vast—mashing happens in one building, lautering in another—but all the pieces are human sized. In terms of scale, it looks like many other much smaller breweries. The way Anheuser-Busch pushes 15 million barrels of beer through this plant every year is not by using titanic equipment, but by choreographing a dance with an intricate matrix of many vessels all working at once. "There are three brewhouses, six of these mash vessels per brewhouse," brewmaster Jim Bicklein explains. By brewhouse, he doesn't mean separate facilities—they're all incorporated into the main brewery. "So I have eighteen mash vessels, and each brewhouse has two lauter tubs, so we have six lauter tubs and six brew kettles." Bicklein schedules fifty to sixty batches every day.

The brewing process is itself completely (and disappointingly) ordinary. Budweiser uses a grist similar to the original beer Adolphus Busch introduced in the 1870s: a blend of two-row and six-row barley and 35 percent rice. The rice is prepared in separate cookers—an arrangement also typical in Belgium—and then fed to the barley mash. Budweiser

High-Gravity Brewing.

The idea behind high-gravity brewing is simple enough: Breweries make a concentrated wort and then water it down before packaging. The practice is fairly widespread among larger breweries, since it saves money and tank space by reducing the volume of beer working its way through a brewery. (Anheuser-Busch doesn't use it for Budweiser or Bud Light, but does for some of their other brands.) Breweries begin with worts that will result in a finished beer of 6% to 8%. Because yeast behaves differently in denser worts, they have to be careful that these stronger beers don't change the profile of the final beer once it has been diluted back down to its appropriate gravity.

uses pellet hops rather than extracts, with an addition at the start and end of the boil. Fermentation is also pretty typical, although "this is when we do get big," Bicklein told me as we stepped into a room with rows of 6,000-barrel fermenters. The yeast is original and only the St. Louis brewery propagates it—that way they can be sure the strains aren't morphing over time. Each day, kegs full of fresh yeast go out on trucks or in airplanes for delivery all over the globe. Budweiser ferments at 52°F for five days and then goes for three weeks to condition—though at the fairly warm temperature of around 50°F.

Of course, it is possible to use more efficient processes to produce huge quantities of beer. Many breweries employ high-gravity brewing or use mash filters (or both). They also save money by shaving days off lagering time. Some of these techniques affect the beer, some don't. But it's important to clarify a point many people misunderstand: Beer is beer. That mass-market lagers are lighter and blander than craft-brewed IPAs is not a function of the brewery design or brewing techniques—it's an intentional decision to make beer that way. It also doesn't mean a brewery doesn't take its

beer incredibly seriously.

Indeed, the thing that charmed me the most about visiting St. Louis was arriving at the beechwood tanks. Spiral strips of beechwood, completely sterilized and stripped of their flavor, are used ostensibly to collect yeast so that circulating beer has more opportunity to be in contact with it. The idea is that it will reduce diacetyl and other off-flavors while the beer slowly conditions. But in a modern brewery, it's a technical antiquity. The microbiologists and chemists at Anheuser-Busch know how to make beer and are certainly competent to address these issues without this old-timey method. But Budweiser has always used beechwood chips, and like breweries that stick with copper kettles and grants, they do it for reasons that can't be explained by chemistry alone. I pressed Bicklein on it, and he said, "We can argue whether it does or it doesn't [affect the flavor profile], but it's something we're not willing to change. It's part of the heritage of Budweiser."

People will decide whether they think beers like Budweiser, Miller, and Coors are great accomplishments in the art of brewing. Those will always be subjective judgments. But breweries like Anheuser-Busch live and breathe beer no less than the Dogfish Heads, Rodenbachs, and Schlenkerlas. They make very different products, but they make it the same way everyone else does—by mashing it, boiling it, and fermenting it. Just, you know, in somewhat larger volumes. ∎

EVOLUTION

ECONOMIST Lisa M. George makes a persuasive case that the shrinking of the planet helped speed the demise of local breweries as national TV advertising appeared at midcentury. According to her analysis, television and the nationalization of beer markets accounted for about a quarter of the decline in local breweries, and trimmed nearly a third of their production.

What effect, then, might the atomization of media in the twenty-first century have on tastes and trends? Craft brewing accounts for more than 10 percent of the total beer market (in dollars) in the United States, and is growing at double-digit rates each year. Meanwhile, demand for the most popular mass-market lagers slips a point or two each year. The United States is on the leading edge of this trend, but it's happening around the world as well. Thirty years ago, the idea of "mass market" was well understood and stable. It is nowhere near as certain what the center of the mass market will look like thirty years from now. Over the course of the twentieth century, beers got lighter and less hoppy. It's possible that this trend could reverse itself and to compete, the large lager breweries will make fuller-bodied, hoppier beers. It's at least conceivable that lagers may lose out to ales eventually. Probably not burly imperial red ales, but pale and wheat ales have found large enough markets that it's possible to envision an ale-dominated future in the U.S.

One thing that does now seem inconceivable is a return to the dominance and consolidation of the 1970s. The big international breweries recognize this and are addressing it by introducing mass-market ales (MillerCoors and the Blue Moon line), purchasing craft breweries (Anheuser-Busch InBev and Goose Island), and product development (Anheuser-Busch and Black Crown).

RIGHT: *Budweiser's signature beechwood chips await in a tank.*

Meanwhile, the "microbreweries" aren't going to remain micro for long. Larger ale companies like Sierra Nevada and New Belgium are following Budweiser's lead and opening up new breweries to increase capacity and improve quality on East Coast shipments. It seems certain that the future will consist of a much more heterogeneous beer landscape marked by more choice and the growth of craft breweries. That will in turn affect the mass market—probably in unforeseen ways. The safest prediction about what will happen? Wait and see. ■

THE BEERS TO KNOW

O NCE UPON A time, partisans would gamely fight over which of the mass-market lagers tasted the best; later, weary beer geeks would dismiss the lot, declaring there wasn't a dime's worth of difference between them. Neither is quite right. As a group, these lagers have more similarities than most styles. In blind tastings, they regularly fool drinkers who think they know how to distinguish among them. But if you step back and consider them region by region it's easier to see their contours. Even in the realm of mass-market lagers, culture exerts an influence: Germany sticks with *Reinheitsgebot*-compliant lagers that are more full-flavored, while Japan goes the opposite direction, drying their beers out with rice. It may not be easy to distinguish a Bud Light from a Coors Light, but Bud from Beck's and Beck's from Foster's—much easier. Below are the regional differences and notes on the major brands.

■ **United States.** Americans were the pioneers of cereal grains, and you can taste the difference if you try **Miller Genuine Draft,** which when cold has a riesling-like crispness, but warms into its corn palate. **Coors** also has a corn note, but it is crisper and more neutral. **Budweiser** is made with rice and the sweetness comes from a combination of low hop bitterness and a touch of ester from comparatively warm conditioning.

■ **Mexico.** Hot-weather countries are ideal for light lagers, which don't dehydrate the drinker as fast. Mexican beers, like those made to the north, often have an undercurrent of corn. **Pacifico** is medium bodied and toasty, but slightly sweet and moreish. **Modelo**

Especial is smooth and clean and has the suggestion of hops. **Dos Equis** is crisp but fades like mineral water on the palate.

■ **Germany.** As a contrast, German lagers are all made with 100 percent barley malt. They are fuller and usually a little less gassy. **Warsteiner** has a soft, grain-y malt base and a sprinkle of peppery hops. **Beck's** is heavier and quite hoppy in comparison to American standards. **Spaten,** the lightest and fizziest, shows how close to the American model a brewery can get without resorting to rice or corn.

■ **Europe.** Expectations vary widely across Europe, and it's interesting to see how different the beers can be. **Carlsberg**

(Denmark), one of the most famous names in the world, is sweet, corny, and watery. **Stella Artois** (Belgium), which markets itself as the sophisticated lager, is clean and crisp like a club soda, but low on actual beer flavors. **Heineken** (the Netherlands), by contrast, is full of flavor, with the dial turned up on sweetness, hoppiness, and body. Of the European lagers, though, **Peroni** (Italy) may well be the overlooked gem; it has rich, bready malts and pronounced herbal-to-spicy hops. You might even mistake it for a German pilsner.

■ **Australasia.** Down under, they make comparatively robust beers. **Foster's** is a full, slightly sweet beer with rich, toasty malts that give it excellent moreishness. In a similar vein New Zealand's **Steinlager** has a fairly full middle and a dry finish, all in a beer with a healthy dose of lemony hops.

■ **Japan.** The 1980s "dry wars" shaped the character of Japanese lagers, which are incredibly crisp and, yes, dry. **Sapporo** is the driest, with just a touch of toast and lychee. **Kirin** is fuller and more tropical with honey malts and a floral, gardenia-like nose. **Asahi**, which kicked off the race for drier beer, has taken things so far their beer now has very little flavor left. ■

Lesser-Known LAGERS

Lager brewing is a relative latecomer in beer evolution, so it contains a smaller warehouse of forgotten traditions and styles—but there are a few. If you travel to the northern fringes of Bavaria, you'll find yourself in a rural area known as Franconia. The city of Bamberg is its spiritual center, a place where breweries make cellar beer (kellerbier), "unbunged" beer (*ungespundet*), and smoked beer (rauchbier). Up in the hills of Franconia, you find unfiltered, rustic lagers, sometimes made in old, rustic

breweries. If you drive east until you approach the Czech Republic, you'll find another lost tradition, communal brewhouses—also ancient—known as *zoigls*. They are essentially active museums of lager brewing. Further south and into neighboring Austria, different farmers used a strange technique of heating stones to boil their wort. This was the birthplace of lagers, so it makes sense that the greatest lode of lost treasure remains there. But there are others, too, some hiding in plain sight right here in America. ∎

UNFILTERED, UNBUNGED, AND CELLARED BEER

THE TYPICAL LAGER is bright and limpid, sparkling in the light as tiny jewels bubble to the surface. One of the central benefits of lagering a beer for weeks at icy temperatures is to precipitate out any haze-causing solids. Most commercial lagers are also filtered, further enhancing their clarity. In parts of Germany and the Czech Republic, however, people enjoy more rustic unfiltered lagers.

In Franconia, the language is specific. "Kellerbier" is the general category of rustic lagers, and it means the beers were aged in a cellar. Cellars keep beers cool, but not frigid, and particles are more likely to stay in suspension. Breweries may also call this beer unfiltered and unpasteurized. (All beers served on tap at little Franconian breweries are likely to be unpasteurized.) There's another, slightly different category of beer called *ungespundet*, which refers to the way the cellared beer was handled. In the romantic days of old, brewers would go down to the cellars and remove the wooden cask's stopper (*spund*) to let the gas escape. The idea was to create a beer with lower carbonation, one that was softer and more gentle to the palate. To prevent spoilage during the period of off-gassing, breweries hopped these kellerbiers more stoutly.

FACING PAGE: *The city of Bamberg—last bastion of rauchbier brewing—sits on the river Regnitz.*

ABOVE: *Mahr's Ungespundet, which the locals call "Ooo," is cloudier than the regular helles.*

Now most lagers, even in Franconia, are aged in steel, but ungespundet beers do have lower levels of carbonation and a more lively amount of hopping. Often they are served directly from the keg *bayrischer anstich*, which means tapped and poured with gravity. Served in this manner, they bear a close resemblance to British cask ales.

These types of beers are becoming more common across the border in the Czech Republic as well. *Nefiltrované pivo* is unfiltered lager, and it's become quite popular. Because many Czech breweries are equipped with refrigeration, nefiltrované *pivo* may be just slightly hazy, though some shimmer a beautiful gold, the color of a Klimt painting. A related beer is known as *kvasnicové*, a lager that gets its cloudiness from yeast added just before packaging.

Cold lagering and filtering do make a beer more gorgeous—that's why so many breweries do them. But they also remove particles that contain aromas and flavors. These may stale bottled beer more quickly, but they also make fresh beer more flavorful and aromatic. Few experiences were more memorable to me than drinking a fresh stein of Mahr's famous Ungespundet in Bamberg or a glass of Únětická 12° near Prague. ■

RAUCHBIER

WHY DO SOME old beers hang on long after they've gone extinct everywhere else? Look at the people drinking them. On my second evening in Bamberg, a clear, warm October night, I happened into Spezial, one of two remaining rauchbier (pronounced *Rowk-beer*) breweries on the planet—the other is crosstown rival Schlenkerla—and it was packed. I spied a few open spaces across the room and worked my way through the crowd, only to find them marked with "Reserved" placards. It wasn't quite seven yet, and the seats of the regulars were waiting for them until then, no matter if it meant Spezial was losing money in the bargain. I crouched by the bar until the clock rang seven and took a seat.

Another explanation was given to me by Matthias Trum, Schlenkerla's sixth-generation owner. He told me how his regulars were the keepers of the rauchbier tradition. "They also defend us against tourists who say, 'Ah, this is terrible—I want a pilsner.' They say, 'If you want a pilsner you have to go elsewhere—we don't have it here.'" He told the story of a scene he witnessed where a tourist had one taste of Schlenkerla and asked for water instead. "The guy at the table next door said, 'How many did you have?'

"'It was my first one,'" Trum said, imitating the tourist.

"'No, you don't get anything else. You empty that first and then we can talk.' He drank it all and then he drank a second." The moral to the story: So long as Bambergers cherish their funny old rauchbier, Bambergers will have rauchbier to cherish.

If you want to experience the taste of

ABOVE: *Matthias Trum demonstrating the wood-fired kiln at Schlenkerla*

beer from several centuries ago, rauchbier is a good place to start. It was for a very long time common for malt to be kilned over flame, a process that infused it with smoke. Malt makers used a variety of sources of fuel, but wood was one of the most common. In Bamberg, Spezial and Schlenkerla continue to make malt this way, smoking it over beechwood. It's not easy to smoke malt—the flavors can easily be too harsh or scorched to be palatable. The breweries guard their secrets, but Schlenkerla's Trum described it in general terms to me: "It depends on the time of the process. [The kiln] starts low and goes up to around 100°C [212°F]. We control very exactly how much wood we put in at what time because we want to have a certain temperature curve for the entire process. It's quite tricky to do it the right way."

Spezial's standard rauchbier is a golden-amber–colored lager with mild smokiness, while Schlenkerla's, a brown beauty the brewery calls a märzen, is much maltier and smokier. A first-timer's encounter with a rauchbier is usually rocky—in Bamberg they say you need three *seidlas* (mugs) to attune your palate to the intensity of the flavor. Part of the problem is that when your brain tastes the smoke, it often confuses it with meat because the flavor is reminiscent of smoke that has suffused familiar meats. This very often leads us to label rauchbier "hammy." (Alaskan Brewing roasts malt over alder for its Smoked Porter, and people confuse it with salmon—which is typically smoked over that wood.) But like ambient noise in a tavern, the mind eventually shifts the flavor to the background. For the regular drinker, "the smokiness steps back in perception," Trum says, "and then the malty notes come out, the bitterness, the smoothness." He's right—Schlenkerla's rauchbier, so smoky at first blush, is in fact quite a rich, malty beer. The sweet notes are there, if you let them emerge.

Rauchbier isn't a style, but a practice. Both Spezial and Schlenkerla brew smoky beers in multiple styles. The *rauchmalt* contributes most of the grist to these beers, but may be supplemented by standard specialty malts for color. The smoke, like dust in a potter's studio, permeates the beer. Even though some beers, like the weizens and Schlenkerla Helles, don't use rauchmalt, they still have hints of smokiness in them. The reason? Yeast scrubs some of the smoke from the beer and carries it with it. When breweries repitch the yeast, it leaves a bit behind in the new beer. ∎

ZOIGL BREWING

ABOUT SIXTY MILES east of Bamberg is a region bordering the Czech Republic known as the Oberpfalz, and scattered across five towns there are the final remnants of communal brewing. It was once common across Europe. A community would collectively own brewing facilities where locals could make a batch of beer and take it home to ferment and ripen. In the mid-1800s, seventy-five towns still had communal breweries in the region, but that number has dwindled to just a handful. Known as *zoigls* (pronounced *Tzoy-guhls*), these old breweries are still used by townspeople, not professional brewers, and they serve the beer out of their homes. The word comes from the pronunciation in the local dialect of the word *zeichen* in German ("sign"), a reference to the six-pointed star brewers hung outside their homes to indicate they had beer available for sale.

The breweries are amazing artifacts from a far earlier time. They employ largely antiquated equipment of wood, iron, and copper—kits that could be moved wholesale straight into museums. They use cool ships and fire their kettles with wood. A brewer from the eighteenth century could easily step into one of these brewhouses and fire up a batch of beer. The brewers make lagers, usually cloudy and golden, but the equipment is so imprecise that batch-to-batch variation is a given. These are handmade beers, treated with care and intention—but they're nevertheless made by nonprofessionals. Some of the beer is reputed to reach a rustic perfection, but some of it is funkier, less refined, and sometimes outright flawed. With zoigl beer, the normal expectation is inverted: A customer expects variability. That's a big part of the charm.

There is much mystique to zoigl beer. Although pubs sometimes have a cask, the real hunt begins when intrepid beer drinkers head off into the villages in search of the six-pointed star hanging from the homes of private citizen brewers, a sign that zoigl beer is inside for the tasting. This is the experience most travelers hope for—stopping into a *zoigl stube* (pub) for a plate of cold meats and a tall mug of cloudy, hoppy, fresh homemade beer. There are a few places online to guide you—mostly in German—and a good place to start is the website zoiglbier.de. ■

STEAM, CREAM, AND CORN: OLD AMERICAN LAGERS

IN THE SECOND HALF of the nineteenth century, beer was really on the move. German immigrants were pouring into North America, dotting the towns of the Midwest and West with new, lager breweries. Pale lagers were streaming out of Bohemia and Austria across Europe. And in America, migrants were sweeping across the continent in search of better lives.

STEAM BEERS

One of the migrants' prime destinations was San Francisco, where they heard the waters ran with gold. In 1848, it was just a small hamlet by the bay, a community of fewer than a thousand souls. But by July of 1850, census workers counted almost 95,000 people—a seething, sweating mass of dreamers and drifters. Franconian entrepreneur Levi Strauss saw them as customers in need of a sturdy pair of pants, but many of his countrymen figured they could use a beer, too. By 1900, the breweries were in place—two

dozen at their peak—making a brew the locals called "steam beer." Taverns bulging with hardworking, thirsty men meant breweries didn't have the time to make proper lager. They brewed with lager malts, generally (though not always) in the German decoction method, but instead of fermenting cool and conditioning the beer for weeks, they pitched lager yeast at ale temperatures, let the wort finish fermenting in wide, shallow "clarifying tanks," and packaged it immediately, without any conditioning. The entire process took less than a week.

The origin of the name "steam beer" is obscure, but there are a couple of decent possibilities. Anchor Brewing, which has kept the style alive through the

Trademarking a Style. In 1981, at the dawn of the American brewing renaissance, Fritz Maytag made the momentous decision to trademark "steam beer." At the time, it was by no means clear which direction American microbrewers might go, and the most valuable name in beer was the one style Americans could claim as their own. Other breweries could brew beer in the same style, but they couldn't call them steam beers.

The decision had two practical effects. First, it gave the kingdom to Maytag. Steam beer remains a revered fragment of Americana, but other breweries have largely eschewed making "California common beer"—the awkward name that came to stand in for Anchor's trademarked style. To this day, few other breweries bother to make an example except as seasonal one-offs. The only style American brewers might have embraced as an indigenous expression is kept in trust by Anchor instead.

The second effect was limiting steam beer's market. Anchor is by far the largest producer of the style, but it doesn't make an especially large quantity of it in absolute terms—the brewery makes about as much beer as Summit Berewing and SweetWater Brewing. Other styles have long surpassed steam beer as American standards. Pale ales, IPAs, amber lagers, and wheat beers are far more prolific than steam beer, and breweries making category-defining examples (Sierra Nevada, Lagunitas, Boston Beer, and Bell's, respectively) sell more than Anchor does. Might steam beer have become a signature U.S. style without a trademark? Hard to say. But if it had, Anchor would have been in a position to reap rewards it hasn't in the last thirty-plus years.

decades, believes the name comes from rooftop cool ships that steamed as the wort cooled. Robert Wahl and Max Henius, writing in 1902 in their *American Handy-book of Brewing, Malting and Auxiliary Trades*, put forward this theory: "This beer is largely consumed throughout the state of California. It is called steam beer on account of its highly effervescing properties and the amount of pressure ('steam') it has in the packages." Whatever the name's origin, Wahl and Henius offer a description of what it might have tasted like: "light in color, hop aroma and bitter taste not very pronounced; very lively and not necessarily brilliant."

Steam beer's popularity suffered mightily with the arrival of refrigeration in the 1890s, which allowed breweries to make lagers even in warm places like San Francisco. It took a further hit with the 1906 earthquake and ensuing fires that destroyed much of the city. A bit more than a decade later, Prohibition came and finished whatever work the fires didn't. Following Prohibition, Anchor Brewing was the sole surviving purveyor of steam beer, and it limped along through more setbacks over the course of the next three decades; by 1965, facing bankruptcy, it planned to shut its doors.

That was when Fritz Maytag, who had a bit of his family's washing-machine money, stepped in and bought a controlling share of Anchor Brewing for $5,000. He didn't buy it outright until 1968, and he spent the intervening years learning the brewing art from colleagues like Bill Leinenkugel and studying Jean de Clerck's *Textbook of Brewing*. In 1969, he bought new equipment and, armed with his new understanding of beer, he

retooled the recipe for steam beer. Over the years, Anchor had succumbed to the same cost-saving shortcuts larger breweries had adopted, and Maytag scrapped them all. He went looking for inspiration in the old tradition of brewing steam beer.

Today Anchor makes steam beer in much the same way that breweries did decades ago. They use wide, open fermenters and a lager yeast strain. Wahl and Henius described the process of kräusening—adding fermenting wort to finished beer to carbonate—to achieve high levels of carbonation, and Anchor does that now, too. The recipe is simple, just pale and caramel malts and Northern Brewer hops, and that's likely how the old San Francisco brewers would have done it. Nothing fancy—just simple, easy beer.

CREAM ALES AND CORN BEERS

Doesn't "cream ale" sound lovely? Rich and smooth, silky in the mouth, perhaps fresh as a pint of organic half-and-half. That's what we think of *now*, with our modern knowledge of things like cream stouts and pale ales. But back in the nineteenth century, when cream ale was sometimes called—obscurely—"present use ale," it was a competitor with pale lagers. Far from heavy and rich, cream ales were actually light, bright, and effervescent. The "cream" was just a poetic touch—no actual cows were involved in the manufacture of cream ales. This was an early example of marketing gloss.

When you look through old sources like Wahl and Henius, one thing jumps out that is peculiarly American: corn. By the last decades of the nineteenth century, pale lagers had arrived in the

Kentucky Common Beer.

One of the most colorful lost styles of beer is a concoction that was made in and around Louisville, Kentucky. It was a strange brew that seems to have been influenced by local bourbon makers who used corn in their wash. Good old Wahl and Henius say that, like steam beer, it was "mainly consumed by the laboring classes." The beer was brewed normally or sometimes started with what sounds like a sour mash ("low mashing temperatures"). Made with 30 percent corn, it wasn't exactly like a bourbon wash, and it also included caramel color or dark malt. Interestingly, the beer was treated like a gose and shipped to taverns still fermenting. The barrels were "placed on troughs, into which the yeast is allowed to work out." Unrefined, the beer usually had a "muddy" appearance, but "a moderately clear article can be obtained if the saloonkeeper lays in a supply so that it can settle a few days before tapping." As it happens, the beer may not be completely lost. A few craft breweries, relying on the descriptions of Wahl and Henius, have attempted revivals; if none of them trademark the name, perhaps it has a future life.

In case you're wondering what other lost treasures Wahl and Henius uncovered, there are a few. "Sparkling" or "brilliant ales" were very clear, effervescent ales made to look like pale lagers, Pennsylvania "swankey" was a very-low-alcohol beer, and "American weissbier" was made to imitate Berliner weisse, but using corn grits, not wheat. The authors frowned on this practice, however. Amusingly: "Undoubtedly the American article could be much improved by employing the materials . . . as grits will under no circumstances yield those albuminoids that give Weiss beer its character, as wheat malt does. . . . [A] brilliant Weiss beer does not seem to catch the fancy of the consumers, who are accustomed to the cloudy, lively article of Berlin fame."

New World and brewers were doing everything they could to lighten the color and increase the clarity of their beers. American six-row barley, dense in protein, made it very hard for brewers to produce elegant translucent beers like those from Bohemia. The addition of adjuncts like corn and rice, usually in proportions of up to 30 percent, made it possible. In style after style—cream ale, pale lager, steam beer, sparkling ale, Kentucky common, and American weissbier—brewers used corn to achieve the effect.

A grist of barley and cereal grains became a marker of American beer. Brewers used a variety of lighteners, including rice and sugar, but corn is the most American of all. And of the pre-Prohibition beers made in the U.S., cream ales might have been the most native of the natives. Cream ales in the nineteenth century were sturdy beers of 14° Plato (1.057 sp. gr.) and 6% alcohol. They were relatively bitter, loaded with more hops than the porters of the era. In the nineteenth century, Cluster hops were king, and they would have added an American flavor to an American beer. Like steam beer, cream ales were made to resemble lagers, but they were fermented variously with ale yeast, lager yeast, or a mixture of yeast strains. Like kölsches, they were crisp and clean, but had a bit of ale fruitiness.

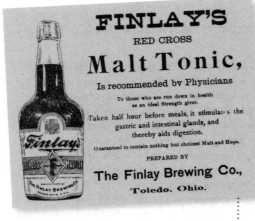

ABOVE: *Among the beers brewed in the early twentieth century were those like low-alcohol Pennsylvania swankey and temperance beer, as well as high-alcoholic "malt tonics" sold through druggists for "medicinal purposes."*

Cream ales reemerged a lesser beer after Prohibition. They had lost both their strength and their bitterness, and by the fifties and sixties were mainly a product of the mid-Atlantic. They're one of those styles that spark nostalgia, but the truth is that they were a diminished thing by the end of the twentieth century. Fortunately, there has been a solid effort to reclaim them in the craft beer era. In some ways, cream ale is a more American product than steam beer ever was. Made with a native grain and a hop that could be called a continental landrace variety, it is the closest thing we have to a nineteenth-century indigenous beer. Revivals aren't made with Cluster hops, but breweries now have a whole new menu of local hops that add local flavor. Sixpoint Sweet Action is a good example of how cream ale might evolve into the twenty-first century. Gentle but full, scented and spiced with sprightly, citrusy hops, it is both easy and pleasurable on a warm afternoon. ∎

BREWING WITH STONES

MY VOTE FOR the most difficult method of producing beer is the one they once used in that magic triangle of Bavaria, Bohemia, and Austria. The technique is this: Take a local shock-resistant variety of stone (in that triangle, it was greywacke), heat for several hours, then immerse in the mash tun and kettle instead of using direct heat. The most common argument advanced is that this dates back to a period of time before brewers had metal vessels, or perhaps was invented by farmers too poor to own metal vessels. But this strains credulity, particularly when you consider that it continued to be used up through the twentieth century.

No, rather, it's clear that brewers continued to make this *steinbier* (stone beer) because of what it did to the end product. The rocks were superheated when they entered the kettle, and caused the wort's sugars to scorch and caramelize. At the Rauchenfels Brewery in Bavaria, the last place to make steinbier commercially, the stones reached 4,500°F. The brewery lowered the rocks through a special chute in the side of the kettle, and the moment of contact was exhilarating: There was a hiss and an explosion of steam as the wort roiled from the stones. (It's possible to see this on old videos.) The stones, having just come from a wood fire, were also coated in smoke and soot. After they cooled, you could see a skin of blackened sugar on the stones; at Rauchenfels, they were added back to the lagering tank where the sugars slowly dissolved, adding body and more toffee-and-soot flavors to the beer.

There's a primitive romance to stone beer, one a few breweries have been unable to resist. Lacking the specialized equipment of Rauchenfels, modern breweries have improvised with cages and drums, mainly aiming to get the caramelization from the stones. (They don't try to actually boil the wort this way.) Because of the drama, they are among the most-documented brews, and you can spend an entertaining hour or two watching videos online of commercial and homebrewed steinbiers being made. ∎

RADLER, RUSS, AND SHANDY

LONG BEFORE SPORTS drinks and the notion of staying hydrated, there was *radler*, a word meaning "cyclist." The background: In 1922, Franz Xaver Kugler, the owner of a Bavarian *gasthaus*, was running low on beer. He had thirsty cyclists and hikers to serve, so he concocted a mixture of dunkel lager cut with lemon-lime soda, which he had in abundance. Voilà! Proto-Gatorade. Now radlers are more often made with pale lagers, but bock and dunkel lagers are used occasionally as well. As low-alcohol and nonalcoholic beers become increasingly popular with German drinkers, breweries have also started bottling radler premixed.

The idea of mixing beer with non-alcoholic beverages is far from novel. Most countries have their own variations. In Germany, when the blend is weizen and soda, it's called *russ*; when it's lager and soda, the nickname is *diesel*. In Britain, however, a diesel is lager, cider, and blackcurrant syrup. And in Britain and its old colonies, a shandy is much the same as a radler; a shandygaff is beer and ginger ale. The variations go on and on and, as the cocktail and craft beer worlds collide, mixologists now regularly dabble in "beer cocktails," a further extension of the idea. ∎

NONALCOHOLIC BEER

THE IDEA OF a beer without the alcohol is at once alluring and dispiriting. Alluring because the idea of a beverage with all the flavor of beer but no mind-clouding alcohol seems ideal for lunch or when you're planning to drive. But for all that, there's the niggling sensation that the whole point of beer is alcohol, the devilish spirit that animates the otherwise wholesome liquid.

It turns out that it's dispiriting in a different way, too; making a beverage with all of the flavor and none of the alcohol can be a tricky business. There are

Hot Scotchy. The name of one of the world's great inventors is lost to the historical record. But he had a kindred spirit in James Horlick, an Englishman and inventor of a product, originally aimed at infants, called "malted milk." Eventually, the powdered version of the product became popular among adults, leading to malted milkshakes, malted milk balls, and other malt-based foods. The heyday of malt lasted for the first half of the twentieth century, though Horlicks malted milk drink is still quite popular throughout Asia. The quality is grainy, like breakfast cereal, sweet, and wholesome. It tastes like something your mother would give you to keep you warm and ward off colds—which, in fact, was pretty much what it became.

Horlick's lost fellow inventor took this comforting concept in a slightly different and more spectacular direction. The idea is much the same. Brewers would draw off a glassful of the mash's first runnings as they issued from the grain bed, fresh and warm. To this they'd add a dollop of Scotch. What happens next is nothing short of mystical. Mash runnings are very sweet and flabby—a bit like Horlicks but without any definition to the flavors. The addition of Scotch somehow reverses all this. Like an electric current, the liquor animates the grains so that you can taste them in high-definition. The Scotch likewise remains a very distinct note, but once enfolded in the warm embrace of the malt, it soothes, not jabs. The liquor has all the flavor of a straight shot, but it's floating amid Mom's comforting malted. A Hot Scotchy is not the easiest cocktail to make at home, but it is one of the most beguiling experiences you'll ever encounter. Homebrewers take note.

two standard practices: either brewing a regular low-gravity beer and stopping fermentation just after it starts, or distilling the alcohol out of regular beer. Neither technique results in a truly convincing lager. Stopping fermentation leaves a beer tasting worty, while distillation can damage subtle flavors. In past decades, distillation made nearly undrinkable beers, but breweries have continued to fine-tune their equipment. It's not going to replace alcohol-rich beer anytime soon, but current nonalcoholic beer is an improvement from the stuff a decade or two back.

Nonalcoholic beer (*alkoholfrei*) is one of the very bright growth areas in Germany, and most production-size breweries offer a version. Adding an alkoholfrei beer to the lineup was one of the reasons Schneider invested in a new brewhouse. Brewer Hans-Peter Drexler described their process when I visited. "It's an evaporation system. We produce a special brew. After the first fermentation we move to this plant. It's heated up to 37° to 38°C [98° to 100°F]. Because it's an evaporation system, we have the pressure down to zero and so the alcohol is distilled out at this low temperature so it's very smooth."

I tried a glass at the pub later than night, and it was definitely a vast improvement on the carbonated malt-water of decades past. But the second I finished it, I hailed the waitress to get a pint of Schneider Weisse; I much prefer the sensual pleasures of fully alcoholic weizenbier. ■

THE BEERS TO KNOW

O DDBALL BEERS are rarely easy to find, but a few get at least occasional distribution. You're more likely to see a rauchbier or cream ale as a seasonal or one-off at your local brewery, so encountering these beers may require serendipity. Following are some examples that are regularly available.

UNFILTERED, UNBUNGED, CELLARED

MAHR'S UNGESPUNDET LAGER

LOCATION: Bamberg, Germany

MALT: Undisclosed

HOPS: Undisclosed

5.2% ABV

H oney-colored, slightly hazy, and frothy—a gorgeous half-liter. The beer, while creamy, has a mineral quality and slightly raw flavor. When served fresh from the cask in Bamberg, it has a liveliness that's lost when it's put in a bottle and shipped, but you still get hints of rawness.

URBAN CHESTNUT ZWICKEL

LOCATION: St. Louis, MO

MALT: Pale, pilsner

HOPS: Hallertauer

5.1% ABV, 1.046 SP. GR., 19 IBU

M any know that before starting Urban Chestnut, Florian Kuplent brewed for hometown giant Anheuser-Busch; fewer know that before *that,* he brewed at the small Brauerei Erharting in his native Bavaria. You can taste the Bavarian kellerbiers he enjoyed then in a glass of Urban Chestnut Zwickel. Bavarian beer is the softest in the world, and the dead giveaway of an American imposter is rough graininess. Zwickel is Bavarian soft, just kissed by delicate German hops, and given rusticity by a haze of yeast. You can buy it by the bottle, but brewery-fresh can't be beat.

RAUCHBIER

AECHT SCHLENKERLA RAUCHBIER

LOCATION: Bamberg, Germany

MALT: Beech-smoked malt (100%)

HOPS: Undisclosed

5.4% ABV, 1.053 SP. GR., 30 IBU

chlenkerla now ships all their beers, and the original rauchbier is labeled "märzen." This is a very intense beer that announces itself with the scent and flavor of a campfire. Underneath, the malts are quite full, nutty and plummy. It has a dry finish, one enhanced by the tannins of the smoke. Buy more than one and have them in a single session. After your second, you should be able to appreciate the flavors; after your third, you'll be hooked.

SPEZIAL RAUCHBIER

LOCATION: Bamberg, Germany

MALT: Smoked malt (40%), pale (60%)

HOPS: Undisclosed

5.0% ABV

ompared to the Schlenkerla freight train, Spezial's rauch seems quite restrained. Using only a portion of smoked malt, Spezial's rauchbier is much lighter, and the smoke tends to inflect the malt flavors, giving them a partly earthy, partly smoky quality. After a few drinks, the smoke all but vanishes.

ALASKAN SMOKED PORTER

LOCATION: Juneau, AK

MALT: Undisclosed

HOPS: Undisclosed

6.5% ABV, 1.068 SP. GR., 45 IBU

moked beers are becoming more popular in the United States, and Alaskan Brewing has a lot to do with it. First released in 1988, the year founder Geoff

Larson decided to partner with a local salmon smoker to smoke his own malt over alder wood, it has been an institution ever since. Like Schlenkerla, Smoked Porter is a malt-forward beer rich in plum and cola—once you acclimatize your palate to the fire. One of the best laying-down beers, it will develop for years.

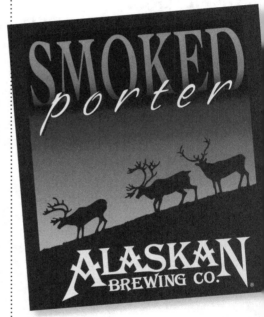

STEAM, CREAM, AND CORN

YAZOO BREWING SUE

LOCATION: Nashville, TN

MALT: Pale, caramel, chocolate, black, cherrywood-smoked

HOPS: Galena, Perle

9.2% ABV, 1.087 SP. GR., 72 IBU

I don't know if Yazoo's brewer Linus Hall was attempting to evoke the old porters of London, but that's what comes to mind with a sip of Sue. A dense, creamy beer with a scent that only hints at the smokiness inside, it opens up into an impressive, sweetly charred beer.

ANCHOR STEAM

LOCATION: San Francisco, CA

MALT: Pale, caramel

HOPS: Northern Brewer

4.9% ABV, 37 IBU

Anchor Steam is a beer sometimes undone by its own titanic legend. It is a rather unassuming copper-colored beverage that doesn't waft heaps of mango hops or vent powerful alcohol fumes. It was never intended to. Instead, it has a welcoming bready base and faintly herbal, woody hopping. It has the crisp smoothness of a lager and was designed to slake thirsts—which is exactly what it does.

SIXPOINT SWEET ACTION

LOCATION: Brooklyn, NY

MALT: Undisclosed

HOPS: Undisclosed

5.2% ABV, 34 IBU

Sweet Action is sometimes dinged for deviating from style by people who associate cream ales with Genessee. But it's actually a reclaimed cream and a really nice example of all-American flavor. The palate is soft and grain-y, like a summer field, and the hops have the tropical fruit flavors of the New World. Cream ales were supposed to be charmingly simple and welcoming, and Sixpoint revives that spirit.

BREWED AND BOTTLED BY ANCHOR BREWING CO., SAN FRANCISCO, CA. FROM ALL BARLEY MALT. ©1968

ANCHOR STEAM BEER

Made in San Francisco since 1896

Schlenkerla

ONE OF THE LAST RAUCHBIER BREWERIES

IN THE TENTH CENTURY, THE DUKE OF BAVARIA TOOK POSSESSION OF THE STEEP HILL IN THE MIDDLE OF BAMBERG AND, IN 1007, WHEN THE DUKE BECAME KING, HE MADE IT THE SEAT OF A BISHOPRIC, WITH PLANS TO TURN BAMBERG INTO A "SECOND ROME." THE CITY WAS LAID OUT LIKE A CROSS WITH CHURCHES AT THE FOUR CARDINAL POINTS, AND THE SEAT OF THE PRINCE-BISHOPRIC WENT THROUGH A PERIOD OF OPULENCE STILL EVIDENT IN THE CHURCH AND RESIDENCE BUILDINGS PERCHED ON THE HIGHEST GROUND. DOWN THE HILL, WHERE THE TOWNSPEOPLE BUSTLED ABOUT THEIR DAILY BUSINESS, A TAVERN OPENED IN 1405 IN A MODEST HALF-TIMBERED BUILDING ALONG WHAT IS NOW A NARROW COBBLESTONE ROAD. THAT TAVERN, WITH EXPOSED WOOD PAINTED IN OXBLOOD, STILL STANDS IN THE SAME SPOT. YOU CAN BUY A KIND OF SMOKY BEER THERE THAT IS REDOLENT OF THE WOOD-FIRED KILNS OF THE FIFTEENTH CENTURY AND LOOK OUT ON A SCENE NOT MUCH CHANGED SINCE THE TIME OF JOAN OF ARC. IN TERMS OF TRADITION, IT'S HARD TO BEAT THE ATMOSPHERE OF AECHT SCHLENKERLA.

In a bit of visual dissonance, the proprietor of this building, Matthias Trum, is not yet forty years old—though he's spent his nearly four decades breathing the history of the Schlenkerla tavern. "Raised by the bottle," he tells me before launching into the deep background of the brewery, which seems threaded with as much history as myth. It involves Andreas Graser, who became the new owner in 1877, and the eventual namesake of the brewery. "According to legend he had an accident in the brewery and he was limping afterwards," Trum began. "In Franconian vernacular when you limp and you dangle your arms, this dangling is called *schlenken*. So a *schlenkerla* is a diminutive or the nickname for a person who dangles, who walks like that—very much like a drunk person would walk. That's the second meaning and why it stuck around. So people say, 'Okay, you drink smoked beers, so you're going to *schlenka*, you're going to dangle.'"

The tavern is the spiritual home of Schlenkerla, but not the location of the actual brewery. That's a few blocks away. Like so many German taverns, Schlenkerla's stretches across several rooms and niches, and spans a courtyard—typically Bambergian—from which drinkers can buy beer to enjoy in the street. Part of the building was once a chapel, and the arches and vaulted ceilings still communicate that it's a sanctified space. To really get the sense of smoked beer, you need to drink in the atmosphere of the tavern while you drink the beer. I prefer the old, original part of the tavern, where the patina of generations seems to coat the walls. This is the place to drink rauchbier.

Trum quotes a proverb: "If you visit Bamberg and have not visited Schlenkerla, you have not visited Bamberg." In six centuries, the pub has taken on its share of rules and rituals, but another—that first-time drinkers should have three glasses to orient their palate—seems especially wise. "At the first sip, the smoke flavor is extremely dominant on your palate. If you're new to the taste, you will notice nothing but the smoked flavor. Only as you go through your first two or three pints does the smokiness step back in perception and then the malty notes come out, the bitterness, the smoothness." Also, "take big sips at the

ABOVE: *Bamberg may be the most pleasant place in the world to enjoy a beer.*

beginning. You have to *drink*. Wash your palate."

We were supposed to be on our way to a tour of the brewery, but two hours on, Trum and I were still busy discussing guild history and the methods of medieval yeast maintenance. He earned an economics degree at the university in Bamberg and then studied brewing at Weihenstephan (see page 403), where he had a focus on brewing history as well as the craft of beer making. Eventually, we managed to connect the threads. At Weihenstephan, "they don't teach you anything about smoking [malt]. They teach you that there is such a thing and they do it in Bamberg. But there is no research or doctoral theses on the details of the smoking process."

It's understandable that the professors in Munich would take little scholarly interest in rauchbier. The tradition—ancient, for sure—is now maintained by just two breweries in the world, both in

Bamberg. Making rauchbier is a family activity. Trum started working in the brewery after college, helping his mother run the tavern. His English is excellent, so he soon transitioned to the export business. After earning the brewing degree, he helped his father in the malthouse and brewery. The elder Trum became an advisor in 2003 and retired fully five years later. Now the secret of rauchbier lives with Matthias.

We did finally make it out of the pub. The brewery proper is typical of a Franconian system—small, tidy, traditional. The cellars, a hundred feet under the brewery, also feature typical horizontal conditioning tanks. The brewing process isn't unusual. Trum conducts a double-decoction mash on the 1930s equipment and cellars the beer at around 41°F. His lager times are on the long side—the standard mid-gravity rauchbier (1.054) goes for eight weeks; the big bock (1.072), twelve. Under Matthias, the Trum family has expanded the range of offerings, although they had to be careful about how they did it.

"When I started, I wanted to do some of the things myself, have some of my own babies. In Germany you of course can't do gueuze or tripel. So in Bamberg I wondered what I could do that was historically accurate on the one hand but inventive on the other hand." He introduced a Lenten beer made with a portion of unsmoked malt, a doppelbock made with malt smoked with oak wood, and a summer beer blended with 10 to 15 percent young beer. Locals have taken to them like old friends, and in distant countries, drinkers probably imagine Schlenkerla's been making them for decades. With a bit of rauch malt, even new styles taste ancient.

I met Trum the day I arrived in Bamberg, where I spent the next three days drinking in the atmosphere and beer from the city's other breweries. A person could easily spend a month exploring the crannies of that lovely old town. But after my wanderings, I kept finding my way back into the old Schlenkerla pub where time had stopped, waiting for me to return. They make venison dishes, great sausage, and a local specialty called a "Bamberg onion" stuffed with a mixture of pork and pork belly. All are tailor-made to accompany the hearty, smoky beer, and I was happy to play matchmaker on my visits. But in truth, the food was just a bonus. I really kept returning for the beer.

LEFT: *Amazing as it seems, the Schlenkerla pub is 600 years old.*

PART FIVE

Tart and Wild Ales

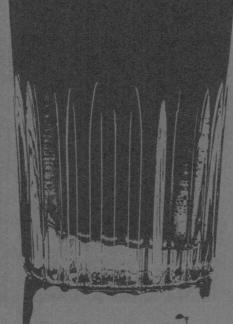

f we think of beer as a taxonomical genus, lagers and ales are the modern species. But what to do with this ancient remnant, once almost extinct—this dinosaur we call clumsily "tart," "sour," or "wild"? These beers are commonly identified by acidic palates, sometimes as puckery as a lemon wedge, though others may be very dry and austere. They are the most ancient beers, and they don't fit neatly into modern categories. Made with regular *Saccharomyces cerevisiae* (ale) yeast, they are later compromised by wild invaders from the sky: *Brettanomyces*, *Pediococcus*, *Lactobacillus*. Most of the styles in this category are throwbacks to an earlier time in brewing, before we "improved" it. But in the last decade or so, some breweries have become so enamored of the bold flavors of these old styles that they're beginning to brew new styles in the old way.

What defines tart ales are wild yeast and bacteria. These rogue microbes are the bane of modern brewing, for they produce all manner of strange compounds. Lactic and acetic acids are two of these, but the total number runs in the scores. The flavors of the resulting beer may be sour or tart but also "leathery," "goaty," "lemony"—and on and on. So they're not ales exactly, and they're not always terribly tart. And yet what else are we to call them?

At one time, all beer was inadvertently inoculated with wild yeast. Brewers didn't understand that the mechanism of fermentation was biological or that yeast lived everywhere. Even when brewers pitched yeast recaptured from previous batches of beer, they didn't realize that wild yeasts were settling on their cooling wort and adding their own unique characteristics. It wasn't until Louis Pasteur conducted fermentation experiments in 1857 that the world finally understood the different agents in alcohol production (yeast) and souring (bacteria). Looking at yeast under a microscope, he saw that domestic and wild yeasts had different shapes, and soon he was able to figure out how beer went sour. Even ignorant of this fact, brewers had nevertheless made

LEFT: *Mort Subite is one of only eight lambic brewers still in existence.*

impressive strides trying to contain the souring properties of wild organisms; while some people enjoyed tart ales, even more people liked sweeter ales that hadn't gone sour. Ale makers knew that beer would spoil in the summer (when wild yeasts and bacteria were most plentiful), and was sweet and largely unpolluted if served fresh. And lager makers kept the temperature of their beer low enough that only their specialized yeasts would work.

There were, however, some brewers who embraced the wild beasts. In eighteenth-century London, porter makers harnessed what they would later learn was *Brettanomyces* to make refined, vinous ales of great complexity. In Belgium, lambic makers learned how to blend different vintages of soured beer to make exceptional, Champagne-like sparkling gueuzes that remain one of the great achievements in brewing. To the west, breweries in Flanders made sweet-and-sour red ales that had the character of balsamic vinegar. Even in Germany, some breweries could be seduced to make tart summer ales as refreshing and sparkling as an Italian soda.

Sour ales are still regarded with a hearty suspicion. Some breweries won't speak of them, and most refuse to allow them to be made in their facilities. They are perhaps not as dangerous as these breweries imagine, but wild yeasts are extremely virulent and can get into other beers if precautions are not taken. But to a minority of breweries and beer drinkers, these odd remnants of an

ABOVE: *Liefmans Goudenband can be aged in the bottle for up to ten years.*

earlier time are the very definition of sublime.

Tart beers are far more complex, varied, and exotic than anything found elsewhere in the beer world. Yeasts are little chemical factories, and they pump out interesting flavors; in addition to acidifying the beer, wild yeasts and bacteria create lush, fruity esters and funky compounds. Until recently mainly the province of Belgian breweries, tart ales have begun to attract fans and converts in the United States, Italy, and beyond, where breweries have embraced the wild. This group of beers will never supplant ales and lagers, but it appears they are no longer bound for extinction, either. ∎

The
LAMBIC FAMILY

Lambics are rare, ancient Belgian beers made through a process of wild fermentation. Every other beer on Earth begins when a brewer pitches cultured yeast, a refinement developed centuries ago. Not lambics. Instead of pitching yeast, the brewery lets freshly boiled wort cool overnight, making it an all-you-can-eat buffet for wild yeasts and bacteria. They happily stream through the open windows, settle on the surface of the wort, and begin gorging. The following morning, the brewer puts the wort in casks where it will

Lambic, Fruit Lambic & Gueuze.

Lambics, the base beer in this august family, are aged one to three years to fully develop the character provided by wild yeasts. Taken from oak casks, they are still and very dry—and at peak sourness. They are refined beers but have widely varying character not only from brewery to brewery, but even cask to cask. Lambic infused with whole fruit becomes kriek (cherry), framboise (raspberry), or any number of other fruity incarnations. The highest expression in the family is gueuze, made by blending younger and older lambics. With towering effervescence and layers of complexity, gueuzes are sometimes called the "Champagnes of Brussels"—and carry with them a similar reputation for quality.

Statistics

Lambic ABV range: 3.5–5%;
IBU: negligible

Gueuze ABV range: 4–8%;
IBU: negligible

Fruit lambic ABV range: 4–6%; IBU: negligible

Serving temperature: 45°–55°F

Vessel: Pleated tumbler (lambic, gueuze); tulip (fruit lambic)

age for years, acting as an eco-system for those now captive wild things.

The rule in other forms of Belgian brewing is no rules: Follow your bliss and make beers that conform to no standards or styles. Lambics are the exception; few beer styles have such a formal, almost ritual brewing process. Yet the beers are the opposite of mannered. Lambics and their variants—gueuze, kriek, framboise, and faro—are vibrant, improvisational beers. Those feral microorganisms are hard to manage, and the beers they make require discipline and consistency. The result is worth the effort—good lambics and

ABOVE: *Family-owned Drie Fonteinen blends an oude gueuze that combines bright lemon-rind notes with contrasting briny, umami flavors.*

especially gueuzes are the most complex beers in the world, and for many people, the most enjoyable. ■

ORIGINS

LAMBICS ARE sometimes described as beers unchanged from ancient times, made in the same manner as they were thousands of years ago. This isn't strictly true. Twenty-first-century lambic breweries have the use of electricity, clean water, and the finest fruits of modern agriculture. Yet it's not entirely wrong, either. Lambics are descendants of an ancient tradition in brewing, and they employ techniques that are at least hundreds of years old. The methods have been refined slightly, but they haven't been abandoned.

Lambics emerged as a style in the area around Brussels—the only home they've ever known. The first mention comes from the early 1300s, but the tradition of farmhouse brewing from which they descend is poorly documented. Lambics are likely much older, or closely related to other much older beers. We know that they have remained largely unchanged for at least 450 years; a document from the town of Halle lists the proper grist ratio as 37 percent wheat, 63 percent barley—a ratio similar to today's beers—and this ordinance refers to an earlier document from the year 1400. These beers are fixtures of the region, ingrained enough in daily life that they were immortalized by the Flemish master Pieter Bruegel the Elder in his paintings of Belgian peasants.

Spontaneous Fermentation.

The word "spontaneous" has several meanings, but the one we're interested in has the sense of "occurring without apparent external influence or cause." Spontaneous fermentation happened when beer appeared to ferment without any action by the brewer. We now know there was a cause, but to brewers before Louis Pasteur's great discovery in 1857, it sure didn't look like it. They took wort straight from the kettle and cooled it in large pan-shaped vessels called cool ships (*koelschip* in Flemish). The brew day ended in the evening, and they just left the beer to sit and cool overnight. In the morning, the brewer put the beer in barrels and called it good. How it went from wort to beer was magical or mystical—in any case, *spontaneous*.

That's still how lambics are made. Now we understand that there are actors involved—millions of them. They are the yeasts and bacteria that teem on the surface of cooling wort, hidden in plain sight. Modern breweries sometimes use fans to help the microorganisms find their way to the wort; others pump outside air through it. But never does a brewery add yeast. There's a related process in which a brewery "pitches" yeast by relying on microorganisms resident in the wooden vessels to do the work—but this is not true spontaneous fermentation. The beasts that inoculate lambics must be free range. Spontaneous fermentation is the most radical kind of brewing because a brewery has no control over the most vital process in beer making. It is dangerous, but also sublime. And when the wrong characters come along instead? (Even for master lambic makers, wild yeasts can sometimes produce unpleasant flavors and aromas.) That's why lambic makers blend their beer, to smooth out the rough edges. (For more on the mechanics and science of spontaneous fermentation, see About the Science, pages 505–507, and Brewing Notes, pages 507–508.)

Even at the low estimate, 700 years, they are one of the oldest styles left on Earth. In that period and earlier, spontaneous fermentation—making beer without pitching yeast—was the standard method for fermenting ale. In what are now Germany and the United Kingdom, breweries moved to pitching yeast as soon as they realized it improved their beer. (Like bakers working with starter, brewers took a pinch of the previous batch of beer to help the next one get going—though they didn't know exactly what they were pitching at the time.)

LEFT: *Cantillon's Lou Pepe beers have a fruity taste that distinguishes them from the brewery's other offerings.*

Belgians were far slower to abandon spontaneous fermentation. Even as late as the end of the nineteenth century, they were making beers using the method, and most Belgian breweries still used flat-cooling vessels rather than the wort chillers the technologically advanced English had been using for a century.

If there is an explanation for why lambics survived in Belgium, it is the fidelity brewers have to traditional methods. Belgians love to tinker with recipes and ingredients and they don't like to copy other beers. Where they are slow to change is technique. Even as German, Bohemian, and British breweries raced to adopt new technologies and dominate growing markets, Belgians stuck to their small-scale, handmade ways. In Hoegaarden, the precursor to witbier survived as a spontaneously fermented ale into the twentieth century. Leuven, the center of advancement in Belgian brewing, was home to another spontaneously fermented beer called dobbel gerst "made like lambic and faro." Lambics survived because many old styles survived.

That doesn't mean lambics didn't change. The Belgian government passed a bizarre tax law in the nineteenth century that assessed a fee based on the size of a brewery's mash tun. Tax laws are often strange, but this was an especially convoluted proxy for the volume of beer a brewery would produce. It gave breweries incentives to use tiny mash tuns no matter how much beer they sold. The result was a type of brewing unique to Belgium wherein breweries packed their small mash tuns with grain and then slowly mashed them over hours. Known as a "turbid mash," this process became the standard still followed today by lambic breweries.

ABOVE: *Faro is effectively extinct; it was once quite popular among the cafés of lambic country.*

For centuries, straight lambic and especially faro were the main products of the lambic breweries. Faro, released green and sweetened with sugar, was a common table beer until recent decades, and could be found, served in pitchers, around Brussels. It has mostly died out. Gueuze, on the other hand, is a more recent innovation, dating to the mid-nineteenth century, when breweries first began to bottle lambic. This presentation wasn't immediately popular, though; a hundred years ago, it accounted for less than 10 percent of lambic sales.

The world wars delivered their usual deleterious blow to lambic makers. In 1910, lambic breweries produced an astounding 1 million hectoliters (850,000 U.S. barrels). Those numbers crashed after the wars, as both German lagers and a debased version of lambic—young, artificially sweetened, and carbonated— began to displace the traditional product. Unlike faro, which preserved lambic's rich character, these modern beverages were designed to capture the attention of the soda drinkers who were beginning to spurn old refreshments for something

RIGHT: *This nineteenth-century equipment may look like a steampunk throwback, but it's state of the art in lambic brewing.*

modern—and they were more like faintly tart sodas themselves than like lambics. By 1965, there were just twenty-seven lambic breweries and about twenty blenders left.

The lambic maker Frank Boon is one of the pivotal figures who helped rescue the style in the 1970s. Boon comes from a brewing family, and he recalls the changes lager brought when it finally penetrated the market. Small breweries abandoned local styles and "switched to cheaper and technically better beer." Lambic makers didn't help their cause, releasing good as well as subpar beer. "It's like the old professor said: 'These old lambic brewers, they sell gueuze like they sell pigs: Everybody wants the best meat, but you have to sell the whole pig.' When customers complained that there was no head on the beer, [breweries] said it was proof that there were no additives in it. If it was cloudy, they said 'See, it's the proof that it's unfiltered.' If it was foamy, they waited until the winter to sell the beer."

"Taste of Summer."

Historically speaking, lambic brewers may not have understood the mechanism of fermentation, but they understood what worked. And fermenting beer in the warm months wasn't it. Writing in 1851, Georges Lacambre, the brewer who documented dozens of Belgian beers, described what happened if fermentation temperatures got too high. The phenomenon even had its own name: *versoemer*.

> The result strongly affected the taste and the more or less nauseating odor is the true character of this kind of alteration. The smell is so characteristic that an experienced man can easily . . . recognize this kind of alteration simply [by] smelling beer that has received the slightest breach of *versoemer* or "taste of summer."

> In order to balance the cooling time and rate of wild inoculation, and avoid the dreaded *versoemer*, lambic breweries still only brew when nighttime temperatures approach freezing—October through April.

By 1970, the lambic maker Belle-Vue (now owned by A-B InBev) went on a buying spree, snapping up every lambic maker in Brussels except Cantillon. The company consolidated the production of traditional gueuze from the acquired breweries to just one site. Traditionalists like Frank Boon, Jean-Pierre Van Roy of Cantillon, and Armand Debelder of Drie Fonteinen refused to let the old styles die, though, and lambics have made a slow comeback since then. The greatest threat now is among companies that slap traditional fruit lambic names on treacly concoctions made with just tiny amounts of actual lambic. Finding a good kriek in Belgium has become hard work (though you can find nice examples by Drie Fonteinen and Oud Beersel on the export market), and the name is now associated with soda-sweet fruit beers. But the traditional breweries, still small by any reasonable standard (Boon, the giant, has only 8,500 barrels of oak-aging capacity—the size of a relatively small craft brewery in the U.S.), are flourishing in the now-tiny market. Lambic blenders, too, work with only small volumes, but they seem to be successful enough so that a new blender, Tilquin, has entered the market. ■

DESCRIPTION AND CHARACTERISTICS

MOST BREWERY TOURS linger over the polished, tiled brewhouses, where the curves of the kettles gleam seductively. By the time you reach the fermenters, you're fairly trotting alongside a brewer who barks out statistics measuring days and temperatures. When I visited Brouwerij Boon, the enigmatic owner, Frank Boon—a combination of the Cheshire Cat and Willy Wonka—marched me through the brewery double time so we could get to the warehouse where dozens of Econoline-sized oak vats rest like sleeping bears. Lambic is a product of time and wood—there is no other way to make it—and that's where the action is.

LAMBIC

Lambic brewers begin with a single recipe that becomes the base beer for all the other permutations falling under the lambic umbrella—gueuze, faro, kriek, and framboise. By tradition, lambics were made with pale barley and unmalted wheat, and that's still true. In 1965, lambics achieved some measure of legal protection for their product as well. Lambic itself is not protected, but because it is the base of gueuze, which is, lambic traditionally adheres to the following rules, now recognized by the European Union:

■ Lambic must contain at least 30 percent unmalted wheat (40 percent was traditional).

■ Lambic must be spontaneously fermented, meaning no yeast has been added.

■ Hops must be aged at least one year (three is usual).

■ Gueuze must be refermented in the bottle.

■ Certain compositional elements must be measurable in a laboratory setting, including the presence of *Brettanomyces*, the absence of isoamyl acetate (a measure of aging), and the presence of certain other volatile acids.

■ Lambic must be aged at least one year in a wooden cask and gueuzes must include one-, two-, and three-year-old beer.

At birth, lambic is a cloudy wheat ale that has something in common with Bavarian weizens and witbiers. *Saccharomyces cerevisiae*—the rough country cousin of standard ale yeast—is the first of the wild yeasts to act on the beer; after a few days, the wort turns into a strange, fruity sludge. This isn't lambic—not yet. Time allows an intricate waltz of the different microorganisms in the wort, each coming in at certain moments and then stepping back to

Pronouncing "Gueuze." There's no single or correct way to pronounce "gueuze." Lambic makers themselves pronounce it differently. *"Gurz"* or *"Gurz-ah"* seem to be the most common, but *"Gooz"* is also acceptable. The vowel sound is similar to "purse," but flatter, as if you're swallowing the word while you're saying it.

make room for others. The beer won't be finished for one to three years, though the subtle effects of age will continue to influence the beer for years after that.

At maturity (typically two years), lambic has exhausted its supply of sugars and is quite dry. Its unique character will be defined by countless factors, from the yeasts and bacteria that inoculated it during fermentation to the interactions of wood, oxygen, and wort that happen inside the cask. Remarkably, a batch of the same lambic spread over multiple casks will evolve differently as the ecosystems within the casks give the contents individual personalities. Some lambic is balanced enough to be packaged and sold straight (Cantillon Grand Cru Broucsella, a three-year-old straight lambic, is the best-known example) or on draft around Brussels. But most lambics will not emerge in perfect balance and will be blended into harmony in gueuze.

GUEUZE

One could be forgiven for imagining gueuze (sometimes rendered "geuze") is an inferior

LEFT: *An exotic presentation for an exotic beer*

version of straight lambic—as blended whisky is to single malt Scotch. The reverse is true. Straight lambics can have depth and character, but they can never approach the symphonic complexity and accomplishment of a well-made gueuze.

Unlike straight lambics, gueuzes are hugely effervescent and tartly refreshing—Belgians like to compare them to sparkling wines. They boil from a bottle as if propelled by heat and pile up gorgeous, thick heads. (In a Belgian café, the server will deliver a bottle of gueuze to your table from the restfulness of a little wicker basket; once he decants the golden bubbly into a rustic, pleated tumbler, he lays the bottle, prone but neck raised, in the basket on your table.) The best examples are at once deeply complex but absolutely approachable, containing within their unassuming appearances everything from the zest of citrus rind to white wine grapes, from earthiness to subtle hints of funkiness. They are tart beers, but those words belie the true nature of gueuzes, which while tart are not vinegar-sour and while beer have more in common with wines. They are like nothing else in the world.

Part of this is age: Gueuze is a blend of vintages. As lambic ages, it expresses different qualities at different moments. First comes the primary alcohol fermentation of regular *Saccharomyces*, which may last a few months. Next, lactic acid fermentation begins, turning the beer very sour, a process that consumes another few months' time. Finally, another stage of alcohol fermentation begins, as the

> "I first taste my old lambic. If I have a mellow lambic with some soft beer, I can work with two- and one-year-old with mild character. If I have an old beer with character, I have to find other types of beer. Each blend is different. From time to time the gueuze is too woody—a woody taste coming from old barrels. Once, when I made the blend I thought the taste would decrease with carbonation. I was wrong! The beer is never the same. Never. You never know what you will discover. That's why lambic is so fun."
>
> —JEAN VAN ROY (SON OF JEAN-PIERRE), BRASSERIE CANTILLON

Brettanomyces becomes active. (Actually, *Brett* is working the whole time; it's just so slow it hasn't built to sufficient numbers to begin producing the compounds that will affect the lambic's flavor.) That *Brettanomyces* will continue to plug along for years, munching sugars and adding flavor and aroma compounds. By mixing different vintages, lambic makers and blenders are taking flavor snapshots from different times and merging them into something wholly new.

Blending has other advantages. Brewers and blenders can never achieve true batch-by-batch consistency (nor would they wish to), but they do want their products to be recognizable. Blending gives Cantillon its lemony character, Boon its smoothness, and Drie Fonteinen its surprising briny center. Blending allows breweries to select single notes from different batches of lambic to construct layers of flavor not possible in single beers. Finally—and functionally—it allows breweries to work with lambics that have gotten too funky, too tart, or that lack the character to be served on their own.

Belgian Blenders. Blenders (*steker* in Flemish) are unique in the world of beer making—and generally misunderstood. They do everything traditional lambic makers do except produce the initial inoculated wort. Instead, they buy lots of inoculated wort from the lambic breweries—largely from Frank Boon, who supplies about 60 percent of the total. From there, blenders age the beer in their own cellars, either blending it from their own barrels later, selling it straight from their barrels, or adding fruit for kriek, framboise, and other fruit lambics. Labels don't always make the distinction between blender and brewer obvious, nor should they. The hard work and the art are in the aging and blending, and the beers that come from blenders such as De Cam, Hanssens, Oud Beersel, and the new blender Tilquin are every bit the equal of the breweries from which they receive their wort. Indeed, the blenders have an additional advantage over the breweries: When they blend their gueuze, they can draw on the production and distinctive characteristics of multiple breweries.

FRUIT LAMBIC

If people outside of Belgium have heard of lambics, it's usually by the name of their fruity incarnations: kriek (cherry, pronounced *creek*) and framboise (raspberry, pronounced *frahm-Bwahz*). These

are the most famous and common varieties, but breweries infuse young lambic with fruit for six months to make cassis (black currant), strawberry, peach, grape, apple, and blueberry lambics.

The effect of fruit on lambic is surprising—its sugars do not sweeten the beer, yet its flavors and aromas are captured seemingly at the moment it was picked. Yeasts have months to consume all fermentable matter, and they leave behind the fruit's essence. In fact, sour beers do a far better job of preserving and presenting that essence than regular beer. Lambics lack the heaviness and malt flavors of other beers; theirs is an almost distillate-like solution.

KRIEK

Beginning at least 400 years ago, villagers near Brussels harvested native sour cherries and delivered them to the city

LEFT: *The Église Royale Sainte-Marie, a parish church in the Brussels neighborhood of Schaerbeek, which was once a small village famous for cherries used in kriek.*

on donkeys. Schaerbeek, nicknamed "the village of donkeys," was the center of cherry cultivation and gave its name to the fruit originally synonymous with kriek. That village is now a neighborhood in Brussels, which gobbled up the fruit trees as it grew and spread out over the countryside. Now most cherries used in kriek lambic come from Poland, which has a similar variety. Nevertheless, among fruit lambics—and Belgian fruit beers generally—kriek is still king.

Cherry's triumph has less to do with regional history or local preference than the way the fruit and beer harmonize. Cherries have a rich flavor that comes from sugar, acid, and the tannins of the pits (which are always used). And color! No other fruit can stain a beer so intensely, and unlike other fruits, cherry's color doesn't fade. The best *oude krieks* (literally "old krieks"—referring to those made the old-fashioned way) are lush beers, scented with fruit so fresh it tastes like it was picked that day; they are tart but rounded, with woody, spicy, or even cinnamon qualities.

Unfortunately, not all krieks are made the same. In the past twenty years, as sugary drinks became increasingly popular, makers began to debase krieks, diluting them with regular beer, filtering them, adding sweeteners and sugars, and/ or using juice or syrups to add flavor. Even some traditional lambic makers followed suit, trying to keep demand and production up. Not only do these beers threaten the far more expensive and temperamental true lambics, but they're absolutely terrible—like limply carbonated cough syrup. One rule that will guide you well in your exploration of authentic lambics is to buy those with "*oude*" in the label—those are made the traditional way. In Belgium, kriek lambic or *kriekenlambik* sometimes appears on draft—it's also the authentic, straight-from-the-brewery good stuff.

FRAMBOISE

Almost as famous as kriek—and possibly older—is raspberry lambic. It is now rarer, however, in part because raspberries aren't as abundant, and in part because the fruit is harder to work with. Framboise is a lighter pink than kriek, and its color fades over time. It is more acidic and drier than kriek, but it also has lighter, springier character.

Look for the Oude. In Flemish, *oude* is "old," and in lambic, old is good. Even though lambics claim only a minuscule share of the Belgian market, the words "kriek" and "gueuze" still have cultural currency—enough that these styles of beer have been repurposed as easy-drinkers, competing with mass-market brands. For decades, lambic makers have tried to protect their product in the courts, and they've managed to carve out some protection for their authentic product. The key is the word "oude." Beers with this designation are made with the requisite unmalted wheat, and they are spontaneously fermented and aged in casks. They are now protected by the EU as "Traditional Specialty Guaranteed." Consider anything else suspect.

BEYOND CHERRY AND RASPBERRY

Any type of fruit may be used to flavor a lambic, and brewers and blenders have experimented with a wide range of them. Lindemans is most associated with the use of fruit in their beers—peaches, apple, cassis—but these aren't authentic lambics. They start out as proper lambics, but after six to eight months, the lambics are mixed with sugar and fruit syrup and then bottled without a secondary fermentation. The beers successfully hide all evidence that lambics were in any way involved in their manufacture.

Cantillon, always one of the most experimental lambic makers, has used a number of different fruits, but in the service of authentic lambic. The Van Roys make lambics with grapes (Vigneronne, St Lamvinus), apricots (Fou' Foune), and blueberries (Blåbær Lambik, sold only in Copenhagen) in addition to making kriek

and framboise. One other beer worth highlighting is Oudbeitje, a strawberry lambic from the blender Hanssens. The color from the berries is long gone by the time you pour out the beer, and the character tends toward the musty/funky quadrant of lambics, yet it is one of the most interesting, unusual fruit varieties made.

OTHER LAMBIC PRODUCTS

In the old triumvirate of lambic types, fruit lambics and gueuze were joined by faro (pronounced *Fah-row*). Until the First World War, faro was the most popular variety of lambic, sold in cafés around Brussels and Pajottenland. Brewed at a lower gravity than its tart cousins, it was sweetened in the cask before serving, often at the café, to stimulate some carbonation—not unlike English cask ale. Today faro is mostly extinct; where it *is* made, it is usually bottled. It's higher in alcohol now, and a strange orphan that satisfies neither the preference for sugary beers that the modern "kriek" offers nor the growing appreciation for traditional, tart lambics.

Lambic makers and blenders sometimes experiment with slightly off-beat products as well. Cantillon has an all-barley lambic called Iris made with regular hops (as opposed to the aged ones typically used). Mort Subite releases very young lambic in a product called Blanche that may well approximate turn-of-the-twentieth-century witbier, a spontaneously fermented ale that was a very close cousin to lambic.

LEFT: *Lindemans is perhaps the best-known fruit lambic producer—even though their "lambics" take liberties with the style.*

One of the most interesting phenomena in the world of tart Belgian beer is the spread of traditional lambic methods to other breweries in the country (and indeed throughout the globe). These lambic-like breweries don't necessarily compete on all the points of tradition, yet they don't skip the important stages: spontaneous fermentation and wood-barrel aging. The West Flanders brewery Bockor spent nearly a hundred years making the oud bruin of the region—another tart beer discussed later—but in 1970 began experimenting with spontaneous fermentation. The beer is aged eighteen months in oak, but is generally blended with nonlambic beer and syrups. The West Flanders brewery Van Honsebrouck, the makers of the Kasteel line, also makes beers from spontaneously fermented stocks, with similar results.

ABOVE: *Faro is still served from a traditional earthenware pitcher at Brasserie Cantillon.*

More interestingly, the craft brewery De Ranke (also in West Flanders) experiments with two blends, half of which they brew themselves. Kriek De Ranke and Cuvée De Ranke are made from a tart Flemish brown ale that the brewery produces. They blend it with Girardin lambic from the traditional maker near Brussels—as well as with cherries in the kriek. ■

ABOUT THE SCIENCE

T**HERE'S AN OLD** episode of *The Simpsons* where Homer's stooped, ancient boss, Montgomery Burns, visits the doctor and learns that he has nearly every disease known to man, but he remains in good health because they all cancel each other out. Lambics are something like that. They are afflicted by *Acetobacter, Enterobacter, Pediococcus, Lactobacillus,* and *Brettanomyces* and other oxidative yeasts; scientists have identified over two hundred organisms at work in lambics. Any of these have the capacity to ruin a beer, yet throw them together under the right circumstances and they all keep each other in a kind of astonishing harmony.

We'll talk about the life cycle of a lambic in a moment, but first a word on acids and esters. When the various microorganisms begin digesting sugars, they produce alcohol—but also acids, and from those acids come related esters. Acids are responsible for the sour flavors and the funky or pungent ones, while esters create fruity aromas and flavors. This is why lambics are so complex—there are dozens of compounds at work. Acetic and lactic acids are two of the compounds that make lambic tart; the esters derived from them are ethyl acetate (which tastes like apple at low levels, like solvent at higher levels) and ethyl lactate (which ranges from fruity to buttery). When we encounter funky notes in lambic, we're picking up these strange compounds. The trick in lambic brewing is finding a balance and concord among them. Fortunately, nature takes care of most of this.

THE LIFE CYCLE OF A LAMBIC

From the moment the sterile, sticky wort leaves the brew kettle and enters the cool ship, a brewer is at the mercy of the tiny beasts of the air to turn it into lambic. Those microorganisms work in waves, each doing its part to transform the beer. The quickest to act are two rough characters known as *Enterobacter* and *Kloeckera apiculata*. The latter may help break down proteins for later stages of fermentation, but *Enterobacter* is dangerously noxious. A source of food spoilage, it causes rotten, vegetal, and fecal-smelling compounds and is an acetic acid (vinegar) engine.

After a few days, the population of *Saccharamyces cerevisiae* cells—regular ale yeast—have multiplied enough to begin alcohol fermentation, overwhelming *K. apiculata*. A couple months down the road, *Enterobacter* will make the environment toxic to itself by lowering the pH. Although *Enterobacter* introduces unpalatable compounds into the beer, it contributes acids critical to making the tartness that characterize lambic. Those off-flavors can overwhelm a beer, but in order to do so they must survive further rounds of chemical changes.

Once primary alcohol fermentation winds down, lactic fermentation kicks in, beginning roughly four months into the lambic's life. While *Lactobacillus* is present in lambics, it is kept in check by hop acids; instead, *Pediococcus* will be the source of lactic acid in lambic. This stage lasts three to six months. (The variation in times is related primarily to temperature.) Lactic fermentation produces what lambic brewers call the "sick" stage—the beer takes on an unsightly oily texture and builds long, mucousy strands. A lambic must be brewed in cold weather so the wild yeasts aren't *too* wild. By the time the cold weather returns again, the sick stage ends and the lactic acid is reabsorbed into the beer. This is the earliest stage at which lambic can be called "complete"— but there's one critical stage left.

The final actor in this drama is the great *Brettanomyces*, the wild yeast that has been very slowly building up its population over the months. In the final months, *Brett* will begin work on the remaining sugars (about 20 percent) and conduct a second alcohol fermentation. During this phase, which can last well over a year, *Brett* will add its own character and give the beer the final array of aromatic and flavor compounds; the beer may also form a pellicle—another unsightly growth that looks like mold on the surface.

The remarkable thing about lambics is that at the end of this protracted process, they don't taste horrible. Throughout their life cycles, the different microorganisms interact differently with the environment—the ambient temperature in the casks, the amount of oxygen that enters through the wooden staves—and these factors produce variations in the levels and amounts of compounds. Most casks won't contain spectacular stand-alone beer, but they will have the qualities that, when blended, will together make spectacular beer. After

These wholly unique beers have no peers or close relatives in the beer world, but American and Italian breweries are experimenting with *wild ales* that have related funky, tart, and dry character. Other distantly related styles include *tart Flemish ales* and *Berliner weisse*.

two years of biochemical change, the various wild yeasts and bacteria will have finally played their part in the theatrics. Lambic will continue to change with the effect of oxygen over the next year, but after two, it has become a stable beer. ■

BREWING NOTES

W**E'VE TALKED** a lot about what happens after the wort reaches the cool ship, but what happens beforehand is nearly as strange and unorthodox. Brewers begin with a mixed grist of at least 30 percent unmalted wheat and conduct a laborious mashing regimen to create wort full of enough proteins and starches to give the various microorganisms something to chew on over the next two years. The "turbid mash" begins with a cool infusion of water and then the brewer raises the temperature by removing, heating, and adding wort back in and so on over the course of hours. The idea is to produce a cloudy wort that will provide fewer active nutrients during the dangerous early stages of fermentation, but more dextrins and starches for the yeast to munch on in the later stages.

The exhausting mash is only the first

Climate Change and Lambic Production. Ideally, a lambic brewer likes the mercury to drop to freezing overnight, a temperature that will result in wort reaching 64° to 68°F by morning. This protects the wort from being infected by dangerous wild yeasts and bacteria. Fifty years ago, lambic breweries could begin brewing in mid-October and continue through the end of April. Now, it takes longer for adequately cold temperatures to arrive in Belgium. Looking at his grandfather's logs, Cantillon's Jean Van Roy has seen the average number of potential brewing days drop by a month—and counting.

half of the marathon; the boil comes next, an hours-long ordeal that recalls methods described in nineteenth-century texts. Periods vary from four to six hours, and the theory holds that beyond reducing the volume to the target gravity, a long boil helps coagulate the raw wheat protein and pulls out the maximum level of antibacterial agents from the aged hops.

(Lambic makers use hops at least a year old but generally three. From these they extract little bitterness, which would get harsh in the long boils, but get those anti-bacterial compounds critical in inhibiting the excesses of wild fermentation.)

From there, the process proceeds through the cooling, aging, and blending stages described already. ■

EVOLUTION

ONE OF THE criteria for producing authentic lambic is that it be made in the small region around Brussels. There's no law protecting this rule, and until a decade ago the question of transgression seemed theoretical at best. But what if a brewery did follow every guideline, particularly the requirement to spontaneously ferment the beer in a cool ship, except that it was brewed outside Brussels—what should that beer be called?

The question is no longer theoretical. Several American and Italian breweries have put their toes in the turbid mash. Out of deference to the Belgian breweries they admire, they don't call their beer lambic—they say "lambic-style" or "spontaneously fermented" or other similar language. Yet some of it meets every criteria except location. Sour beers have become a serious niche in both countries—not huge in absolute terms, but popular enough to support a growing segment in those countries. To avoid confusion with the classic production of the lambic region, these beers are described in a subsequent chapter. Make no mistake, though: The taste for lambics has reached other countries and now there's not enough of it to go around. Belgian breweries and blenders must turn away foreign requests. As a result, breweries elsewhere are learning the old ways and making spontaneously fermented beers themselves. ■

BREWED AND BOTTLED BY UPLAND BREWING COMPANY, BLOOMINGTON, IN

Upland Brewing Co.

BLUEBERRY LAMBIC
Belgian-Style Ale
Aged in oak with whole blueberries

LEFT: *Upland Brewing in Indiana includes a variety of fruited lambic-style beers in their sour ale program.*

THE BEERS TO KNOW

ONLY EIGHT LAMBIC brewers still exist: Boon, Cantillon, De Troch, Girardin, Lindemans, Mort Subite, Timmermans, and Drie Fonteinen. The last suspended brewing in 2009 after a brewery accident and spent the next three years blending lambics. The world was fortunate when Armand Debelder put together funds sufficient to buy new equipment in 2012, so Drie Fonteinen is a brewer again. In addition, there are another four blenders: De Cam, Hanssens, Oud Beersel, and Tilquin. The volume of authentic lambic that these breweries and blenders produce is small enough that very little is available to export markets.

All of the authentic lambic and gueuze produced by these breweries is exceptional, but there are some imposters lurking. De Troch makes the "Chapeau" line of fruit lambics, all of which are syrup-sweetened and inauthentic. Lindemans fruit lambics, the most widely distributed, are also syrupy and should be avoided; however, the brewery makes an authentic gueuze called Cuvée René as well as an oude kriek that are wholly traditional. Timmermans, though sweetened, retains some sharpness.

The very best products come from Boon, Cantillon, Drie Fonteinen, and Girardin, and all the brands made by these brewers are reliably authentic and—more important— extraordinarily good. Because the process includes variability, the vintages are never exactly the same, so I haven't included specific reviews here; they only serve to capture a snapshot of a point in time. I highly recommended them all.

Brasserie Cantillon and Brouwerij Boon

IN THE VALLEY OF THE LAMBICS

LAMBIC BREWING IS BY DESIGN AN ANCIENT PRACTICE, BUT EVEN AMONG LAMBIC BREWERIES, CANTILLON IS THE MOST IMPERVIOUS TO TIME. THE EQUIPMENT, THE BREWERY, THE METHODS—EVERYTHING COULD HAVE COME STRAIGHT FROM THE NINETEENTH CENTURY. CANTILLON HAS A MUSEUM AT THE BREWERY AS WELL, BUT IF YOU VISIT, YOU'LL FIND THAT THIS IS A BIT REDUNDANT: CANTILLON *IS* A MUSEUM.

I scheduled my visit to coincide with a day brewer Jean Van Roy would be brewing—a practice limited by the cramped cask space in what is now a nondescript urban neighborhood in Brussels. Cantillon's equipment is steampunk old, and very hands-on. When I arrived, Van Roy was elbow deep in a vessel that looked a bit like a hop back, shoveling out material that had been reduced to mulch.

Van Roy has a disarmingly democratic approach to visitors: *mon brasserie, votre brasserie.* He told me just to go wander around if I wanted to see the rest of the place—he had no time to offer a tour. Cantillon has the feel of a warehouse, with anemic lighting and tight spaces. I went up wooden stairs to the kettle room and up another flight to where the casks rest in shadows. The cool ship hovers on a loft above the cask room, where open windows let in the Brussels air. It's up one last flight of stairs, walled in by white-painted brick, and accessed by a rough-hewn door on a landing. On a chilly day, the steaming wort creates clouds of ethereal mist that waft through the rafters, and I spent probably fifteen minutes communing with this scene. For an American lambic fanatic, this was ground zero for one of the most remarkable events in brewing.

In the romantic story of lambic brewing, you always hear about the pastoral Senne Valley just south of Brussels, laden with fruit trees and populated by farmers smilingly working the fields. My mind conjured a kind of rural preserve where the wild yeasts were pristine and untroubled by modern life. In the case of Cantillon, I was all wrong. The brewery is in the middle of a gritty urban tableau and those wild yeasts have definitely been slumming with some streetwise elements.

But the yeasts outside the brewery are only part of the equation. Cantillon, the museum, is rife with life. Nothing is disturbed, lest the inner ecosystem be thrown out of balance. "You have to create your own atmosphere in the building," says Van Roy. I had heard tales of even cobwebs left intact—and indeed, on the old casks and beams where the lambic aged, there they were.

After his brew day, Van Roy was ready for a beer. He disappeared and returned with a small pitcher of the kind that faro was once regularly served in. Again he disappeared, and this time returned with a bottle of five-year-old gueuze and one of the traditional wicker serving baskets. I asked him about his process, and he approached the subject with the imprecision of a theologian. "When we taste such a lambic we are so proud—for me, but also for the product itself. No one, no brewers on the earth can have the same rapport, the same feeling with his beer. In French we have a sentence. We say, *Tout est dans tout.* If I translate it: 'Everything is in everything.' In this brewery, everything is playing a role in the final product. Everything." He continued: "I

ABOVE: *Cantillon brewer Jean Van Roy has an almost spiritual approach to the art of making lambic.*

know my beer. I feel my product. The beer is alive. I really have contact with the beer. I feel, I smell what the beer will accept or not." Van Roy has a monkish manner to go with his theological descriptions—eloquent when he is finally coaxed into speech, and firm in his convictions.

Cantillon is perhaps the most admired lambic brewery in the world, not just for its beer, but because the Van Roys—Jean and his father, Jean-Pierre—have been at the leading edge of preserving the art. It does not hurt that Jean is generous and welcoming and has helped breweries in the U.S. and Italy experiment with spontaneous fermentation. But mainly, he is the face of lambic to the world, and when the world thinks of a lambic brewery, it envisions Cantillon.

Just a few miles south of that famous brewery is the small town of Lembeek, where lambic was born. It is also the home of Brouwerij Boon, which I visited the day after my trip to Cantillon. It was a fascinating contrast of styles. The brewer, Frank

TOP: *Brouwerij Boon is the last of the lambic-makers still located in Lembeek.*

MIDDLE: *Frank Boon pulling a sample of two-year-old lambic*

BOTTOM: *Casks bound for blenders bear the brewery's mark.*

a suburb. Boon told me that valleys were historically important for lambic brewers—and dangerous for regular breweries, which prefer high ground. Valleys create pools of still air, and microorganisms collect there. River valleys are even better, because the fog and humidity help keep the wild buggies from drifting away. Even though the Boon brewery is only a few miles from Cantillon, the wild yeasts are definitely different there—as anyone who's tasted beer from the two can readily attest.

Boon, is emphatically not a museum brewer; in fact, he's one of the most microbiologically sophisticated beer makers I encountered in Europe. He currently has a traditional old brewery, but is in the process of upgrading everything—well, almost everything. He will install the world's first modern lambic brewhouse, purpose-built to accommodate the rigors of turbid mashing, but designed to create absolutely consistent worts batch after batch. The traditional part of the process—cool ship, wood aging, and blending—will continue in the centuries-old traditional method.

The Boon brewery is located in sight of the famous Senne River, but again my expectations were thwarted. The river is tiny—a stream one could ford on foot. It's a much more rural location than Cantillon's, but it's still just thirteen miles from Brussels's Grand Place—located, essentially, in what Americans would call

Another area where Boon and Cantillon differ is their casks. Cantillon uses wine barrels, but Boon uses vats—twenty to forty times bigger than wine barrels. This has a substantial effect on the beer. The percentage of beer exposed to wood is greater in a smaller barrel, which affects the density of resident microorganisms and the amount of air that permeates the staves. I mentioned to Boon that I've seen some published analyses of which yeasts become active in the life cycle of lambic and asked if his followed the same pattern. Boon has been working with a university microbiologist to learn more about his yeasts—likely the most far-reaching studies into the biology of lambic ever done. He gave me an enigmatic grin and said that those charts don't apply to his yeasts—but he wasn't prepared to divulge how his lambic differs.

This wasn't the first time I recognized the difference between Boon's approach and Van Roy's. Again and again, Boon discussed the science of lambic, the ways in which some of the wild variability of the microbiology could be tamed. Observing his new brewery, he pointed out what traditional once meant: "You don't make better beer with cast-iron mash tuns. We had them because 120 years ago the oak mash tuns were stirred by hand. The old systems were okay when there was nothing else." Everything is made to Boon's specifications, even the pilsner malt he uses. (The German malts he once used are grown and dried too hot, and introduced compounds he didn't like into his beer.)

Yet Boon does take time to practice some craft. When old staves rot and need to be replaced, Boon does the work himself. It's the one remaining area where he has a completely hands-on role in the brewery. When we concluded our tour, he looked at his tuns of aging beer, resting quietly. "The finest flavors, the best esters, are built slowly. It takes time. Time, time, time. It's a time-consuming way of making beer."

Lambics, and especially gueuzes, live in that strata of artistic accomplishment that includes stinky cheeses, opera, and abstract painting. It's very difficult to come to a gueuze cold and appreciate what's going on with it. Once you get past the shock of the experience, you begin to understand the flavors and how they work together. Moreover, sampling bottles from different breweries makes it instantly clear what role the wild yeasts play. Gueuzes are a bit like dog breeds—they are distinctive and unique, and people have their preferences. I have discussed gueuzes with lambic fans and know some so devoted to Boon, Cantillon, Drie Fonteinen, or Girardin that they consider the preference for others a minor blasphemy. That kind of devotion is a testament to just how profound these beers can be. Is it a reflection of the approach of the brewer? Is that essence a part of the nature of the beer? In the case of lambics, almost certainly.

"If your brewery is on the top of the hill, you will always have less wild yeast. Temperatures in the night, for one reason, and also the wind. If you look at it from another side, the old English books will tell you if you're going to build a new brewery, put it on the top of a hill and make the opening of your cellars from the north. To keep the wild bugs out. So if you put it close to the river and put the openings to the south, you will have much more wild yeasts. If you count wild yeasts in the air, you will find much more wild yeasts near a river than at the top of a hill; if you count bacteria, it's about the same. And that is very interesting. Some people forget it's spontaneous fermentation, not spontaneous acidification. The idea is to make a wheat beer that ferments with wild yeast."

—FRANK BOON, BROUWERIJ BOON

The Tart Ales of
FLANDERS

Belgium is divided along cultural and linguistic lines, the north occupied by speakers of Flemish (a variant of Dutch), the south by French speakers. Brussels is a crossroads for both. The top half of the country is known as Flanders; the bottom, Wallonia. So far, so good. The trouble is that the western half of Flanders was once a part of the French house of Valois, a region of Burgundy. If you sail past Belgium's hop fields in the province of West Flanders, you enter French Flanders. And though they speak Flemish in the Belgian municipality of Poperinge, a few miles down the road in the Dutch-named Steenvoorde, France, they speak French.

★ ★ ★

Tart Ales of Flanders.

If you were to devise a product equally as attractive to beer geeks and oenophiles, it would look a great deal like the "Burgundies of Belgium." These brownish-red (or is it reddish-brown?) beers are bright and acidic, yet fruity and often slightly sweet. Once there were dozens of these regional specialties and it made sense to differentiate between the schools known as Flemish red and brown beers. Now there are a dwindling number and their differences are far less significant than their similarities.

As a class, these beers are dark, balanced, vinous, and tart—sometimes sharply so. Yet they have a comforting layer of sweetness that balances them out. They're quite versatile with food, matching nicely with the regional cuisine of mussels and sweet-and-sour Flemish carbonnade.

STATISTICS

★ ★ ★

ABV range: 4.5–6%
Bitterness: 5–20 IBU
Serving temperature: 45°–50°F
Vessel: Tulip

Confused yet? It would be a relief to explain that the native beers exhibit none of the region's entanglements, but alas, it's not so. The beers made in Flanders are just as confusing. The balsamic ales characterized by Rodenbach are a dark red-brown but are by tradition called "red ales." Their close relatives, known locally as *oud bruins*—sweet and sour and slightly meaty—which are brown with amber highlights, are called "browns." Still other breweries make beers that share characteristics of both, and some qualities of neither. Unfortunately, the distinction grows ever more academic: These exquisite beers, echoes of the distant past,

ABOVE: *A street view in Oostvleteren, typical of the small villages that dot the countryside in West Flanders*

are slowly dying out. Even more than lambics, their future rests in the survival of a shrinking handful of producers. ■

ORIGINS

TART FLEMISH ALES date back centuries in Flanders, where they have long been a regional specialty, extending as far east as Mechelen (just north of Brussels). But unlike their sour cousins near Lembeek, the group never formed a cohesive or enduring style the way lambics did. Writing in the 1850s, Georges Lacambre clustered them together out of convenience, acknowledging that they came "in a number of varieties. . . . It varies greatly from place to place and sometimes in the same locality; often in the same town there are not two brewers whose beers are the same."

Throughout Flanders, people prized these beers and regarded their deep color a marker for quality. Remarkably,

brewers achieved it not through the use of dark malts or sugars, but through slow caramelization of the wort over exceptionally long boils. Ten to twelve hours was the standard for the famous beers of Mechelen, and in West Flanders they were longer—sometimes an astonishing twenty hours. These intense boils must have produced heavy, concentrated beers loaded with caramel flavor. Of course, such a boil was arduous and expensive, so some breweries cheated, adulterating their beer with the mineral lime.

Current Flemish tart ales get their character from aging in wooden casks, and that practice goes back centuries. Practices varied in West Flanders, where the beer was considered ripe and palatable after

LEFT: *Rodenbach's beer has a pure, sharp tartness.*

regional favorites into the sixties and seventies. Only larger, wealthier breweries were able to maintain large cellars full of foeders, however, and the number of breweries making wood-aged tart ales dwindled as cheaper lagers became popular. One of the great champions of these beers arrived in the 1970s and remained a fierce advocate until his death: the writer Michael Jackson. He was the first to attempt to place the dizzying variety of Belgian beers into categories or "styles," and decided to split the Flemish tart ales in two. He didn't have an especially good reason for this, though there is perhaps an admission hidden in this passage from *Beer Companion*:

> *The sweet-and-sour character is common to the brown ales of East Flanders and the 'red' of the West, and the two are brother brews.*
> *. . . Both interpretations have their origins in wood at ambient temperatures, before either stainless steel or refrigeration became available. Each is geographically in the corner of its country, and they have somehow survived.*

three months. In Mechelen, breweries aged their beers up to ten months and, much as the famous producer Rodenbach does today, blended old stock with fresh beer. Interestingly, Rodenbach traces their own practice of blending beer to Britain. In 1872, a third-generation Rodenbach, Eugène, returned from a stint in England where he learned the secrets of porter brewing. Although vat aging was known to Flemish breweries, Rodenbach apparently wasn't doing it. Eugène collected the first huge vats (*foeder* in Flemish, *foudres* in French) and began to age Rodenbach to achieve the kind of vinous acidity for which porters had become famous. (There may be another connection. Eugène's grandmother, Regina Wauters, was a brewer's daughter from Mechelen.)

Tart ales remained popular well into the twentieth century. Following the wartime devastation, tart ales rebounded in the late 1940s and were still considered

For each style, the famous old breweries in Roeselare in West Flanders (Rodenbach) and Oudenaarde in East Flanders (Liefmans) stood as standard bearers for "the brown ales of East Flanders and the 'red' of the West" but they had less and less company. Jackson's patronage may have saved these breweries, but his distinction between them stylistically is now hard to argue. (Even the east–west distinction might look strange to visitors noting that the breweries are separated by only twenty-five miles.)

Tart ales were seriously endangered when Riva, a large consortium of breweries, bought Liefmans in the early 1990s. The new owners quit the quirky old brewery in Oudenaarde and moved production to nearby Dentergem. In 2007, Liefmans was saved from liquidation by Duvel Moortgat. In an effort to find a wider audience, Liefmans has been cleaned up and some find the character has gotten less complex. A handful of other Flanders breweries, led by Verhaeghe, Bockor, and Van Honsebrouck, have kept the tradition alive, if barely. Verhaeghe is the only brewery besides Rodenbach and Liefmans devoted to this type of beer, while Bockor and Van Honsebrouck make just one example. These are desperate times for the style—even the Americans, reliable rescuers of lost styles, have had a hard time replicating the quality of the originals—and it may well dwindle further. A twinkle of possibility yet remains: Revivalists at De Dolle and De Struise, two modern Flanders craft breweries, have made impressive, accomplished twenty-first-century tart Flemish ales. ■

DESCRIPTION AND CHARACTERISTICS

PEOPLE HAVE SPENT well over a hundred years trying to categorize the differences among the brown ales of Flanders, but the beers have perpetually shifted and changed. In recent decades, writers have focused on two breweries as exemplars of style—Rodenbach and Liefmans—but this gave false coherence to a shaggy collection of different products. Looking at the survivors that still manage to produce beers in the lineage of tart dark ales, you see almost as many unique examples as there are breweries—the idea of "styles" isn't much use to us in a consideration of tart Flemish ales.

The region's most important brewery is Rodenbach, and not just because it's the most famous. Rodenbach uses a mixed culture of yeasts, and ages their beer in immense vats—the largest are 8,000 gallons—for up to two years. During that time it acidifies to a pH even more extreme than lambic's. Until the

RIGHT: *Of the tart ales of Flanders, Bellegems Bruin is the smoothest and least sour.*

ABOVE: *Flemish red? Flanders oud bruin? A rose by any other name . . .*

1970s, Rodenbach used a cool ship and fermented their beer spontaneously, and until Palm acquired the brewery in 1998, it supplied its multistrain yeast to many of the area's breweries—Verhaeghe, De Dolle, Liefmans, and Strubbe along with others that no longer make soured browns. The shift to "mixed fermentation" signaled a change at Rodenbach, and the breweries dependent on Rodenbach's yeast changed when they could no longer procure fresh cultures. Even in the past few decades, the "traditional" beers have evolved.

Let's start with Rodenbach. The brewery selects the very best lots to bottle separately (a rare practice) but mainly uses wood-aged beer to blend with fresh ale. Regular Rodenbach uses 25 percent vintage ale, and Grand Cru 75 percent. The former is a quite sweet ale lightly kissed by tartness, a versatile partner for food. (After tastes changed, Rodenbach had to sweeten this blend, and some older fans still chafe at the decision.) Grand Cru depends on what brewer Rudi Ghequire calls the "triangle of taste"—sweetness, dryness, and acidity. The dryness and acid come from the aged ale, which can reach 98 percent attenuation. Fresh beer provides a bit of the sweetness and effervescence, but equally important are esters that develop during the long maturation. The esters give Rodenbach Grand Cru the unmistakable flavor of balsamic vinegar that comes from acetic and lactic acids as well as their associated esters.

Brouwerij Verhaeghe in Vichte, just southeast of Roeselare, follows a similar process to produce its signature Duchesse de Bourgogne; Verhaeghe also produces a dry, woody, unblended product called Vichtenaar. As with Rodenbach, the nature of the sour is distinctly balsamic.

Liefmans old brown ales are also similar, but there is one noteworthy difference. The brewing is handled off-site; fermentation, carried out in the old location at Oodenaarde, happens in open fermenters with mixed fermentation. The biggest difference from the beers brewed in Roeselare and Vichte is that Liefmans is aged in steel. Blends of Oud Bruin are made from three-to-four-month-old beer; Goudenband is aged at least a year.

But others approach their beers in completely different ways. Brouwerij Bockor, in Bellegem, makes their beer by blending a brown lager with spontaneously fermented ale aged eighteen months. The character for this beer oscillates between a smooth, neutral brown and a lightly sour ale. The Van Honsebrouck brewery also makes a brown called Bacchus using this method. By contrast, Bavik ages a strong pale beer for two years in oak tuns. That beer becomes Petrus Aged Pale, but the brewery also blends some in with a lighter, fresh brown ale to make Oud Bruin. Finally, De Dolle Brouwers have experimented with a number of different methods to make Oerbier, but currently use a very traditional (read: nineteenth-century) brewing method that involves a long boil, settling the trub (sediment) in a cool ship, and sour aging in steel.

All of these beers bear some resemblance, but they are distinctive.

Verhaeghe and Rodenbach have vinegar notes and pure, sharp tartness. Bockor Bellegems Bruin has a similar nose, but is smoother and lacks the balsamic sour of Rodenbach. De Dolle is a huge, deep beer with a dry, austere finish. Liefmans has a sweet-and-lactic-sour character that is less complex but more comforting. Bavik Petrus Oud Bruin is woody and bitter, but has a nonbalsamic vinegar note that sharpens the palate. Their differences make them one of the most interesting families of beers, and each deserves to be sampled once. ■

BREWING NOTES

WE'VE ALREADY TOUCHED on some of the variation in methods, but it's useful to drill down and look at a couple of important (if not universal) aspects in brewing tart Flemish ales: mixed fermentation and wood aging. Spontaneous fermentation isn't limited to the area around Brussels—brewers in Flanders still do it to make tart ales, and Rodenbach's legendary strain of yeast originally derived from spontaneous methods. Most breweries now used a process called "mixed fermentation"—a blend of wild cultures pitched rather than harvested wild in open cool ships.

No one can describe the process better than Rodenbach's brewer, Rudi Ghequire.

In our process, we work with a yeast culture with eight different yeast strains and also a little bit of lactic bacteria. During the first week,

we have an alcoholic fermentation from the yeast cells, and after one week the lactic bacteria take over. During the lagering time [four to five weeks] we reduce the yeast cells in the beer by precipitation, and then we send a nearly bright, young beer to the wood. The big difference between spontaneous fermentation and mixed fermentation is with spontaneous you send wort to wood and we send young beer. Beer has an alcoholic protection, so it is less risky. When you reuse yeast from spontaneous fermentation, you have arrived at "mixed fermentation."

The process of aging beer on wood induces subsequent changes that give these tart ales their unique quality. Although the oak tuns contain resident wild yeasts and bacteria, they only

ABOVE: *Goudenband is aged at least a year.*

reproducing the balance of acids and esters that give Belgian beers, aged in foeders, their rich complexity. Wine barrels activate the *Brettanomyces*, which dry the beer out, reducing the perception of sharp acid typical in foeder-aged Flemish beer. A few breweries have found larger European wine tuns (Boulevard, Tröegs, and New Belgium, to name a few), but it is hard to find the fine-grained European oak vessels favored by brewers. Those two elements—mixed fermentation with wild yeasts and bacteria, and slow aging in large foeders—are key to these beers.

Recipes for tart Flemish ales are fairly similar. Pale or Vienna malts, caramel, corn, and sugar are common. Hopping is used for its antibacterial qualities, not for bitterness or flavor. In most Flemish tart ales, hops fall below the flavor threshold. The beers enjoy relatively long boils of two hours or more—which, while long by modern standards, is well below the boil lengths for lambics.

The beer resting in the foeders is judged ready not when it reaches a certain age, but when the brewer determines it tastes complex and ripe—a moment that may come months apart for different batches in different tuns. When the beer is ready, brewers blend various batches of aged beer into a single mother-batch that itself gets blended with younger beer, or in some cases sold as is. Even in highly technical breweries like Rodenbach, this is still done by tasting, though chemical analysis confirms their work. ■

inflect the already inoculated beer. Rather, it's the action of oxygen that makes the difference. Some microorganisms are anaerobic, working in the absence of oxygen, while others, like *Brettanomyces*, are aerobic. Wood is porous and allows oxygen to feed aerobic yeasts and inhibit anaerobic bacteria. But equally important is the amount of oxygen entering the beer—a factor dependent on the size of the foeder and the thickness of the oak slats. The larger the tun, the less beer will be in contact with oxygen; the thicker the stave, the less oxygen. Standard-size wine barrels let in about ten times the amount of oxygen as Rodenbach's massive tuns.

This is one of the reasons American breweries have had such a hard time

EVOLUTION

THE TART ALES of Flanders suffer from misunderstanding, obscurity, and general weirdness, but at least brewers have more latitude in their methods than do lambic makers. This may be their salvation. More than thirty years ago, De Dolle Brouwers—the "mad brewers"—became pioneers in resurrecting old brewing styles. Indeed, they resurrected a nearly lost brewery, acquiring a creaky old place in Esen, near the French border, that dates back to the 1840s. They could be called one of the first Belgian craft brewers—one of the first craft brewers, period—but the partners are more like cultural archivists, saving and preserving tradition. Their first beer was, appropriately, a tart Flemish ale. They called it Oerbier, where "oer" has the same sense as the German *ur*—original. It was their original beer, but the meaning really suggests the original beer of the region, the ur-Flemish brown.

Oerbier has gone through several incarnations, originally using yeast from Rodenbach. When that became unavailable, Oerbier became a regular strong brown—"like a Trappist," says founder and brewer Kris Herteleer. Now Oerbier goes through a separate mixed fermentation, though in steel tanks. One small batch, Oerbier Reserva, was put on cask and it was a huge success; the brewers hope to do more in the future.

The beer goes through a classic long boil of up to three hours before resting for an hour in a cool ship—not to attract wild yeasts (the beer is too hot), but to settle out particulates. It's a technique Lacambre lauded in the mid-nineteenth century, one he felt didn't have the disadvantages of the newfangled English chillers that failed to remove the trub. Much like the nineteenth-century brewers, De Dolle's Harteleer is also a big fan of long boils, which "thank much of their flavor to the . . . [Maillard] reactions" that caramelize the malt. (Maillard reaction describes a chemical process of browning that gives seared steak, baked bread, and dark ales their tasty flavors.) But for De Dolle Brouwers, the long boils produce richer malt flavor and a deeper bitterness. In a wry aside, Harteleer admitted that brewing scientists now think long boils damage a beer's shelf life and "with their new testing machinery, they are even able to prove it." Harteleer is unpersuaded, and it's hard to argue with the highly praised beers De Dolle makes.

Another new brewery steeped in the region's history is De Struise Brouwers—"The Sturdy Brewers." The brewery was originally founded at an ostrich farm, and the word for "sturdy" is a play on the Flemish word for "ostrich"—and why an ostrich appears on their official seal. De Struise makes a much larger line than De Dolle and wanders more readily into modern craft beer styles like imperial stouts. Its flagship is Pannepot, a beer with a personal connection to the brewery. The beer takes its name from a small fishing vessel of a type owner Carlo Grootaert's great-grandfather once used to ply the waters near De Panne for herring. It is fashioned on an old homebrew made by the wives in the family.

They had a unique system of mulling it by plunging a red-hot poker from the fire into the beer, which had the secondary effect of caramelizing it. De Struise approximates that homebrew with the thick Pannepot. "The label is actually my great-granddad's boat, the B-50," he told me.

But De Struise's greatest brewing achievement is a rare one, limited by their cask capacity. Called Aardmonnik, it is a strong brown ale with a pronounced tartness, aged two years in wine barrels inoculated with lactic bacteria—no *Brettanomyces*. The final product is blended to produce a complex beer of sharp sour and rich, sweet malt. Like the brewers at De Dolle, the Sturdy Brewers are keen to revive old traditions.

These types of beers have not been brewed to distinction outside Flanders—with one notable exception. Colorado's New Belgium Brewing produces a beer called La Folie that has all the complexity and depth of the originals. It's not surprising. The brewer at New Belgium, Peter Bouckaert, came there from Rodenbach. A part of the Lips of Faith series, La Folie is a beer worthy of a Rodenbach brewer. ∎

THE BEERS TO KNOW

VEN PITCHING the largest tent under which all these ales might gather, they constitute a sadly short list. Some of these beers are readily available, though, and are musts for anyone unfamiliar with the tradition. They're also handy to have around when you have wine drinkers visiting, especially those who maintain a distance from beer—give them a tart ale from Flanders and see how their opinions change.

RODENBACH GRAND CRU

LOCATION: Roeselare, Belgium

MALT: Undisclosed variety of pale malt, roasted barley, corn grits

HOPS: Locally grown (varieties change year to year)

6% ABV

It's worth beginning with a bottle of regular Rodenbach, containing 25 percent aged stock, so you can triangulate when you try 75 percent old stock Grand Cru. The latter is obviously more sharply tart, but what surprises are the higher levels of fruity esters, which fool some people into believing cherries have been added. Grand Cru is a dry beer, but esters fool the palate into thinking it's sweeter—this is the chemistry that makes the style sing. From time to time, Rodenbach releases single-*foeder*, undiluted stock—a beer with nearly no remaining sugars that is nevertheless rich and tastes of cherry. Grand Cru is one of the world's great beers, and every beer fan should try it at least once.

VERHAEGHE DUCHESSE DE BOURGOGNE

LOCATION: Vichte, Belgium

MALT: Undisclosed

HOPS: Undisclosed

6.2% ABV, 1.065 SP. GR.

The Duchesse de Bourgogne is Verhaeghe's answer to Rodenbach Grand Cru—but the brewery offers a slightly lighter, sweeter take. Many of the elements are consistent with Rodenbach and yet the Duchesse is more vinous, with a wine-skin astringency. If you're trying to convert wine-loving friends to beer, this is the one to start with.

Flemish Art of Brewing

DUCHESSE DE BOURGOGNE

Verhaeghe Vichte

VERHAEGHE ECHTE KRIEK

ooooooooooooooooooooooooooooooooooooooo

LOCATION: Vichte, Belgium

MALT: Undisclosed

HOPS: Undisclosed

OTHER: Limburg Province cherries

6.8% ABV, 1.065 SP. GR.

One way to assure consumers you're not using flavoring syrups is to call your beer "Real Cherry"—as does Verhaeghe, in Flemish, with Echte Kriek. One of the only remaining examples of a once-common variation, Verhaeghe's illustrates how well the elements of brown ales, acid, and cherries come together. Even more than lambics, the chocolatey malts in a brown ale really allow the cherries to pop—and everyone knows what a great combination cherries and chocolate are. Drying tannins attest to the presence of actual fruit.

DE STRUISE AARDMONNIK

ooooooooooooooooooooooooooooooooooooooo

LOCATION: Oostvleteren, Belgium

MALT: Undisclosed

HOPS: Undisclosed

8.0% ABV

The balsamic aroma wafting off Aardmonnik marks it as an authentic Flemish tart ale, but the scent is somewhat deceptive—on the palate there's far more chocolate, wood, and malt. It's quite a bit darker and richer than the typical Flemish; an almost stout-like quality that adds balance to drying acid. A rare beer released in small lots, this is one of the finest examples from the region.

LIEFMANS GOUDENBAND

ooooooooooooooooooooooooooooooooooooooo

LOCATION: Oudenaarde, Belgium

MALT: Undisclosed

HOPS: Undisclosed

7.9% ABV, 1.075 SP. GR., 6 IBU

Goudenband has long stood as the "oud bruin" counterpoint to the "Flemish red" of Rodenbach. They are different. Goudenband has much more fresh malt character, sweet and raisin-like, cosseting the tart balsamic notes. It's something like Chinese sweet-and-sour sauce; where the currents cross you find a cinnamon and port. The body of this brown is surprisingly light and effervescent. Liefmans is less intensely sour than Rodenbach and has a light, candy-like sweetness that makes it more approachable.

DE DOLLE BROUWERS OERBIER

ooooooooooooooooooooooooooooooooooooooo

LOCATION: Esen, Belgium

MALT: Undisclosed

HOPS: Poperinge-grown Whitbread Golding

OTHER: Dark solid candi sugar

9.0% ABV, 1.083 SP. GR., 30 IBU

Oerbier is a strong brown ale acidified slightly by *Lactobacillus*. It doesn't possess the characteristic balsamic note of some Flemish tart ales, nor is the tartness aggressive. Rather, the beer is smooth, coruscating, and mildly tart. It's woody, dry, and fairly hoppy as well. Oerbier, De Dolle's bid for an ur-tart ale, may or may not be the original Flemish ale; with luck, it could be Flemish ale's future.

Rodenbach

THE ART OF WOOD AGING

THE TOWN OF ROESELARE SEEMS MORE MODERN AND BUSTLING THAN MANY OF THE SLEEPY, MEDIEVAL TOWNS THROUGHOUT WEST FLANDERS. THERE'S A REASON FOR THIS: ROESELARE, LOCATED ON THE FRONT LINES IN WORLD WAR I, WAS LARGELY WIPED OUT. AFTER THE WARS, THE CITY REBOUNDED AND IS NOW A HUB OF INDUSTRY AND TRADE. FOR NEARLY TWO CENTURIES, THE RODENBACH FAMILY HAS BEEN AT THE CENTER OF COMMERCE, AND FOR NEARLY AS LONG, RODENBACH HAS KEPT ALIVE THE MOST TRADITIONAL METHODS OF FLANDERS BREWING.

When Rudi Ghequire, the master brewer at Rodenbach, took me on a tour of the brewery, we spent less than ten minutes in the actual brewhouse. We spent a similar amount of time on the history of the brewery (even though history is a *big* deal at Rodenbach) and a few minutes on fermentation. But our tour lasted two hours.

The remainder of our time? We spent it inside the maze of cellars that contain the massive vats of aging beer.

LEFT: *The old maltings building, now a museum*

RIGHT: *Except for the mustaches, little has changed at Rodenbach in the last 100 years.*

This is not incidental. Rodenbach takes care making its beer—the new owners, Palm, spent a boatload of money on a beautiful new brewery after purchasing it in 1998—but what happens in the mash tun and kettle aren't the main event. The real action happens in those famous oaken foeders. There are 294 of them altogether, and they're housed in ten vast cellars that can hold up to thirty-three each. The smallest are 120 hectoliters (roughly 100 barrels or 3,200 gallons) and the largest are a whopping 650 hectoliters (550 barrels/1,700 gallons). Many of them are very old—the brewery says "older than 150 years" but they've been saying that for a while. The three oldest date back to the 1830s. The brewery has its own cooperage, not for building the vats

but for maintaining them. This is how their version of an acidified red ale has been made for well over a century. Inside the vats, a happy little colony of wild yeasts work away for months, adding lactic acid to the beer and dropping the pH. This is where Rodenbach is truly made.

When it comes time to bottle the beer, Ghequire leads a team of tasters who blend the vintage beer to get the character they want. They taste the beer in each foeder and begin to construct a blend from a combination of vats that have the proper character. Each vat is its own ecosystem, so the beer coming out will taste different

TOP LEFT: *Brewer Rudi Ghequire*

TOP RIGHT: *A line of foeders*

RIGHT: *Oak drying in the cooperage*

FACING PAGE: *The new glass-walled brewhouse is ultra-modern, but the beer becomes Rodenbach in the cellars below.*

vat to vat. On the day I visited, Ghequire pulled out a "key" that opened the valve on the foeders. We tried samples in different cellars and of different ages. One was so sour it made me cough. Another was chocolatey. In one, Ghequire tasted the kiss of *Brettanomyces*—a flavor that doesn't appear in Rodenbach's beers. It was too subtle for me to detect, but he made a mental note of it. "We'll have to blend that out," he said. Once they have a final blend of vintage stocks, they will combine that back with fresh beer to make Rodenbach and Grand Cru.

Rodenbach's baroque production methods would only be worthy of a footnote if the beer were ordinary. Of course, it's not. Regular Rodenbach is a lovely session tipple that has surprising versatility with food and Grand Cru, a blend of two-year-old foeder-aged beer (75 percent) and young beer (25 percent), is simply one of the world's best beers. Americans are adept at re-creating most styles, but approximating Rodenbach is tough; Ghequire believes this is entirely due to the wood. Without the interaction of wild yeasts and the tiny bit of oxygen that permeates the grain, beer can't develop the depth and character Rodenbach has. Those giant tuns are central to the process, too. Because very little of the beer is in contact with oxygen-permeable wood, it ages very slowly. It's much harder to do this kind of beer with small tuns or wine-sized casks. Ghequire says the 180-hectoliter vessels are ideal.

Of all the breweries there are to visit in the ancient brewing countries of Great Britain, Belgium, Germany, and the Czech Republic, Rodenbach may be the most awesome. Every older brewery I visited discussed the balance between tradition and efficiency—an important consideration for a commercial enterprise. But Rodenbach is off the charts in terms of the expense and inefficiency it takes them to produce a single bottle of beer. No modern company would or could consider the Rodenbach model. The vats alone cost thousands of dollars, never mind the cellar space. Add to that the notion of vatting beer for two years—an absurdly expensive venture. And yet here the brewery is, putting beer in vats and then trying to compete in a marketplace where industrial lagers can be made in a fraction of the time and for a tiny fraction of the cost.

It's no surprise that the tart beers of Flanders are on the endangered species list. Very few brewers make authentic ones, and none make them the way Rodenbach does. It is almost impossible to imagine any brewery will join Rodenbach in the near term, either. If we could designate breweries as "World Heritage" sites that would never fail because of commercial pressures, I'd put Rodenbach at the front of the list. In the world of beer, there's nothing like it, and we are fortunate indeed that it has survived the vagaries of wars, depressions, and modernization. Fortunately, we can all act to protect this institution by drinking a bottle of Grand Cru now and again.

Wild ALES

magine you're the brewer at a modern facility, standing in front of a gleaming steel conditioning tank. Do you marvel at the technological advancement that has allowed you to make the purest beer in the long history of brewing? Do you silently praise the caustic chemicals that return your equipment to laboratory cleanliness? Do you sing hosannas because, unlike your predecessors from centuries past, you no longer have to contend with souring

Wild Ales.

The category of wild ale includes any beer that derives its central character from wild yeast and bacteria. There are no boundaries of color or strength, and many wild ales—following the tradition of sour fruit beers of Belgium—are made with fruit. Despite this huge range, wild ales have an unmistakable unifying quality. Acidity is almost always half the equation, though it may be experienced as dryness or sourness depending on the beer; "funk" is the other half, a constellation of flavors that range from the fruity and citric to the decomposing and animal-like. The acidity of these beers makes them excellent partners for rich, decadent foods.

The funk can bring out the earthiness of a Gruyère or the creaminess and herb of a blue cheese, and one of the best pairings in the beer world is a fruit sour and dark chocolate.

Wild ales constitute a method far more than a style. As beers, they are impossible to catalogue: They may have very little alcohol or a great deal; be light-colored or dark; or made with wheat or fruit.

microorganisms that will quickly spoil your beer? You do not.

Instead, you wonder what it would be like to brew beer as they did during the Thirty Years War, using techniques that would surely produce tart and funky beer unpalatable to the great majority of twenty-first-century beer drinkers. Sure, the process is slow and expensive—but it's unpredictable, too! Bizarrely enough, this roughly describes the thinking that led to a growing number of strange and wonderful beers made in the United States and Italy. ■

ORIGINS

THE MODEST Dan Carey does not claim to have single-handedly reintroduced tart ales to the modern world—but he probably could. It was actually the reason he and his wife, Deb, founded New Glarus Brewing in Wisconsin in 1993, though his love of acidic beers goes back to the previous decade and a continent across the sea. "When I was an apprentice in Germany, my wife and two daughters and I were living there and we rented a car and drove across the border into Belgium on vacation. That was 1986." By chance, he stopped in at the Lindemans brewery where he encountered the magic of lambic brewing. It was then "a rustic farmhouse brewery and [René Lindemans] was very open and he showed us how he brewed the beer. We thought it was just cool."

Dan tried to figure out how Lindemans did it, but it took him years. Working in Oregon at brewery fabricator JV Northwest, he tested out different practices on a 15-gallon system he cobbled together from the company's scrap pile. When describing the period, he pauses for two or three beats before allowing, "It was difficult. It was difficult to figure out how to brew it, that's for sure." But figure it out he did, and afterward he turned to his wife and said, "Let's move back home to Wisconsin and start a brewery." Carey launched New Glarus on the strength of the lagers he learned to brew in Germany—a more familiar tipple to the region's heavily German population—but released Wisconsin Belgian Red, a kriek made with famous Door County cherries, in 1995. It instantly started winning awards (and irritating Belgians), and piqued consumers interest across the country.

None of the Americans knew how to make wild beers, though. This wasn't a thing they taught you in brewing school, and the techniques weren't known in the U.S. In the 1990s, lots of people tried to get Carey to explain how he did it, but he guarded his techniques. Beginning in the 2000s, breweries became more adept at barrel aging and pitching wild yeasts. Some experimented with sour mashes and lactic fermentations, and eventually even began exploring spontaneous fermentation. In Maine, Allagash's Rob Tod embarked on the most audacious journey into the world of wild ales in 2008, when he added a new building and cool ship for spontaneous fermentation; others, like Ron Jeffries at Jolly Pumpkin in Michigan, also played with these techniques.

The Brett Pack. In 2006, a group of five American brewers decided to take a trip to Belgium to see how many secrets they might prize from the methods of the old country. A lot, as it turned out. When they returned stateside, full of inspiration and excitement, each one launched some kind of wild ale program; the brewers now form a who's who of wild-ale brewing: Adam Avery (Avery Brewing), Tomme Arthur (Port Brewing/Lost Abbey), Sam Calagione (Dogfish Head), Vinnie Cilurzo (Russian River Brewing), and Rob Tod (Allagash). A group of five guys fueled by charisma and beer—on a mission to understand the secrets of *Brettanomyces*—the name was almost too perfect. But which one is Joey Bishop?

Americans led the way in this revival, but soon brewers from other countries joined in. Belgians, perhaps feeling a bit proprietary about the methods Americans were happily appropriating, were among the first. Craft breweries like De Proef and De Struise jumped in to reclaim their national heritage. But the Italian brewers have most quickly adopted the methods of wild fermentation. In fact, wild beers form a much more central part of the emerging Italian brewing canon than they do in either Belgium or the United States, where wild ales are at most a niche interest. Italian brewhouses like Birra del Borgo, Baladin, LoverBeer, Panil, and Ducato all have been making stellar examples. ■

DESCRIPTION AND CHARACTERISTICS

I**F YOU VISIT** at the right time of year, you might find flats of apricots stacked around the Cascade Barrel House in Oregon. Brewer Ron Gansberg likes to make a trip down the Columbia River Gorge from Portland to personally select the fruit he'll put in his barrel-aged sour beer. (He also uses cherries, blackberries, blueberries, raspberries, figs—whatever catches his fancy, really.) But Gansberg, whose biography includes a stint in the wine industry, is a firm believer that *Brettanomyces* is the bane of good beer. When his hand-selected apricots find a barrel, they'll encounter only *Lactobacillus* acidifying the beer.

If, however, you visit the cellars of Chad Yakobson's Denver-based Crooked Stave, you enter the Sanctum of *Brett*. A lot of brewers use *Brettanomyces* in their beers, but no one is as committed to the wild yeast as Yakobson. In brewing school, he wrote a detailed master's thesis on the famous English fungus and went on to found a brewery where all beers are pitched exclusively with various strains of *Brett*.

These are but two examples of two brewers, both holding as close to perfectly opposing views as brewers could have. The point is: With wild ales, there are no rules, no general guidelines, no standard practices. To brewers, this is one of the beers' central attractions. The frontier of tart, acidic beers is tabula rasa and there is no theology to blaspheme. New Belgium's Peter Bouckaert, a pioneer in barrel-aged beers, says, "If I find a better way to make better beer, I'll make a better beer." A Belgian who came to Colorado via Roeselare and Rodenbach, he knows of what he speaks. New Belgium's system evolved from wine barrels to large wine vats, like Rodenbach, but in Fort Collins they make their famous La Folie using a "solera" system developed by sherry makers. It's a beer compared to Rodenbach, but the production method is quite a bit different. "What is traditional?" Bouckaert asks. "I'm not stuck in tradition—I'm not a museum. I want to continue to learn."

Wild ales may be only lightly acidic or puckeringly sour; they may be any strength or color; and they may be made without fruit or, more often, with. The dazzling range of beers and production methods make this vein of brewing very difficult to categorize. It includes a beer called

Buddha's Brew from Austin's Jester King. The brewery racks raw wort into barrels, pitches yeast and bacteria, and after a gestation period of nine months, bottles it with a fresh infusion of kombucha (a tea made with *Acetobacter* and yeasts). It is just 4.7% ABV, and the flaxen hue of witbier. The category also includes Cascade's Bourbonic Plague, a beer aged in three different types of barrels and blended with a separate batch that had been aged with cinnamon sticks and vanilla beans. Blended together, they spend another fourteen months on dates. That beer is 12% and black as an oil slick. And, too, the group includes Allagash Coolship Red (5.7%), a spontaneously fermented beer flavored with raspberries, and Double Mountain Devil's Kriek (9%), made with the cherries picked from brewer Matt Swihart's orchards. And . . . well, the list is hundreds of beers long, and no two are alike.

If there is a proclivity that distinguishes the new wild ales from those brewed in Belgium and Germany, it has to do with strength and intensity. Tart ales are by their own measure "extreme"—at least when compared with standard lagers and ales. American breweries tend to accentuate that by brewing them strong. The best-known examples from Russian River, The Lost Abbey, New Belgium, and Cascade Brewing are mostly stronger than 7%. Moreover, the flavors tend to be bolder than their European counterparts. The *Brettanomyces* character is drier and more leathery, the lactic acids sharper and more pronounced. Oregon State University measured these qualities when they compared tart ales from Flanders with

LEFT: *Wild and aged in bourbon barrels, Cascade's deep black Bourbonic Plague proves that wild ales defy typecasting.*

How Sour Is Too Sour? In one extraordinary twenty-four-hour period, I sampled lambics and gueuzes from the breweries/blenderies at Cantillon, Drie Fonteinen, and Boon in and around Brussels. When I was sitting down to a gueuze from my fourth producer, Girardin, I had a bolt of insight. None of the many different sour beers I'd been drinking was violent. They may have been brightly tart, but the flavors harmonized beautifully. In the United States, where "extreme" is a prized characteristic, tart ales can sometimes pack the punch of a raw habanero.

It should not be so. In many American wild ales, the acidity is as unyielding as vinegar and the "funk" tastes of diapers, burned rubber, and nail polish remover. To stake out a bold position, let me argue that a glass of vinegar that smells like burned rubber and used nappies is a mistake, not a beer. Too often, Americans forgive offensive aromas and flavors so long as they're suitably loud. Because tart ales contain so many weird flavors, drinkers often think these unpleasant qualities are intentional. Making good beer with wild yeasts and bacteria is one of the biggest challenges in brewing and, done right, produces a beverage almost anyone can appreciate—if not love. The drink will contain unfamiliar flavors and sensations, but they won't be innately unpleasant. Plenty of American breweries make beers to rival those in Brussels—even more reason we should refuse to tolerate those that don't.

American beers. Reporting the findings, OSU pilot brewery manager Jeff Clawson summarized the differences this way: "The American beers were perceived as quite a bit more sour, more astringent, more bitter, more salty, more stale/moldy, briny, dusty/earthy. Again, it's a character the American brewers are looking for." The Belgian beers, he said, were "less sour, a lot sweeter, lower in alcohol, not very bitter, and just very mellow, easy-to-drink sour beers."

Hypertartness is not the rule with Italian wild ales, however. It's a hallmark of Italian brewing that nothing is made to the extremes. With their focus on harmonizing beverage with cuisine, the hoppy ales are never too hoppy, and the wild ales are never too wild. LoverBeer, from just outside Torino, uses local barbera grapes to inoculate the wort—and those cultures have since inoculated the brewery's small wooden tuns—but the effect is a supple, rounded tartness. Farther east, in Allesandria, Birrificio Montegioco also makes delicate wild ales aged in wine barrels. They can have earthy, savory, herbal, or tropical highlights, and they finish with a tingle, not an electric shock of sour. ∎

BREWING NOTES

UNTIL THEY TASTED Dan Carey's marvelous tart ales, most American brewers hadn't spent a lot of time considering how to replicate the feat. Once they began scratching around, though, they found a trove of old and *really* old techniques from decades—and centuries—gone by. They began experimenting. Do you need to make a turbid mash, as the lambic makers do? Some breweries use them (Allagash), others don't (Russian River). Do you need to use aged hops? What about malted versus unmalted wheat? Personally I don't know of any brewery that attempted the twelve-hour boils Georges Lacambre described from the mid-nineteenth century (see page 246), but I wouldn't be shocked to learn they've been reprised.

American brewers have different equipment and ingredients, and make ad hoc adjustments to account for the changes in the modern brewery. They have to improvise, and in many cases don't have anyone to consult. At New Belgium, Peter Bouckaert realized that he was having a problem with yeast accumulation in his foeders. He came up with a clever solution. "Now what we do is a lager fermentation and we then filter the yeast out warm and then put it on wood." Lagering and filtration—modern innovations they never used in Lembeek.

Russian River's Vinnie Cilurzo and Lost Abbey's Tomme Arthur—two *Brett* Packers—modified their systems for spontaneous fermentation after that fateful trip to Belgium and Cantillon. "That's when Tomme and I came up with the idea to do the mash tun," Cilurzo said, "because we didn't have a cool ship." After doing a sour mash on Friday evening, he ran the wort out of the mash tun, cleaned it, and returned the wort. "We would . . . let it sit overnight in the mash tun so it would pick up all the little bugs and critters that [grew] during the sour mash the night before. And then we come in

> Wild ales are modern re-creations of *lambics, tart Flemish ales*, and *Berliner weisses*—and those are all good places to turn if you're craving something in the puckery spectrum.

Sunday and pump the beer over to the barrels. Then it would go through a spontaneous fermentation." (Russian River has upgraded to a stand-alone cool ship.)

Taken together, the techniques used in the United States and Italy form a living museum of wild ale brewing. Following is a short list of the most common methods.

■ **Spontaneous fermentation.** This is the granddaddy of all wild ale techniques, both the most expensive and the least predictable. Belgian lambic breweries have the advantage of tradition; they have had decades to perfect their techniques. When breweries like Allagash began using completely wild inoculation, they weren't sure whether the wild yeasts around their breweries would produce palatable beers—and not all of them have. But some—and Allagash is the charter member—have found their local yeasts to be wonderful partners in producing spontaneous beers. Now several American breweries make beer this way—more than do it in Belgium.

■ **Spontaneous via media.** Wild yeasts and bacteria are airborne, but they also live on the surfaces of objects. Brewers in Belgium speculate that one of the reasons lambic breweries have had such healthy, flavorful yeasts is because the bugs took flight from nearby fruit trees. LoverBeer, in Italy's northern wine country, decided to skip the airborne stage; brewer Valter Loverier adds yeast-covered grapes straight to his cooled wort instead. This is how vintners sparked fermentation for centuries, and it works for beer, too.

■ **Solera.** In the production of balsamic vinegar and certain wines like sherry, a solera consists of a series of wooden casks. The solera is a way of progressively aging the liquid; a portion is taken out of each cask at regular intervals and moved to the next cask, which contains an older mixture, so that by the time liquid is removed from the final cask, it contains a blend of aged liquids. In beer production, each cask is its own solera.

The most prominent practitioner of this technique is New Belgium, which has a system of large oak vats from 1,600 to over 5,200 gallons where beer is aged. Some of the vats contain pale base beer (named Felix), others dark (Oscar, of course), and they both ripen for the better part of two years. When it comes time to produce a beer like La Folie, the master blender, Lauren Salazar, begins tasting the lots from different vats and making a mother blend. Afterward, the brewery tops off each vat with fresh beer and the process repeats. Over time, each vat becomes a distinct ecosystem for populations of different microorganisms, and the beer each one produces is unlike the next.

■ **Barrel inoculation.** Another way of working with native populations of yeast and bacteria is to nurture them in barrels and inoculate fresh wort by putting it in these funky casks. Wineries and breweries used to spend time and money making sure the critters stayed out of the barrels, but this is a way of taking advantage of barrels where they have taken up residence. As in New Belgium's solera system, each wild barrel will develop its own characteristics.

■ **Pitched wild yeasts.** The easiest and most common way to introduce wild yeast and bacteria to fresh wort is in the form of laboratory-produced pure culture. American companies like White Labs and Wyeast have cultured different strains, and they are a (relatively) safe way to sour beer. Still, the effects are not predictable: Once introduced into a wooden cask, the effects of oxygen, temperature, and other organisms will affect each batch differently. For brewers who want more control, steel reduces the variables even more.

These are just the most common methods, and they are often used in combination. Cilurzo, for example, distinguishes between the kind of spontaneous fermentation he conducts and the process used in Belgium. "There has been a lot of spontaneous [fermentation] in there, but there have also been a lot of barrels that we pitched. You know, bacteria spilled on the floor." Those pitched, spilled bacteria and yeasts now inhabit the barrel room and form part of the microbiology of the "spontaneous" environment. Most breweries have similar small modifications in their own processes. ■

EVOLUTION

THE **REINTRODUCTION** of wild ales into captivity is less than two decades along. Since the methods of making them had been long abandoned (willfully, in most cases), brewers are still in the formative, tinkering stage. Each year, a brewery comes out with a new interpretation to add to the growing canon. As of this writing, the ratings site *BeerAdvocate* lists about seven hundred commercial examples—about twice the number of helles bocks and schwarzbiers. The tide has only begun to rise. ∎

THE BEERS TO KNOW

UNLIKE MOST production beers, it's nearly impossible to reproduce the flavors in wild ales consistently. This year's La Folie may be deep with red fruits, while last year's was heavier on persimmon. More like wine vintages, good wild ales reflect the conditions of the year. The temperature, variety of ambient microorganisms, quality of fruit—who knows, possibly even the position of the moon—all these things will result in gamier or softer or drier examples from year to year.

Fruited ales can be drunk as soon as you find a bottle, while others might evolve for a year or more in the bottle—acidity and alcohol are excellent preservatives, so even delicate fruit aromas remain bright longer in these types of beers. Whenever wild yeasts are involved, beers may continue to change as the vigorous *Brettanomyces* continues to consume sugars; the beers will become stronger and drier. The "wild" in wild ales is meant to indicate the nature of the yeast, but it could as easily point to the beers themselves. They are not predictable, and drinkers who enjoy this type of beer will have to venture without a map . . . into the wild.

NEW BELGIUM LA FOLIE

○○○

LOCATION: Fort Collins, CO

MALT: Pale, Munich, carapils, caramel, chocolate

HOPS: Target

6% ABV, 18 IBU

The foeders of New Belgium have decidedly different character from one another, and some of them ripen beer into extremely tart liquids. Brewed very roughly in the mode of Rodenbach, La Folie is more acetic and less lactic than Roeselare's finest. It also has some dry tannins that make it distinctive. These spikier elements are balanced by a sumptuous sweetness that comes from various blends. It's not a subtle beer, but with many facets of different sweet, sour, and bitter flavors that produce a different vintage each year, it rewards careful attention.

ALLAGASH COOLSHIP RESURGAM

LOCATION: Portland, ME

MALT: Undisclosed

HOPS: Undisclosed

6% ABV

Resurgam is a blend of brews of different ages, like a gueuze; the batch I tried contained two-year-old, eighteen-month-old, and six-month-old vintages. The mark of Belgian gueuzes is their balance and approachability, and Allagash meets this standard. It is a lemony, peppery beer with a wheat softness and mild acidity. The brewery is working to increase its volume, and Resurgam should continue to evolve in complexity as Allagash has more beer to work with.

NEW GLARUS WISCONSIN BELGIAN RED

LOCATION: New Glarus, WI

MALT: Pale, Munich, wheat, caramel

HOPS: Aged Hallertau

OTHER: Door County Montmorency cherries

4% ABV, 1.052 SP. GR.

I remember when this Belgian Red first appeared, I couldn't believe how tart it seemed. The market has since pushed flavors to the extreme, and now this lovely little kriek seems a perfect balance of lush fresh cherries dried by acid crispness. It's the kind of beer even those wary of sourness will enjoy.

RUSSIAN RIVER BEATIFICATION

LOCATION: Santa Rosa, CA

MALT: Undisclosed

HOPS: Undisclosed

5.5% ABV, 1.050 SP. GR.

Beatification is a beer that seems to vary from the sour to the extremely sour—a sere, leathery sensation that overwhelms even the sharp vinegar notes. It takes a swallow or two to acclimatize the palate, and then a curious thing happens: Beatification opens up with light, springing lemon and grapefruit-rind flavors. Bubbling carbonation invigorates the beer and animates it.

CASCADE APRICOT ALE

LOCATION: Portland, OR

MALT: Franco-Belgian pilsner, pale

HOPS: Aged Golding

OTHER: Hood River apricots

7.3% ABV, 1.065 SP. GR., 8 IBU

Cascade brewer Ron Gansberg has a fleet of excellent sour ales—Noyeaux, The Vine, Bourbonic Plague, and more—so here we'll let Apricot stand in for all of them. Gansberg's careful selection of fruit leads to dense, sweet aromatics and the scent of fruit blossoms. The beer itself, though alcoholic, is light bodied and apricot hued, summery and refreshing. The acidity preserves the fruit flavors and aromas, and there is enough residual sweetness to add body and balance; a Champagne-like spume of bubbles further enlivens it.

THE LOST ABBEY CUVEE DE TOMME

LOCATION: San Marcos, CA

MALT: Pale, wheat, light and dark caramel, Special B, chocolate

HOPS: Challenger, East Kent Golding

OTHER: Dextrose, raisins, candi sugar, sour cherries

11% ABV, 1.092 SP. GR.

This beer really speaks of the American craft-brewing instinct. Pushed and prodded to the extremes on every dimension, it is hugely alcoholic and packed with intense flavors that begin as fruit and sugars—cherries for sure, but they have to battle treacle and dark fruit for top billing. The *Brettanomyces* gives the beer just enough acid for balance.

JOLLY PUMPKIN LA ROJA

LOCATION: Dexter, MI

MALT: Pilsner, pale, Munich, dark caramel, black, and wheat malt

HOPS: Tettnang, Strisselspalt

OTHER: Dextrose

7.2% ABV, 1.054 SP. GR., 25 IBU

La Roja takes its inspiration from tart Flemish ales, but is distinctly American. Brewer Ron Jeffries blends one-year-old, six-month-old, and one-month-old beer. Even with the fresher beer, the *Brettanomyces* turns this to an incredibly dry, stony beer—a more parched presentation than you'd ever find in Brussels. Some nuttiness and wood tannins give it depth.

DESTIHL ST. DEKKERA ALES

LOCATION: Normal, IL

MALT: Varies

HOPS: Varies

ABV, SP. GR., IBU: Varies

Dekkera is another name for *Brettanomyces*, but the ales in the brewery's series are actually spontaneously wood fermented and contain a lambic-like variety of microorganisms. The beers rotate and change. A sampling I tried in 2011 included a violent framboise but two lovely milder ales, one with strawberry and a tart Flemish that had nutty malt character to balance sharper tart notes and tons of fruity esters.

Allagash

PAJOTTENLAND WEST

IF YOU WALK AROUND THE OUTSIDE OF THE ALLAGASH BREWERY, AN INDUSTRIAL WAREHOUSE FACILITY IN PORTLAND, MAINE, YOU RUN INTO AN ODD SIGHT—ANOTHER, MUCH SMALLER BUILDING ATTACHED LIKE A RUMBLE SEAT. A PIPE RUNS FROM THE MAIN BREWERY TO A BROAD, FLAT TANK THAT FILLS MOST OF THE INSIDE OF THE LITTLER STRUCTURE, AND DELIVERS WORT STRAIGHT FROM THE BREW KETTLE. THE TANK WILL HOLD THE WORT FOR TWELVE HOURS WHILE WILD YEASTS FROM THE CLEAN MAINE AIR DRIFT THROUGH OPEN WINDOWS AND "INFECT" THE BEER. THIS IS THE MOST ELEMENTAL FORM OF BREWING, MILLENNIA OLD, AND WHEN OWNER ROB TOD INSTALLED THE COOL SHIP IN 2008, HE HAD NO IDEA WHETHER IT WOULD WORK.

When I asked whether they had done any tests to gauge its viability, Tod and head brewer Jason Perkins said nope, that wasn't really possible. "We considered it," Perkins said, "but truthfully it wouldn't have been— well, it might have been partially accurate, but we needed to build the room first. We could have just put a bucket out there in the woods to see what would happen, but it wouldn't have been the same effect." They had some inkling the project would work, though. One of the brewery's barrels had already picked up some wild yeast, and instead of dumping the contents and hosing down the facility, they nurtured it. At first, Tod and Perkins weren't even certain what it was, but thought the character indicated *Brettanomyces*. Eventually they had it isolated at Wyeast Labs and found it was *Brett*. "It was not a strain they've ever seen before, different character," Perkins said. "So it's resident to this area, certainly. It has since gotten into a couple of our other barrels over time, some of our real long-aging barrels, unintentionally."

The second factor was the location. They looked at the maps and found that Maine is actually south of Brussels, but despite extremes in the hottest summer and coldest winter months, the weather

wheat malt and conduct something like a traditional turbid mash. Perkins pulls out a portion to bring to a boil in the kettle before returning it, raising the temperature in a Belgian version of decoction. Later he adds aged hops to avoid bitterness and puts the wort through a marathon four-hour boil. Like the lambic brewers in Belgium's Pajottenland, the wort overnights in the cool ship and then spends months aging in barrels before being blended and packaged. In every way that matters, Tod has re-created a lambic brewery in the United States.

is actually very similar. "March through June and late October through December, they're identical weather," Perkins said.

It was still a pretty radical decision. Tod was a member of the famous *Brett* Pack of American brewers who traveled to Belgium in 2006. Like his cohorts, he got really excited at the prospect of wild brewing—but later reconsidered. "When I got back I thought, 'It's too much work, it's too risky having all those microbes in the brewery. Let's just focus on the other Belgian-style beers we do.'" The enthusiasm returned, though, and later on "we all just looked at each other and we're like 'F**k it, let's build a cool ship.' That was basically what it came down to."

The gods of brewing smile on Allagash. The Atlantic air that blows across their cooling wort carries a rich habitat of healthy microorganisms that produce excellent lambic-style beer. The wild ales of Allagash are characterized by light and balanced tartness. Like those of Cantillon, they have a bit of lemon rind that adds citrus and bitterness. These Portland wild ales have a balanced acidity with none of the harsh chemical flavors wild yeasts sometimes produce.

In deference to the originals in Belgium, Allagash doesn't call their beer a lambic—but they could. They use raw

It's difficult to see how the spontaneous project will generate much in the way of revenue, but that's the wrong way to think about it. Breweries making this kind of beer, such as New Belgium, Russian River, Destihl, and others, do it because they love the flavors the ales contain. Because spontaneous and wild ales are a small portion of the breweries' bottom line, they don't have to pencil out financially. Breweries enjoy making them and customers get excited to buy them—which doesn't hurt the reputation of the brewery. But there are tangible benefits, too, and more and more breweries are recognizing them. Allagash's initial dalliance with *Brettanomyces* was risky and not obviously profitable. Yet it gave them a wonderful yeast they now use in Confluence, Interlude, Gargamel, and others. Their courage has resulted in a ton of good press—none of which hurts the sale of the flagship, White Ale—and their experiments are yielding unexpected possibilities. It's an exciting time.

PART SIX

Enjoying Beer

L est we forget, beer contains booze . . . Lovers of beer can spend hours extolling its wonderful qualities—sensual, social, healthful, and historical. But we must concede that the main reason it has burrowed so deeply into society has to do with its more active properties. Old English 800 Non-Alcoholic? That was never going to be a big seller. There is something inborn in humans that enjoys altered states of consciousness. Coffee, tea, tobacco, and alcohol (and in some places, legalized marijuana) account for billions of dollars of legal trade a year. Illegal efforts to trip, buzz, and get high are worth billions more.

And it was always so. From eating plants with psychotropic properties to eating slightly fermented ripe fruit, humans have tried to alter their consciousness as far back as we can see. Beer does have wonderful qualities—not the least of which was saving the lives of millions when water was unsafe to drink—but they are not its central lure. We drink beer because it tastes wonderful *and* provides a euphoric thrumming at the back of our brain pans. More dilute than wine or liquor, it makes an excellent social lubricant, keeping drinkers loose and happy without sending them immediately into stumbling drunkenness.

Because of this, beer is a fairly safe way to reach a companionable buzz—and therefore an excellent way to heighten already fun activities. Dining and pub going, beer festivals, tailgating, parties, and games are all made more enjoyable with the addition of a splash of beer. And these need not be mere pleasures of the flesh—the ancient ritual of toasting has divine connotations, and monks have, for thirteen centuries, been serving beer to pilgrims who visit their monasteries. There is something innately redeeming in the human impulse to experience collective exhilaration. Beer has long been a magic potion people used to help them in this endeavor, and it's worth at least skimming the social side of this wonderful merry-making beverage. ■

Serving and STORING BEER

There is an old debate. Bavarian wheat beers are bottled with extraordinary effervescence, both to create a lively body and to a give the beer a dense pile of snowy head. The trick is to get the beer from the bottle into the glass with two or three fingers of head—not half the glass.

There are two methods to accomplish this—two schools, even. Practitioners of the more traditional approach pour the bottle at a slow trickle, holding the glass at a 45-degree angle. Even this gentle technique is enough to rouse a billowing head. Other, more show-offy types place the glass over the bottle and then flip it so the bottle is held directly above the vertical glass. The pourer raises it slowly as the beer gurgles out. It takes talent to hold the lip of the bottle just above the rising surface, and failure results in an unwanted geyser. Both camps agree that the ritual is complete only when the dregs of the bottle have been deposited on the head, and the feet of the glasses have been clinked against each other in cheery salute. (I suppose that when you spend idyllic afternoons in the dappled sunlight of a Bavarian biergarten, you need something to debate.) *Prost!*

Do you need to pour a beer in such a prescribed manner? Must it be decanted in a weissbier vase? What about the yeasty lees—do you *have* to cloud your beer with them? The short answer is no.

Select any style of beer, and there will be rules governing how it should be served. The package it arrives in, the temperature it's supposed to be served at, the glassware appropriate to highlight its features, and the manner of pouring—some or all of these will be resident in the high ritual of service. A properly educated beer geek should know his weizen glass from his pleated lambic tumbler, and it's actually a lot of fun to understand the science and cultural expectations (which are sometimes presented as science) behind them. But all these rituals have one ultimate purpose: to accentuate the sensual enjoyment of drinking a beer. Although someone will inevitably tell you you're drinking your beer "wrong" (no matter how you're doing it), it's a good idea to learn how the manner in which it is served affects its appearance, aroma, and taste—and then go ahead and follow your bliss. ■

PACKAGING

UNLIKE MOST BEVERAGES, beer comes to us not only in different packages, but in a variety of different *states*. It may be naturally carbonated and "alive" (or, more precisely, containing live yeast), as in cask ale or container-conditioned beers. It might be artificially carbonated, as in keg beer. Or it might be enlivened with a nitrogen mixture rather than straight carbon dioxide. Any discussion of how to serve beer begins with how that beer comes to us, so here's a brief rundown on common states and packaging.

■ **Cask Ale.** The most elemental and ancient style of beer is "conditioned" right in the cask. The beer actually goes into the cask—once wooden but now usually metal or plastic—before it has completely finished fermenting. As the yeasts continue to munch away, they expel carbon dioxide, naturally carbonating the beer. The casks arrive at the pub, where a cellarman will let them settle and finish fermenting. When the yeast has fallen out of suspension, the beer can be tapped. In most traditional setups and throughout Britain, the cask takes on air as it drains, limiting it to a very short life—a few days at most. After that, the beer will turn sour. Modern systems do exist that replace the cask's empty space with sterile CO_2, but traditionalists frown on this practice.

■ **Bottle-Conditioned Beer.** The same principle applies here. Beer is packaged before it has completely finished fermenting, or is primed to start a secondary fermentation. Bottle-conditioned beer will have a dusting of yeast in the bottom. Once you open the container, that yeast will slowly be roused by the bubbling carbonation, so it's usually best to decant it immediately.

Pasteurization and Sterile Filtration.

Breweries have to make a calculation when they bottle their beer. On the one hand, they want to inhibit the action of beer-spoiling microorganisms, while on the other, they want to lengthen shelf life. Pasteurization accomplishes the first goal. There are two methods. "Tunnel pasteurization" exposes packaged beer to a ten-minute spray of 140°F (60°C) water; in "flash pasteurization," breweries heat the beer to 160°F (71°C) for less than a minute before rapidly chilling it back down.

Pasteurizing beer has two big downsides. Heating actually accelerates the aging process, so pasteurized beer stales faster. It also dulls delicate flavors and aromas, which may be the highlight of some specialty or craft-brewed beers. Some breweries use a process called "sterile filtration" to split the difference. In this process, also called "cold sterilization" or "draft filtering," breweries use an extremely fine filter to remove the cells of yeast and microorganisms. It doesn't change the chemistry of the beer like pasteurization, but it does remove flavor- and aroma-carrying particulates.

■ **Regular Bottles.** Bottles are the earliest form of take-home packaging, and they're still going strong. They continue to have a more exalted status than lowly cans, in spite of the fact that they don't do quite as good a job protecting the beer from harmful light.

■ **Cans.** Cans have some advantages over bottles. They are lighter, which not only makes them more convenient, but they require less energy during shipping. They protect beer completely from light. And for small breweries, canning lines are cheaper to install. Despite old prejudices, the metal in no way affects the flavor of beer—modern cans are lined.

■ **Kegs.** This is the big innovation that largely displaced cask ale. Beer in kegs is artificially carbonated and pressurized with CO_2 to stay unspoiled indefinitely. Stored at cold temperatures, kegs preserve the beer best, but it will eventually suffer the ravages of time like any beer.

■ **Nitrogen ("nitro") Beer.** Because yeasts naturally produce carbon dioxide, it is the most common way to carbonate beer. In the 1950s, however, Guinness discovered that beer could also be enlivened by nitrogen gas. Guinness fans know what the gas does to beer: It produces a unique cascade of bubbles that eventually form into an extremely tight, mousse-like head. Any beer may be nitrogenated, even when sold in bottles or cans.

■ **Growlers.** Brewpubs and craft beer bars commonly sell half-gallon jugs known as "growlers." The system dates back to at least the nineteenth century as a way for patrons to take beer home with them from the pub. Publicans pour the beer straight from the tap, and the jug will remain fresh and carbonated for several days—though it will quickly flatten after it's opened the first time. ■

TEMPERATURE

THE AVERAGE REFRIGERATOR is set to about 36°F (2°C), the ideal temperature for a frosty one. The problem is, you don't want a frosty one. Of all the things that affect the presentation of a beer, temperature is the most profound. Each style has an ideal range that allows the beer to express the flavors and aroma the brewer intended. Cold inhibits these qualities—and anesthetizes the tongue to boot. Of course, beer can be too warm, too, with predictably sticky, heavy results. Beyond flavor and aroma, temperature affects carbonation as well as texture and mouthfeel.

Most chapters in this book have a recommendation of serving temperature appropriate to style, but there are some general rules of thumb. English ales, which have delicate flavors that unfurl as they shake off the cold, should be served at the warm end, around 55°F. Lagers, on the other hand, have clarion notes of malt and hop that should come across without distortion. The cold—around 40°F— helps showcase these elements. Intensely scented hoppy beers—America's specialty—must be a bit warmer to showcase their aromas. Summery light beers are thirst quenchers, built for being served chilled.

No matter what temperature your beer is when it enters the glass, it'll warm up as you drink it. Notice how its properties change. Cold can help conceal faults in a beer, but if you're in a mood for diagnosis, you might like to let the beer reach room temperature. Any faults will be on vivid display then. Temperatures affect flavors and aromas predictably, but the way we react to those flavors and aromas are individual. Experiment, and find out what the right temperature is for your tastes. ■

GLASSWARE

THE HISTORY OF pale beers is usually told through the lens of malting innovation. Before the seventeenth century, malts were crusted with heat and smoke and the beers they made were nut-colored to coal-black. True enough, but why then did it take so long for paler beers to catch on? They required a parallel innovation—the mass production of clear glassware. Before clear glass came along, drinking vessels were made of opaque materials like pottery, wood, leather, or metal. But with glass, punters could finally get a good look at what they were drinking: chunky, murky, river-water stuff—some of the brown beers at the time must have failed to impress (and that's being generous). So when pale ales and lagers came along, refracting golden light through their sparkling clarity, people were magnetized by the sight of them. Beer was

(continued on page 550)

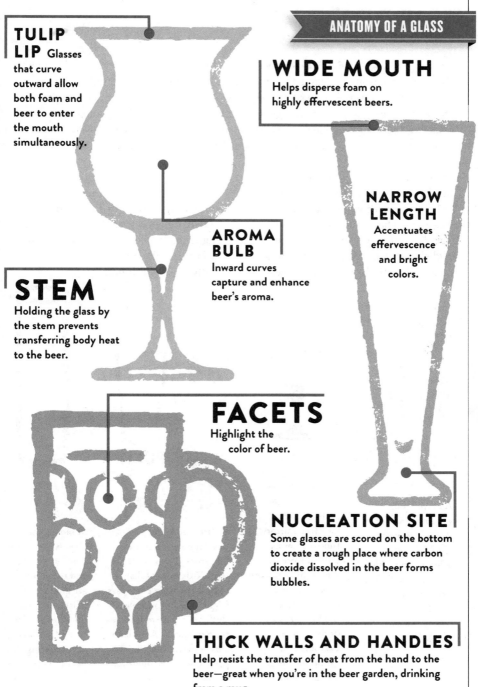

TULIP LIP Glasses that curve outward allow both foam and beer to enter the mouth simultaneously.

WIDE MOUTH
Helps disperse foam on highly effervescent beers.

NARROW LENGTH
Accentuates effervescence and bright colors.

AROMA BULB
Inward curves capture and enhance beer's aroma.

STEM
Holding the glass by the stem prevents transferring body heat to the beer.

FACETS
Highlight the color of beer.

NUCLEATION SITE
Some glasses are scored on the bottom to create a rough place where carbon dioxide dissolved in the beer forms bubbles.

THICK WALLS AND HANDLES
Help resist the transfer of heat from the hand to the beer—great when you're in the beer garden, drinking from a mug.

GLASS TYPES

THE VISUAL ELEMENTS of beer aren't limited to color; it foams and bubbles like a cauldron and leaves tracery on the side of the glass. To highlight these features, breweries have been designing proprietary glasses for decades. In some cases, glasses were designed by pub owners for durability and ease of use. Whatever the origin, a collection of a dozen or so glasses have become standardized for serving a style or category of beer styles. The most important are listed below.

It is worth mentioning that while the glasses are effective at highlighting their corresponding beer styles, it's not necessary to have a different glass for every beer. It may even be overly fussy. English and American pint glasses do a great job with the majority of beers.

A smaller glass like a snifter, tulip, or goblet—or even a wineglass—is nice for stronger specialty beers, and a tall, slender glass is great for pilsners and light golden ales. On the other hand, you can really impress guests with a fully stocked cabinet!

GERMAN MUG
(seidel/krug)

A more modern version of ancient stoneware mugs, ideal for festive drinking. Handles and thick walls keep beer cold in warm weather—and aid hearty toasts.

Tulip

Although they look like snifters, tulip glasses are quite different. The stem keeps the beer cold, and the outward flare at the lip allows the drinker to receive beer and head simultaneously. Use particularly for highly effervescent Belgian ales.

NONICK / TULIP
PINT GLASSES

British publicans developed the nonick ("no-nick") glass (left) in the 1960s as a stackable vessel. The tulip pint glass (right) hails from Ireland. Both are great workhorses for British and American ales, and the tulip in particular is excellent for conserving aromatics.

GERMAN STANGE

Stange is the German word for "rod" or "stick," and these glasses are common for kölsch and have qualities similar to a pilsner glass, accentuating the beer's clarity and bead. Alts use a similar glass called a becher.

PILSNER

A classic design that showcases a pilsner's golden clarity, sparkling effervescence, and snow-capped head.

SNIFTER

Snifters were developed for digestifs like brandy—and they do a great job with similar high-alcohol beers that open when they're warmed by the hand.

STEMMED POKAL

A straight-lined, Teutonic version of the tulip. Perfect for strong, sipping lagers like doppelbocks.

GOBLET

Designed for effervescent abbey ales, goblets prevent overfoaming and exaggerate deep colors; often enlivened with nucleation sites. They vent rich alcohol aromas and promote sipping.

WEISSBIER

Although it looks like a pilsner glass, the bulb-like top accommodates a towering head and, later, captures aroma. A good weiss "vase" has a thick foot to tap during toasts.

SHAKER PINT

Actually developed as a shaker for mixed drinks, this durable pint glass is nearly ubiquitous in pubs. Unfortunately, it's ugly and suppresses aromas.

flute

A specialty glass for special beers, particularly effervescent beers and fruit ales. Like a pilsner glass, it conserves carbonation and highlights color.

ENGLISH DIMPLED

Once common throughout the pubs of England, this pint glass now has the look of the past. It's quite useful, though—the handle keeps the beer cold (and hand warm), and the facets highlight the beer's color.

TUMBLER

Used for rustic styles like witbier, saison, and lambics. By tradition, lambic breweries typically use a pleated tumbler, while witbiers are served in chunkier jelly jar–style glasses.

Frosted Glasses. **It used to be common for nicer restaurants and bars to store beer glasses in a specialized freezer that coated them with a layer of cloudy ice. On the theory that no beer could be too cold, these glasses protected against thermal loss—and turned the figurative "frosty" mug into the literal. As a function of serving ritual—and visual panache—the idea has a lot of merit. As a way to serve the needs of the beer, not so much. Not only do frosted glasses help keep icy beer icy, they actually add ice to and water down the beer. The crime is not so great when committed against a mass-produced light lager, but with any other beer, a frosted glass will appreciably diminish the experience. Request a regular glass instead.**

(continued from page 546)

never the same again. We mainly use our noses and mouths to explore beer, but glassware finally gave us the chance to use our eyes.

An energetic writer could devote an entire book to glassware; because glasses have evolved in tandem with beer to highlight the virtues of local specialties, there are nearly as many glass shapes as there are styles of beer. The proper glass for an abbey tripel is a wide, stemmed goblet. Kölsches call for the opposite—narrow, rod-straight glasses called stanges. I'll spare you a full volume devoted to the ins and outs of glassware, but I have highlighted some of their most important features and offer up a few essential types: see pages 547 and 548–549, respectively. ■

POURING

THE ACT OF POURING out a beer—*decanting*, if you prefer—is not rocket science. On the other hand, if you're not paying attention, you may end up with a mug full of foam or a glassy-topped beer with no head at all. Some styles, like Irish stouts or Bavarian wheat beers, practically demand to be poured out, and publicans have to learn the proper way to do so. (Decanting helps rouse the yeast in a wheat beer and release the strong carbonation; and Irish stouts are served on nitrogen, which comes boiling out of solution when the bottle or can is opened.) But every style looks good with at least a skiff of foam, and a finger or two is a good mark to shoot for.

When you begin to pour out a beer, though, you may not have any idea how carbonated it is. (Carbonation is itself not constant—it's far more difficult to encourage a head in a beer of 38°F than at 55°F.) Before you pour without reservation, test the beer: Hold the glass at a 45-degree angle and begin pouring very slowly down the near side of the glass. Highly carbonated beers will begin to foam, while flatter beers will drizzle down without any sign of head. If you've got a highly carbonated beer, keep pouring down the side. You can moderate the

Honest Pints. Imagine you went to a gas station where the advertised price looked like a bargain, but where the pumps were calibrated to deliver 105-ounce gallons. At another station, the price was higher, but the gallons were a standard 128 ounces. In essence, this is the situation in which American pubgoers find themselves. When we go out for a beer, we may be getting anywhere from 12 to 20 ounces in glasses all called "pints."

The main culprit is the nearly ubiquitous shaker pint, the thick, conical vessel favored by bars for its durability. Most are 16 ounces, but some—with the same dimensions—have thick bottoms and hold only 14 ounces. These are the infamous "cheater pints" that sparked a nationwide project to bring transparency to glass sizes. (Full disclosure: I was one of its founders, though I'm no longer involved.) The problem goes beyond deception, though. Some pubs serve 20-ounce imperial pints, and some even serve 23-ounce imperial pints—on the assumption that with headspace, they will give a full 20 ounces of liquid.

Other countries regulate glassware measurements, but the United States leaves it to the retailer. As a consumer, one thing you can do is ask your server how large their glasses are. If you're suspicious, ask them to switch to "honest pints." In the absence of agreed-upon standards, customers have to be vigilant.

amount of head you create by pouring more or less vigorously.

If the beer looks fairly still, hold the glass vertically and lift the bottle six or eight inches high, pouring directly and vigorously into the middle of the glass. You don't have to pour fast, and in fact, if the liquid comes out in glugs, it will make large, unattractive splash bubbles. It's better to hold the bottle farther away from the glass so the beer plunges into the center, an act that will encourage it to release its carbon dioxide and form a head.

A final note: Before you pour, have a look at the label or bottom of the bottle to see if the beer contains yeast sediment. If it does, you have a decision to make: If you pour out the entire bottle, the last bit will be hazy with yeast and it will cloud your beer. If you don't, you leave a mouthful of precious beer remaining in the glass. A dilemma! My solution is simple: I pour out most of the beer, leaving enough behind so that I don't cloud the beer. Done right, the residue amounts to just about a swallow—delicious. ■

STORING AND AGING

THE MOMENT BEER leaves the brewery, it begins to change. The effects are minor at first and vary depending on the type of beer, what it was packaged in, and how it was stored. In science-y terms this is because, according to Belgian researcher Bart Vanderhaegen, "the constituents of freshly bottled beer are not in chemical equilibrium." And that is because, as you already knew, "thermodynamically, a bottle of beer is a closed system and will thus strive to reach a status of minimal energy and maximal entropy." In other words, the chemical compounds that create a perfectly fresh, vivid-tasting beer are not stable.

It is therefore almost axiomatic that beer is better the fresher it is. Almost. There's a small category of beer—strong, usually dark—that is actually improved by those chemical changes. Or if not improved, altered in interesting and pleasant ways. Left alone in a cool cellar for months or years, these beers develop rich, plummy depths—and pulling them out for a special occasion can be a real pleasure.

In most aging beer, certain compounds that taste like cardboard, sherry, honey, and red fruit increase, while others like subtle fruity notes and bitterness decrease. These effects are accelerated at warm temperatures and in the presence of oxygen—which means packaging type and control is critical. Because beers differ chemically, the changes aren't consistent across types. Ales change more than lagers. The act of roasting malt creates a chemical change, the Maillard reaction (see page 521), and in beer with roasted malt these compounds behave differently. A similar dynamic is at play with alcohol, which increases the sensation of liquor-like notes of sherry or whisky with age.

RIGHT: Brett *beers like lambics and gueuzes ripen with age, making them interesting candidates for cellaring.*

At first, it's difficult to get a cellar up and running—delayed gratification is not a beer drinker's strong suit. But if you can manage to put a few bottles away every year, it won't be long until you're holding tasting parties just to clear out more space. Patience! If all of this sounds intriguing, you're ready to start building a cellar, which really just needs to be an undisturbed space that's cool and dark (say, behind the basement stairs or in a wine chiller with the racks removed). Store beer below 60°F, but don't refrigerate it—that will slow the aging process too much. Some temperature fluctuation won't hurt, but if your cellar regularly gets warmer than room temperature, that's a problem. The best choices for cellaring are those beers with an alcohol percentage above 8% ABV—they'll age even better if they're north of 10%.

If the date is not marked on the bottles, note the year and month each beer was made. Place capped bottles standing upright and corked bottles on their side. Bottle-conditioned beer ages best, so look for bottles that have a layer of yeast on the bottom (but don't rule out those that

Stocking Your Cellar.

Any well-stocked cellar has a few of the classics—imperial stouts, barley wines, strong dark abbey ales. These kinds of beers were designed for storage and in some cases, actually *need* a few months to coalesce. Beers made with *Brettanomyces* will definitely change. Even a beer as light as Orval (bottled at 6.2% ABV) will change markedly over the course of a year. Bigger beers last even longer. In that same vein, lambics and particularly gueuzes will also ripen nicely as the wild yeasts continue to slowly eat away remaining sugars. Some beers don't need a lot of time—just enough to smooth a bit. American craft breweries often rush winter warmers to market, and you might find that buying them in October and saving them for the Christmas feast is ideal.

If you're considering cellaring beer, there are a few rules of thumb to keep in mind. For beers without wild yeasts, only consider aging those stronger than 8% ABV—the higher the alcohol content, the longer it is likely to improve. Among these stronger beers, two considerations are color and hops. It's best to age beers with some color, though they don't have to be black (amber-colored barley wines seem to do fine). Hoppy beers are trickier. Extremely bitter beers may need some time to soften, but beers with delicate, fleeting aromas and flavors will lose their most important qualities. So dry-hopped double IPAs should not be aged, but bitter American barley wines should.

Beers made with wild yeast and bacteria (lambics, wild ales) are another category that generally ages very well, even at modest strengths like 5% ABV. Because the yeast is active, it continues to consume sugars and—crucially—oxygen. The evolving biochemical changes help preserve these beers. There is one note of caution, though: Consider buying more than one bottle of wild beer if you plan to cellar it. As the *Brettanomyces* continue their work in your aging bottle, they may take it beyond the point you find most pleasant. Try a bottle periodically to make sure it is still palatable.

don't—see Stocking Your Cellar, above). Finally, buy several of each beer you wish to cellar; that makes it possible to hold periodic tastings with several vintages of the same beer.

What you're looking for in aged beer is a depth of flavor. Eventually, every beer will begin to lose integrity and the flavors will become thin and flat. A beer with "good age" will have a hearty resonance. The flavors will seem almost a bit stewed—all the sharp edges worn off, replaced by burnished, refined, rounded flavors. Oxidation has a distinctive

aroma and flavor; at low levels it's like the smell of old books—pleasantly musty—but once it gets too strong, it has the quality of wet cardboard. Most aged beers will take on some oxidation—it's part of what gives them their "aged flavors," but it should enhance the caramel and dark fruit flavors or give the beer a sherry-like refinement, not overwhelm the beer. If you try a particular vintage and like the results, consider drinking the remaining beers—it's a minor tragedy to wait too long and have a beer wimp out on you. ■

Pairing Beer WITH FOOD

"**S**o Firestone Walker Wookey Jack." Chef Paul Kasten, who has developed a specialty of hosting brewers dinners, was beginning a description of his method of pairing food and beer on the menu. It was a remedial lesson, for I am by no means a foodie. "Break down the flavors: You got some roasty, you got some earthy/peppery notes from the rye, the hops with piney/citrusy and some earthy character, some grassy-green character, and of course bitter." Even though he's a chef, Kasten starts with the beer, literally creating a map of its flavors and then assembling his dish by placing, one by one, flavors to match those he finds in the beer. In front of him was a legal pad full of diagrams,

like sentences broken out on a classroom blackboard.

"Each component of the dish is hitting a number of the flavors in the beer." He had paired Wookey Jack (a black rye IPA) with a dish of tandoor-roasted pork loin. "The roasted potatoes, they'll match up with the roasty flavors of the beer; they'll get a little char on them, bitterness. On to the morels—they'll pick up the earthy notes from the rye and hops. Guajillo *jus*—the spiciness of it, the toasty and lightly smoky flavor to it—will hit the peppery rye, it will line up with the bitterness of the hops. I've got a little bit of gremolata—basically chopped parsley, garlic, and lemon zest—on top just to brighten it up. That will hit your green notes from the hops, the citrus, the raw garlic, the peppery quality to it."

At some point in our discussion, I asked, "It's not like white wine with fish, and red with beef, is it?" He looked at me sadly. ■

THE ALCHEMY OF FLAVOR

MATCHING FOODS can be trickier than it looks. The reason has to do with the alchemical nature of flavor, which doesn't follow the rules of simple addition. Combining one thing with another doesn't necessarily give you a blend of flavors—as Cody Morris, who crafts his Epic Ales specifically to be food-friendly, explains. "Beer pairings work best when you try the beer and it tastes like one thing; you try the food and it tastes like another; you try them together and they taste like a third thing altogether."

Because of these quantum effects, food pairing can produce unexpected flavors. I was recently served a dish of three types of roasted vegetables that I paired with a crisp, balanced German pilsner. With the savory potatoes, the pilsner harmonized with fresh herbs, and the malt's sweetness drew out the potato skins' earthiness. But with the tart, pickled onion, it was the pilsner that popped, crisp and dry. The final vegetable, bitter greens, didn't work well at all. The sweetness of the malt seemed to sharpen the vegetable's bitterness, which in turn clashed with the beer's spicy hopping.

French food chemist and author Hervé This gives one example of why this happens, on a molecular level. "A glass of vinegar is undrinkable," he writes in *Molecular Gastronomy*, "but it becomes palatable if one adds a large amount of sugar to it. Yet the pH—the acidity of the vinegar measured in terms of hydrogen atoms—is unchanged. Why is the sensation of acidity weakened? Because the perception of tastes depends on the environment in which taste receptors operate." When I paired the German pils with savory, tart, and bitter flavors, a similar kind of chemistry happened in the mouth.

And herein lies the silver lining: Once you understand these interactions, they are predictable. The example of sugar and acid is one case. When Paul Kasten begins to design a pairing, he starts with the beer's constituent elements and works backward from there. His diagrams help him match the elements to those he'll put in his dishes. When we're sitting down to a meal, we can do the same thing. The result will be alchemical, but it doesn't have to be random. ■

TOWARD A GOOD PAIRING

BEER HAS MANY elements. Carbonation levels vary widely, and texture ranges from watery to syrupy. Some beers are dry and crisp—an indication of the attenuation—while others are heavier and sweeter. Beers have very different intensities, from those that whisper to screaming punk songs of flavor. And of course, beers have a huge range of flavors—far more than wine.

When we sit down to dinner at a restaurant or open the fridge, there's one obvious question: Which beer will go with this meal? People have been putting their brains to this puzzle for some years now. It has been more than a decade since Brooklyn Brewery's brewmaster, Garrett Oliver, and food writer Lucy Saunders first published books on the subject. Thanks to their work, along with a few pioneering chefs across the country, people have begun to take seriously the idea that beer is as good a partner on the dinner table as wine. Beer has slowly been losing its second-class status as people discover how versatile it is. Experts have developed certification programs like those offered by Cicerone and Master Brewers Association of the Americas (MBAA) to train people to match beer with food. Chefs have been developing their own pairing methods through trial and error. There is a growing pool of knowledge that you can dip your toe into to quickly improve your odds of making a good match. The theories are largely complementary and overlapping—they just organize the concepts differently. Try them out and find the one that works for you.

THE BASICS

Drinking beer with a meal is something like adding a condiment—you're tinkering with the food. The results can either be harmonious, discordant, or a hash where the two don't relate in a meaningful way. It's no different for beer than chili sauce. One basic rule of thumb, then, is to match intensities. Chili sauce can easily overwhelm a dish, and so can intense beers like lambics or IPAs. The reverse is true, too; fiery or rich dishes require a beer that won't taste like water by comparison.

Another handy rule of thumb is to think about the role the beer will play. Are you looking for the flavors to meld together and complement each other—roasted meat and a roasty beer—or act as a contrast, like a sweetly malty beer with a spicy enchilada? Some beers also help cut through richness or heat, or help cleanse the palate along the way. These three concepts are known as the "Three Cs."

■ **Complement.** These are flavors that harmonize through similar elements. The sweetness of malts accentuates sweetness in meat; the herbal flavor of hops seasons herbal dishes.

■ **Contrast.** In good contrasting pairings, elements harmonize by putting each other into sharp relief. Roasted malts balance sweetness (think coffee and dessert); hop bitterness, by comparison, contrasts nicely with some sweeter meats. Sweetly malty beers contrast nicely with oil-and-vinegar dressings, and so on.

■ **Cut (or Cleanse).** One of the best uses for a beer is to cut through intense food flavors. When approaching rich food, hops, carbonation, and acidity are excellent tools. Acidity is also great at cutting saltiness.

Don't forget to consider regional specialties and classic pairings. When beer and food come from the same place, they will often go hand in glove with one another. The smoky, rich meats of Bavaria are perfect with dunkel lagers; Flemish carbonnade is a triumph with tart Flanders ales; and the sweet and briny flavors in raw oysters are wonderful with roasty Irish stouts or charred porters.

Alcohol stimulates the appetite. As an aperitif, you want a beer that isn't heavy and filling, and also one that won't coat your tongue or wreck your palate. Dry, lightly bitter, effervescent, and acidic beers fit the bill, including fruit lambics or gueuzes, saisons, pilsners, and effervescent pale ales. You want the opposite when looking for a digestif—those beverages like brandy and Port that come after the meal. Here, too, certain styles are excellent, like barley wines, old ales, strong abbey ales, and doppelbocks. They are heavy, satiating, and alcoholic—a dessert unto themselves.

These few basics are a great foundation. To dig a little deeper and begin to get an intuitive sense of good pairings, it's useful to consider the different elements of beer and cuisine. There are a few systems out there, and taken together, they can greatly improve your odds of making that perfect pairing.

CONSTITUENTS OF FLAVOR

Folks at the Master Brewers Association have reconfigured beer types away from style and regional tradition, focusing instead on flavor. When beer washes over our tongue and its aroma fills our nostrils, style is secondary to experience; our immediate impressions are sensory, not intellectual. The Master Brewers divided beer into four categories based on the dominant flavor: 1) malt, 2) hops, 3) fermentation flavors, and 4) added flavors like fruit or smoke.

MALT FLAVORS

In pairing foods, understanding the dominant flavor is critical—it will be the main driver of success or failure. Malt-driven flavors have a range that goes from the very sweet to the acrid—they will inflect food very differently. When considering a malty beer, think about how those flavors will express themselves.

MALT TYPE	DOMINANT IN	FLAVORS
Pale malts	Pale lagers, English bitters, pale Belgian ales	Grain, bread, scone, biscuit
Caramel malts	American pale ales and amber ales	Candy, toffee, caramel, honey, dark fruit
Medium malts	Amber lagers, mild and brown ales	Nuts, toast, bread crust, caramel
Black/ roasted malts	Porters, stouts, schwarzbier	Dark chocolate, coffee, char, roast

HOP FLAVORS

Hops are more complex and pose more of a challenge. When we say a beer is hoppy, we are actually referring to three separate qualities: bitterness, flavor, and aroma. One hoppy beer may be very bitter but have little in the way of hop flavors or aromas (some altbiers are like this). Other hoppy beers may not be especially bitter, but have tons of flavor or aromas—like many pale ales. The real trouble comes when trying to figure out the nature of the hops. Are they woody or citrusy? Paul Kasten creates his menus so that his dishes "borrow" the flavors of hops, using them like seasoning. Offering the example of a dish containing prosciutto, goat cheese, apricot, and balsamic vinaigrette, he says, "Say you've got a beer with a distinct apricot flavor—why not use that to replace the apricot in your dish?" In order to do this kind of matching, you need to consider which family of flavors your hoppy beer falls into.

FLAVOR FAMILY	MAY TASTE LIKE
Herbal	Pepper, hay, mint, anise, sage, juniper, dill, marijuana
Woody	Cedar, pine, earthy, resin, incense
Citrusy	Grapefruit, bergamot, lemon, passion fruit, lemongrass
Floral	Lavender, jasmine, geranium, apple blossom
Fruity	Apricot, mango, melon, black currant, quince, peach

FERMENTATION FLAVORS

The category of fermentation flavors is the most unfamiliar, but it is in many ways the most precise. Yeast produces flavor and aroma compounds that are more concrete—empirical, measurable—than the more impressionistic and poetic qualities malts and hops produce. Once you begin to feel comfortable with the concepts, the flavors become easier to distinguish than, say, whether a hop is more piney or grapefruity. Those beers that are driven by fermentation characteristics—rustic ales, weizens, tart and wild ales—are regularly cited by sommeliers and chefs as the easiest to pair with food, too, so getting to know these flavors will come in handy in your own pairings.

CHARACTERISTICS	MAY TASTE LIKE
Esters (fruity)	Apple, anise, banana, pear, pineapple, honey, rose
Phenols (spicy)	Pepper, clove, smoke, vanilla
Wild yeasts (tart)	Balsamic vinaigrette, yogurt, leather, barnyard, compost

ADDED FLAVORS

The final group includes those beers driven by flavors contributed by other ingredients like fruit and spices. It also includes smoked malts and barrel-aged beers, which pick up flavors from whiskey or wine. Pairing foods with these types of beers is more intuitive because the flavors are distinctive and recognizable. Beers keyed by the addition of cherries can be paired as you would the fruit; smoky beers can inflect the flavor of meats the way barbecue does.

THE SEVEN FLAVOR CATEGORIES

Washington, D.C.–based beer sommelier Greg Engert developed a similar method to the Master Brewers', but as a sommelier, he thinks of flavors through the lens of the layman's incomplete sense of beer. "The first mission of the flavor profiles is to start with a beer you're interested in," he says. As he was developing his system of categories, he kept encountering people who had strong opinions about beers they didn't like—but misunderstood what it was about the beer they objected to. This "backward" way of getting at flavor had the advantage of using all the customer's experiences. He came up with his categories to help customers learn as they went. "Rather than just having a beer list that was inaccessible to the average guest, I wanted something that was coachable."

Engert's seven categories are arranged in increasing intensity, and each flavor is divided into different types.

Crisp	Delicate fruit; malt-accented; and brisk hoppiness
Hop	Earthy and dry; malty backbone; and bold, herbal, and citric
Malt	Toasty; nutty; fruit; toffee
Roast	Soft and silky; dark and dry
Smoke	Subdued smolder; spicy and meaty
Fruit and spice	Bright; dark
Tart and funky	Delicate; fruity and vinous; earthy

By organizing them from least intense to most, Engert gives diners a yardstick to begin with. His subcategories are pretty good guides for channeling the type of beer to the right food. Which hoppy beer to try with a hard cheese? Probably one that is earthy and dry will work better than a heavier malty one. An ale that is delicately fruity like a kölsch is probably not a great fit for spicy cuisine—try a malt-accented crisp beer like a Vienna lager, instead.

RICHNESS, BITTERNESS, AND ROASTINESS

Paul Kasten has a simple system. For him, everything starts with richness, on both the food and beer sides: "Richness and richness is a general rule." This is a slightly different dimension from intensity; a beer can be intensely bitter but not rich, and a dish might be, say, intensely spicy but not rich.

Once he's established a beer's richness, Kasten thinks about two other elements. Bitterness is one. His approach is to pair spice with hops. "Some pairing experts say that you should beat the beer into submission with the food," a practice designed to showcase food at beer's expense. He prefers using the beer to add layers of flavor to food. Finally, he looks at the malts and their roastiness or toastiness. Roast works well with heavier smoky or roasted meats, while toastiness can accentuate complementary nutty or toasty notes. After considering these three major flavor elements, Kasten turns to the specifics of individual flavor and begins matching.

PUTTING IT ALL TOGETHER

T DOESN'T MATTER particularly if you think of beer in terms of having three, four, or seven categories. Every expert I spoke to—brewer, chef, or sommelier—repeated the same message: "Beer is complex." You have intensity, texture, density, and richness to consider along with flavors. The challenge is to keep all that in mind as you begin to experiment with pairing beer with foods. But don't despair—the homework is as fun as any you'll get. As the flavors blend and transmute, notice what's happening, whether it works or not. Pretty soon, you'll begin to understand the alchemy on an intuitive level. The pleasure is in the experimentation and discovery, but everyone can use a bit of a road map to help them get pointed in the right direction. What follows is a "rule-of-thumb" guide that will help you get started. But remember—rules are meant to be broken.

IF THE BEER IS HOPPY AND/OR BITTER . . .

■ Bitterness is a natural ally of salty foods. The two flavors are intense, but they help calm one another. Salt inhibits bitterness, and the bitterness quenches after a salty wash.

■ Bitterness helps cut through rich foods. It reduces the satiating effect of fat on the palate, working equally well with heavy meats and cheeses.

■ Consider using the flavor of the hops to complement herbs in food, especially those that are citrusy, fruity, spicy, or green-tasting.

IF THE BEER IS SWEET . . .

■ Sweetness is an excellent contrasting element, adding depth to salty dishes and tempering sour ones.

■ Sweetness is a useful tool in soothing the fiery assault of spicy foods. The viscosity of sweet beer will help temper the fires, as well.

■ Matching sweetness in beer and food can bring out the rich tones in both, but keep intensities in mind—extremely sweet beers may cloy when paired with sweet dishes.

IF THE BEER IS TART . . .

■ Acidity is one of the best ways to cut through rich cream or cheese, oils, or fats. Tart beers are especially nice with funky cheeses.

■ Salt helps neutralize acid, so tart beers will be dulled by salty food.

■ When pairing with tart ales, consider secondary characteristics like fruit flavors or esters, which may complement sweet notes in food.

IF THE BEER IS ROASTY . . .

■ Meats are an obvious choice for roasty beers like porters and stouts, but pay attention to the intensity and richness of both beer and meat and match accordingly.

■ Some roasty beers have a smoky component that works nicely with barbecue, game, or dishes with mushrooms or truffles.

■ Like coffee, roast can be used to nice effect to contrast rich, creamy, or sweet dishes.

IF THE BEER IS MALTY . . .

■ Malty beers are generally low intensity, so pair them with milder foods like pizza and roasted root vegetables.

■ German beers, including kölsch and altbier, are excellent partners for meat dishes, including those with tangy or smoky qualities.

■ Consider darker, sweeter malty beers with well-spiced dishes like stews and mole sauces.

IF THE BEER IS ALCOHOLIC OR STRONG . . .

■ Strong beers are nearly always intense, and must be served with robust foods.

■ Treat sweeter strong beers like Belgian ales as you would dessert wines, serving them with either hard, salty cheeses or desserts.

■ High levels of alcohol intensify the sense of spicy heat, so don't serve lighter-bodied strong Belgian ales with fiery dishes.

IF THE FOOD IS BITTER . . .

■ Choose a sweet beer to balance the bitterness in vegetables, but a light one that won't overwhelm the veggies' delicacy.

■ Dressed salads offer interesting pairing opportunities. With sweeter dressings, crisp or tart beers will complete the triangle, but for vinegar dressings, a sweeter beer or a crisp one are better choices.

■ The intensity of dark chocolate is a good match for a heavy, sweet beer like old ale or a sweeter barley wine.

IF THE FOOD IS SWEET . . .

■ Light, crisp beers work well with lightly sweet dishes, since the carbonation cuts and the crispness cleanses.

■ To contrast the sweetness of fresh fruit, try a tart or crisp beer. Tartness will contrast fruit's sugars while the esters harmonize. Crisp beers will enliven fruit.

■ Beer works surprisingly well with desserts. Dark, roasty beers accentuate chocolate, caramel, dark fruit, and spice, while acidic, crisp beers cleanse the richness and density of creamy or buttery desserts.

IF THE FOOD IS TART OR SOUR . . .

■ Citrus is a wonderful match for bright, crisp beers, especially those with citrusy hop notes.

■ Consider fruit ales as a contrasting element to sour foods.

■ Malty beers like helles are a natural pair for pickled dishes (including sauer-kraut). The sweet malts temper tartness.

IF THE FOOD IS MEATY . . .

■ The Maillard reactions in malt and meat harmonize nicely, and dark beers and roasted meats are a classic combo.

■ Dark, light-bodied beers like porter and schwarzbier can make subtly sweet notes—such as those in pork or shellfish—pop.

■ Lighter-colored malty beers like American wheats and Scottish ales are nice with lighter meats like poultry and dishes with spice, like Mexican and Thai.

IF THE FOOD IS SALTY . . .

■ Salty foods exaggerate booziness, so choose lower-alcohol beers, especially with salty snacks that encourage sipping.

■ Tart beers offset saltiness, and sweet beers add a toothsome contrast—but remember to match intensities.

■ Avoid roasty beers, which clash with the flavor of salt.

IF THE FOOD IS SPICY . . .

■ Bitter beers may accentuate the heat in spicy foods, but the flavors of hops may also be used to harmonize where spices have a citrus or floral component.

■ The same nerves that detect spice also recognize carbonation, so for very fiery dishes, skip highly effervescent beers. Instead, use sweeter, thicker beers to douse the pain.

■ Consider taking a drink *before* you chomp down on that chile; the beer will coat your tongue and help balance the lick of flame that comes roaring through.

AT THE PUB

If ever there was a place designed to soothe and cheer, it was the humble corner pub. On a chill night, a pub means warmth and conviviality; on a hot summer day, the patio is a wonderful place to enjoy a cold one. The notion of drinking together seems to go back as far as Sumer—to the original brewing culture—when drinkers sat around a vase of beer with straws outstretched, drawing it in communally. The Celts maintained pubs, and Romans established roadside watering holes for travelers during their occupation of Britain—an auspicious activity that the natives have happily maintained ever since.

In the United States, taverns have their own illustrious—and notorious—reputation. Boston's Green Dragon, established in 1654, was peopled by luminaries like Paul Revere and John Hancock, and it was there that locals overheard British soldiers discussing the attacks on Lexington and Concord. Like a good fish story, it doesn't actually matter if it is true—a tavern tale is affirmed by its deliciousness. Philadelphia's elegant City Tavern served as an unofficial meeting place for the First Continental Congress. And of course, New York was home to legendary speakeasies like Chumley's, where the phrase to "86" someone or something was born (it referred to the entrance at 86 Bedford Street, out of which boozy scofflaws fled). Other famous pubs have been home to mobsters, working girls, poets, and presidents—every town's history is more entertaining when told through the lens of its pubs.

Unfortunately, the pub as institution fell on hard times after Prohibition, and before craft brewing came along, had often been relegated to the margins—a smoky, windowless box made to protect the "respectable" public from sight of the drinkers

RIGHT: *The storied White Horse Tavern in New York City's Greenwich Village has been in business—largely unchanged—since the 1880s.*

We call them dive bars now, but in the 1970s and '80s, they were just bars. This state of affairs reflected another aspect of the American experience—our long, conflicted relationship with booze. As a culture, we're not completely comfortable with alcohol. Someone's always trying to consume it, and others are trying to inhibit its consumption. The windowless pub was a way to sequester the drinkers from the nondrinkers, but it meant that pubs remained haunts mainly of men, with doors decorated by "no minors allowed" signs.

By the time the twenty-first century rolled around, things had changed again. Windows are back, and with them, women and children. Drinkers are interested in the alchemy of food commingling with beverage in the mouth, and go to pubs to eat as well as drink. One recent manifestation of this is the "gastropub"—a high-end pub where the menu and taplist are selected to complement one another.

The arrival of good beer has brought flavor back into the equation and, perhaps with a little help from drunk-driving laws, moderation as well. Only one in ten beers is served on draft, but for the first time in decades, that number is ticking upward, not down. Pubs have come back into American lives, at least for a time, and conviviality is back on the agenda. ■

THE FOREIGN PUB

ONE OF THE more interesting things about foreign travel is how the unnoticed, little aspects of life we take for granted shift and change when we cross the sea. Going to a bar involves all kinds of specialized knowledge that we've long forgotten, but visit another country and we're reminded of just how many little social agreements there are. Take, for example, the word

"bar." This is an Americanism, and it isn't specific. We may use it as shorthand to describe a place with no food, but with a pool table and cheap beer—or it could refer to the brass-and-oak taproom at a high-end restaurant with twenty-dollar entrees and eight-dollar pints. (Oh, "entrees"? In French that means first course, not main course. See what I mean?) We use "pub," "tavern," "bar," "lounge," and "brewpub" to describe different kinds of drinking establishments, and we know that they can mean slightly different things. Imagine the confusion to a foreign visitor.

It turns out that ordering a pint always involves interacting with local culture, expectations, and mores. It would take a book—a lovely, gorgeous book—to describe the practices of every country, but here are notes on the habits in those most famous of brewing countries.

BRITAIN

In Britain, the standard unit of measure is a pub. Unlike the convoluted naming system we use in the U.S., in Britain a pub is a pub is a pub. Some are very elegant, with dark wood covering the walls, crystal lights, and polished brass, while others are more spartan. But from the lowliest to the most elegant, British pubs have a cozy, welcoming feel. Chatting is encouraged, even among complete strangers. Ask the bloke next to you at the bar about the beer he's drinking and you'll be off to the races. In no place on Earth is the act of buying a beer a more genial experience.

Everything is very straightforward. You walk up to the bar, order your pint, and take it back to your table (or enjoy it right there at the bar). You order food at the bar as well—but someone will bring it back to you. When drinking with friends, it's typical to buy beer in rounds, a process that encourages one

RIGHT: *A quintessential British pub*

to stay on past the first pint. (When it's your turn say, "It's my shout," for extra points.) Tipping is not typical, but if you spend a whole evening in one pub, you might throw in a pound or two after the final round for thanks. In an enormously controversial move, the U.K. government banned smoking as of 2006 and 2007 (Scotland was first, England last), but pubs seem to have survived the shock.

In the south of England, a pint will be served au naturel, straight from the cask. This method has the virtue of authenticity—you're getting unadulterated, pure beer this way. Detractors note that the method produces a thin, big-bubbled head of little beauty. In the north, they use a "sparkler" to produce a creamy head, much like one from a nitrogen tap. Critics of this method feel that in frothing the beer, the sparkler changes the experience of the pint. The sparkler is the subject of intense debate that shows no signs of letting up.

If you do walk into a pub, don't be surprised to see a preponderance of men. Beer drinking is still the purview of men, perhaps a cultural artifact of the pub. If

you do see women, they're as likely to be drinking wine as beer. Beer companies are trying to rectify this by introducing "women's beer"—froufy products masquerading as white wine—but the image of an old codger sitting at the bar is the real culprit. As in the United States, women have embraced craft beer, and this may be the thing that finally turns the tide. The progress has been slow to date.

BELGIUM

Beer is ubiquitous in Belgium, and so the difference between a restaurant and a bar is slim indeed. "Café" is a more common word than pub. As in the United States, you can choose to sit at the bar, but if you sit at a table, you order through a server. Belgian beer cafés are not quite as uniform as British pubs. Most are airy and bright, with a greater emphasis on the table than bar. One fascinating cultural proclivity involves wall ornamentation—beer paraphernalia, photos, magazine covers, shelves with tchotchkes. Sometimes I was less certain I was in a bar than in a museum.

Unlike Britain, in Belgium the majority of specialty beer is sold in bottles, not on tap. That's largely a function of the beer itself, much of which goes through a secondary fermentation in the bottle. Because of this, presentation is a big part of the experience, and the server plays no small role in the ritual of decanting a beer. The procedure begins with the proper glass: Not only does every brewery have its own specially shaped design, but a brewery may have a glass for every style of beer it brews. Lambics are the most baroque; a gueuze

may be poured from its own little basket and the bottle left to recline with its neck raised, while faro is transferred to an earthenware pitcher. The server is aware of the level of carbonation—variation is tremendous—and decants the beer to produce the perfect head. Because Belgian beers are bottle conditioned, they contain a skiff of yeast at the bottom of the bottle; the server will stop before the entire beer is emptied to keep the yeast in place. You may add it yourself, clouding the beer, or drink it separately. Finally, the server will deposit the bottle in front of you, turning it so you can read the label. As in Britain, tipping is not expected.

In Belgium, women drink beer. In cafés and restaurants, women are equally likely to be drinking a goblet of tripel as their dining companion—who may be a woman drinking a tulip of blond. In fact, everyone drinks beer. It was even the case that children were served beer at school—"child's beer" was a form of *bière de table*—though that tradition foundered in recent decades. Even now, children over sixteen may enjoy a glass at a restaurant with their parents. Smoking, partially banned in 2007, was fully abolished in 2011.

GERMANY

I entered my first German tavern, Zum Schlüssel in Düsseldorf, groggy after an international flight. Drawn in by the cozy (but full) room visible from the street, I made my way back around the bar and discovered a cavernous pub spread across a few rooms. It wasn't unusual; the central feature of the German beer hall is its immensity. Some

LEFT: *Munich's formidable Hofbräuhaus welcomes thousands of imbibers.*

oldest institutions around.) There is region-to-region variation, and no place is as distinctive as Bavaria, where it seems like every place has blond wood tables, antlers on the wall, and dark paneling throughout.

In Germany, everyone drinks beer. Taverns are gathering spots, and it seems like the whole city can be found inside them. Young people, old people, men and women—everyone enjoys a pint (make that a half-liter) down at the pub. Pubs are so much the center of community life that they often reserve tables for regulars. In towns like Bamberg, this is mystifying to the tourist. I walked into Spezial Brewery a little before seven o'clock one Friday night and found the place thrumming with life. When I tried to sit in one of the three or four vacant seats, locals gave me a firm talking-to. Those tables were reserved for regulars who, right on cue, showed up to claim their seats just before seven. I had a half-liter and milled around by the bar to drink it.

Servers are attentive, but not intrusive, and habits have evolved to make sure people get their beer. The practice of bringing fresh glasses and adding a tick mark to the patron's coaster is codified in Cologne and Düsseldorf, but other places use the tick-mark system as well. Usually a simple nod of the head to the server is enough to ensure a fresh pour. At the end of the session, though, you do have to summon your server. Unlike in the U.S., he will never

are honeycombed with smaller rooms and niches, but some are as vast as ballrooms. It turns out Schlüssel, which seats four hundred, isn't an especially big place—Munich's Hofbräuhaus seats three thousand. But beyond size, German taverns are suffused with ritual, culture, and local custom.

Walking into an unfamiliar German tavern can be disorienting. Even the small pubs are likely to be spread out across more than one room, so finding a seat usually means exploring. Rarely will someone seat you, though servers are happy to help you find a place if it's busy. The typical pub has large tables, and parties sit where there are free seats. In Germany, sharing tables is part of the community vibe. In the pub at Füchschen Brewery, I was joined by a group of three drinkers at a standing table the size of a large pizza. We put our glasses on the table and stood back to make room for each other. Taverns have a distinctly ecclesiastical feel about them—stained glass is common, and I was amazed by how many crucifixes I found. (Maybe this shouldn't be surprising; brewing and the church are the leave a bill unless you request it. More commonly, the server will have a sturdy belt with pouches holding cash and each patron's tab and will make change on the spot. It is customary to offer a small tip, usually by rounding up—you would pay 25 euros on a tab of 22.5. In Germany, smoking is regulated by the state, so check before you light up.

CZECH REPUBLIC

There are many ways in which the Czech Republic and Britain are kindred spirits. The use of floor malts, for one, and the devotion to zesty little session beers is another. The pub is the most obvious connection, though. Like the British, Czechs favor a comfortable and inviting little nook. No two pubs are alike, but they have a feng shui that makes you want to settle in and never leave. Publicans favor cozy spaces, wooden paneling, and pleasingly worn seats.

Navigating to a seat can be a slightly mystifying process. Czech public houses do have bars, but they're not the center of attention—sometimes you can't even sit at them. Instead, look for a free table—as in Germany, the pubs often sprawl across connected rooms, so wander around. As you circle looking for a table, you may also discover signs on free tables marked "reserved." Apparently, back in the days of Communist rule, staff would sometimes scatter these around the pub to limit the number of tables they had to tend, and I've felt that same practice was at work on a couple of occasions even recently. More often, it's a way of herding the crowd into a manageable cluster. And as in Germany, sometimes tables are permanently reserved for regulars.

Once seated, you're golden. Czech servers are responsive and warm. I once found a pub in Prague that had a wonderful little back room. It was midafternoon and I was the only one in the room and yet, every time my mug started to reach a dangerously low level, my waitress magically appeared. The Czech language is a bear to learn (I never really mastered the word for "thank you," *děkuji*—which is pronounced something like *Dye kooye*), but the servers are willing to work with you—by semaphore if necessary. Smoking *is* allowed in Czech pubs, but often only in the evenings. Although Czechs don't tip, the koruna ("crown") is worth so little that you can safely round up without offending your server. ■

TOASTING YOUR HEALTH

IMAGINE THE SCENE: You're out with a group of friends and the publican has just dropped fresh, foamy mugs of beer in front of you. What's the next thing that happens? In a good many places around the world, some sort of toast or salute. In some, to skip this step would be freighted with tons more meaning than stopping to acknowledge it. I have sat around tables where drinkers merely nod to one another, and others where clinking glasses with your neighbor is adequate. In yet others, each person must clink glasses with every other drinker, making eye contact with each. Sometimes, we clink the base of our glasses. "Cheers!" we trill, or *Sláinte*, or *Na zdraví*, or *Prost!* Have you ever wondered why?

It starts with the human instinct toward ritual. We often think of rituals as religious, but they are just as often social. We shake hands or kiss each other's cheeks in greeting; hand out cigars at childbirth; sing songs at birthdays. They reaffirm our connections and help us mark important milestones. We use ritual in life's most significant moments, but also its most prosaic.

Throughout the world and across the centuries, a great many of our celebrations and commemorations involve alcohol. Rites of passage—to adulthood, at weddings, graduations, and funerals—often involve alcohol. We christen boats with bottles of Champagne (I've seen breweries get the same treatment—but of course with bottles of rare beer), and in some cultures the purchase of a new home means breaking out the bubbly.

There's a reason we use alcohol. Although different alcoholic beverages have status associations (Champagne high, beer typically low), in general we think of alcohol as a social leveler. People go to public places to drink, and in them, the status differential between a business owner and his line workers falls away. The mood-altering effects of alcohol help facilitate bonding, which in turn helps integrate diverse groups. And, because it is spirituous, alcohol has a quality of power and transformation. We could mark special occasions with lemon soda, but alcohol is an accelerant, a way of magnifying our celebratory joy. It has potency.

Our tradition of "toasting" one another goes back more than a thousand years, starting with the drinker's salute in Middle English, *wæs hæil*—a wish to be healthy or fortunate. We get the word "wassail" from this, and that term goes back as far as *Beowulf*:

> *The rider sleepeth,*
> *the hero, far-hidden; no harp resounds,*
> *in the courts no wassail, as once was*
> *   heard.*

There is a beverage historically associated with this salute, and with it we near the origin of our word. Traditionally the drink was warmed, and contained at least a portion of beer among its ingredients. In those very early days of Middle English, there were no hops, so the beer was spiced and usually spiked with liquor or mead. As hopping came along, the preparation depended on mulling without boiling, lest the potion get too bitter. Different wassail recipes called for all manner of varying ingredients, from fruit and sugar to eggs—and usually something stronger for added booziness. The Georgian- and Victorian-era British had to suffer through winters without central heating, so they found their warmth in liquid form. They used special bowls to serve the mixture, adding a communal and ritual flair. One of the most common ingredients, as early as the thirteenth century, was crisped bread floated on top of the bowl. In other words: toast. The combination of wishing people well and drinking from a common vessel eventually became codified, linguistically at least, to our practice of toasting one another's good health.

HOW TO SAY "CHEERS!"

Given the breadth of different cultural rituals, the expressions for "cheers" have a lot in common. In Romance and Slavic languages, drinkers toast to health. German and Dutch have a similar sense taken from the Latin. In China and Japan, the notion is closer to "bottoms up." All of which are familiar enough—even if the sounds of the words aren't, to English-speaking ears. ■

sláinte!
(Slawn-cha, "health")
IRISH GAELIC

CHINESE
Gan bēi!
(Gan bay, literally "dry glass" as in "empty your glass")

SALUTE!
(sah-Loo-tey, "health")
ITALIAN

CZECH
Na zdraví!
(nahz Drah-vee, literally "to health")

Kanpai!
(kahn-Pie, "dry glass")
JAPANESE

DANISH, SWEDISH, NORWEGIAN
SKÅL!
(Skole, literally "bowl" or old drinking vessels)

Na zdrowie!
(nahz Drov-ya, "to health")
POLISH

DUTCH
Proost!
(proohst, from "may it benefit [you]")

salud!
(sah-Lood, "health")
SPANISH

GERMAN
PROST!
(prohst, also from "may it benefit")

PUB GAMES

BEFORE THE ADVENT of the abomination known as the sports bar, people went almost exclusively to pubs to drink. To pass the hours, they invented games, interactive ones that the drinkers played, rather than games they watched with mouths agape. Some of these—Shove Ha'penny, Aunt Sally, and Toad in the Hole—are in what we'd call *declining status*. Others, like darts, shuffleboard, and pool, are going strong. Pub quizzes have, in recent years, become the rage across the country. Following are the rules for some barroom classics.

DARTS

The most iconic of all the pub games involves beer and sharpened projectiles—obviously a winning combination. If darts earns demerits for anything, it's the reliance on math, which slows the game in later rounds. The goal is simple. Beginning with 501 or 301 points, players take turns trying to reduce the total to zero, subtracting the amount where their dart lands on the board. Each player is given three darts a turn, and the final throw must land either in the bull's-eye or doubles segments (a rule novices often spurn). The board is divided into twenty slices, each marked with a value. There is a narrow band at the outer edge worth double the value, and a thin band about halfway between the edge and the bull's-eye worth triple the amount. The bull's-eye has an inner pupil and outer iris worth, respectively, 50 and 25 points. The fewest throws a good darts player

ABOVE: *The game of skittles is bowling's great-grandfather. Inconveniently played outdoors, punters figured a way to turn it into a pub game.*

needs to reach 501 is nine. How many do you require?

POOL

Sophisticates refer to it as billiards, but in a standard-issue American bar, everyone else calls it pool. In the days before craft brewing, pool was ubiquitous in barrooms across the country. The only thing to do in bars was drink, so shooting pool helped pass the time. Although pool sharks may play games like nine-ball or straight pool, the game invariably played by the average pubgoer is eight-ball. The rules are so simple most kids know them—you're either stripes or solids, and the first one to knock in all her balls plus the black eight ball wins—which accounts for a large part of pool's popularity.

Pool tables take up a lot of space, and they are an increasing rarity in urban bars where each square foot costs a king's ransom. As a result, bars with pool tables maintain a kind of louche credibility—they become markers of a blue collar, drinking-man's environment. Facility at the pool table is another marker of barroom credibility, and a time-honored system ensures that the best players hold the table at busy bars. Newcomers can ask to play the winner, but lose to the local king and you're back to your pitcher of Pabst Blue Ribbon.

In rare cases, you might encounter a gigantic table with a bunch of red balls. This is snooker, an English game. Like cricket, no one knows how it's played.

SHUFFLEBOARD

My choice for best beer-drinking diversion is the noble game of shuffleboard. Apparently the world doesn't share my opinion, because the number of tables has been on a steep decline since I first came of age. Let us hope for a retro revival (I've heard tales of one in certain cities). The easiest of all the games by far, the goal is to rack up twenty-one points by sliding weighted disks down an alley scattered with silicone beads. Four disks, and throwers alternate to facilitate defensive play, knocking a foe's weight off the table with a satisfying clack. Some sticklers demand that only the farthest disk scores points (or disks if there are multiples of the same color). But in the majority of barrooms where I've played, we just tot them all up. After a good whacking, there are often few pucks to consider, anyway.

DRINKING GAMES

Once, during the longueurs of summer in between my freshman and sophomore years of college, friends and I invented a game in which we tossed a soccer ball into a laundry basket. If the shooter made his shot, the other player had to take a drink of beer. This is sort of the essence of the drinking game: a very basic activity that ensures people keep sipping their beer (it was also a very rudimentary form of beer pong). Some versions are played in teams, others with cards, some while watching television. Some are incredibly simple, some are abstruse. Some are played mainly for their social value, others are more brutalist activities to facilitate getting drunk fast. What follows is a sampling of some of the enduring favorites.

BOAT RACES
AKA FLIP CUP

A team competition that requires plastic cups and an equal number of players (minimum six total). To play, the plastic cups are filled and distributed among the teams. One member on each team drinks his beer as quickly as possible. In boat races, the drinker puts the cup upside down on his head before the next team member can begin drinking. In flip cup, the drinker must put the vessel on the edge of table and flip the overhanging edge so the cup lands upside down on the table. Only then can the next member continue.

BEER PONG

In beer pong, another team event, six or ten plastic cups are arranged like bowling pins on either end of a longish table (often a ping-pong table—hence the name). Players throw ping-pong balls at the opposing glasses. If they land a ball in a cup, members of the other team have to drink the contents. There are many variations and house rules to beer pong.

BULLSHIT

There are many card games, but bullshit has both strategic and social elements, elevating it above some of the others. A deck of cards is distributed to participants. The first player discards all her aces, the second all her twos, and so on. The object of the game is to get rid of all your cards. One may lie and discard the wrong cards in an effort to win the game. However, if someone shouts "bullshit" and the player *has* lied, she must pick up the pile of discards and drink. If she was telling the truth, the accuser must pick up the pile and drink.

QUARTERS

The implements of this game are a quarter dollar and a shot glass. Players take turns trying to bounce the quarter off the table and into the glass. If successful, the shooter selects one of the other participants, who then must drink.

Drinking games are *legion*. The list gives a sense, but partisans for Master of the Thumb or Zoom Schwartz Profigliano will surely say it is incomplete. New games are born constantly, and perhaps you have invented your own. In the best of cases, they're simple and fun and great as icebreakers. You might even give the old soccer-ball-and-laundry-basket game a go; I recommend a bouncy ball.

FEATS OF SPEED, CONSTITUTION, AND CAPACITY

Who was the first man—it had to be a man—ever to say to his companion: "I can drink my beer faster than you"? Probably the man who invented beer. Feats of speed, constitution, and capacity are just human nature, so naturally, the beer world is littered with them. In the 1970s, Guinness World Records clocked Steven Petrosino drinking a liter—nearly 34 ounces—in 1.3 seconds. It seems gravity was his greatest obstacle. Englishman Eric Lean set a record for capacity in 2003 when he downed 7.75 imperial pints in five minutes. That's more than an entire half-case to you Yanks. The late

LEFT: *Shuffleboard originated in the pubs of England.*

Andre the Giant once drank an astounding 119 twelve-ounce beers over the course of six hours. (Guinness has since discontinued record keeping on feats related to alcohol, an interesting irony given that it was the managing director of the eponymous brewery who started the whole thing.)

It goes without saying that these are unhealthy and in most cases dangerous practices. It also goes without saying that people know this and engage in them anyway. The allure of getting booze into the belly fast is as timeless as it is ubiquitous. When I was in my tender drinking years, we played quarters to while away our time; today beer pong dominates. There's no point in going very deeply into these practices, except to note a few that have survived the centuries. They have achieved something like cultural acceptability and can do the standing-in for more disreputable practices like shot-gunning, boat-racing, and beer-ponging, all of which are well documented across the Internet.

YARD OF ALE

The name is admirably direct: An ale yard is a glass vessel, trumpet-ended on one side, fish-bowled on the other, that runs one yard's length. The old chestnut holds that these devices were used to whet the whistles of thirsty Victorian coach drivers. Their length facilitated handing up to the driver, who apparently was so busy he didn't have time to scramble down to drink a pint. Like so many of the tales we tell of the nineteenth century, it's almost certainly not true—contemporary accounts of coach travel never mentioned them—and the yard was rather, as it is today, a test of one's drinking mettle.

The notion is to drink the whole thing in one go. Part of the difficulty is volume; a yard contains around 50 ounces (more than three pints) of liquid. Part of it is technique. The devilish design, which narrows to a thumb's width just before opening into a wide globe at the bottom, creates problems with air movement. As the liquid struggles past the narrows and into the globe, it dislodges a wave of beer, which douses the drinker—to the pleasure of everyone else in the bar. The trick is to go slowly and gradually spin the yard, which allows air to sneak in. That is, of course, if you can manage to drink two and a half imperial pints of ale without stopping.

BOOT OF BEER

Closely related to the yard is the beer boot or *bierstiefel*. Another vessel with a forthright name, this is a glass boot that usually contains two liters of tasty German lager. As with the yard, the origins of the boot are murky and they tend toward the unlikely. The more believable story is that they, like the yard, were part of drinking-game fun. There's a potential booby trap for the first-time boot chugger, but it's easier to overcome. The toe of the boot must not be facing skyward, or the vessel will burp in

ABOVE: *A challenger partakes in the time-honored tradition of chugging a boot of beer.*

the same manner as a yard, sending a disgorgement of beer out and into the face of the drinker. If the toe points down until most of the beer is gone and then the drinker slowly rotates it to the horizontal position, gushing beer is no worry. ■

Alcoholism. By sheer numbers, alcohol is one of the most deadly substances on Earth. The World Health Organization estimates that it kills 2.5 million people a year and is the third largest risk factor for disease. In the United States, drunk drivers are responsible for over ten thousand deaths a year. Long-term alcohol abuse leads to a host of physical ailments and mental health problems. Alcohol abuse is the second leading cause of dementia. It has profoundly malign effects culturally, affecting far more than just the drinker; alcohol abuse leads to violence, child neglect and abuse, and accidents. One does not have to develop a moral paradigm to recognize the impact alcohol has on society.

That alcohol is a mind- and mood-affecting drug is one of the reasons humans consume it, but it comes with the further danger of addiction. Definitions for alcohol dependency vary by culture, but the phenomenon is obviously real—as are the withdrawal symptoms, which are so severe they may be fatal. Everyone enjoys the occasional merry evening, and even extreme behavior like drinking from a yard or boot can be fun and harmless. But it's important to acknowledge that alcohol consumption has its dangers. These are all the more acute when the intention is focused on drunkenness.

Beer
TOURISM

Traveling to wine country is such a well-established practice that it has its own name—*enotourism*. Anyone traveling to Scotland at least considers the idea of stopping in at a whisky distillery. For reasons good and bad, breweries seem to have a weaker magnetic pull. To the extent that breweries are less artisans of place than are vintners and whisky distillers, it makes sense. There's not a lot of terroir exerting its influence at the average brewery. On the other hand, there are some very good reasons to visit the places where beer is made.

Here's an example or three. The Brussels air turns chill in October, reliably so in November. That's when lambic brewing starts. If you watch the Facebook page of Brasserie Cantillon, you'll notice what appear to be obscure updates: "Next brews on Tuesday 19th and Thursday 21st." These are actually subtle invitations to fans to drop by the brewery and see brewer Jean Van Roy in action. And in Pilsen, an hour and a half by train from Prague, you can sample wood-aged lager in the cellars beneath

Pilsner Urquell—the only place on Earth that's possible. Or how about London? The stately, wisteria-draped Griffin Brewery, home to Fuller's, is just next to the Thames and contains a living museum of Victorian brewing relics. Fuller's sometimes offers special deals, like a tour that ends with an eight-year-old bottle of Vintage Ale from the brewery's private cellars.

There's no better way to get a rich sense of a brewery than by visiting it. Breweries regularly have special beers available that you can't easily find anywhere else. And if you're a little pushy, you can sometimes arrange to speak with a brewer, get a more specialized tour, or even get the brewery to pour out a splash of ripening beer from one of the conditioning tanks. If you have a deep interest in a brewery's beer, let them know—they are often happy to try to welcome passionate customers. Call or email ahead and see how they might accommodate you.

But even if you just want a more casual experience, plan ahead and take a public tour. If you've never been inside a brewery, you'll find it fascinating and revealing. If you *have* been inside a brewery—or even fifty—you'll probably be surprised, too. I have been in scores of breweries across Europe and the U.S., and every time I've walked into an unfamiliar one I've found something unexpected. To get you started, here's a tour of some of the classics from around the world. (But don't be afraid to explore online and chart your own course.) ◼

Use this key to locate notable places of interest on the following tourism maps.

—∘ KEY ∘—

🛢 BREWERY

🍴 RESTAURANT

🍺 PUB

☕ CAFÉ

🍾 ABBEY

🛢 BREWPUB

BELGIUM

FROM THE CENTRAL city of Brussels, you're no more than two hours in any direction from the country's 130 breweries. That opens up a wide vista for travel planning. You have to make a decision whether you wish to go deeply into a particular type of brewing or would rather sample here and there from Belgium's great buffet. Lambic brewing happens in the Brussels area, and sourheads often make it a point to do a circuit of the

RIGHT: *A glimpse at the historic cellars beneath Pilsner Urquell*

area's breweries and blenderies, such as Boon, Cantillon, De Cam, Drie Fonteinen, Girardin, Hanssens, Lindemans, Mort Subite, or Oud Beersel. Others like to make the rounds of the Trappist breweries. An additional question you want to ask is how well beer tourism fits in with general tourism. Belgium's sights, including Bruges and Ghent, are pretty spectacular. You don't want to miss the forest for the trees. (And anyway, no matter where you go, you'll find a brewery or two.)

WHERE TO GO

Consider these a starting point of excellent experiences and go from there. If you start in Brussels, **Cantillon** is a great

debut (cantillon.be). You can schedule a guided tour in advance or drop in during open hours—which are expansive. The brewery is a funky little space that looks like an auto shop from the outside—and a bit like that on the inside, too—so put on your game face. Be sure to stop into one of the two **Moeder Lambi**c pubs for a chance to try many more beers from lambic land. If you have time, **Drie Fonteinen** and **Oud Beersel** are just south of Brussels in the village of Beerseland and are easy to visit (3fonteinen.be; oudbeersel.com).

South of Brussels, in the tiny town of Le Rœulx, is one of the most picturesque breweries in the world—rustic **St. Feuillien** (st-feuillien.com). Although

BELGIAN BREWERIES TO SEE

DE DOLLE BROUWERS • BRUGES
ESEN GHENT
IN DE VREDE RODENBACH
ROESELARE
ANTWERP
FLANDERS
BRUSSELS ★ CANTILLON
MOEDER LAMBIC
DRIE FONTEINEN
OUD BEERSEL BEERSEL
SINT SIXTUS
WESTVLETEREN
LE RŒULX
ST. FEUILLIEN
CHARLEROI

there's a bigger production brewery elsewhere, you'll tour the old tower that served the Friart family, proprietors for over a century.

Much of the best action is west of Brussels in Flanders. One of the top five most awesome brewery experiences is standing next to towering oaken foeders in the thirty-odd cellars of **Rodenbach** (rodenbach.be). The entire brewery is gorgeous, and goes from state-of-the-art modern to nineteenth-century traditional.

One of the reasons some people visit Belgium is to secure a bottle from the most reclusive monks of **Sint Sixtus** at Westvleteren (sintsixtus.be)—and the only place to do it is the abbey in the town of the same name. Stop in at **In de Vrede,** the little café (indevrede.be), and have a thick slab of cheese with a goblet of beer. You can't visit the brewery, but you can walk around the grounds a bit and down the lovely Wandelpad to an outdoor shrine (sintsixtus.be).

Finally, **De Dolle Brouwers** offers a tour of their brewery every Sunday afternoon. Even though the company is relatively young, you'll find wonderfully funky old equipment gathered up by the "Mad Brewers"—and enjoy a great beer afterward (dedollebrouwers.be).

WHEN TO GO

Beer is so closely woven into the fabric of Belgian culture that there's no bad time to visit. Rather, set your itinerary based on what you wish to see. To see a lambic brewery in action, you have to go between November and March. Summer, however, allows you to bike around the tiny village roads and through fields of sprouts and hops (in Flanders, anyway). But don't forget September, when Belgian Beer Weekend turns Brussels's Grand Place into a spectacle of brewing ritual and history. ■

GERMANY

W ITH GERMANY you don't have the luxury of proximity. The country is large and diverse, and unfortunately—or fortunately, depending on your perspective—for the beer tourist, there are a lot of excellent places to visit. The two cities of the Rhine, Düsseldorf and Cologne, are absolutely wonderful beer towns. They have beer drinking culture unique in the world (see Ales of the Rhine, starting on page 229), and a tour of Uerige, one of Germany's most traditional breweries, is worth a trip all on its own. But the force

of gravity inevitably draws the tourist south, to Franconia and Bavaria, the seat of lager brewing and the heart of the German tradition. The majority of the country's breweries are located there, as well as many of the most famous. If you go to Germany looking for beer, you go to Bavaria.

WHERE TO GO

If you go one place in Germany for beer, make it Franconia and the city at its heart, Bamberg. Bamberg is itself an

BRANDENBURG GATE

HAMBURG

BERLIN

BRAUEREI RITTMAYER HALLERNDORF

DÜSSELDORF

COLOGNE

COLOGNE CATHEDRAL

BRAUEREI HARTMANN

WÜRGAU BAYREUTH

FRANKFURT BAMBERG

SCHINNER

MAHR'S MAISEL

SCHLENKERLA

AMBRÄUSIANUM AKTIEN BECHER BRÄU

SPEZIAL

WEIHENSTEPHAN

FREISING SPATEN

PAULANER BREWERY

MUNICH

HOFBRÄUHAUS

KLOSTER ANDECHS AUGUSTINER

AYINGER BREWERY

incredible jewel, a wholly intact town with stunning half-timbered medieval architecture and history everywhere you look. In fact, UNESCO declared the entire old town a World Heritage site in 1993. It also has nine local breweries—impressive for a town of 70,000 people—including **Mahr's, Schlenkerla, Ambräusianum,** and **Spezial,** where the breweries make the local specialties of rauchbier and *ungespundet.* The Bamberg breweries don't offer tours, but the pubs are the real show, anyway. You could easily spend a week and never leave Bamberg's old city, but if you want to go on road trips, **Brauerei Hartmann** in neighboring Würgau is a good bet, and they do tours, as well (brauerei -hartmann.de). South of Bamberg in Hallendorf is **Brauerei Rittmayer** (rittmayer.de), another excellent outing. If you're looking to go farther afield, take a jaunt to Bayreuth, home to **Aktien, Becher Bräu, Maisel** (which has a museum), and **Schinner** (aktienbrauerei.de; becherbraeu.de; maisel.com; buergerbraeu-schinner.de).

Only barely behind Bamberg in terms of interest is the grand brewing city of Munich. It's impossible to overstate Munich's importance in brewing, and best of all for the visitor, much of the tradition lives on in an unbroken lineage. The famous old breweries like **Paulaner, Spaten, Hacker-Pschorr, Augustiner,** and the **Hofbräuhaus** are still brewing their famous lagers and weisses. Most offer tours, so check websites for information (paulaner.com; spatenbeer.com; hacker-pschorr.com; augustiner-braeu.de; hofbraeu-muenchen .de).

Just outside Munich are two other important destinations. Near the airport north of town is **Weihenstephan** in Freising (weihenstephaner.de). Brewing has been conducted continuously on this site longer than any other in the world, and the state-owned brewery doubles as a university and anchors the most important brewing programs in the world. If you take a tour there, one of the students will act as your guide. It is situated on a leafy campus and there's a cozy little pub near the brewery.

Another must-see is the monastic brewery **Andechs** (andechs.de), just southwest of Munich. It's a gorgeous abbey, with a classic Bavarian onion-dome spire and steep-roofed buildings, situated on a hill next to Lake Ammer—an easy day trip from the city. You can spend time seeing the abbey, touring the brewery, and of course, spending a few euros in the enormous beer garden afterward.

WHEN TO GO

With something going on most of the year, the only real downtime in Germany is the period between the New Year and spring (but even then, snuggling up in a warm pub with sausages and a dark lager has its allure). Munich's Oktoberfest is staged the last two weeks in September and the first week of October. Bock tappings happen across Franconia from September through December. And then there's summer, which as we all know was the season invented to enable sipping helles bier in beer gardens. ∎

CZECH REPUBLIC

FAR TOO FEW beer tourists put the Czech Republic on their wish list—and they cheat themselves by ignoring this amazing brewing oasis. The remarkable thing is: It's getting better. Craft brewing fever hit the Czech Republic in the past several years, and now it's as easy to find a good pint in Prague as in Pilsen. In fact, for the first time in decades, Prague has become a vital piece of the country's brewing scene. Bohemia, the Czech Republic's western half, is only about twice as big as tiny Belgium (one-seventh the size of Germany), which makes it a manageable destination.

CZECH BREWERIES TO SEE

WHERE TO GO

It is still very much worth traveling to Pilsen to see **Pilsner Urquell** (prazdroj visit.cz). There's something momentous about walking through the huge anniversary gate and into the brewery that changed the face of brewing across the world. It's a great tour, offered in Czech, English, or German, and finishes with that famous tipple of wood-aged pilsner. Pilsen also has a nice brewing museum near the cathedral, and two small brewpubs, **Purkmistr** and **Groll** (purkmistr.cz; pivovargroll.cz), have had the temerity to open up in the shadow of Urquell. Pilsen is just sixty miles west of Prague, an easy train ride. Ninety miles south of the capital, in Budweis (České Budějovice) is the other famous national brewery, **Budvar** (budejovickybudvar.cz). Tours run Monday through Friday in multiple languages from April through November.

Prague is one of the great cities of the world, at times the seat of emperors and kings, and budget-minded travelers have enjoyed seeing the city of spires for prices half that of lesser cities in Western Europe. While Prague isn't home to a surfeit of ancient, famous breweries to match Pilsen and Budweis, it is now a beery destination in its own right. What changed everything was the rise of independent pubs with multiple taps from a variety of breweries (called *čtvrtá pípa* or "fourth tap"). Much as is happening elsewhere, these places offer a wide selection of beers, including ales. They're actually the places to go to find a wide selection of the country's beer.

Try **Zlý Časy** (zlycasy.eu), which has the look of a neighborhood pub but perhaps the largest taplist in the city; **Tramway,** where you can sit in an actual old tram and where the concept of fourth tap was born (prvnipivnitramway.cz); and **U Sadu** (usadu.cz), with a riot of weird objects on the walls, some local ales, and even vegetarian food—and an English-language menu!

Prague also has some good breweries to consider. In town, **U Fleků** (ufleku.cz) is an institution, dating back hundreds of years, and you'll want to try their dark lager. For a contrast, try one of the newest breweries in town, **Únětický Pivovar** (unetickypivovar.cz). It's actually located about seven miles north of Prague Castle, and getting there via public transportation can be a bit of a challenge. Persevere. The brewery only makes two beers, both pale lagers, and they were the best I had in the Czech Republic. Ask around and they might show you their tiny brewery. Finally, **Pivovarský Dům** (pivovarskydum .com) is a good stop; it illustrates how the country is changing. Owned by a company that recently started a new brewery in an old monastery, they make the usual lineup of lagers but have recently introduced strange potions like sour cherry and nettle beers.

WHEN TO GO

There's no bad time to visit the Czech Republic. If you're hardy, the winter can be enchanting under a blanket of snow. And nothing warms quite so well as a cozy pub. ∎

BRITAIN

THE ISLAND OF Great Britain is about the size of Minnesota, and yet it feels much bigger. Even the spans of northern and southern England seem vast. This means that getting around feels more arduous than it is (not so great), but also that different regions reward travelers with a whole different slate of local beers (great). Breweries in England and Scotland are pretty good about offering tours, but you have to schedule ahead. It's mandatory to see some of the old breweries, which stand as a record of decades past and will help you understand why cask ale remains a national trust. But it's also mandatory to spend a goodly time in pubs as well—that's where British beer culture thrives. What follows is a smattering of wonderful old breweries to visit; they are spread out across the country. I recommend, however, that you select a location and really get to know it rather than traipsing across the island without delving deeply into any one place.

WHERE TO GO

The following breweries are arranged in such a way that if you were to ignore my advice and do a grand tour, this would do nicely. If you *do* take my advice and camp out in one place, poke around the Internet and see what famous breweries are nearby—this list is only a starting point. Note that the price of most of the tours includes a pint at its conclusion.

A few of the old breweries have retained nineteenth-century traditions like employing coopers and delivering beer by dray horse. One is **Wadworth** (wadworthvisitorcentre.co.uk), a brewery in Wiltshire, in southwest England. The tour takes you to both the cooperage and stables. **Hook Norton** (hooky.co.uk) is located in nearby Oxfordshire, and is possibly *the* signature Victorian tower brewery—at least among those open for touring. Not only does it have many of the old fixtures found elsewhere, but Hook Norton also maintains the last of the country's steam engines.

London is eighty miles southeast of Hook Norton, and there you'll find **Fuller's** (www.fullers.co.uk). Fuller's also runs some of the most handsome pubs around, and you find them scattered across the city—don't hesitate to pop in for a pint. London's also a wonderful place to drink, and one of the best places to find newer craft beers. **The Rake,** at Borough Market (utobeer.co.uk/the-rake) and **Craft Beer Company** in Clerkenwell and other neighborhoods (thecraftbeerco .com/pubs) are two of the best known. If you've read Pete Brown's book *Shakespeare's Local*, you can also look for the venerable pub in Southwark. While in London, you might be interested in newer breweries as well, and both **The Kernel,** at the Spa Terminus in Bermondsey (thekernelbrewery.com), and **Meantime,** in Greenwich (meantimebrewing.com), are worth seeking out.

To the southeast, in hop country, you'll find **Shepherd Neame** (shepherd neame.co.uk), Britain's oldest brewery. Heading north you come to the picturesque little town of Bury St Edmunds in Suffolk and England's largest ale brewery, **Greene King** (greenekingshop.co.uk).

BRITISH BREWERIES TO SEE

LOCH NESS MONSTER

BALMORAL CASTLE

CALEDONIAN BREWERY

EDINBURGH CASTLE

DUNBAR

BELHAVEN BREWERY

GLASGOW

EDINBURGH

SCOTLAND

HADRIAN'S WALL

ENGLAND

THEAKSTON BREWERY

BLACK SHEEP BREWERY

MASHAM

YORK

TREMBLING MADNESS

BRADFORD

LIVERPOOL

SHEFFIELD

BURTON UPON TRENT

WALES

MARSTON'S

GREENE KING

NATIONAL BREWERY CENTRE

BIG BEN

BURY ST EDMUNDS

HOOK NORTON BREWERY

LONDON

CARDIFF CASTLE

OXFORDSHIRE

WADWORTH BREWERY

WILTSHIRE

KENT

SHEPHERD NEAME

STONEHENGE

THE RAKE

THE GEORGE INN

CRAFT BEER COMPANY

MEANTIME BREWING

THE KERNEL BREWERY

FULLER'S BREWERY

Farther north, in the West Midlands, you'll find **Marston's** (marstons.co.uk), one of the remnants of the great brewing tradition of Burton upon Trent. Visiting offers an opportunity to see the last of the old wood-barrel–based Burton Union fermenting systems in action. And while in Burton, be sure to check out the **National Brewery Centre** museum.

The north of the country awaits, and if I had to visit only one location, I might make it Yorkshire. The ancient city of York is worth the entire trip to England—you can visit the **Trembling Madness** pub (tremblingmadness.co.uk), with its bizarre collection of hunted heads, including the family rodentia, on the wall—but stray north a bit more until you come to Masham. There you'll find 200-year-old **Theakston** (theakstons .co.uk), maker of Old Peculier, employer of a cooper, and brewer of traditional ales. Almost across the street is another brewery owned by a rogue Theakston family member—hence the name **Black Sheep Brewery** (blacksheepbrewery.com). When he founded the brewery in 1987, Paul Theakston found old equipment, right down to proper Yorkshire squares,

and assembled the equipment in an old malthouse to make what looks like—but isn't—an old brewery.

People visiting Scotland normally look for a different kind of malt. Should you wish to leaven your whisky tour with a brewery visit, I recommend **Caledonian** (caledonianbeer.com), which is right in Edinburgh and has a wonderfully odd and funky brewhouse, where bell-shaped copper kettles are fed by long copper pipes around which brewers must duck and dodge. **Belhaven** (belhaven.co.uk) is in nearby Dunbar if one traditional Scottish brewery fails to slake your thirst.

WHEN TO GO

If you really want to immerse yourself in British beer, the Great British Beer Festival, in August, is a grand way to do it. Summer in general is nice—whether you're biking the rolling hills and picturesque villages of the Cotswolds (good for building a thirst) or strolling through the moors of the Peak District. Mild ale fans might like May, when there's a month-long celebration. ∎

UNITED STATES

XCEPT FOR A handful of exceptions, the United States does not offer up sumptuous old breweries as eye candy. The vast, vast majority of our breweries are modern, utilitarian, and appear industrially unremarkable. The reason people bother to travel is for the beer, not the breweries. Much as

has happened in other large(ish) beer countries like Germany and the United Kingdom, America has begun to develop beer regions. Most breweries don't ship their beers farther than a state or three away, and so even very famous beers like those made by New Glarus, Russian River, and Shipyard are not available too far from their home bases. Improvisation and experimentation is America's niche in the world of beer, and visiting far-flung cities becomes an Easter egg hunt to find the latest release or newest nanobrewery.

WHERE TO GO

As I write this, there are roughly 3,000 breweries in the United States—twice as many as there were a decade earlier. There are breweries in every state, and most citizens live no more than a few miles from one. If you have a local brewery and haven't checked under the hood, ask around—most are happy to show you how things work. When you travel, you might do the same, especially with smaller breweries. But the main event happens in the glass. Wherever possible, drink small glasses so you can maximize your sampling.

If you want to get a taste of the breadth of American brewing, there are several cities to explore. On the East Coast, Portland, Maine, will give you a good sense of the impressive New England scene. **Geary's** (gearybrewing .com) and **Allagash** (allagash.com) are two of the nation's finest, and samples of **Shipyard** (shipyard.com) and **Gritty McDuff's** (grittys.com) will clue you in to the (old) English roots of this scene. The Newcomer **Maine Brewing** (mainebeer company.com) may show its future.

The other great East Coast city— and one with a credible claim to be the nation's best—is Philadelphia. This is one of America's oldest beer towns, in one of the only states to survive Prohibition with a few breweries, and it's now a craft beer leader. There are some venerable pioneers

in and around the city—**Dock Street** (dockstreetbeer.com), **Yards** (yardsbrew ing.com), **Flying Fish** (flyingfish.com), **Victory** (victorybeer.com), and **Sly Fox** (slyfoxbeer.com)—along with a new crop that includes **Philadelphia Brewing** (philadelphiabrewing.com) and **Earth Bread + Brewery** (earthbreadbrewery .com). Add good-food pubs like **Monk's Cafe** (monkscafe.com) and you've got a lot on your plate.

The middle of the country doesn't yet have must-see cities like the coasts, but Chicago is coming along. The old guard consists largely of **Goose Island** (gooseisland.com), which held down the fort for years until reinforcements could arrive. And arrive they have—nearly twenty at last count. Where Chicago really exceeds is food, starting with nationally renowned **Publican** (thepublicanrestau rant.com). Add gastropubs like **Hopleaf** (hopleaf.com), **The Bristol** (thebristol chicago.com), and **Longman and Eagle** (longmanandeagle.com), and Chicago stands as the city most interested in placing good beer and good food on the same table.

Denver is also in the country's middle, but as far as brewing is concerned it arrived a long time ago. Home of the Brewers Association and Great American Beer Festival (GABF), Denver's the kind of town that loves beer so much it would elect a brewer as mayor. (They did—John Hickenlooper—and then elected him governor.) Some of the classics are here, including **Great Divide** (greatdivide.com) and **Wynkoop** (the governor's place; wynkoop.com), and just down the road in Boulder are **Avery** (averybrewing.com) and **Boulder Beer** (boulderbeer.com).

The West Coast is lousy with beer

AMERICAN BREWERIES TO SEE

FREMONT BREWING
ELYSIAN BREWING
PIKE BREWING
PYRAMID BREWERIES

SEATTLE
SPACE NEEDLE
OLYMPIA

WA

BRIDGEPORT BREWING
UPRIGHT BREWING
CASCADE BREWING BARREL HOUSE
PORTLAND

HOOD RIVER
FULL SAIL BREWING
DOUBLE MOUNTAIN BREWERY & TAPROOM

HAIR OF THE DOG BREWING
WIDMER BROTHERS BREWING

SALEM
BEND

DESCHUTES BREWERY

OR

BEAR REPUBLIC BREWING
HEALDSBURG
SANTA ROSA
PETALUMA

RUSSIAN RIVER BREWING
LAGUNITAS BREWING

SACRAMENTO

GOLDEN GATE BRIDGE

ANCHOR BREWING
21ST AMENDMENT BREWERY

MAGNOLIA GASTROPUB & BREWERY

BOULDER BEER
AVERY BREWING
GREAT DIVIDE BREWING
WYNKOOP BREWING

BOULDER
DENVER

SAN FRANCISCO

CA

AZ

CO

FOUR PEAKS BREWING
TEMPE

TX

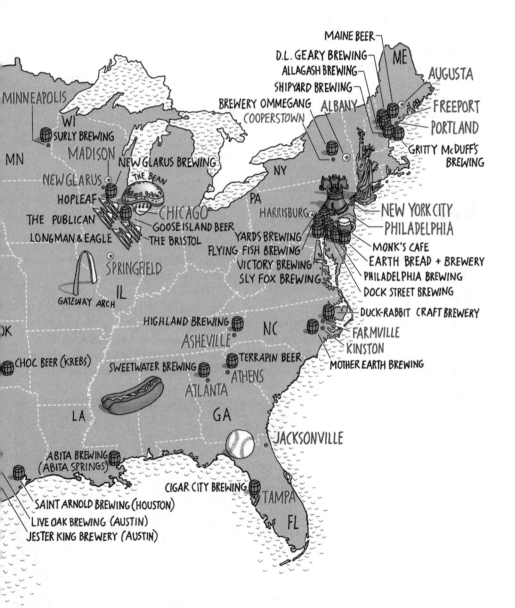

MAINE BEER
D.L. GEARY BREWING
ALLAGASH BREWING
SHIPYARD BREWING
BREWERY OMMEGANG
COOPERSTOWN
ALBANY
ME
AUGUSTA
FREEPORT
PORTLAND
GRITTY McDUFF'S
BREWING

MINNEAPOLIS
WI
SURLY BREWING
MN
MADISON
NEW GLARUS BREWING
NEW GLARUS
THE BEAN
HOPLEAF
THE PUBLICAN
LONGMAN & EAGLE
CHICAGO
GOOSE ISLAND BEER
THE BRISTOL
NY
PA
HARRISBURG
YARDS BREWING
FLYING FISH BREWING
VICTORY BREWING
SLY FOX BREWING

NEW YORK CITY
PHILADELPHIA
MONK'S CAFE
EARTH BREAD + BREWERY
PHILADELPHIA BREWING
DOCK STREET BREWING
DUCK-RABBIT CRAFT BREWERY

SPRINGFIELD
IL
GATEWAY ARCH

HIGHLAND BREWING
ASHEVILLE
NC

FARMVILLE
KINSTON
MOTHER EARTH BREWING

OK
CHOC BEER (KREBS)
SWEETWATER BREWING
TERRAPIN BEER
ATHENS
ATLANTA
LA
GA

JACKSONVILLE

ABITA BREWING
(ABITA SPRINGS)
CIGAR CITY BREWING
TAMPA
SAINT ARNOLD BREWING (HOUSTON)
LIVE OAK BREWING (AUSTIN)
JESTER KING BREWERY (AUSTIN)
FL

cities, including Seattle (20+ breweries), Portland, Oregon (50+), San Francisco (20+), and San Diego (40+, depending on how generous you are with city boundaries). Each has claimed—with justification—to be the nation's best beer city, and they all have something in common. San Francisco is probably the foodiest, Portland the funkiest, San Diego the hoppiest, and Seattle, well, the rainiest. A visit to any of these cities will leave you wishing you had more time, no matter how long you stay.

WHEN TO GO

American cities, following Philadelphia's lead, have taken to hosting "beer weeks" to showcase their local breweries. Those are excellent times to visit: San Francisco in February, Chicago and Seattle in May, Philly in June, and San Diego in November. Denver's beer week is really the nation's beer week—when the GABF comes to town in October. The best time to visit Portland, Oregon, and Seattle is during the harvest, when the fresh-hop beers are in season—from late September through October. ∎

BEER FESTIVALS

WHAT'S BETTER than a sprawling tavern full of beer drinkers? How about a sunny, picnic table–strewn park full of them? The idea is not a new one. Munich has hosted a fairly well-known October festival for more than 200 years—you may have heard of it. But these so-called Oktoberfests have evolved. When people started to get interested in new-fangled offbeat beers back in the 1980s, breweries realized that festivals created a great way for people to sample their beer. The most famous example is the Great American Beer Festival, an event that helped legitimize the new "microbreweries" that were cropping up then, but the Oregon Brewers Festival and Great Taste of the Midwest have

become summer fixtures in Portland and in Madison, Wisconsin.

These American beer events take a slightly different approach from the Oktoberfest model; their focus is more on sampling and tasting a broad spectrum of beers, rather than downing liters of the same festbier. As the decades have passed,

RIGHT: *The Great American Beer Festival as viewed through a glass*

the fests have grown more and more specialized. There are fests for cask ales, for winter beers, for imports, even for things as esoteric as fruit beer and beers made with freshly picked hops. Cities host rolling ongoing week-long parties, and many countries have national showcase festivals like Wellington, New Zealand's Beervana Festival; the Great Japan Beer Fest; Belgian Beer Weekend; and on and on. Michigan-based beer writer Paul Ruschmann maintains a website with listings for fests around the world, beerfestivals.org, and he was tracking more than 1,300 at last count. If you can imagine a type of festival, someone's probably already hosting one.

Festivals aren't just a way to get a lot of beer into your belly. Well-curated fests are enormously interesting. In an afternoon's time, a drinker can try a dozen samples of beer. The first witbier I ever tried was at the Oregon Brewers Festival in the early 1990s. Belgian ales were at the time an obscure oddity, and I had never heard of witbier. Even the idea— "white" beer—was strange. But on that balmy July afternoon, I thought I had never tasted an ale as good as that wheaty tipple. In subsequent years I tried my first bourbon barrel–aged beer, my first braggot, and my first black IPA at beer festivals. For the beer curious, nothing satisfies like a good festival.

Following is a small selection of festivals, roughly organized by month, to give you a sense of their breadth. For people planning vacations, they make wonderful focal points.

■ **SAVOR** (Washington, D.C., in May or June). Hosted by the Brewers Association, Savor is the premier fest to highlight pairings of beer and food. Attendees sample beer alongside cuisine prepared to match each pour. There are educational salons and area beer events that take advantage of the unique marriage of food and beer.

■ **GREAT TASTE OF THE MIDWEST** (Madison, WI, in August) and **OREGON BREWERS FESTIVAL** (Portland, OR, in July). These are the two grand old regional fests of the United States, founded in 1986 and 1988, respectively. The Great Taste is held in Olin Park, on the edge of Madison's Lake Monona. The Fest is frustratingly short—just five hours on one Saturday in August—but boasts an insane variety of beers that fans navigate with phone apps or a dense guide running over a hundred pages. The Oregon Brewers Fest runs from Wednesday through Sunday and has a more modest selection of predominantly local beers. Held on the bank of the Willamette River in downtown Portland, it attracts 100,000 visitors a year.

■ **GREAT BRITISH BEER FESTIVAL** (London in early August). Organized by the Campaign for Real Ale, the venerable British organization devoted to promoting traditional ales, this is the world's great celebration of cask ale. It includes beers and ciders from around the globe, but there are hundreds of local products on cask—pure heaven for lovers of British ales. This is the fest where judges crown an annual "champion beer of Britain"— the only event in the world where mild ales regularly win. As craft breweries have become ale rivals to old cask-ale breweries, they have introduced their own fest, also held in London in August: the London Craft Beer Festival.

representatives of all the major Belgian beer styles.

■ GREAT AMERICAN BEER FESTIVAL (Denver, CO, in October).

The American corollary to the GBBF features nearly twice as many beers from hundreds of breweries across the United States. It is easily the best single place to go to sample beer from small breweries, all found in the cavernous Colorado Convention Center in downtown Denver. Since most have no distribution beyond their local region, it's a great way to take a tour of the country's beers, organized by region. The venue itself is a little grim, but the weekend of the fest becomes a rolling party all across Denver, with scads of events held in the crisp early autumn weather.

■ OKTOBERFEST (Munich in September and October).

A force of nature. People go to Oktoberfest as much for the throngs in dirndls and lederhosen as the beer—but beer remains at the center of the festivities. Only six breweries can sell their beer there—Augustiner, Hacker-Pschorr, Löwenbrau, Paulaner, Spaten, and the Hofbräuhaus—and they have the exclusive right to call it Oktoberfestbier. Munich is deluged with people—a million of them attend each year—and it's wise to book up to six months in advance.

■ BELGIAN BEER WEEKEND (Brussels in September).

Held in the spectacular Grand Place in Brussels, this fest features four dozen Belgian breweries amid lots of Old World pomp and grandeur, including the strange and wonderful parade of the Knighthood of the Brewers' Mash Staff—it includes a procession of historic beer trucks and men wearing odd, medieval-looking costumes. Like the Great British Beer Festival, this is a premier assemblage of Belgian breweries, including

■ FRESH-HOP FESTIVALS (Hood River, OR, and Yakima, WA, in October).

Made with freshly picked, undried hops, fresh-hop ales (see pages 332–337) are made only once a year. Extremely perishable, they last only a few weeks before their flavors fade. The very best way to sample them is at one of these two festivals, which tend to focus on beers from their home states. Both held outdoors under skies that have in past years turned liquid, they nevertheless attract throngs of hopheads who wait all year for these rare, evanescent beers.

■ THE FESTIVAL (Date and location changes).

Hosted by importer Dan

Shelton, this new fest, founded in 2012, is looking to become the premier venue for imports. Not only does it feature a wide selection of beer styles from around the world, but the brewers are on hand to talk about their products and methods. Based on the first couple years, it's doing an excellent job. ■

Appendixes

GLOSSARY

NOTE: Words in *italics* in the definitions also appear as entries in this glossary.

ABBEY ALE: A style brewed in the Belgian tradition; made with sugar for a lighter *body*, greater strength, and a *dry* finish.

ABV: Alcohol by volume, expressed as a percentage. A measure of the strength of an alcoholic beverage, based on the volume of alcohol relative to total volume.

ADJUNCT: Any fermentable substance added during the brewing process besides barley, hops, *yeast*, and water. Adjuncts usually refer to corn or rice—typically considered cheap ingredients—but can also refer to fruits and sugars.

ALE YEAST: See *top-fermenting yeast*.

ALTBIER: An ale associated with Düsseldorf, Germany, with dark, woody malts and insistent bitterness.

AMERICAN ALE: A style characterized by robust strengths and a saturation of hop flavor, aroma, and bitterness from distinctive native hop strains.

AMERICAN STRONG ALE: A style with intense hop aroma and flavor.

ATTEMPERATION: The method of controlling temperature, usually by running water through pipes to cool hot *wort*.

ATTENUATION: The percentage of residual sugars that have been converted to alcohol and carbon dioxide during *fermentation*. The more sugars converted, the *drier* the beer and the more highly attenuated.

BARLEY WINE: A style of very strong ale.

BARREL: A unit of measurement equaling 31.5 gallons or two standard *kegs*.

BAUDELOT: A device that chills beer by running cold water through hot *wort*.

BEAD: The bubbles in a beer, or the cascade of bubbles that rise to the surface.

BELGIAN ALE: A variable style; usually has light *body*, low bitterness, and a distinctive yeastiness that may be spicy, fruity, or funky.

BELGIAN WITBIER: A style that blends pale barley, wheat, oats, and spices to produce a straw-colored beer with white haze.

BERLINER WEISSE: A tart German wheat ale known for its effervescence and wine-like appearance.

BITTER: A well-hopped British ale; comes in a range of strengths.

BOCK: A strong, refined, and elegant beer with rich maltiness and alcoholic warmth.

BODY: The weight or thickness of a beer. A thin beer is called "light-bodied," while a thick beer is "full-bodied."

BOTTLE-CONDITION: To allow a beer to further ferment after it has been bottled. See also *conditioning*.

BOTTOM-FERMENTING YEAST: So called because it sinks to the bottom of the beer during *fermentation*. A synonym for *lager yeast*.

BRETTANOMYCES: A genus of *wild yeast* used to produce a distinctive aroma and taste.

BREW KETTLE: The vessel in which the *wort* is boiled with *hops*.

BRIGHT: Describes a beer from which the *yeast* has been filtered out or has settled to the bottom of the conditioning tank.

BRIGHT BEER TANK (CONDITIONING TANK): A vessel in which beer is allowed to mature further after the initial *fermentation*. This secondary fermentation causes carbonation and clarification.

BROWN ALE: A style with an emphasis on malt flavor and the gentle fruitiness of *ale yeast*.

BURTON UNION: A method of *fermentation* in which a number of casks are linked together, allowing excess *yeast* to be removed from the beer. This method also allows the development of a stable strain of yeast over time.

CAMRA: Campaign for Real Ale, an organization created in Britain in 1971 to preserve traditional brewing techniques and cask ale.

CASK-CONDITIONING: The British practice of *fermenting* beer a second time in a cask, with a second dose of *yeast*. Beer that has been cask-conditioned (cask ale) is sometimes referred to as "real ale."

CHESTNUT BEER: A style that originated in Italy, where a portion of the barley malt is replaced by chestnut flour.

CHILL HAZE: Cloudiness caused by proteins in the beer. Can occur at low temperatures, but does not affect flavor.

CHIT: During *malting*, grain is germinated to begin the production of malt sugars and soluble starch; the tiny rootlets that develop are known as "chits."

COLD BREAK: The proteins and polyphenols that precipitate out from *wort* at chilling; these will contribute to *chill haze* if left in the wort.

CONDITIONING: Aging that follows the initial *fermentation*, during which the beer matures and clarifies.

CONTRACT BREWING: A business arrangement in which a brewery produces at least one beer to be marketed and sold by a different company.

COOL SHIP (*KOELSCHIP*): A flat vessel used for cooling *wort* during the brewing process.

COPPER: A British term for the *brew kettle*.

CRAFT BEER: A term with different meanings in different countries. In the United States, it refers to any beer that is neither a mass-market lager nor an import, usually made by a small, independent brewery.

CZECH *TMAVÉ*: A dark Czech lager.

DECOCTION: A method of *mashing* in which some of the *wort* is removed, heated, then returned to the *mash*.

DORTMUND EXPORT: A pale lager, once a burly, brassy beer but now lighter and less assertive.

DRY: Describes a beer with low levels of malt sweetness; a synonym is "highly-*attenuated*."

DRY-HOPPING: The practice of adding dry hops to a brew after the initial *fermentation* period has ended.

DUNKEL: A smooth, dark lager characterized by sweet malts and a hint of roastiness.

EBU: A measure of bitterness. See *IBU*.

ESTER: A flavor compound that occurs naturally during *fermentation* and results in a fruity aroma.

FERMENTATION: A step in the brewing process in which *yeast* consumes sugar and produces alcohol and carbon dioxide.

FIRST RUNNINGS: *Wort* drained during the beginning of the runoff process, high in sugar content.

FLOOR MALTING: A traditional method of *malting*, in which the grain is spread on a large stone floor and encouraged to germinate, then moved to a kiln room where furnaces heat the floor from below.

FOEDER: A large oak aging barrel, ranging in size from 60 to 250 hectoliters.

FREEZE-DISTILLATION: A process in which beer is lowered to a temperature at which water will freeze but alcohol will not. The frozen material is then removed, leaving the beer with a higher alcohol content.

FRENCH ALE: A family of ales characterized by malt smoothness; the use of spices and local ingredients and the ease of pairing with food are also common elements.

FRESH-HOP ALE: A style made with *fresh hops* for an earthy and wild flavor.

FRESH (WET) HOPS: Hops that have just been harvested and not kilned or dried; often used in making seasonal fall brews.

FRUIT LAMBIC: A style that infuses young *lambic* beer with fruit.

GARDE: A French term meaning "to age."

GERMAN WEIZEN: A wheat ale of Bavaria, served cloudily unfiltered, with vigorous carbonation. Characterized by spicy, clove-like phenols and banana *esters*.

GOSE: A tart German wheat ale with a soft, delicate palate accented by coriander and salt.

GRANT: A vessel located between the *lauter tun* and kettle; used to control the flow of *wort*.

GRIST: The grain or combination of grains that have been *milled* and are ready for brewing.

GRUIT: A mixture of herbs and spices used for brewing that predated the use of hops. Now used to describe a beer that does not use hops in the brewing process.

GUEUZE: A beer made with blends of different vintages of *lambic*.

HELLES: A pale lager similar to pilsner but emphasizing more soft maltiness.

HIGH-GRAVITY BEER: Beer *fermented* to a high alcohol content, which is then weakened to the desired strength by the addition of water.

HOGSHEAD: A type of cask holding 54 imperial gallons (243 liters).

HOP BACK: A strainer or sieve used to filter hops out of the *wort*. Can also be filled with fresh hops through which the wort then passes, to increase its flavor.

HOPS: A creeping vine whose flowers are dried and used in the brewing of most beers to create flavor, aroma, and bitterness.

HOT BREAK: The point during boiling at which protein resins, assisted by hops, coagulate and precipitate out of the *wort*.

IBU: International Bittering Unit; the accepted system for describing the hop bitterness of a beer.

INDIA PALE ALE: A strong, hoppy style, originally brewed by the British.

KEG: Equal to one-half *barrel* or 15.5 U.S. gallons.

KILNING: The step in the *malting* process of heat-drying germinated grain.

KÖLSCH: Pale ale brewed in the city of Cologne. Delicate and balanced with spicy hops, subtle fruitiness, and smooth malts.

KRÄUSEN: To add a small amount of partially fermented *wort* to an already fermented beer, inducing *secondary fermentation.*

LACTOBACILLUS: Bacteria that convert sugar into lactic acid. Some brewers add lactobacillus intentionally to create a sour flavor in certain styles of beer.

LAGERING: The process of storing *bottom-fermenting* beers at cold temperatures, for maturation and clarification.

LAGER YEAST: See *bottom-fermenting yeast.*

LAMBIC: A style aged in wooden vessels for one to three years to fully develop the character provided by *wild yeasts.*

LAUTER TUN: A vessel used for lautering, the process of removing the sweet *wort* from the grains by straining.

LEES: *Yeast* deposits from *secondary fermentation* in the bottle.

LIGHT-STRUCK: Describes beer that has reacted to UV light, creating a skunky smell and flavor.

LIQUOR: Hot water used in the brewing process.

MAILLARD REACTION: The natural browning that occurs between sugars and protein when food or *wort* is heated. This happens to roasting malt or beer brewed over an open flame.

MALT: Grain (usually barley) that has been germinated, then dried or *kilned* to create the base ingredient for brewing.

MALT BILL: The combination of grains used in the *mash.*

MALTING: The process during which grain (usually barley) is steeped in water, allowed to sprout, then dried or roasted. See *malt.*

MÄRZEN: An amber lager.

MASH: A mixture of warm water and milled or crushed grain.

MASHING: The process of soaking milled or crushed malt in warm water in order to convert starches to sugars that *yeast* can consume and turn to alcohol.

MASH TUN: A vessel used for *mashing*, with a perforated bottom so liquid can be strained out.

MICROBREWERY: Originally used to refer to the small breweries that started opening in the 1970s. Now can refer to a brewery that produces less than 15,000 *barrels* of beer per year.

MILD ALE: A low-alcohol, low-hopped British beer style.

MILLING: Grinding or crushing the grain before *mashing.*

MIXED FERMENTATION: A process that uses a blend of yeast and bacteria to create alcohol and lactic fermentations in a beer, typical of the tart ales of Flanders.

MOREISH: An English term describing a beer that retains its interest and ease of drinkability over the course of two or three pints.

MOUTHFEEL: Qualities of beer other than the flavor; includes *body* and amount of carbonation.

NANOBREWERY: An imprecise term; refers to very small breweries, often not much bigger than homebrew systems.

NITROGENATED BEER (NITRO): Beer in which nitrogen is used in addition to carbon dioxide to create a silky, creamy form of carbonation. Nitrogenated beers—often *stouts*, such as Guinness—contain approximately 70 percent nitrogen and 30 percent carbon dioxide.

NOBLE HOPS: The four traditional European varieties of hops: Hallertauer, Tettnanger, Spalt, and Saaz. They are generally characterized by an aromatic flavor and low bitterness.

OLD ALE: An English beer style, usually dark and strong; may include sherry-like notes produced during wood aging.

ORIGINAL (STARTING) GRAVITY: An expression of the amount of dissolved sugars in *wort* before *fermentation*. See *specific gravity*.

PALE ALE: A hop-forward style that relies on a foundation of malt sweetness and expressive hop flavors and aromas.

PARTI-GYLE: A method of brewing in which the runnings from a *mash* are collected separately, boiled, and later blended to create multiple beers of different strengths.

PASTEURIZE: To sterilize using heat.

PHENOL: A chemical compound that, in beer, causes spicy, smoky, or sometimes medicinal or Band Aid–like aromas.

PILS (PILSNER): A pale lager first brewed in the 1840s in the Czech Republic town of Plzen (Pilsen).

PITCH: To add *yeast* to *wort* after it has cooled.

PORTER: Dark ales of modest strength and medium body, characterized by roasty flavors.

REINHEITSGEBOT: The Bavarian law dating to 1516 that restricted the ingredients in beer to water, malted barley, and hops.

SAISON: A rustic ale exhibiting interesting grain character, hazy appearance, spiciness, and/or *dryness*.

SCHWARZBIER: A dark lager marked by smoothness, with a range in flavor from cocoa and vanilla to licorice and coffee.

SCOTCH ALE: A style created by Americans who misunderstood Scottish ale. Scotch ales are generally strong, and always contain peat-roasted malt.

SCOTTISH ALE: Scottish ales may be light-bodied and *sessionable* like English ales, or strong and malt-forward (wee heavy).

SECONDARY FERMENTATION: Another term for bottle- or cask-conditioning, when yeast and/or sugar are added to create a secondary fermentation and naturally carbonate a beer.

SESSION BEER: Beer that has a light *body* and a relatively low alcohol content, therefore easy to consume in larger quantities (sometimes described as "sessionable"). In Britain, to have multiple beers at one sitting is known as a "session."

SHANDY: A mixture of beer and British-style lemonade, ginger beer, or citrus soda.

SORGHUM: A grain high in sugar, often used in the production of gluten-free beer.

SPARGE: To sprinkle grain with water at the end of *mashing*, to rinse off all remaining sugars.

SPECIFIC GRAVITY: A measure of the density of solid materials in the beer, as compared to the density of water.

STIFF: Describes the quality of a beer made with minerals, particularly calcium, that limns flavors with a harder edge.

STOUT: A dark ale with a pronounced roast note.

TART FLEMISH ALE: A style of brownish-red beer, bright and acidic, fruity, and often slightly sweet.

TERMINAL (FINAL) GRAVITY: The *specific gravity* of the beer at the end of *fermentation*.

TERROIR: The unique soil, climate, and topography, among other characteristics, of a crop's geographic location, which affect the finished product. Often used in reference to wine and the grapes used to make it, but occasionally also used in descriptions of hops or, more rarely, barley.

TOP-FERMENTING YEAST: A synonym for ale yeast, so named because the cells rise to the surface of the fermenting *wort*; they are sometimes skimmed off the surface for later re-use.

TORREFIED WHEAT (PUFFED WHEAT): The word "torrefy" refers to heating or scorching; wheat treated with high heat puffs the kernel, breaking down the cellular structure to make the starches more fully available during fermentation.

TRAPPIST ALE: Beer made under the direct supervision of a strict order of monks in Trappist monasteries, principally in Belgium.

TRUB: Sediment formed when proteins and hop resins precipitate out of the *wort* during boiling and chilling.

TUN: A large vessel used in brewing beer, often where the *mash* is steeped.

TURBID: Hazy; the appearance of cloudy beer. Can also refer to a type of traditional *mash* used in Belgium.

VIENNA LAGER: A type of amber lager.

VINOUS: Characteristics that recall wine; typically refers to tart, dry, alcoholic notes or grape-like flavors.

WHIRLPOOL: A vessel that stirs the *wort* until a vortex forms, allowing easier removal of the *trub*.

WILD ALE: Any beer that derives its central character from *wild yeast* and/or bacteria.

WILD YEAST: *Yeast* collected from the environment that has not been domesticated, but may have been cultured by a brewery or yeast company. *Brettanomyces* is a typical variety.

WORT: The liquid extracted from the *mash* and fermented into beer.

YEAST: A one-celled fungus that, when exposed to the sugars in the *wort*, produces carbon dioxide, alcohol, and flavor and aroma compounds like phenols and esters.

YORKSHIRE SQUARES: Square-shaped slate brewing vessels.

STYLE ORIGIN MAPS

NEARLY ALL OF the surviving styles of beer—continental ales, lagers, and the British and Irish ales—originated in three fairly concentrated regions. If you trace a line from Lille, France, through Belgium and on to Berlin, Germany, you set a course through some of the most famous ale-producing regions in the world. It covers just over 500 miles, about the distance between Atlanta, Georgia, and Richmond, Virginia, and farther than San Francisco is from Portland, Oregon. That proximity helps explain the existence of all those German ales—Cologne, after all, is only 130 miles from Brussels, but 350 from Munich. In a similar fashion, France's old brewing traditions were centered around Lille, right on the border with Belgium, and those beers were and remain ales. Farther south, Strasbourg became the center of lager-producing

France in the 20th century (which makes sense: Strasbourg is far closer to Bavaria than Bruges).

Lagers were even more concentrated. Bavaria and Bohemia share a lagering tradition going back centuries. Munich and Pilsen, two of the most famous beer cities in the world, aren't much farther apart than Boston and New York. Vienna is a longer trek, but the triangle that joins these three brewing cities would form a country the size of Belgium.

British brewers communicated with the continent, and their ales were not born in a vacuum. Still, the famous styles produced in Great Britain and Ireland are yet a third concentration of the world's great beers.

Draw a rough circle around these three areas and you've captured something on the order of 80 percent of all existing beer styles brewed in the world.

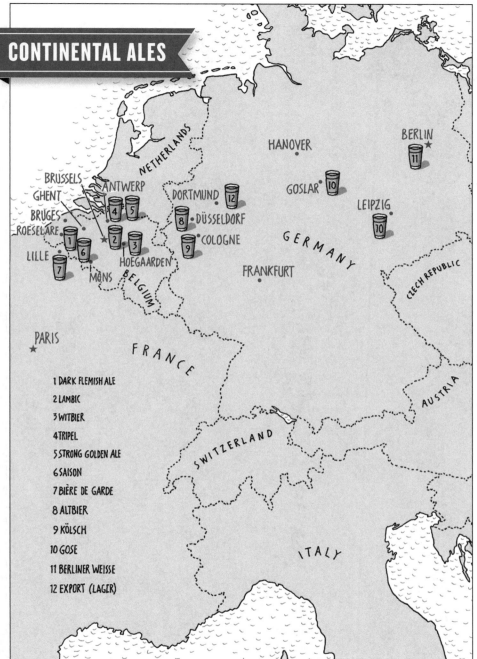

CONTINENTAL ALES

1 DARK FLEMISH ALE

2 LAMBIC

3 WITBIER

4 TRIPEL

5 STRONG GOLDEN ALE

6 SAISON

7 BIÈRE DE GARDE

8 ALTBIER

9 KÖLSCH

10 GOSE

11 BERLINER WEISSE

12 EXPORT (LAGER)

LAGERS

1 RAUCHBIER
2 HELLES
3 MÄRZEN
4 DUNKEL LAGER
5 BOCK
6 SCHWARZBIER
7 WEISSBIER (ALE)
8 PILSNER
9 VIENNA LAGER

BRITISH AND IRISH ALES

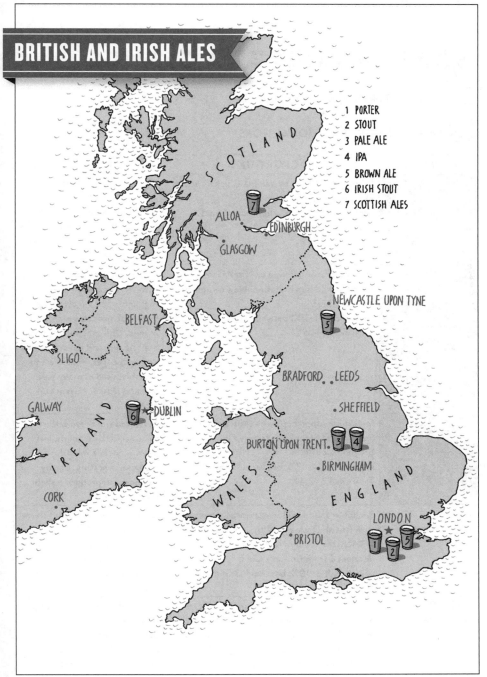

1 PORTER
2 STOUT
3 PALE ALE
4 IPA
5 BROWN ALE
6 IRISH STOUT
7 SCOTTISH ALES

SCOTLAND

ALLOA
EDINBURGH
GLASGOW

NEWCASTLE UPON TYNE

BELFAST

SLIGO

BRADFORD LEEDS

SHEFFIELD

GALWAY

IRELAND

DUBLIN

BURTON UPON TRENT.

BIRMINGHAM

WALES

ENGLAND

CORK

LONDON

BRISTOL

HOP VARIETIES AT A GLANCE

▇ PROPRIETARY OR PATENTED HOPS

▇ LANDRACE OR TRADITIONAL HOPS

HOP VARIETY	BACKGROUND	AROMA AND FLAVOR
AHTANUM United States	Private strain bred by Yakima Chief Ranches, of unknown parentage. Alpha acid: 5.5–6.5%, beta acid: 5–6.5%. Total oils 0.8–1.2%	Charter member of the American family, but with a more floral aroma and herbal-to-piney flavors than the purely citrusy character that typifies other U.S. hops.
AMARILLO United States	Was discovered growing on Virgil Gamache Farms, a wild hop mutation. Now owned by Yakima Chief. Alpha acid: 8–11%, beta acid: 6–7%. Total oils 1.5–1.9%	Classically American hops with vibrant orange-citrus highlights and sweet, fruity flavors of apricot, peach, and mango. Unlike some American hops, is soft and flavorful, with no harsh edges. Versatile and mutable; used in many pale ales and IPAs for flavor and aroma.
BRAVO United States	Superhigh-alpha hops with principally Zeus and Nugget parentage, released by S. S. Steiner in 2006. Alpha acid: 14–17%, beta acid: 3–5%. Total oils 1.6–2.4%	Most find the Bravo bitterness to be relatively smooth, but like Chinook, a minority find it coarse or grating. Earthy to spicy; can produce a slight tangerine flavor.
BREWER'S GOLD United States	Seedlings found wild in Manitoba, crossed with British strains in 1919, and released in 1934. Many modern high-alpha hops were developed from Brewer's Gold. Alpha acid: 8–10%, beta acid: 3.5–4.5%. Total oils 1.6–1.9%	Distinctive black currant flavor characteristic of older strains. Like Cluster, Brewer's Gold has an unfashionable flavor some find rough, others strangely fruity.
CASCADE United States	The first commercial hops from the USDA breeding program at Oregon State University, bred in 1956 but not released for cultivation until 1972. Obtained by crossing an British Fuggle with a plant that originated from the Russian variety Serebrianka. Alpha acid: 4.5–7.0%, beta acid: 4.5–7.0%. Total oils 0.6–0.9%	One of the world's great hops: versatile, clean, and elegant. Exhibits some of the citrus typical of American hops, but is more noted for its floral scent, reminiscent of gardenias.

HOP VARIETY	BACKGROUND	AROMA AND FLAVOR
CENTENNIAL United States	Bred in 1974 and released in 1990, this variety is three-quarters Brewers Gold, with Fuggle, East Kent Golding, and other unknown stock. Alpha acid: 9.5–11.5%, beta acid: 3.5–4.5%. Total oils 1.5–2.5%	Classic citrus hops with an almost candy-like fruit quality, but in high concentrations it can be pungent and peppery.
CHALLENGER United Kingdom	Bred at Wye College in England in the 1960s of German hop parentage. Popularized when Bass used it in the 1970s. Alpha acid: 6.5–8.5%, beta acid: 4.0–4.5%. Total oils 1.0–1.7%	Smooth, clean bitterness and a sharp flavor tending toward marmalade.
CHINOOK United States	Developed in the early 1980s in Washington State by the USDA as a variant of Golding. Alpha acid: 12–14%, beta acid: 3–4%. Total oils 0.7–1.2%	An aggressive strain; has a character of pine or spruce with hints of citrus. Some people find it gives a harsh, grinding bitterness, but it is one of the best strains for dry-hopping, offering a clean, herbal quality.
CITRA United States	Another of the recent proprietary strains, relatively high–alpha dual-use hops. Purported parentage includes Hallertauer, American Tettnanger, and East Kent Golding. Alpha acid: 11–13%, beta acid: 3.5–4.5%. Total oils 2.2–2.8%	Versatile, with the potential to produce a wide range of fruit flavors, heavy on the tropical—passion fruit and lychee, but sometimes peach and apricot. Fruit, fruit, and more fruit. Used for either bittering or aroma.
CLUSTER United States	America's great original hops, at one time king in the U.S., accounting for 90 percent of the country's crop. Production is now dwindling almost to extinction. Alpha acid: 5.5–8.5%, beta acid: 4.5–5.5%. Total oils 0.4–0.8%	Has an antiquated black currant flavor and comparatively rough bitterness.
COLUMBUS/ TOMAHAWK/ ZEUS ("CTZ") United States	The parentage of the hops known individually as Columbus, Tomahawk, and Zeus—believed to be genetically very similar or identical—is one of the great mysteries in hop breeding. One parent may have been Brewer's Gold, but the ultimate varieties were the result of crossbreeding with unknown plants. Alpha acid: 14.5–16.5%, beta acid: 4–5%. Total oils 2–3%	Among the most distinctive and assertive of American hops, producing a skunky/ marijuana aroma and a sticky, resinous flavor. To some people, they can seem to have a savory garlic or onion note, while others find them intensely fruity. Work best blended with others.

HOP VARIETY	BACKGROUND	AROMA AND FLAVOR
CRYSTAL United States	Developed in 1983 in Corvallis, Oregon, and released a decade later. Derived from German Hallertau, a half-sister of Mt. Hood and Liberty. Alpha acid: 4–6%, beta acid: 5.0–6.7%. Total oils 0.8–2.1%	Offers a very clean, neutral hopping that at high rates can take on a pleasant spiciness.
FIRST GOLD United Kingdom	Dwarf variety (bines only grow to eight feet) developed in England, derived from a dwarf male and a Whitbread Golding variety. Alpha acid: 6.5–8.5%, beta acid: 3–4%. Total oils 0.7–1.5%	Similar to East Kent Golding: spicy, earthy hops that at high levels offers intense, sharp bitterness.
FUGGLE United Kingdom	Introduced in the 1870s, of unknown parentage. One of England's two most famous hops, Fuggle once constituted 78 percent of the country's crop. Sadly not hardy, and is slowly dying out. Alpha acid: 3.0–5.5%, beta acid: 2–3%. Total oils 0.7–1.4%	The loss is a shame, because its woody, earthy character is unmatchable—and as English as Earl Grey tea.
GALAXY Australia	Proprietary strain developed by Hop Products Australia in 1994, of undisclosed parentage. Crossover hops, high in alpha acids, often used in late- and dry-hopping. Alpha acid: 13–16%, beta acid: 5–6%. Total oils 2.4–2.7%	Intense, pungent strain with tropical-to-stone-fruit and black currant. Some people pick up fresh vegetable notes like celery or cucumber.
GALENA United States	Made from an open pollination crossed with Brewer's Gold in Idaho in 1968. Alpha acid: 11–13.5%, beta acid: 7–8.5%. Total oils 0.9–1.3%	Produces a clean, neutral, pleasant bitterness. Flavors sit somewhere between citrus and wood but are not pronounced.
GLACIER United States	Bred by researchers at Washington State University and released in 2000, promising for good yield and low cohumulone content. Parentage is half Alsatian Elsasser crossed with several other European varieties. Alpha acid: 4.5–9.5%, beta acid: 6–9%. Total oils 0.7–1.6%	Similar to Crystal in its clean, neutral character. Tends toward earthiness with a subtle peach note.
HALLERTAUER MITTELFRÜH Germany	German landrace hops, the source of countless hybrids grown in the Hallertau region north of Munich. Hallertau Tradition is a modern cultivar bred to possess Mittelfrüh's qualities, and a regular substitute. Alpha acid: 3.5–5%, beta acid: 3.5%. Total oils 0.7–1.3%	Many people consider Mittelfrüh the king of hops for its very elegant herbal, spicy flavors and aromas. Delicate and gentle.

HOP VARIETY	BACKGROUND	AROMA AND FLAVOR
HERKULES Germany	Bred at Hüll, Germany, by the Hop Research Center in 2006 from Hallertauer Taurus and an unnamed Hüll male. The latest in the line of high-alpha German hops, following Northern Brewer and Magnum. Alpha acid: 12–17%, beta acid: 4–5.5%. Total oils 1.6–2.4%	Used mainly for bitter charges, but has an intense, resinous and spicy flavor.
HERSBRUCKER Germany	Classic German landrace variety from the region just outside Nuremburg. Another of the hops that define German brewing. Alpha acid: 2–4%, beta acid: 2.5–6%. Total oils 0.5–1.0%	Elegant and delicate like Hallertauer Mittelfrüh; spicy and herbal with a light fruity essence.
KENT GOLDING United Kingdom	Developed in the late 1700s of unknown parentage. Alpha acid: 4–6.5%, beta acid: 2–3%. Total oils 0.4–0.8%	Very gentle, smooth hops fused with the identity of British ales—at turns floral, lemony, lightly spicy, and, in some cases, savory.
LIBERTY United States	Product of the USDA's breeding program in Corvallis, Oregon, with all-German heritage including triploid Hallertauer Mittelfrüh, released in 1991. Bred to be a replacement for Hallertauer Mittelfrüh that would grow in the U.S. Alpha acid: 3–5%, beta acid: 3–4%. Total oils 0.6–1.2%	Gentle herbal, earthy flavors and aroma similar to the original. Like its relative Crystal, is clean and neutral when used for bittering.
LUBLIN/ LUBELSKI Poland	Polish landrace hops likely descended from Saaz, which it closely resembles. Grown in the region from Pulawy to Lublin, southeast of Warsaw. Alpha acid: 3–4.5%, beta acid: 3–4%. Total oils 0.5–1.1%	Similar to Saaz hops, with spicy, herbal quality. Can also produce floral, lavender-like aromas. The other common Polish hops, Marynka, also produces a rich, aromatic floral aroma.
MAGNUM Germany	Another project of the Hop Research Center in Hüll, Germany. Developed in the 1980s from German stock including Hallertauer Mittelfrüh. Until very recently the most popular high-alpha hops; now being replaced by Herkules. Alpha acid: 11–16%, beta acid: 5–7%. Total oils 1.6–2.6%	Very neutral hops with low aroma, designed to be used as bittering hops.

HOP VARIETY	BACKGROUND	AROMA AND FLAVOR
MOTUEKA New Zealand	Bred in 1997 in the "hops with a difference" program. Like its sister, Riwaka, a cross of one-third Saaz and two-thirds New Zealand stock. Alpha acid: 6.5–7.5%, beta acid: 5–5.5%. Total oils 0.8%	A charter member of the tropical-fruit club of New Zealand hops, leaning toward lemon-lime.
MT. HOOD United States	Another USDA hybrid of Hallertauer Mittelfrüh and Early Green, from the 1980s. Named for the conical mountain near Portland, Oregon. Alpha acid: 4–7%, beta acid: 5–8%. Total oils 1.2–1.7%	Versatile hops with multiple dimensions, from earthy and piney to herbal and spicy. Clean, with gentle character.
NELSON SAUVIN New Zealand	Bred entirely of New Zealand stock, including the Smoothcone variety. Alpha acid: 12–13%, beta acid: 6–8%. Total oils 1.0–1.2%	Incredibly powerful; can be used to produce subtle mango or white wine flavors ("Sauvin" refers to sauvignon blanc). Also prone to overly intense, saturated flavors that can begin to taste musky or "sweaty."
NORTHERN BREWER United Kingdom (originally)	Originally bred in 1934 of Golding stock; now grown across Europe and in the U.S. Alpha acid: 7–10%, beta acid: 3–5%. Total oils 1.0–1.6%	Character really depends on where it is grown. German Northern Brewer is spicier and more herbal, U.S. varieties wilder and more woody.
NUGGET United States	A complex hybrid developed in Corvallis, Oregon, in the 1980s by the USDA, consisting of a majority of Brewers Gold with Early Green, Golding, and German stock. Alpha acid: 11–14%, beta acid: 3–6%. Total oils 0.9–2.2%	One of the earlier high-alpha hops still popular for its herbal, fresh, and "green" aroma and clean bitterness. Commonly used as a base bittering hops in American ales.
PERLE Germany	Another Hüll, Germany, hop bred from Northern Brewer and an unnamed German hop. Alpha acid: 5–9%, beta acid: 2.5–4.5%. Total oils 0.5–1.5%	Versatile hops that can be used at any point in the boil. Have a peppery, spicy flavor; some people locate a hint of mint. Have the delicacy of classic German hops with a bit more intensity.
PRIDE OF RINGWOOD Australia	Bred in Melbourne in the 1960s from English Pride of Kent hops and open pollination. Was the king of Australia for decades, and the highest-alpha hops at release. Alpha acid: 7–11%, beta acid: 4–6%. Total oils 0.9–2.0%	Has a citrus quality but is rougher than American hops; sometimes a fruity, berry-like flavor emerges.

HOP VARIETY	BACKGROUND	AROMA AND FLAVOR
PROGRESS United Kingdom	Developed at Wye College, England, in the 1950s of Golding and wild American stock in an effort to find a replacement for Fuggle. Alpha acid: 7–11%, beta acid: 4–6%. Total oils 0.9–2.0%	One of the classically fruity English hops, with a marmalade-to-sweet-lime flavor and even a touch of fresh spruce.
RIWAKA New Zealand	Produced during the same breeding trials as Motueka in 1997; a one-third Saaz, two-thirds New Zealand cross. Alpha acid: 4.5–6.5%, beta acid: 4–5%. Total oils 0.8%	Far spicier hops than the fruity Motueka, with a quality part pine and part bergamot. Unusual and quite distinct from American varieties.
SAAZ (ŽATEC) Czech Republic	Czech landrace hops grown since the Middle Ages in the Žatec region northwest of Prague. Closely related to Spalt and Tettnanger. Over 80 percent of the acreage in the Czech Republic is devoted to this quintessential pilsner hops. Alpha acid: 3–6%, beta acid: 4–6%. Total oils 0.4–1.0%	Distinctive flavor, with a tangy cedar crispness and an undertone of tarragon or rosemary.
SANTIAM United States	Developed by the USDA in Corvallis, Oregon, from German Tettnanger and Hallertauer stock as a replacement for imported hops. Released commercially in 1997. Alpha acid: 5–7%, beta acid: 6–8%. Total oils 1.3–1.7%	Very close in characteristics to the German originals. Tettnanger is famous for its delicate aroma, and Santiam has a similar character. However, instead of the spicy German qualities, Santiam has a characteristically American citrus-orange flavor. Regularly used in American ales.
SAPHIR Germany	Developed in Hüll, Germany, at the Hop Research Center. Bred of Mittelfrüh and other stock. Alpha acid: 2–4.5%, beta acid: 4–7%. Total oils 0.8–1.4%	Versatile, at times flowery, fruity, or woody. Flavor is gentle enough that Anheuser-Busch InBev made it the feature hops in Beck's Sapphire.
SIMCOE United States	Proprietary strain bred by Yakima Chief, released in 2000. Alpha acid: 12–14%, beta acid: 4–5%. Total oils 2–2.5%	One of the most popular and distinctive American hops, lending its intense pungent, piney, and grapefruit aromas and flavors to IPAs and pale ales.

HOP VARIETY	BACKGROUND	AROMA AND FLAVOR
SORACHI ACE Japan	Originally bred in Japan in 1988 of Brewer's Gold and Saaz stock. In U.S. fields, Sorachi Ace fails to get the very high alpha levels attained in Japan. Alpha acid: 10–16%, beta acid: 6–7. Total oils 2–2.8%	For a majority of drinkers, Sorachi Ace tastes distinctly of lemon, with a slight herbal undertone; a minority of drinkers, however, taste dill.
SPALT SELECT Germany	A more widely grown strain than the original Spalter it was designed to replace. Introduced by the Hop Research Center in 1993. Alpha acid: 3–6.5%, beta acid: 2.5–5%. Total oils 0.6–0.9%	Similar in character to Spalt Spalter but with more woody, spicy tang.
SPALT SPALTER Germany	Very old German variety closely related to Saaz and Tettnanger, cultivated in the region around the town of Spalt, near Nuremberg. The three are nearly identical genetically, but have become distinct as they adapted to different environments. Alpha acid: 2.5–5.5%, beta acid: 3–5%. Total oils 0.5–0.9%	Despite its low alpha acids, delivers an intense bitterness. Flavors and aromas are gentle, with a fruity, woody character.
STERLING United States	Designed to mimic Saaz's flavors for domestic production in the United States. Contains Saaz, Cascade, and other European hop parentage. Released in 1998. Alpha acid: 6–9%, beta acid: 4–6%. Total oils 1.3–1.9%	A much closer doppelganger for Czech Saaz than American-grown Saaz, which tends to be much more citrusy. Contains the same cedary, herbal flavors as Czech Saaz.
STRISSELSPALT France	French landrace hops, originally grown in Alsace. Alpha acid: 2–4%, beta acid: 3–5.5%. Total oils 0.6–0.9%	Evokes the country with floral, lemon zest aromas and flavors. Once used widely in lagers, but works well with Belgian yeast, particularly in rustic styles.
STYRIAN GOLDING Slovenia	Grown by farmers to replace disease-ravaged fields in the 1930s. In a case of mistaken identity, they thought they were planting Golding stock, but used Fuggle instead. Alpha acid: 4–6%, beta acid: 2–4%. Total oils 0.5–1.0%	Earthy with an herbal-to-spicy, white pepper character. Not assertive, but versatile.
SUMMIT United States	Hedgerow or low-trellis hops developed by the American Dwarf Hop Association. Alpha acid: 14–18%, beta acid: 4–6%. Total oils 1.5–2.5%	Extremely assertive; can, in some cases, have deep tangerine and grapefruit. Can also produce onion or durian fruit flavors and aromas—equally intense. A hop that divides beer drinkers.

HOP VARIETY	BACKGROUND	AROMA AND FLAVOR
TARGET United Kingdom	One of the first higher-alpha hops, bred in 1972 by Wye College in England. Parentage includes Northern Brewer and Eastwell Golding. Alpha acid: 8–13%, beta acid: 4.5–6%. Total oils 1.2–1.4%	Provides a clean bitterness with a touch of earthiness and English marmalade bending ever so slightly toward citrus.
TETTNANGER Germany	Very old German variety, closely related to Saaz and Spalt, cultivated in the region around the town of Tettnang. Alpha acid: 2–5.5%, beta acid: 3–5%. Total oils 0.8–1.4%	Classic German hops are marked by a smooth sophistication, and Tettnanger is no exception. But where other German varieties have spice as their principle note, Tettnanger has wood, chocolate, and berries as well. Lovely hops.
TETTNANGER (U.S.) United States	For years growers took this to be a descendant of the German landrace strain, until researchers began to doubt this, as its elements bore a strong resemblance to Fuggle—which is how the USDA now classifies it. Alpha acid: 4–5%, beta acid: 3.5–4.5%. Total oils 0.4–0.8%	Has a spicy woodiness that seems related to German varieties, but is also similar to Willamette hops, which are almost entirely Fuggle.
WARRIOR United States	Bred by Yakima Chief, related to Simcoe. Released in 2001. Alpha acid: 15–17%, beta acid: 4.5–5.5%. Total oils 1.0–2.0%	Like Simcoe, dances the line between pine and grapefruit; may express sweeter floral notes when used in late additions.
WILLAMETTE United States	One of the first hops developed by the USDA, beginning in the 1960s and ultimately released in the 1970s. Made almost exclusively of English Fuggle stock and, interestingly, is being introduced back to England to replace the disease-prone Fuggle. Alpha acid: 5–10%, beta acid: 3–5.%. Total oils 1.0–1.5%	Even in the U.S., retains its European character. Has a mild earthy-to-spicy flavor that works in both lager and English-style ales. Lacks the floral and citrusy flavors that characterize other American varieties.

BIBLIOGRAPHY

Bahnson, Maximiliano. *Prague: A Pisshead's Pub Guide*. lulu.com, 2011.

Baker, Julian L. *The Brewing Industry*. London: Methuen, 1905.

Bamforth, Charles. *Beer: Tap Into the Art and Science of Brewing*, 3rd edition. New York: Oxford University Press, 2009.

Barnard, Alfred. *The Noted Breweries of Great Britain and Ireland*, Volumes I–V. London: Joseph Causton and Sons, 1889–91.

"Beer Statistics." Brussels, Belgium: The Brewers of Europe, 2010.

Belau, Ken. "Acidification in the Brewhouse." Presentation at the Master Brewers Association of the Americas Winter Conference, January 14, 2011.

Bilger, Burkhard. "A Better Brew: The Rise of Extreme Beer." *The New Yorker*, November 24, 2008.

Booth, David. *The Art of Brewing*. London: Baldwin and Cradock, 1829.

Bostwick, William and Jesse Rymill. *Beer Craft: Six-Packs from Scratch*. Emmaus, PA: Rodale, 2011.

Boulton, Chris and David Quain. *Brewing Yeast and Fermentation*. Malden, MA: Blackwell, 2006.

Brewers Almanac 2010. Washington, DC: The Beer Institute, 2011.

Bryson, Lew. March 2004 interview with Sam Calagione. LewBryson.blogspot.com.

Capecka, Ewa, Anna Mareczek, and Maria Leja. "Antioxidant activity of fresh and dry herbs of some *Lamiaceae* species." *Food Chemistry*, volume 93, issue 2, November 2005.

Chartier, Francois. *Taste Buds and Molecules*. Hoboken, NJ: John Wiley and Sons, 2012.

Child, Samuel. *Every Man His Own Brewer*. London: Burlington House, 1768.

Combrune, Michael. *The Theory and Practice of Brewing*. London, 1762.

Cook, Charles Henry, John Greville Fennell, and J. M. Dixon. *The Curiosities of Ale and Beer* [published pseudonymously under the name John Bickerdyke]. London: Swan Sonnenschein & Company, 1889.

Cornell, Martyn. *Amber, Gold & Black: The History of Britain's Great Beers*. Stroud, England: The History Press, 2010.

Cornell, Martyn. Assorted entries, 2008–2012. Zythophile.wordpress.com.

Damerow, Peter. "Sumerian Beer: The Origins of Brewing Technology in Ancient Mesopotamia." Berlin: Max Planck Institute for the History of Science, 2011.

Daniels, Ray. *Designing Great Beers*. Boulder, CO: Brewers Publications, 1998.

De Clerck, Jean. *A Textbook of Brewing*. London: Chapman & Hall, 1957.

De Keukeleire, Denis. "Fundamentals of Beer and Hop Chemistry." *Química Nova*, volume 23, number 1, January/February 2000.

Delwiche, Jeannine. "Interactions in Flavor." *Tasting Science* (tastingscience.info).

Dineley, Merryn and Graham Dineley. "Neolithic Ale: Barley as a source of sugars for fermentation." *Plants in Neolithic Britain and Beyond*. Edited by Andrew S. Fairbairn. Oxford: Oxbow Books, 2000.

Donnachie, Ian. *A History of the Brewing Industry in Scotland*. Edinburgh: John Donald Publishers, 1979.

Dunn, Barbara, and Gavin Sherlock. "Reconstruction of the genome origins and evolution of the hybrid lager yeast *Saccharomyces pastorianus*." *Genome Research*, volume 18, number 10, October 2008, e-published September 11, 2008.

Engert, Greg. "The Seven Flavor Categories of Beer: What They Are, How to Pair Them." *The Splendid Table* (splendidtable.org), March 23, 2013.

Evans, R.E. "The Beers and Brewing Systems of Northern France." *Journal of the Institute of Brewing*, Volume 11. Birmingham, England: Harrison and Sons, 1905.

Figuier, Louis. *Les merveilles de l'industrie, ou Description des principales industries modernes*, Volume 4. Paris: Furne, Jouvet et Cie. Editeurs, 1860.

Fimrite, Peter. "Joseph Owades: brewmaster, created light beer." *San Francisco Chronicle*, December 20, 2005.

Gaab, Jeffrey S. *Munich: Hofbräuhaus and History—Beer, Culture, and Politics*. New York: Peter Lang Publishing, 2006.

Glaser, Greg. "The Late Great Ballentine." *Modern Brewery Age*, March 27, 2000.

"Gold Rush Chronology 1846–1849." Museum of the City of San Francisco, SFMuseum.org.

"Gold Rush Chronology 1850–1851." Museum of the City of San Francisco, SFMuseum.org.

Goldstein, Evan. *Perfect Pairings*. Berkeley: University of California Press, 2006.

"Government Review of Alcohol Taxation." London: British Beer and Pub Association, 2010.

Hanlon, Mike. "Extreme Beer: Man's Favourite Drink Suddenly Gets Much Stronger." Gizmag.com, May 28, 2010.

Hanni, Tim and Virginia Utermohlen. "Beverage Preferences, Attitudes, and Behavior of 'Sweet' versus 'Tolerant' Wine Consumers." Prepared for the Consumer Wine Awards, October 2010.

Hayden, Rosannah. "Brewing with Rye." *Brewing Techniques*, September/October 1993.

Hieronymus, Stan. *Brewing With Wheat*. Boulder, CO: Brewers Publications, 2010.

Hieronymus, Stan. *Brew Like a Monk*. Boulder, CO: Brewers Publications, 2005.

Hieronymus, Stan. *For the Love of Hops*. Boulder, CO: Brewers Publications, 2012.

Holle, Stephen R., editor. *Beer Steward Handbook: A Practical Guide to Understanding Beer*. St. Paul: Master Brewers Association of the Americas, 2012.

Hornsey, Ian. *A History of Beer and Brewing*. London: Royal Society of Chemistry, 2003.

Jackson, Michael. *Beer Companion*, 2nd edition. Philadelphia: Running Press, 1997.

Jackson, Michael. *Great Beers of Belgium*, 3rd edition. Philadelphia: Running Press, 1998.

Jackson, Michael. *Pocket Guide to Beer*. New York: Simon and Schuster, 1994.

Jackson, Michael. *Ultimate Beer*. New York: DK Publishing, 1998.

Jackson, Michael. *World Guide to Beer*. Philadelphia: Running Press, 1977.

Khatchadourian, Raffi. "The Taste Makers." *The New Yorker*, November 23, 2009.

Kumar, Vivek, and R. R. Rao. "Some interesting indigenous beverages among the tribals of Central India." *Indian Journal of Traditional Knowledge*, volume 6, number 1, January 2007.

Lacambre, Georges. *Traité de la Fabrication des Bières et de la Distillation des Grains*. Brussels: Librairie polytechnique d'Aug, 1851.

LaFrance, Peter. "The True Story of the First Pumpkin Beer." BeerBasics.blog.com, December 6, 2007.

MacNeil, Karen. *The Wine Bible*. New York: Workman Publishing, 2001.

Markowski, Phil. *Farmhouse Ales*. Boulder, CO: Brewers Publications, 2004.

Mathias, Peter. *The Brewing Industry in England, 1700–1830*. Cambridge: Cambridge University Press, 1959.

Meussdoerffer, Franz G. "A Comprehensive History of Brewing." *Handbook of Brewing: Processes, Technology, Markets*. Edited by Hans Michael Esslinger. Hoboken, NJ: Wiley-VCH, 2009.

Mosher, Randy. *Radical Brewing*. Boulder, CO: Brewers Publications, 2004.

Mosher, Randy. *Tasting Beer*. North Adams, MA: Storey Publishing, 2009.

Nelson, Max. *The Barbarian's Beverage: A History of Beer in Ancient Europe*. London: Routledge, 2005.

Nicholson, Paul and Ian Shaw. *Ancient Egyptian Materials and Technology*. Cambridge: Cambridge University Press, 2000.

Noonan, Gregory J. *Scotch Ale*. Boulder, CO: Brewers Publications, 1993.

Ogle, Maureen. *Ambitious Brew: The Story of American Beer*. Pleasanton, CA: Harvest Books, 2007.

Oliver, Garrett, editor, *Oxford Companion to Beer*. New York: Oxford University Press, 2012.

Ott, Cindy. *Pumpkin: The Curious History of an American Icon*. Seattle: University of Washington Press, 2012.

Page, Karen and Andrew Dornenburg. *The Food Lover's Guide to Wine*. New York: Little, Brown and Company, 2011.

Pasteur, Louis. *Studies on Fermentation, the Diseases of Beer, Their Causes, and the Means of Preventing Them*. Translated by Frank Faulkner and D. Constable Robb. London: Macmillan and Company, 1879.

Pattinson, Ronald. *Scotland!* Amsterdam: Kilderkin, 2012.

Pattinson, Ronald. Assorted entries, 2007–2012. *Shut Up About Barclay Perkins* (barclayperkins.blogspot.com).

Protz, Roger. *Classic Stout and Porter*. London: Trafalgar Square Publishing, 1997.

Pryor, Alan. "Indian Pale Ale: an Icon of Empire." *Commodities of Empire Working Paper No. 13*. Milton Keynes, England: The Open University, 2009.

Rail, Evan. *Good Beer Guide Prague and the Czech Republic*. St. Albans, England: CAMRA Books, 2008.

Rail, Evan. "On the Founding of Pilsner Urquell, Parts 1–3." *Beer Culture*, August/ September 2012.

Rajotte, Pierre. *Belgian Ale*. Boulder, CO: Brewers Publications, 1992.

Ridgely, Bill. "Gold of the Aqllakuna: the Story of Chicha." *BarleyCorn*, May 1994.

Roach, John. "9,000-Year-Old Beer Re-Created From Chinese Recipe." *National Geographic*, July 18, 2005.

Sambrook, Pamela. *Country House Brewing in England, 1500-1900*. London: Hambledon Press, 1996.

Shepherd, Gordon M. *Neurogastronomy: How the Brain Creates Flavor and Why It Matters*. New York: Columbia University Press, 2012.

Sinclair, Thomas R., and Carol Janas Sinclair. *Bread, Beer, and the Seeds of Change*. Wallingford, England: Centre for Agricultural Bioscience International, 2010.

"A Single System for Taxing Alcoholic Beverages." Oxford: Oxford Economics, August 2010.

"Social and Cultural Aspects of Drinking." Report to the European Commission. Oxford: Social Issues Research Centre, March 1998.

Stack, Martin H. "A Concise History of America's Brewing Industry." *Journal of Macromarketing*. Volume 30, number 1, March 2010.

Steel, Mitch. *IPA: Brewing Techniques, Recipes and the Evolution of India Pale Ale*. Boulder, CO: Brewers Publications, 2012.

Swinnen, Johan F. M., editor. *The Economics of Beer*. Oxford: Oxford University Press, 2011.

Taylor, Alan. "The Brewing of Pilsner Beers." Presentation at the Master Brewers Association of the Americas Spring Meeting, May 14, 2010.

This, Hervé. *Molecular Gastronomy: Exploring the Science of Flavor*. New York: Columbia University Press, 2006.

Thompson, Jennifer Trainer. *The Great American Microbrewery Beer Book*. Berkeley: Ten Speed, 1997.

Tuck, John. *The Private Brewer's Guide*. London: Simpkin and Marshall, 1822.

Tucker, Abigail. "The Beer Archaeologist." *Smithsonian*, July-August, 2011.

Unger, Richard W. *Beer in the Middle Ages and the Renaissance*. Philadelphia: University of Pennsylvania Press, 2004.

Ure, Andrew, and Robert Hunt. *Ure's Dictionary of Arts, Manufactures and Mines*. London, 1867.

Van den Steen, Jef. *Geuze & Kriek: The Secret of Lambic Beer*. Tielt, Belgium: Lannoo, 2012.

Vanderhaegen, Bart, Hedwig Neven, Hubert Verachtert, and Guy Derdelinckx. "Chemistry of Beer Aging, A Critical Review." *Food Chemistry*, volume 95, number 3, April 2006.

Wahl, Robert and Max Henius. *American Handy-book of the Brewing, Malting and Auxiliary Trades*. Chicago: Wahl-Henius Institute, 1902.

Warner, Eric. *German Wheat Beer*. Boulder, CO: Brewers Publications, 1992.

Webb, Tim. *Good Beer Guide Belgium*. St. Albans, England: CAMRA Books, 2009.

Webb, Tim. *Lambicland*. Lavenham, England: Cogan & Mater, 2010.

White, Chris, and Jamil Zainasheff. *Yeast, the Practical Guide to Beer Fermentation*. Boulder, CO: Brewers Publications, 2010.

Woods, John, and Keith Rigley. *The Beers of France*. Winscombe, England: The Artisan Press, 1998.

Wright, I. A., A. J. I. Dalziel, R. P. Ellis, and S. J. G. Hall. "The Status of Traditional Scottish Animal Breeds and Plant Varieties and the Implications for Biodiversity." Government of Scotland, December 2002.

Zacharof, M. P., R. W. Lovitt, and K. Ratanaponglek. "The importance of *Lactobacilli* in contemporary food and pharmaceutical industry." Proceedings of 2010 International Conference on Chemical Engineering and Applications (CCEA 2010).

TOURS AND INTERVIEWS

Adnams, Jonathan and Fergus Fitzgerald (Adnams Brewery, UK), tour, November 9, 2011.

Barrett, Steve (Samuel Smith's Brewery, UK), tour, November 13, 2011.

Bexon, John (Greene King Brewery, UK), tour, November 8, 2011.

Bicklein, Jim (Anheuser-Busch, St. Louis, USA), tour, April 12, 2013.

Bogaert, Stéphane (Brasserie St. Germain, France), tour, November 21, 2011.

Boon, Frank (Brouwerij Boon, Belgium), tour, November 17, 2011.

Bouckaert, Peter (New Belgium Brewery, USA), interview, June 14, 2012.

Bravi, Andrea (Birrificio di Como, Italy), tour, October 4, 2012.

Břevnovský Pivovar (Czech Republic), tour, October 29, 2012.

Brocca, Alessandra (Birrificio Lambrate, Italy), tour, October 31, 2012.

Brož, Adam (Budweiser Budvar, Czech Republic), tour, October 26, 2012.

Buchanan, Alex, Matt Clark, Rob Lovatt, and Caolan Vaughan (Thornbridge Brewery, UK), tour, November 11, 2011.

Carey, Dan (New Glarus Brewing, USA), interview, February 18, 2013.

Carilli, Bruno (Birra Toccalmatto, Italy), tour, October 3, 2012.

Cilurzo, Vinnie (Russian River Brewing, USA), interview, March 7, 2012.

Dedeycker, Olivier (Brasserie Dupont, Belgium), tour, November 24, 2011.

De Harenne, François (Brasserie d'Orval, Belgium), tour, November 27, 2011.

Drexler, Hans-Peter (G. Schneider and Sohn, Germany), tour, October 18, 2012.

Emmerson, James (Full Sail Brewing, USA), tour, January 10, 2012 and interview, January 4, 2013.

Engert, Greg (Neighborhood Restaurant Group, Washington, DC), interview, April 16, 2013.

Fish, Gary (Deschutes Brewery, USA), interview, November 30, 2009.

Forster, John (Brauerei Aying, Germany), tour, October 23, 2012.

Falce, Loïc (Brasserie Castelain, France), tour, November 21, 2011.

Friart, Dominique (Brasserie St. Feuillien, Belgium), tour, November 25, 2011, and correspondence.

Geary, David (Geary's Brewery, USA), interview, July 7, 2011.

Ghequire, Rudi (Brouwerij Rodenbach, Belgium), tour, November 20, 2011.

Grootaert, Carlo (De Struise Brouwers, Belgium), visit, November 22, 2011.

Grossman, Ken (Sierra Nevada, USA), interview, August 9, 2011.

Hook, Alastair (Meantime Brewery, UK), tour, November 7, 2011.

Howell, George (Belhaven Brewery, UK), tour, November 14, 2011.

Kasten, Paul (formerly of Wildwood Restaurant, Portland, OR), interview, August 27, 2012.

Keeling, John, and Derek Prentice (Fuller's Brewery, UK), tour, November 6, 2011.

Kehoe, Tom (Yards Brewery, USA), interview, December 30, 2011.

Kemper, Will (Chuckanut Brewery, USA), interview, January 7, 2013.

King, Tyler (The Bruery, USA), interview, January 13, 2013.

Knöller, Jürgen (Bayern Brewery, USA), interview, February 12, 2013.

Leinhart, Phil (Brewery Ommegang, USA), interview, March 14, 2012.

Lemay, Marc and Hugues Dubuisson (Brasserie Dubuisson, Belgium), tour, November 24, 2011.

Loverier, Valter (LoverBeer, Italy), tour, November 1, 2012.

Mareš, David (Pivovar Ferdinand, Czech Republic), tour, October 28, 2012.

Murray, Fergal (Guinness, Ireland), interview, March 27, 2012.

Musso, Teo, with translation by Fabio Mozzone (Birrificio Baladin, Italy), tour, November 2, 2012.

Ockert, Karl (BridgePort Brewery, USA), interview, August 5, 2011.

O'Hara, Ross (Caledonian, UK), tour, November 14, 2011.

Palm Brewery (Belgium), tour, November 17, 2011.

Paulaner Brewery (Germany), tour, October 24, 2012.

Plzeňský Prazdroj/Pilsner Urquell (Czech Republic), tour, October 25, 2012.

Reed, Paul, and Mark Tranter (Dark Star Brewery, UK), tour, November 8, 2011.

Santos, Gumer (Brasserie Rochefort, Belgium), tour, November 27, 2011.

Schnitzler, Michael, and Sebastian Degen (Hausbrauerei Uerige, Germany), tour, October 15, 2012.

Stecken, Jens (Brauerei Reissdorf, Germany), interview, October 16, 2012.

Stecken, Jens, and Frank Hasenkrug (Brauerei Reissdorf, Germany), tour, October 16, 2012.

Swihart, Matt (Double Mountain Brewery, USA), tour, July 16, 2011.

Taylor, Alan (Zoiglhaus, USA), interview, September 3, 2012.

Tod, Rob and Jason Perkins (Allagash Brewery, USA), tour, November 25, 2008.

Trum, Matthias (Aecht Schlenkerla Rauchbier, Germany), tour, October 19, 2012.

Úněticky Pivovar (Czech Republic) tour, October 29, 2012.

Van Roy, Jean (Brasserie Cantillon, Belgium), tour, November 16, 2011.

Weihenstephan (Germany) tour, October 23, 2012.

Welch, Darron (Pelican Brewery, USA), interview, September 14, 2011.

Index

CREDITS

All photographs by Jeff Alworth unless noted below.

Cover Photograph: volff/fotolia

age fotostock: Tony Briscoe p. ix; EKA p. 380 (bottom); English Heritage p. 86; Steven Morris p. 48; Clement Philippe p. 41; SuperStock p. 565. **American Society of Chemists:** reproduced, by permission, from the Beer Flavor Wheel, American Society of Chemists, St. Paul, MN: p. 69. **Alamy:** Peter Alvey p. 574 (bottom left); Phillip Bond p. 5; Carl Clark p. 357; Steve Cukrov p. 593; Daily Mail/Rex p. 574 (top right); FoodCollection.com p. 542; Arunas Gabalis p. 544; Gareth/Stockimo p. 141; Hemis pp. 552, 554; Kuttig-Travel-2 p. 152; Moon Yin Lam p. 567; Lordprice Collection p. 571; Niday Picture Library p. 424; Trinity Mirror/Mirrorpix p. 575; Leon Werdinger p. 3; Zigzag Mountain Art p. 42 (right). **Fotolia:** jovannig p. 143; primopiano p. 74; Aleksey Sagitov p. 594; volff p. i. **Getty Images:** Josh Haunschild/MLB Photos p. 573; Huw Jones p. 564; Holger Leue/Lonely Planet Images p. 153.

Courtesy Photos: Abita Brewing Co., LLC: p. 139 (top). **Alaskan Brewing Co.:** p. 486. **Anchor Brewing Company:** p. 487. **Anchorage Brewing Company:** p. 7. **AS Aldaris:** p. 158. **Avery Brewing Company:** pp. 8, 137. **Frank Bauer/München Tourismus:** p. 443 (bottom). **B.B.N.P. Brewery:** pp. 432, 435. **Bear Republic Brewing Company, Inc.®:** p. 115. **beer-coaster.eu:** pp. 92, 117, 135, 159, 203, 237, 255, 412, 458 (both). **Bell's Brewery, Inc.:** p. 209. **Birrificio Italiano®:** p. 328. **Blue Moon Brewing Co.:** p. 386. **Bob Kay Beer Labels:** p. 450. **The Boston Beer Company:** pp. 446, 448. **Boulder Beer Company:** p. 171. **Boulevard Brewing Co.:** p. 275. **Brasserie Cantillon:** p. 496. **Brasserie Castelain:** p. 291. **Brasserie Dupont:** p. 274. **Brasserie Rochefort:** p. 307. **Brasserie St. Germain:** p. 296 (middle). **Brooklyn Brewery:** p. 138. **Brouwerij Drie Fonteinen:** p. 491. **Brouwerij Kerkom:** p. 261 (left). **Brouwerij Moortgat:** pp. 76, 493. **Brouwerij Rodenbach:** pp. 17, 516, 525 (right). **Brouwerij Verhaeghe Vichte:** p. 523. **Cascade Brewing:** p. 531. **Tim Cederman-Haysom:** p. 380 (top). **Chuckanut Brewery & Kitchen:** p. 430. **Cigar City Brewing/artwork by Eric Swanson:** p. 185. **Cölner Hofbräu P. Josef Früh KG:** p. 238. **Dark Star Brewing Co.:** p. 102. **Christian Deglas:** p. 381. **De Ranke Brewery:** p. 261 (right). **Deschutes Brewery:** p. 157. **Diageo–Guinness USA:** pp. 150, 160. **Dogfish Head Craft Brewery:** pp. 349, 359. **The Duck-Rabbit Craft Brewery, Inc.:** p. 161. **European Beer Museum, Stenay, France:** pp. 282, 283 (top), 457. **Fat Head's Brewery:** p. 114. **Firestone Walker Brewing Company:** p. 91. **Full Sail Brewing Company:** p. 184. **Fuller's Brewery:** p. 90. **Geary Brewing:** p. 103. **Goose Island Beer Company:** p. 277. **Ground Breaker Brewery:** p. 352. **Harviestoun Brewery:** p. 224. **Frank Heinrich, Leipzig:** p. 394. **John Warner Photography:** p. 350. **Erin Joy:** p. 354. **Kent Life:** p. 81. **Kiuchi Brewery:** pp. 356, 387. **Kout na Šumavě Brewery:** p. 428. **Katherine Longly & France Dubois/Brasserie de la Senne:** p. 259. **LoverBeer Brewery:** p. 330. **Mahrs-Bräu:** p. 485. **Maple Leaf Auctions:** p. 148. **Merchant du Vin:** pp. 460, 461, 462 (left), 509. **Mikkeller/artwork by Keith Shore:** p. 178. **Moorhouse's Brewery:** p. 129 (bottom left). **Mother Earth Brewing:** p. 411. **New Glarus Brewery:** p. 447. **Ommegang Brewery:** pp. 44, 276, 313, 388. **Orkney Brewery:** p. 223. **Orval Brewery:** pp. 244, 317. **Pilsner Urquell:** p. 577. **Jeff Renfro:** p. 16. **Ritterguts Gose GmbH:** p. 398. **B. Roemmelt/München Tourismus:** pp. 439, 443 (top). **Louisa Salazar:** p. 355. **Sly Fox Brewing Co.:** p. 433. **Patricia Smith:** p. 273. **Smuttynose Brewing Co.:** p. 139 (bottom). **Southampton Publick House:** p. 293. **Spoetzl Brewery:** p. 456. **St. Peter's Brewery:** p. 351. **Struise Brouwers:** p. 522 (top right). **Studio Schulz:** p. 537. **Summit Brewing Company:** p. 104. **Surly Brewing Co.:** p. 130. **Daniel Thiriez:** p. 286. **Thornbridge Brewery:** p. 116. **Toccalmatto Brewery:** p. 329. **Mathew Trogner/Allagash Brewing Company:** p. 539. **Upland Brewing Co.:** p. 508. **Weihenstephan Breweries:** p. 373. **Widmer Brothers Brewing:** p. 186. **Workman Publishing:** Michael Di Mascio pp. 311, 473 (both); Bobby Walsh pp. 6, 540–541. **Xingu Brewery:** p. 413. **Yards Brewing Company:** p. 129 (top right).

Maps by Susan Hunt Yule (pp. 578, 580, 582, 585, 588–589, 603, 604, 605).

Infographics by James Williamson (pp. 39, 54–55, 344, 547, 548–549, 570).

ABOUT THE AUTHOR

JEFF ALWORTH has been writing about beer for more than 15 years. He is the author of *The Beer Tasting Toolkit* and *Cider Made Simple*, and has also written for *Draft*, *All About Beer*, *BeerAdvocate*, *Sunset*, and more, as well as for his popular site, Beervana. He lives in Portland, Oregon, in the heart of the craft beer revival, the Pacific Northwest.